*L*OST *V*OICES OF *W*ORLD *W*AR *I*

'This large and appropriately well-produced anthology . . . Altogether the project is a noble and worthy one. Moving by its very nature, it is also an extraordinarily absorbing guide to both the passions and the techniques which dominated the literature of the early part of our disastrous century, and the ways in which individual writers responded to the idea – and the fact – of all-out war. The selection of fifty-nine writers has been singularly well-judged'
– MARTIN SEYMOUR-SMITH, *Independent*

'Remarkable . . . more generously wide-ranging than any other similar collection; its Introduction and Conclusion by Robert Wohl sensibly discuss general cultural issues; and its lead-ins to each writer are usefully – and in some cases vitally – informative' – ANDREW MOTION, *Observer*

'Tim Cross's engrossing anthology . . . This is a valuable book, often cutting deep' – PETER VANSITTART, *Daily Telegraph*

'An exceptional and thought-provoking book' – DEREK MAHON, *Irish Times*

'The editor and publishers must be congratulated for printing the original texts even when they are in Breton or Armenian, opposite the translation'
– JAMES JOLL, *New York Review of Books*

'Its method and format seem exactly right for its leading idea; even its incongruities and occasional puzzles add to the general historic flavour . . . How many of us, for instance, have heard of Stramm or Löns, Baum or Flex? But they are, or were, as notorious in their homeland as Brooke in our own; and when Cross introduces us to their lives and works they become as alive as Sorley, Ledwidge and their other English opposite numbers admirably presented by Jon Stallworthy. Ian Higgins has done an equally good job for the young Frenchmen or Belgians . . .' – JOHN BAYLEY, *London Review of Books*

'Remarkable and ambitious . . . Peter Read's essay of Apollinaire is one of the treasures of the book . . . The choices are terrible and funny, gentle and wild . . . The most telling and impressive aspect of the anthology is the manner in which a dead writer is presented via a brief life, a critique, a photograph and a translation which is truly eye-opening' – RONALD BLYTHE, *Punch*

AN INTERNATIONAL ANTHOLOGY OF WRITERS, POETS & PLAYWRIGHTS

THE LOST VOICES OF WORLD WAR I

TIM CROSS

BLOOMSBURY

First published 1988

This edition first published 1998

Bloomsbury Publishing Plc, 38 Soho Square, London W1V 5DF

A CIP catalogue record is available from the British Library

ISBN 0 7475 4276 7

10 9 8 7 6 5 4 3 2 1

Typeset by Columns, Reading
Printed in Great Britain by Butler & Tanner Limited, Frome

*T*O THE *L*OST *V*OICES OF *A*LL *W*ARS

Acknowledgments

This book has its genesis in the Armistice Festival commemorating the seventieth anniversary of the end of World War I. Under the aegis of Sir Yehudi Menuhin, I devised an artistic programme of concerts, exhibitions and readings to be held in London in November 1988, exclusively concerned with the works of composers, artists, poets, playwrights and writers who had lost their lives in the many conflicts which made up the hostilities of 1914–18. The wide range of literary accomplishment in this anthology was complemented in the creative spheres of music and fine art. The impact of such an array of burgeoning talents (but in most cases in full flower) was, and in the case of this anthology, should still be disturbing. That the Armistice Festival was an international venture was reflected in the patronage of HRH The Duke of Kent together with that of the Ambassadors and High Commissioners of twenty-two nations. Funding for the Festival likewise came from many different sources, and these have been acknowledged in material relating directly to the Festival. Commitment by the Festival's Board of Directors to the raising of funds on which the Festival as well as this book depended was unwavering, and I count myself fortunate to have had recourse to the Board's advice and support on the long road from gestation to fruition, and, in some cases, well beyond. Original material for this book has been commissioned by the Armistice Festival with the generous support of Cecile Lantz-Nichols with the help of the legacy of the late Flora Calcutt-Nichols. Assistance is gratefully acknowledged from Waterstone and Company. The Kantvlead Bleimor has subsidized the section on Jean-Pierre Calloc'h.

Due to the exigencies of producing this volume in time for the Festival, many of these articles and translations had to be commissioned at very short notice. My gratitude is due to all contributors, writers of articles and translators alike who undertook to complete their sections with such speed and care. I am particularly indebted to Dr Ian Higgins, to whom fell the lion's share in terms of original research. In compiling the French, Belgian and Breton sections he in turn would like to thank those who contributed and who gave advice and support, namely: Ann Cottrell, Adrian Gratwick, Nicky Haxell, Claude Henry, Sándor Hervey, Humphrey Humphreys, Louis Le Bras, Graham Martin, Roy Owen, Siân Reynolds, Susan Rowe, Malcolm Scott and Adèle Walker.

Acknowledgments to those individuals and publishing houses who have kindly consented to give permission to reproduce from already published sources are credited in the appropriate bibliographical section in the body of the book. Special mention must be made of those individuals who so very generously waived reproduction fees for these contributions: Janet Adam Smith for the late Michael Roberts' biographical sketch on T.E. Hulme; Samuel Beckett for his translation of Guillaume Apollinaire's *Zone*; Eckhard Faul for his piece on Hans Leybold; Professor Patrick Bridgwater for his perceptive analysis of German war poetry from which I have quoted extensively; Michael Hamburger (whose enthusiasm for the concept of the book has been so encouraging) for his translations of Georg Trakl and Alfred Lichtenstein; Professor Christopher Middleton for the use of his translations of Trakl; Michael Patterson for granting permission to use substantial extracts from his chapter on Sorge in *The Revolution in German Theatre 1900-33*; Professor J.M. Ritchie for his translation of August Stramm's play *Erwachen*; and Professor Jon Stallworthy for his specially revised articles on Rupert Brooke, Charles Hamilton Sorley, Isaac Rosenberg, Edward Thomas and Wilfred Owen, as well as for his staunch support of the project from its inception. I am very fortunate to have met with so many contributors who have lent time and effort to the successful completion of this book without expectation of any remuneration: Dr Philip Mann for his translations of Hans Leybold poems; George Gömöri, Dr Bernard Johnson, Jacek Laskowski, Dr Harry Leeming and Dr V. Nersessian for their contributions to the Hungarian, Serbian, Polish, Slovene and Armenian sections respectively. Likewise I am greatly indebted to the resourcefulness of Dr Robert Pynsent and the staff of the School of Slavonic and East European Studies; Dr Georgi Papantchev and Peter Sherwood for their articles and translations on the Czech, Bulgarian and Hungarian sections; and also to Dr Peter Shopov of the Bulgarian Embassy, Mario Mikolic of the Czech Embassy and Henryk Ziętek of the Polish Cultural Institute in London.

The avoidance of the great majority of authors' and printers' errors has been accomplished with the help of copy- and proof-editors Nancy Deuin and Kelly Davis as well as, at various stages in the book's compilation, Jacques Bergier, Robin Davidson and Gwen West. My special thanks go to Valerie West, the General Manager of the Armistice Festival, for her devotion to this whole project.

Tim Cross
1 August 1988

Contents

*I*NTRODUCTION

Now, God be thanked Who has matched us with His hour . . .
Rupert Brooke, August 1914

August 1914. For aspiring writers and artists born during the last two decades of the 19th century, it was, if not the best, certainly the most exhilarating of times. Europe was in the throes of a cultural transmutation so unsettling that many young men and women felt that they were about to witness the dawn of a new age. This helps to explain the mixture of impassioned enthusiasm and repressed anxiety with which they greeted the news of war. One culture was passing; another was about to be born. No wonder they wept with joy and marvelled at their incredible good fortune. To how many generations was it given to witness the coming of a new era?

But for those same young people it would also soon become the worst of times, a nightmare from which all too many would never awaken. Some who had already given gauges of their talent, and countless others who were on the verge of doing so, would lose their lives in a long and destructive war that blew to smithereens the comfortable world into which they had been born. Others would emerge from the war mutilated in body or mind – disillusioned, confused, disoriented and prey to the destructive political ideologies that would dominate European politics in the 1920s and 1930s. These survivors would, in their great majority, live to fight, or suffer from, the war of 1939–45. In their minds, the Great War would always divide their lives into a *before* of innocence and laughter and an *after* of hopelessness and loss. Many would experience the postwar years as a 'waste-land' (T.S. Eliot) or a 'flight without end' (Joseph Roth).

To be young and gifted in 1914 was, for males and females alike, a tragic fate. They were condemned to live in a world for which their youth had not prepared them. Nor would the new civilization be the one whose outlines they had glimpsed before 1914. Yet from their fate, the men and women of 1914 would wring a formidable cultural legacy. For war and culture in early 20th-century Europe entered into a complex relationship of stimulus and counter-stimulus that defied the theories of pacifists and warmongers alike and made for unexpected results. War destroyed culture and it destroyed countless human beings who were endowed with the gifts to contribute to its further development and transformation. But war also created a spur to cultural production because it provided an experience, an object of reflection and a complex of powerful emotions which have proven capable of outliving those who underwent it. As paradoxical as it may seem, the war of 1914–18 became a major cultural event.

How could this be so? War, the Spanish philosopher José Ortega y Gasset (1883–1955) noted in 1916, enters the soul of men and expands them.

> It puts us in contact with the profound and essential reality and, before it, all other everyday things appear as the transitory creations they deserve to be and lose their authority and solidity. War renders fluid all human things. The soft and almost liquid material of life yields to the pressure of enterprising hands. Everything is possible, everything is possible!

To put Ortega's idea more prosaically, war heightens emotions, breaks up the humdrum rhythms of everyday life and makes possible ruptures and innovations. It both accelerates and gives a new direction to change.

The Great War, then, did not in itself *create* culture. The German writer Gerrit Engelke (1890–1918) was no doubt right when he said that war was 'the negation . . . of the spiritual, and the furthering of the power of the material world'. The war of 1914–18 did, however, create circumstances that gave rise to cultural production. And to understand that culture, we must probe back into the period before 1914, those ten or so years following the turn of the century when the future combatants first encountered their civilization and developed the attitudes towards it that they would take to war.

The Old Cultures and the New

There are those whose character is not so far developed as their mind; these are the breakers of values.
But those whose minds are less developed than their characters; these are the conservers of values.
And he alone, in whom mind and character are one, is the Creator of new Values.

Ferenc Békássy (1893–1915), 'Aphorisms'

First, however, let us identify our protagonists in generational terms. The writers commemorated in this volume were born between 1852 (Franc Maselj-Podlimbarski) and 1895 (Charles Sorley and Gaston de Ruyter). The majority belong to what I (and others) have called the generation of 1905. These men were mostly born in the 1880s and had launched their careers well before the outbreak of the war. A second contingent – consisting of men born in the late 1880s and early 1890s – had little time to make their mark in cultural life before the war swept them up in its maelstrom. They are properly called the 'generation of 1914'. Despite all the differences between these two age groups, for the purposes of this introduction I intend to group the two together and refer to them as the 'generations of 1914', as indeed they tended to do themselves.

How did the generations of 1914 first encounter culture? To begin with, they quickly discovered that it came packaged in different forms, which co-existed and competed for their attention. First, there was the official culture which was consecrated by academies, taught in schools and performed in state theatres, concert halls and opera houses. This consisted of elements taken from the Greek and Roman classics; selected fragments of Christianity, often presented in secularized forms; and those literary and artistic works which had been certified over the centuries as 'great' and 'representative' of the national spirit – for example, Racine's *Phèdre* in France, Dante's *Divina Commedia* in Italy, Goethe's *Faust* in Germany and Shakespeare in England. By 1900, official culture had integrated many elements of late 19th-century science – above all, the conviction that society, like nature, could be understood in terms of the metaphor of 'law' – and was strongly oriented towards the needs and aspirations of the middle classes. Hence it was often referred to (or dismissed) as 'bourgeois' culture.

Co-existing with official culture, though normally regarded as inferior to it, was popular culture: the traditional culture of the peasants and artisans who made up the *Volk*. These residues from a distant past, sometimes recently rediscovered or invented, consisted of melodies, dances, dress, furniture, architectural forms, festivals and tales passed on from one generation to the next, often through an oral tradition. This type of culture exercised a particular attraction on young people from rural areas, but it also held a special charm for urban youth who felt that Europe's new cities were destroying regional and national cultural identities. Many members of the generations of 1914 – including the musicians Béla Bartók (1880–1945) and George Butterworth (1885–1916) and the writers Walter Flex (1887–1917) and Edward Thomas (1878–1917) – would flee their native cities in search of folk culture, or write, as their contemporary Charles Péguy (1873–1914) did, with passion and nostalgia about the traditional cultures that were being lost.

In sharp contrast to popular culture was the newly emerging mass culture, as much a culture of the city as popular culture was of the land. Mass culture could be found in newspapers, illustrated magazines, cabarets, music halls, circuses, vaudeville and – above all – in the newest art, the cinema. In 1914, the status of these forms of entertainment and distraction as culture was still uncertain; but they had the immense advantage that they were more fun and gave more immediate pleasure than their pedigreed competitors. To the great consternation of their elders, many talented members of the generations of 1914, especially those of the second contingent born after 1890, would devote themselves to mass culture and help to win for it, even if belatedly, recognition as authentic art.

That this would occur was, however, not at all clear in the years before 1914; for the form of culture that was capturing the attention of many of the men commemorated in this volume was what we today would call the 'culture of the avant-garde' or the 'culture of modernism'. This is because it was the culture of the New. And the culture of the New had identified itself and was identified with 'Youth', a term that had taken on a special meaning and power for the generations of 1914.

The foundations of the culture of modernism had been laid during the last two decades of the 19th century by men who could have been the fathers and uncles of the generations of 1914 – or, more often, their older brothers. Many of the founders of modernist culture had fallen prey to the programme of the 'decadents', which invited artists and writers to revel in the sensual charms of language, music, movement, colour and form as ends in themselves, to be savoured as the world outside collapsed or went up in flames. But though some members of the generations of 1914, like the Czech writer Miloš Marten (1883–1917), continued to dabble in decadent art, the majority pulled back from the abyss of sensuality and self-indulgence and looked to the example of such early modernist masters as Claude Debussy (1862–1918), Frank Wedekind (1864–1918), Wassily Kandinsky (1866–1944) and André Gide (1869–1951), who were creating new languages for expressing new feelings and states of mind and, in the process, revolutionizing the meaning of a work of art.

The generations of 1914 did not create the New Culture; it was already in place when they appeared on the scene. Instead, they discovered it as an adolescent or a young man might receive an unexpected legacy beyond his wildest dreams. Such a legacy, of course, could also be experienced as frightening or dangerous; and many members of the generations of 1914 would react against modernist culture and seek refuge in the certainties of official or popular culture. But no aspiring writer or artist growing up during the years before 1914 could ignore the modernist challenge.

It was also true that, between 1905 and 1914, the cause of modernism was confined to small groups of avant-garde intellectuals and artists who gathered in cafés and cabarets, and clustered around reviews whose subscriber lists were short, amazingly so by the standards of the late 20th century: Charles Péguy's *Cahiers de la Quinzaine* (*Fortnightly Review*), Franz Pfemfert's *Die Aktion* (*Action*), Herwarth Walden's *Der Sturm* (*Storm*), Giuseppe Prezzolini's *La Voce* (*The Voice*), Georg Lukács's *A Szellem* (*Spirit*) and Wyndham Lewis's *Blast* seldom printed more than a few thousand copies. For young intellectuals growing up in pre-1914 Europe, the élitist quality of these journals was part of their charm: it confirmed these young men and women in thinking that they and their friends had a monopoly on the New. Yet the influence the journals achieved would reach far beyond the limited clienteles whose support they mobilized; and the ideas they championed would make their way, by strange and convoluted paths, into some of the most important cultural and political movements of 20th-century Europe.

Die Neue Kunst

Franz Henseler (1883-1918): Design for *Die Neue Kunst*, 1912.
Dr Joachim Hensinger von Waldegg, Mannheim

Before 1914, the capital of modernist culture was Paris, the city of Baudelaire, Manet and Debussy; and every enlightened member of the generations of 1914 followed, as closely as he or she could, what was happening in the City of Light and dreamed of one day going there to stroll the lanes of Montmartre and conceive masterpieces in some intellectuals' café while sipping strong drink. But before the turn of the century, modernism had begun to put down roots in other European cities: Vienna, Florence, Munich, Barcelona, Berlin, Brussels, Budapest – and even along Europe's periphery, in St Petersburg, London, Dublin and Madrid. By 1905, the culture of the New had become truly European, and before long, it would cross the Atlantic to take up quarters in New York.

The culture of modernism differed from one country to another, and any attempt to describe it outside of the urban and national contexts in which it developed is doomed to failure. Indeed, the term 'modernism' can itself be misleading; for in some countries, the culture of the pre-1914 avant-garde developed as a reaction against late 19th-century movements that had called themselves 'modernist'. But the word itself is unimportant: what matters is that perceptive young urban men and women all over Europe were aware that culture was undergoing a deep and radical change; and it was the awareness of this change that encouraged them to believe that their generation was somehow special and charged with a unique cultural mission. 'History,' wrote Ortega in 1914, 'is trembling to its very roots, its flanks are torn apart convulsively, because a new reality is about to be born.'

Modernism, then, was not so much a movement as a sensibility or a mood that could give rise to movements of very different kinds. And central to this sensibility were three ideas. The first was that 'truth' was not an absolute that could be seized and encapsulated by the human mind, but rather a perspective, which, chameleon-like, would change with the situation of the person seeking knowledge. Applied to literature, this meant that stories could be narrated in a multiplicity of voices, with none being given the privilege of omniscience. Readers might finish a story or a novel no more enlightened about the 'truth' of what had really happened than they had been when they began it. Nor could one be sure what narrators had actually seen or experienced and what they had imagined. Applied to painting, multi-perspectivism meant that there was no longer a single point around which the space represented by a canvas could be organized. Though the idea sounds quite innocent – and we take it for granted today – it meant that the viewer of a picture might no longer be able to make sense of lines and colours that seemed to go off senselessly in all directions. And applied to one's own life, to the realm that late 19th-century middle-class Europeans would have called 'morality', multi-perspectivism suggested that everyone was free – indeed, condemned – to improvise his or her own values. Regardless of how one sought to apply it, the discovery that the world was not a single reality that could be grasped, but a multiplicity of points of view that must remain forever relative was both liberating and profoundly disturbing.

The second idea that inspired much of the New Culture was the belief that knowledge of the world was to be gained not through analysis or reasoning – least of all through science – but rather through action, insight, intuition and instinct. 'Reason,' the French writer Maurice Barrès (1862–1923) mused in a phrase that seemed profoundly true to many of his younger readers, is a 'tiny thing on the surface of ourselves'. If it is misleading to claim that modernist writers and artists scorned reason and sought to substitute for it unreason, as Barrès often appeared to do, it is none the less indisputable that they wished to reform reason, dethrone it and demote its role in culture. Behind much modernist literature and art was the conviction that reason had become a substitute for, or an obstacle to, life. Hence the determination of early 20th-century writers and artists to probe beneath the veneer of convention and to explore and release the energies and passions that 19th-century civilization had hidden and repressed. They were ready to heed the advice of the French philosopher Henri Bergson who counted many disciples – including the British writer T. E. Hulme (1883–1917) and the Pole Jerzy Żuławski (1874–1915) – among the generations of 1914: 'You must take things by storm; you must thrust intelligence outside itself by an act of will.' Our distance from these generations is dramatized by the fact that they would have known – or would have thought they knew – exactly what Bergson meant by this (to us) cryptic exhortation.

The third idea was that life, history and culture are not governed by knowable laws, but by chance, caprice and the action of determined individuals who impose their will on the masses. Vitality, energy, passion, *élan* were the human fuel that drove the engines of history; virtue, understood in the bourgeois sense of the discipline and repression of the senses, seemed incompatible with cultural creation; progress was not a certainty, on which one could comfortably count, but a goal that had to be achieved through heroic effort which might fail. What ascended in history also fell; decadence constantly lurked around the corner; history took the form of jumps and leaps rather than of reliable and constant evolution; cultural values were themselves fictions which had constantly to be renewed and reinvented.

Attitudes like these were bound to produce a different form of art and literature; and the ten years before 1914 were, in the field of culture, among the most revolutionary in the history of Europe. Cubism and Futurism shattered century-old conventions of how forms and motion should be represented on a flat surface; Schoenberg (1874–1951) and Stravinsky (1882–1971) redefined melody and abandoned tonic resolution in favour of music that was meant to shock, discombobulate and confound the senses; Proust (1871–1922), Mann (1975–1955) and Kafka (1883–1924) began to experiment with novels that confused inner and outer time and swept their readers into a subjective world in which feelings need not necessarily be related to any firm external reality.

The style of these works, of course, was new; but their impact on those who saw, heard or read them went far beyond that caused by the novelty of stylistic innovation. For what made these works revolutionary, disquieting and exhilarating was that they called into question the very function of culture. The new literature, music and art had given up the attempt to represent an external reality that could be assumed to be common to all cultivated people. It had turned inwards to plumb the depths of the soul; and at the same time, it made no effort to disguise that its products were cultural inventions rather than representations of nature. Picasso (1881–1974) put it well:

> Art is a lie that makes us realize truth, at least the truth that is given to us to understand. The artist must know how to convince others of the truthfulness of his lies . . . Through art we express our conception of what nature is not . . . That those lies are necessary to our mental selves is beyond any doubt, as it is through them that we form our aesthetic view of life.

This was not a view of art that the official culture, based on the concepts of the Beautiful, the Good and the True, could easily accept. But Picasso's paradoxical play on the 'truth' of artistic 'lies' would have been savoured by the painter's staunchest advocate Guillaume Apollinaire (1880–1918) and the pre-1914 avant-garde.

Picasso's sketch of Apollinaire.

THE BATTLE OF THE GENERATIONS

We smash through the power and topple the thrones of the old reign . . . on our heads the crowns of young messiahs we wear.
Ernst Wilhelm Lotz (1890–1914) 'Uprising of Youth'

During the pre-war decade, the modernist sensibility gave rise to many movements, ranging from Cubism in France to Futurism in Italy and Vorticism in England. It would be futile, and misleading, to attempt to reduce these disparate groups to a single programme. Yet underlying their artistic experiments was a common conviction that gave them and their adversaries the impression that they represented a unified camp; and that was their deeply felt belief that the official culture of late 19th-century Europe was exhausted, and that it was on the verge of being replaced by a new culture whose outlines could only be grasped dimly through the fog that enveloped the phase of cultural reconstruction.

In retrospect, this belief that one age was coming to an end and another was about to be born seems exaggerated. To be sure, many changes would occur during the 20th century; but the continuities between the 20th century and the late 19th century are also striking. Contrary to what many intellectuals believed or claimed to believe during the years before 1914, Science, Reason, Truth, Liberty, Freedom, Equality and Beauty have not lost their power as ideals; the 'illusions of progress' have not completely died. But both before and after the war, the expectation of cultural palingenesis had serious consequences. The first was a determination to hasten the work of cultural demolition: to expose, undermine and destroy the values underlying official culture. The second was a belief that it was the mission of Youth to lay the foundations for the culture of the New.

This, rather than any sudden collapse of relations between children and their parents, explains, I think, why the theme of generational revolt became so prominent in pre-war culture. It is certainly true that many young men born in the 1880s and early 1890s chose, as the French writer Ernest Psichari (1883–1914) did, to break with the values of their parents and grandparents and to cultivate a style of life that their parents found difficult to accept. For the great majority of Europeans, it would have been easier to make such a break between 1900 and 1914 than it would have been 30, 100 or 200 years before. Industrialization, the rapid growth of the European economies, the creation of new occupations, the invention of faster means of transport, and imperial expansion into previously unexplored corners of the world had made movement away from the place and the social station into which one had been born easier than ever before. Psichari, like many other young Europeans, took a steamship from France to find himself and reforge his values in French colonial Africa.

Paul Wegener as the insane Father in *Der Bettler* by Reinhard Sorge (1892-1916) from a lithograph by Bruno Paul of the original production mounted by Max Reinhardt in 1917.

But the theme of generational revolt, which is so prominent in the literature of pre-1914 and postwar Europe, expressed not just an individual's frustration with anachronistic parents (as in Reinhard Sorge's play *Der Bettler*) or the conflict of egotisms (as Adrian Consett Stephen's play *Echoes* suggests), but also the collective belief that 19th-century European civilization was moribund and inadequate to the demands of 20th-century life. Nowhere was this motif more aggressively developed than in Central Europe where it became a standby of Expressionist poetry and drama. Though one is tempted to relate its prevalence and power to the nearly contemporary psychoanalytic discoveries of Sigmund Freud (1856–1939) and his disciples, it is probably more illuminating to view this phenomenon as a result of the radical social dislocations that the newly created German state was undergoing at this time. Within fifty years, Germany had passed from being a number of loosely linked states filled with small and picturesque towns to become one of the most urbanized and industrialized of Europe's great powers. Tradition was a victim of this process; and modernism flourished in Germany's greatest cities, as it did in neighbouring Vienna where it became a formidable adversary of the official culture. Many German and Austrian writers and artists from the generations of 1914 – for example, August Stramm (1874–1915) and Georg Trakl (1887–1914) – were drawn towards modernist movements, chiefly Expressionism; but others, like Walter Flex (1887–1917), felt impelled to defend tradition against the onslaught of the urban world. Post-war German culture would continue to experience this schism, and it was not until Hitler came to power that the traditionalists would achieve a decisive, if ephemeral, victory over 'decadent' literature and art.

The Impact of Technology

At nightfall when the factories close the main street is filled with people. They walk slowly or in the middle of an alley they stop and stand.
They are blackened with work and engine soot.
But their eyes uphold Earth still, the tough power of the soil and the festive light of the fields.

Ernest Stadler (1883–1914)

If tradition seemed so problematic to young intellectuals and artists between 1900 and 1914, either requiring relentless attack or desperate defence, it was because the world into which they had been born was in the process of violent upheaval. The world, Péguy lamented in 1913, had changed less since the birth of Jesus Christ than it had during the previous thirty years. To someone born around 1885, whose adolescence had coincided with the century's turn, Péguy's hyperbole appeared a simple statement of fact.

The most visible agent of this transformation was a rapidly advancing technology that seemed capable of unlimited and Promethean innovations. The years of the late 19th and early 20th centuries were an era when newly invented machines challenged or called into question many certainties with which Europeans had lived for hundreds of years. The electric light erased the age-old distinction between day and night. The telephone and the wireless made it possible for people to communicate across enormous distances. The bicycle, the motorcar and the steamship accelerated the speed with which people could move through the world, and enlarged the range of their effective action. The cinema offered the imagination a new way of telling stories, in which sequence could be replaced by simultaneity and in which space and time could be manipulated at will. And after 1909, the aeroplane opened up to human locomotion the dimension of the heavens, a realm formerly reserved for birds, angels and God.

Such prospects were exhilarating, and in 1909 in Paris, F. T. Marinetti (1876–1944) and a group of like-minded friends who called themselves 'Futurists', issued an appeal calling for an art and literature that would correspond to the era of speed, machines, violence and danger that they sensed was dawning.

> *We shall sing of great crowds agitated by work, by pleasure and by rebellions; we shall sing of the multicoloured and polyphonic waves of revolutions in modern capital cities; we shall sing of the vibrating nocturnal fervour of arsenals and shipyards ablaze with violent electric moonlight; of greedy railway stations which devour smoking serpents; of workshops hanging from the clouds by the twisted wires of their smoke; of bridges, similar to gigantic gymnasts, which leap over rivers, shining in the sun like glistening knife blades; of adventurous steamers that sniff the horizon; of locomotives with broad chests that paw their rails like enormous steel horses bridled with pipes; and of the slipping flight of aeroplanes whose propellers flutter in the wind like flags and seem to applaud like enthusiastic crowds.*

Writers and artists all over Europe responded to this demand for a new form of culture. Futurists groups formed in cities as widely separated as Milan, London and St Petersburg. Three of the most talented of these Futurists – the painter and sculptor Umberto Boccioni (1882–1916), the architect Antonio Sant'Elia (1888–1916) and the Russian artist Vladimir Burlyuk (1886–1917) – would die in the war.

But many European writers and artists of the generations of 1914 responded to the machine age with less enthusiasm, seeking in the still untransformed countryside traces of a simpler, purer, less agitated form of life. This seems to have been the case especially in the British Isles where the poetry of Edward Thomas (1878–1917), Rupert Brooke (1887–1914) and the Irishman Francis Ledwidge (1891–1916) evoked arcadian scenes of rural tranquillity, far removed from the frantic neurasthenia of Europe's cities, where (as in Boccioni's famous painting of Milan) not even private residences could protect their inhabitants from the predatory invasion of the street. Indeed, it was often in the city, 'sweating, sick and hot', that poets such as Brooke remembered and captured in verse the country's 'sleepy grass', 'kindly winds', 'bosky' woods, 'unkempt' roses and 'mysterious' streams, 'green as a dream and deep as death'.

Umberto Boccioni (1882-1916): *The Noise of the Street enters the House* (1911). *Sprengel Sammlung, Hanover*

THE LURE OF POLITICS

We love Trieste for the restless soul she gave us. She takes us away from out little sorrows and makes us her own, makes us brothers of all those who have to fight for a homeland. She has reared us for struggle and for duty. . . . We love you and bless you because we are happy even to die in your fire.

Scipio Slataper (1888–1915)

Politics was another form in which the transformation of the world presented itself to the generations of 1914. Ruling élites were everywhere under pressure to open the political system to groups who had formerly been excluded from political participation. Where universal male suffrage did not exist – and that was in the great majority of European countries – it was demanded. Where it did exist or had nearly been realized, an increasing number of voices insisted that it be extended to women. Patterns of deference by the lower to the higher orders of society, long taken for granted as being in the nature of things, and sanctified by tradition, were called into question, or ignored. Workers struck against their employers; peasants offered resistance to their lords; artisans organized against the banks and the 'interests'. The cry for revolution, variously interpreted, was heard all over Europe. In short, it was an unsettling time for those with a vested interest in the status quo.

Socialism was the great movement of the day. Socialist parties mobilized workers, summoned them to demonstrations, organized their strikes, instructed them in national and international politics and, where the suffrage was sufficiently broad, appealed to them for their votes. Of these organizations, by far the strongest, richest and most numerous was the German Social Democratic Party. Other socialist parties could hope to become, as the German party had, the most formidable parliamentary force in their land. Most pursued, as the Germans did, a policy of revolutionary reformism: that is, they assumed that the struggle for political and economic reform would one day bring about a revolutionary transformation of society. What that transformation would consist of, they seldom bothered to define.

Such a vision, especially when articulated by someone like the great French socialist and spellbinding orator Jean Jaurès (1859–1914), could appear extraordinarily attractive. But during the decade preceding 1914, socialism lost much of its power to excite intellectual youth. There were several reasons for this. The entry of socialist parties into the rough and tumble of democratic politics, where they had that option, tarnished their revolutionary image. To cite Péguy and twist (but not distort) his famous phrase, the *mystique* of socialism had turned to *politique*. Socialism was no longer a religion; for many, it had become a career. Moreover, the kind of

Jean Jaurès, the socialist orator who was assassinated on 31 July 1914.

parliamentary and reformist *politique* that socialists pursued lacked appeal for young people drawn towards modernist and avant-garde culture. The revolution they yearned after had nothing to do with votes, hours and wages or literacy rates: it was moral and internal. A revolution of the spirit, like the one that Nietzsche had preached, and one not attainable by the masses. It is revealing, I think, that few of the figures commemorated in this volume took up the socialist cause; and those who did, such as Rupert Brooke, often interpreted socialism in a highly personal manner that had little to do with the day-to-day struggle of socialist parties.

The nation was another matter. Europe, during the years before the war, was still composed primarily of multinational states. The Russian empire, the Austro-Hungarian empire, the German empire, even the United Kingdom and Spain, all brought together peoples of different racial backgrounds, languages, religions and historical experiences. One of the legacies of the 19th century had been the belief that every ethnic group that desired independence and possessed a language should have its own state. This belief was all the more deeply held in those regions of Europe, like Ireland, Bosnia, Catalonia, Finland, Poland, where the inhabitants felt that they were being exploited by the nationality that controlled the central government. The perception of exploitation could arise from contemporary political, economic, educational or religious policies aimed at creating a more centralized and homogeneous state, but this perception was almost always exacerbated by bitter historical memories of oppression, thus rendering it all the more potentially explosive.

Towards the end of the 19th century, nationalist movements arose to lead the struggle for independence and a separate cultural and political identity among those European peoples who had not, like the Italians and the Germans, recently succeeded in creating unified national states. At the same time, 'nationalist' parties emerged dedicated to maintaining the integrity of the nation and safeguarding it against its internal and external enemies. Both xenophobic and anti-democratic, the leaders of these parties did not hesitate to proclaim that the health of the nation might have to be achieved through war.

Socialist doctrine declared that class struggles must take precedence over all other conflicts. The Second International, which united in a single organization the world's most important socialist parties, was founded on that belief. 'Workers of the world unite and turn your wrath against your upper-class exploiters,' socialist leaders admonished their supporters. But the same socialists who gave voice to these internationalist slogans often expressed doubts about this aspect of their official programme; and intellectuals from the generations of 1914 certainly showed themselves susceptible to patriotic feelings and the appeal of nationalist parties.

Whether they were drawn towards parties of national independence or parties of national revival and national defence depended upon the country in which they lived. But nationalism would probably never again exert a stronger pull in Europe than it did on men born between 1880 and 1895. It was a Bosnian nationalist Gavrilo Princip (1894–1918) who assassinated the Archduke Ferdinand of Austria in Sarajevo on 28 June 1914, thus putting into motion the process that led to the outbreak of a general European and later world war; and many writers from the generations of 1914 began their careers, as did the Italian Scipio Slataper (1888–1915) and the Serbian Milutin Bojić (1892–1917) with books or poems evoking the uniqueness of their land and their people. Those, like Gustav Sack (1885–1916), author of *The Objector*, who felt no allegiance to the nation and who were willing to let it 'go to the dogs', were the exceptions.

Attitudes Towards War

For when all's said and done, every Frenchman will do his duty in time of war. I mean every *Frenchman – even those who claim at present that they won't, who may in the event prove more zealous than anyone else.*

Ernest Psichari (1883–1914)

Whatever their sympathy for the underprivileged members of society or the cause of the nation, most members of the generations of 1914 (including the writers commemorated in this volume) felt no compulsion to join a political party during the years preceding the outbreak of the war. They felt free to devote themselves to the exploration of their homelands and the stimulation of foreign travel; to the plumbing of their psyches and the plotting of their sexual identities; to the discovery of the new literature and the cultivation of their talent; or, as in the case of that fascinating figure Ernest Psichari, to a revaluation of old and discredited institutions such as the army and the Church. In most European countries, politics was still a pursuit that could be safely left by intellectuals to politicians. The revolution that mattered was the one taking place in culture – in literature, music and art.

But there was one public issue that could not so easily be avoided; and that was the possibility of a general European war. Most of the writers in this anthology had done their military service sometime between 1900 and 1914. Some were reserve officers, and proud of it. Whatever their rank, they had been trained to defend their countries, and they knew that one day they might be asked to risk and perhaps give up their lives in war. Most of them accepted the idea of this sacrifice and considered it necessary, just, even noble, though the vast majority of them came from middle-class families not noted for their military traditions or, as in Psichari's case, from one associated with opposition to the army and assumed to be of pacifist inclinations. Like the German student of law, Franz Blumenfeld (1891–1914), they were ready to give their lives, 'gladly and willingly'.

To be sure, war, though said to be inevitable, appeared unlikely. It was in the shadow of this paradox that the majority of young European men lived during the decade before 1914. Their insouciance seemed justified: repeatedly, between 1905 and 1914, serious crises between the major powers had been resolved without armed conflict. The wars that Europeans fought during these years occurred on the periphery of Europe – in the Balkans – or in the colonial world. There was no compelling reason to suppose that this would not continue to be the case. This helps to explain why war, when it came, though long predicted, was experienced as a surprise, a bolt from the blue of one of Europe's most beautiful and cloudless summers.

It was also true that the war these men imagined and accepted was not the war they were going to fight. Most European wars since the middle of the 19th century had been short and – in the collective memory of the period – progressive in their effects. The Crimean War of 1853–6 had resulted in the containment of reactionary Russia. The Franco-Austrian War of 1859 had made possible the unification of Italy. Bismarck's wars against Austria and France between 1866 and 1871 had left as their legacy a unified German state. Even the Russo-Japanese War of 1904–5 had forced the Tsar to grant his people a parliament. Why not assume, as many people did, that another European war would round off the uncompleted democratic and national agenda of the 19th century? Moreover, prestigious men of letters had argued convincingly that a long, destructive war would be incompatible with the type of advanced industrial economy that prevailed in the major European countries after 1900. Even military planners assumed that war, if and when it came, would be decided rapidly, with a single knockout blow. They had made no preparations for the long war of attrition they would be compelled to fight.

Few young men of military age would have given much thought to such considerations. They might instead imagine war in terms of a great adventure, a test of manhood, an opportunity to demonstrate their love of country – or perhaps, in some cases, a chance to use the new technology that writers such as the Frenchman Émile Driant (1855–1916) had described in novels aimed at boys and young men. Such motivations were not limited to pre-war European youth. But there was among some young people of the period a mood or cluster of feelings that was peculiar to the generations of 1914: a strange and sinister belief that war might save Europe from decadence and revitalize its flagging creative energies. Such an idea seems strange to us; but it followed logically from one of the premisses of much European avant-garde culture: if bourgeois civilization were moribund and yet at the same time resistant to its own transformation or demise, was it not reasonable to think that war might accomplish what revolutionary politics, of both the right and left varieties, had failed to achieve? War could be conceived as a rite of purification that would complete the demolition of the Old and open the way for the breakthrough to the New. 'We want to glorify war – the world's only hygiene – militarism, patriotism, the anarchists' destructive gesture, the beautiful idea for which one dies . . . ' Marinetti wrote in his first Futurist manifesto of 1909. This confused jumble of nationalist and anarchist ideas expressed the apolcalyptic mood of feverish expectation that possessed the minds of many young Europeans during the years before 1914. The odour of death was in the air, and many proponents of the new culture sometimes seemed to have a morbid fascination with the prospect of Armageddon.

Attitudes like these were, of course, confined to intellectuals and artists; they scarcely touched the masses. Nor is there any evidence that they played a role in the chain of events that brought about the war. But they were strongly felt within an élite of the sort that is represented in this book, and they help us to understand the immediate cultural response to the war. The idea that war could purify and elevate European civilization would die hard; and it sustained many intellectuals who continued to nourish visions of cultural revival during the worst moments of the conflict.

As the final crisis developed in July 1914, and as the possibility and then the likelihood of war became apparent, attitudes towards war seem to have differed from one country to another. In France, the mood was one of relief, resignation and grim determination. In Germany, feelings of exhilaration, release and the fulfilment of destiny were often expressed. In Britain, long-building sentiments of hostility against German ambitions and aggressiveness quickly multiplied and mutated overnight into moral outrage. On the periphery of Europe, inhabitants of the smaller nations watched the conflict grow and reflected on their own impotence to influence the unfolding of events that would determine their future. Eventually, all but a handful of European nations would be drawn into the conflict; and even those that were not, like Spain and Sweden, would experience the reverberations of the war's events.

It is also likely that attitudes towards the coming war differed considerably among the highly differentiated classes of 1914 Europe. It may be that enthusiasm for war was greater within the middle classes, the social stratum from which almost all the writers represented in this volume came. This is what F. Scott Fitzgerald believed and what he tried to express in his novel *Tender is the Night*, published in 1934:

> This western-front business couldn't be done again, not for a long time . . . This took religion and years of plenty and tremendous sureties and the exact relation that existed between the classes . . . You had to have a whole-souled sentimental equipment going back further than you could remember. You had to remember Christmas, and postcards of the Crown Prince and his fiancée, and little cafés in Valence and beer gardens in Unter den Linden and weddings at the *mairie*, and going to the Derby, and your grandfather's whiskers . . . Why, this was a love battle – there was a century of middle-class love spent here.

Whether the war can be linked in some way to the history and 'sentimental equipment' of Europe's middle classes is – and may forever remain – speculation. But it is illuminating to think of the war in its early stages in terms of the release of highly charged emotions and erotic energies. Despite the radical differences separating Europeans of different classes, the initial effect of the war was to unite them. Indeed, this may have been one of the secret attractions that the war had and may explain the outburst of belligerent enthusiasm in countries that, before August 1914, had been deeply divided internally over issues of foreign affairs. 'But let us go forward!' Renato Serra (1884–1915) wrote in what is one of the most probing and honest of self-examinations carried out by members of the generations of 1914 before going to war.

> Behind me, those that follow are all brothers, even if I do not see them or know them well . . . After the first miles of our marching, all differences will have fallen drop by drop like the sweat from our downward-cast faces . . . There is no time for remembering the past or for thinking a great deal when we are moving shoulder to shoulder, and there are so many things to be done, or rather, one thing only between us all.

In any case, the generations of 1914 responded to the outbreak of war with genuine enthusiasm. Many volunteered for service before they were called; and some of Europe's most promising writers had died before the end of the year. Nor did the horror of the war, once it was revealed, diminish their zeal to participate. Even after the scale of the slaughter was known, many chose to share the fate of the combatants, knowing it was likely that they themselves would die. Why did they go? Did they know? Some, among them the Irishman Thomas Kettle (1880–1916), thought they did.

> Know that we fools, now with the foolish dead,
> Died not for flag, nor King, nor Emperor.
> But for a dream, born in a herdsman's shed,
> And for the secret Scripture of the poor.

But the great majority went because they believed that it was right and just, because the others had gone, and because they felt it was their destiny.

ROBERT WOHL

The Hood Battalion at Blandford Camp before departure to Gallipoli, April 1915. The poet Rupert Brooke is standing second from left in the second row; third and fourth along are the composers W. Denis Browne (1888-1915) and F.S. Kelly (1880-1916). The Battalion also contained the scholars Patrick Shaw Stewart (1888-1917) and Charles Lister (1887-1915).

Imperial War Museum, London

*H*ECTOR *H*UGH *M*UNRO '*S*AKI' 1870–1916

'It seems almost too good to be true that I am going to take an active part in a big European war.'
Letter to his sister Ethel, 7 November 1915

Hector Hugh Munro has always been better known as 'Saki', the pen-name he adopted in 1900 for his first satires. The name apparently derived from Fitzgerald's translation of the *Rubáiyát*, in which Saki is the impressive 'Cypress-slender Minister of Wine' at life's garden party. The young men in Munro's stories certainly know how to liven up a party, often in alarmingly unexpected ways. Like Saki-Munro himself, they are handsome, immaculately dressed story-tellers with a taste for practical jokes. When a Clovis or a Reginald arrives, the foundations of polite society seem suddenly frail: at any moment, a revolution might break out, or the bishop might decide to massacre the local Jews. Reginald talks of writing a drama in which the sound of wolves would be 'a sort of elusive undercurrent in the background that would never be satisfactorily explained'. Clovis introduces a wolf into a dinner party. In 'Gabriel–Ernest' (1909), one of the earliest stories to show Munro's full originality, the beautiful youth is more subversive still, turning up naked in a respectable drawing-room and actually becoming a wolf at sundown. When Munro was in the trenches in 1916, he thought of living in Siberia, wolf-country, after the war; he had never felt entirely at home in the England he had satirized.

Animals, especially dangerous ones, often figured in his life and then in his writing. He was born on 18 December 1870 in Burma, where his father held a senior post in the police. His mother took her three children home to the safety of Devon, where she died in 1872 after a cow charged at her. The children were brought up thereafter by two disagreeable aunts, on whom Munro seems to take vengeance in some of his best stories. In 'The Story-Teller' (1913), a bachelor – who might be the adult Munro – humiliates an aunt by telling the three children in her charge about a little girl who was so good that she was eaten by a wolf. In 'Sredni Vashtar', sometimes said to be Munro's masterpiece, the sickly orphan Conradin seems to be a portrait of his author's young self, silently enduring a guardian's cruelty.

> Mrs De Ropp would never, in her honestest moments, have confessed to herself that she disliked Conradin, though she might have been dimly aware that thwarting him 'for his good' was a duty which she did not find particularly irksome. Conradin hated her with a desperate sincerity which he was perfectly able to mask.

H.H. Munro photographed by E.O. Hoppé.
The Mansell Collection, London

The boy keeps a caged but murderous ferret: 'And one day, out of Heaven knows what material, he spun the beast a wonderful name, and from that moment it grew into a god and a religion.' When Mrs De Ropp investigates the cage, Sredni Vashtar answers his worshipper's one prayer. Like Conradin, Munro was a spinner of names as well as a pagan. In his stories, the peace of the countryside (always lushly Devonian) is an illusion through which sudden violence may crash like a maddened stag. It is characteristic of him that one of his very few descriptions of the Western Front should be about bird-life under shell-fire.

He was slow to discover his creative talent. His father returned from the East, freeing the children from their torment and taking them travelling in Europe for several years. Munro was persuaded to join the Burma police, but fever soon sent him home again. He decided to become a writer in London, first attempting history and then journalism, but he did not make his mark until 1900, when he began a series of topical satires for the *Westminster Gazette*. Each piece parodied a scene from Lewis Carroll as, for example, in 'Alice Has Tea at the Hotel Cecil' (November 1901). The Conservative government was sometimes referred to as the Hotel Cecil because it contained several allegedly idle members of the Cecil family, including the Prime Minister, Lord Salisbury (the Dormouse), and the Leader of the Commons, A. J. Balfour (the March Hare). The Mad Hatter represents the Secretary of State for the Colonies, Joseph Chamberlain. The Boer War is dragging on and Irish MPs are causing trouble in the House. Munro attacks the government for doing nothing, a common complaint against administrations in the pre-war period. While the *Alice* versions were still appearing, Munro started writing comic sketches for the *Westminster* about an exquisite young man called Reginald. 'Saki' had found his medium.

Munro was too restless to settle down at once to story-writing. Little is known about his personal life, but his dapper appearance concealed a man at odds with social convention. His politics were always strongly Tory, patriotic and spartan, unsympathetic to the mild Conservatism of the day. Christianity struck him as absurd. He was homosexual, apparently from his teens; discretion in such matters was essential, but taking risks was part of the game. The homosexual implications in many of his stories would have passed unnoticed by most readers; to those who shared his tastes and were in the know, that may have seemed the funniest of all his practical jokes. His stories are rarely kind to women, although a few of his best narrators are female; his opinion of suffragettes may be guessed at from 'The Gala Programme' and the less ferocious 'Hermann the Irascible'. His affairs with men seem to have been numerous but short-lived. Perhaps there were rumours about him; at any rate, he seems never to have been much more than a guest on the fringes of the society which he mocked.

In 1902, he went on his travels again, this time as correspondent for the *Morning Post* in the Balkans, St Petersburg and elsewhere. He reported on Bulgarian resistance to Turkish rule and witnessed the 1905 massacre in St Petersburg, condemning absolutist repression but not losing his belief in firm government. It was not until 1909 that he finally settled in London. Nearly all the work on which his reputation rests appeared in the Tory press during the next few years.

Munro's best stories were brilliantly original without being innovative. Other short-story writers of the period included James Joyce and D. H. Lawrence, but he took no notice of new movements in the arts except to satirize them occasionally. Perhaps the only contemporary author to influence him was Kipling. His own influence has been mainly on other comic writers, such as A. A. Milne and Noel Coward, and his admirers have always regarded themselves as a select band of connoisseurs. His settings remained Edwardian, his style was unashamedly derived from Oscar Wilde, and his delight in reflecting life in reverse was learned from Lewis Carroll. When the odious Tarrington claims to have met Clovis at luncheon with his aunt, the reply comes from looking-glass land with Wilde's quickness of repartee:

> 'My aunt never lunches,' said Clovis; 'she belongs to the National Anti-Luncheon League, which is doing quite a lot of good work in a quiet, unobtrusive way. A subscription of half a crown per quarter entitles you to go without ninety-two luncheons.'
>
> 'This must be something new,' exclaimed Tarrington.
>
> 'It's the same aunt that I've always had,' said Clovis coldly.

Munro's methods are simple: characterization by means of a name and a few deft phrases ('Constance Broddle . . . one of those strapping florid girls that go so well with autumn scenery or Christmas decorations in church'); bizarre comparisons ('a family whose individual members went through life . . . with as much tact and consideration as a cactus-hedge might show in going through a crowded bathing-tent'); reversals of normality, followed through with merciless logic and often accompanied by, as it were, the sound of wolves (a leopard in the spare bedroom, or an assassination squad of Boy Scouts in the shrubbery, preferably to the discomfiture of a clergyman). Names are important: Clovis Sangrail, Bertie van Tahn ('so depraved at seventeen that he had long ago given up trying to be any worse'), the Grobmayer child ('It certainly *looked* very like a pig'), Septimus Brope ('I believe he comes from Leighton Buzzard'), Morlvera (for an evil-looking doll), Filboid Studge (for a breakfast cereal which sells in huge quantities, thanks to its name and posters of celebrities in hell above the slogan 'They cannot buy it now'). The compression imposed by a newspaper column was invaluable, demanding a ruthless economy of words which matched the ruthlessness of Munro's humour. When he wrote at greater length, the lack of feeling which is so entertaining in the stories was exposed as a genuine deficiency. He was a master of the very short narrative.

His two novels are inferior work but not without interest. Comus Bassington, the hero of *The Unbearable Bassington* (1912), is another Pan-like youth, green-eyed and untameable, but he is not the triumphant figure of the stories. As A. J. Langguth suggests, the final description of Comus in colonial exile may be the nearest Munro ever came to a self-estimate, a confession of longing for the mother and family life he had never known:

> . . . he was the outsider, the lonely alien, watching something in which he could not join, a happiness in which he had no part or lot. He would pass presently out of the village and his bearers' feet would leave their indentations in the dust: that would be his most permanent memorial in this little oasis of teeming life. And that other life, in which he once moved with such confident sense of his own necessary participation in it, how completely he had passed out of it! Amid all its laughing throngs, its card-parties and race-meetings and country-house gatherings, he

'The martial trappings, the swaggering joy of life, the comradeship of camp and barracks, the hard discipline of drill yard and fatigue duty, the long sentry watches, the trench digging, forced marches, wounds, cold, hunger, makeshift hospitals, and the blood-wet laurels – these were not for them. Such things they might only guess at, or see on a cinema film, darkly; they belonged to the civilian nation.'
From When William Came

> was just a mere name, remembered or forgotten . . . He had loved himself very well and never troubled greatly whether anyone else really loved him, and now he realized what he had made of his life. And at the same time he knew that if his chance were to come again he would throw it away just as surely, just as perversely. Fate played with him with loaded dice; he would lose always.

Munro's sense of alienation finds more general expression in *When William Came* (1913), one of the last of many invasion novels in the pre-war period. The book was warmly approved by Lord Roberts, who had been campaigning for years in favour of conscription and strong defences against Germany. In Munro's version of what would happen when Kaiser William came, Britain's inadequate forces have already suffered swift defeat and now, without any pressure from the conquerors, London society is beginning to acquiesce in the *fait accompli*. It is soon obvious that some of his earlier humour had been based on prejudices as popular then as they are unattractive now. The foreign names and references to Jews in his stories, for example, become an open statement that London's Englishness has been undermined by the international character of modern art and by the presence of foreigners, especially cosmopolitan German-Jews. The final humiliation comes in an Imperial decree, which is expected to impose military service; in a twist typical of Saki, Berlin forbids the British to be armed at all, politely drawing attention to their dislike of military preparations before the war. Henceforth Britain will be the 'civilian nation' in the German Empire, working to earn the wealth needed for Imperial defence.

Munro heard Sir Edward Grey's famous speech in the House of Commons on 3 August 1914. Like most people, he was relieved that the government had decided not to tolerate the invasion of Belgium. Although he was over-age, with a history of serious illness, he enlisted in the ranks on 25 August, refusing all offers of a commission. By the autumn, he was in training with the 22nd Battalion, Royal Fusiliers, taking stern pleasure in the rigours of army life. He continued to write articles, some of them harshly critical of pacifists, businessmen, shirkers and the ' "Boys of the Lap-dog Breed" '. His biographer regards this as a betrayal of his earlier self, but the pre-war stories had never shown respect for such people. Clovis – and Conradin, had he been old enough – would surely have enlisted, and Comus would have redeemed himself on the battlefield; it is the feebler characters, such as Van Cheele, who would have stayed at home.

Munro was sent to France in November 1915. He seems not to have been disheartened by the trenches. Patrolling no man's land at night reminded him of games when he and his niece 'were wolves and used to go prowling after fat farmers' wives'. After nearly a year in the war zone, with one short break in England, he fell ill with malaria. The safety of a hospital bed induced the guilt often felt by soldiers under such circumstances when their comrades were still in the line. Hearing that a 'show' was expected, Munro discharged himself on 11 November and returned to the trenches. The 22nd was among the many units being briefed for an assault in the northern Somme sector, where Beaumont Hamel and other strongholds had been resisting capture ever since the great offensive in July. The Battle of the Ancre began at dawn on 13 November. Men advanced through mud, often sinking to their waists. Talking and smoking were forbidden. The ground was littered with rotting corpses, still unburied after the wasted carnage of July. Some lessons had been learned from that disaster; this time, Beaumont Hamel fell and the line was pushed beyond it. The 22nd went into action during the afternoon. Early next morning, they went forward again, in a chill fog. During a brief rest, a man absent-mindedly lit a cigarette, a mark for a sniper. Lance-Sergeant Munro's last words were 'Put that bloody cigarette out.' The Battalion gained its objective and was back in billets two days later.

DOMINIC HIBBERD

Texts
The Complete Works of Saki (Bodley Head, London, 1980).

Secondary sources
A. J. Langguth, *SAKI: a life of Hector Hugh Munro* (Hamish Hamilton, London, 1981). The fullest available biography of Saki. Contains six short stories never before collected.

Alice has Tea at the Hotel Cecil

The March Hare and the Dormouse and the Hatter were seated at a very neglected-looking tea-table; they were evidently in agonized consideration of something – even the Dormouse, which was asleep, had a note of interrogation in its tail.

'No room!' they shouted, as soon as they caught sight of Alice.

'There's lots of room for improvement,' said Alice, as she sat down.

'You've got no business to be here,' said the March Hare.

'And if you had any business you wouldn't be here, you know,' said the Hatter; 'I hope you don't suppose this is a business gathering. What will you have to eat?' he continued.

Alice looked at a long list of dishes with promising names, but nearly all of them seemed to be crossed off.

'That list was made nearly seven years ago, you know,' said the March Hare, in explanation.

'But you can always have patience,' said the Hatter. 'You begin with patience and we do the rest.' And he leaned back and seemed prepared to do a lot of rest.

'Your manners want mending,' said the March Hare suddenly to Alice.

'They don't,' she replied indignantly.

'It's very rude to contradict,' said the Hatter; 'you would like to hear me sing something.'

Alice felt that it would be unwise to contradict again, so she said nothing, and the Hatter began:

Dwindle, dwindle, little war,
How I wonder more and more,
As about the veldt you hop
When you really mean to stop.

'Talking about stopping,' interrupted the March Hare anxiously, 'I wonder how my timepiece is behaving.'

He took out of his pocket a large chronometer of complicated workmanship, and mournfully regarded it.

'It's dreadfully behind the times,' he said, giving it an experimental shake. 'I would take it to pieces at once if I was at all sure of getting the bits back in their right places.'

'What is the matter with it?' asked Alice.

'The wheels seem to get stuck,' said the March Hare. 'There is too much Irish butter in the works.'

'Ruins the thing from a dramatic point of view,' said the Hatter; 'too many scenes, too few acts.'

'The result is we never have time to get through the day's work. It's never even time for a free breakfast-table; we do what we can for education at odd moments, but we shall all die of old age before we have a moment to spare for social duties.'

'You might lose a lot if you run your business in that way,' said Alice.

'Not in this country,' said the March Hare. 'You see, we have a Commission on everything that we don't do.'

'The Dormouse must tell us a story,' said the Hatter, giving it a sharp pinch.

The Dormouse awoke with a start, and began as though it had been awake all the time: 'There was an old woman who lived in a shoe –'

'I know,' said Alice, 'she had so many children that she didn't know what to do.'

'Nothing of the sort,' said the Dormouse, 'you lack the gift of imagination. She put most of them into Treasuries and Foreign Offices and Boards of Trade, and all sorts of unlikely places where they could learn things.'

'What did they learn?' asked Alice.

'Painting in glowing colours, and attrition, and terminology (that's the science of knowing when things are over), and iteration (that's the same thing over again), and drawing –'

'What did they draw?'

'Salaries. And then there were classes for foreign languages. And such language!' (Here the March Hare and the Hatter shut their eyes and took a big gulp from their tea-cups.) 'However, I don't think anybody attended to them.'

The Dormouse broke off into a chuckle which ended in a snore, and as no one seemed inclined to wake it up again Alice thought she might as well be going.

When she looked back the Hatter and the March Hare were trying to stiffen the Dormouse out into the attitude of a lion guardant. 'But it will never pass for anything but a Dormouse if it will snore so,' she remarked to herself.

' "You've told me stories about grand-dukes and lion-tamers and financiers' widows and a postmaster in Herzegovina," said the Baroness, "and about an Italian jockey and an amateur governess who went to Warsaw, and several about your mother, but certainly never anything about a saint." '

'The Story of St Vespaluus'

The Story-Teller

It was a hot afternoon, and the railway carriage was correspondingly sultry, and the next stop was at Templecombe, nearly an hour ahead. The occupants of the carriage were a small girl, and a smaller girl, and a small boy. An aunt belonging to the children occupied one corner seat, and the further corner seat on the opposite side was occupied by a bachelor who was a stranger to their party, but the small girls and the small boy emphatically occupied the compartment. Both the aunt and the children were conversational in a limited, persistent way, reminding one of the attentions of a housefly that refused to be discouraged. Most of the aunt's remarks seemed to begin with 'Don't,' and nearly all of the children's remarks began with 'Why?' The bachelor said nothing out loud.

'Don't, Cyril, don't,' exclaimed the aunt, as the small boy began smacking the cushions of the seat, producing a cloud of dust at each blow.

'Come and look out of the window,' she added.

The child moved reluctantly to the window. 'Why are those sheep being driven out of that field?' he asked.

'I expect they are being driven to another field where there is more grass,' said the aunt weakly.

'But there is lots of grass in that field,' protested the boy; 'there's nothing else but grass there. Aunt, there's lots of grass in that field.'

'Perhaps the grass in the other field is better,' suggested the aunt fatuously.

'Why is it better?' came the swift, inevitable question.

'Oh, look at those cows!' exclaimed the aunt. Nearly every field along the line had contained cows or bullocks, but she spoke as though she were drawing attention to a rarity.

'Why is the grass in the other field better?' persisted Cyril.

The frown on the bachelor's face was deepening to a scowl. He was a hard, unsympathetic man, the aunt decided in her mind. She was utterly unable to come to any satisfactory decision about the grass in the other field.

The smaller girl created a diversion by beginning to recite 'On the Road to Mandalay'. She only knew the first line, but she put her limited knowledge to the fullest possible use. She repeated the line over and over again in a dreamy but resolute and very audible voice; it seemed to the bachelor as though someone had had a bet with her that she could not repeat the line aloud two thousand times without stopping. Whoever it was who had made the wager was likely to lose his bet.

'Come over here and listen to a story,' said the aunt, when the bachelor had looked twice at her and once at the communication cord.

The children moved listlessly towards the aunt's end of the carriage. Evidently her reputation as a story-teller did not rank high in their estimation.

In a low, confidential voice, interrupted at frequent intervals by loud, petulant questions from her listeners, she began an unenterprising and deplorably uninteresting story about a little girl who was good, and made friends with everyone on account of her goodness, and was finally saved from a mad bull by a number of rescuers who admired her moral character.

'Wouldn't they have saved her if she hadn't been good?' demanded the bigger of the small girls. It was exactly the question that the bachelor had wanted to ask.

'Well, yes,' admitted the aunt lamely, 'but I don't think they would have run quite so fast to her help if they had not liked her so much.'

'It's the stupidest story I've ever heard,' said the bigger of the small girls, with immense conviction.

'I didn't listen after the first bit, it was so stupid,' said Cyril.

The smaller girl made no actual comment on the story, but she had long ago recommenced a murmured repetition of her favourite line.

'You don't seem to be a success as a story-teller,' said the bachelor suddenly from his corner.

The aunt bristled in instant defence at this unexpected attack.

'It's a very difficult thing to tell stories that children can both understand and appreciate,' she said stiffly.

'I don't agree with you,' said the bachelor.

'Perhaps *you* would like to tell them a story,' was the aunt's retort.

'Tell us a story,' demanded the bigger of the small girls.

'Once upon a time,' began the bachelor, 'there was a little girl called Bertha, who was extraordinarily good.'

The children's momentarily aroused interest began at once to flicker; all stories seemed dreadfully alike, no matter who told them.

'She did all that she was told, she was always truthful, she kept her clothes clean, ate milk puddings as though they were jam tarts, learned her lessons perfectly, and was polite in her manners.'

'Was she pretty?' asked the bigger of the small girls.

'Not as pretty as any of you,' said the bachelor, 'but she was horribly good.'

There was a wave of reaction in favour of the story; the word horrible in connection with goodness was a novelty that commended itself. It seemed to introduce a ring of truth that was absent from the aunt's tales of infant life.

'She was so good,' continued the bachelor, 'that she won several medals for goodness, which she always wore, pinned on to her dress. There was a medal for obedience, another medal for punctuality, and a third for good behaviour. They were large metal medals and they clicked against one another as she walked. No other child in the town where she lived had as many as three medals, so everybody knew that she must be an extra good child.'

'Horribly good,' quoted Cyril.

'Everybody talked about her goodness, and the Prince of the country got to hear about it, and he said that as she was so very good she might be allowed once a week to walk in his park, which was just outside the town. It was a beautiful park, and no children were ever allowed in it, so it was a great honour for Bertha to be allowed to go there.'

'Were there any sheep in the park?' demanded Cyril.

'No,' said the bachelor, 'there were no sheep.'

'Why weren't there any sheep?' came the inevitable question arising out of that answer.

The aunt permitted herself a smile, which might almost have been described as a grin.

'There were no sheep in the park,' said the bachelor, 'because the Prince's mother had once had a dream that her son would either be killed by a sheep or else by a clock falling on him. For that reason the Prince never kept a sheep in his park or a clock in his palace.'

The aunt suppressed a gasp of admiration.

'Was the Prince killed by a sheep or by a clock?' asked Cyril.

'He is still alive, so we can't tell whether the dream will come true,' said the bachelor unconcernedly; 'anyway, there were no sheep in the park, but there were lots of little pigs running all over the place.'

'What colour were they?'

'Black with white faces, white with black spots, black all over, grey with white patches, and some were white all over.'

The story-teller paused to let a full idea of the park's treasures sink into the children's imaginations; then he resumed:

'Bertha was rather sorry to find that there were no flowers in the park. She had promised her aunts, with tears in her eyes, that she would not pick any of the kind Prince's flowers, and she had meant to keep her promise, so of course it made her feel silly to find that there were no flowers to pick.'

'Why weren't there any flowers?'

'Because the pigs had eaten them all,' said the bachelor promptly. 'The gardeners had told the Prince that you couldn't have pigs and flowers, so he decided to have pigs and no flowers.'

There was a murmur of approval at the excellence of the Prince's decision; so many people would have decided the other way.

'There were lots of other delightful things in the park. There were ponds with gold and blue and green fish in them, and trees with beautiful parrots that said clever things at a moment's notice, and humming birds that hummed all the popular tunes of the day. Bertha walked up and down and enjoyed herself immensely, and thought to herself: "If I were not so extraordinarily good I should not have been allowed to come into this beautiful park and enjoy all that there is to be seen in it," and her three medals clinked against one another as she walked and helped to remind her how very good she really was. Just then an enormous wolf came prowling into the park to see if it could catch a fat little pig for its supper.'

'What colour was it?' asked the children, amid an immediate quickening of interest.

'Mud-colour all over, with a black tongue and pale grey eyes that gleamed with unspeakable ferocity. The first thing that it saw in the park was Bertha; her pinafore was so spotlessly white and clean that it could be seen from a great distance. Bertha saw the wolf and saw that it was stealing towards her, and she began to wish that she had never been allowed to come into the park. She ran as hard as she could, and the wolf came after her with huge leaps and bounds. She managed to reach a shrubbery of myrtle bushes and she hid herself in one of the thickest of the bushes. The wolf came sniffing among the branches, its black tongue lolling out of its mouth and its pale grey eyes glaring with rage. Bertha was terribly frightened, and thought to herself: "If I had not been so extraordinarily good I should have been safe in the town at this moment." However, the scent of the myrtle was so strong that the wolf could not sniff out where Bertha was hiding, and the bushes were so thick that he might have hunted about in them for a long time without catching sight of her, so he thought he might as well go off and catch a little pig instead. Bertha was trembling very much at having the wolf prowling and sniffing so near her, and as she trembled the medal for obedience clinked against the medals for good conduct and punctuality. The wolf was just moving away when he heard the sound of the medals clinking and stopped to listen; they clinked again in a bush quite near him. He dashed into the bush, his pale grey eyes gleaming with ferocity and triumph, and dragged Bertha out and devoured her to the last morsel. All that was left of her were her shoes, bits of clothing, and the three medals for goodness.'

'Were any of the little pigs killed?'

'No, they all escaped.'

'The story began badly,' said the smaller of the small girls, 'but it had a beautiful ending.'

'It is the most beautiful story that I ever heard,' said the bigger of the small girls, with immense decision.

'It is the *only* beautiful story I have ever heard,' said Cyril.

A dissentient opinion came from the aunt.

'A most improper story to tell young children! You have undermined the effect of years of careful teaching.'

'At any rate,' said the bachelor, collecting his belongings preparatory to leaving the carriage, 'I kept them quiet for ten minutes, which was more than you were able to do.'

'Unhappy woman!' he observed to himself as he walked down the platform of Templecombe station; 'for the next six months or so those children will assail her in public with demands for an improper story!'

Gabriel-Ernest

'There is a wild beast in your woods,' said the artist Cunningham, as he was being driven to the station. It was the only remark he had made during the drive, but as Van Cheele had talked incessantly his companion's silence had not been noticeable.

'A stray fox or two and some resident weasels. Nothing more formidable,' said Van Cheele. The artist said nothing.

'What did you mean about a wild beast?' said Van Cheele later, when they were on the platform.

'Nothing. My imagination. Here is the train,' said Cunningham.

That afternoon Van Cheele went for one of his frequent rambles through his woodland property. He had a stuffed bittern in his study, and knew the names of quite a number of wild flowers, so his aunt had possibly some justification in describing him as a great naturalist. At any rate, he was a great walker. It was his custom to take mental notes of everything he saw during his walks, not so much for the purpose of assisting contemporary science as to provide topics for conversation afterwards. When the bluebells began to show themselves in flower he made a point of informing everyone of the fact; the season of the year might have warned his hearers of the likelihood of such an occurrence, but at least they felt that he was being absolutely frank with them.

What Van Cheele saw on this particular afternoon was, however, something far removed from his ordinary range of experience. On a shelf of smooth stone overhanging a deep pool in the hollow of an oak coppice a boy of about sixteen lay asprawl, drying his wet brown limbs luxuriously in the sun. His wet hair, parted by a recent dive, lay close to his head, and his light-brown eyes, so light that there was an almost tigerish gleam in them, were turned towards Van Cheele with a certain lazy watchfulness. It was an unexpected apparition, and Van Cheele found himself engaged in the novel process of thinking before he spoke. Where on earth could this wild-looking boy hail from? The miller's wife had lost a child some two months ago, supposed to have been swept away by the mill-race, but that had been a mere baby, not a half-grown lad.

'What are you doing there?' he demanded.

'Obviously, sunning myself,' replied the boy.

'Where do you live?'

'Here, in these woods.'

'You can't live in the woods,' said Van Cheele.

'They are very nice woods,' said the boy, with a touch of patronage in his voice.

'But where do you sleep at night?'

'I don't sleep at night; that's my busiest time.'

Van Cheele began to have an irritated feeling that he was grappling with a problem that was eluding him.

'What do you feed on?' he asked.

'Flesh,' said the boy, and he pronounced the word with slow relish, as though he were tasting it.

'Flesh! What flesh?'

'Since it interests you, rabbits, wild-fowl, hares, poultry, lambs in their season, children when I can get any; they're usually too well locked in at night, when I do most of my hunting. It's quite two months since I tasted child-flesh.'

Ignoring the chaffing nature of the last remark Van Cheele tried to draw the boy on the subject of possible poaching operations.

'You're talking rather through your hat when you speak of feeding on hares.' (Considering the nature of the boy's toilet the simile was hardly an apt one.) 'Our hillside hares aren't easily caught.'

'At night I hunt on four feet,' was the somewhat cryptic response.

'I suppose you mean that you hunt with a dog?' hazarded Van Cheele.

The boy rolled slowly over on to his back, and laughed a weird low laugh, that was pleasantly like a chuckle and disagreeably like a snarl.

'I don't fancy any dog would be very anxious for my company, especially at night.'

Van Cheele began to feel that there was something positively uncanny about the strange-eyed, strange-tongued youngster.

'I can't have you staying in these woods,' he declared authoritatively.

'I fancy you'd rather have me here than in your house,' said the boy.

The prospect of this wild, nude animal in Van Cheele's primly ordered house was certainly an alarming one.

'If you don't go I shall have to make you,' said Van Cheele.

The boy turned like a flash, plunged into the pool, and in a moment had flung his wet and glistening body half-way up the bank where Van Cheele was standing. In an otter the movement would not have been remarkable; in a boy Van Cheele found it sufficiently startling. His foot slipped as he made an involuntary backward movement, and he found himself almost prostrate on the slippery weed-grown bank, with those tigerish yellow eyes not very far from his own. Almost instinctively he half raised his hand to his throat. The boy laughed again, a laugh in which the snarl had nearly driven out the chuckle, and then, with another of his astonishing lightning movements, plunged out of view into a yielding tangle of weed and fern.

'What an extraordinary wild animal!' said Van Cheele as he picked himself up. And then he recalled Cunningham's remark, 'There is a wild beast in your woods.'

Walking slowly homeward, Van Cheele began to turn over in his mind various local occurrences which might be traceable to the existence of this astonishing young savage.

Something had been thinning the game in the woods lately, poultry had been missing from the farms, hares were growing unaccountably scarcer, and complaints had reached him of lambs being carried off bodily from the hills. Was it possible that this wild boy was really hunting the countryside in company with some clever poacher dog? He had spoken of hunting 'four-footed' by night, but then, again, he had hinted strangely at no dog caring to come near him, 'especially at night'. It was certainly puzzling. And then, as Van Cheele ran his mind over the various depredations that had been committed during the last month or two, he came suddenly to a dead stop, alike in his walk and his speculations. The child missing from the mill two months ago – the accepted theory was that it had tumbled into the mill-race and been swept away; but the mother had always declared she had heard a shriek on the hill side of the house, in the opposite direction from the water. It was unthinkable, of course, but he wished that the boy had not made that uncanny remark about child-flesh eaten two months ago. Such dreadful things should not be said even in fun.

Van Cheele, contrary to his usual wont, did not feel disposed to be communicative about his discovery in the wood. His position as a parish councillor and Justice of the Peace seemed somehow compromised by the fact that he was harbouring a personality of such doubtful repute on his property; there was even a possibility that a heavy bill of damages for raided lambs and poultry might be laid at his door. At dinner that night he was quite unusually silent.

'Where's your voice gone to?' said his aunt. 'One would think you had seen a wolf.'

Van Cheele, who was not familiar with the old saying, thought the remark rather foolish; if he *had* seen a wolf on his property his tongue would have been extraordinarily busy with the subject.

At breakfast next morning Van Cheele was conscious that his feeling of uneasiness regarding yesterday's episode had not wholly disappeared, and he resolved to go by train to the neighbouring cathedral town, hunt up Cunningham, and learn from him what he had really seen that had prompted the remark about a wild beast in the woods. With this resolution taken, his usual cheerfulness partially returned, and he hummed a bright little melody as he sauntered to the morning-room for his customary cigarette. As he entered the room the melody made way abruptly for a pious invocation. Gracefully asprawl on the ottoman, in an attitude of almost exaggerated repose, was the boy of the woods. He was drier than when Van Cheele had last seen him, but no other alteration was noticeable in his toilet.

'How dare you come here?' asked Van Cheele furiously.

'You told me I was not to stay in the woods,' said the boy calmly.

'But not to come here. Supposing my aunt should see you!'

And with a view to minimizing that catastrophe Van Cheele hastily obscured as much of his unwelcome guest as possible under the folds of a *Morning Post*. At that moment his aunt entered the room.

'This is a poor boy who has lost his way – and lost his memory. He doesn't know who he is or where he comes from,' explained Van Cheele desperately, glancing apprehensively at the waif's face to see whether he was going to add inconvenient candour to his other savage propensities.

Miss Van Cheele was enormously interested.

'Perhaps his underlinen is marked,' she suggested.

'He seems to have lost most of that, too,' said Van Cheele, making frantic little grabs at the *Morning Post* to keep it in its place.

A naked homeless child appealed to Miss Van Cheele as warmly as a stray kitten or derelict puppy would have done.

'We must do all we can for him,' she decided, and in a very short time a messenger, dispatched to the rectory, where a page-boy was kept, had returned with a suit of pantry clothes, and the necessary accessories of shirt, shoes, collar, etc. Clothed, clean, and groomed, the boy lost none of his uncanniness in Van Cheele's eyes, but his aunt found him sweet.

'We must call him something till we know who he really is,' she said. 'Gabriel-Ernest, I think; those are nice suitable names.'

Van Cheele agreed, but he privately doubted whether they were being grafted on to a nice suitable child. His misgivings were not diminished by the fact that his staid and elderly spaniel had bolted out of the house at the first incoming of the boy, and now obstinately remained shivering and yapping at the farther end of the orchard, while the canary, usually as vocally industrious as Van Cheele himself, had put itself on an allowance of frightened cheeps. More than ever he was resolved to consult Cunningham without loss of time.

As he drove off to the station his aunt was arranging that Gabriel-Ernest should help her to entertain the infant members of her Sunday-school class at tea that afternoon.

Cunningham was not at first disposed to be communicative.

'My mother died of some brain trouble,' he explained, 'so you will understand why I am averse to dwelling on anything of an impossibly fantastic nature that I may see or think that I have seen.'

'But what *did* you see?' persisted Van Cheele.

'What I thought I saw was something so extraordinary that no really sane man could dignify it with the credit of having actually happened. I was standing, the last evening I was with you, half-hidden in the hedge-growth by the orchard gate, watching the dying glow of the sunset. Suddenly I became aware of a naked boy, a bather from some neighbouring pool, I took him to be, who was standing out on the bare hillside also watching the sunset. His pose was so suggestive of some wild faun of pagan myth that I instantly wanted to engage him as a model, and in another moment I think I should have hailed him. But just then the sun dipped out of view, and all the orange and pink slid out of the landscape, leaving it cold and grey. And at the same moment an astounding thing happened – the boy vanished too!'

'What! Vanished away into nothing?' asked Van Cheele excitedly.

'No; that is the dreadful part of it,' answered the artist; 'on the open hillside where the boy had been standing a second ago, stood a large wolf, blackish in colour, with gleaming fangs and cruel, yellow eyes. You may think –'

But Van Cheele did not stop for anything as futile as thought. Already he was tearing at top speed towards the station. He dismissed the idea of a telegram. 'Gabriel-Ernest is a werewolf' was a hopelessly inadequate effort at conveying the situation, and his aunt would think it was a code message to which he had omitted to give her the key. His one hope was that he might reach home before sundown. The cab which he chartered at the other end of the railway journey bore him with what seemed exasperating slowness along the country roads, which were pink and mauve with the flush of the sinking sun. His aunt was putting away some unfinished jams and cake when he arrived.

'Where is Gabriel-Ernest?' he almost screamed.

'He is taking the little Toop child home,' said his aunt. 'It was getting so late, I thought it wasn't safe to let it go back alone. What a lovely sunset, isn't it?'

But Van Cheele, although not oblivious of the glow in the western sky, did not stay to discuss its beauties. At a speed for which he was scarcely geared he raced along the narrow lane that led to the home of the Toops. On one side ran the swift current of the mill-stream, on the other rose the stretch of bare hillside. A dwindling rim of red sun showed still on the skyline, and the next turning must bring him in view of the ill-assorted couple he was pursuing. Then the colour went suddenly out of things, and a grey light settled itself with a quick shiver over the landscape. Van Cheele heard a shrill wail of fear, and stopped running.

Nothing was ever seen again of the Toop child or Gabriel-Ernest, but the latter's discarded garments were found lying in the road, so it was assumed that the child had fallen into the water, and that the boy had stripped and jumped in, in a vain endeavour to save it. Van Cheele and some workmen who were nearby at the time testified to having heard a child scream loudly just near the spot where the clothes were found. Mrs Toop, who had eleven other children, was decently resigned to her bereavement, but Miss Van Cheele sincerely mourned her lost foundling. It was on her initiative that a memorial brass was put up in the parish church to 'Gabriel-Ernest, an unknown boy, who bravely sacrificed his life for another'.

Van Cheele gave way to his aunt in most things, but he flatly refused to subscribe to the Gabriel-Ernest memorial.

ADRIAN CONSETT STEPHEN 1892–1918

'The man who cannot play chorus to his own drama is not worthy to be on this stage at all.'

Adrian Consett Stephen. *University of Sydney*

Adrian Consett Stephen was as successful in civilian life as in war. He was born in 1892 in Sydney, New South Wales. His father was a solicitor, and Adrian Consett Stephen followed in his father's footsteps by taking up law at Sydney University. Graduating with honours in 1915 was the culmination, but not the sum, of Stephen's achievements at St Paul's College. His contributions to student life were substantial: he edited two university magazines, was a leading member of the Undergraduates' Association, the Union Board and the Law Society. He was secretary and chief actor of the Sydney University Drama Society for which he wrote and produced four plays. According to a colleague he was endowed with 'ready eloquence, a trenchant wit, rare insight into human nature, sympathy and unfailing humour' which 'combined to make him a charming companion, a brilliant raconteur and debater, an actor of great promise and a literary genius'. What promised to be a formidable career either in the theatre or at the Bar – although it would have surprised none of his contemporaries had he chosen to follow both at once – was interrupted by the war. He joined the army at the age of 23, and was killed in action less than three years later, on 14 March 1918, at Zillebeke near Ypres.

What made his military career distinctive was not only the decorations he received. The Croix de Guerre *avec palme* was awarded to him for his work on the Somme in June 1917, followed by the Military Cross at Passchendaele Ridge in October that year. He was promoted from Second Lieutenant to Lieutenant and during that year of 1917 was acting-Major in command of his battery. Stephen was proud to be one of the few Australians serving in a British regiment – the Royal Field Artillery: 'This War has made me feel how grand it is to be an Australian. I only hope that the little part I play in this big affair may make me not unworthy to be classed (in all but name) as a real Anzac.' The fact that Stephen was not a fellow 'pom' may have been important to him and his comrades-at-arms, but clearly created little impression on the *indigènes* of the host nation: 'We told them we were Australians; but that conveyed nothing to them. They would merely ask us if we were British. For the French, Australia does not exist.' Yet Stephen, true to form, knew how to ingratiate himself with his hosts by means other than the flaunting of nationality. As he wrote home in a letter in March 1916: 'I am sitting in the sun – yes, in the sun, on a deck-chair in a little vegetable garden . . . A French dame has just thrust her head out of the window and regarded me with disfavour. I suddenly realized that my chair was planted on her lettuce patch, so I smiled sweetly, and murmured *Bonjour* in the inimitable way that has so often won eggs and butter from apparently disapproving sources.'

Stephen arrived on the Western Front one year after the front line had been established, when trench warfare had long acquired a stultifyingly monotonous pattern. Even days which in peacetime would have been marked by some special event merited little attention in the continual war of attrition: 'Today is the 25 December. It is not Christmas, for Christmas does not exist out here. There are no Christmas greetings, and any fraternizing between the armies has been strictly forbidden. The day commenced with a steady artillery duel uncomfortably close to our gun that I was firing. For five minutes this morning the sun came out and one bird presumed to sing. After that unprecedented occurrence things returned to their normal course, i.e. mud and rain'.

Before the major battles of 1917 it is not surprising that Stephen should have retained a longing for the thrills of theatrical violence as opposed to that of battle: 'The stage has more sensations than war. The war has many fears, but never the sweet keen fear before I stepped on

'From the soldier's point of view the real curse of this war is stagnation.'

October 1915

the stage for the wild speech about "murder" or the stealthy whispered scene outside the chamber . . .'

Stephen's whole mind turned toward the humorous and the dramatic. The former trait was wholly reserved for his numerous contributions to the *Sydney Morning Herald.* These brief articles covered all aspects of life on the front, of which 'The Trench Mortar Officer' is a good example of the wry good humour so necessary in preserving a sense of perspective when conducting a life so near to death. The four short plays that were published posthumously treat topical social themes in an earnest manner. In particular *Echoes*, with its subtitle 'A Play of Today' seeks to lend the generational conflict polemical expression. The verbal sparring of father and son is clearly evidence of Stephen's legal and inquisitorial mind at work. The arguments postulated in *Echoes* serve as a better indication of the success Stephen might have made of a courtroom drama rather than of a domestic wrangle. Nevertheless Adrian Consett Stephen can claim to have been the most promising dramatic talent of the British Empire whose career was cut short in the war in which he was so proud to have played a part.

TIM CROSS

Texts

Four Plays (W. C. Penfold, Sydney, 1918).

Stories, Burlesques and letters from Hermes (W. C. Penfold, Sydney, 1918).

An Australian in the RFA (W. C. Penfold, Sydney, 1918) Letters and diary.

ECHOES

A Play for Today

The FATHER's business is failing. He is plagued by the thought that he will have no legacy, leave no monument to posterity of his life's work. Only his SON (Selwyn), soon to complete his university training, can rescue and carry on the ailing family business. The MOTHER on the other hand is sceptical that the uneven partnership of FATHER and SON will bring about either success or satisfaction. She does not want to see her SON embroiled in her husband's all-consuming work which was the cause of the disintegration of her marriage. The SON arrives unexpectedly to announce to his MOTHER that he has abandoned his university career in favour of a career in journalism. The MOTHER's revelation that his FATHER is financially ruined prompts the SON to relent – but the MOTHER urges him to commit himself to his new-found plans of a future independent of his FATHER. This leads to the central confrontation between FATHER and SON.

With ominous deliberation the father closes the door, and then with a half-smile surveys the form of Selwyn. Slowly he strolls to the centre table, taking his time about it, for he is trying to enjoy the situation. The bitterness and wrath within him find their first expression in a spirit of cruel gaiety. He lifts up the untasted glass of whisky and speaks banteringly.

FATHER. I regret that the beverage of the father is not approved of by the son. Come, it will perk you up for the interview. Teetotaller?

SELWYN. No.

FATHER. H'm. And to what are we indebted for this well-timed and cheerful visit?

SELWYN. Father – I feel a cad.

FATHER. You look it.

SELWYN. Don't goad me.

FATHER [*raising his eyebrows*]. Will it bite? Is it dangerous? And so – and so – you've left the University?

SELWYN [*starting*]. How did you know?

FATHER. I am not without my inspirations.

SELWYN. I thought to strike out alone – I simply had to.

FATHER. And the exams?

SELWYN. I can't go back now. [*Sits L. table.*] I'm sorry – I didn't know –

FATHER [*contemptuously*]. Stand up and answer like a man! Stop playing the Prodigal Son and Mary Magdalene in that chair! Stand up! [*Selwyn obeys;) the father folds his arms and regards his son with grim humour.*] Question No. 1 – Are you my son?

SELWYN. For pity's sake –

FATHER. Yes or no, sir?

SELWYN [*faintly*]. Yes.

FATHER [*bowing in mockery*]. You flatter me. For the moment I had a doubt. I am reassured at your generous statement. I thank you.

SELWYN [*miserably*]. Let's talk straight. For God's sake drop this pantomime.

FATHER [*in surprise*]. Pantomime! So far the situation seemed devoid of frivolity. Perhaps I cannot aspire to your keenness of humour. However, since you tire of this method, perhaps you will be so good as to take one of your father's chairs.

Selwyn sits at table R. Then, like a flash, his father's mood changes and his voice becomes harsh and bullying.

FATHER. How long have you been home?

SELWYN. Ten minutes.

FATHER. Time enough for your mother to tell you the state of affairs?

SELWYN. Yes.

FATHER. What do you say?

SELWYN. I – I don't know.

FATHER. Your opinion?

SELWYN. I haven't decided.

FATHER. Not got one?

SELWYN. No.

FATHER. So much the better. I have; and one opinion is ample for this house.

SELWYN. I'm very sorry – of course, father.

FATHER [*brusquely*]. Wipe that father and son sentiment off the slate. You'll have to earn your daily bread now.

SELWYN [*quietly*]. I've made provision for that.

FATHER. In your mind – good.

SELWYN. In fact.

FATHER. Eh?

SELWYN. I didn't mean to come home empty-handed. I was prepared in case you –

FATHER. In case I – well?

SELWYN. Turned nasty.

FATHER. Oho! and what, pray, is an example of a father 'turning nasty'?

SELWYN [*rising*]. Your conduct for the last ten minutes.

FATHER. It *can* bite. So you came prepared – for what?

SELWYN. To defend my independence.

FATHER [*roaring*]. Independence! [*Stamps down L.*] So you're soaked in that modern jargon, are you? – The claims of temperament, the realization of the soul! Independence, indeed! Only those who have faced the struggle and the strife can claim that prize – only those who have found a god in themselves, one who never stoops to forgiveness, a god sterner than any of the figures men have made out of their dreams. When you have found him and can face him you may claim your independence. It is not for boys or women, so wipe the word from your vocabulary!

SELWYN [*quietly*]. I was armed for this, too.

FATHER [*sneering*]. You bristle with defences.

SELWYN. In a letter I wrote my mother –

FATHER. I know.

SELWYN. How? You open her letters?

FATHER. She read it aloud.

SELWYN. With you standing over her.

FATHER [*calmly*]. I was standing by the fireplace.

SELWYN. She read it *all*?

FATHER. Yes – er – almost.

SELWYN. I mentioned that I had been offered a position as a journalist –

FATHER [*snapping*]. A scurrilous scribbler – wandering about the streets with long hair, the emptiness of the pocket only equalled by that of his head! You refused, of course; you said so.

SELWYN [*firmly*]. Yesterday – I accepted.

The effect is electrical. With the roar of a beast his father rushes at him.

FATHER. Accepted! Smash my life, would you? – You little –

Selwyn does not move, but something in his attitude and the levelness of his eye checks his father. Selwyn's manhood has leapt up with the instinct of physical preservation. He is master of the scene.

SELWYN [*steadily*]. You've smashed your own life now – every word sent a castle tumbling.

FATHER [*realizing his disadvantage*]. I – the instinct of the moment, the shock, and – and so on.

SELWYN [*curtly*]. Don't apologize.

FATHER [*savagely*]. You clutch any excuse.

SELWYN [*strongly*]. I want no excuse; you asked me to stand up and answer like a man. As a dutiful son I obey. You get your wish and its consequences. We're level, now – man to man – not son to father. There's a difference. That sounds irony, but there's truth in it, nevertheless.

FATHER [*damping his oratory*]. H'm! – why this – er – pantomime?

SELWYN [*retorting*]. The situation is fast gaining in frivolity.

FATHER [*coming to facts*]. What's your plan? – expound it.

SELWYN. Simply that I have accepted the offer. I return to work immediately, unless –

FATHER. Well?

SELWYN. Unless I change my mind. [*Walks fireplace.*]

FATHER. Ah! [*He clutches at this straw and rallies himself to the simple task of changing his son's mind.*] It's a hard life, Selwyn.

SELWYN. My eyes are wide open.

FATHER. The rewards are negligible.

SELWYN. Rewards measure nothing.

FATHER. Only the young say that. The work is heavy.

SELWYN. I've faced that.

FATHER. Do you call that 'liberty'?

SELWYN. There are different liberties.

FATHER. You will have no social position, or obedience from others.

SELWYN [*with finality*]. I have chosen.

FATHER [*breaking out*]. And what right have you to choose? How can you – a mere unit – put a whim against generations?

SELWYN. The monument has crumbled.

FATHER. You can rebuild it. [*Walks up to him.*] Have you no pride in you – doesn't your blood call to you? The name you carry into the future – your family and the things they've done, and the big ambitions that drove them – What does all that mean to you?

SELWYN [*turning*]. Nothing.

FATHER [*bitterly*]. I suppose that is what your mother would call 'human nature'. *In*human.

SELWYN [*calmly*]. Because I don't agree with my father?

FATHER. Where would you be without your father? Answer me that.

SELWYN [*unruffled*]. I admit that by the cruel laws of Nature a father of some sort is a necessity, but only cowards make a *virtue* of necessity.

FATHER. I gave you life.

SELWYN. In an outburst of generosity: Life – that was your unconditional gift. I accept it. It's mine now – to waste, to make – Mine to fashion as I will.

FATHER [*snapping*]. Take it, and go to the devil with it!

SELWYN. Yes, I'd sooner go to the devil my own way than to heaven your way – or anybody else's for that matter.

The father decides on a change of tactics.

FATHER. Come, now; what's your objection to my business?

SELWYN [*walks front table*]. To me it spells torture – prison – I'm not an unpractical dreamer either. But I've seen other men who were weak enough to drift or to be led from their own path and to follow somebody else's – perhaps for the same sentimental reasons that you advocate. What's been the result? They've gradually become like beasts in a cage, peering out at what they might have been, beating themselves crazy against the bars until they're too tired even for that – and then for the rest of their wasted lives pacing up and down, up and down. No cage for me! [*Crosses R.*]

FATHER. H'm! You didn't always think that. Doesn't take long for the rats to desert the sinking ship.

SELWYN. I feel it no duty to spend my life in keeping afloat the ship you've mismanaged.

FATHER [*throwing up his hands*]. What a son! A nice investment you've been!

SELWYN [*smiling*]. Ah! I thought I was more of an investment than a son. In future, you must find other souls to gamble with.

FATHER. You talk to your father like that! I sent you to the University in the fond hopes they might turn out a gentleman.

SELWYN. I turned myself out – that's some recommendation.

FATHER [*subsiding into sentiment*]. Selwyn – I – Selwyn, my boy –

SELWYN [*coldly*]. Wipe that father and son sentiment off the slate.

FATHER [*quietly*]. You're scoring now. But, listen, I counted on you. [*Laying a hand on his shoulder.*] I want you. I'm getting old and on you rests my happiness. Well?

SELWYN [*quietly*]. You've had your share of happiness. It's my turn now.

FATHER [*breaking out*]. Good God, man, you can't leave me stranded. You can't do it.

SELWYN [*motionless*]. I go my own way.

The father looks at him and again shifts his ground.

FATHER. Have some supper. Draw up. Fill your pipe. Let's yarn. [*They sit at table.*] Of course, from the business point of view –

SELWYN. The *personal* point of view, if you please.

FATHER. Even there the advantages –

SELWYN. Are in going one's own way.

FATHER. And dragging your father's grey hairs –

SELWYN [*curtly*]. Let's taboo the 'grey hairs' argument. It's overdone.

FATHER. I appeal to you as your father.

SELWYN [*quaintly*]. I was afraid you'd do that. If you appeal to my better feelings you must win. [*After a moment's thought.*] Well, there's my life – I give it you.

FATHER. But I won't take it.

SELWYN. What now?

FATHER [*proudly*]. I don't appeal to any man's better feelings.

SELWYN. Well, what is to decide the question?

FATHER. Why be ashamed to let selfishness decide?

SELWYN [*back at table; rising and speaking with deep force*]. That's it! It's my egotism against yours, selfishness against selfishness. And why not? All the other causes worth fighting for have been lost. We have only *ourselves* to champion now. You crave for power to mould others at your will; I – for power to mould myself at my own will. We are fighting desperately *with* our egotism *for* our egotism. Our battle is the same. It is only the battle-cry that differs.

FATHER [*strongly*]. Mine is the best.

SELWYN. Prove it.

FATHER. There's no argument you'll listen to.

SELWYN. There's *one* argument.

FATHER. At last! The dawn of sanity.

SELWYN. Listen! I am following in your footsteps – in the way of selfishness. Will you admit to me now that your life, your way, has been *wrong*? Admit it, and my faith is shattered. That is the one argument. Well?

FATHER [*hedging*]. What – admit that all I've done – my work –

SELWYN [*pressing him*]. Admit it.

FATHER. But the circumstances –

SELWYN. Admit it.

FATHER. No.

SELWYN [*quietly*]. I've won.

Pause.

FATHER [*smiling*]. But the triumph is mine. [*Rises.*]

SELWYN [*surprised*]. What illusion have you got now?

FATHER. It's *you* who are under the illusion – you flatter yourself that you have beaten me with your own words and your own thoughts. Fool! The voice you use is mine; the thoughts that have coloured yours are mine; the blood that rebels in you is mine. You see, it is a father's victory!

SELWYN. A father's illusion.

FATHER [*defiantly*]. Shatter it if you can.

SELWYN [*slowly choosing his words*]. Easily! Looking back over this interview – getting – as it were – outside ourselves – I see that the voice I used was not altogether mine, certainly not yours.

FATHER [*contemptuously*]. A pretty excuse. Be proud of your voice, sir. It is the oldest of all; the voice that created the world; the voice of Ego – Ego.

SELWYN [*grimly*]. A paternal inheritance – you know no other.

FATHER. I am not ashamed of it.

SELWYN. You have no shame.

FATHER. Ah! That's my strength.

Pause.

SELWYN [*slowly*]. I admire – you.

FATHER [*regaining his good humour at the touch of flattery*]. You admire your own father! Strange sentiments for a modern son!

SELWYN [*gravely*]. But you are not a modern father.

FATHER. Indeed! Of what age am I, pray?

SELWYN. You're a relic of the age of inventions, machinery and all that. You fondly imagined that your son would be a continuation of yourself, and another link in the chain, eh? You forgot that I belonged to another age, that in reality you were begetting a new generation, with different ideas and that spoke in a voice strange to you. [*Vaguely.*] Perhaps I have caught its echo.

FATHER [*contemptuously*]. You spoil your victory with that admission. Claim the voice yourself.

SELWYN. Who can tell where his voice comes from? [*Sternly.*] But this I do know: there is another behind me, the voice of one whose thoughts, like yours, have coloured mine; whose blood, like yours, runs in my veins. Have you forgotten that other? My rebellion is hers too.

They look at one another.

FATHER. Your mother?

SELWYN [*nodding*]. So you have a conscience.

FATHER [*blustering*]. And how dare you treat your mother as though she were an ordinary woman?

SELWYN. A crime of which you will never be accused.

FATHER. What do you mean? She's free.

SELWYN [*quickly*]. To leave you.

FATHER. She's not a prisoner. The door stands open.

SELWYN. Will you *tell* her that?

FATHER. She knows. I'm not a gaoler.

SELWYN. Ah, but will you hold the door open for her?

FATHER. You're trying to frighten me.

SELWYN. No need.

FATHER [*fiercely*]. Why should I tell her? Answer me that!

SELWYN [*slowly*]. Because you – *must.*

FATHER [*bowing*]. The son commands; the father obeys.

SELWYN. It's yourself who will command. You said you were a god unto yourself. Well, a god can admit no fear. You will tell her.

FATHER. That's a bold reliance.

SELWYN [*smiling*]. I have faith in your Ego.

FATHER [*furious*]. Idiot!

SELWYN [*quietly*]. We shall see. [*He turns to the window, and the atmosphere of the scene relaxes.*] What a night!

FATHER. Stormy?

SELWYN. When I sneaked home the stars were as clear as crystals – Yes, they are still shining.

FATHER [*surprised*]. Are they? Cold though! [*Crosses to fireplace.*]

SELWYN. Grand thought! There is always a dawn for those who go out to meet it.

FATHER. It'll be a bitter dawn for you, leaving your father's house. To your last hour you'll have remorse for this.

SELWYN [*turning*]. It's worth it.

FATHER. You don't know remorse.

SELWYN [*quickly*]. Do *you?*

FATHER. No!

SELWYN. Ah, so far you are only a god unto yourself. The Judge and Jury have yet to come.

He turns and picks up his hat and coat, then comes back to his father.

SELWYN [*quietly*]. I'm sorry, father, for what I've said tonight, but I'm not sorry for what I'm doing, and I never shall be.

FATHER. Nor I.

SELWYN. I wonder.

The Trench Mortar Officer

A Field Impression

'Seven o'clock, sir. Shall I get breakfast?'

'What is there for breakfast?'

'Bacon, sir.'

The TMO turned over on his wire bed and surveyed his servant dreamily. 'Bacon' he repeated. 'I think I have heard that word before.' His voice hardened. 'It seems to pursue me down a long vista of mornings. You might say the word cheerfully as though the bacon really weren't all fat. If you can't vary the breakfast at least vary your tone. Dismiss.'

The TMO crawled gingerly out of his sleeping bag and proceeded to wash in a canvas bucket outside his dug-out.

'Here's a shell coming, sir,' shouted the servant.

'Well, stop the blooming thing; can't you see I'm busy?' He returned to the dug-out in time to support one corner of the roof, which was drooping suspiciously as a result of the shell.

He spent an acrobatic breakfast supporting his home with one hand and eating the bac— (no I won't say the beastly word) with the other. 'Life,' he muttered 'is not worth living.' He was rescued from pessimism by a frenzied messenger who announced breathlessly that an Infantry officer had thought he saw a German in the enemy's front trench. Would the TMO come at once and fire a 50 lb bomb at him (i.e. the German.) The TMO received the news with masterful self-control.

'Jones,' he shouted to his sergeant, 'come and hold the dug-out up while I go down to the trenches.'

'Perhaps, sir,' suggested Jones, 'I could prop it up with something.'

'A distinct idea, Jones. Masterful fellow; I always said you had brains.'

The TMO dragged on his thigh gumboots and set off to his gun, which was in the reserve trench, a matter of ten minutes' walk from the dug-out.

At the commencement of the trench he paused. 'Why don't the bally infantry clean their trenches for me?' he queried to the world at large. The next moment he trod on nothing and a sump hole received him. He swam ashore in time to see a sergeant gravely saluting him.

'Did I notice you smiling, Sergeant?' he spluttered.

'Oh no, sir.' (A liar, obviously, but a tactful one).

'If it had been a Staff officer, sir,' commenced the sergeant. Their eyes met – and twinkled.

The TMO reached his gun looking like a slab of animated trench. He called the gun detachment together, and prepared for action.

An Infantry officer sauntered into sight. 'I'm afraid that German beggar has gone,' he said to the TMO. 'In fact he wasn't a German at all; he was a stump; but I rather want to see how your jolly old mortar works.' The TMO did not lose his temper – he was a perfect gentleman. Taking the gun to pieces he explained it thoroughly.

'Thank you,' said the Infantry officer, who had been watching an aeroplane during the demonstration. 'I don't understand a word you've said; perhaps if you were to fire a round from the old bus.'

The TMO put the gun together. 'Range 500, fuze 11,' he ordered.

Just then a captain strolled along.

'Hullo, that's a new sort of mortar, isn't it? Ugly-looking beast; what? How does it work?'

After another exhaustive explanation the captain suggested that the 'old jigger' should be fired.

The TMO placed two sticks on top of the trench in line with a German sap, and proceeded to sight the gun on to the sticks. 'Bring out a bomb' he thundered in his best martial voice.

But a Staff officer appeared on the scene. 'Good morning, is this the trench mortar? Very interesting. Now how does it work? Can you explain?'

The TMO drew a long breath.

'Perhaps if you took it to pieces' suggested the Staff officer. When the gun had been dismantled to its smallest detail, the Staff officer confessed, with the usual modesty of his tribe, that he didn't quite follow the explanation. Would the TMO please fire a round? Once again the gun was prepared for action. At that moment a brigadier-general joined the group. 'A mortar, eh,' he exclaimed. 'How does it –'

'Excuse me, sir,' hurriedly broke in the TMO, but the Boches invariably drop their Minnenwerfers just where you are standing, and at about this time too.'

The audience then remembered that it had business elsewhere, and went on its way with an alacrity that only duty can inspire.

'What target, sir?' asked the number one gunner.

'Target,' panted the TMO mopping his brow, 'any old target, only for heaven's sake fire and get it over.'

A loud bang, a huge watermelon bomb sailing through the sky; a dull thud in the enemy trench, and then – silence. The bomb had not exploded. A dud! A dud!

A messenger ran up to the TMO. 'Please sir, the Staff captain wants your ammunition report, showing how many rounds expended, and how many exploded.'

The TMO waved him away and buried his face in his hands. Was it all a ghastly joke? 'Shall I fire again, sir?' asked the gunner.

'Not now,' groaned the TMO. 'Some other time; some other war.' He set off for his dug-out. A salvo of shells and four Minnenwerfer bombs fell in the trenches around him, making the earth rock. They were a peevish hint that the efforts of mortars are not appreciated by the Teutonic mind.

He hardly noticed them. He was wondering whether a certain sump hole could have possibly engulfed those exalted personages who had just preceded him. After all a sump hole is no respecter of rank. Thus he wondered, and wondering thus, fell into the sump hole himself.

'Life,' he gurgled, 'is not worth living.'

After lunch his sergeant confronted him with a pile of army forms.

'There is one form here, sir, that asks how many English, French, Russian, Belgian and Italians there are in the battery.'

'What about Germans?'

'They are not officially on the strength, sir.'

'Well,' concluded the TMO with dignity, 'please inform the Staff captain that this is a battery, and not a foreign opera company.'

The sergeant placed the pile of forms on the table. 'Those must be filled in by 4 o'clock, sir.' An ominous silence. 'Hand me the whisky' commanded the officer in funereal tones. 'Do not disturb me till 4 o'clock. If by that time I have not mastered these forms, you will find my body hanging from the roof.'

'The roof is not too strong, sir.'

'Leave me.'

The sergeant tiptoed out, feeling that he was a party to the making of tremendous history.

When evening came the officer stepped from his dug-out, pale yet triumphant, yet he looked older, much older. Army forms have that effect. Around him were the charred rafters and the lonely, jagged walls of a ruined town. The moon shining through this skeleton turned its desolation into beauty – the spectral beauty of memories and of dreams.

Softly through this dead silence floated the sounds of music, bringing haunting visions of the past and gay hopes for the future.

'Life,' murmured the TMO, 'is worth living after all – even here.'

GEORGE CALDERON 1868–1915

'I'm off on a new and unknown adventure, but it either ends ill or very well, and no thought can alter it. So rejoice in the colour and vigour of the thing, and drink deep with jolly friends while it's doing –.'
Letter, 10 May 1915, before Gallipoli

The loss of George Calderon in the ill-fated assault on Achi Baba at Gallipoli on 4 June 1915 was greeted in *The Times* as 'the heaviest blow which struck English drama during the war'. However, this claim seems hardly justified in view of the few performances of Calderon's plays after his death. The fact is that George Calderon's abilities were not confined to drama alone. George Leslie Calderon came from a distinguished artistic background, his family descending from the great Spanish dramatist Calderón de la Barca. Born in London on 2 December 1868, Calderon himself was the fifth son of the painter Philip H. Calderon who later became Keeper of the Royal Academy. His younger brother, Frederick Elwyn Calderon (1874–1916) (q.v.), was a portrait painter who was killed fighting with the First Canadian Contingent at St Eloi on 3 April 1916. George Calderon was also an artist, creating caricatures for his first novel, *Downy V. Green*, which told of the curious adventures of an American Rhodes scholar at Oxford. As well as being an able musician, he was also an actor, a theatre director, a political commentator, a travel writer (*Tahiti*) and an expert on the Slavonic languages. It is arguable that Calderon's protean qualities, while giving him this enviable versatility, were the cause of his lack of lasting success as a playwright, and that the self-imposed haphazardness of his career prevented him from developing a distinctive enough style or voice which might have set him apart from his contemporaries. Calderon's first play *The Fountain* received two performances in 1909, by the Stage Society at the Aldwych Theatre, and by Alfred Wareing's Glasgow Repertory Theatre. Critics compared this socially critical piece, exposing the absurdities of the Poor Laws, unfavourably with G. B. Shaw's *Heartbreak House*. In the same year, he directed the first British production of a Chekhov play, *The Cherry Orchard*, in his own translation. Social iniquities were again the subject of his final full-length drama *Revolt*, produced by Lewis Casson with Sybil Thorndike in 1912. Here, Calderon questioned on the one hand, the rights of a trade union to hamper the progress of industry and an inventor's rights, and on the other hand, the power of the monied class to manipulate the inventor's research. The inventor Gregory, who discovers nuclear fuel as an alternative source of energy, at first appears optimistic that his talents will

Calderon photographed by Frederick Hollyer. *The British Library*

provide him with limitless opportunities: 'What is the past? Heaven's rough draft for the future!' However, his idealism is gradually worn down, the first indications of which are revealed at a garden party hosted by the wealthy industrialist:

> GREGORY. I love to see the rich in the country.
> HARRY. They look so sleepy and good-natured.
> GREGORY. Like tigers between two meals.

The one-act plays are simple but effectively structured illustrations of morals and fables. *Derelicts* is a wistful tale of two middle-aged people who, on finding themselves in surroundings somewhat conducive to romance one fine summer evening, come close to avoiding solitude in old age by tentatively broaching the possibility of marriage. Although initially tempted by union, the woman rejects her suitor, recognizing that 'Two egotisms do not make a love . . .' In the one-act play *Peace* (q.v.), Calderon, in the style of a vaudeville farce, exposes the double-standards employed by many pacifists before the war.

The Little Stone House (1911) is evidently the result of his fascination for the Slavonic taste in melodrama, and is set with a meticulous attention to realistic detail. Calderon had spent two years in St Petersburg between 1895–7, working as a journalist in order to supplement his income after being called to the Bar in 1894. He returned from Russia with a profound knowledge of the Slavonic languages and literature which he then applied as a member of staff at the British Museum. The public results of his work were translations of two Chekhov plays and *Reminiscences* by Tolstoy's son. A comprehensive study of Slavonic religions and folklore was in preparation when the war broke out.

Despite being married, and despite the fact that at 46 he was well over-age for active service, George Calderon resolved to reach the fighting-line. Joining the Inns of Court OTC at the first available opportunity – on 3 August 1914 – he secured a post as an interpreter in France. After recovering from wounds he had received in 1915, he was sent, with a commission in the 9th Battalion of the Oxfordshire & Buckinghamshire Light Infantry, to Gallipoli. From the peninsula, he wrote letters fully describing what it was like to live at a front so unlike the Western one he had already experienced, and referring rather respectfully to the Turk as 'Him':

> Since lunch I have been attending an instruction in bomb-throwing from trench to trench; very interesting. It is strange, this careless, rather amused life at leisure in the sunshine, in full view of Him on the big mole-heap. Surely it must discourage him to see the tip-end of a big civilization leisurely going about the routine of life while it closes up to swallow him.

TIM CROSS

Texts

The Fountain: a comedy in three acts (Gowans & Gray, London, 1911).
Eight One-Act Plays (Grant Richards, London, 1922). Includes *The Two Talismans*, *Derelicts*, *Peace*, *The Little Stone House* (which was also published separately in 1913), *Geminae* and *Longing: a subjective drama in two scenes*.
The Adventures of Downy V Green, Rhodes Scholar at Oxford (Smith, Elder, London, 1902). Contains humorous illustrations by the author.
Dwala: a romance (Smith, Elder, London, 1904).

Secondary sources

Percy Lubbock, *George Calderon: a sketch from memory* (Grant Richards, London, 1921). This gives an assessment of the public personality of Calderon; it is, however, short on factual references nor does it deal with his deeper motivations.

PEACE

Enter SIR BLENNERHASSETT POSTLETHWAITE *in dressing-gown and night-cap, carrying a bedroom candle.*

POSTLETHWAITE. It's useless trying to sleep; I'm too nervous and excited. Nervous, because I'm entirely alone in the flat; no one to protect me; my wife's away; and excited, because tomorrow, tomorrow is the greatest day of my life. I'm going to be called upon to take the chair at the Meeting of the Peace Society. The Society of Universal Peace. No Army; no Navy; no more violence; the reign of amity begins at last. They are going to present me with a cup. Here it is. My Secretary chose it. Very nice cup. I shall have to make a speech; an impromptu. I have been the whole week trying to get it off by heart. My Secretary wrote it. Think of them there in their thousands, in their serried ranks applauding me. I shall have the wittiest answers ready in reply to all interruptions. My Secretary will do the interruptions. I should like to run through some of the most telling passages only there's no one to hear me. However, I'll try. I imagine that an audience sits before me, a large and intelligent audience. It's a great effort, but I'll try to imagine it. Ahem! –

Ladies and Gentlemen – Five minutes ago I assure you I had not the faintest idea of what was before me. This elevated position is one for which I was totally unprepared. Then as if by chance I shall lay my hand on the case of exhibits which I am giving to the Society: relics of barbarism: weapons of the past. Ladies and Gentlemen [*Holding up the revolver*] – In the fifteenth century the gun replaced the bow and arrow. There was to have been a gun, but it was too long for the case. But in the twentieth the olive branch (Exhibit No. 15) has replaced the gun. Progress marches before us with the Lamp of Learning in one hand [*Holding up the candle*] and the Cap of Liberty in the other [*Holding up the nightcap*]. Although we wish for peace Englishmen are not afraid. Their noble bosoms do not harbour such miserable sentiments as those of fear. [*Noise at the window;* BURGLAR *knocks over something*] Gracious goodness! What was that? [*Seizing revolver*] Somebody attacking the house! Infernal miscreants! It was like them to choose the moment when my wife was away. [*Blows out the candle and hides*]

Enter BURGLAR *by window and pulls up ladder after him which he leans against the high bookcase.*

BURGLAR. I'd best pull the ladder up after me. Somebody might see it from the outside. Now let's see what we have here. Ha! That'll be the plate chest! [*Seeing* POSTLETHWAITE] Good Lord! What's that? A man?

POSTLETHWAITE. Yes, I'm a man, what are you?

BURGLAR. Can't you see? I'm a burglar.

POSTLETHWAITE. A burglar! O Lord! [*Aside*] And my wife's away ... Get away! Get away from here or I'll shoot you.

BURGLAR. Lord! He's armed. [*Runs away, puts lamp on low revolving bookcase and hides*] Now then, fire away. I'm not afraid. [POSTLETHWAITE *fires three shots and the lamp falls*] Ow! You've killed me!

POSTLETHWAITE. Killed you! Are you sure? [*Turns up electric light and walks over to* BURGLAR] Where did I hit you?

BURGLAR. Right through the ... through the ... come closer ... right through the wick. [*Seizing* POSTLETHWAITE *and taking the pistol from him*] You Juggins! You didn't suppose I was holding the lamp, did you? Now then it's my turn ... Jump, you beggar, jump ... [*Fires twice at* POSTLETHWAITE'S *feet.* POSTLETHWAITE *jumps and runs up ladder on to the top of the bookshelf*]

POSTLETHWAITE. [*Looking over*] Pax!

BURGLAR. That's all very well. You shot at me first.

POSTLETHWAITE. I was within the law. You put me in fear of my life.

BURGLAR. What about me, then?

POSTLETHWAITE. You're only a burglar; I'm a respectable householder.

BURGLAR. Well, I'm not blood-thirsty, I'm only cautious ... cautious ... [*Moving ladder*] Now you stay up there, Mr Respectable Householder, while I go through your things and see what's worth keeping.

POSTLETHWAITE. Aren't you ashamed of yourself to come to another person's house in the middle of the night and put him in fear of his life?

BURGLAR. I didn't come here to put you in fear of your life. I simply came for the stuff. I never wanted this fracas. You ought to have been in bed at this time of night. I like people to be regular. Were you lying in wait for me? Did you know I was coming?

POSTLETHWAITE. No; if I had I shouldn't have been here at all, I should have gone out.

BURGLAR. Then what were you doing?

POSTLETHWAITE. I was preparing my speech for tomorrow.

BURGLAR. Speech! Are you going to make a speech tomorrow?

POSTLETHWAITE. Yes; would you like to hear it? I was wanting an audience. 'Ladies and Gentlemen, – Five minutes ago I assure you I had not the faintest idea of what was before me ...'

BURGLAR. I dare say not.

POSTLETHWAITE. 'This elevated position is one for which I was totally unprepared ...'

BURGLAR. Stop or I'll shoot you!

POSTLETHWAITE. But you don't know what my speech is about yet.

BURGLAR. I don't want to, an idea has occurred to me. I'm going to make a speech myself.

POSTLETHWAITE. What, do *you* make speeches?

BURGLAR. No, never; there's the trouble. I'm a member of the Walworth Parliament.

POSTLETHWAITE. You! But I thought you were a burglar.

BURGLAR. So I am at night, but what do you suppose I do all day? Do you imagine we have no private life? We meet every Saturday night.

POSTLETHWAITE. But Saturday night isn't in the daytime. You ought to be burgling on Saturday night. I like people to be regular.

BURGLAR. You show your ignorance, Sir, we're not allowed to burgle on Saturday nights.

POSTLETHWAITE. Who by, the police?

BURGLAR. No, trade union.

POSTLETHWAITE. What, do burglars have a trade union?

BURGLAR. Naturally; we must have someone to protect us. Saturday night is our day off.

POSTLETHWAITE. But a night can't be a day.

BURGLAR. Silence, Sir! I'm going to make a speech.

POSTLETHWAITE. But this isn't the time or the place; if you've come here to burgle – burgle. You're keeping me in suspense.

BURGLAR. I shall choose my own time and place for speaking.

POSTLETHWAITE. Why not choose Saturday night in Walworth?

BURGLAR. Because I can't. I don't know how it is, but somehow I can never catch the Speaker's eye. This is the first time I have ever got my audience, so to speak, in hand. '*Semper ego auditur tantum num quamque reponam.*'

POSTLETHWAITE. No Latin quotations, Sir, I beg. It's old-fashioned.

BURGLAR. I'm an old-fashioned man, I shall do what I like. '*Honi soit qui mal y pense*,' Mr Speaker, Sir . . .

POSTLETHWAITE. What is it on? Politics?

BURGLAR. Of course; I'm a strong Imperialist.

POSTLETHWAITE. O Lord, I might have guessed it! The party of violence.

BURGLAR. What's that you say?

POSTLETHWAITE. I was only talking to myself.

BURGLAR. No asides, they're old-fashioned. I expect assent and applause, do you understand? What I need is help and encouragement.

POSTLETHWAITE. I suppose I'd better humour him . . . Hear, hear!

BURGLAR. What is Society founded on?

POSTLETHWAITE. On love.

BURGLAR. On violence.

POSTLETHWAITE. On love.

BURGLAR. On violence. Don't interrupt me.

POSTLETHWAITE. But you asked me a question.

BURGLAR. The question was rhetorical and didn't require an answer. Who made the poor poor and the rich rich? [*Bis*] Why don't you answer?

POSTLETHWAITE. I thought your question was rhetorical and did not need an answer.

BURGLAR. Don't prevaricate, but answer me at once. Who made the rich rich?

POSTLETHWAITE. The which which?

BURGLAR. Who made the rich rich?

POSTLETHWAITE. The rich.

BURGLAR. You're wrong, the poor made the rich rich. How?

POSTLETHWAITE. By violence.

BURGLAR. No, Sir; by industry. And who made the poor poor?

POSTLETHWAITE. The poor.

BURGLAR. Wrong again; it was the rich made the poor poor.

POSTLETHWAITE. Poor poor!

BURGLAR. How did the rich make the poor poor?

POSTLETHWAITE. By industry.

BURGLAR. Wrong again. By violence. How is this to be righted? How are we to make the rich poor and the poor rich?

POSTLETHWAITE. By industry.

BURGLAR. No, Sir; by violence. And if the poor man comes to the rich man to make himself rich, and the rich man poor, how does the rich man meet him?

POSTLETHWAITE. By v-v-v-

BURGLAR. That's right.

POSTLETHWAITE. By violence.

BURGLAR. And if one nation comes against another nation, how must the nation meet the nation?

POSTLETHWAITE. By violence.

BURGLAR. Come, I want a little more enthusiasm say it again.

POSTLETHWAITE. By violence.

BURGLAR. That's right. And how is England to be ready to repel violence with violence? By having a strong army and a strong navy. Loud applause.

POSTLETHWAITE. Ha! ha! Hear! hear!

BURGLAR. Come, I'm glad to find that we're both of the same way of thinking. When the Germans take up arms, what must we do?

POSTLETHWAITE. We must take up arms.

BURGLAR. And when the Germans lay down a new keel, what must we do?

POSTLETHWAITE. We must lay down our arms.

BURGLAR. Look here, Mr Speaker, I don't know if you're fooling me . . .

POSTLETHWAITE. No, no; I'm nervous, that's all. You're so quick I can't get the right answer ready.

BURGLAR. I've had two shots at you already.

POSTLETHWAITE. How many shots did you say?

BURGLAR. Two.

POSTLETHWAITE. And how many did I have at you?

BURGLAR. You? Three.

POSTLETHWAITE. Let's see; two and three is five.

You're quite sure it was two?

BURGLAR. Quite. I still owe you one.

POSTLETHWAITE. Well, you'll have to go on owing it because there aren't any more cartridges. There were only five to start with. I counted 'em.

BURGLAR. We'll soon see about that. [*Click*]

POSTLETHWAITE. Yah!

BURGLAR. I don't care, I'm going on with my speech.

POSTLETHWAITE. I won't listen to you.

BURGLAR. You won't, won't you? There, take that! [*Firing arrow which sticks into the wall*]

POSTLETHWAITE. Yah! There's only one arrow.

BURGLAR. Gentlemen, *Carthago est delenda.*

POSTLETHWAITE. No Latin.

BURGLAR. '*Si pacem vis para bellum.*'

POSTLETHWAITE. Ireland for ever!

BURGLAR. '*Primus inter pares.*'

POSTLETHWAITE. Votes for Women! Votes for Women! Votes for Women! Votes for Women!

BURGLAR. Very well, if you won't listen I shall just go on with what I came for. What's this?

POSTLETHWAITE. That's a work-box.

BURGLAR. Yours?

POSTLETHWAITE. No, my wife's.

BURGLAR. Good Lord, have you got a wife?

POSTLETHWAITE. Rather.

BURGLAR. Why the devil didn't you say so before?

POSTLETHWAITE. She's asleep, don't make such a noise.

BURGLAR. Where? In there?

POSTLETHWAITE. No; in Cornwall.

BURGLAR. Old buffoon. [*He begins hunting for something in his tool bag*]

POSTLETHWAITE. O Lord, if I could only telephone to the police. [*Reaches down for the telephone*] I can't reach the damn thing.

BURGLAR. What are you doing?

POSTLETHWAITE. Ju-jit-su! I must have something to keep me warm. [*Tries to loop the telephone up with the rope of his dressing-gown. He pulls up the telephone and then the telephone book, which hangs by a long chain*] Now for the number of the police station.

BURGLAR. What are you doing?

POSTLETHWAITE. Nothing.

BURGLAR. What is that book?

POSTLETHWAITE. Bradshaw. I must have something to read . . . Here we are. 2304 Mayfair; 2304 Mayfair.

BURGLAR. What's that you're saying?

POSTLETHWAITE. Nothing; it's the time of the train. Saturdays only. Refreshment room, telegraph at the station. [*Exit* BURGLAR *to bedroom while he is talking*] Wrong number. O Lord! Send for the Supervisor. I shall write to *The Times*. Try again. Ho! for the Lord's sake, come quick; I'm all alone with a burglar in my flat. Is he armed? Yes, he has got a pistol, my pistol. What's that you say? The officer will be here in a quarter of an hour. But I don't want an officer, an ordinary private is good enough for me. I can't wait, he's murdering me. What's that you say? You like things done regular. Oh! take your time. Don't be late for the inquest. Bring the undertaker and some mutes. O Lord, quarter of an hour, and I'm getting so cold and so dusty up here. I must speak to Mary about it. [*Re-enter* BURGLAR *wearing fur coat and top hat of wrong size and carrying dressing-bags, dressing-cases, etc.*] Have you got all you want?

BURGLAR. Pretty well, now, I think. [*Helping himself to a whisky and soda*]

POSTLETHWAITE. Sure there's nothing else? Got my mother-o'-pearl studs and the hairbrushes, and the nailbrushes, and the toothbrush? Then you'd better be going.

BURGLAR. Oh, there's no hurry.

POSTLETHWAITE [*Looking at his watch*]. But there is. I've telephoned for the police.

BURGLAR. You've telephoned for the police! You scoundrel! [*Pointing pistol at him*] Come down and have it out like a man.

POSTLETHWAITE. No, thanks, I prefer to stay up here.

BURGLAR. Where's the door?

POSTLETHWAITE. That's it, that square thing in the wall.

BURGLAR. No, I might meet them on the stairs. I'll go by the window.

POSTLETHWAITE. You might meet them in the street.

BURGLAR. Well, I'll go one way or the other. Hullo! What's that?

POSTLETHWAITE. That's my cup.

BURGLAR. 'Presented to Sir Blennerhassett Postlethwaite.' How did you come by this? Now come, don't prevaricate. Do you know Sir Blennerhassett?

POSTLETHWAITE. Know Sir Blennerhassett! I am Sir Blennerhassett.

BURGLAR. The MP?

POSTLETHWAITE. The MP.

BURGLAR. The famous one?

POSTLETHWAITE. O Sir!

BURGLAR. The notorious blatherskite who preaches universal peace?

POSTLETHWAITE. Haven't I been preaching it for the last half-hour?

BURGLAR. And the police are coming?

POSTLETHWAITE. Yes, you'd better be off.

BURGLAR. No, on seconds thoughts I'll stay.

POSTLETHWAITE. But I shall give you in charge.

BURGLAR. No, you won't; you daren't.

POSTLETHWAITE. I daren't!

BURGLAR. Because I shall ruin your reputation.

POSTLETHWAITE. How?

BURGLAR. Because I shall tell the magistrate how you received me with a pistol.

POSTLETHWAITE. He won't care.

BURGLAR. But the public will. I shall make a speech.

POSTLETHWAITE. Another?

BURGLAR. In court; the papers will be full of it. By the time you get up at your blessed meeting it'll be in all the evening papers.

POSTLETHWAITE. But the meeting's in the afternoon.

BURGLAR. But the evening papers come out in the morning.

POSTLETHWAITE. But it's all right, you can go; the police won't be here for another ten minutes. I won't open the door till you're gone.

BURGLAR. But I refuse to go.

POSTLETHWAITE. You can keep your swag, I don't want it.

BURGLAR. This isn't enough.

POSTLETHWAITE. What more do you want?

BURGLAR. A cheque.

POSTLETHWAITE. Let me down then. [BURGLAR *brings ladder*] How much?

BURGLAR. A thousand pounds.

POSTLETHWAITE. I can't do it.

BURGLAR. You must.

POSTLETHWAITE. Where's my chequebook? Who am I to make it out to?

BURGLAR. It's not for me. [*Grandiloquently*] It's for the Navy League.

POSTLETHWAITE. The Navy League! I can't do it.

BURGLAR. You must. [POSTLETHWAITE *signs cheque*]

POSTLETHWAITE. O Lord, there are the police banging at the door. They'll break it in. Get out by the window.

BURGLAR. Not at all, I mean to go like a gentleman.

POSTLETHWAITE. If they find you here I shan't know what to say!

BURGLAR. Say I'm a friend of yours.

POSTLETHWAITE. I can't.

BURGLAR. You must. Open the door. [POSTLETHWAITE *opens the door*]

POLICEMAN. Good evening, Sir, you sent for me, I think.

POSTLETHWAITE. Did I?

POLICEMAN. Did you! Don't you know if you did?

POSTLETHWAITE. Oh yes, I remember, I-I-I- This is a friend of mine.

POLICEMAN. [*To* BURGLAR] Good evening, Sir. I think I know your face.

BURGLAR. Oh dear, yes, lots of people know my face. This gentleman rang you up . . .

POLICEMAN. What's the charge?

BURGLAR. Oh dear, no, no charge; entrance free.

POLICEMAN. [*To* POSTLETHWAITE] What did you want me for?

POSTLETHWAITE. This gentleman was going away, and I rang you up . . . to ask if you'd mind calling a taxi for him.

POLICEMAN. A taxi!

POSTLETHWAITE. Yes. The fact is we've lost our whistle. And if you want a drink here's a quid for you.

POLICEMAN. Very good, Sir. [*Turning to* BURGLAR *and picking up dressing-case*] Is this yours?

BURGLAR. Yes, it's mine. It was his but it is mine. It's sometimes his and sometimes mine. Perhaps you wouldn't mind carrying it down to the cab for me.

POLICEMAN. No more luggage, Sir? [*Exit* POLICEMAN]

BURGLAR. Why, bless my soul, I was nearly forgetting . . . my christening cup! [*Taking up the silver cup*] Goodbye, old chap, I'll look in again some time. Don't be cast down; whatever you have done this evening has been done for the sake of peace.

POSTLETHWAITE. Scoundrel! Tell me your name that I may curse you!

BURGLAR. Oh, my name's Peace, Charlie Peace.

CURTAIN

ALAN SEEGER 1888–1916

'If it must be, let it come in the heat of action. Why flinch? It is by far the noblest form in which death can come. It is in a sense almost a privilege . . .'
Letter, 22 May 1915

Alan Seeger at Harvard, 1910.

Alan Seeger died at Belloy-en-Santerre on 4 July 1916. Had any of his Harvard contemporaries from the class of 1910 – T. S. Eliot, Walter Lippmann, John Reed – died so young, there would have been little for the public to have noted. Seeger proclaimed himself indifferent to worldly ambition and lived to the full an anachronistic dream of heroism and high art; for a moment, he spoke to the heart of his countrymen. His passionate advocacy of the cause of France, and the enthusiasm with which he served for twenty-two months in the French Foreign Legion, made poems such as 'I Have a Rendezvous with Death' poignant and effective contributions to the cause dear to his heart: the entrance into the war of the United States on the side of the Allies.

Seeger's death may, in small measure, have strengthened a certain idealistic enthusiasm for the war, a sentiment given ironic expression by another Harvard man, John Dos Passos, in an early novel: *Three Soldiers* (1921). When Seeger was killed, his regiment was supporting the massive British attack on the Somme, a battle which brutally withered the idealism of a generation of volunteer soldiers. He died before disillusionment with the war became widespread, and thus, like Rupert Brooke, whose posthumous fame he envied, and whose 1914 sonnet 'Peace' he alludes to in his 'Ode in Memory of the American Volunteers Fallen for France', Seeger belongs to the mentality of the pre-war world. He welcomed war, he felt redeemed by the chance to die heroically and, like so many of his European contemporaries, from Barrés to Stefan George, saw in war the chance to turn away from the *anomie* of everyday life and rediscover community. Seeger's poems, letters and diaries repeatedly emphasize that, through war, a 'new companionship', an 'intrepid brotherhood', was being forged which would remake the world:

Craonne, before thy cannon-swept plateau,
Where like sere leaves lay strewn September's dead,
I found for all dear things I forfeited
A recompense I would not now forgo.

For that high fellowship was ours then
With those who, championing another's good,
More than dull Peace or its poor votaries could,
Taught us the dignity of being men.

From 'The Aisne (1914–15)'

Although Seeger was born in New York City, his family lived in a semi-rural setting on Staten Island. Business difficulties in the aftermath of the Spanish–American war caused the Seeger family to move to Mexico City in 1900, where he remained for two years before being sent back to Tarrytown, New York, to continue school. He entered Harvard in 1906. He was a tall, handsome young man but, to contemporaries, seemed to be without the gift of sociability: he could be rude, arrogant and selfish. Through John Reed, he met the small band of Harvard rebels and nonconformists, but Seeger declined to become one of their number. He was a loner who, though he lived the life of a poet, occupied a private world of his own and refused to show anyone his work. He studied Dante, Celtic sagas and medieval romances, and affected disdain for commerce and contemporary life. After graduating in 1910, he lived for two years in Greenwich Village where, again, he declined to seek advancement. He lived on money borrowed from friends, wore a romantic black cloak, and attended the salon of Mabel Dodge.

His parents, dismayed at their handsome son's aimless life and scruffy appearance, sent him in 1912 to continue his studies in Paris. There he lived on the Left Bank, desultorily attended lectures at the Sorbonne, and fell in with other young Harvard men who were not yet ready to assume their rightful place on the great American treadmill. Seeger assembled his poems in 1914, gave the manuscript the title 'Juvenilia', and found French publishers unreasonably doubtful about their commercial prospects. When the war broke out, he was in London. Hurrying back to Paris, he stopped in Bruges and left the manuscript with a publisher. His friends in Paris were in a frenzy of enthusiasm for the war, and Seeger, carrying erect an American flag, was with the first body of American volunteers who marched through Paris at the end of August.

American nationals could not swear allegiance to France, and were thus, at this stage of the war, only able to serve in the Foreign Legion. Seeger was assigned to the 1st Company, Battalion C, 2nd Regiment *Étrangère*, and sent off to Rouen to undergo basic training. There was tension in the Legion between the *anciens* and the American volunteers, and considerable frustration at the tedium of training. Seeger ignored the problems and, in his letters to his mother, and in articles in the New York press, wrote as one who was utterly fulfilled by the chance to serve his chosen cause. His *Letters and Diary*, published posthumously in 1917, make strange reading. He was convinced that the war was just and good, and assured his mother that 'this life agrees with me' (22 December 1914). Seeger dreamed, during quiet moments in the trenches, of leading glorious advances through the enemy lines and liberating the occupied territories of France. Kept largely in reserve duties, Seeger envied those of his friends who took part in the fighting around Arras in July 1915, and expressed his 'great regret' at the 'hard luck' which kept his regiment out of the cauldron of Verdun. The battle of Champagne in September was his baptism by fire, but the inconclusive result of the furious French assault, and the staggering cost in lives lost, seem to have left Seeger annoyed that a chance for heroic triumph had been missed. He began to go out alone on night patrol (it was the only way to get a Croix de Guerre) and filled his letters home with reflections on the 'bright side' of soldiers' lives. He rebuked his countrymen for their pusillanimous attitude towards the war, and accepted with exaltation the idea of death in combat.

In 1917, his countrymen read Seeger's poems for their touching idealism, and then, when general disillusionment set in about the war and its aftermath, chose not to read him at all. Seeger was not even mentioned in Louis Untermeyer's *The New Era in American Poetry* (1919). He was not untalented as a poet, but the exalted language of his idealism seemed out of place in the age of Imagism and *The Waste Land*. T. S. Eliot, who had known Seeger at Harvard, reviewed the *Poems* anonymously in *The Egoist* in December 1917:

> Seeger was serious about his work and spent pains over it. The work is well done, and so much out of date as to be almost a positive quality. It is high-flown, heavily decorated and solemn, but its solemnity is thorough going, not a mere literary formality. Alan Seeger, as one who knew him can attest, lived his whole life on this plane, with impeccable poetic dignity; everything about him was in keeping.

ERIC HOMBERGER

Texts

Alan Seeger, 'As a Soldier thinks of War', *The New Republic*, iii (22 May 1915, pp. 66–8).

Poems (Constable, London, 1917). With an introduction by William Archer.

Letters and Diary of Alan Seeger (Constable, London, 1917).

Secondary sources

Harrison Reeves, 'The Tragedy of Alan Seeger', *The New Republic*, x (10 March 1917, pp. 160–2).

[T. S. Eliot], Review of Seeger, 'Poems', *The Egoist*, iv (December 1917, pp. 172).

T. Sturge Moore, 'Soldier Poets (iv): Alan Seeger', *English Review*, xxvii (September 1918, pp. 199–207).

Edward Eyre Hunt, 'Stelligeric: a Footnote on Democracy', *Essays in Memory of Barrett Wendell by his Assistants* (Harvard University Press, Cambridge, Ma, 1926, pp. 303–20).

Irving Werstein, *Sound No Trumpet: the Life and Death of Alan Seeger* (Thomas Y. Crowell, New York, 1967).

Alan Seeger in the French Foreign Legion, 1915.

SONNET I

Sidney, in whom the heyday of romance
Came to its precious and most perfect flower,
Whether you tourneyed with victorious lance
Or brought sweet roundelays to Stella's bower,
I give myself some credit for the way
I have kept clean of what enslaves and lowers,
Shunned the ideals of our present day
And studied those that were esteemed in yours;
For, turning from the mob that buys Success
By sacrificing all Life's better part,
Down the free roads of human happiness
I frolicked, poor of purse but light of heart,
And lived in strict devotion all along
To my three idols – Love and Arms and Song.

I HAVE A RENDEZVOUS WITH DEATH

I have a rendezvous with Death
At some disputed barricade,
When Spring comes back with rustling shade
And apple-blossoms fill the air –
I have a rendezvous with Death
When Spring brings back blue days and fair.

It may be he shall take my hand
And lead me into his dark land
And close my eyes and quench my breath –
It may be I shall pass him still.
I have a rendezvous with Death
On some scarred slope of battered hill,
When Spring comes round again this year
And the first meadow-flowers appear.

God knows 'twere better to be deep
Pillowed in silk and scented down,
Where Love throbs out in blissful sleep,
Pulse nigh to pulse, and breath to breath,
Where hushed awakenings are dear . . .
But I've a rendezvous with Death
At midnight in some flaming town,
When Spring trips north again this year,
And I to my pledged word am true,
I shall not fail that rendezvous.

The Aisne (1914–15)

We first saw fire on the tragic slopes
Where the flood-tide of France's early gain,
Big with wrecked promise and abandoned hopes,
Broke in a surf of blood along the Aisne.

The charge her heroes left us, we assumed,
What, dying, they reconquered, we preserved,
In the chill trenches, harried, shelled, entombed,
Winter came down on us, but no man swerved.

Winter came down on us. The low clouds, torn
In the stark branches of the riven pines,
Blurred the white rockets that from dusk till morn
Traced the wide curve of the close-grappling lines.

In rain, and fog that on the withered hill
Froze before dawn, the lurking foe drew down;
Or light snows fell that made forlorner still
The ravaged country and the ruined town;

Or the long clouds would end. Intensely fair,
The winter constellations blazing forth –
Pursues, the Twins, Orion, the Great Bear –
Gleamed on our bayonets pointing to the north.

And the lone sentinel would start and soar
On wings of strong emotion as he knew
That kinship with the stars that only War
Is great enough to lift man's spirit to.

And ever down the curving front, aglow
With the pale rockets' intermittent light,
He heard, like distant thunder, growl and grow
The rumble of far battles in the night, –

Rumours, reverberant, indistinct, remote,
Borne from red fields whose martial names have won
The power to thrill like a far trumpet-note, –
Vic, Vailly, Soupir, Hurtelise, Craonne . . .

Craonne, before thy cannon-swept plateau,
Where like sere leaves lay strewn September's dead,
I found for all things I forfeited
A recompense I would not now forgo.

For that high fellowship was ours then
With those who, championing another's good,
More than dull Peace or its poor votaries could,
Taught us the dignity of being men.

There we drained deeper the deep cup of life,
And on sublimer summits came to learn,
After soft things, the terrible and stern,
After sweet Love, the majesty of Strife;

There where we faced under those frowning heights
The blast that maims, the hurricane that kills;
There where the watch-lights on the winter hills
Flickered like balefire through inclement nights;

There where, firm links in the unyielding chain,
Where fell the long-planned blow and fell in vain –
Hearts worthy of the honour and the trial,
We helped to hold the lines along the Aisne.

*F*RANCIS *L*EDWIDGE 1887–1917

'I look forward to poetry and fame after the war and feel that by joining I am helping to bring about peace and the old sublimity of which the world has been robbed.'

1914

'If I survive the war, I have great hopes of writing something that will live. [. . .] My book has had a greater reception in England, Ireland and America than I had ever dreamt of, but I never feel that my name should be mentioned in the same breath with my contemporaries. You ask me what I am doing. I am a unit in the Great War, doing and suffering, admiring great endeavour and condemning great dishonour. I may be dead before this reaches you, but I will have done my part. Death is as interesting to me as life. I have seen so much of it from Suvla to Serbia and now in France. I am always homesick. I hear the roads calling, and the hills, and the rivers wondering where I am. It is terrible to be always homesick.'

In just over six months, on 31 July 1917, Francis Ledwidge was blown to bits by a shellburst at Ypres.

The land for which he felt such longing was Ireland, more specifically the fields and roads along the banks of the Boyne in County Meath where he grew up. Born on 19 August 1887 in Slane, Ledwidge was the eighth child of an evicted tenant-farmer Patrick Ledwidge. He was later to claim that he was 'of a family who were ever soldiers and poets . . .' Leaving school at 12, he began work in the fields and in domestic service, ending up as an overseer of roads for the Slane area. His first attempts at verse were published in the *Drogheda Independent*, and it was not until June 1912, when he sent copies of his poems to the poet Lord Dunsany, that he secured an introduction to the literary world. His formal influences were Keats and Yeats, but his inspiration was the countryside and the travails of his own heart. Lord Dunsany was 'astonished by the brilliance of that eye that had looked at the fields of Meath and seen there all the simple birds and flowers, with a vividness that made those pages like a magnifying glass, through which one looked at familiar things seen thus for the first time.' Together they prepared Ledwidge's first book of poetry, *Songs of the Fields*.

Ledwidge's concern for his immediate surroundings prompted his interest in local affairs. He became secretary of the County Meath farm labourers' union, served on Navan District Council and was the county's insurance commissioner. He also joined and helped

Ledwidge in the uniform of a lance-corporal of the Royal Inniskilling Fusiliers.

organize the Slane corps of the Irish Volunteers. Ledwidge was a nationalist, but not a member of Sinn Fein. Finding himself isolated after the Volunteers split over the political dilemma of whether to fight for Britain in the war, he enlisted in the Royal Inniskilling Fusiliers in Dublin:

> Some of the people who know me least imagine that I joined the Army because I knew men were struggling for higher ideals and great emprises, and I could not sit idle to watch them make for me a more beautiful world. They are mistaken. I joined the British Army because she stood between Ireland and an enemy common to our civilization and I would not have her say that she defended us while we did nothing at home but pass resolutions.

Another reason for wanting to leave his home was his rejection by the girl he had hoped to marry, intimated in the poem 'After My Last Song'. *Songs of the Fields* was published while Ledwidge was serving in Salonika in autumn 1915. The press received the volume favourably, and Edward Marsh published three poems – 'A Rainy

Day in April', 'The Lost Ones', and 'The Wife of Llew' – in the second issue of *Georgian Poetry*.

After suffering from rheumatism in the winter, Ledwidge managed to secure a passage home. The interest he had shown in Turkish culture was evinced by his letter of 8 March 1916 to Lord Dunsany: 'By the way, I have great respect for the Turks. They fought us a clean fight, and we must admit they are brave soldiers. In my admiration for them, I have read the Koran. Mahomet nearly equals you in finding a simile for the moon. You have said: "When she is old, she hobbles away from the hills." Mahomet says: "She is twisted and broken like an old palm branch." '

The shock of the Easter Uprising in Dublin overshadowed his work. He wrote a total of twenty poems on the insurrection. The summer of 1916 was spent in County Derry, where he lost his lance-corporal's stripes after a 'bit of a night out'. There were several of these for, as Ledwidge began to recover physically, his mood grew blacker. War to him seemed an increasingly futile exercise. Even after his transfer to the Western Front, the war never featured overtly in his poems. That did not stop him writing about his experiences on the Western Front in his letters to Edward Marsh. Barely a month before his death he wrote: 'If you visit the front, don't forget to come up the line at night to watch the German rockets. They have white crests which throw a pale flame across no-man's-land and white bursting into green and green changing into blue and blue bursting and dropping down in purple torrents. It is like the end of a beautiful world.'

TIM CROSS

Text
The Complete Poems of Francis Ledwidge (Alice Curtayne (ed.), Brian & O'Keefe, London, 1974). This is the fullest available collection of Ledwidge's poems. It supersedes Lord Dunsany's edition of 1955.

Secondary source
Alice Curtayne, *Francis Ledwidge: a life of the poet* (Brian & O'Keeffe, London, 1972). Contains an extensive bibliography.

THE LOST ONES

Somewhere is music from the linnets' bills,
And thro' the sunny flowers the bee-wings drone,
And white bells of convolvulus on hills
Of quiet May make silent ringing, blown
Hither and thither by the wind of showers,
And somewhere all the wandering birds have flown;
And the brown breath of Autumn chills the flowers.

But where are all the loves of long ago?
Oh, little twilight ship, blown up the tide,
Where are the faces laughing in the glow
Of morning years, the lost ones scattered wide?
Give me your hand, Oh brother, let us go
Crying about the dark for those who died.

SOLILOQUY

When I was young I had a care
Lest I should cheat me of my share
Of that which makes it sweet to strive
For life, and dying still survive,
A name in sunshine written higher
Than lark or poet dare aspire.

But I grew weary doing well;
Besides, 'twas sweeter in that hell,
Down with the loud banditti people
Who robbed the orchards, climbed the steeple
For jackdaw's eggs and made the cock
Crow ere 'twas daylight on the clock.
I was so very bad the neighbours
Spoke of me at their daily labours.
And now I'm drinking wine in France
The helpless child of circumstance.
Tomorrow will be loud with war.
How will I be accounted for?

It is too late now to retrieve
A fallen dream, too late to grieve
A name unmade, but not too late
To thank the gods for what is great;
A keen-edged sword, a soldier's heart,
Is greater than a poet's art.
And greater than a poet's fame
A little grave that has no name,
Whence honour turns away in shame.

The Wife of Llew

And Gwydion said to Math, when it was Spring:
'Come now and let us make a wife for Llew.'
And so they broke broad boughs yet moist with dew,
And in a shadow made a magic ring:
They took the violet and the meadowsweet
To form her pretty face, and for her feet
They built a mound of daisies on a wing,
And for her voice they made a linnet sing
In the wide poppy blowing for her mouth.
And over all they chanted twenty hours.
And Llew came singing from the azure south
And bore away his wife of birds and flowers.

After My Last Song

Where I shall rest when my last song is over
The air is smelling like a feast of wine;
And purple breakers of the windy clover
Shall roll to cool this burning brow of mine;
And there shall come to me, when day is told
The peace of sleep when I am grey and old.

I'm wild for wandering to the far-off places
Since one forsook me whom I held most dear.
I want to see new wonders and new faces
Beyond East seas; but I will win back here
When my last song is sung, and veins are cold
As thawing snow, and I am grey and old.

Oh paining eyes, but not with salty weeping,
My heart is like a sod in winter rain;
Ere you will see those baying waters leaping
Like hungry hounds once more, how many a pain
Shall heal; but when my last short song is trolled
You'll sleep here on wan cheeks grown thin and old.

The Coming Poet

'Is it far to the town?' said the poet,
As he stood 'neath the groaning vane,
And the warm lights shimmered silver
On the skirts of the windy rain.
'There are those who call me,' he pleaded,
'And I'm wet and travel-sore.'
But nobody spoke from the shelter,
And he turned from the bolted door.

And they wait in the town for the poet
With stones at the gates, and jeers,
But away on the wolds of distance
In the blue of a thousand years
He sleeps with the age that knows him,
In the clay of the unborn, dead,
Rest at his weary insteps,
Fame at his crumbled head.

After Court Martial

My mind is not my mind, therefore
I take no heed of what men say,
I lived ten thousand years before
God cursed the town of Nineveh.

The Present is a dream I see
Of horror and loud sufferings,
At dawn a bird will waken me
Unto my place among the kings.

And though men called me a vile name,
And all my dream companions gone,
'Tis I the soldier bears the shame,
Not I the king of Babylon.

The Dead Kings

All the dead kings came to me
At Rosnaree, where I was dreaming,
A few stars glimmered through the morn,
And down the thorn the dews were streaming.

And every dead king had a story
Of ancient glory, sweetly told.
It was too early for the lark,
But the starry dark had tints of gold.

I listened to the sorrows three
Of that Eire passed into song.
A cock crowed near a hazel croft,
And up aloft dim larks winged strong.

And I, too, told the kings a story
Of later glory, her fourth sorrow:
There was a sound like moving shields
In high green fields and the lowland furrow.

And one said: 'We who yet are kings
Have heard these things lamenting inly.'
Sweet music flowed from many a bill
And on the hill the morn stood queenly.

And one said: 'Over is the singing,
And bell bough ringing, whence we come;
With heavy hearts we'll tread the shadows,
In honey meadows birds are dumb.'

And one said: 'Since the poets perished
And all they cherished in the way,
Their thoughts unsung, like petal showers
Inflame the hours of blue and grey.'

And one said: 'A loud tramp of men
We'll hear again at Rosnaree.'
A bomb burst near me where I lay.
I woke, 'twas day in Picardy.

France, 7 January 1917

In a Café

Kiss the maid and pass her round,
Lips like hers were made for many.
Our loves are far from us tonight,
But these red lips are sweet as any.

Let no empty glass be seen
Aloof from our good table's sparkle,
At the acme of our cheer
Here are francs to keep the circle.

They are far who miss us must –
Sip and kiss – how well we love them,
Battling through the world to keep
Their hearts at peace, their God above them.

11 February 1917

Home

A burst of sudden wings at dawn,
Faint voices in a dreamy noon,
Evenings of mist and murmurings,
And nights with rainbows of the moon.

And through these things a wood-way dim,
And waters dim, and slow sheep seen
On uphill paths that wind away
Through summer sounds and harvest green.

This is a song a robin sang
This morning on a broken tree,
It was about the little fields
That call across the world to me.

Belgium, July 1917

*T*OM *K*ETTLE 1880–1916

'If I live, I mean to spend the rest of my life working for perpetual peace. I have seen war and faced modern artillery and know what an outrage it is against simple men.'

1916

Tom Kettle was an Irish patriot, a resolute advocate of Home Rule for a united Ireland. Yet he volunteered for military service and was killed fighting for Britain in the Somme offensive of September 1916. The incongruity of an Irish Nationalist in British uniform was made all the more pointed after the Easter rising of 1916. When Kettle's friend and brother-in-law Frank Sheehy-Skeffington was executed summarily by the British forces, Kettle bitterly remarked, 'These men will go down to history as heroes and martyrs and I will go down – if I go down at all – as a bloody British officer.'

The man who embodied this paradox was born on 9 February 1880 in Artane, County Dublin. Thomas Michael Kettle was the third son of Andrew J. Kettle, a wealthy farmer, and Margaret MacCourt. His intellectual and oratorical powers were already in evidence at the Christian Brothers' School, and he was marked for scholarship at the Clongowes Wood College. However overwork and the emotional stress induced by the death of a brother interrupted his university career. He was prompted to undertake a *Wanderjahr* to restore his health.

This trip to Europe helped to establish in Kettle's mind the proper place within Europe's comity of nations and cultures for a troubled Ireland, 'a civilization shaken by Norse invasion before it had quite ripened; swept by Anglo-Norman invasion before it had quite recovered; a people plunged in an unimaginable chaos of races, religions, ideas, appetites, and provincialism; brayed in the mortar without emerging as a consolidated whole; tenacious of the national idea, but unable to bring it to triumph; riven and pillaged by invasion without being conquered – how could such a people find leisure to grow up, or such a civilization realize its full potentialities of development and discipline?'

The European tour was to bring Kettle to a closer understanding of the German and French cultures: 'If everyone could afford to travel there would be no wars. People would discover their neighbours to be so remarkably human.' Yet his distrust of the German 'will to power' mentality remained in the form of his distaste for the German philosopher Nietzsche who 'made Germans dance as before him only Heine had done'. With the French on the other hand, Kettle sensed a rapport with the Irish spirit and mind. Both were 'lucid, vigorous and positive'. This affinity was later – in 1914 – to extend to the Belgians and provide the motivating force for Kettle's eagerness to take up arms in their defence.

Tom Kettle.

For Kettle 1901 was a formative year. He was never to be more than a lay poet but his poetic imagination, the source of metaphoric strength for much of his later political oratory, was already evident. His travel notes contain vivid evocations of urban centres at night, where 'the lamps like captive moons or monstrous pearls' were 'strung about the lustful throat of the city'.

The next years saw Tom Kettle first called to the Bar but then switch to journalism, to politics and finally to an academic career. Although a firm Irish patriot, Kettle disavowed revolutionary tactics. He was a parliamentarian, a constitutionalist and a staunch believer in the ability to persuade the British of the necessity for Home Rule for Ireland by reason and not by force. The ten years from 1906 were spent primarily advocating this cause: 'There is in liberty a certain tonic inspiration, there is in the national idea a deep fountain of courage and energy not to be figured out in dots and decimals; and unless you can call these psychological forces into action your Home Rule Bill will be only ink, paper, and disappointment. In one word, Home Rule must be a moral as well as a material liquidation of the past.'

After Tom Kettle married Mary Sheehy in 1909 he was appointed Professor of National Economics at the National University in Dublin. His academic duties came into conflict with his parliamentary responsibilities and he resigned as MP for East Tyrone in 1910. As a Nationalist politician Kettle had made a great impression. His rhetorical skills, his charm, wit and command of repartee, had served women's suffrage and Irish Home Rule well. His commitment to Home Rule for an Ireland which was to include the northern province of Ulster continued outside a parliamentary career. The continued prevarication of the Westminster Parliament on this issue forced upon Kettle the realities of the dilemma: to seek Home Rule on a constitutional basis, or to establish a force which could counter the British presence. The Irish Volunteers was founded and Kettle was dispatched to Europe in the summer of 1914 to purchase arms on its behalf. A greater conflict was to overtake the growing friction in Ireland. Tom Kettle found himself in Brussels on 2 August 1914, the day of the German ultimatum to Belgium. The arms buyer quickly switched to his former occupation of journalism and wrote bulletins for the *Daily News*, describing his outrage at the subsequent desecration of places of worship and learning by the invading German army: 'Our duty is not to banish the memories of war as we have experienced it, but to burn them in beyond effacement every lie and trait, every dot and detail.'

Belgium was the key to Kettle's behaviour in the next two years. Belgium as an oppressed smaller nation became analagous to Ireland. He resolved to fight for a liberty he regarded as sacred: 'I care for liberty more than I care for Ireland.' Liberty for Ireland, he believed, would temporarily have to take a back seat to that of Belgium. Kettle felt the need to play a more intimate role in the fight. Journalism was not enough: 'I would rather see the war through as a sixth-rate soldier than as a first-rate man of letters.' His scorn for anyone who shirked this duty was biting. A minor Australian poet who argued that men of letters should keep out of the war and hand on the torch of culture to the future generation with the statement, 'I would rather be a tenth-rate minor poet than a great soldier,' was treated to a characteristic Kettle retort, 'Well, aren't you?'

Kettle volunteered for active service, but his health and his oratorical abilities better fitted the uniform of a recruiting officer. He made over 180 speeches up and down the country using Belgium as tinder for igniting Irishmen's enthusiasm: 'Come and help Belgium, the latest and greatest of evicted tenants . . . Call it a paradox, but the absentee at the present time is the man who stays at home . . . I cannot help hoping that when Catholics and Covenanters, Unionist and Nationalist, have written in blood their joint acceptance of this bill of honour on the continent they may possibly find an easier way of settling their differences at home.'

> *'If I were an English poet like that overpraised Rupert Brooke, I should call it, no doubt, the Gethsemane before the climb up the Windy Hill, but phrase-making seems now a very dead thing to me . . .'*
>
> *On leaving for the front, July 1916*

The events of the first two years of the war did not make it easy for Kettle to reconcile his ideals. The continued ambiguous stance of the British Government towards Home Rule prompted him to denounce what seemed a gross lack of generosity and understanding: 'England goes to fight for liberty in Europe and for junkerdom in Ireland.' Kettle also had misgivings about Britain's motives for continuing the war after the stalemate of 1915: 'It is time for somebody to say quite brutally that this is a struggle to destroy Prussian militarism, not to establish British Protectionism.'

Matters came to a head with the Easter Rising in Dublin in 1916. Kettle was not involved, and abhorred the violence on both sides. The murder of his wife's pacifist brother, Frank Sheehy-Skeffington, affected him deeply. But the rising gave the British Prime Minister, H. H. Asquith, and his Minister of Munitions, Lloyd George, the much-needed impetus to seek a resolution to the problem quickly. The offer of a *temporary* separation of Ulster from the rest of Ireland was a compromise which Kettle and the Nationalists accepted as a necessity. Kettle now felt free to fight in France and joined the Irish Brigade. Lloyd George's duplicity in offering *permanent* separation from the rest of Ireland to the Unionists in Ulster did not become apparent until Kettle was at the front. Kettle's disillusionment with the machinations of the British Government and the handling of the war, witnessed now at first hand, led to his strongest indictment of the whole conflict:

> Morality begins where hedonism ends. Truly the scourge of war is more terrible, more apocalyptic in its horror than even the most active imagination could have pictured. When the time comes to write down in every country a plain record of it, with its wounds and weariness and flesh stabbing and bone pulverizing and lunacies and rats and lice and maggots, and all the crawling festerment of battlefields, two landmarks in human progress will be revealed. The world will for the first time understand the nobility, beyond all phrase, of soldiers, and it will understand also the foulness, beyond all phrase, of those who compel them into war.

Kettle wrote in his essay 'The Ways of War', 'War has long been accepted as our best aid to the teaching of geography! Blood is an expensive marking fluid for maps, but it is vivid and indelible.' Lieutenant Kettle added his blood to the map of the Somme when shot dead by a bullet in the chest during the attack mounted at Ginchy on 9 September 1916.

In literature Kettle has survived only as the model for the character Hughes in *Stephen Hero*, James Joyce's evocation of his Dublin youth. Yet Kettle's sonnet to his daughter, composed only five days before his death, remains one of the prime exemplars of the Christian perspective of war.

The loss of Tom Kettle was an expensive one for Ireland, although he was troubled by alcoholism in the later stages of his short lifetime and it can be legitimately questioned whether he would have found the emotional strength to continue the struggle for a united Ireland after the war. Kettle's importance as a national leader would in any case have been founded on his vision of an Ireland at parity with Britain as a free European nation: 'My only programme for Ireland consists, in equal parts, of Home Rule and the Ten Commandments. My only counsel to Ireland is, that in order to become deeply Irish, she must become European . . .'

TIM CROSS

Texts

Poems and Parodies (Dublin & London, 1916).
The Ways of War (London & New York, 1917). Essays, with a memoir by Mary S. Kettle.
The Day's Burden and Miscellaneous Essays (Dublin & London, 1918, 1939).
An Irishman's Calendar: a quotation from the works of T. M. Kettle for every day in the year (Mary S. Kettle (ed.), Dublin, 1916).

Secondary source

J. B. Lyons, *The Enigma of Tom Kettle, Irish Patriot, Essayist, Poet, British Soldier 1880–1916* (Glendale Press, Dublin, 1983). This scrupulously researched biography contains a full list of manuscript sources, published essays, pamphlets, introductions, translations, articles, reviews and secondary sources.

On Leaving Ireland

The pathos of departure is indubitable.
I never felt my own essay 'On Saying Good-Bye' so profoundly aux tréfonds du coeur. *The sun was a clear globe of blood which we caught hanging over Ben Edar, with a trail of pure blood vibrating to us across the waves. It dropped into darkness before we left the deck. Some lines came to me, suggested by a friend who thought the mood cynical.*

As the sun died in blood, and hill and sea
Grew to an altar, red with mystery,
One came who knew me (it may be overmuch)
Seeking the cynical and staining touch,
But I, against the great sun's burial
Thought only of bayonet-flash and bugle-call,
And saw him as God's eye upon the deep,
Closed in the dream in which no women weep,
And knew that even I shall fall on sleep.

14 July 1916

To My Daughter Betty, The Gift of God
(Elizabeth Dorothy)

In wiser days, my darling rosebud, blown
To beauty proud as was your mother's prime,
In that desired, delayed, incredible time,
You'll ask why I abandoned you, my own,
And the dear heart that was your baby throne,
To dice with death. And oh! they'll give you rhyme
And reason: some will call the thing sublime,
And some decry it in a knowing tone.

So here, while the mad guns curse overhead,
And tired men sigh with mud for couch and floor,
Know that we fools, now with the foolish dead,
Died not for flag, nor King, nor Emperor,
But for a dream, born in a herdsman's shed,
And for the secret Scripture of the poor.

In the field, before Guillemont, Somme, 4 September 1916

*T. E. H*ULME 1883–1917

'. . . A German victory means an end of Europe as we know it, as a comity of nations; the whole framework would be changed.'
'Inevitability inapplicable', 29 January 1916

'Creative effort means new images . . . Thought is the joining together of new analogies, and so inspiration is a matter of an accidentally seen analogy or unlooked for resemblance.'

Thomas Ernest Hulme was born on 16 September 1883, at Gratton Hall, Endon, North Staffordshire. In January 1894, he entered the High School, Newcastle-under-Lyme. Those who knew him at this time say that he was original, humorous and speculative. His best subject was mathematics, but he also took a keen interest in the school debating society and in natural history.

As an Exhibitioner at St John's College, Cambridge, in 1902 he would entertain his friends with his persistent examination of every idea they expressed. A good deal of his criticism took the form of banter, and most of it was destructive, but there was no malice or superiority in his manner. 'I liked Hulme though some didn't,' says one of his friends of that period. 'He was entirely without side, and however provocative he might be, he was always entertaining and kind, and at bottom serious.' Hulme's fundamental seriousness was not apparent to the college authorities, but they observed the perpetual rows in his rooms. Hulme himself was a teetotaller, but some of his friends were drunken rowdies. There were disturbances at the local theatre, where Hulme with his Staffordshire voice corrected the pronunciation of the actors, and in March 1904 he was sent down, together with other undergraduates, for 'over-stepping the limits of the traditional licence allowed by the authorities on Boat Race night'. According to J. C. Squire, Hulme was given 'the longest mock funeral ever seen in the town'.

In July 1906 he went to Canada, working his way out and back, and doing labouring work on farms and in lumber-camps for eight months. He came back to England with £70 in his pocket: his physique had become first-rate; he was 6 ft 2 in and weighed about 13½ stone. He stayed in England only a few weeks, and early in 1907 went to Brussels, where for seven months he taught English and learned French and German. When he returned to London, he began a more systematic study of aesthetics and the history of philosophy, and in 1909, he published a number of essays on the philosophy of Henri Bergson, who saw existence as a struggle between the 'life force' (perceived through intuition) and the material world (perceived through the use of the intellect). From this time onwards, Hulme lived mainly on a small allowance from one of his relatives. In April 1911, he attended the Philosophical Congress at Bologna, and spent the next three months travelling in Italy. At

T.E. Hulme, photographed by G.C. Beresford *c.*1916.
Richard Cork

Bologna, Hulme hesitated whether to go and hear Professor Enriques's opening paper on 'Reality' or to stay and hear the bands and watch the dignified, brown-cloaked crowds that were waiting to welcome the Duke of the Abruzzi. 'I regard processions as the highest form of art. I cannot resist even the lowest form of them. I must march even with the Salvation Army bands I meet accidentally in Oxford Street on Sunday night.'

After his return to England, Hulme published a series of articles on Bergson in *The New Age* in October and November 1911, and about this time he wrote some short poems, five of which were printed in *The New Age* (25 January 1912) under the heading, *The Complete Poetical Works of T. E. Hulme.* They were meant to convey clear visual images rather than romantic emotions, and they used cadence rather than metre. This was the kind of thing that Hulme thought young poets ought to be doing; and the poems were typical of what afterwards came to be known as Imagism. There is a story that Hulme wrote them all in about three minutes, to show how easy it was; but this seems to be belied by his manuscripts, which show very careful corrections and improvements.

Hulme was already beginning to make the acquaintance of a number of critics and philosophers. His views were now taking a definite form: Bergson's doctrine of intuition, and the anti-romanticism common to the syndicalists and the neo-royalists, were combining in Hulme's mind to form a new compound: '. . . I can find a compromise for myself, however, which I roughly indicate by saying that I think time is real for the individual, but not for the race' – a statement that recalls Baudelaire's argument that there is no real progress, that is to say moral progress, except for the individual. At this time Hulme seems to have shared the anti-democratic views of syndicalists and royalists, and he rejected the arguments of those who found support for the democratic ideal in Bergson's philosophy: 'Bergson no more stands for Democracy than he stands for paper-bag cookery.' Later, in his articles on the war, Hulme tried to dissociate the democratic ideal from the romantic faith in personality and the inevitability of progress.

Early in 1912, he was readmitted to St John's, partly on the personal recommendation of J. C. Squire, and partly owing to a letter from Bergson.

Hulme had already given a course of lectures on Bergson at a private house in Kensington (November and December 1911), and at Cambridge he gave a lecture on the same subject to a society in Girton. In the same month (February 1912), he addressed the Heretics on 'Anti-romanticism and Original Sin'. He remained at Cambridge only a short time; something happened again, and down he came once more, without taking a degree. He next spent nine months in Berlin, where he attended the Berlin Aesthetic Congress and talked with Worringer. Rupert Brooke (q.v.) happened to be in Berlin at the same time; Hulme did not like him very much because he did not like any romantics, but the two used to meet and talk at the Café des Westens.

After Hulme's return to London, he became interested in the new geometrical art of Picasso, Wyndham Lewis, David Bomberg, William Roberts and Jacob Epstein. It seemed to him that this art was the expression of an attitude very like his own. It was anti-romantic, and had nothing to do with vitality and delight in nature. According to P. G. Konody's report of one of Hulme's lectures, Hulme maintained that this new art 'creates certain geometrical abstract shapes, rigid lines and crystalline forms, which are the refuge from the confusion and accidental detail of existence'.

Romantic art, as Hulme saw it, was an expression of faith in man's natural power of development. Classical art expressed a sense of man's limitations and a feeling for the *tension* that is fundamental to all valuable activity. Romantic art, being divorced from this sense, was slack and disorganized: it was based on a false view of human nature, and it recklessly indulged in emotion for emotion's sake without criticizing the quality of the emotion itself.

'A man cannot write without seeing at the same time a visual signification before his eyes. It is this image which precedes the writing and makes it firm.'

Notes on Language and Style

In April and May 1914, a series of lectures on new developments in art and literature was given at Kensington Town Hall, and at one of these meetings, Hulme read a paper on modern poetry. Despite the fact that he was more impressive in his conversation and his casual writing than in the lecture-hall, Hulme's knowledge and critical sensibility combined with his personal charm and his brilliance as a talker to make him a centre of the new movements in art and criticism. Among those who went to the weekly discussions at 67 Frith Street were Epstein and Gaudier-Brzeska (q.v.), Ezra Pound, J. C. Squire, Ashley Dukes, Wilfrid Gibson and Middleton Murry. Edward Wadsworth and C. R. W. Nevinson often came to these meetings, and Rupert Brooke also turned up once or twice. Hulme's talk bubbled with imagery. Sometimes he would lead people up the garden-path, make them agree to things, and then leave them in the lurch, simply for the fun of the thing; but he was intolerant of affectation and obscurantism, and Edward Marsh, another of the visitors to Frith Street, tells how 'There was a fashion at that time for nosing out unexpected racial strains in the pedigrees of great men, and crediting these with their qualities – Hulme was ridiculing this with his usual energy and finished up with comical gusto: "I decline to revise my opinions on the basis that Dostoevsky was an Italian." '

Hulme was at his best in monologue: 'I have seen him in the clutches of a little university professional, with Kant at his fingertips, whom he had provoked by his dialectical truculence,' says Wyndham Lewis. 'Hulme floundered like an ungainly fish, caught in a net of superior academic information.'

Against this, we may set the story of Hulme emphasizing an argument with Lewis himself by holding him upside down on the railings in Soho Square. This was early in 1914, about the time when Gaudier-Brzeska was threatening to sock Bomberg on the jaw, and Epstein and Bomberg were engaged in a quarrel that ended with a ceremonial kiss of reconciliation in the Goupil Galleries. Hulme persuaded Gaudier-Brzeska to make him a knuckleduster, carved out of solid brass, and this he afterwards carried about with him wherever he went. He was interested in the quarrels, but more concerned to illustrate his own theories of aesthetics, even when dealing with knuckledusters. In the course of some articles in *The New Age*, he defined his own position as a critic:

As in these articles I intend to skip about from one part of my argument to another, as occasion demands, I might perhaps give them a greater appearance of shape by laying down as a preliminary three theses that I want to maintain.
1. There are two kinds of art, geometrical or abstract, and vital and realistic art, which differ absolutely in kind from the other. They are not modifications of one and the same art, but pursue different aims and are created to satisfy a different desire of the mind.
2. Each of these arts springs from, and corresponds to, a certain general attitude towards the world. You get long periods of time in which only one of these arts and its corresponding mental attitude prevails. The naturalistic art of Greece and the Renaissance corresponded to a certain rational humanistic attitude towards the universe, and the geometrical has always gone with a different attitude of greater intensity than this.
3. The re-emergence of geometrical art at the present day may be the precursor of the re-emergence of the corresponding general attitude towards the world, and so of the final break-up of the Renaissance.

Epstein's drawing, 'The Rock Drill', as well as his carvings in flenite, and some of the early sculpture of Gaudier-Brzeska, might be taken to show the influence of these theories. Hulme had a genius for harnessing the energies of other people: just as he cajoled or bullied his friends into doing most of the work of his translations, so he tried to persuade the sculptors to do work that would illustrate his theories, and he was annoyed when Epstein spent much of his time modelling realistic busts. Hulme's relations with Ezra Pound and Wyndham Lewis were sometimes strained, but he always liked and admired Gaudier, and his enthusiasm for Epstein was unbounded. He persuaded A. R. Orage to reproduce some of the drawings of Epstein, Gaudier, Nevinson, Roberts and Bomberg in *The New Age*, and later he wrote a book about Epstein, but this was lost in 1917.

When the war broke out, Hulme joined the Honourable Artillery Company, and on 29 December 1914, he went to France. For a few days he was stationed at a rest camp, 'a fearful place, deep in mud, where we have to sleep in tents, which makes me very depressed . . . I thoroughly enjoy all the events, like being seen off at the docks, except that there were only about ten people to cheer us as the ship left the side, but it's all very amusing – and the girls at the windows.' Early in January, his battalion was moved up nearer to the Front: 'In the evening I went round to see some of the people I used to know in the 1st Battalion. All looked very different, their faces and clothes a sort of pale mud colour, all very tired of it and anxious to get back.'

Before the end of the month, he was in the trenches. At first, their part of the line was quiet, and on 27 January, Hulme wrote in his diary:

> I had to crawl along on my hands and knees through the mud in pitch darkness, and every now and then seemed to get stuck altogether. You feel shut in and hopeless. I wished I was about four feet. This war isn't for tall men. I got in a part too narrow and too low to stand or sit and had to sit sideways on a sack of coke to keep out of the water. We had to stay there from about 7 p.m. till just before dawn next morning, a most miserable experience. You can't sleep and you sit as it were at the bottom of a drain with nothing to look at but the top of the ditch slowly freezing. It's unutterably boring. The next night was better because I carried up a box to sit on and a sack of coke to burn in a brazier. But one brazier in a narrow trench among twelve men only warms about three. All through this night we had to dig a new passage in shifts. That in a way did look picturesque at midnight – a very clear starry night, this mound all full of passages like a molehill and three or four figures silhouetted on top of it using pick or shovel. The bullets kept whistling over it all the time, but as it's just over the crest of a hill most of them are high, though every now and then one comes on your level and is rather uncomfortable when you are taking your turn at sentry. The second night it froze hard, and it was much easier walking back over the mud.
>
> In reality there is nothing picturesque about it. It's the most miserable existence you can conceive of. I feel utterly depressed at the idea of having to do this for forty-eight hours every four days. It's simply hopeless. The boredom and discomfort of it exasperate you to the breaking point.

Hulme found nothing romantic or attractive in the war, and he had no liking for the technical business of warfare; but since the job had to be done, he thought it might as well be done efficiently. In his diary, he speaks of inefficiency and muddle, but there is no personal complaint; and when he mentions that the tennis-player, Kenneth Powell, has been killed carrying up corrugated iron, he says: 'It seems curious the way people realize things. I heard a man say: "It does seem a waste, Kenneth Powell carrying up corrugated iron." You see, he was interested in games.'

At times, Hulme wrote with the detachment of a poet or a painter, describing actual physical sensations that everybody shared:

> The only thing that makes you feel nervous is when the star shells go off and you stand out revealed quite clearly as in daylight. You have then the most wonderful feeling as if you were suddenly naked in the street and didn't like it . . . It's really like a kind of nightmare, in which you are in the middle of an

'I admit that the new order of society will be different from the old; the old was breaking up before; the war did not cause the decay, it merely announced the fact on a hoarding.'
'The kind of rubbish we oppose', 5 February 1916

> enormous saucer of mud with explosions and shots going off all round the edge, a sort of fringe of palm trees made of fireworks all round it.

The censor complained of the length of these letters, but Hulme went on writing sketches of life behind the line and in the trenches:

> We had to spend the night in the open air as there were very few dug-outs. There was a German rifle trained on a fixed part of the trench just where we were. It's very irritating to hear a bullet time after time hit the same spot on the parapet. About lunch-time this rifle, continually hitting the same place, spattered dirt from the parapet over my bread and butter. It gets very irritating after a time and everybody shouts out 'Oh stop it.' It showed however that it was a dangerous corner . . .

On 10 February, they came under heavy shell-fire:

> It was a dangerous trench for shelling because it was very wide and gave no protection to the back. An NCO told us to shift to a narrower part of the trench. I got separated from the others in a narrow communication trench behind with one other man. We had seen shells bursting fairly near us before and at first did not take it very seriously. But it soon turned out to be very different. The shells started dropping right on the trench itself. As soon as you had seen someone hurt, you began to look at shelling in a very different way. We shared this trench with the X Regiment. About ten yards away from where I was a man of this regiment had his arm and three-quarters of his head blown off – a frightful mess, his brains all over the place, some on the back of that man who stands behind me in the photograph. The worst of shelling is, the regulars say, that you don't get used to it, but get more and more alarmed at it every time. At any rate, the regulars in our trenches behaved in rather a strange way. One man threw himself down on the bottom of the trench shaking all over and crying. Another started to weep. It lasted for nearly one and a half hours and at the end of it parts of the trenches were all blown to pieces. It's not the idea of being killed that's alarming, but the idea of being hit by a jagged piece of steel. You hear the whistle of the shell coming, you crouch down as low as you can, and just wait. It doesn't burst merely with a bang, it has a kind of crack with a snap in it, like the crack of a very large whip. They seemed to burst just over your head, you seem to anticipate it hitting you in the back, it hits just near you and you get hit on the back with clods of earth and (in my case) spent bits of shell and shrapnel bullets fall all round you. I picked up one bullet almost sizzling in the mud just by my toe. What irritates you is the continuation of the shelling. You seem to feel that twenty minutes is normal, is enough – but when it goes on for over an hour, you get more and more exasperated, feel as if it were 'unfair'. Our men were as it happened very lucky, only three were hurt slightly and none killed. They all said it was the worst experience they have had since they were out here. I'm not in the least anxious myself to repeat it, nor is anyone else I think. It was very curious from where I was; looking out over the back of the trench, it looked absolutely peaceful. Just over the edge of the trench was a field of turnips or something of that kind with their leaves waving about in a busy kind of way, exactly as they might do in a back garden. About twelve miles away over the plain you could see the towers and church spires of an old town very famous in this war. By a kind of accident or trick, everything was rather gloomy, except this town which appeared absolutely white in the sun and immobile as if it would always be like that, and was out of time and space altogether. You've got to amuse yourself in the intervals of shelling and romanticizing the situation is as good a way as any other. Looking at the scene, the waving vegetables, the white town and all the rest of it, it looks quite timeless in a Buddhistic kind of way and you feel quite resigned if you are going to be killed to leave it just like that. When it ceased and we all got back to our places everybody was full of it.

Early in March, Hulme was wounded, and sent home; and two months later Gaudier-Brzeska was killed at Neuville Saint-Vaast. Hulme had been one of Gaudier's nearest friends: he was the first to hear of his death, and it was he who sent Mrs Bevan to break the news to Sophie Brzeska. After Hulme had recovered from his wound, he was 'lost' by the War Office for some months, and walked about London telling his friends that he didn't see why he should go back till they asked him. Meanwhile, however, he was trying to get a commission in the Royal Marine Artillery. He did not want a commission in the infantry, that would have been 'too much the same thing', nor did he want to go on serving in the ranks.

> It would be extremely depressing to me to start again as a private at this stage of the war. It was very different in the first months of the war, when one was excited about the thing. Besides, even

> impersonally, I do think I am suited to have a commission of this kind. Mathematics was always my subject and I should pick up the theoretical part, the calculations, etc., of which there is quite a lot in connection with the very big guns of the RMA, more easily than most people, and should enjoy the work. I am also about the build for heavy gun work . . .

In a series of 'war notes' published in *The New Age* (November 1915 to March 1916) and *The Cambridge Magazine* (January to March 1916) – including 'Why we are in favour of this war' – over the signature 'North Staffs', Hulme put forward a temperate and reasoned defence of the war based not on any liking for the excitement of war, and not on any belief that the war would achieve any great positive good, but on his conception of 'the heroic values' and his dislike of the prospect of German domination in Europe. In the course of these articles, he engaged in a controversy with Bertrand Russell and other pacifists, and tried to show that their arguments rested on a romantic conception of progress and an over-valuation of 'life' as against the absolute ethical values that make life worthwhile.

The commission came in March 1916, and Hulme spent the next six months in barracks at Portsmouth, going up to London frequently to sit for Epstein. About this time, he published his translation of Sorel's *Réflexions sur la violence* together with an introduction that he had already printed in *The New Age* (14 October 1915).

It would be ridiculous to judge Hulme's work mainly in the light of his passion for processions, knuckledusters and suet pudding. It is always interesting to trace the relation between a man's conduct and his ideas, but if the ideas have any value at all, they must be judged on their own merits. To some of his friends, it seemed that Hulme was a genius, but without the faith that makes geniuses think it worthwhile to express themselves and justify themselves. To others, it seemed that all his public truculence and exhibition of ingenuity for ingenuity's sake was nothing more than youthful exuberance. They believed that there was another side to Hulme, a side that seldom appeared in argument but found expression sometimes in his writing and sometimes when he was talking to one or two friends in Mrs Bevan's house at Hampstead or in his old room above Harold Monro's Poetry Bookshop. 'He had a very powerful brow and nose, and then a mouth kind and small compared to the other features, and a chin that did not reinforce the brow and nose. His eyes had a quick, almost projecting, glance, and the lids could become heavy and the eyes veiled in contemplation, giving him quite a different expression.

Hulme believed that the work he was doing was important, but he knew that he had added very little to the ideas he had borrowed, and that his real work remained to be done.

His outlook as expressed in his notes was incomplete and perhaps not wholly self-consistent, and the papers that he left behind ranged from 'a collection of hundreds of loose notes, varying in size from pieces of paper no bigger than a postage-stamp to complete folios of notes on one subject'. A 'Notebook on Notebooks' gave some clue to the use to which he intended to put these notes, but the work was never completed. He went back to the Front towards the end of 1916, taking the book on Epstein with him, and still full of the work that he was going to do. The batteries of the Royal Marine Artillery were situated at Oost-Duinkerke Bains, on the coast behind Nieuport, and they confined themselves to shelling German long-range batteries near Ostend, mostly at regular and conventional hours. Ashley Dukes, who was with the 1st Division when it came into that part of the line in June 1917, says that Hulme viewed this entry with great disfavour because the coastal sector had been quiet under the French, and Hulme preferred a quiet war. 'He had never in fact walked up as far as Nieuport, a mile in front of his guns, because he objected to coming under rifle fire. He explained the barbarous character of close-range warfare and one evening when we were walking together up the road because I had to go into the line, he turned back at a ruined dairy and said that was the utmost limit of his constitutional.'

Perhaps this was nothing more than the usual pose of the artilleryman, but those who met Hulme when he came home on leave say that his outlook was greatly changed: 'I remember Hulme remarking that the war had made him more tolerant, and that he was growing more and more democratic. I thought it wiser to ask no question on this remark as the knuckleduster was near at hand.' Certainly Hulme was as disputatious as ever. 'What a man!' said an officer who met him while he was serving with his battery. 'He'd argue a dog's hind leg off.' On 28 September, just when everybody seemed to have knocked off for lunch, there was an unexpected burst of shell-fire, and Hulme was killed.

MICHAEL ROBERTS

Texts
Speculations (Herbert Read (ed.), Routledge, Kegan Paul, London, 1924).
Further Speculations (Samuel Hynes (ed.), London, 1955).
Notes on Language and Style (Haskell House, USA). A reprint of the 1929 edition.

Secondary sources
Michael Roberts, *T. E. Hulme* (Carcanet, Manchester, 1982). The article by Michael Roberts is an abridged version of the 'Biographical Sketch' which first appeared in this 1938 edition of this thorough study of Hulme's thoughts on philosophy and literature. The above passage is reproduced with the kind permission of Janet Adam Smith and Carcanet New Press. The 1982 edition contains an introduction, evaluating Roberts's response to Hulme, by Anthony Quinn.
Alun R. Jones, *The Life and Opinions of T. E. Hulme* (Gollancz, London, 1960).

Why We Are in Favour of This War

[. . .] Reasons which are sufficient to make us reject 'pacifist philosophy' are *not* sufficient to make us accept this *particular* war. The fact, for example, that a high value should be attached to military heroism, has nothing to do with the justification of a particular event in which such heroism may be displayed. This is an absolutely different question.

There are, moreover, at this moment, a class of pacifists who do not accept 'a pacifist philosophy', and whose reasons for objecting to the war are based on the nature and causes of *this* war itself. I was talking recently to a pacifist of this type, and what he said threw a good deal of light – for me, personally, at any rate, on the nature of a certain opposition to the war. He had no objection to killing; and conveyed the impression that he was quite prepared to fight himself in some more 'ideal' type of struggle – one with some positive and definite aim – in a war, for example, which would bring about the final disappearance of capitalism. But he was not prepared to fight in *this* war, which, in as far as it was not an entirely unnecessary stupidity, was concerned with interests very far removed from any which had any real importance for the individual citizen, and more definitely the individual workman.

I admit that this attitude, if we *agree to certain tacit assumptions*, does seem justified. As the attitude is very real and fairly widespread it is perhaps worthwhile examining the nature of these assumptions. Though it may not be very conscious or formulated, I think it demonstrable that there is floating before the mind of the man who makes this objection a certain false conception of the character of human activities. What makes the objection possible and gives force to it is the conception of Progress. By that I do not mean merely the hope that capitalism will ultimately disappear. It is rather that progress is looked upon as *inevitable* in this sense – that the evils in the world are due to definite oppressions, and whenever any particular shackle has been removed, the evil it was responsible for has disappeared for ever, for human nature is on the whole, good, and a harmonious society is thus possible. As long as you hold this conception of the nature of history, you are bound, I think, to find nothing in *this war* which makes it worthwhile. But this is a false conception; the evil in the world is not merely due to the existence of oppression. It is part of the *nature* of things and just as man is not naturally good and has only achieved anything as the result of certain discipline, the 'good' here does not preserve itself, but is also preserved by discipline. This may seem too simple to be worth emphasising, but I think this way of treating the objection justified, for it really does spring from this quite *abstract* matter, this false conception of the nature of evil in the world. It is only under the influence of this false conception that you demand an *ideal* war where great sacrifices are for great ends.

So it comes about that we are unable to name any great *positive* 'good' for which we can be said to be fighting. But it is not necessary that we should; there is no harmony in the nature of things, so that from time to time great and useless sacrifices become necessary, merely that whatever precarious 'good' the world has achieved may just be preserved. These sacrifices are as negative, barren, and as *necessary* as the work of those who repair sea-walls. In this war, then, we are fighting for no great *liberation* of mankind, for no great jump upward, but are merely accomplishing a work, which, if the nature of things was ultimately 'good,' would be useless, but which in this actual 'vale of tears' becomes from time to time necessary, merely in order that bad may not get worse.

This method of stating the question avoids the subterfuges to which those who hold the optimistic conception of man are driven – of inventing imaginary positive 'goods' which the war is to bring about 'to end war' and the rest. But if this argument is to have any effect it must be possible to give a clear account of the definite evils that would follow our defeat.

We are fighting to avoid (1) a German Europe, (2) the inevitable reactions which would follow this inside the beaten countries.

The consequences of such a defeat seem so perfectly clear and definite to us, that we think that if we could only for once actually *focus* the attention of the pacifist on them we should convince him. But we are mistaken; to perceive things is not enough; it is necessary to attach weight to the things perceived. It is not sufficient that you shall merely *perceive* a possible German hegemony; it is necessary that you shall have a vivid realisation of what it means. It is like the distinction which writers on religion are accustomed to make, between assent to some proposition, and real *faith* – leading to action. There are many pacifists, who will assent to what you say about German hegemony – they agree verbally, but . . . it is as if you pointed out to an old lady at a garden party, that there was an escaped lion about twenty yards off – and she were to reply, 'Oh, yes,' and then quietly take another cucumber sandwich.

But it won't do to ignore these consequences of defeat. If you are sitting in a room carrying on a discussion with another man, on some very abstract subject, and suddenly you notice that the floor is beginning to tilt up, then you have to pay attention to the fact. In comparison with the abstract discussion it interrupts, it may be a low, material fact, but it has to be dealt with. This is exactly the position many pacifists are in. Trying to indicate to them the consequences of German hegemony is like trying to show a cat its reflection in a mirror. It isn't interested, its mind is full of other interests . . .

In approaching the subject (the consequences of German hegemony) I feel at once the presence of certain difficulties. The people one wishes to convince seem instinctively inclined to *discount* what one says in advance. Before going into any detail, then, it is best to deal with the reasons which prevent due weight being attached to these things.

(1) They seem disinclined to consider reasons drawn from the consequences of German hegemony, because they think that reasons we give are not the real causes of our actions. We are in favour of the war because we are moved by certain impulses of national pride and aggressiveness, and we then desire to *find* good reasons to justify our attitude. This scepticism has a good deal of force because it does describe accurately the position of many people. Many people are moved not only by the impulses mentioned above, but by a certain instinct which makes men want life at a higher pitch and intensity (the instinct that makes a man seek the excitement to be got from gambling) – and they imagine that war will provide them with this. Under these circumstances we might deceive ourselves; we should tend to think the issues at stake were much more important than we shall think them in peacetime. There is, then, something unreal about the justification we give for the war, because our action is really not dependent on the reasons we give.

I do not say that I was not moved by such impulses at the beginning of the war; but I am writing now at a period when any such bellicose impulses in us, any exuberance in this direction, have been cured by experience; I don't think I have an ounce of bellicosity left. I probably have quite as intense a *desire* for peace as any pacifist. I am fully aware of the wretched life led by those in the trenches – practically a condition of slavery – and would like to see it ended at once. It is true that if I read in a German paper some vainglorious boasting over our coming defeat, I should at once feel a very strong revival of these impulses of aggressiveness, and pride, and a desire to humiliate at all costs, the people who have written these things. But putting such moments out of court, I can honestly say that my convictions about the consequences of defeat, whether right or wrong, are founded on observation, and not on *impulses*.

(2) There is another way in which such reasons may be misleading. People who can read foreign newspapers, and who take an interest in foreign policy, tend to acquire certain special interests, which they often mistake for the real interests of their country. They tend to look on these things as a kind of drama, and wish their own country to play a distinguished part. If I know the whole history of a certain disputed part of Africa, if I am fully aware of the secret designs of some other country, I have a great longing then to see my own country intervene at all costs. I then attach an undue importance to the matter for my special interest in the subject is out of all proportion to the country's real interest. It is like the passion which may be aroused in a game of chess. The pacifist who wishes to think of all these problems in terms of individual welfare rather than national glory, tends to treat all reasoning of this kind with a smile and tolerant disdain – 'funny little German professors who write about Welt-politik . . . these dreams of writers on foreign politics are not very real when compared with the actual interests of the workman.'

The answer I make is the same as in the first case. The fears I have about German hegemony have nothing whatever to do with the concern of the man interested in foreign policy. The things at issue are realities which will affect very strongly the life of the ordinary citizen.

(3) This last objection has proved more effective than either of the other two. The usual presentment of the consequences of German hegemony as it might be given, for example, by the *Morning Post*, is soaked with false reasons, which make it seem entirely unreal to you. It is based on assumptions – Imperialist and others – which you do not share. But many false reasons can be given for true things. The two should be carefully distinguished here. I share most of your assumptions. I have no disguised reactionary motives. I am not in favour of the war, because I think all wars favour reaction. I am, on the contrary, inclined to think that this war will hasten the disappearance of the rich. I think it possible to state the reasons based on the probable reactions that would follow German hegemony in a way that should be convincing to the democrat.

From The Cambridge Magazine, *12 February 1916*

Henri Gaudier-Brzeska (1891-1915): Knuckleduster for T.E. Hulme.

The Poet

Over a large table, smooth, he leaned in ecstasies,
In a dream.
He had been to woods, and talked and walked with trees.
Had left the world
And brought back round globes and stone images,
Of gems, colours, hard and definite.
With these he played, in a dream,
On the smooth table.

Autumn

A touch of cold in the Autumn night
I walked abroad,
And saw the ruddy moon lean over a hedge
Like a red-faced farmer.
I did not stop to speak, but nodded;
And round about were the wistful stars
With white faces like town children.

In the City Square

In the city square at night, the meeting of the torches.
The start of the great march,
The cries, the cheers, the parting.
Marching in an order
Through the familiar streets,
Through friends for the last time seen.
Marching with torches.

Over the hill summit,
The moon and the moor,
And we marching alone.
The torches are out.

On the cold hill,
The cheers of the warrior dead
(For the first time re-seen)
Marching in an order
To where?

Trenches: St Eloi

Over the flat slope of St Eloi
A wide wall of sand bags.
Night,
In the silence desultory men
Pottering over small fires, cleaning their mess-tins:
To and fro, from the lines,
Men walk as on Piccadilly,
Making paths in the dark,
Through scattered dead horses,
Over a dead Belgian's belly.

The Germans have rockets. The English have no rockets.
Behind the line, cannon, hidden, lying back miles.
Before the line, chaos:

My mind is a corridor. The minds about me are
corridors.
Nothing suggests itself. There is nothing to do but
keep on.

*R*UPERT *B*ROOKE 1887–1915

' "War declared with Austria. 11.9." There was a volley of quick low handclapping – more a signal of recognition than anything else. Then we dispersed into Trafalgar Square, and bought midnight war editions, special. All these days I have not been so near tears. There was such tragedy, and such dignity, in the people.'

12 August 1914

Rupert Chawner Brooke was born on 3 August 1887. His father was a housemaster at Rugby School, and Rupert and his two brothers grew up in the comfortable security of a home dedicated to the ideals of 'godliness and good learning'. Having discovered the power of poetry – from a chance reading of Browning – at the age of 9, Rupert entered his father's school in 1901. From the start, he did well both in the classroom and on the playing field; for although early on he adopted the pose of the decadent aesthete, winning the school poetry prize in 1905, he found time to play in the cricket XI and the rugger XV.

Just under 6 feet tall, he was strikingly handsome, and people would turn in the street to watch him pass under a tossing mane of red-gold hair. This physical presence was matched by a sharpness of intellect, a charm and vitality of manner that affected everyone with whom he came into contact. Popular and successful at Rugby, he was even more so at King's College, Cambridge, where he went as a scholar in 1906. He read more voraciously than ever, he threw himself into acting (playing the parts of Mephistopheles in Marlowe's *Dr Faustus* and the Attendant Spirit in Milton's *Comus*) and into the activities of the University Fabian Society, of which he became president. His circle of friends soon included Frances Cornford, E. M. Forster, Hugh Dalton, George Leigh Mallory, Geoffrey and Maynard Keynes, and Virginia Stephen (later to make her name as Virginia Woolf). When Henry James visited Cambridge in 1909, he too fell under the spell of the golden-haired young man who punted him down the Cam, although the pole was unfortunately allowed to fall on the Master's bald head. Told that Rupert Brooke wrote poetry, but that it was no good, he replied: 'Well, I must say I am relieved, for with that appearance if he had also talent it would be too unfair.'

Talent, however, there was. This and an unswerving dedication to poetry were producing poems in which, by the end of that year, a modern voice was making itself heard through the period diction:

One of the famous portraits of Rupert Brooke executed by Sherril Schell.

The damned ship lurched and slithered. Quiet and
 quick
 My cold gorge rose; the long sea rolled; I knew
I must think hard of something, or be sick;
 And could think hard of only one thing – *you*!
You, you alone could hold my fancy ever!
 And with you memories come, sharp pain, and
 dole.
Now there's a choice – heartache or tortured liver!
 A sea-sick body, or a you-sick soul!

Do I forget you? Retchings twist and tie me,
 Old meat, good meals, brown gobbets, up I
 throw.
Do I remember? Acrid return and slimy,
 The sobs and slobber of a last year's woe.
And still the sick ship rolls. 'Tis hard, I tell ye,
To choose 'twixt love and nausea, heart and belly.

Having gained a second class in the Cambridge Classical Tripos, Brooke established himself in Grantchester at the Old Vicarage (afterwards made famous by his poem 'The Old Vicarage, Grantchester') and began to work at a dissertation on Webster and the Elizabethan dramatists. His pastoral existence, however, was interrupted by an unhappy love affair, and in 1912 he travelled through France and Germany in search of peace of mind. It was in the Café des Westens, Berlin, that he composed 'Grantchester'.

Partially recovered, he returned to England and was elected to a Fellowship at King's. He divided his time between Cambridge and London, where through Eddie Marsh, a prominent civil servant with literary tastes, he met such poets as Lascelles Abercrombie, Wilfrid Gibson, John Drinkwater and Edward Thomas (q.v.), and made friends in social and political circles centred on Violet Asquith, the Prime Minister's brilliant and attractive daughter.

Falling in love again, this time with the actress Cathleen Nesbitt, Brooke decided that he needed a change of scene while considering what to do with his life, and in May 1913 he sailed for America. He had been commissioned by the *Westminster Gazette* to write a series of articles on his impressions of the United States and Canada, and over the coming months sent back a dozen such dispatches. His friends received a stream of vivid, entertaining, and frequently ribald letters that showed the poet revelling in his role of Byronic self-exile. Christmas 1913 found him in New Zealand, reached by way of Hawaii, Samoa, and Fiji, and a month later he was in Tahiti. This he decided was 'the most ideal place in the world' and, finding in this Pacific paradise an Eve (called Taatamata), he wrote a number of happy poems such as 'Tiare Tahiti':

> *Taü here*, Mamua,
> Crown the hair, and come away!
> Hear the calling of the moon,
> And the whispering scents that stray
> About the idle warm lagoon.
> Hasten, hand in human hand,
> Down the dark, the flowered way,
> Along the whiteness of the sand,
> And in the water's soft caress,
> Wash the mind of foolishness,
> Mamua, until the day.
> Spend the glittering moonlight there
> Pursuing down the soundless deep
> Limbs that gleam and shadowy hair,
> Or floating lazy, half-asleep.
> Dive and double and follow after,
> Snare in flowers, and kiss, and call,
> With lips that fade, and human laughter
> And faces individual,
> Well this side of Paradise! . . .
> There's little comfort in the wise.

Brooke left Tahiti in April 1914, writing to Cathleen Nesbitt:

> It was only yesterday, when I knew that the Southern Cross had left me, that I suddenly realized that I'd left behind those lovely places and lovely people, perhaps for ever. I reflected that there was surely nothing else like them in this world and very probably nothing in the next . . .

Four months later, the outbreak of war prompted a general resurgence of what he termed 'grandiose thoughts about the Destiny of Man, the Irresistibility of Fate, the Doom of Nations, the fact that Death awaits us All, and so forth'. In South Africa, Isaac Rosenberg (q.v.), envisioning an exhausted civilization rejuvenated by conflict, ended his poem 'On Receiving News of the War' (q.v.):

> O! ancient crimson curse!
> Corrode, consume.
> Give back this universe
> Its pristine bloom.

In France at the same time, Wilfred Owen (q.v.) also used 'bloom' to develop a similar natural image in the sestet of his sonnet '1914':

> For after Spring had bloomed in early Greece,
> And Summer blazed her glory out with Rome,
> An Autumn softly fell, a harvest home,
> A slow grand age, and rich with all increase.
> But now, for us, wild Winter, and the need
> Of sowings for new Spring, and blood for seed.

In England, Brooke began work on the first of the 1914 sonnets that were to make his name. Paradoxically entitled 'Peace', it celebrates the discovery of a cause, a vision resembling Owen's and Rosenberg's: the regeneration of 'a world grown old and cold and weary'. The solemnity of the occasion prompted grandiose thoughts and, forsaking Marvellian tetrameters for Tennysonian pentameters, Brooke yielded to the temptations of a high style that in his better poems he had resisted. Despite the change of style, however, his subject remains the same: the place of life and laughter after death. His fourth sonnet, 'The Dead', comes to the same conclusion as 'Tiare Tahiti':

> These had seen movement, and heard music; known
> Slumber and waking; loved; gone proudly friended;
> Felt the quick stir of wonder; sat alone;
> Touched flowers and furs and cheeks. All this is ended.
> There are waters blown by changing winds to laughter
> And lit by the rich skies, all day. And after,

Frost, with a gesture, stays the waves that dance
And wandering loveliness. He leaves a white
Unbroken glory, a gathered radiance,
A width, a shining peace, under the night.

What is new in this is the closing metaphor's implication that human laughter has returned to its natural source, is now a part of nature. Although 'Frost, with a gesture, stays the waves that dance', sun and moon will in time release them and the changing winds blow them to laughter once again.

Brooke's fifth and most famous sonnet reverts, in its sestet, to the Platonic position he had so often mocked:

And think, this heart, all evil shed away,
A pulse in the eternal mind, no less
Gives somewhere back the thoughts by
England given . . .

'The Soldier' would not have been as successful as it was if it were not, in its way, a good poem, but some of the unease that over the years has crept into its readers' response may well be related to a lack of conviction on the part of its author as he tried to convince himself of the existence of an afterlife in which he did not believe. The irony is, of course, that whether or not Brooke *is* now 'A pulse in the eternal mind', he *does* give back, in the best of his poems,

the thoughts by England given;
Her sights and sounds; dreams happy as her day;
And laughter, learnt of friends; and gentleness,
In hearts at peace, under an English
heaven.

Brooke is not a war poet. He is a poet of peace, a celebrant of friendship, love, and laughter, such as he shared with his fellow officers in March 1915 on the troopship destined (though they did not know it) for Gallipoli. On the voyage, he contracted first heatstroke, then dysentery, and finally blood-poisoning, of which he died on 23 April. That evening he was buried on the Greek island of Skyros.

England at this time needed a focal point for its griefs, ideals and aspirations, and the valediction that appeared in *The Times* over the initials of Winston Churchill, the First Lord of the Admiralty, sounded a note that was to swell over the months and years that followed:

> The thoughts to which he gave expression in the very few incomparable war sonnets which he has left behind will be shared by many thousands of young men moving resolutely and blithely forward into this, the hardest, the cruellest, and the least-rewarded of all the wars that men have fought. They are a whole history and revelation of Rupert Brooke himself. Joyous, fearless, versatile, deeply instructed, with classic symmetry of mind and body, he was all that one would wish England's noblest sons to be in days when no sacrifice but the most precious is acceptable, and the most precious is that which is most freely proffered.

In due course, another friend – the poet Frances Cornford – was to speed the transition of man into myth – man into marble – with her quatrain:

A young Apollo, golden-haired,
Stands dreaming on the verge of strife,
Magnificently unprepared
For the long littleness of life.

Brooke's *1914 and Other Poems* was published in June 1915, and over the next decade, this and his *Collected Poems* sold 300,000 copies.

It is important to distinguish, however, between the man and the myth; important to avoid the facile and dishonest juxtaposition of Brooke's *1914* sonnets with, say, the later poems of Wilfred Owen. Brooke may have seen himself and others of his generation turning, at the outbreak of war, 'as swimmers into cleanness leaping', but he was not alone in envisioning an exhausted civilization rejuvenated by war. It should be remembered that, in 1914, Wilfred Owen was himself writing:

O meet it is and passing sweet
To live in peace with others,
But sweeter still and far more meet,
To die in war for brothers.

Had Brooke lived to experience the Gallipoli landings or the trenches of the Western Front, it is hard to imagine that the poet of 'A Channel Passage' would not have written as realistically as Owen and Sassoon.

JON STALLWORTHY

Texts

The Collected Poems (Sidgwick & Jackson, London, 1987).
Letters from America (Sidgwick & Jackson, London, 1987).
The Letters of Rupert Brooke (Geoffrey Keynes (ed.), Faber, London, 1968). Extracts by kind permission of Faber and Faber Ltd.

Secondary sources

Christopher Hassall, *Rupert Brooke, a biography* (Faber, London, 1984).
Paul Delaney, *The Neo-Pagans: friendship and love in the Rupert Brooke circle* (Macmillan, London, 1987).

1914

I. PEACE

Now, God be thanked Who has matched us with His hour,
And caught our youth, and wakened us from sleeping,
With hand made sure, clear eye, and sharpened power,
To turn, as swimmers into cleanness leaping,
Glad from a world grown old and cold and weary,
Leave the sick hearts that honour could not move,
And half-men, and their dirty songs and dreary,
And all the little emptiness of love!

Oh! we, who have known shame, we have found release there,
Where there's no ill, no grief, but sleep has mending,
Naught broken save this body, lost but breath;
Nothing to shake the laughing heart's long peace there
But only agony, and that has ending;
And the worst friend and enemy is but Death.

II. SAFETY

Dear! of all happy in the hour, most blest
He who has found our hid security,
Assured in the dark tides of the world that rest,
And heard our word, 'Who is so safe as we?'
We have found safety with all things undying,
The winds, and morning, tears of men and mirth,
The deep night, and birds singing, and clouds flying,
And sleep, and freedom, and the autumnal earth.

We have built a house that is not for Time's throwing.
We have gained a peace unshaken by pain for ever.
War knows no power. Safe shall be my going,
Secretly armed against all death's endeavour;
Safe though all safety's lost; safe where men fall;
And if these poor limbs die, safest of all.

III. THE DEAD

Blow out, you bugles, over the rich Dead!
There's none of these so lonely and poor of old,
But, dying, has made us rarer gifts than gold.
These laid the world away; poured out the red
Sweet wine of youth; gave up the years to be
Of work and joy, and that unhoped serene,
That men call age; and those who would have been,
Their sons, they gave, their immortality.

Blow, bugles, blow! They brought us, for our dearth,
Holiness, lacked so long, and Love, and Pain.
Honour has come back, as a king, to earth,
And paid his subjects with a royal wage;
And Nobleness walks in our ways again;
And we have come into our heritage.

IV. THE DEAD

These hearts were woven of human joys and cares,
Washed marvellously with sorrow, swift to mirth.
The years had given them kindness. Dawn was theirs,
And sunset, and the colours of the earth.
These had seen movement, and heard music; known
Slumber and waking; loved; gone proudly friended;
Felt the quick stir of wonder; sat alone;
Touched flowers and furs and cheeks. All this is ended.

There are waters blown by changing winds to laughter
And lit by the rich skies, all day. And after,
Frost, with a gesture, stays the waves that dance
And wandering loveliness. He leaves a white
Unbroken glory, a gathered radiance,
A width, a shining peace, under the night.

V. THE SOLDIER

If I should die, think only this of me:
That there's some corner of a foreign field
That is for ever England. There shall be
In that rich earth a richer dust concealed;
A dust whom England bore, shaped, made aware,
Gave, once, her flowers to love, her ways to roam,
A body of England's, breathing English air,
Washed by the rivers, blest by suns of home.

And think, this heart, all evil shed away,
A pulse in the eternal mind, no less
Gives somewhere back the thoughts by England Given;
Her sights and sounds; dreams happy as her day;
And laughter, learnt of friends; and gentleness,
In hearts at peace, under an English heaven.

The Old Vicarage, Grantchester

Just now the lilac is in bloom,
All before my little room;
And in my flower-beds, I think,
Smile the carnation and the pink;
And down the borders, well I know,
The poppy and the pansy blow . . .
Oh! there the chestnuts, summer through,
Beside the river make for you
A tunnel of green gloom, and sleep
Deeply above; and green and deep
The stream mysterious glides beneath,
Green as a dream and deep as death.
– Oh, damn! I know it! and I know
How the May fields all golden show,
And when the day is young and sweet,
Gild gloriously the bare feet
That run to bathe . . .
Du lieber Gott!

Here am I, sweating, sick, and hot,
And there the shadowed waters fresh
Lean up to embrace the naked flesh.
Temperamentvoll German Jews
Drink beer around; – and *there* the dews
Are soft beneath a morn of gold.
Here tulips bloom as they are told;
Unkempt about those hedges blows
An English unofficial rose;
And there the unregulated sun
Slopes down to rest when day is done,
And wakes a vague unpunctual star,
A slippered Hesper; and there are
Meads towards Haslingfield and Coton
Where *das Betreten*'s not *verboten*.

ἔθε γενοιμην . . . would I were
In Grantchester, in Grantchester! –
Some, it may be, can get in touch
With Nature there, or Earth, or such.
And clever modern men have seen
A Faun a-peeping through the green,
And felt the Classics were not dead,
To glimpse a Naiad's reedy head,
Or hear the Goat-foot piping low: . . .
But these are things I do not know.
I only know that you may lie
Day-long and watch the Cambridge sky,
And, flower-lulled in sleepy grass,
Hear the cool lapse of hours pass,
Until the centuries blend and blur
In Grantchester, in Grantchester . . .
Still in the dawnlit waters cool
His ghostly Lordship swims his pool,
And tries the strokes, essays the tricks,
Long learnt on Hellespont, or Styx.

Dan Chaucer hears his river still
Chatter beneath a phantom mill.
Tennyson notes, with studious eye,
How Cambridge waters hurry by . . .
And in that garden, black and white,
Creep whispers through the grass all night;
And spectral dance, before the dawn,
A hundred Vicars down the lawn;
Curates, long dust, will come and go
On lissom, clerical, printless toe;
And oft between the boughs is seen
The sly shade of a Rural Dean . . .
Till, at a shiver in the skies,
Vanishing with Satanic cries,
The prim ecclesiastic rout
Leaves but a startled sleeper-out,
Grey heavens, the first bird's drowsy calls,
The falling house that never falls.

God! I will pack, and take a train,
And get me to England once again!
For England's the one land, I know,
Where men with Splendid Hearts may go;
And Cambridgeshire, of all England,
The shire for Men who Understand;
And of *that* district I prefer
The lovely hamlet Grantchester.
For Cambridge people rarely smile,
Being urban, squat, and packed with guile;
And Royston men in the far South
Are black and fierce and strange of mouth;
At Over they fling oaths at one,
And worse than oaths at Trumpington,
And Ditton girls are mean and dirty,
And there's none in Harston under thirty,
And folks in Shelford and those parts
Have twisted lips and twisted hearts,
And Barton men make Cockney rhymes,
And Coton's full of nameless crimes,
And things are done you'd not believe
At Madingley, on Christmas Eve.
Strong men have run for miles and miles,
When one from Cherry Hinton smiles;

Strong men have blanched, and shot their
wives,
Rather than send them to St Ives;
Strong men have cried like babes, bydam,
To hear what happened at Babraham.
But Grantchester! ah, Grantchester!

There's peace and holy quiet there,
Great clouds along pacific skies,
And men and women with straight eyes,
Lithe children lovelier than a dream,
A bosky wood, a slumbrous stream,
And little kindly winds that creep
Round twilight corners, half asleep.
In Grantchester their skins are white;
They bathe by day, they bathe by night;
The women there do all they ought;
The men observe the Rules of Thought.
They love the Good; they worship Truth;
They laugh uproariously in youth;
(And when they get to feeling old,
They up and shoot themselves, I'm told) . . .

Ah God! to see the branches stir
Across the moon at Grantchester!
To smell the thrilling-sweet and rotten
Unforgettable, unforgotten
River-smell, and hear the breeze
Sobbing in the little trees.

Say, do the elm-clumps greatly stand
Still guardians of that holy land?
The chestnuts shade, in reverend dream,
The yet unacademic stream?
Is dawn a secret shy and cold
Anadyomene, silver-gold?
And sunset still a golden sea
From Haslingfield to Madingley?
And after, ere the night is born,
Do hares come out about the corn?
Oh, is the water sweet and cool,
Gentle and brown, above the pool?
And laughs the immortal river still
Under the mill, under the mill?
Say, is there Beauty yet to find?
And Certainty? and Quiet kind?
Deep meadows yet, for to forget
The lies, and truths, and pain? . . . Oh! yet
Stands the Church clock at ten to three?
And is there honey still for tea?

Menelaus and Helen

I

Hot through Troy's ruin Menelaus broke
To Priam's palace, sword in hand, to sate
On that adulterous whore a ten years' hate
And a king's honour. Through red death, and smoke,
And cries, and then by quieter ways he strode,
Till the still innermost chamber fronted him.
He swung his sword, and crashed into the dim
Luxurious bower, flaming like a god.

High sat white Helen, lonely and serene.
He had not remembered that she was so fair,
And that her neck curved down in such a way;
And he felt tired. He flung the sword away,
And kissed her feet, and knelt before her there,
The perfect Knight before the perfect Queen.

II

So far the poet. How should he behold
That journey home, the long connubial years?
He does not tell you how white Helen bears
Child on legitimate child, becomes a scold,
Haggard with virtue. Menelaus bold
Waxed garrulous, and sacked a hundred Troys
'Twixt noon and supper. And her golden voice
Got shrill as he grew deafer. And both were old.

Often he wonders why on earth he went
Troyward, or why poor Paris ever came.
Oft she weeps, gummy-eyed and impotent;
Her dry shanks twitch at Paris' mumbled name.
So Menelaus nagged; and Helen cried;
And Paris slept on by Scamander side.

1909

Fragment

I strayed about the deck, an hour, tonight
Under a cloudy moonless sky; and peeped
In at the windows, watched my friends at table,
Or playing cards, or standing in the doorway,
Or coming out into the darkness. Still
No one could see me.

I would have thought of them
– Heedless, within a week of battle – in pity,
Pride in their strength and in the weight and firmness
And link'd beauty of bodies, and pity that
This gay machine of splendour 'ld soon be broken,
Thought little of, pashed, scattered . . .

Only, always,
I could but see them – against the lamplight – pass
Like coloured shadows, thinner than filmy glass,
Slight bubbles, fainter than the wave's faint light,
That broke to phosphorus out in the night,
Perishing things and strange ghosts – soon to die
To other ghosts – this one, or that, or I.

April 1915

Heaven

Fish (fly-replete, in depth of June,
Dawdling away their wat'ry noon)
Ponder deep wisdom, dark or clear,
Each secret fishy hope or fear.
Fish say, they have their Stream and Pond;
But is there anything Beyond?
This life cannot be All, they swear,
For how unpleasant, if it were!
One may not doubt that, somehow, Good
Shall come of Water and of Mud;
And, sure, the reverent eye must see
A Purpose in Liquidity.
We darkly know, by Faith we cry,
The future is not Wholly Dry.
Mud unto mud! – Death eddies near –
Not here the appointed End, not here!
But somewhere, beyond Space and Time,
Is wetter water, slimier slime!
And there (they trust) there swimmeth One
Who swam ere rivers were begun,
Immense, of fishy form and mind,
Squamous, omnipotent, and kind;
And under that Almighty Fin,
The littlest fish may enter in.
Oh! never fly conceals a hook,
Fish say, in the Eternal Brook,
But more than mundane weeds are there,
And mud, celestially fair;
Fat caterpillars drift around,
And Paradisal grubs are found;
Unfading moths, immortal flies,
And the worm that never dies.
And in that Heaven of all their wish,
There shall be no more land, say fish.

Rupert Brooke succumbing to sunstroke in Egypt after having dragged his 'slow length about the desert sands on the first day like a wounded alexandrine'. *King's College, Cambridge*

CHARLES HAMILTON SORLEY 1895–1915

'There is no such thing as a just war. What we are doing is casting out Satan by Satan.'

May 1915

Charles Hamilton Sorley was a Scot, born to an academic family on 19 May 1895. In one of his last letters, he wrote: ' "Sorley" is the Gaelic for "wanderer". I have had a conventional education: Oxford would have corked it. But this [the war] has freed the spirit, glory be. Give me *The Odyssey*, and I return the New Testament to store. Physically as well as spiritually, give me the road.' His 'conventional education' included Marlborough, where he wrote a number of poems, one of the earliest being 'Banbury Camp', about a pre-Roman hill-fort on the Marlborough Downs, which begins:

> We burrowed night and day with tools of lead,
> Heaped the bank up and cast it in a ring
> And hurled the earth above. And Caesar said,
> 'Why, it is excellent. I like the thing.'
> We, who are dead,
> Made it, and wrought, and Caesar liked the thing.

Here it can be seen that the imagination of yet another public-school boy has been stamped with the martial insignia of a classical education. A later stanza employs a phrase – a concept – curiously close to the 'joy of battle' of Julian Grenfell (q.v.), but uses it in a very different context:

> So, fighting men and winds and tempests, hot
> With joy and hate and battle-lust, we fell
> Where we fought. And God said, 'Killed at last then?
> What!
> Ye that are too strong for heaven, too clean for hell,
> (God said) stir not.
> This be your heaven, or, if ye will, your hell.'

The ghosts of Sorley's Roman soldiers live on in their native landscape as, he imagines in a later poem, will the soldiers marching to a later war.

He was in Germany when that war broke out. Having won a scholarship to Oxford in December 1916, he decided to spend the two terms before he went up learning German – and independence. He learned both, to the extent that his first feelings of patriotism were towards Germany. He was out for a walk in February 1914 when he heard a group of German soldiers singing, as he said, 'something glorious and senseless about the Fatherland':

Sorley in the uniform of a captain, Suffolk Regiment.

> And when I got home, I felt I was a German, and proud to be a German: when the tempest of the singing was at its loudest, I felt that perhaps I could die for Deutschland – and I have never had an inkling of that feeling about England, and never shall.

That emotion died with the cessation of the singing, but the affection and admiration he had acquired for the Germans continued after they became 'the enemy'. He recognized, however, that he had to choose between the two countries and seems to have had no hesitation in making his choice, but because of his conflicting feelings, he is critical of anything that smacks of 'jingoism'. 'England –' he writes, 'I am sick of the sound of the word. In training to fight for England, I am training to fight for that deliberate hypocrisy, that terrible middle-class sloth of outlook and appalling "imaginative indolence" that has marked us out from generation to generation.'

He is particularly critical of the jingoistic strain in Rupert Brooke, and a letter to his mother about Brooke's death in 1915 highlights the principal difference between these two poets:

> That last sonnet-sequence of his, of which you sent me the review in the *Times Lit. Sup.*, and which has been so praised, I find (with the exception of that beginning 'Their hearts were woven of human joys and cares . . .' which is not about himself) overpraised. He is far too obsessed with his own

> sacrifice regarding the going to war of himself (and others) as a highly intense, remarkable and sacrificial exploit, whereas it is merely the conduct demanded of him (and others) by the turn of circumstances, where the non-compliance with this demand would have made life intolerable. It was not that 'they' gave up anything of that list he gives in one sonnet: but that the essence of these things had been endangered by circumstances over which he had no control and he must fight to recapture them. He has clothed his attitude in fine words: but he has taken the sentimental attitude.

As this shows, Sorley was far from sentimental. Brooke had also spent time in Germany before the war, but whereas his most famous sonnet, 'If I should die', invokes the noun 'England' no less than four times, Sorley wrote a sonnet (some months earlier) entitled 'To Germany'. It begins:

> You are blind like us. Your hurt no man designed,
> And no man claimed the conquest of your land . . .

The sestet moves from present blindness to a prophetic vision of future sight that has an interesting relation to the piercing recognition and reconciliation of Englishman and German in Owen's poem 'Strange Meeting'. Sorley is much more optimistic:

> When it is peace, then we may view again
> With new-won eyes each other's truer form
> And wonder. Grown more loving-kind and warm
> We'll grasp firm hands and laugh at the old pain,
> When it is peace. But until peace, the storm
> The darkness and the thunder and the rain.

Much as one may admire the attitudes expressed in that poem, it has to be said that its impact is diminished by the euphemistic metaphor with which it ends – 'But until peace, the storm/The darkness and the thunder and the rain . . .' – especially when one remembers other poems in which he writes exultantly of wind and rain – what Robert Graves was to call 'Sorley's weather'.

There are no such euphemisms, however, in the sonnet found in his kit after his death on the Western Front in October 1915:

> When you see millions of the mouthless dead
> Across your dreams in pale battalions go,
> Say not soft things as other men have said,
> That you'll remember. For you need not so.
> Give them not praise. For, deaf, how should they
> know
> It is not curses heaped on each gashed head?
> Nor tears. Their blind eyes see not your tears flow.
> Nor honour. It is easy to be dead.
> Say only this, 'They are dead.' Then add thereto,
> 'Yet many a better one has died before.'
> Then, scanning all the o'ercrowded mass, should you
> Perceive one face that you loved heretofore,
> It is a spook. None wears the face you knew.
> Great death has made all his for evermore.

Sorley was one of the first poets to get the numbers right – there were '*millions* of the mouthless dead' – and, responding perhaps to Brooke's 'If I should die' (one of those sonnets Sorley had criticized for their excessive concern with *self*), there is no first-person pronoun, no 'I', in his poem. Where Brooke had urged his reader to 'think only this of *me*', Sorley tells us to

> Say not soft things as other men have said,
> That you'll remember. For you need not so.

Those negatives are followed by others, as with unsparing irony he punctures the platitudes of consolation:

> Give them not praise. For, deaf, how should they
> know
> It is not curses heaped on each gashed head?
> Nor tears. Their blind eyes see not your tears flow.
> Nor honour. It is easy to be dead.

In November 1914, writing to the Master of Marlborough, Sorley had quoted a line from the *Iliad* spoken by Achilles – 'Died Patroclus too who was a far better man than thou' – adding, 'no saner and splendider comment on death has been made.' As his last sonnet enters its sestet, he echoes that Homeric line with another instruction to his reader:

> Say only this, 'They are dead.' Then add thereto,
> 'Yet many a better one has died before.'

Sorley's dead are blind, deaf, gashed. They are not heroic Homeric shades, garlanded with glory, but an indistinguishable 'o'ercrowded mass'. He did not live long enough to acquire the technical skills of an Owen or a Sassoon, but Sorley understood the truth about the war – and found words for it – before they did. He stands as an attractive transitional figure between the first wave of poets and those of the second wave.

JON STALLWORTHY

Texts

Marlborough and Other Poems (Cambridge University Press, 1916).

The Collected Poems of Charles Hamilton Sorley (Jean Moorcroft Wilson (ed.), Cecil Woolf, London, 1985).

The Collected Letters of Charles Hamilton Sorley (Jean Moorcroft Wilson (ed.), Cecil Woolf, London, 1985).

Secondary sources

Jean Moorcroft Wilson, *Charles Hamilton Sorley: a biography* (Cecil Woolf, London, 1985).

All the Hills and Vales Along

All the hills and vales along
Earth is bursting into song,
And the singers are the chaps
Who are going to die perhaps.
O sing, marching men,
Till the valleys ring again.
Give your gladness to earth's keeping,
So be glad, when you are sleeping.

Cast away regret and rue,
Think what you are marching to,
Little give, great pass.
Jesus Christ and Barabbas
Were found the same day.
This died, that, went his way.
So sing with joyful breath.
For why, you are going to death.
Teeming earth will surely store
All the gladness that you pour.

Earth that never doubts nor fears
Earth that knows of death, not tears,
Earth that bore with joyful ease
Hemlock for Socrates,
Earth that blossomed and was glad
'Neath the cross that Christ had,
Shall rejoice and blossom too
When the bullet reaches you.
Wherefore, men marching
On the road to death, sing!
Pour gladness on earth's head,
So be merry, so be dead.

From the hills and valleys earth
Shouts back the sound of mirth,
Tramp of feet and lilt of song
Ringing all the road along.
All the music of their going,
Ringing swinging glad song-throwing,
Earth will echo still, when foot
Lies numb and voice mute.
On marching men, on
To the gates of death with song.
Sow your gladness for earth's reaping,
So you may be glad though sleeping.
Strew your gladness on earth's bed,
So be merry, so be dead.

Two Sonnets

I

Saints have adored the lofty soul of you.
Poets have whitened at your high renown.
We stand among the many millions who
Do hourly wait to pass your pathway down.
You, so familiar, once were strange: we tried
To live as of your presence unaware.
But now in every road on every side
We see your straight and steadfast signpost there.

I think it like that signpost in my land,
Hoary and tall, which pointed me to go
Upward, into the hills, on the right hand,
Where the mists swim and the winds shriek and blow,
A homeless land and friendless, but a land
I did not know and that I wished to know.

II

Such, such is Death: no triumph: no defeat:
Only an empty pail, a slate rubbed clean,
A merciful putting away of what has been.

And this we know: Death is not Life effete,
Life crushed, the broken pail. We who have seen
So marvellous things know well the end not yet.

Victor and vanquished are a-one in death:
Coward and brave: friend, foe. Ghosts do not say
'Come, what was your record when you drew breath?'
But a big blot has hid each yesterday
So poor, so manifestly incomplete.
And your bright Promise, withered long and sped,
Is touched, stirs, rises, opens and grows sweet
And blossoms and is you, when you are dead.

12 June 1915

*E*DWARD *T*HOMAS 1878–1917

'All I can tell is, it seemed to me that either I had never loved England, or I had loved it foolishly, aesthetically, like a slave, not having realized that it was not mine unless I were willing and prepared to die rather than leave it as Belgian women and old men and children had left their country.'
From 'This England', September 1914

'Yesterday, too, we had a coloured sunset lingering in the sky and after that at intervals a bright brassy glare where they were burning waste cartridges. The sky, of course, winks with broad flashes all round almost all night and the air flaps and sags.'
Description of the trenches, 4 April 1917

Philip Edward Thomas was born at Lambeth on 3 March 1878 and spent most of his childhood in London where his father was a staff clerk in the Board of Trade. A stern man, who had worked his way up in the world, he had temperamentally little in common with Edward, the oldest of his six sons. 'Almost as soon as I could babble,' the poet was later to write, 'I "babbled of green fields",' and he was never happier than in his school holidays spent with his aunt or grandmother in Swindon. There he discovered his lifelong passion for the countryside and its creatures, for country people and country pursuits.

His father introduced him to literature, first of all to the prose writers who celebrated the country and its ways, Izaak Walton and Richard Jefferies, and when he was 15 he began to read poetry for pleasure. By then he was at St Paul's School, Hammersmith, where his natural shyness was increased by the greater confidence of the other boys, who for the most part came from more prosperous middle-class homes. He had recently begun writing seriously – in the manner of Richard Jefferies – and found an ally and encourager in James Ashcroft Noble, a 50-year-old journalist and author. Thomas left St Paul's in 1895 and went up to Oxford, ostensibly reading for the Civil Service examination, but in fact extending his knowledge of literature and writing a book of his own, *The Woodland Life* (1897). This was dedicated to Noble, who had died the previous year, and to whose daughter Helen he was secretly engaged. In 1899, following a courtship movingly described in her *As It Was*, they were married – secretly because of the disapproval of their parents. A year later, with a second-class degree, a baby son, and high literary ambitions, Edward Thomas left Oxford for slum lodgings in Earlsfield.

Edward Thomas, photographed by E. O. Hoppé.

Reviewing and literary journalism were hard to find and, when found, exhausting and poorly paid. 'I now live – if living it may be called – by my writing,' he told a friend, ' "literature" we call it in Fleet Street (derived from "litter") . . . . It's a painful business, and living in this labyrinth of red brick makes it worse.' Unable to resist the lure of the country, the Thomases moved to Kent in 1901. Their spirits rose only to be dashed by the discovery that Helen was again pregnant. She wrote: 'It means more anxiety for Edward and more work for him. Home will become unendurable to him. Even now poverty, anxiety, physical weakness, disappointments and discouragements are making him bitter, hard and impatient, quick to violent anger, and subject to long fits of depression.'

A melancholy inherited from his much-loved mother became more marked over the difficult years that followed. He was reviewing up to fifteen books a week and, though he hated the drudgery, reviewing them conscientiously and with discernment. The meagre income that it brought him he supplemented by selling his review copies and writing one book after another. Thirty were published between 1897 and 1917, and during those twenty years he also edited sixteen anthologies and editions. Everything was done hurriedly, but nothing was slovenly, and he was able to find delight – and communicate it with freshness and charm – in even the most unpromising 'hack' assignment.

His great gifts as a literary critic appeared to best advantage in his reviewing of poetry, and he was the first to salute such new stars in the literary firmament as W. H. Davies the 'Super-Tramp', Robert Frost and Ezra Pound. Coming up to London, usually in search of work – a search that with his proud modesty he hated – he met many of the leading writers of the day: Edward Garnett, Hilaire Belloc, Ivor Gurney, John Masefield, Joseph Conrad, Walter de la Mare, Rupert Brooke (q.v.) and D. H. Lawrence.

Frost and Thomas met in October 1913 and began a friendship that would be of central importance to them both. It was Frost who first urged Thomas to try his hand at poems, on the grounds that some of his prose was essentially poetry. Thomas was full of self-doubt, however, and made no serious attempt to turn from the prose that was earning him the money he so desperately needed until November or December 1914. Then, under the stress of deciding whether or not to enlist in the army, poems suddenly began to pour from his pen: 'Up in the Wind', 'November', 'March', 'Old Man' and 'The Sign-Post' between 3 and 7 December, and at least five more before the end of the month. On New Year's Day 1915 he sprained his ankle so badly that he was lame for nearly three months, during which time the stream of poetry flowed more swiftly and more richly than ever. From 7 to 9 January, for example, he wrote 'A Private', 'Snow', 'Adlestrop', 'Tears' and 'Over the Hills'.

While his ankle was recovering, he considered emigrating to America where his friend Robert Frost had offered to find him work, but decided against it and in July 1915 enlisted in the Artists' Rifles. When a friend asked him if he knew what he would be fighting for, he bent down, picked up a pinch of earth and, crumbling it between his fingers, said: 'Literally, for this.'

A responsible family man of 37, he was much older than most of his fellow recruits and his greater maturity was soon recognized by the award of a lance-corporal's stripe. In the intervals between drilling, weapon training, cleaning his equipment and instructing a squad in map-reading, he was still writing poems. One of the best of them, 'Rain', illustrates a common and curious feature of his work:

> Rain, midnight rain, nothing but the wild rain
> On this bleak hut, and solitude, and me
> Remembering again that I shall die
> And neither hear the rain nor give it thanks
> For washing me cleaner than I have been
> Since I was born into this solitude.
> Blessed are the dead that the rain rains upon:
> But here I pray that none whom once I loved
> Is dying tonight or lying still awake
> Solitary, listening to the rain,
> Either in pain or thus in sympathy
> Helpless among the living and the dead,
> Like a cold water among broken reeds,
> Myriads of broken reeds all still and stiff,
> Like me who have no love which this wild rain
> Has not dissolved except the love of death,
> If love it be for what is perfect and
> Cannot, the tempest tells me, disappoint.

Three years before, in his prose book *The Icknield Way*, he had written:

> I am alone in the dark still night, and my ear listens to the rain piping in the gutters and roaring softly in the trees of the world. Even so will the rain fall darkly upon the grass over the grave when my ears can hear it no more. I have been glad of the sound of rain, and wildly sad of it in the past; but that is all over as if it had never been; my eye is dull and my heart beating evenly and quietly; I stir neither foot nor hand; I shall not be quieter when I lie under the wet grass and the rain falls, and I of less account than the grass . . .
>
> Black and monotonously sounding is the midnight and solitude of the rain. In a little while or in an age – for it is all one – I shall know the full truth of the words I used to love, I knew not why, in my days of nature, in the days before the rain: 'Blessed are the dead that the rain rains on.'

His deepest loyalties and preoccupations, his love of England and her seasons celebrated so long in prose, rise again distilled to a purer form in his poems. His awareness of the natural world, its richness and beauty, is now intensified by a sense of impending loss and the certainty of death – his own and others'. Thomas's 'war poems' are those of a countryman perceiving the violence done by a distant conflict to the natural order of things. In his poem 'In Memoriam (Easter, 1915)', he wrote:

> The flowers left thick at nightfall in the wood
> This Eastertide call into mind the men,
> Now far from home, who, with their sweethearts, should
> Have gathered them and will do never again.

In January 1917, the countryman was called to the Front and, on 9 February, reached Arras, where a massive build-up for the Easter offensive was in progress. There he heard that three of his poems had been accepted by the magazine *Poetry* and, on 4 April, was heartened to read an enthusiastic review in the *Times Literary Supplement* of his contribution to *An Annual of New Poetry*. Five days later, Easter Monday, the Battle of Arras began with a deafening artillery barrage, and in the opening minutes, in a forward observation post, Edward Thomas was killed by the blast of a shell.

JON STALLWORTHY

Texts
The Collected Poems of Edward Thomas (ed. R. George Thomas, Oxford University Press 1985).
The Childhood of Edward Thomas: a fragment of autobiography (Faber, London, 1983).

Secondary sources
R. George Thomas, *Edward Thomas, a portrait* (Oxford University Press, 1985).
Andrew Motion, *The Poetry of Edward Thomas* (Routledge, London, 1980).

This is No Case of Petty Right or Wrong

This is no case of petty right or wrong
That politicians or philosophers
Can judge. I hate not Germans, nor grow hot
With love of Englishmen, to please newspapers.
Beside my hate for one fat patriot
My hatred of the Kaiser is love true:–
A kind of god he is, banging a gong.
But I have not to choose between the two,
Or between justice and injustice. Dinned
With war and argument I read no more
Than in the storm smoking along the wind
Athwart the wood. Two witches' cauldrons roar.
From one the weather shall rise clear and gay;
Out of the other an England beautiful
And like her mother that died yesterday.
Little I know or care if, being dull,
I shall miss something that historians
Can rake out of the ashes when perchance
The phoenix broods serene above their ken.
But with the best and meanest Englishmen
I am one in crying, God save England, lest
We lose what never slaves and cattle blessed.
The ages made her that made us from dust:
She is all we know and live by, and we trust
She is good and must endure, loving her so:
And as we love ourselves we hate her foe.

As the Team's Head-Brass

As the team's head-brass flashed out on the turn
The lovers disappeared into the wood.
I sat among the boughs of the fallen elm
That strewed the angle of the fallow, and
Watched the plough narrowing a yellow square
Of charlock. Every time the horses turned
Instead of treading me down, the ploughman leaned
Upon the handles to say or ask a word,
About the weather, next about the war.
Scraping the share he faced towards the wood,
And screwed along the furrow till the brass flashed
Once more.
The blizzard felled the elm whose crest
I sat in, by a woodpecker's round hole,
The ploughman said, 'When will they take it away?'
'When the war's over.' So the talk began –
One minute and an interval of ten,
A minute more and the same interval.
'Have you been out?' 'No.' 'And don't want to, perhaps?'
'If I could only come back again, I should.
I could spare an arm. I shouldn't want to lose
A leg. If I should lose my head, why, so,
I should want nothing more . . . Have many gone
From here?' 'Yes.' 'Many lost?' 'Yes, a good few.
Only two teams work on the farm this year.
One of my mates is dead. The second day
In France they killed him. It was back in March,
The very night of the blizzard, too. Now if
He had stayed here we should have moved the tree.'
'And I should not have sat here. Everything
Would have been different. For it would have been
Another world.' 'Ay, and a better, though
If we could see all all might seem good.' Then
The lovers came out of the wood again:
The horses started and for the last time
I watched the clods crumble and topple over
After the ploughshare and the stumbling team.

Roads

I love roads:
The goddesses that dwell
Far along invisible
are my favourite gods.

Roads go on
While we forget, and are
Forgotten like a star
That shoots and is gone.

On this earth 'tis sure
We men have not made
Anything that doth fade
So soon, so long endure:

The hill road wet with rain
In the sun would not gleam
Like a winding stream
If we trod it not again.

They are lonely
While we sleep, lonelier
For lack of the traveller
Who is now a dream only.

From dawn's twilight
And all the clouds like sheep
On the mountains of sleep
They wind into the night.

The next turn may reveal
Heaven: upon the crest
The close pine clump, at rest
And black, may Hell conceal.

Often footsore, never
Yet of the road I weary,
Though long and steep and dreary,
As it winds on for ever.

Helen of the roads,
The mountain ways of Wales
And the Mabinogion tales
Is one of the true gods,

Abiding in the trees,
The threes and fours so wise,
The larger companies,
That by the roadside be,

And beneath the rafter
Else uninhabited
Excepting by the dead;
And it is her laughter

At morn and night I hear
When the thrush cock sings
Bright irrelevant things,
And when the chanticleer

Calls back to their own night
Troops that make loneliness
With their light footsteps' press,
As Helen's own are light.

Now all roads lead to France
And heavy is the tread
Of the living; but the dead
Returning lightly dance:

Whatever the road bring
To me or take from me,
They keep me company
With their pattering,

Crowding the solitude
Of the loops over the downs,
Hushing the roar of towns
And their brief multitude.

Man and Dog

' 'Twill take some getting.' 'Sir, I think 'twill so.'
The old man stared up at the mistletoe
That hung too high in the poplar's crest for plunder
Of any climber, though not for kissing under:
Then he went on against the north-east wind –
Straight but lame, leaning on a staff new-skinned,
Carrying a brolly, flag-basket, and old coat, –
Towards Alton, ten miles off. And he had not
Done less from Chilgrove where he pulled up docks.
'Twere best, if he had had 'a money-box',
To have waited there till the sheep cleared a field
For what a half-week's flint-picking would yield.
His mind was running on the work he had done
Since he left Christchurch in the New Forest, one
Spring in the 'seventies, – navvying on dock and line
From Southampton to Newcastle-on-Tyne, –
In 'seventy-four a year of soldiering
With the Berkshires, – hoeing and harvesting
In half the shires where corn and couch will grow.
His sons, three sons, were fighting, but the hoe
And reap-hook he liked, or anything to do with trees.
He fell once from a poplar tall as these:
The Flying Man they called him in hospital.
'If I flew now, to another world I'd fall.'
He laughed and whistled to the small brown bitch
With spots of blue that hunted in the ditch.
Her foxy Welsh grandfather must have paired
Beneath him. He kept sheep in Wales and scared
Strangers, I will warrant, with his pearl eye
And trick of shrinking off as he were shy,
Then following close in silence for – for what?
'No rabbit, never fear, she ever got,
Yet always hunts. Today she nearly had one:
She would and she wouldn't. 'Twas like that. The
bad one!
She's not much use, but still she's company,
Though I'm not. She goes everywhere with me.
So Alton I must reach tonight somehow:
I'll get no shakedown with that bedfellow
From farmers. Many a man sleeps worse tonight
Than I shall.' 'In the trenches.' 'Yes, that's right.
But they'll be out of that – I hope they be –
This weather, marching after the enemy.'
'And so I hope. Good luck.' And there I nodded
'Good-night. You keep straight on,' Stiffly he plodded;
And at his heels the crisp leaves scurried fast,
And the leaf-coloured robin watched. They passed,
The robin till next day, the man for good,
Together in the twilight of the wood.

Lights Out

I have come to the borders of sleep,
The unfathomable deep
Forest where all must lose
Their way, however straight,
Or winding, soon or late;
They cannot choose.

Many a road and track
That, since the dawn's first crack,
Up to the forest brink,
Deceived the travellers,
Suddenly now blurs,
And in they sink.

Here love ends,
Despair, ambition ends;
All pleasure and all trouble,
Although most sweet or bitter,
Here ends in sleep that is sweeter
Than tasks most noble.

There is not any book
Or face of dearest look
That I would not turn from now
To go into the unknown
I must enter, and leave, alone,
I know not how.

The tall forest towers;
Its cloudy foliage lowers
Ahead, shelf above shelf;
Its silence I hear and obey
That I may lose my way
And myself.

A Private

This ploughman dead in battle slept out of doors
Many a frozen night, and merrily
Answered staid drinkers, good bedmen, and all bores:
'At Mrs Greenland's Hawthorn Bush,' said he,
'I slept.' None knew which bush. Above the town,
Beyond 'The Drover', a hundred spot the down
In Wiltshire. And where now at last he sleeps
More sound in France – that, too, he secret keeps.

*A*RTHUR *G*RAEME *W*EST 1891–1917

'To defy the whole system, to refuse to be an instrument of it – this I *should have done.'*

1916

Arthur Graeme West was an exception to popular conceptions of public school boys' attitudes to war. He was conspicuously unathletic. He preferred the unorthodox study of caterpillars to that of the rugby tackle, and was victimized by his school contemporaries as a result. It is, therefore, hardly surprising that the disciplined camaraderie forced upon him in the army did not appeal:

> The army is really the most anti-social body imaginable. It maintains itself on the selfishness and hostility of nations, and in its own ranks holds together, by a bond of fear and suspicion, all anti-social feeling. Men are taught to fear their superiors, and *they* suspect the men. Hatred must often be present, and only fear prevents it flaming out.
>
> My feeling of impotent horror, as of a creature caught by the proprietors of some travelling circus and forced with formal brutality to go through meaningless tricks, was immensely sharpened by a charcoal drawing of C...'s called 'We want more men!' showing Death, with the English staff cap on and a ragged tunic, standing with a jagged sickle among a pile of bleeding, writhing bodies and smoking corpses – a huge gaunt figure that haunted me horribly.

Yet West, despite reservations about the rightness of what he was doing, enlisted – or at least tried to, having been rejected for a commission owing to his defective eyesight. He managed to join the army as a private in one of the Public Schools Battalions in February 1915, and, by November, was in the trenches. Crawling around on the ground in search of caterpillars was one thing; crawling in the filth of the trenches was another. He detested the front-line existence and particularly the attitudes instilled in and adopted by his fellow soldiers. 'Tonight I said something about my being a respectable atheist, to which it was promptly answered that there could be no such thing: and people said, "You aren't really an atheist, are you?" Thus we see how men cannot get out of their minds "the horrid atheist" idea – the idea that intellectual convictions of this sort must of necessity imply some fearful moral laxity.'

West experienced great doubts about his Christian faith while in the trenches. He also questioned the value

The only known photographic portrait of A.G. West.
The Bodleian Library, Oxford

of the war in which he found himself fighting. Despite his public school background, and keen reading of the classics, there was never any possibility that he might have expressed the sentiments of the 'first wave' of poets. This was forcibly iterated in his rejoinder to H. Rex Freston's (q.v.) attitude 'that God is good, amused, rather, at us fighting'. Freston's arrogant lines, 'I know that God will never let me die./He is too passionate and intense for that.' was debunked in West's 'God! How I hate you, you young cheerful men!' Nor did West adopt the euphemistic imagery of his contemporaries. Instead he 'read the *Odyssey* and enjoyed it for itself and for the really novel exercise of making out the meaning of the lives and the new interest it gave to war.'

In the spring of 1916, West was sent home to be trained for a commission. 'We had a lecture on behaviour – i.e. not to go into pubs; this could be done in France, where officers and men were not sharply distinguished; we were not to go about with obvious tarts, nor get drunk. We could, however, do all these things if we would get

'I suppose it is the suddenness and the threat of unusually terrible destruction, when war comes, that makes men respond willingly to this singularly uninspiring appeal when they will not listen to the Socialist.'

1916

into mufti – the usual assumption that all civilians somehow fall short of gentility.'

In August of that year he was given a commission in the 6th Oxford & Bucks Light Infantry and sent back to France. He was not at all sure that he had made the right decision and was plagued by his conscience:

> I have mentioned the feeling against conscientious objectors, even in the minds of sentimental and religious people. Even R. speaks sneeringly of Bertrand Russell; no one is willing to revise his ideas or make clear to himself his motives in joining the war; even if anybody feels regret for having enlisted, he does not like to admit it to himself. Why should he? Every man, woman and child is taught to regard him as a hero; if he has become convinced of wrong action it lands him in an awkward position which he had much better not face. So everything tends to discourage him from active thinking on this important and, in the most literal sense, vital question.
>
> They are, as one knows, many of them worthy and unselfish men, not void of intelligence in trivial matters, and ready to carry through this unpleasant business to the end, with spirits as high as they can keep them, and as much attention to their men as the routine and disciplinary conscience of their colonel will permit.
>
> They are not often aggressive or offensively military. This is the dismal part of it: that these men, almost the best value in the ordinary upper class that we have, should allow themselves to suppose that all this is somehow necessary and inevitable; that they should give so much labour and time to the killing of others, though to the plain appeals of poverty and inefficiency in government, as well national as international, they are so absolutely heedless. How is it that as much blood and money cannot be poured out when it is a question of saving and helping mankind rather than of slaying them?

Towards the end of 1916, West analysed his fear:

> I feel afraid at the moment. I write in a trench that was once German, and shells keep dropping near the dug-out. There is a shivery fear that one may fall into it or blow it in.
>
> Yet *what* do I fear? I mind being killed because I am fond of the other life, but I know I should not miss it in annihilation. It is not that I fear.
>
> I don't definitely feel able to say I *fear* the infliction of pain or wound. I cannot bind the fear down to anything definite. I think it resolves itself simply into the realization of the fact that being hit by a shell will produce a new set of circumstances so strange that one does not know how one will find oneself in them. It is the knowledge that something may happen with which one will not be able to cope, or that one's old resolutions of courage, etc. will fail one in this new set of experiences. Something unknown there is. How will one act when it happens? One may be called upon to bear or perform something to which one will find oneself inadequate.

West also feared he lacked the 'martyr stuff' to carry his objection through, and so remained at the front until hit by a chance sniper's bullet as he was leaving his trench at Bapaume on 3 April 1917.

TIM CROSS

Text
The Diary of a Dead Officer, being the posthumous papers of Arthur Graeme West (Allen & Unwin, London, 1918).

God! How I Hate You, You Young Cheerful Men!

God! How I hate you, you young cheerful men,
Whose pious poetry blossoms on your graves
As soon as you are in them, nurtured up
By the salt of your corruption, and the tears
Of mothers, local vicars, college deans,
And flanked by prefaces and photographs
From all your minor poet friends – the fools –
Who paint their sentimental elegies
Where sure, no angel treads; and, living, share
The dead's brief immortality.
                                        Oh Christ!
To think that one could spread the ductile wax
Of his fluid youth to Oxford's glowing fires
And take her seal so ill! Hark how one chants –
'Oh happy to have lived these epic days' –
'These epic days'! And *he'd* been to France,
And seen the trenches, glimpsed the huddled dead
In the periscope, hung in the rusting wire:
Choked by their sickly fœtor, day and night
Blown down his throat: stumbled through ruined hearths,
Proved all that muddy brown monotony,
Where blood's the only coloured thing. Perhaps
Had seen a man killed, a sentry shot at night,
Hunched as he fell, his feet on the firing-step,
His neck against the back slope of the trench,
And the rest doubled up between, his head
Smashed like an egg-shell, and the warm grey brain
Spattered all bloody on the parados:
Had flashed a torch on his face, and known his friend,
Shot, breathing hardly, in ten minutes – gone!
Yet still God's in His heaven, all is right
In the best possible of worlds. The woe,
Even His scaled eyes *must* see, is partial, only
A seeming woe, we cannot understand.
God loves us, God looks down on this our strife
And smiles in pity, blows a pipe at times
And calls some warriors home. We do not die,
God would not let us, He is too 'intense',
Too 'passionate', a whole day sorrows He
Because a grass-blade dies. How rare life is!
On earth, the love and fellowship of men,
Men sternly banded: banded for what end?
Banded to maim and kill their fellow men –
For even Huns are men. In heaven above
A genial umpire, a good judge of sport,
Won't let us hurt each other! Let's rejoice
God keeps us faithful, pens us still in fold.
Ah, what a faith is ours (almost, it seems,
Large as a mustard-seed) – we trust and trust,
Nothing can shake us! Ah, how good God is
To suffer us be born just now, when youth
That else would rust, can slake his blade in gore,
Where very God Himself does seem to walk
The bloody fields of Flanders He so loves!

The End of the Second Year

One writes to me to ask me if I've read
Of 'the Jutland battle', of 'the great advance
Made by the Russians', chiding – 'History
Is being made these days, these are the things
That *are* worthwhile.'
                                        These!
                                                Not to one who's lain
In Heaven before God's throne with eyes abased,
Worshipping Him, in many forms of Good,
That sate thereon; turning this patchwork world
Wholly to glorify Him, point His plan
Towards some supreme perfection, dimly visioned
By loving faith: not these to him, when, stressed
By some soul-dizzying woe beyond his trust,
He lifts his startled face, and finds the Throne
Empty, and turns away, too drunk with Truth
To mind his shame, or feel the loss of God.

The Night Patrol

Over the top! The wire's thin here, unbarbed
Plain rusty coils, not staked, and low enough:
Full of old tins, though – 'When you're through, all three,
Aim quarter left for fifty yards or so,
Then straight for that new piece of German wire;
See if it's thick, and listen for a while
For sounds of working; don't run any risks;
About an hour; now, over!'
And we placed
Our hands on the topmost sand-bags, leapt, and stood
A second with curved backs, then crept to the wire,
Wormed ourselves tinkling through, glanced back, and
dropped.
The sodden ground was splashed with shallow pools,
And tufts of crackling cornstalks, two years old,
No man had reaped, and patches of spring grass.
Half-seen, as rose and sank the flares, were strewn
With the wrecks of our attack: the bandoliers,
Packs, rifles, bayonets, belts, and haversacks,
Shell fragments, and the huge whole forms of shells
Shot fruitlessly – and everywhere the dead.
Only the dead were always present – present
As a vile sickly smell of rottenness;
The rustling stubble and the early grass,
The slimy pools – the dead men stank through all
Pungent and sharp; as bodies loomed before,
And as we passed, they stank: then dulled away
To that vague fœtor, all encompassing,
Infecting earth and air. They lay, all clothed,
Each in some new and piteous attitude
That we well marked to guide us back: as he,
Outside our wire, that lay on his back and crossed
His legs Crusader-wise; I smiled at that,
And thought on Elia and his Temple Church.
From him, at quarter left, lay a small corpse,
Down in a hollow, huddled as in bed,
That one of us put his hand on unawares.
Next was a bunch of half a dozen men
All blown to bits, an archipelago
Of corrupt fragments, vexing to us three,
Who had no light to see by, save the flares.
On such a trail, so lit, for ninety yards
We crawled on belly and elbows, till we saw,
Instead of lumpish dead before our eyes,
The stakes and crosslines of the German wire.
We lay in shelter of the last dead man,
Ourselves as dead, and heard their shovels ring
Turning the earth, then talk and cough at times.
A sentry fired and a machine-gun spat;
They shot a flare above us, when it fell
And spluttered out in the pools of No Man's Land,
We turned and crawled past the remembered dead:
Past him and him, and them and him, until,
For he lay some way apart, we caught the scent
Of the Crusader and slid past his legs,
And through the wire and home, and got our rum.

France, March 1916

*I*SAAC *R*OSENBERG 1890–1918

'It's a fearful nuisance, this war, I think the perfect place is at the front – we'll starve or die of suspense anywhere else . . .'

1914

Rosenberg as a private. *Imperial War Museum, London*

Isaac Rosenberg was born in Bristol on 25 November 1890, of parents who had emigrated from Russia some years before. When he was 7, the family moved to the East End of London in search of better-paid work, but they were not successful and the boy, whose health had never been good, developed a lung ailment. From the Board School of St George's in the East, he went on to Stepney Board School, where his natural gift for drawing and for writing so impressed the headmaster that he allowed him to spend most of his time on them. Out of school, he used to read poetry and draw with chalks on the pavements of the East End.

Obliged to leave school at 14, he was apprenticed to the firm of Carl Hertschel, engravers, in Fleet Street. His parents hoped that this might prove a stepping-stone to a painter's career, but Isaac hated the work, writing in a letter: 'It is horrible to think that all these hours, when my days are full of vigour and my hands craving for self-expression, I am bound, chained to this fiendish mangling machine, without hope and almost desire of deliverance'. He wrote poems in his lunch-hours, and in the evenings attended classes in the Art School of Birkbeck College. At last, his apprenticeship completed, he was free, and in 1911, three generous Jewish women undertook to pay his tuition fees at the Slade School of Fine Art. There he came to know the painters Gertler, Bomberg, Kramer, Roberts, Nevinson and Stanley Spencer, but increasingly found art and poetry incompatible and himself drawn towards poetry. 'Art is not a plaything,' he wrote, 'it is blood and tears, it must grow up with one; and I believe I have begun too late.' Even so, he was a capable draughtsman and painted some good pictures, a few of which were exhibited at the Whitechapel Gallery. Leaving the Slade, he considered going to Russia, but it was difficult for a Jew to get a passport and he abandoned the idea. He had hoped to earn a living from his portraits but, in 1914, was told that his lungs were weak and advised to seek a warmer climate. Having a married sister in Cape Town, he sailed for South Africa in June. There he painted some pictures, gave a series of lectures on modern art, and published a few articles and poems, but he was far from happy, as he made clear in a letter to that patron of the arts, Eddie Marsh:

> I am in an infernal city by the sea. This city has men in it – and these men have souls in them – or at least have the passages to souls. Though they are millions of years behind time, they have yet reached the stage of evolution that knows ears and eyes. But these passages are dreadfully clogged up: gold dust, diamond dust, stocks and shares, and Heaven knows what other flinty muck.

His reactions to the outbreak of war were complex and found their way into a poem 'On Receiving News of the War':

> Snow is a strange white word.
> No ice or frost
> Has asked of bud or bird
> For Winter's cost.
>
> Yet ice and frost and snow
> From earth to sky
> This Summer land doth know.
> No man knows why.
>
> In all men's hearts it is.
> Some spirit old
> Hath turned with malign kiss
> Our lives to mould.

Red fangs have torn His face.
God's blood is shed.
He mourns from His lone place
His children dead.

O! ancient crimson curse!
Corrode, consume.
Give back this universe
Its pristine bloom.

He perceives the approaching violence more distinctly than many other poets; it is an 'ancient crimson curse', but he hopes it may have a purging effect and restore the universe to its original prelapsarian innocence and beauty.

In 1915 he returned to England where he published a small pamphlet of poems, *Youth*, and, in November or early December, enlisted in the Bantam Regiment; being, as he said, 'too short for any other'. He took that decision purely to help his family, having been told that half his pay could be paid to his mother as a separation allowance.

From the first he hated the army, and the army, in the person of his 'impudent schoolboy pup' of an officer, disliked him. The Rosenbergs were 'Tolstoyans' and Isaac, himself the most vulnerable of men, hated the idea of killing. However, after a period of training at Bury St Edmunds and at Farnborough, he crossed the Channel early in 1916 with the King's Own Royal Lancaster Regiment. He had not been long at the front when he sent Eddie Marsh 'a poem I wrote in the trenches, which is surely as simple as ordinary talk':

The darkness crumbles away –
It is the same old druid Time as ever.
Only a live thing leaps my hand –
A queer sardonic rat –
As I pull the parapet's poppy
To stick behind my ear.
Droll rat, they would shoot you if they knew
Your cosmopolitan sympathies.
Now you have touched this English hand
You will do the same to a German –
Soon, no doubt, if it be your pleasure
To cross the sleeping green between.
It seems you inwardly grin as you pass
Strong eyes, fine limbs, haughty athletes
Less chanced than you for life,
Bonds to the whims of murder,
Sprawled in the bowels of the earth,
The torn fields of France.
What do you see in our eyes
At the shrieking iron and flame
Hurled through still heavens?
What quaver – what heart aghast?
Poppies whose roots are in man's veins
Drop, and are ever dropping;
But mine in my ear is safe,
Just a little white with the dust.

'. . . About the army I think the world has been terribly damaged by certain poets (in fact any poet) being sacrificed in this stupid business. There is certainly a strong temptation to join when you are making no money.'
Apparently unfinished letter to Ezra Pound, 1915

Critics locate this poem, 'Break of Day in the Trenches,' in the tradition of the pastoral elegy and call attention to a number of elegiac literary echoes, the most significant being the lines from George Herbert's peom 'Virtue':

Sweet rose, whose hue angry and brave
Bids the rash gazer wipe his eye,
Thy root is ever in its grave,
And thou must die.

Although Rosenberg has absorbed – and in 'Break of Day' looks back on – the great tradition of pastoral poetry, his tone is different: lighter, more informal and ironic. As the curtain goes up, 'The darkness crumbles away . . .' like the dusty edge of the trench-parapet that is the speaker's horizon. In the strange sentence that follows – 'It is the same old druid Time as ever' – we can *see* the figure of Old Father Time personified as a druid (standing perhaps before a druidic sacrificial altar), and can *hear* an alternative and complementary meaning: it is a customary time for druidic sacrifice – dawn. The colloquial setting of this image saves it from portentousness, and there is a wry good humour (altogether foreign to the great pastoral elegies) in the entrance on stage of the poem's protagonists:

Only a live thing leaps my hand –
A queer sardonic rat –
As I pull the parapet's poppy
To stick behind my ear.

. . . just where a bullet might be expected to open another red flower if he were to lift his head above the parapet. But he does not, because in this world of anti-pastoral, the roles of man and rat are reversed: the man hiding as the rat commutes between the British and German lines. The creature is imagined as inwardly grinning – in vengeful mockery, perhaps? – as it passes the bodies of its former hunters, now 'Sprawled in the bowels of the earth, /The torn fields of France.' Man and Nature personified have both been *torn*. The poppy, too, has been torn from its root 'in man's veins' and, when we're told that the flower 'in my ear is safe, /Just a little white with the dust', we know that, far from being safe, poppy and man are ever dropping towards the charnel dust. Not the least astonishing thing about this poem is its impersonality, the total absence of the bitterness and

'I am determined that this war, with all its powers for devastation, shall not master my poeting.'
Letter to Laurence Binyon, autumn 1916

indignation characteristic of Owen's poems. In this and such other 'Poems from Camp and Trench' as 'Returning We Hear the Larks' and 'Dead Man's Dump', Rosenberg succeeded in his intention of writing 'Simple *poetry*, – that is where an interesting complexity of thought is kept in tone and right value to the dominating idea so that it is understandable and still ungraspable.'

On 28 March 1918 he ended a letter to Eddie Marsh: 'I think I wrote you I was about to go up the line again after our little rest. We are now in the trenches again, and though I feel very sleepy, I just have a chance to answer your letter, so I will while I may. It's really my being lucky enough to bag an inch of candle that incites me to this pitch of punctual epistolary. I must measure my letter by the light . . .'

The day before this letter was postmarked 2 April, Isaac Rosenberg was dead.

JON STALLWORTHY

Text
The Collected Works of Isaac Rosenberg (Ian Parsons (ed.), Chatto & Windus, London, 1979). Contains his poetry, prose, letters, paintings in full colour reproduction, and drawings.

Secondary source
Joseph Cohen, *Journey to the Trenches Isaac Rosenberg 1890–1918*, Robson Books, London.
Jean Moorcroft Wilson, *Isaac Rosenberg, Poet and Painter* (Cecil Woolf, London, 1975).

LOUSE HUNTING

Nudes – stark and glistening,
Yelling in lurid glee. Grinning faces
And raging limbs
Whirl over the floor one fire.
For a shirt verminously busy
Yon soldier tore from his throat, with oaths
Godhead might shrink at, but not the lice.
And soon the shirt was aflare
Over the candle he'd lit while we lay.

Then we all sprang up and stript
To hunt the verminous brood.
Soon like a demons' pantomime
The place was raging.
See the silhouettes agape,
See the gibbering shadows
Mixed with the battled arms on the wall.
See gargantuan hooked fingers
Pluck in supreme flesh
To smutch supreme littleness.
See the merry limbs in hot Highland fling
Because some wizard vermin
Charmed from the quiet this revel
When our ears were half lulled
By the dark music
Blown from Sleep's trumpet.

1917

RETURNING, WE HEAR THE LARKS

Sombre the night is.
And though we have our lives, we know
What sinister threat lurks there.

Dragging these anguished limbs, we only know
This poison-blasted track opens on our camp –
On a little safe sleep.

But hark! joy – joy – strange joy.
Lo! heights of night ringing with unseen larks.
Music showering our upturned list'ning faces.

Death could drop from the dark
As easily as song –
But song only dropped,
Like a blind man's dreams on the sand
By dangerous tides,
Like a girl's dark hair for she dreams no ruin lies there,
Or her kisses where a serpent hides.

1917

Dead Man's Dump

The plunging limbers over the shattered track
Racketed with their rusty freight,
Stuck out like many crowns of thorns,
And the rusty stakes like sceptres old
To stay the flood of brutish men
Upon our brothers dear.

The wheels lurched over sprawled dead
But pained them not, though their bones crunched,
Their shut mouths made no moan,
They lie there huddled, friend and foeman,
Man born of man, and born of woman,
And shells go crying over them
From night till night and now.

Earth has waited for them
All the time of their growth
Fretting for their decay:
Now she has them at last!
In the strength of their strength
Suspended – stopped and held.

What fierce imaginings their dark souls lit
Earth! have they gone into you?
Somewhere they must have gone,
And flung on your hard back
Is their souls' sack,
Emptied of God-ancestralled essences.
Who hurled them out? Who hurled?

None saw their spirits' shadow shake the grass,
Or stood aside for the half-used life to pass
Out of those doomed nostrils and the doomed mouth,
When the swift iron burning bee
Drained the wild honey of their youth.

What of us, who flung on the shrieking pyre,
Walk, our usual thoughts untouched,
Our lucky limbs as on ichor fed,
Immortal seeming ever?
Perhaps when the flames beat loud on us,
A fear may choke in our veins
And the startled blood may stop.

The air is loud with death,
The dark air spurts with fire
The explosions ceaseless are.
Timelessly now, some minutes past,
These dead strode time with vigorous life,
Till the shrapnel called 'an end!'
But not to all. In bleeding pangs
Some borne on stretchers dreamed of home,
Dear things, war-blotted from their hearts.

A man's brains splattered on
A stretcher-bearer's face;
His shook shoulders slipped their load,
But when they bent to look again
The drowning soul was sunk too deep
For human tenderness.

They left this dead with the older dead,
Stretched at the cross roads.
Burnt black by strange decay,
Their sinister faces lie
The lid over each eye,
The grass and coloured clay
More motion have than they,
Joined to the great sunk silences.

Here is one not long dead;
His dark hearing caught our far wheels,
And the choked soul stretched weak hands
To reach the living word the far wheels said,
The blood-dazed intelligence beating for light,
Crying through the suspense of the far torturing wheels
Swift for the end to break,
Or the wheels to break,
Cried as the tide of the world broke over his sight.

Will they come? Will they ever come?
Even as the mixed hoofs of the mules,
The quivering-bellied mules,
And the rushing wheels all mixed
With his tortured upturned sight,
So we crashed round the bend,
We heard his weak scream,
We heard his very last sound,
And our wheels grazed his dead face.

1917

Through These Pale Cold Days

Through these pale cold days
What dark faces burn
Out of three thousand years,
And their wild eyes yearn,

While underneath their brows
Like waifs their spirits grope
For the pools of Hebron again –
For Lebanon's summer slope.

They leave these blond still days
In dust behind their tread
They see with living eyes
How long they have been dead.

1918

*W*ILFRED *O*WEN 1893–1918

'I came out in order to help these boys – directly by leading them as well as an officer can; indirectly, by watching their sufferings that I may speak of them as well as a pleader can. I have done the first.'
October 1918

Wilfred Owen photographed by John Gunston. *Imperial War Museum*

Wilfred Edward Salter Owen was born in Oswestry on 18 March 1893. His parents were then living in a spacious and comfortable house owned by his grandfather, Edward Shaw. At his death two years later, this former mayor of the city was found to be almost bankrupt, and Tom Owen was obliged to move with his wife and son to lodgings in the backstreets of Birkenhead. They carried with them vivid memories of their vanished prosperity, and Susan Owen resolved that her adored son Wilfred should in time restore the family to its rightful gentility. She was a devout lady, and under her strong influence, Wilfred grew into a serious and slightly priggish boy. At school in Birkenhead and later in Shrewsbury – where Tom Owen was appointed Assistant Superintendent of the Joint Railways in 1906 – he worked hard and successfully, especially at literature and botany. He had begun writing poems when he was 10 or 11, and soon fell under the spell of Keats, who was to remain the principal influence on his work.

Leaving school in 1911, Owen took up a post as lay assistant to the vicar of Dunsden in Oxfordshire. He was to help the vicar with his parish work and receive in return coaching for the university entrance examination that he hoped in due course to sit. Removed from his mother's influence, he became less enamoured of evangelical religion and more critical of the role of the Church – as represented by the vicar of Dunsden – in society. His letters and poems of this period show an increasing awareness of the sufferings of the poor and the first stirrings of the compassion that was to characterize his later poems about the Western Front. He attended botany classes at Reading University and was encouraged by the professor of English to read and write more poetry. In February 1913, on the verge of a nervous breakdown, he left Dunsden and, when he had recovered, crossed to France where he taught at the Berlitz School of Languages in Bordeaux.

He was in the Pyrenees, acting as tutor in a cultivated French household, when war was declared. A visit to a hospital for the wounded soon opened his eyes to the true nature of war, but it was not until September 1915 that he finally decided to return to England and enlist. For several months, he and Edward Thomas (q.v.)

were privates, training at Hare Hall Camp in Essex, but there is no evidence that they ever met. Commissioned into the Manchester Regiment, Owen crossed the Channel on 30 December 1916 and, in the first days of January, joined the 2nd Manchesters on the Somme near Beaumont Hamel. His letters to his mother tell their own story:

> I have not been at the front.
> I have been in front of it.
> I held an advanced post, that is, a 'dug-out' in the middle of No Man's Land.
> We had a march of 3 miles over shelled road then nearly 3 along a flooded trench. After that we came to where the trenches had been blown flat out and had to go over the top. It was of course dark, too dark, and the ground was not mud, not sloppy mud, but an octopus of sucking clay, 3, 4, and 5 feet deep, relieved only by craters full of water. Men have been known to drown in them. Many stuck in the mud and only got on by leaving their waders, equipment, and in some cases their clothes.
> High explosives were dropping all around us, and machine guns spluttered every few minutes. But it was so dark that even the German flares did not reveal us.
> Three quarters dead, I mean each of us ¾ dead, we reached the dug-out, and relieved the wretches therein. I then had to go forth and find another dug-out for a still more advanced post where I left 18 bombers. I was responsible for other posts on the left but there was a junior officer in charge.
> My dug-out held 25 men tight packed. Water filled it to a depth of 1 or 2 feet, leaving say 4 feet of air.
> One entrance had been blown in and blocked.
> So far, the other remained.
> The Germans knew we were staying there and decided we shouldn't.
> Those fifty hours were the agony of my happy life.
> Every ten minutes on Sunday afternoon seemed an hour.
> I nearly broke down and let myself drown in the water that was now slowly rising over my knees.
> Towards 6 o'clock, when, I suppose, you would be going to church, the shelling grew less intense and less accurate: so that I was mercifully helped to do my duty and crawl, wade, climb and flounder over No Man's Land to visit my other post. It took me half an hour to move about 150 yards.
> I was chiefly annoyed by our own machine guns from behind. The seeng-seeng-seeng of the bullets reminded me of Mary's canary. On the whole I can support the canary better.
> In the Platoon on my left the sentries over the dug-out were blown to nothing. One of these poor fellows was my first servant whom I rejected. If I had kept him he would have lived, for servants don't do Sentry Duty. I kept my own sentries halfway down the stairs during the more terrific bombardment. In spite of this one lad was blown down and, I am afraid, blinded.

That last experience was to find its way into Owen's poem 'The Sentry', more than a year and a half later.

In March 1917 he fell into a cellar and suffered concussion, and some weeks later, after fierce fighting near St Quentin, was invalided home with shell-shock. At Craiglockhart War Hospital on the outskirts of Edinburgh, he met Siegfried Sassoon, whose first 'war poems' had just appeared in *The Old Huntsman and Other Poems*. Under their influence and with the encouragement and guidance of the older poet, Owen was soon producing poems far superior to any he had written previously. Sassoon not only helped him to purge his style of its early excessive luxuriance, but introduced him to such other poets and novelists as Robert Graves, Arnold Bennett, H. G. Wells and Osbert Sitwell.

It was probably in August 1917 that Owen read the anonymous 'Prefatory Note' to the anthology, *Poems of Today* (1916), which began:

> This book has been compiled in order that boys and girls, already perhaps familiar with the great classics of the English speech, may also know something of the newer poetry of their own day. Most of the writers are living, and the rest are still vivid memories among us, while one of the youngest, almost as these words are written, has gone singing to lay down his life for his country's cause . . . there is no arbitrary isolation of one theme from another; they mingle and interpenetrate throughout, to the music of Pan's flute, and of Love's viol, and the bugle-call of Endeavour, and the passing bell of Death.

It is not difficult to imagine him, stung by those sentiments, sitting down to write his 'Anthem for Doomed Youth':

> What passing-bells for these who die as cattle?
> Only the monstrous anger of the guns.
> Only the stuttering rifles' rapid rattle
> Can patter out their hasty orisons.
> No mockeries now for them; no prayers nor bells;
> Nor any voice of mourning save the choirs, –
> The shrill, demented choirs of wailing shells;
> And bugles calling for them from sad shires.
>
> What candles may be held to speed them all?
> Not in the hands of boys but in their eyes
> Shall shine the holy glimmers of goodbyes.
> The pallor of girls' brows shall be their pall;

Their flowers the tenderness of patient minds,
And each slow dusk a drawing-down of blinds.

Those who die as cattle in a slaughterhouse die in such numbers that there is no time to give them the trappings of a Christian funeral that Owen remembers from his Dunsden days. Instead, they receive a brutal parody of such a service: 'the stuttering rifles' praying (presumably) that they will kill them; the 'choirs . . . of shells' wailing as they hunt them down. The bugles may sound the 'Last Post' for them, but they had previously called them to the colours in those same 'sad shires'. So, bitterly but obliquely, Owen assigns to Church and State responsibility for their deaths.

The turn at the end of the octave brings us home, across the Channel, and the sestet opens with a question paralleling the first: 'What candles may be held to speed them all?' It is a gentler question than 'What passing-bells for these who die as cattle?', preparing for the gentler answer that, instead of the parodic rituals offered by rifle, shell and bugle, those who love the soldiers will mark their death with observances more heart-felt, more permanent, than those prescribed by convention:

The pallor of girls' brows shall be their pall;
Their flowers the tenderness of patient minds,
And each slow dusk a drawing-down of blinds.

Many of Owen's other poems spring from a similarly indignant response to a prior text. They, too, are protest poems, directed against many of the same targets as Sassoon's – notably the *old* men of the Army, Church and Government who send *young* men to their death – but, as imaginative and musical structures, they are more complex and reverberant than Sassoon's. Owen's poems also have an important relation to the pastoral tradition of English poetry.

Discharged from Craiglockhart in October, Owen was posted to the 5th Manchesters in Scarborough and there wrote 'The Show' and probably 'Exposure' and 'Strange Meeting'. In March 1918, he was transferred to Ripon. 'The Send-Off', written during this period, is typical of his later work in the way it makes its bitter statement with brilliant economy, its calm surface mined with ironies:

Down the close darkening lanes they sang their way
To the siding-shed,
And lined the train with faces grimly gay.

Their breasts were stuck all white with wreath and spray
As men's are, dead.

Dull porters watched them, and a casual tramp
Stood staring hard,
Sorry to miss them from the upland camp.
Then, unmoved, signals nodded, and a lamp
Winked to the guard.

So secretly, like wrongs hushed-up, they went.
They were not ours:
We never heard to which front these were sent.

Nor there if they yet mock what women meant
Who gave them flowers.

Shall they return to beatings of great bells
In wild train-loads?
A few, a few, too few for drums and yells,

May creep back, silent, to still village wells
Up half-known roads.

At the end of August, Owen was certified 'fit to proceed overseas' and, a month later, was again in action. He was awarded the Military Cross for his part in a successful attack on the Beaurevoir–Fonsomme Line and, before sunrise on the morning of 4 November, led his platoon to the west bank of the Sambre and Oise Canal. They came under murderous fire from German machine guns behind the parapet of the east bank, and at the height of the ensuing battle, Owen was hit and killed while helping his men bring up duck-boards at the water's edge.

In Shrewsbury, the Armistice bells were ringing when his parents' front-door bell sounded its small chime, heralding the telegram they had dreaded for two years.

JON STALLWORTHY

Texts
The Complete Poems and Fragments (Jon Stallworthy (ed.), Chatto & Windus, 1983, 2 vols). Authoritative new edition.
Selected Letters (John Bell (ed.), Oxford University Press, 1985).

Secondary sources
Jon Stallworthy, *Wilfred Owen* (Chatto & Windus, London, 1974).
Dominic Hibberd, *Owen the Poet* (Macmillan, London, 1986).

MINERS

There was a whispering in my hearth,
A sigh of the coal,
Grown wistful of a former earth
It might recall.

I listened for a tale of leaves
And smothered ferns,
Frond-forests, and the low sly lives
Before the fauns.

My fire might show steam-phantoms simmer
From Time's old cauldron,
Before the birds made nests in summer,
Or men had children.

But the coals were murmuring of their mine,
And moans down there
Of boys that slept wry sleep, and men
Writhing for air.

And I saw white bones in the cinder-shard,
Bones without number.
Many the muscled bodies charred,
And few remember.

I thought of all that worked dark pits
Of war, and died
Digging the rock where Death reputes
Peace lies indeed.

Comforted years will sit soft-chaired,
In rooms of amber;
The years will stretch their hands, well-cheered
By our life's ember;

The centuries will burn rich loads
With which we groaned,
Whose warmth shall lull their dreaming lids,
While songs are crooned;
But they will not dream of us poor lads,
Left in the ground.

DULCE ET DECORUM EST

Bent double, like old beggars under sacks,
Knock-kneed, coughing like hags, we cursed through
sludge,
Till on the haunting flares we turned our backs
And towards our distant rest began to trudge.
Men marched asleep. Many had lost their boots
But limped on, blood-shod. All went lame; all blind;
Drunk with fatigue; deaf even to the hoots
Of tired, outstripped Five-Nines that dropped behind.

Gas! GAS! Quick, boys! – An ecstasy of fumbling,
Fitting the clumsy helmets just in time;
But someone still was yelling out and stumbling,
And flound'ring like a man in fire or lime . . .
Dim, through the misty panes and thick green light,
As under a green sea, I saw him drowning.

In all my dreams, before my helpless sight,
He plunges at me, guttering, choking, drowning.

If in some smothering dreams you too could pace
Behind the wagon that we flung him in,
And watch the white eyes writhing in his face,
His hanging face, like a devil's sick of sin;
If you could hear, at every jolt, the blood
Come gargling from the froth-corrupted lungs,
Obscene as cancer, bitter as the cud
Of vile, incurable sores on innocent tongues, –
My friend, you would not tell with such high zest
To children ardent for some desperate glory,
The old Lie: Dulce et decorum est
Pro patria mori.

THE NEXT WAR

Out there, we walked quite friendly up to Death, –
Sat down and ate beside him, cool and bland, –
Pardoned his spilling mess-tins in our hand.
We've sniffed the green thick odour of his breath, –
Our eyes wept, but our courage didn't writhe.
He's spat at us with bullets, and he's coughed
Shrapnel. We chorused if he sang aloft,
We whistled while he shaved us with his scythe.

Oh, Death was never enemy of ours!
We laughed at him, we leagued with him, old chum.
No soldier's paid to kick against His powers.
We laughed, – knowing that better men would come,
And greater wars: when every fighter brags
He fights on Death, for lives; not men, for flags.

Mental Cases

Who are these? Why sit they here in twilight?
Wherefore rock they, purgatorial shadows,
Drooping tongues from jaws that slob their relish,
Baring teeth that leer like skulls' teeth wicked?
Stroke on stroke of pain, – but what slow panic,
Gouged these chasms round their fretted sockets?
Ever from their hair and through their hands' palms
Misery swelters. Surely we have perished
Sleeping, and walk hell; but who these hellish?

– These are men whose minds the Dead have ravished.
Memory fingers in their hair of murders,
Multitudinous murders they once witnessed.
Wading sloughs of flesh these helpless wander,
Treading blood from lungs that had loved laughter.
Always they must see these things and hear them,
Batter of guns and shatter of flying muscles,
Carnage incomparable, and human squander
Rucked too thick for these men's extrication.

Therefore still their eyeballs shrink tormented
Back into their brains, because on their sense
Sunlight seems a blood-smear; night comes
blood-black;
Dawn breaks open like a wound that bleeds afresh.
– Thus their heads wear this hilarious, hideous,
Awful falseness of set-smiling corpses.
– Thus their hands are plucking at each other;
Picking at the rope-knouts of their scourging;
Snatching after us who smote them, brother,
Pawing us who dealt them war and madness.

Cramped in That Funnelled Hole

Cramped in that funnelled hole, they watched the dawn
Open a jagged rim around; a yawn
Of death's jaws, which had all but swallowed them
Stuck in the bottom of his throat of phlegm.

They were in one of many mouths of Hell
Not seen of seers in visions; only felt
As teeth of traps; when bones and the dead are smelt
Under the mud where long ago they fell
Mixed with the sour sharp odour of the shell.

Strange Meeting

It seemed that out of battle I escaped
Down some profound dull tunnel, long since scooped
Through granites which titanic wars had groined.

Yet also there encumbered sleepers groaned,
Too fast in thought or death to be bestirred.
Then, as I probed them, one sprang up, and stared
With piteous recognition in fixed eyes,
Lifting distressful hands, as if to bless.
And by his smile, I knew that sullen hall, –
By his dead smile I knew we stood in Hell.

With a thousand pains that vision's face was grained;
Yet no blood reached there from the upper ground,
And no guns thumped, or down the flues made moan.
'Strange friend,' I said, 'here is no cause to mourn.'
'None,' said that other, 'save the undone years,
The hopelessness. Whatever hope is yours,
Was my life also; I went hunting wild
After the wildest beauty in the world,
Which lies not calm in eyes, or braided hair,
But mocks the steady running of the hour,
And if it grieves, grieves richlier than here.
For by my glee might many men have laughed,
And of my weeping something had been left,
Which must die now. I mean the truth untold,
The pity of war, the pity war distilled.
Now men will go content with what we spoiled,
Or, discontent, boil bloody, and be spilled.
They will be swift with swiftness of the tigress.
None will break ranks, though nations trek from
progress.
Courage was mine, and I had mystery,
Wisdom was mine, and I had mastery:
To miss the march of this retreating world
Into vain citadels that are not walled.
Then, when much blood had clogged their chariot-
wheels,
I would go up and wash them from sweet wells,
Even with truths that lie too deep for taint.
I would have poured my spirit without stint
But not through wounds; not on the cess of war.
Foreheads of men have bled where no wounds were.

'I am the enemy you killed, my friend.
I knew you in this dark: for so you frowned
Yesterday through me as you jabbed and killed.
I parried; but my hands were loath and cold.
Let us sleep now . . .'

The Parable of the Old Man and the Young

So Abram rose, and clave the wood, and went,
And took the fire with him, and a knife.
And as they sojourned both of them together,
Isaac the first-born spake and said, My Father,
Behold the preparations, fire and iron,
But where the lamb, for this burnt-offering?
Then Abram bound the youth with belts and straps,
And builded parapets and trenches there,
And stretched forth the knife to slay his son.
When lo! an Angel called him out of heaven,
Saying, Lay not thy hand upon the lad,
Neither do anything to him, thy son.
Behold! Caught in a thicket by its horns,
A Ram. Offer the Ram of Pride instead.

But the old man would not so, but slew his son,
And half the seed of Europe, one by one.

Exposure

Our brains ache, in the merciless iced east winds that
knive us . . .
Wearied we keep awake because the night is silent . . .
Low, drooping flares confuse our memory of the
salient . . .
Worried by silence, sentries whisper, curious, nervous,
But nothing happens.

Watching, we hear the mad gusts tugging on the wire,
Like twitching agonies of men among its brambles.
Northward, incessantly, the flickering gunnery rumbles,
Far off, like a dull rumour of some other war.
What are we doing here?

The poignant misery of dawn begins to grow . . .
We only know war lasts, rain soaks, and clouds sag
stormy.
Dawn massing in the east her melancholy army
Attacks once more in ranks on shivering ranks of grey,
But nothing happens.

Sudden successive flights of bullets streak the silence.
Less deathly than the air that shudders black with snow,
With sidelong flowing flakes that flock, pause, and renew;
We watch them wandering up and down the wind's
nonchalance,
But nothing happens.

Pale flakes with fingering stealth come feeling for our
faces –
We cringe in holes, back on forgotten dreams, and stare,
snow-dazed,
Deep into grassier ditches. So we drowse, sun-dozed,
Littered with blossoms trickling where the blackbird fusses,
– Is it that we are dying?

Slowly our ghosts drag home: glimpsing the sunk fires,
glozed
With crusted dark-red jewels; crickets jingle there;
For hours the innocent mice rejoice: the house is theirs;
Shutters and doors, all closed: on us the doors are closed, –
We turn back to our dying.

Since we believe not otherwise can kind fires burn;
Nor ever suns smile true on child, or field, or fruit.
For God's invincible spring our love is made afraid;
Therefore, not loath, we lie out here; therefore were born,
For love of God seems dying.

Tonight, this frost will fasten on this mud and us,
Shrivelling many hands, puckering foreheads crisp.
The burying-party, picks and shovels in shaking grasp,
Pause over half-known faces. All their eyes are ice,
But nothing happens.

GERRIT ENGELKE 1890–1918

'The greatest task which faces us after the war will be to forgive our enemy, who has, after all, been our neighbour on earth ever since Creation.'

In Gerrit Engelke's notebook, there is an entry dating from the end of 1913:

> A chapter could perhaps be written about me divided into the following three parts (one knows oneself the best):
> I The Man of the World (city and world poems)
> II The Artist (simple poems and songs)
> III The Phantasist (cosmic poetry)

Although Engelke wrote little poetry actually inspired by the war, a single poem 'An die Soldaten des Grossen Krieges' ('To the Soldiers of the Great War') would necessitate the addition of a fourth section: 'The Soldier-Poet'. However, by 1917, he did not regard himself as such: 'The war, in which I have served since '14, has rendered me virtually speechless. I have created no "war poetry". And it is only after the war, when we can breathe out again after such intense pressure that I hope, as with others, to be able to reach new and consummate heights.' A year later, Engelke composed the tribute to his close freind August Deppe, 'An die Soldaten des Grossen Krieges'.

In 1914, Engelke had embarked on an ambitious prose treatment of the Don Juan legend, but the war interrupted the process, and it remained in a fragmentary form: 'My intention (if I can even talk of such a thing at all) was to place a Faustian being of unfulfilled longing in our times and ultimately lead him to atonement.' This departure from his usual verse form might have led to the creation of a fifth, substantially different section. However well Engelke's work can be subdivided in this way, his work as a whole permits no categorization: 'If one is not ex- or im-pressionist enough nor radical enough for the people on the *Sturm*, then one is too wild for the other camp. So there is only one course: to ignore one's admirers and critics and be only aware of where one's own point of reference is and choose a straight path from there.' The great German poet Richard Dehmel confined his appraisal of Engelke to 'A genius – greater than us all!' But even this reference was not enough to save Engelke from a neglect which was virtually total until the 1970s.

Gerrit Engelke, 1912. *Gerrit-Engelke-Gedächtnis-Stiftung, Hanover*

Gerrit Engelke was born on 21 October 1890 to a small-time salesman in Hanover who emigrated to the United States ten years later. His wife and daughter were to follow, leaving Gerrit Engelke behind in Germany to complete his military service. This abandonment by his family induced a sense of isolation and spiritual yearning in Gerrit Engelke that was to feature in much of his earlier poetry.

Engelke is often cited as an *Arbeiterdichter* (workers' poet) in current reference works. This is inaccurate. He certainly earned his living as a house decorator and painter from time to time, and was brought up in close proximity to the industrial centre of a major town, but he had no associations with the proletarian art world, and little that could be construed as class-consciousness appears in his writings. The epithet is derived from two misreadings of his work and life. Central to much of Engelke's poetry is the industrial image: the descriptions of smoking chimney stacks, the pulse and beat of machinery works, the pounding of the steam hammer, the rattle and rolling of the locomotives are powerful, but objective. Engelke did not share the Futurists' unqualified

'Art has a single purpose: to elevate man. It does this through joy as it does through sorrow. Its prime aim can only ever be to touch man to his innermost core.'

enthusiasm for all things modern: 'Why such a hue and cry about the Futurists and Cubists? They only impart an imperfect art, a dazzling one-sidedness. They give us chaotic content without a cohesive form of life and movement . . .' Nor was Engelke a precursor of the *Industriekunst* of the post-war period. In a letter of 1917:

> Let us beware industrialism to the exclusion of all else! They would love to tar us all with the same brush, shove us in the pigeon-hole of 'industrial art' . . . We sing of the modern work conditions because that is where we have come from and we have to live with them. We do not, however, see it as something all-embracing, only a part of the whole which God created called our World. A higher aim is the task for us to sing of the nature of being a true European, to sing of humanity.

This attitude did not prevent Engelke from being an overawed witness of Germany's militarization in May 1913 in a letter to his father:

> Some time ago in Hamburg, the biggest ship in the world, the *Imperator* ran down the slips, and somewhat later the even larger *Vaterland*! I was in Hamburg (and Blankensee) about eight weeks ago and saw the *Imperator* in the harbour: completely done in red lead – without funnels: an overpowering hulk! Then I also saw (on a harbour tour) the great iron-railed structure in which the two ships had been constructed – a forest of iron. Then: the swimdocks of a length of about 200 metres, and: the largest crane in the world.

The second cause for the misapplication of *Arbeiterdichter* to Gerrit Engelke was his strong and valuable friendship with Jakob Kneip, through whom Engelke came into contact with a group of artisan poets: the *Werkleute auf Haus Nyland*. Although Engelke exchanged many ideas with Kneip and his associates, there seems to be very little evidence that the group's aim to create a new type of poetry derived from the living folk heritage of working people influenced his writing. In fact, two-thirds of Engelke's *oeuvre* was already complete by the time he met Kneip in the spring of 1914.

Instead, Engelke the poet remained highly individual, drawing on moral inspiration rather than poetic influence from his friendships with Richard Dehmel, August Deppe and Martin Gulbrandsen of Denmark. It is rather the hymnal quality of Walt Whitman's 'compassionate realism' that colours the mood of Engelke's later war poetry.

When the war broke out in August 1914, Engelke was not in Germany but with Gulbrandsen in neutral Denmark. Parallel to the experience of the conscientious objector Gustav Sack (q.v.), Engelke was unwilling to return:

> Even though I 'ought' really to go 'home', I have remained here. Not because I'm afraid. The man-in-the-street has as his purpose in life to be of use to himself and others in his time. Should men fall in the war, then they have fulfilled their purpose. The man of genius, however, is only one in a thousand. He alone has the duty not to serve just himself, but always to aim to affect mankind beyond his time and inspire and lead the sons and daughters of the future. So I do not want to do my country the minor service of sacrificing my bones, but rather do my people the major service of increasing the intellectual worth of the German Empire.

The 'major service' with which Engelke hoped to justify his special treatment was to provide posterity with the completed novel of *Don Juan*. But like Sack, financial pressures induced him to return to Germany and accept his fate: 'I realize I should have left immediately . . . Everything goes its way as it should. One struggles for a little while believing that one can govern one's own destiny – only to be pushed back on to the wheel of fortune and circumstance again – whether with or without one's consent. I know I am going to end up where I belong and that is why I am confident and full of hope.'

This optimistic fatalism carried Engelke through four years of a war towards which he remained ever sceptical:

> My feelings still struggle instinctively against the war. Were it not for the fact that we were acting in defence, I would have refused outright, and remained where the grass grows green. Mark this! No people hates the other – it is the powerful speculators without a conscience who manage the war. And so it is even now. But – after all, even they, like all criminals, do not act of their own accord, but are only doing what they have to. No man can manufacture such a war – it is always the giant, unseen hand of fate, of God, the power over heaven and earth – or call it what you will.

Engelke experienced war on the front-line at Langemarck, St Mihiel, the Somme, Champagne, Dünaberg and Verdun. In 1916 he was awarded the Iron Cross for swimming the flooded Yser on the German-Belgian border. The following year, he was wounded. In this last period of recuperation and reprieve from front-line life, he met and became engaged to a war-widow, and when he had to return to fight in May 1918, copious love letters followed. His friends attempted to have him transferred from the front-line, much to Engelke's annoyance: he resisted all attempts to remove him from the company of his front-line comrades. However, before a transfer could be considered, Engelke was badly wounded in a successful British assault on 11 October. He was discovered by the British troops the next day and taken to a field hospital. The following day he was dead.

Throughout the war, Engelke's attitude to the motivations and bloody results remained steadfast:

> Our war is lacking in a soul – just consider the thread which binds here with over there as the three threads of capitalism, party politics and diplomacy. As a concept, this war will surely only ever be portrayed in the arts as a time-dictated great and insanely bloody event . . . War is the negation or at least the undermining of the spiritual, and the furthering of the power of the material world.

TIM CROSS

Texts

Rhythmus des neuen Europa, das Gesamtwerk (Postskriptum, Hanover, 1979). Paperback reprint of 1960 edition (Paul List, Munich) with a newly revised introduction by Hermann Blome. The complete works contain: 132 poems; notes and essays; *Don Juan*, fragment of a novel; *Wala*, fragmentary dramatic scenes; 'The Fort', a short story; war diary; letters.

Secondary sources

Kurt Morawietz, *Mich aber schone, Tod: Gerrit Engelke 1890–1918* (Postskriptum, Hanover, 1979). Companion to the complete works. Clears many misconceptions concerning Engelke's status within German literary history. Documents Engelke's output as a graphic artist. Full bibliography. Photographic illustrations.

Kurt Morawietz heads the Gerrit-Engelke-Gedächtnis-Stiftung (Leinstr. 17, D-300 Hanover, West Germany) with whose kind permission the photograph above is reproduced. Originally printed in *die horen, Zeitschrift für Literatur, Kunst & Kritik*, issue 117 (K. Morawietz (ed.), Hanover, 1980).

AN DEN TOD

Mich aber schone, Tod,
Mir dampft noch Jugend blutstromrot, –
Noch hab ich nicht mein Werk erfüllt,
Noch ist die Zukunft dunstverhüllt –
Drum schone mich, Tod.

Wenn später einst, Tod,
Mein Leben verlebt ist, verloht
Ins Werk – wenn das müde Herz sich neigt,
Wenn die Welt mir schweigt, –
Dann trage mich fort, Tod.

TO DEATH

But spare me, Death;
I am still in the first flush of youth,
My life-work is still unaccomplished,
The future is still wrapped in a haze –
Therefore spare me, Death.

Sometime later, Death,
When my life has been lived, when it has burned away
Into my work – when the tired heart is waning,
When the world has nothing more to say to me,
Then carry me off, Death.

PROSE TRANSLATION BY PATRICK BRIDGWATER

THE FORT

I

All was quiet. The rampart of the communication trench, which looked like the long crest of a hill, stretched away and disappeared darkly into the night. The hazy, reddish new moon hung low, casting a pale light on the soldiers sleeping in the trench; here and there rifle barrels gleamed.

Marks, lying with his back to the rampart, squinted into the massive ring of light and then tried to make out the distant range of the Vosges mountains. The longer he looked the more everything swam before his eyes; and as soon as he thought he could distinguish something it melted away and the night rose before him like an endless black wall. He had been lying like this since nine o'clock, unable to sleep. He was usually quite composed but the certain knowledge that the main assault was to be launched at two a.m. had made him apprehensive. Apart from a few minor skirmishes he had, in fact, not been through anything, and this was to be the first big engagement of the war. Unbidden thoughts came gnawing at his brain and his ears were buzzing.

It was only six months since he had completed the compulsory year of military service; after that he had immediately resumed his medical studies in Göttingen. And then war broke out. He and several other students who did not want to remain temporarily inactive members of their units at once volunteered for front-line duty. They had been drafted into this company to supplement it as its strength had dwindled in the first, bloodily repulsed assault on the southern forts of the stronghold. After the failure of the attack the infantry had dug in around the fortress. Heavy howitzers had been brought up. For five days the bombardment had roared unceasingly. The siege troops had already become apathetic as a result of the incessant thundering. They had noticed with amazement that in the past two nights the smoking iron muzzles had fallen silent and the encircled enemy also made no response. Since the day before yesterday the northern fort had been quiet for long periods and, in between, its fire had been weak and irregular. It was assumed that here was the weak point and so, after the arrival of some Bavarian reinforcements, nearly all forces were concentrated in front of this fort throughout the day. Only the reserves and artillery were left behind in the vacated entrenchments. Their task was to deceive the enemy by keeping up a brisk fire. In the afternoon, despite the unpleasant light artillery fire from the fort, the sappers had to dig new, narrow trenches further ahead to shorten the way up the endangered glacis which would be exposed to the worst hail of bullets during the night assault. Gradually, all troops moved forward into the new positions. Then, at nine p.m. Taps was sounded and, at last, there was quiet. Up there in the fieldworks right at the front, only the sappers, those tired lads, were trying to catch a few hours' sleep. The infantry were lying behind them.

Suddenly, with a start, Marks grabbed his rifle – he could hear the muffled sound of something sliding and metal clanking nearby. He looked intently: it was only a soldier who had lain too far up against the rampart and had slithered down in his fitful sleep. His helmet had rolled over his shoulder strap and rifle but the man did not wake up. Marks pulled out his watch and held it up towards the moon: ten o'clock exactly! Slowly he turned round and heaved himself up – he saw a blurred silhouette, spreading darkly: the elevation on which the fortress was situated. From somewhere he heard the sentry's footsteps but could not see anybody. Quietly he slid down again, squeezed past the sleeping men, turned on his side, shut his eyes and tried to go to sleep. But it did not work; his hearing was becoming too acute and his ears were singing – heavy breathing, now and then some involuntary movement or confused stammering born of tormented dreams, then again deep, exhausted breathing all around. He could hear an indeterminate scraping sound and a jangling noise – probably the horses of the supply vehicles or the light guns, he thought. The snore of the man next to him, with its rattling and eerie groans, was getting worse. Marks yawned, yet he was not tired; his temples twitched and pounded. His neighbour was snoring terribly and somewhere another man began to gurgle spasmodically. Marks sat up and, annoyed, looked to his side but he nearly laughed at the silly, helplessly twisted face of the sleeper from whose mouth, gaping like a dark cave, constant eruptions burst like big air bubbles. It sounded as if a fist was squeezing his throat and he was about to choke. Marks rolled over on his right side and noticed two wide-awake eyes peering at him. 'Well now,' he thought, 'can't he sleep either?'

They looked at each other for a while. Gradually, Marks realized that this was the pessimistic young teacher who had been allotted to this unit and placed close beside him. He, too, was a replacement but had been drafted a day later than Marks himself.

'Hey!' Marks called in a low tone.

The teacher crept nearer, climbed over the man lying next to him, squatted by Marks's side and shook hands. They looked at one another – and each knew that the other was worried.

'Well, thank God, we'll be going into action at last, tomorrow.' When the teacher did not reply Marks gave him a sidelong glance – he thought he could detect water in his eyes.

'Yes –', the teacher sighed at last, 'it is awful.'

'Awful?', asked the student. 'Are you scared?'

'Oh no, that's not it,' the young teacher smiled wistfully. 'Have you written to your parents and relations?'

'What for?' Marks said equably; 'they'll learn soon enough whether I'm above or beneath the earth.'

'I haven't written either – maybe it's better that way.'

They said no more. Marks looked around. The snorer had fallen silent and lay there, the moon shining on his peaceful face. He had pulled up his knees; the two polished brass buttons at the top of his tunic shimmered in the light.

Further up a soldier flailed his arms about and the neighbour who had been hit let out a dull groan.

Deep breathing.

The moon stood high now and looked a yellowish silver.

'Yes,' the younger man resumed, 'in drowsy peace-time one's blood becomes too thick and sated – anyway, we had stored up too much strength in the peaceful years since 1870; now it will and must explode again.' He had raised his hand emphatically and kept beating the air to lend force to his main argument as he continued: 'What grey creatures we have become! We are shopkeepers and traders, industrialists and suchlike – but we no longer have that great urge for the faraway, the wild lust for adventure, for conquest, which our forefathers had. We don't want to accept the fact that our blood is always seeking struggle, always! A ready fist to fight with!'

While Marks was holding forth so loudly the teacher tapped his arm repeatedly but he had not noticed it; now and then he was puffing out his breath as though he were sweating.

'We mustn't talk so loud,' the teacher said. A little bewildered, Marks looked both ways – but nobody stirred.

'It's all very well, the way you put it,' the older man remarked calmly. 'But why not a peaceful struggle: prudence versus prudence – instead of these barbaric wars that are fed by the basest, primal instincts of man? This is no longer a battle: strength against strength, fist against fist as it used to be – it is a mechanized massacre; machine-guns, rapid-fire guns, armoured airships and mines raging against each other. The struggle is impersonal, it has become gigantic and terrible – and ends in limitless destruction of all life. Do you realize that by winning his battles the victor – that is he who most skilfully mows down the youth of the enemy state – destroys its entire future for a hundred years, maybe for centuries?'

The student reflected in silence; he drummed his fingers mechanically on the bayonet strap.

'I have no time for sentimental pity for the vanquished; the strongest alone has a right to life. You can see this everywhere in nature and among humans. And after tomorrow we'll see who is the strongest, the victor and architect of the future.'

The teacher pulled up his knees, wrapped his elbows around them and said, as if talking to himself: 'I suppose we'll have to fight this war; but later on things should be better. No armies, no lunatic armament races.'

'Still, that is what puts money in people's pockets,' Marks interjected.

'Certainly, the people do make money but it could be used to more humane ends. Yes, later – there ought to be only police forces and courts which uphold law and order and a single great court of arbitration for the whole world that settles any budding dispute between states and will banish war from this earth. All wars must be avoided – even this one could have been prevented in time – but now it's too late.' The teacher suppressed a sigh.

'And if your beautiful dream comes true,' said Marks, 'all mankind can go to sleep in peace.' Immediately regretting his irony, he added: 'No – seriously; surely you, too, know that great ideals are never realized, at least not fully.'

'True . . . unfortunately not, but hope springs eternal and we still believe that we are at the beginning and . . .'

Marks pulled his arm: 'The sentry!'

Both threw themselves down. Marks, lying on his stomach, looked up. Out of the corner of his eye he saw the black silhouette of the soldier coming to a halt, motionless; his rifle slung, the fixed bayonet gleaming. Then he resumed his walk; his heavy steps died away softly. For a while the two men stared into the dark.

'Well,' the teacher whispered cautiously, 'I reckon we ought to get a few more hours' sleep.'

'Yes.' Marks was holding up his watch. 'It's ten past eleven, we've only got another three hours.'

For a laden moment both were silent.

'Goodnight,' said Marks.

'Till we meet again,' the other one replied meaningfully, as he pressed Marks's hand and so crept quietly to his place.

Deep breathing all around; here and there some snoring. The moon has moved up high; its light is strange and peaceful.

II

Marks felt an odd, dull, rocking sensation – there it was again – he opened his eyes wide: someone had shaken him by the shoulder to wake him; the man had already moved on. The whole place was swarming with soldiers jumping to their feet or creeping upwards. Marks looked up, collecting his thoughts. The moon had slid far down to the side. A little further away Marks heard a voice: 'Get up! Up!' – I suppose I'll have to, he thought. He stood up, his legs were stiff, he was freezing. He rolled up the grey greatcoat on which he had lain, tied it round the pack and tossed the heavy rucksack over his back. Coat, tunic and pack – everything was damp and clammy. He shook himself and slapped his arms a few times across his chest. 'Fall in! Dress off!' someone yelled behind him. He grabbed his rifle, climbed over the rampart and leapt forward, joining a dark mass of men. Buttons and weapons flashed, a subdued murmur buzzed all around, commands shrilled far into the night. He tried to find his way around the teeming mass, someone came up to him – it was the teacher – no, he recognized his lance-corporal, Möller: 'Damn dark,' he said. Marks had not heard properly and moved towards him. One by one, the men slowly formed a long line. Some coarse loudmouth was showing off. Marks looked around but he could not identify anyone among the restlessly treading throng of soldiers; down the line the tops of helmets flashed above luminous faces.

'Quiet!' came a roar from the front. As if cut off, all fell silent.

'Attention!' – a single, dull jerk shot through their limbs all along the line. Nothing moved.

'Shoul-der arms!' – a single clashing crash; a few rifles continued to clatter. Officers ran feverishly ahead of the front, shouting disjointed orders. Marks could not make them out.

Low down in front of him, close to the black ground stretching away, he saw tiny lights moving in the distance: sappers, he thought.

'At ease! Forward, March!'

(The same orders were shouted to the left and right.) The leaden-dark mass of men tramped heavily along, slowly pushing its way into the darkness.

Advancing step by step. From time to time Marks would stumble.

Onwards, step by step. He heard the lance-corporal next to him yawn loudly and then curse.

The ground rose in irregular undulations. A few shadows flitted ahead of the line – they were the NCOs and lieutenants; their grey uniforms made them almost invisible in the dusk.

Brrrr – there was a sound – Marks listened; he thought it came from the fort. Brrrr – it was getting nearer, but coming from the rear; travelling forward across the marching troops, a strong metallic drone. Marks saw something black. It cast a fleeting shadow like a big bat. The plane must be flying fairly high; the usually sharp chatter of individual detonations turned into a blurred, faint whirring, then nothing more could be heard.

Now they were advancing through a vineyard; vines, half a man's height, snapped under the stumbling soldiers' heavy boots and were trampled. Onward!

Marks had a feeling that they would have to march on like this into eternity – step by step, by step – on and on and on.

There was some movement from the direction of the left wing; 'Onward' – the call leapt from man to man, and one after the other each took off his heavy helmet. The man to his left shouted 'Cover helmets!' Marks took his off, passed on the word to the right, pulled the grey cloth cover from his trouser pocket and slipped it over the betraying gleam of the helmet.

There was some disarray but as soon as the helmets were firmly on all heads the feet resumed their usual heavy tread.

The advance was getting more arduous. At short intervals, piles of earth and blocks, sometimes separated by holes in the ground, rose from the dewy, slippery grass. You had to watch your step. This exertion, the oppressive darkness and the uncertainty facing them had made the troops hot. The smell of sweat drifted from man to man and, from the mass of humans on the move with their heavy packs, a kind of warm mist rose into the chilly, damp night air. Marks was no longer freezing; his tunic, in fact all his clothes, smelt musty, like things do in the rain. His pack was beginning to press hard as the contents had shifted and each time he moved they would slide to the left; he pulled the pack over to his right shoulder. He was getting bored with the monotonous trudge and, in a low tone, started to hum 'Toreador, now guard thee'; but he soon stopped again though he did not know why. He was panting: the slope was getting steep. The ranks were breaking here and there; the men jumped, walked, crawled, dragged up a leg, marched another few steps – forwards, ever forwards.

What was that? – a long streak of light played on the night clouds, descended and, slowly scanning the ground, crept nearer . . . 'Down!' yelled the man next to Marks and he, in turn, shouted the word to his right-hand neighbour. Panting, they all lay motionless on their stomachs in the wet field.

'Must be cabbage,' Marks thought as he nervously fingered some big, coarse leaves. The beam of the searchlight flashed eerily, shining more sharply from the side – now! – Marks jerked and squeezed his eyes shut; when he opened them again a second later he was still completely dazzled. A large pool of light spread before him but the beam had travelled on and was now probing into the darkness, far to the right.

They all set off again, forwards.

And now – that muffled drone, it was coming from the fort up there; they must have noticed something. At fairly long intervals the blurred rumble and thud of distant guns; they were probably firing in another direction.

From the rear, a shrill trumpet signal blared out. 'Sections, Halt!'

'Halt,' shouted the NCOs in front of every row.

'Packs off! Fix, bayonets!' came the next order. A forest of well-honed knives flashed on the gun barrels; the packs tossed off the men's backs crashed to the ground.

For a moment, expectant silence – the whole line stood man to man; their hearts furiously pounding. The spasmodic rumbling from the fort was getting stronger.

Phweee! – bright red Very lights whistling up into the blackness before them: the signal for general attack.

Everywhere, at the back among the massed troops, ahead of the front, to the left and right and far up on the right – the shrill, piercing sound of the section leaders' whistles:

'Attack! At the double, March, March!'

Impetuously they surged forward and up the slope, like a huge, grumbling herd.

An incessant thunder was dinning in their ears; the defenders of the fort were firing as if possessed. Shells were whizzing past, close over the attackers' heads; circles of fire flashed like lightning up above; the whole dark night let out a roar. It was thundering, murderous chaos.

Then – Bang! A shell landed right among them – a spattering, screaming fountain of earth, flesh and smoke erupted skywards. Marks and men next to him were hurled to the ground by the tremendous blast of air – he pulled himself up; he felt nothing; he started to run again, forwards, forwards! Shell splinters were raining down on the helmets.

They had to get through this zone of fire as fast as possible. Instinctively they all ran like mad; why? what for? No one knew. Storm ahead – that was all. Quick! Quick!

They must be fairly close to the fort now for the din of the guns was ear-splitting. Blindly, they ran through smouldering, stinging, dense gunpowder-smoke as through thunderclouds.

And now a new, gnawing rumble started up everywhere in the distance, becoming a drone, the darkest undertone in the cacophony of whizzing, crashing and crackling: the 42 cm siege guns had resumed their sinister work. All forts were being kept under fire. The thick air, whisked up by the smoke and smell of gunpowder, was cut by the roar of guns, screaming shells and explosions high above. The hail of shells intensified; they were hitting closer, tearing horrifying holes in the surging ranks before furiously boring into the ground.

Up ahead, soldiers were falling on either side. Marks kept on running, between the men, jumping over one, pushing aside another who had been hit and was keeling over towards him. One thought alone was burning more fiercely in his brain than the fever in all his limbs as he groped his way forward. *Forward!* Nothing else. What's this? He bounced back, others tumbled. Barbed wire was barring the way. Sappers leapt forward, cleaved a way through the hazardous obstacle with big wirecutters – and Marks was through! He did not even notice the large bloody scratch right across his hand. But only ten paces on he flung himself back with all his might, falling with a thud. Several others stepped on him: at the last moment he had spotted a sinister pit, a trap filled with spiked stakes and wire. Screaming and groaning could be heard, many must have fallen into it. – 'Timbers over!' someone commanded – and the massed troops surged over the planks and boards which the sappers had thrown across.

Now they stood at the foot of the rampart; it rose before them like a black wall.

Above, the machine-guns kept up a violent, monotonous chatter, spraying down bullets by the sackful, like peas.

The result was dreadful: one third of the men were mown down as they ran.

'*Forwards, attack! hurrah!*' . . . the officers' shouts, almost swallowed up by the noise of gunfire, could be heard through the smoke. With a wild roar of '*Hurrah*!' all race on, push upwards – creeping on all fours, jumping, falling. *Hurrah! Hurrah!* and into the hand-to-hand fighting on the rampart.

Ten men tumble down backwards – twenty others push on, gritting their teeth – ten more, their bodies shot through, plummet down sweeping other comrades with them – but another thirty leap on to the rampart with bloodcurdling, hoarse *Hurrahs* – and yet more to come – hundreds of them!

The defenders withdraw to the centre of the fort, behind walls, into the armoured turrets, into the ruins of the casemates – some jumping, others running, all over the place. The attackers, crouching behind the humps of the ramparts, fire into the terrible devastation of the fort spreading before them. Time and again Marks presses the trigger; the barrel is already getting hot, his right shoulder hurting from the continual recoil of the butt. The blood pounding in his head to near bursting point represses every thought and blurs consciousness; he feels as if he is lying in the hot sun and sweating profusely. Mechanically he pulls the cocking handle, inserts another clip into the chamber – six more bullets from the barrel which he aligns with feverishly cramped fingers – lower handle – new clip in – another six shots – endlessly.

The defenders of the fort have fled into the interior. Their fire is getting lighter. The dead are piling up between the gaps in the ruins of concrete and masonry; they have fallen all over each other. Wounded men may still be groaning deep beneath them.

At several points the attackers, in a single great leap from the ramparts, are pushing towards the centre of the fort.

Suddenly, ten men rush out from behind the shattered armoured turret. With fixed bayonets they dash with crazy bravado towards the rampart and the detested attackers. But before they have covered a few metres, nine of them, riddled by bullets, collapse like scarecrows into one another – the last one stumbles on, fitfully gurgling some unintelligible sounds as if trying to sing – then he, too, tumbles slowly backwards; a leg twitches and he lies still.

The fort is taken. The last man has fallen.

Amidst the ruins the conquerors stand around in groups, one after the other shouting 'Hurrah!', as if drunk. Marks, too, wanted to call out but the word caught in his throat. He slid away and sat on a slab of masonry in a corner. He was not feeling tired, only thirsty. He drank the black coffee from his cloth-covered metal flask, without once setting it down.

A few orders; a loud clatter of boots; the occupation guards were posted; the others were to have a rest at last. Totally exhausted, most of the soldiers sank into a confused, blood-filled doze, wherever they happened to stand or sit, some with faces feverishly reddened, others a pale green.

From the other forts which looked like large molehills in the dull-grey distance the muffled, perfunctory boom of guns continued. Occasionally there was a sharp bang; then it got quieter. An oppressive weariness had settled everywhere.

Two bodies lay by Marks's side: across the face of one of them blood was still oozing from a wound in the forehead as from a tiny spring; at the edges it was a black crust. Nauseated, Marks turned round and peered outside through a large breach in the rampart. Silently, day was dawning with a hazy, dullish-grey, shivering brightness across the entire sky; at one spot it was turning greenish-violet and below, deep down, it was already glowing yellow.

. . . And here he sat; one of the victors. He did not know whether to be glad or filled with sadness – aimless thoughts ebbed and flowed through his brain; he felt so empty and really quite useless. He could see how in the capital, in all towns in the homeland, people would be crowding around the poster pillars, thronging in front of newspaper offices eagerly reading telegrams of victory – and then: the yelling and shouting and jubilation of victory! But who would spare a thought for the countless fallen conquerors, for the dead who, too, had won the victory?

After all, the lists of losses were always published much later. Doubts and wistful apprehension were shrinking his heart: '. . . this war . . . this war!' He groaned. He raised his fixed stare from the stony ground and looked into the far distance again. The sphere of the sun glowed scarlet amidst the little clouds tinged with red.

There it hung, like a bloody lump; hideously red as if it had soaked up all the blood swimming down there. He felt as if the distant mountain peaks, the long sloping fields and vineyards trampled to destruction – as if the whole morning sky and he himself were drenched in blood, roaring blood! He sensed that he was going to be sick; he felt giddy – he got up and wanted to . . . there! – his foot knocks against the other corpse – and – this is – the teacher! He begins to sway, reaches into the air and collapses with a stifled groan.

And a glorious, still morning shone like gold.

TRANSLATED BY R. P. HELLER

AN DIE SOLDATEN DES GROSSEN KRIEGES

In memoriam August Deppe

Herauf ! aus Gräben, Lehmhöhlen, Betonkellern,
Steinbrüchen!
Heraus aus Schlamm und Glut, Kalkstaub und
Aasgerüchen!
Herbei! Kameraden! Denn von Front zu Front, von Feld
zu Feld
Komme euch allen der neue Feiertag der Welt!
Stahlhelme ab, Mützen, Käppis! und fort die Gewehre!

Genug der blutbadenden Feindschaft und Mordehre!

Euch alle beschwör ich bei eurer Heimat Weilern und
Städten,
Den furchtbaren Samen des Hasses auszutreten, zu jäten,
Beschwöre euch bei eurer Liebe zur Schwester, zur
Mutter, zum Kind,
Die allein euer narbiges Herz noch zum Singen stimmt.
Bei eurer Liebe zur Gattin – auch ich liebe ein Weib!
Bei eurer Liebe zur Mutter – auch mich trug ein
Mutterleib!
Bei eurer Liebe zum Kinde – denn ich liebe die Kleinen!
Und die Häuser sind voll von Fluchen, Beten, Weinen!

TO THE SOLDIERS OF THE GREAT WAR

Rise up! Out of trenches, muddy holes, concrete bunkers.
quarries.
Up out of mud and fire, chalk dust and stench of corpses!

Come along! Comrades! For from front to front, from
battlefield to battlefield,
May the world's new red-letter day come to you all!
Off with your steel helmets, caps, képis! And away with
your rifles!
Enough of this bloody enmity and murderous sense of
honour.

You all I implore by your country's villages and towns

To stamp out, to weed out the monstrous seeds of hatred,
Implore you by your love of your sisters, mothers,
children,
Which alone still disposes your scarred heart to sing.
By your love of your wife – I too love a woman!
By your love of your mother – a mother's body bore
me too!
By your love of your child – for I love little ones!
And the houses are full of cursing, praying, weeping!

Lagst du bei Ypern, dem zertrümmerten? Auch ich lag dort.
Bei Mihiel, dem verkümmerten? Ich war an diesem Ort.
Dixmuide, dem umschwemmten? Ich lag vor deiner Stirn
In Höllenschluchten Verduns, wie du in Rauch und Klirrn;
Mit dir im Schnee vor Dünaburg, frierend, immer trüber,
An der leichenfressenden Somme lag ich dir gegenüber.
Ich lag dir gegenüber überall, doch wußtest du es nicht!
Feind an Feind, Mensch an Mensch und Leib an Leib, warm und dicht.

Ich war Soldat und Mann und Pflichterfüller, so wie du,
Dürstend, schlaflos, krank – auf Marsch und Posten immerzu.
Stündlich vom Tode umstürzt, umschrien, umdampft,
Stündlich an Heimat, Geliebte, Geburtsstadt gekrampft
Wie du und du und ihr alle. –
Reiß auf deinen Rock! Entblöße die Wölbung der Brust!
Ich sehe den Streifschuß von fünfzehn, die schorfige Krust,
Und da an der Stirn vernähten Schlitz vom Sturm bei Tahüre –
Doch daß du nicht denkst, ich heuchle, vergelt' ich mit gleicher Gebühr:
Ich öffne mein Hemd: hier ist noch die vielfarbige Narbe am Arm!
Der Brandstempel der Schlacht! von Sprung und Alarm,
Ein zärtliches Andenken lang nach dem Kriege.
Wie sind wir doch stolz unsrer Wunden! Stolz du der deinigen,
Doch nicht stolzer als ich auch der meinigen.

Du gabst nicht besseres Blut und nicht rötere Kraft,
Und der gleiche zerhackte Sand trank unsern Saft! –
Zerschlug deinen Bruder der gräßliche Krach der Granate?
Fiel nicht dein Onkel, dein Vetter, dein Pate?
Liegt nicht der bärtige Vater verscharrt in der Kuhle?
Und dein Freund, dein lustiger Freund aus der Schule? –
Hermann und Fritz, meine Vettern, verströmten im Blute,
Und der hilfreiche Freund, der Jüngling, der blonde und gute.
Und zu Hause wartet sein Bett, und im ärmlichen Zimmer
Seit sechzehn, seit siebzehn die gramgraue Mutter noch immer.
Wo ist uns sein Kreuz und sein Grab! –

Franzose du, von Brest, Bordeaux, Garonne,
Ukrainer du, Kosak vom Ural, Dnjestr und Don,

Österreicher, Bulgaren, Osmanen und Serben,
Ihr alle im rasenden Strudel von Tat und von Sterben –
Du Brite, aus London, York, Manchester,

Were you at Ypres, ruined Ypres? I too was there.
At Mihiel, stricken Mihiel? I was there.
At Dixmuide, surrounded by floods? I was out in front of you.
In Verdun's hellish defiles, in the smoke and din like you,
With you in the snow outside Dünaburg, freezing and getting more and more depressed,
At the necrophagous Somme I was opposite you.
I was opposite you everywhere, but you did not know it!
Enemy beside enemy, man beside man and body beside body, warm and close together.

I was a soldier and a man and did my duty, just like you,
Thirsty, sleepless, sick – always on the march or on guard.
Hourly surrounded by falling, screaming, smoking death,
Hourly aching for home, loved ones, one's own town,
Like you and you and all of you. –
Tear open your tunic! Bare your barrel of a chest!
I see the grazing shot dating from '15, the scab,

And there on your forehead the sewn-up gash from the attack at Tahüre –
But so that you will not think I'm putting it on, I'll repay you in the same coin:
I open my shirt: here is the multi-coloured scar on my arm!
Battle's brand! Long after the war
A fond souvenir of scramble and alarm.
How proud we are of our wounds.
You proud of yours,
But no prouder than I am of mine.

You did not give better blood nor greater vitality,
And the same churned-up sand drank our vital juices! –
Did the dreadful crump of that shell blow your brother to blazes?
Did not your uncle fall, your cousin, your godfather?
Does not your bearded father lie buried in his grave?
And your friend, your jolly friend from school?
Hermann and Fritz, my cousins, bled to death,

And my helpful friend, the young one, the one who was fair-haired and kind.
And at home his bed is waiting for him, and in her shabby room
His mother, grey with grief, has been waiting ever since '16, '17;
Where is his cross and his grave? –

Frenchman, from Brest, Bordeaux, Garonne;
Ukrainian, Cossack from the Urals, from Dnjestr and Don;
Austrians, Bulgarians, Turks and Serbs,
All of you in the raging whirlpool of action and dying –
Britisher, from London, York, Manchester,

Soldat, Kamerad, in Wahrheit Mitmensch und Bester –

Amerikaner, aus den volkreichen Staaten der Freiheit:
Wirf ab: Sonderinteresse, Nationaldünkel und Zweiheit!
Warst du ein ehrlicher Feind, wirst du ein ehrlicher
Freund.
Hier meine Hand, dass sich nun Hand in Hand zum
Kreise binde
Und unser neuer Tag uns echt und menschlich finde.

Die Welt ist für euch alle groß und schön und schön!
Seht her! staunt auf! nach Schlacht und Blutgestöhn:
Wie grüne Meere frei in Horizonte fluten,
Wie Morgen, Abende in reiner Klarheit gluten,
Wie aus den Tälern sich Gebirge heben,
Wie Milliarden Wesen uns umbeben!
O, unser allerhöchstes Glück heiß: Leben! –

O, daß sich Bruder wirklich Bruder wieder nenne!
Daß Ost und West den gleichen Werk erkenne:
Daß wieder Freude in die Völker Blitzt:
Und Mensch an Mensch zur Güte sich erhitzt!

Von Front zu Front und Feld zu Feld,
Laßt singen uns den Feiertag der neuen Welt!
Aus aller Brüsten dröhne *eine* Bebung:
Der Psalm des Friedens, der Versöhnung, der Erhebung!
Und das meerrauschende, dampfende Lied,
Das hinreißende, brüderumarmende,
Das wilde und heilig erbarmende
Der tausendfachen Liebe laut um alle Erden!

Soldier, comrade-in-arms, truly fellow human being and
best of men –
American, from the populous states of freedom:
Throw away partisanship, national pride and antagonism!
If you were an honourable enemy, become an honourable
friend.
Here is my hand, so that hand in hand may now be linked
together
And our new day find us sincere and humane.

For all of you the world is great and beautiful!
Look! Marvel! After battle and blood's groaning:
How freely green seas flow into their horizons;
How mornings and evenings glow in pure brightness,
How mountains rise up out of the valleys,
How billions of living beings tremble all around us!
Oh, our greatest blessing of all is: life! –

Oh, that brother may again really be called brother!
That east and west may recognize the same values!
That joy may again flash into all nations,
And man be roused to goodness by man!

From front to front and battlefield to battlefield,
Let us sing the birthday of the new world!
Out of every chest let a *single* tune ring forth:
The psalm of peace, of reconciliation, of revolt!
And may the surging, radiant song,
The thrilling, brother-embracing,
The wild and divinely compassionate song
Of thousandfold love ring out around the earth!

PROSE TRANSLATION BY PATRICK BRIDGWATER

Franz Marc (1880-1916):
The Creation II.
Staatliche graphische Sammlung, Munich

GUSTAV SACK 1885–1916

'We, the "good soldiers", fight because we are soldiers and are here to save our skins and want to survive at all costs. We are not fighting for an aim, nor for the Fatherland, nor for a united Germany – that is all stuff and nonsense.'

Gustav Sack led a dissolute life. The scars on his face bore witness to the countless fencing duels he had provoked after nights of student debauchery, of which also his failure to complete his academic studies was a direct result. Success as a writer in his brief lifetime also eluded him. Therefore the enthusiastic reception which greeted the posthumous publication of his novels became an irony that Sack had, characteristically, anticipated. After completing his final work in 1916, he declared to his wife: 'Now would be the time for me to fall. Then the books will get published, you would be all set up, and everything will be dandy.' Within four months, on 5 December 1916, Gustav Sack was dead, shot in an attack at Finta Mare during the advance on Bucharest. And his books were indeed published. Despite extreme paper shortage immediately after the war, Sack's first novel had reached sales figures of 20,000 in three editions by 1918.

Gustav Sack was born on 28 October 1885 in the small provincial town of Schermbeck near Wesel in the Niederrhein in western Germany, and he started his literary activity at an early age. This, combined with the carousing of his student days, served to interrupt his haphazard academic career (he read philosophy, natural science and literature), with the result that he failed to matriculate in 1910. When, in 1913, it had become clear to his parents that their maverick son would never complete his studies, they disowned him. It thus became imperative for Sack to make a success of his chosen career, and he was to spend the next six years in the vain attempt. Although his student days may not have resulted in academic distinction, they did provide him with material for the novel which was to prove such a success after the war: *Ein verbummelter Student* (*An Idle Student*).

Sack embodied paradoxes in his life as much as in his writings. For example, he relished soldiering, yet was an anti-militarist. He was frequently in conflict with the authorities during the periods of military training to which all men in Germany were subject. The resulting detentions were, however, further opportunities for Sack to continue producing novellas, essays and poems. The torrid *Der Rubin* (*The Ruby*, 1913) is set against the background of army barracks life. Sack was a loner, but compulsory military service inevitably led to companion-

Gustav Sack. *Schiller Nationalmuseum, Marbach*

ships. A fellow trainee, Hans Harbeck, became an important link in Sack's life. Sack met and fell in love with Harbeck's sister Paula, who in turn brought his first novel to the attention of the famous publisher Hans W. Fischer, although this contact failed to produce any material results during Sack's lifetime. However, while the continual rejection of his works by publishers in Germany may have made Sack depressed and embittered, it did not curb his industry. In the winter of 1912–13 there followed his second novel *Ein Namenloser* (*One Without a Name*), which again was based on recent personal experience.

Sack's isolationist tendency in the army was compounded by his failure to find acceptance among the literary circles in Munich, where he moved in 1913. He stayed in the same house as Hans Leybold (q.v.) who, together with the future Dadaist Hugo Ball, wrote humorous poems for the avant-garde periodical *Die Aktion*. Sack's arrogance became the subject of Leybold's article 'Der Zynismus unserer Jüngsten' ('The Cynicism of our Youth'), and his contempt for the *'Literaten'* – the socialites who passed for intellectuals – won him no friends in what he regarded as the superficiality of big city life. Nor did it win him publishing contracts. After a year in Munich, he resolved to leave Germany. Following further military service, he married Paula Harbeck, but in July 1914, he set off for Switzerland – alone.

In the Swiss Alps, he collected additional ideas for his third novel. Stylistically, *Paralyse* remains his most complex achievement, its non-narrative style having been compared to that of James Joyce. However the outbreak of war interrupted this last experiment, and subsequent events prevented its completion. Thomas Mann later commented: 'It is always to be regretted that this audaciously conceived work will remain a torso – admittedly, a torso more compelling than many a completed work.'

At the outbreak of war, the essential nature of Sack's principles was exposed and challenged by his legal obligation to report immediately to his command in Germany. (Conscription in Germany was compulsory.) Yet Sack, in neutral Switzerland, refused to leave. His future publisher Fischer remarked curtly: 'Refusing to join up – what idiocy!' Later, he analysed Sack's standpoint with greater insight: 'He felt no allegiance to the State. He had no need to fear the reproach of cowardice from anyone who knew him. The whirl of patriotism appeared to him merely as a despicable situation which was redeemed only by its comic side. He refused to submit to any moral pressure.'

This 'despicable situation', its comic overtones and the expostulation of his protest became the subject of Gustav Sack's final summation of his life's work: *Der Refraktär* – the refractor, or objector. This *Refraktär* was intended for the stage; its production was also meant to provide Sack with sufficient funds to survive the duration of the war in voluntary exile. In a letter to his wife, dated 31 August: '*The Objector* is progressing superbly well – the first act is finished! I am convinced that this is what will pull us through once and for all.' However, the stark economics of his impoverishment could not be overcome without remunerative employment; work in Switzerland in 1914 proved impossible to come by, and Sack had run up debts at the village inn where he was staying. His father-in-law was unsympathetic to his stand against conscription and refused to produce the outstanding portion of Paula Sack's dowry.

This great dilemma – to write or to fight – became the setting for a polemical drama. In the play, the objector Egon is deserted by friends and family, and resorts to the solitude of nature where he ultimately finds his death. Sack himself was less idealistic. When an amnesty was declared for pre-emptive deserters in September 1914, there seemed no other realistic way out: Sack was compelled to return. 'At least the war offers a chance of survival . . .' he wrote. 'It is a great shame that I cannot complete the play. In three weeks, it would have been done. But we simply lack all funds.'

However, the opportunity to complete the play did eventually materialize. The manuscript lay untouched for the fifteen consecutive months Sack spent on the Western Front, then in January 1916, he suffered a nervous breakdown. While recuperating from shellshock, he settled down to revising and reconstructing the story of his conscientious objector.

On one level, the theme of conscientious objection to the war serves only as a forum for Sack's debate on the importance of language, and the artist as its moral guardian. In the character of the journalist Dr Jakob Vogel, Sack exposes the despised '*Literat*' of his Munich experience. Vogel's decision to join the protagonist Egon in his refusal to fight threatens to undermine Egon's integrity. By announcing this decision to the assembled community, Vogel attempts to place himself on the same level as Egon, as an objector, and he even uses the same label – '*Herr Co-Refraktär*' – as if they were brothers with the same intent. Egon sees through the braggart: he knows, from Vogel's use of language, that it is not a decision arrived at from conviction, but an attempt to hide behind a label. While Egon embodies the Nietzschean ideal of the artist independent of society, Vogel succeeds in trivializing the artist's status.

Egon's main contrivance is to unmask Vogel's pretence. By a cunning ruse, he traps Vogel into marriage with the girl he has made pregnant, and Egon then tricks Vogel into accepting another label under which he can march off to war – as 'carefree cannon-fodder'. Now free to resume his stand, Sack allows his anti-hero to seek Nietzschean fulfilment by having him hurl himself off the mountain top at the play's melodramatic conclusion: 'in death I regain my world, my Ego . . . Then time is vanquished.' Yet the sentiment of the play remains ambiguous, as Sack explained in a letter to his wife: 'At first, I wanted to have Egon give himself up and was in a quandary for quite some time. But as the mountain scenes flowed so well, I have now added the finishing touches and he hurls himself off into the void.'

Der Refraktär is Gustav Sack's central work, but its structural weaknesses do not give the best indication of the standing of his *œuvre.* The play is better understood in the light of Sack's prose and poetry, as it contains numerous references to previous novels, poems and experiences. These culminate in the great fantastical scene in Act IV, when Egon the writer is isolated in a mountain hut. Egon's quest for moral independence has only led to physical isolation which in turn proves to be merely a prelude to spiritual solitude – loneliness. Thus ostracized by his community, Egon is confronted by characters from his other works who step out of the conflagration of his fevered mind and mock him with this futile attempt to survive outside society. As Walter H. Sokel, in his chapter 'The Writer *in extremis*' remarks, 'Egon's work, for the sake of which he has accepted loneliness, appears to him, in the end, as nothing more noble than the sublimation of his needs.' The sudden

'This war is the strangest of all wars; for the greatest war which has ever been fought, is, for us no more than the battle against the dirt and the rain and that overbearing thing, bellowing at us from all fronts: boredom.'

realization of this prompts Egon to destroy all his precious manuscripts and seek his end on the icy heights.

Sack occupies no definable position in German literary history. His existence has barely been acknowledged by any but the most enterprising germanists, and in reference books he is generally dismissed as a self-obsessed atheistic follower of Nietzsche. Any desire by students of literature to categorize Sack is confounded by the fact that he never belonged to any group or had any meaningful contact with any contemporary artists. In fact, he was, by and large, scornful of contemporary writing. For example, he wrote this about the war poetry of the time:

> Compare a poem of 1813 with those of today. We might as well chuck it all in. It makes me bitterly disappointed. I am furious with myself. My rage is as radical as hell & I wish we had stayed in Zurich. On the other hand: the basic feeling among the people is doubtless sincere, but how unbelievably pathetically it is expressed by its 'designated muses'!

Sack's ideas were among the most radical of his time, but his anarchism was not so much politically motivated as socially and culturally. Sack's widow speculated that, had they remained in Zurich, Sack, in so far as he was capable of forming an association with any particular group, may have attached himself to the Dadaists of the Café Voltaire. However, while his political attitudes were indeed shared by Hugo Ball, considering his differences with Ball's friend Leybold, an association with the group would have been unlikely. His viewpoint may have been extreme, but as is seen from the almost Shavian discourse of *Der Refraktär*, it was conventional in execution.

What can be said about Gustav Sack's place in German literature is that he merits re-evaluation as one of the most strikingly individual voices of pre-war expressionism. As one of the 'angry young men' of 1914, he is one of the few who genuinely succeeded in confronting the issues raised by the war, both in life and in literature.

TIM CROSS

Texts

Paula Sack (ed.), *Gesammelte Werke* (S. Fischer, Berlin, 1920). This remains the definitive collection of Sack's *œuvre*. It contains a memoir by Hans W. Fischer; the complete novels *Ein verbummelter Student* and *Ein Namenloser*, the poems first issued under the title *Die drei Reiter*, the juvenile work *Prometheus*; the fragmentary novel *Paralyse*; novellas; the drama *Der Refraktär*, and the war diary *In Ketten durch Rumänien*.

Prosa/Briefe/Verse (Albert Langen, Munich, 1962). Contains previously unpublished letters, but some editorial discrepancies appear in the republication of the prose works.

Paralyse/Der Refraktär (Fink, Munich, 1971). Contains a full bibliography, chronology and notes to the texts by Karl Eibl.

Hans Harbeck (ed.), *Gustav Sack, eine Einführung in sein Werk und eine Auswahl* (Steiner, Wiesbaden, 1958). Appeared in the series 'Verschollene und Vergessene' by the Akademie der Wissenschaften und der Literatur. Contains an introduction by Sack's brother-in-law Hans Harbeck; a selection of 17 poems; 12 short stories, including 'Im Heu'; one article 'Etwas mehr Philosophie'; an extract from the war diary originally published in 1920 as *In Ketten durch Rumänien*; a brief biography.

The Gustav Sack papers are held in their entirety at the Deutsche Literaturarchiv, Marbach am Neckar, West Germany.

Secondary source

Paula Sack, *Der verbummelte Student: Gustav Sack* (Munich, 1971). An essential accompaniment to the understanding of Sack's ideology and approach to his work, compiled by his widow.

Quark

Man frißt sich so durch seine Jahre
und wird mit jedem Jahre älter
und ist am Ende ohne Haare
doch immer noch ein Hinterhälter.

Man ißt und trinkt und man poussiert,
zeugt unfreiwillig ein paar Kinder,
indes die Jahre exaltiert
fortsausen Tag für Tag geschwinder.

Man packt sich aus, man streckt sich hin
und macht sich reuevoll ans Sterben,
um so als letzten Reingewinn
sich einen Nachruf zu erwerben.

Piffle

Year after year, you gnaw your way
through life, the years elude your clutch,
and in the end, your hair is grey
and still you don't amount to much.

You eat and drink and court a girl,
get children too, the Lord knows why,
while Time, pursuing its mad whirl,
faster and faster rushes by.

You lay you down to end your days
a penitent; you thus obtain
fine tributes to your worthy ways,
and so chalk up one last net gain.

TRANSLATED BY ANTHEA BELL

The Ruby

Around the time when the lime-trees blossom on the coast, Volunteer Cadet Greenhorn sat astride the wall encircling the barracks. Apart from the three-day imprisonment and his demotion to lance-corporal, the punishment meted out to him for his blatant act of moral decadence consisted of house-arrest. For that reason he had to slip out of the dormitory he shared with his company each night; had to sneak along the hallway, down the echoing steps and through the lurking shadows of the barrack square, and then swing himself over the wall to freedom. Awaiting him there was the blonde Madelon, with whom he would hurriedly disappear into his apartment in the town.

With a grating sound, the old clock drew breath into its rusty lungs and called out twelve rattling chimes into the night, and the nail-studded boots of the patrolling guard plodded dully and hard on the stone floor or glided slowly and insidiously over the crunching gravel. Round about, the fog spread out in white pools and lakes, out of which the peaks of the elms and lime-trees protruded like bulbous basilisk heads and the headlamps of a train stared like the red eyes of a cockroach. And in the middle of the starless night the moon hung like a highly polished brass lantern. A handful of sounds drifted aimlessly through the air and quivered dreamily between the red-brown buildings and sank with a whine into the sombre mists.

'Stop!'

A red hairy fist gripped his foot with brutal force and yanked him down. But with a curse, he tore himself back up, furiously kicking the bloke in the face so that he stumbled backwards, staggering to the ground with helmet and rifle. He swung himself over.

'O Madelon!'

Thick and nebulous, the fragrance from the lime-tree blossoms poured into the room. The shadows, fringed with brown, hung down from the ceiling into the red light which stood at the centre of the four walls like a giant ruby. And if you can picture the ruby, then you will be able to imagine the quivering grey column of smoke which rose from a bluish ashtray – spreading itself like a mushroom and breaking up into fantastical acanthus decorations and curling arabesques – as a vertical crack or an imperfection in the gemstone. And not so much an imperfection, rather its innermost secret, the core of the gem. You will have to regard the carafe of oily wine which glows a deep purple from time to time as the pulsating heart of the red ruby. But the tall white flame, the sensual burning spirit of the stone must surely be Madelon, as with unabashed nakedness she walked over to the bedstead on to which her lover had thrown himself.

'Do you not want to get undressed?'

'No. You look all the more white and silken against the sparkling buttons on the dull blue and the bright red of this – huh! – tunic of honour! O Madelon!'

Then he drew her to him and asked her to sit astride his chest. Thereupon he clasped her hands and searched her eyes and sank into their glittering blue as if in an increasingly fathomless sea.

'Did you see out there, the way the moon hung in the starless night, a lamp, glowing all on its own, like some forgotten lantern? That is how I am, helpless and lonely, suspended in the indescribable meaninglessness and the eternal brutality of this world. [. . .] To forget the world I look elsewhere: to ecstasy, strictly ignoring everything other than submerging myself in your red-hot love and your silken body.

'You beautiful, effervescent wave, called to life by the storm outside and driven on in a roar, never allowed to subside until by splashing up foam and froth, the rock which you caress subsides into your white embrace.

'Do you not feel you are in a church, in whose dim arches and recesses the fumes of incense and the organ notes are caught? Won't you have a sip? Look, the wine is so red, as red as the nipples on your proud breasts.

'O Madelon, your love is the only way I can see the world as a painting whose brightness and rich palette of colour I can enjoy without having to question its purpose, origin and content. Sweet aster, red wine and silken body, oh gushing wave, my long-lost happiness and that violet smile in the corner of your – you – my God!'

Then her body gave a shudder, and she lowered herself over him so that his head lay between her breasts.

When Volunteer Cadet Greenhorn was hauled out of bed the next day by the sergeant and heard that he was to be punished with ten days' arrest and loss of his stripes, his mate took him aside: 'I don't understand you! For a girl who is so blatantly betraying you! This very morning I saw how she went up to someone else's place three blocks along from here. And the fact that she only comes to you at midnight, isn't that so? And to think that you could not have guessed –'

Then the Volunteer Cadet Greenhorn went back up to his apartment, undressed himself at a leisurely pace and lay down on the pillows which still held the warmth from her body. Then he waited until the patrol arrived to collect him. And in the moment the door burst open, he shot a bullet into his mouth.

'Will you admit now, that you were carrying on with him? Will you?'

As she said nothing and only whimpered, doubled over in front of him, the whip came down with a crack on her back.

'Scandalous! To shoot oneself for the likes of a whore such as this! At least admit it! D'you hear?'

As she still failed to say anything and still whimpered kneeling before him, the dog-whip cracked down once, twice, three times over her bare back. Then he let go of her hands, causing the woman squatting in front of him to collapse and hit her forehead on the edge of the stool. She remained prostrate in that position. But he strode about wheezing. The room smelled of stale beer and cigarette smoke. He brandished the whip and finally threw it down on the striped back of the blonde Madelon with a 'You ass!' Then he stepped to the window, opened it, and wiped the sweat from his brow.

The quavering night air fluttered in and caressed Madelon's tangled hair, and suspended the image of the dark ruby and its purple heart before her sobbing eyes.

But when the student felt the breath of air on his troubled brow, he tore the duelling blade off the wall and leapt into a fencing posture and began to work over the oven pipe in threatening lunges.

At that, Madelon forgot the red ruby and her tears and started to smile to herself; and when the tireless man threw the sabre into the corner with a clatter, dragged a crate of beer to the sofa and began to drink, her eyes regained their sparkle and only waited for the 'Well, kid, let's make up.' And when at last it came, she slid over on her knees towards him and flung her arms around his drunken body.

Then she pulled off his boots and socks and pressed her lips to his foot.

At nine the next morning the heat of the sun lay on the street like a malevolent white beast, pouncing with its glass claws and with its suffocating breath upon everyone who stepped outside from the cool of the night; then it pressed down into his lungs, bit deep and scorchingly into his eyes and weighed him down like lead around his feet. And the higher the sun rose, the larger the beast grew and the whiter its glassy pelt, the higher it clambered up the walls of the houses and climbed in through windows and lolled about the rooms, foul and heavy and sultry. But it felt most at home swelling with pleasure in the room with the dented oven pipe, where the jagged sabre lay on the ground next to the empty beer bottles. There it soaked up the sweaty beer-laden vapours in deep breaths, heating them until they glowed within its chest and, with a devilish grin, belching them back out again over the two sleeping forms.

This is what woke Madelon. And as she caught sight of the brightness of the day and the white sun-beast, she turned over and woke up her lover and passed her tender blue eyes over his ruddy bloated face, his sleep-encrusted eyes and his half-open mouth out of which there rose the sickly-stale smell of alcohol. Then she pressed herself down on his warm damp body and felt how a sticky sweat broke out suddenly from all his pores.

'Oh darling, now you are no longer angry.'

Then one, two, three salvoes echoed in the morning air.

'Now they've buried him.'

But she shook her hair with a reluctant smile. Her delicate features shone suddenly with a sweet tenderness. And as she clung feverishly to the man, who was grunting with pleasure, she whispered into his red ass's ears, 'What is it that makes me love you so?'

TRANSLATED BY TIM CROSS

THE OBJECTOR

EGON's (the objector's) pivotal speech in Act II Scene 2, followed by his brother ALBERT's reasoned response in Scene 4, and finally the loyalist HERBERT's counter-argument in Scene 5.

EGON. It hardly matters whether you know this or not – but do not think for a moment that I am blind! Do not think that any of the reasons that have driven you to war together like an over-enthusiastic herd of sheep have had any bearing on me. Do not think I do not know who the masters of our political destiny are: it is not the people, but the élite cliques of marketeers, stocktraders and industrialists. Corrupt exporters are running the show, and the ambassadors are their gaily caparisoned circus horses. The people do not have a clue about what is happening, what will happen to them and why. They do not realize that the blood of several million people serves as nothing more than the bank-balance for the marketing of railway lines, wool, alcohol and money. They do not realize that, with the bloody and damnable phrases 'Honour, Fatherland, Civilization and Culture', their blood supply is being placed on tap. They do not realize that it is only to boost the dividends of Krupp and Creusot that they are marching to their deaths! They just don't realize – – But that's not true! They *do* realize! They know damn well about their dollar- and consumer-hungry oligarchs. The few who don't realize, who still haven't seen through the fatuous slogans – they can go to hell! But the majority *does* realize. And it is the majority which is off marching in spite of knowing full well that they are giving up their lives to preserve a system that, should they survive, will only serve to exploit them even further. These doomed people, are well aware that their enemy, right from the start, is the almighty industrialist who ordains what they should eat and drink every hour of the day. In spite of all that, they still march off. And why? Out of a pathetic and timid sheep-mentality. And, by intoxicating themselves in waves of atavistic patriotism, delude themselves of their true fate. And that is the despicable and single most depressing thing about this war that robs me of all hope and makes me denounce it: it has destroyed all my faith in mankind's ability to arrive at any kind of self-determination. They can die for their personal freedom with pleasure for all I care. But here they die reluctantly, yet obediently, and in doing so only too well aware that they are merely endorsing their enslavement. They are slaves, and are condemned to stay slaves for ever. But that is not the end of the story! For are these men who wield so much power, these oligarchs who crave for consumers rather than subjects, are they even fit to play ringmaster in this war? Are they fit to be the master butcher of these millions of slaves and their souls? Have they the right to instigate a bloodbath for their own profit? Are their 'profits' worth this? Are they such exemplary specimens of the human race that their purity cannot be sullied by this sea of blood? Are they bathed in their reflected glory to such an extent, so exalted that this sea, its spray and foam cannot bespatter them? Or will this bloody ocean also rise to that brilliant height? Just take a look at them! Look at the books they read, the houses they live in. Just take a look at the clothes they wear! Their amusements, their charades, their music. Take a look at the women they keep. But most of them are just under-sexed family men. Take a look at their faces. They go to church – even they go to church. They even take to the pulpit themselves!

But I know what you are going to say: 'This is all past history. You must not look back. The war is here and here now. Like a typhoon which has unleashed some sort of evil spirit on the world, there is no avoiding it. What ought to be done now is to save what can still be saved. Help your people, to whom you owe your language and everything that is worthwhile, so they will not go under. Save the beauty and blessings your heritage has bestowed on us from being rent asunder. Or at least help deflect this evil on to another people. Once the war is over, avoid it, run away from it, never have to confront it again, roam stateless as you will; but right now, help bear the destruction to another nation.'

But let me tell you this: This nation that was so cowardly that anything worthwhile I had to *wrest* from it; so shameful that it shunned like the plague all the blessings that *I* wanted to bestow on it; a nation that was too cowardly and incompetent to guide its own destiny, and so cowardly that, despite recognizing the lie in its patriotic war-cry, it still marched off to war – let it go to the dogs! The human race is about as inextinguishable as the common flea. What the hell does it matter if a portion of the earth is depopulated and laid to waste? In thirty years, no one will be able to tell the difference. And that is why there is not a single inch of ground which I can share with you. This war has nothing to do with me. I had nothing in common with you before and even less now. I condemn it outright. How much blood will be spilled, what the outcome may be, what it will destroy – I couldn't care less.

ALBERT. I only want to ask you one thing: Why are you a writer? You say you don't want anything to do with your country, with our world. Why do you write then? Surely you write for us. And only for us. You would let your books be published. Just for yourself, by any chance? You want to improve your fellow-man – for you are and remain human – and so deepen his understanding. You probably don't really know yourself what you want to communicate to him. But you want to be read, acknowledged. Whether it is today, or in the future, that's irrelevant here. But you do want to get closer to him, be part of him. But now? Your countrymen are in need. They don't want to read. They want you. Your fist. Your feet. You also want to be famous. Some day or other. Famous. But then – I'm sorry – but it is pretty bad form to expect, to demand, to beg, for fame and fortune when you won't stand by those who will give it to you, in their hour of need. Therefore you've got to choose: either you cut yourself off entirely from the world, stand isolated, cocoon yourself in your own solitary existence – but then you can no longer write and expect anything from us in return – *or* you belong to us and write *and fight*!

EGON [*sullenly*]. I write in order to discover myself.

ALBERT. I see. To discover yourself, eh? Dear boy, the time will come when you will remember what I have said.

EGON. As if you did not already know: here it is a case of to what extent I am to bow before the State. Because it is a question between me and State, not between me and the people, as my clever brother claims. It is a question of to what extent I should bow before the State, that hybrid creation, half the time a nanny and half the time an avaricious monster which knows and acknowledges nothing outside itself. Unless you happen to stuff some greasy gristle, the fattiest, greasiest gristle down its gullet. You know I have chosen to stand outside it. I have withdrawn from it as far as I could, and only conceded as much as my self-respect would allow. But now, where it inconsiderately demands that I defend with my blood the very thing I condemned – and that is not race, nation or order – but the bestial disregard for the individual . . . then I *cannot* act differently. It would betray my very essence. The State is an essential protection and harness for the mediocre majority. But it should draw a line between those who need to be protected and harnessed and those who wish to go their own way and who would not dream of depriving that well-behaved fenced-in herd of sheep of a single jot of their pathetic complacency. That may sound like anarchism, and the State has a right to stamp out this enemy wherever it finds him. But – and this you know all too well: I do not *preach* anarchism. These principles I apply only to myself! I forbid anyone else to adopt them! And that is why the public, the State, should let me apply them. Because I never put them to any use which could undermine the State or its members. I am no preacher. Nothing is more obnoxious than a preacher. I am not out to preach platitudes to the masses. And what I write, I am writing for myself. That's right! Only for me to fathom who I really am. True, the State is not in a position to draw the line between those who need to depend on the State and those who do not. It has no means of judging that, and therefore has the right, and duty to its members, to treat everyone the same. But then I have got exactly the same right and exactly the same duty: the duty to preserve myself from all encroachments, inducements and attempts to undermine my individuality –

HERBERT. So that's your final word?

EGON. It is.

HERBERT (*thoughtfully*). You could be right. But what do we mean by what's 'right' here? Right is who is in control. Sure, thre is no ultimate reason or justice, and the State is hardly the highest manifestation of either. If one were to speak of ultimate reason at all, then the nearest would the ultimate right of the race.

EGON (*laughing*). The race? There aren't any more races left in Europe. At most, the race of capitalists. Were I to take up arms at all, it would be against the embodiment of capitalism – at most, against the British.

HERBERT. Well, what are you waiting for?

EGON (*laughs, shaking his head*).

HERBERT. No my boy. Power prevails over right. And as the State has all the power between heaven and hell, it will crush you to death. So you are sticking to it? Then (*taking his hand*) good luck on your downfall.

TRANSLATED BY TIM CROSS

DER SCHREI

Aus dieser steingewordenen Not,
aus dieser Wut nach Brunst und Brot,

aus dieser lauten Totenstadt,
die sich mir aufgelagert hat

härter als Erz, schwerer als Blei,
steigt meine Sehnsucht wie ein Schrei

quellend empor nach Meeren und Weiten
und ungeheuren Einsamkeiten,

aus all dem Staub und Schmutz und Gewimmel
nach einem grenzenlosen Himmel.

THE CRY

Out of this adamantine need,
out of this rage to eat and breed,

out of this loud city of death
weighing me down, quenching my breath,

iron-hard, lead-heavy, up on high
my longing rises like a cry

climbing towards oceans, distant spaces
climbing towards vast, lonely places,

above dust, dirt and noise to rise
on, up, into the boundless skies.

TRANSLATED BY ANTHEA BELL

*E*RNST *W*ILHELM *L*OTZ 1890–1914

'Everything that one fills with desire, lives!'

Lotz's breezy nature was best summed up by his close friend, the expressionist painter of apocalyptic cityscapes Ludwig Meidner:

> German enthusiast, a Romantic, in love with clouds and wind. Slim and tall, taking great fiery strides through the confusion of the streets. Delighting in street life, singing with hands aloft the praises of the sea that is the city. Forever dancing, swimming, sailing through the blue alleyways. All sadness of the world was shaken off with his hips. With feverish intent showing in his face, craning forward, he breathed the air of the tumultous day into his buoyant lungs, gamely acting on his impulse, and would pull the inspiration, when it came, as impetuously into his arms as he would a girl.

This youthful spirit was born on 6 February 1890 in Culm an der Weichsel. He was at first headed for a military career, and had attained the rank of officer before he switched to sales training in 1911. As with many budding poets of his day, his first fruitful encounter with the literary world was with Richard Dehmel in 1912 in Hamburg. The only collection of Lotz's poetry published in his lifetime was a verse flysheet called *Und schöne Raubtierflecken*, in 1913.

The greatest influence on Lotz was not, however, Richard Dehmel but Ernst Stadler (q.v.). He even penned an adulatory poem – *An Ernst Stadler* – praising the inspiration of the older poet's *Bruderverse*. Stadler's collection of poems entitled *Der Aufbruch* has been (as Michael Hamburger points out in *A Proliferation of Prophets*) 'interpreted too literally as a prophecy and glorification of war'. In particular, the military imagery of the title poem 'has little to do with actual warfare, much more with the poet's own personal and literary situation in 1911 and 1912, when he evolved his own style . . . The war-like imagery of *Der Aufbruch* is one of liberation from outworn conventions.' Likewise Lotz's poetry carries with it powerful descriptive passages illustrative of the generational conflict arising from the resentment by the young of the restrictive practices of the old. Although the *Aufbruch der Jugend* – the uprising of youth which Lotz advocates – is all-consuming, its social and political aims are unclear. They can at best be thought of as symptomatic of the spirit of the times – the overturning of the old to make way for the new, a sentiment expressed by many of the modernist writers of that period in Germany.

Ludwig Meidner and E. W. Lotz. *Schiller Nationalmuseum*

The adventure of a major war was seemingly just the sort of experience that Lotz had been advocating. The war would change things, and, as Meidner described, with 'Reason tucked in his coat pocket like a snuffbox intended for only occasional use', Lotz went to war. On 26 September 1914, he was killed at Bouconville on the Aisne.

TIM CROSS

Texts
Wolkenüberflaggt. Gedichte (Kurt Wolff, Munich, 1917).
Und schöne Raubtierflecken . . . Ein lyrisches Flugblatt (Hellmut Draws-Tychsen (ed.), 1968).
Prosaversuche und Feldpostbriefe, aus dem bisher unveröffentlichten Nachlass (H. Draws-Tychsen (ed.), Huber, Diessen, 1955).

Secondary source
K. L. Berghahn, 'Ernst Wilhelm Lotz: Aufbruch der Jugend', *Literatur ist Utopie* (1978).

Glanzgesang

Von blauem Tuch umspannt und rotem Kragen,
Ich war ein Fähnrich und ein junger Offizier.
Doch jene Tage, die verträumt manchmal in meine
Nächte ragen,
Gehören nicht mehr mir.

Im großen Trott bin ich auf harten Straßen
mitgeschritten,
Vom Staub der Märsche und vom grünen Wind besonnt.
Ich bin durch staunende Dörfer, durch Ströme und alte
Städte geritten,
Und das Leben war wehend blond.

Die Biwakfeuer flammten wie Sterne im Tale
Und hatten den Himmel zu ihrem Spiegel gemacht,
Von schwarzen Bergen drohten des Feindes Alarm-
Fanale,
Und Feuerballen zersprangen prasselnd in Nacht.

So kam ich, braun von Sommer und hart von
Winterkriegen,
In große Kontore, die staubig rochen, herein,
Da mußte ich meinen Rücken zur Sichel biegen
Und Zahlen mit spitzen Fingern in Bücher reihn.

Und irgendwo hingen die grünen Küsten der Fernen,
Ein Duft von Palmen kam schwankend von Hafen
geweht,
Weiß rasteten Karawanen an Wüsten-Zisternen,
Die Häupter gläubig nach Osten gedreht.

Auf Ozeanen zogen die großen Fronten
Der Schiffe, von fliegenden Fischen kühl überschwirrt,
Und breiter Prärien glitzernde Horizonte
Umkreisten Gespanne, für lange Fahrten geschirrt.

Von Kameruns unergründlichen Wäldern umsungen,
Vom mörderischen Brodem des Bodens umloht,
Gehorchten zitternde Wilde, von Geißeln der Weißen
umschwungen,
Und schwarz von Kannibalen der glühenden Wälder
umdroht!

Amerikas große Städte brausten im Grauen,
Die Riesenkräne griffen mit heiserm Geschrei
In die Bäuche der Schiffe, die Frachten zu stauen,
Und Eisenbahnen donnerten landwärts vom Kai.

So hab ich nachbarlich alle Zonen gesehen,
Rings von den Pulten grünten die Inseln der Welt,
Ich fühlte den Erdball rauchend sich unter mir drehen,
Zu rasender Fahrt um die Sonne geschnellt.

Song of Glory

In a coat of blue, red-collared, a handsome sight,
I was a cadet, I was an officer,
But those days, revisiting me in dreams by night,
Are mine no more.

At a brisk trot, I travelled the hard high road,
Weathered by the dust of the march and the green air.
Through awestruck villages, over rivers, past towns we
rode,
And life rippled free and fair.

Campfires burned, shining like stars in the valley
Making themselves a mirror of the sky,
From dark hills echoed the enemy's reveille,
Fireballs exploded, sending sparks flying high.

So brown with summer, hard with winter campaigning,
I went
Into counting-houses, dusty of smell and of look.
Over the ledgers now my back was bent
As I entered figures carefully in a book.

Yet somewhere lay the green shores of distant lands
The scent of palms came wafting up from the bay,
Caravans rested, white, beside wells in desert sands
Pious heads turned East to pray.

The prows of mighty ships still sailed the sea,
Surrounded by flying fish, cool, skimming the surf,
And over the glittering prairies, fast and free
Ran teams of horses thundering on the turf.

With Cameroon's vast forests around them singing,
In the murderous, heavy stench of the soil,
Trembling natives bent to the white man's lash, fearing
Cannibals from the sultry jungle amid their toil.

Under grey-hung skies, America's cities roared
As giant cranes, hoarsely creaking, reached with ease
Into the bowels of ships, lowering freight to be stored,
While railway trains thundered landward from the quays.

And so I saw the whole world at second hand,
About my desk the earth's green islands spun,
I felt the smoking globe turn under me, sea and land,
Racing on in its journey around the sun.

Da warf ich dem Chef an den Kopf seine Kladden!
Und stürmte mit wütendem Lachen zur Türe hinaus.
Und saß durch Tage und Nächte mit satten und glatten
Bekannten bei kosmischem Schwatzen im Kaffeehaus.

Und einmal sank ich rückwärts in die Kissen,
Von einem angstvoll ungeheuren Druck zermalmt.
Da sah ich: Daß in vagen Finsternissen
Noch sternestumme Zukunft vor mir qualmt.

I rose and threw my boss's books at his head!
I stormed out of the door with angry laughter.
I sat in the café, to chat of the cosmos with friends
instead,
With sleek, smooth friends, for days and nights thereafter.

And once, of a sudden, I sank back in my chair
Crushed by a monstrous pressure, boding ill,
For I saw through the vague shapes in the dark air
The future looming before me star-silent still.

TRANSLATED BY ANTHEA BELL

Pen sketch of Lotz by Ludwig Meidner.

*E*RNST *S*TADLER 1883–1914

'The only guarantee against the war lasting all that long is the economic upheaval, under which surely all nations must suffer equally, and the horrendous losses to both sides.'

1914

Ernst Stadler was European. Shortly after his death, Hermann Hesse wrote in the *Neue Zürcher Zeitung*, 'He is an early, isolated example of the budding European spirit, one who tied the bond of friendship between the Germanic–Gothic and the romantic–classical spirit.' Born in the bilingual region of the Alsace, Stadler was equally at home in Germany, in France, whose philosophers Jammes and Péguy (q.v.) he translated, or in England, where he had studied as a Rhodes scholar in Oxford. Therefore the war provided Stadler with a fearsome dilemma, illustrated by the occasion of a literary meeting at the beginning of August 1914. A messenger burst in to announce the news that Germany had declared war on France. The Alsatian poets stood up and launched into the national anthem. But the words were not German. They sang 'La Marseillaise'.

Ernst Stadler photographed by Thea Sternheim, July 1914.
Schiller Nationalmuseum, Marbach

The poet Ernst Stadler was born in Colmar, in the Alsace, on 11 August 1883. Like most of his fellow students at Strasburg University, he was influenced by Nietzsche. The German philosopher's principle that suffering was the source of all achievement was regarded as an endorsement of life by Stadler and his colleagues: 'That is why Zarathustra is the advocate of suffering, because he is the advocate of life.' With his colleague René Schickele, he founded a periodical *Der Stürmer* in which most of his early poems were published; when the paper failed in 1902, Stadler underwent his obligatory military service.

It was clear that he was set for an academic career, and by 1906, he had won a Rhodes scholarship to Oxford. He emerged from Magdalen College – to which he referred as that 'dear old place' – two years later, to all external appearances an Englishman. In England, his fascination for Shakespeare had grown immeasurably, and the great playwright was made the subject of his most substantial academic work, *The History of Literary Criticism of Shakespeare in Germany*. However, from 1910, Stadler's academic seat was the Université Libre in Brussels and was to remain so until 1914. Stadler continued publishing in Alsatian periodicals such as *Das Neue Elsaß* and the *Cahier Alsaciens*, as well as the avant-garde *Die Aktion*, based in Berlin.

As a literary figure, Stadler commands the status of Georg Heym and Georg Trakl (q.v.) but, with his exhortation *'Mensch, werde wesentlich!'* ('Acquire essence, man!'), differed substantially in outlook to the introspective expressionism of these prophets of the apocalypse. Stadler's sensitivity is rooted in the real, everyday experience, not in the brooding of the soul. Like Walt Whitman, his verse contains a humble dedication to the external and a profound sympathy with the suffering and underprivileged among his fellow men – as can be seen in his 'Kinder vor einem Londoner Armenspeisehaus'. As Michael Hamburger details in his essay '1912' in *A Proliferation of Prophets*, the poem 'Fahrt über die Kölner Rheinbrücke bei Nacht' likewise 'renders an actual experience – the crossing of a railway bridge at night – but gives such a vast extension of meaning to the experience that one cannot even be sure that the descriptive details – housefronts, lights, and chimneys, for instance – are that and no more. As in Surrealist poetry and that of Dylan Thomas, one image generates another; but all the disparate images are swept in one direction by the dynamism of feeling. Stadler's poem re-creates an

'Scepticism can only lead to the end of all creative power, to decadence. The truly creative man, on the other hand, is he who can create the world anew, who imposes his new and different idea of the world on to the created world as it is; the man with a teleological direction, not the one who merely counts up [existing phenomena] on his fingers.'

immediate experience; far from being "emotion recollected in tranquility", it approximates as closely as poetry can to the bewildering moment of sensation. This would be easy enough if the writing of a poem could be synchronized with the experience that occasioned it; but, at its most immediate, poetry is emotion generated in retrospect. Stadler's apparent spontaneity, therefore, was the result of deliberate and skilful application.

'In the first few lines of the poem, realistic imagery preponderates; one attributes their dynamism to the actual speed of the express train. Yet they prepare the reader for the larger symbolism that emerges more clearly later; for the journey is one into the "entrails of night"; and there is an allusion to a descent into the subconscious, symbolized by the mine gallery. It is only the connection between the river of the poem, the Rhine at Cologne, and the sea that establishes a primarily symbolic significance. When the poet writes of "Salut von Schiffen über blauer See", we are suddenly aware that these ships are not part of the actual setting of the poem; his imagination has travelled with the river to the sea. And it is the extraneous image of the sea that dominates the whole poem; for the whole poem is a glorification of the flux of life itself; and the sea is the destination of that flux.

'Symbolically, Stadler's poem affirms only life itself – and death. The poem ends with the word "Untergang", submergence or extinction; it does so because the utmost intensity of feeling burns itself out. Just as the river's motion comes to rest in the sea, Stadler's ecstatic awareness of being alive culminates in the extinction of consciousness. The last line makes the connection, frequent in Stadler's love poems also, between the total fulfilment of individuality and its total dissolution.

'Stadler goes far in the breaking up of regular syntax, for his vitalism was impatient of conventional restrictions. For the same reason, he was much more apt to coin new combinations of words. Examples in this poem are "nachtumschient" ("railed round with night") and "nachtentrissene Luft" ("air snatched away from night"). Because of their extreme dynamism, his poems have a rhetorical effect; but it is private rhetoric, as it were, not aimed at the reader in the manner of many of the later Expressionists. Only his excellent craftsmanship saved Stadler from other dangers. Few poets would have got away with the long succession of asyntactic words – most of them abstract and general – in the last two lines; one would expect them to read like a parody of the new style, quite apart from the inclusion of prayer in the list, between the ecstasy of procreation and self-extinction in the sea. Stadler brings off these verbal and mental leaps, just as he manages to keep his long line from spilling over into prose, and makes his rhymes all the more effective for being delayed.'

Stadler's most famous and most frequently anthologized poem is 'Der Aufbruch', a jubilant greeting extended to a new age expressed in the martial imagery of a rain of bullets, bugle calls, fanfares and harnessed horses. Although written before 1913, the poem came to symbolize, albeit falsely, the enthusiasm which greeted the war in August 1914. Nothing could have been further from Stadler's mind. He viewed the idiocies which war brought in its wake with a distancing irony, as he commented on in a letter of 4 August: 'During the night a German hunting patrol accidentally shot two German border guards from Schlettstadt. *C'est la guerre*. Already a few human lives are beginning to become worthless.'

The award of the Iron Cross in October 1914 to Lieutenant Stadler came as a surprise to the humanist poet. He admitted in his last letter, dated 9 October and addressed to Thea, the wife of Carl Sternheim, that, 'One is, after all, too full of nerves and feelings to possess those soldierly virtues which are popularly supposed to exist as a matter of course, and which perhaps do exist from time to time. Or do I see things differently because I find this sort of bravado somewhat wanting, and because I would imagine and wish for myself another object in life other than to have a grenade blow me into little bits? . . .'

It was a British grenade exploding at Zandvoorde a few weeks later, on 30 October, during the first Battle of Ypres, which ended Ernst Stadler's life.

TIM CROSS/MICHAEL HAMBURGER

Text
Klaus Hurlebusch & Karl Ludwig Schneider (eds), *Dichtungen, Schriften, Briefe* (Beck, Munich, 1983). Critical edition of Stadler's complete works collected for the first time. Contains poems, essays, translations, war diary and comprehensive bibliography.

Secondary source
Michael Hamburger, *A Proliferation of Prophets*, in series 'Modern German Literature' (Carcanet, Manchester, 1983). Passage from '1912' reproduced with kind permission of the author.

FAHRT ÜBER DIE KÖLNER RHEINBRÜCKE BEI NACHT

Der Schnellzug tastet sich und stößt die Dunkelheit entlang.
Kein Stern will vor. Die ganze Welt ist nur ein enger, nachtumschienter Minengang,
Darein zuweilen Förderstellen blauen Lichtes jähe Horizonte reißen: Feuerkreis
Von Kugellampen, Dächern, Schloten, dampfend, strömend . . . nur sekundenweis . . .
Und wieder alles schwarz. Als führen wir ins Eingeweid der Nacht zur Schicht.
Nun taumeln Lichter her . . . verirrt, trostlos vereinsamt . . . mehr . . . und sammeln sich . . . und werden dicht.
Gerippe grauer Häuserfronten liegen bloß, im Zwielicht bleichend, tot – etwas muß kommen . . . oh, ich fühl es schwer
Im Hirn. Eine Beklemmung singt im Blut. Dann dröhnt der Boden plötzlich wie ein Meer:
Wir fliegen, aufgehoben, königlich durch nachtentrissne Luft, hoch übern Strom. O Biegung der Millionen Lichter, stumme Wacht,
Vor deren blitzender Parade schwer die Wasser abwärts rollen. Endloses Spalier, zum Gruß gestellt bei Nacht!
Wie Fackeln stürmend! Freudiges! Salut von Schiffen über blauer See! Bestirntes Fest!
Wimmelnd, mit hellen Augen hingedrängt! Bis wo die Stadt mit letzten Häusern ihren Gast entläßt.
Und dann die langen Einsamkeiten. Nackte Ufer. Stille. Nacht. Besinnung, Einkehr. Kommunion. Und Glut und Drang
Zum Letzten, Segnenden. Zum Zeugungsfest. Zur Wollust. Zum Gebet! Zum Meer. Zum Untergang.

1913

ON CROSSING THE RHINE BRIDGE AT COLOGNE BY NIGHT

The express train gropes and thrusts its way through darkness. Not a star is out.
The whole world's nothing but a mine-road the night has railed about
In which at times conveyors of blue light tear sudden horizons: fiery sphere
Of arc-lamps, roofs and chimneys, steaming, streaming – for seconds only clear,
And all is black again. As though we drove into Night's entrails to the seam.
Now lights reel into view . . . astray, disconsolate and lonely . . . more . . . and gather . . . and densely gleam.
Skeletons of grey housefronts are laid bare, grow pale in the twilight, dead – something must happen . . . O heavily
I feel it weigh on my brain. An oppression sings in the blood. Then all at once the ground resounds like the sea:
All royally upborne we fly through air from darkness wrested, high up above the river. O curve of the million lights, mute guard at the sight
Of whose flashing parade the waters go roaring down. Endless line presenting arms by night!
Surging on like torches! Joyful! Salute of ships over the blue sea! Star-jewelled, festive array!
Teeming, bright-eyed urged on! Till where the town with its last houses sees its guests away.
And then the long solitudes. Bare banks. And silence. Night. Reflection. Self-questioning. Communion. And ardour outward-flowing
To the end that blesses. To conception's rite. To pleasure's consummation. To prayer. To the sea. To self's undoing.

TRANSLATED BY MICHAEL HAMBURGER

Ex Aetheribus

Den Duft der Gletscher möcht' ich in meine Verse
 zwingen,
Hinuntergießen in eure Täler in einem einzigen wilden
 Feuerrausch,
Die Nacht der Felsen und den Glast der Firnen,
Die Kraft der Schneelawinen, die zu Tale donnern
Und den schweren Traum tiefgrüner Alpseen . . .

O Berge, Berge der Einsamkeit!
Da ich im Tale wandelte, wie war ich schwach,
Unfrei und unfroh. Nun jauchzt meine junge Seele
Zum goldnen Morgenduft, da purpurn alle Spitzen
Die weiße Stirn mit Flammenlaub umwinden:
Nun kam die Sonne erst und kam der Tag.

O Berge, meine Berge! – Wenn das große Schweigen
 des Mittags
Seine goldbraunen Fäden über die Arvenkronen
 spinnt
Und die grünen Matten und die schimmernden
 Schneehalden –

O Berge, meine Berge! – Wenn der Tag
 verdämmert
Und das Licht der Firnen lischt,
Und die Schroffen in trüben, rostigem Rot funkeln –

O Berge, meine Berge! – Wenn mein Auge wieder
In eure Abgrundtiefen schauernd trinkt,
Ihr meine besten Freunde, meine wahrste Welt –

Goldenem Flammentau gleich brause euer Atem durch
 meine Gesänge,
Ewiger Kraft und Schönheit leuchtend Mal,
Ewiger Jugend!

1903

Ex Aetheribus

The scent of glaciers would I like to force into my
 verses,
Pouring down into your valleys in a single wild fiery
 frenzy,
The night of the rocks and the glaze of the snows,
The force of the avalanches, which thunder into the valley
And the heavy dream of deep green alpine lakes . . .

O mountains, mountains of solitude!
How weak was I when I wandered in the valley,
Unfree and unjoyed. Now my young soul exults
In the golden morning air, as all the purple summits
Encircle my white brow with flaming greenery:
Now only has the sun come, and now the day.

O mountains, my mountains! – When the great midday
 silence
Spins golden-brown threads over the tips of the stony
 pine
And the green meadows and the shimmering
 snowslopes –

O mountains, my mountains! – When then the day
 glimmers
And the light on the high snow fades,
And the precipices sparkle in dull, rusty red –

O mountains, my mountains! – When my eyes
Shudder and drink in again your deep ravines,
You, my best friends, my truest world –

May your breath like a golden dewy flame fill out my
 songs,
Eternal strength and beauty's shining goal,
Eternal youth!

TRANSLATED BY JEREMY ADLER

Der Aufbruch

Einmal schon haben Fanfaren mein ungeduldiges Herz blutig gerissen,
Daß es, aufsteigend wie ein Pferd, sich wütend ins Gezäum verbissen.
Damals schlug Tambourmarsch den Sturm auf allen Wegen,
Und herrlichste Musik der Erde hieß uns Kugelregen.
Dann, plötzlich, stand Leben stille. Wege führten zwischen alten Bäumen.
Gemächer lockten. Es war süß, zu weilen und sich versäumen,
Von Wirklichkeit den Leib so wie von staubiger Rüstung zu entketten,
Wollüstig sich in Daunen weicher Traumstunden einzubetten.
Aber eines Morgens rollte durch Nebelluft das Echo von Signalen,
Hart, scharf, wie Schwerthieb pfeifend. Es war wie wenn im Dunkel plötzlich Lichter aufstrahlen.
Es war wie wenn durch Biwakfrühe Trompetenstöße klirren,
Die Schlafenden aufspringen und die Zelte abschlagen und die Pferde schirren.
Ich war in Reihen eingeschient, die in den Morgen stießen, Feuer über Helm und Bügel,
Vorwärts, in Blick und Blut die Schlacht, mit vorgehaltnem Zügel.
Vielleicht würden uns am Abend Siegesmärsche umstreichen,
Vielleicht lägen wir irgendwo ausgestreckt unter Leichen.
Aber vor dem Erraffen und vor dem Versinken
Würden unsre Augen sich an Welt und Sonne satt und glühend trinken.

1913

Setting Out

There was a time before, when fanfares bloodily tore apart my own impatient brain,
So that, up-rearing like a horse, it bit savagely at the rein.
Then tambourines sounded the alarm on every path
And a hail of bullets seemed the loveliest music on earth.
Then, suddenly, life stood still. Different paths were leading between the old trees.
Rooms were tempting. It was sweet to linger and sweet to rest at ease,
And, unchaining my body from reality, like some old dusty armour,
To nestle voluptuously in the down of the soft dream-hour.
But then one morning through the misty air there rolled the echo of the bugle's ring.
Hard, sharp, whistling like a sword-thrust. As if suddenly on darkness lights had started shining.
As if, through the tented dawn, trumpet-jolts had roused the sleeping forces,
The waking soldiers leapt up and struck their tents and busily harnessed their horses.
I was locked into lines like splints that thrust into morning, with fire on helmet and stirrup,
Forward, with battle in my blood and in my eyes, and reins held up.
Perhaps in the evening, victory marches would play around my head.
Perhaps we all would lie somewhere, stretched out among the dead.
But before the reaching out and before the sinking,
Our eyes would see their fill of world and sun, and take it in, glowing and drinking.

Translated by Jeremy Adler

DÄMMERUNG

Schwer auf die Gassen der Stadt fiel die
Abenddämmerung.
Auf das Grau der Ziegeldächer und der schlanken
Türme,
Auf Staub und Schmutz, Lust und Leid und Lüge der
Großstadt
In majestätischer Unerbittlichkeit.

Aus Riesenquadern gebrochen dunkelten die
Wolkenblöcke
Brütend, starr . . . Und in den Lüften lag's
Wie wahnwitziger Trotz, wie totenjähes Aufbäumen –
Fern im West verröchelte der Tag.

Durch die herbstbraunen Kastanienbäume prasselte der
Nachtsturm,
Wie wenn Welten sich zum Wachen wecken
Und zur letzten, blutigen Entscheidungsschlacht.

Trotz im Herzen und wilde Träume von Kampf und Not
und brausendem Sieg,
Lehnt' ich am Eisengitter meines Balkons und sah
Die tausend Feuer blecken und die roten Bärte flackern,
Sah den wunden Riesen einmal noch das
Flammenbanner raffen.

Einmal noch das alte, wilde Heldenlied aufhämmern
In wirbelnden Akkorden –
Und zusammenstürzen
Und vergrollen
Dumpf –
Fern . . .

Auf der Strasse Droschkenrasseln. Musik. Singende
Reservisten.
Jäh fahr ich auf –
Über Türmen und Dächern braust die Nacht.

1902

TWILIGHT

Heavily on to the streets of the town fell the evening
twilight.
On to the grey of the tiled toofs and the slender
towers,
On to the dust and dirt, the joy and pain and lie of the
city,
In inexorable majesty.

Broken out of giant slabs, the cloud-blocks
darkened,
Brooding, rigid . . . And in the air there seemed to hang
Some mad defiance, like dead, abrupt rebellion –
Far in the west, the day ended, gasping.

The night-storm pattered through the autumn-brown
chestnut trees,
As when worlds awake to rise
To the last, bloody, decisive battle.

With defiance in my heart and wild dreams of war and
want and heady victory,
I leaned on the iron railings of my balcony and saw
The thousand fires grimace and the red beards flicker,
Saw the wounded giant once again gather up the flaming
banner.

And once again he hammered out the old heroic song
In whirling chords –
And collapsed
And rumbled
Muffled –
Far . . .

Carriages clatter on the street. Music. Singing.
Conscripts.
Suddenly I started –
Over towers and roofs, the night rages.

TRANSLATED BY JEREMY ADLER

Kinder vor einem Londoner Armenspeisehaus

Ich sah Kinder in langem Zug, paarweis geordnet, vor einem Armenspeisehaus stehen.
Sie warteten, wortkarg und müde, bis die Reihe an sie käme, zur Abendmahlzeit zu gehen.
Sie waren verdreckt und zerlumpt und drückten sich an die Häuserwände.
Kleine Mädchen preßten um blasse Säuglinge die versagenden Hände.

Sie standen hungrig und verschüchtert zwischen den aufgehenden Lichtern,
Manche trugen dunkle Mäler auf den schmächtigen Gesichtern.
Ihr Anzug roch nach Keller, lichtscheuen Stuben, Schelten und Darben,
Ihre Körper trugen von Entbehrung und früher Arbeitsfrohn die Narben.

Sie warteten: gleich wären die andern fertig, dann würde man sie in den großen Saal treten lassen,
Ihnen Brot und Gemüse vorsetzen und die Abendsuppe in den blechernen Tassen.
Oh, und dann würde Müdigkeit kommen und ihre verkrümmten Glieder aufschnüren,
Und Nacht und guter Schlaf sie zu Schaukelpferden und Zinnsoldaten und in wundersame Puppenstuben führen.

1914

Children in Front of a London Eating-House for the Poor

I saw children in a long line, ordered in pairs, standing in front of an eating-house for the poor,
They were waiting, silent and tired, until it was their turn for supper, and they could go through the door.
They were filthy and ragged and they pressed against the walls of the building.
Little girls held their thin pale babies close, in hands that were weak and fading.

They stood hungry and frightened under the lights that went on around the place.
Some had dark spots and moles that grew on a gentle face.
Their clothes smelled of scolding and starving, of light-shy rooms and of the cellar.
Their bodies were scarred by compulsory early work, and by suffering's deep pallor.

They waited: soon the others would be finished, and then they too would be allowed to go into the great hall,
Where bread and vegetables and the evening soup in tin mugs would be set in front of them all.
Oh, and then a big tiredness would come along and loosen their limbs' contorted gloom,
And the night and a good long sleep would lead them to rocking-horses, and tin soldiers, and a dolls' house with an amazing room.

TRANSLATED BY JEREMY ADLER

Die Rosen im Garten

Die Rosen im Garten blühn zum zweiten Mal. Täglich schießen sie in dicken Bündeln
In die Sonne. Aber die schwelgerische Zartheit ist dahin,
Mit der ihr erstes Blühen sich im Hof des weiß und roten Sternenfeuers wiegte.
Sie springen gieriger, wie aus aufgerissenen Adern strömend,
Über das heftig aufgeschwellte Fleisch der Blätter.
Ihr wildes Blühen ist wie Todesröcheln,
Das der vergehende Sommer in das ungewisse Licht des Herbstes trägt.

1914

The Roses in the Garden

The roses in the garden are blossoming again. Daily, they shoot up in thick bundles.
Into the sun. But that luxuriant tenderness is gone,
With which their earlier blossom trembled in the yard of white and red starry fire.
They leap more lustily, as if pouring from lacerated veins
Over the heftily swollen flesh of leaves.
Their wild blossoming is like the gasp of death
That the passing summer carries on into the uncertain light of the fall.

TRANSLATED BY JEREMY ADLER

Kleine Stadt

Die vielen kleinen Gassen, die die langgestreckte
Hauptstraße überqueren
Laufen alle ins Grüne.
Überall fängt Land an.
Überall strömt Himmel ein und Geruch von Bäumen
und der starke Duft der Äcker.
Überall erlischt die Stadt
in einer feuchten Herrlichkeit von Wiesen,

Und durch den grauen Ausschnitt
niederer Dächer schwankt
Gebirge, über das die Reben klettern,
die mit hellen Stützen in die Sonne leuchten.
Darüber aber schließt sich Kiefernwald: der stößt
Wie eine breite dunkle Mauer an die rote Fröhlichkeit
der Sandsteinkirche.

Am Abend, wenn die Fabriken schließen,
ist die große Straße mit Menschen gefüllt.
Sie gehen langsam
oder bleiben mitten auf der Gasse stehn.
Sie sind geschwärzt von Arbeit und Maschinenruß.
Aber ihre Augen tragen
Noch Scholle, zähe Kraft des Bodens
und das feierliche Licht der Felder.

1914

Small Town

The many narrow alleys that cut across
the long through mainstreet
All run into the country.
Everywhere the green begins.
Everywhere the sky pours in and fragrance of trees
and the strong scent of ploughland.
Everywhere the town stops
in a moist magnificence of pastures,

And through the grey slit between
low roofs hills lean
With vines that climb over them and shine
with bright supporting poles in the sunlight.
Still higher the pinewood closes in: like a thick dark
Wall to border on the red rejoicing
of the sandstone church.

At nightfall when the factories close,
the mainstreet is filled with people.
They walk slowly
or in the middle of an alley they stop and stand.
They are blackened with work and engine soot.
But their eyes uphold
Earth still, the tough power of the soil
and the festive light of the fields.

Translated by Michael Hamburger

Gegen Morgen

Tag will herauf. Nacht wehrt nicht mehr dem Licht.
O Morgenwinde, die den Geist in ungestüme Meere
treiben!
Schon brechen Vorstadtbahnen fauchend in den Garten
Der Frühe. Bald sind Straßen, Brücken wieder von
Gewühl und Lärm versperrt –
O jetzt ins Stille flüchten! Eng im Zug der Weiber, der
sich übern Treppengang zur Messe zerrt,
In Kirchenwinkel knien! O, alles von sich tun, und nur in
Demut auf das Wunder der Verheißung warten!
O Nacht der Kathedralen! Inbrunst eingelernter
Kinderworte!
Gestammel unverstandner Litanein, indes die Seelen in
die Sanftmut alter Heiligenbilder schauen . . .
O Engelsgruß der Gnade . . . ungekannt im Chor der
Gläubigen stehn und harren, dass die Pforte
Aufspringe, und ein Schein uns kröne wie vom Haar von
unsrer lieben Frauen.

1913

Towards Morning

Day wants to rise. Night no more opposes light.
O morning breezes, that drive the spirit on into
impetuous seas!
The suburban trains are hissing, breaking into the garden
Of dawn. Soon the streets, bridges will be blocked by
crowds and noise –
O, to flee now into the stillness! Packed in the throng of
women pressing over the stairway to Mass,
To kneel in a church corner! Oh, to leave everything, and
humbly await the wonder of annunciation!
O cathedral night! Fervour of remembered childhood
words!
Stammering of uncomprehended litanies, while meek
souls watch the ancient images of saints . . .
O angelic grace and greeting . . . to stand and wait
unknown amid the choir of believers, that the gate
Might burst open, and a light crown us, as if from the
hair of our beloved women.

Translated by Jeremy Adler

*F*RANZ *J*ANOWITZ 1892–1917

*'Oh son of war, illuminate my night!
Choose love, and so renounce your might.'*

'It is the earthly mission of poetry to grasp and make visible not just the idea, but the enemy of the idea, too. Philosophy forgoes this. It seeks the truth. But poetry finds truth, and confronts it with the lie.'

Franz Janowitz. *Brennerarchiv, Innsbruck*

Franz Janowitz conflicts with the received idea of the best German war poets. Neither realistic, nor ironic nor properly expressionistic, while he excoriated the battlefield that the whole world had become, he still preserved a faith in nobility, innocence and song. Forced into maturity by the war, his poetic voice never lost a certain childlike note – indeed, in some of his best poems, naïvity and wisdom co-exist to an almost paradoxical degree. Such poetry was fired by a vision of a transcendental realm that lay beyond conflict, but never sought to exclude death. His 25 years, the last four of which were spent in the army, scarcely left him time to develop a wholly independent voice, but his work displays an increasing mastery of form and deepening of vision. His small *oeuvre* consists of *Novellen*, essays, aphorisms and a handful of the best German poems connected with the Great War.

Janowitz's style was derived from the late neo-Romanticism already exploited by Hofmannsthal and the young Rilke, and this, perhaps, has meant that he has remained comparatively unknown. His lyricism does not suit militant pacifists, who prefer tougher depictions of the fighting; and his images of war do not suit the lyricists. Moreover, he shares the fate of so many writers born in what is now Czechoslovakia: they no longer have a living, German-speaking hinterland to promote their work.

On 28 July 1892, Janowitz was born, the youngest of four children, into a Jewish home in the small Bohemian town of Poděbrady on the Elbe, and spent his early childhood there. It was an artistic family. One brother, Otto, became a musician, and another, Hans, also became a poet and the author of several screenplays, including (with Carl Mayer) *The Cabinet of Dr Caligari*. Janowitz senior was a musician, but illness had forced him to give up a promising career; instead he became a farmer, and eventually took over the family business. Franz attended the *Gymnasium* in Prague, and then studied chemistry, and later, philosophy in Leipzig and Vienna. In 1913, at the age of 21, he joined the Second Tiroler Landschützen-Regiment as an *Einjährig Freiwilliger*. In the war, on 24 October 1917, Lieutenant Janowitz was hit by machine-gun fire during an assault on Monte Rombon, and died of his wounds on 4 November 1917.

The young poet's talent was first recognized by Max Brod, who in 1913 published fourteen poems in his *Arcadia* yearbook, alongside the first printing of Kafka's *Das Urteil* (*The Judgement*). A second crucial contact was the satirist and poet Karl Kraus. Franz's brother Otto was Kraus's musical accompanist, and it was apparently through Kraus's championship that Kurt Wolff agreed to publish Franz's one collection of poems *Auf der Erde* (*On the Earth*) in 1919 (it has never been reprinted). Franz prepared the volume for the press, but did not survive to see it appear. It consists of 51 poems, several of which relate explicitly to the war, and begins with a bitter elegiac sonnet by Karl Kraus.

Nature provides one of the constant themes in

Janowitz's work, and in nature trees as one of his commonest subjects. Before the war, he describes quasi-magical experiences: 'I am transformed . . .am tree or flower, meadow and field . . .' The Eastern Front brought a harsh awakening, as shown by a poem such as 'The Galician Trees' (summer 1915). War proves to be a crime not just against man, but against nature, and the images recall Goya's *Horrors of War*:

'Trees in the clouds:
See the bodies rent asunder,
see our fragmented limbs,
see the branches now stripped bare,
see the roots all torn off!'

Man, who should act as God's representative on earth, has abrogated his responsibility towards creation, and thus incurs a triple guilt: towards himself, towards other beings and towards the Almighty. This metaphysical dimension underpins Janowitz's view of the external world.

As with the mature Rilke, the outer world must be related and elevated to a corresponding inner realm, described in the masterly 'Was innen gehet . . .' ('What goes within . . .'), written in the summer of 1915. Here, the vision of a fallen world gains added urgency through a sense of immanent horror. The war itself remains unstated, but yet informs the experience.

By early 1916, Janowitz had attained greater stylistic precision, and as his powers grew, so did his ability to integrate shock and anger into his work. In poems like 'Sei, Erde, wahr!' ('Be, Earth, true!') written in the summer of 1916, the imagery becomes vivid and apocalyptic. The ideal stretches almost to breaking point: the unspoken experience seems to lie accusingly between the poignantly succinct stanzas, bodying forth an inexplicable world.

JEREMY ADLER

Texts
Auf der Erde: Gedichte (Kurt Wolff Verlag, Munich, 1919).
'Der tägliche Tag' in *Der Brenner* (VI/6, 1920, pp. 424–36).
'Der steinerne Tag' in *Der Brenner* (VII/1, 1922, pp. 41–2).
'Verwandlungen des Winters' in *Der Brenner* (VIII, 1923, pp. 107–9).
'Der Glaube und die Kunst: Aphorismen' in *Der Brenner* (XI, 1927, pp. 88–100).
'Der jüngste Tag' in *Der Brenner* (XII, 1928, pp. 117–19).

Secondary sources
Christina Czuma, 'Franz Janowitz' in Walter Methlagl et al (eds), *Untersuchungen zum Brenner: Festschrift für Ignaz Zangerle zum 75. Geburtstag* (Otto Müller, Salzburg, 1981).
Jürgen Serke, *Böhmische Dörfer. Wanderungen durch eine verlassene literarische Landschaft* (Paul Zsolnay, Vienna & Hamburg, 1987).

WAS INNEN GEHET . . .

Was innen gehet und gehalten wird
von enger Brust in tiefster Stunde Stille:
Es sprengt die Türe deines Zimmers und
du blickst hinüber zu den Menschentischen.

Was deine Kehle würgt, erlöst sie auch:
Es springt hervor, gewandelt und doch treu,
nun ist's im Raume und im See der Luft,
und landet schon in den bereiten Häfen.

Ein Bild nur ist dein Bruder. Aber wie
der Vogel auf die Luft vertraut im Absprung,
wirft sich das Wort ihm zu mit wilden Flügeln.

Doch alles Sprechen hat und alles Singen
des Wahnsinns Miene. – Nahe kommt
dem Wort, um das die Welt sich dreht, nur Schweigen.

WHAT GOES WITHIN . . .

What goes within and there can be contained
by a narrow breast in deepest hour still:
Now bursts the doorway of your room, and so
you glance across to the human tables.

What chokes your throat, will also bring release:
It will leap out, transformed, but faithful yet,
now in your room, now in the sea of air,
and now it lands, in well-prepared harbours.

Your brother but an image is. Yet as
the bird trusts in the air when taking off,
the word flies at him with its angry wings.

But every speaking has, and every song,
the face of madness. Only silence
approaches the word on which the whole world turns.

TRANSLATED BY JEREMY ADLER

SEI, ERDE, WAHR!

So sei noch dieser Trost als Wahn gebüsst,
der aus dem All mit seinen Lichtern grüsst!

Denn scheinst auch du nicht lieblich, finstrer Stern,
den Wesen dort als angestrebte Fern'?

Blickst milde nicht durchs Laub der Liebesnacht?
Verhehlst im Leuchten, was dich schrecklich macht?

Schwört nicht bei uns, o weltenweit Entrückte,
nicht diesem Stern, wenn er euch tief entzückte!

Du Stern des Kriegs, verdunkle deine Glut,
tauch' auf in Sphären als ein Ball von Blut!

So rauchend, wie du rauchst, erscheine dort!
Häng' deinen Namen aus, und heisse Mord!

Ein wütend Auge schiele du ins Nichts,
erschreck' im All ein jedes Kind des Lichts!

Ein wandelnd Zeichen künde Müttern Not!
Zu Häupten dich, mal sich die Welt den Tod!

Heiss' Unheil der Geburt, Unruh der Brust!
Sei Lampe alles Mords, und ihm nur Lust!

Gespiegelt in der Pfütze, beb' vor dir,
auf Trank verzichtend, ahnungsvoll das Tier!

Doch ahnt ein Wesen hier bewohnte Tage,
sei's möglich nur, dass es uns tief beklage!

Sei, Erde, wahr im Bild, wie wir's nicht sind!
So sei, – wie wären wir's! – des Alls ein Kind!

Einst glüht ein Strich. Sie starren, was dort brennt.
Ein Blitz der Freude zuckt durchs Firmament.

Die Flur des Himmels strahlt von Schrecken frei.
Sie stehn und schauen, staunend, was es sei.

BE, EARTH, TRUE!

So let this comfort as madness be contrite
that greets the universe with distant light.

For do you not shine gentle, gloomy star,
the inspiring goal of human life so far?

Don't you look kindly through night's loving twigs?
Cover in shining, what makes fear grow big?

Swear not by us, who are removed from earth,
not to this star, when it enjoyed your worth!

You star of war, now cover up your flood,
rise up in spheres as a ball of blood!

As smoking, as you smoke, appear in shame!
Hang out your sign, let murder be your name!

A raging eye, you gaze on nothingness,
to every child of light you bring distress.

A wandering sign announcing mothers' woe,
you at the head, the world must die below.

Prove fatal at each birth, breasts rent by fire!
Be lamp at every kill, and sole desire!

Then, mirrored in a puddle, see him pall,
renouncing drink, the knowing animal!

But if some Being should sense earth's living days,
if he be real, let him lament our ways!

Be, earth, true to the form that we disgrace,
and be – for how could we! – a child of space!

One day, a light will streak. But what is meant?
A joying flash will cross the firmament.

The fields of heaven shine, from terror free.
Man stands and stares, amazed at what can be.

TRANSLATED BY JEREMY ADLER

*G*EORG *T*RAKL 1887–1914

'Too little love, too little justice and compassion, and evermore too little love; far too much harshness, haughtiness and all manner of criminality – that is what I am.'
Letter to his patron, Ludwig von Ficker, 1913

'A few days ago I was quite ill, I think from untold sorrow. Today I am glad because we are almost certain to march north and in a few days may already be passing through into Russia.'
October 1914

Georg Trakl was born at Salzburg on 3 February 1887. His mother, *née* Halik, was the second wife of Tobias Trakl, a prosperous ironmonger who belonged to a Protestant family long established in this Roman Catholic city. Both the Trakl and Halik families were of Slav descent; the Trakls had originally come from Hungary, the Haliks – much more recently – from Bohemia. The family house at Salzburg, with its old furniture, paintings and statuary, as well as the family garden in a different part of the city, contributed images to many of Trakl's poems, especially to the sequence *Sebastian im Traum*. The whole of Salzburg – or Trakl's vision of it – is present in much of his work; it is the 'beautiful city' of his earlier poems, a city in decay because its present does not live up to its past.

It is difficult to say whether Trakl's childhood was as melancholy and as lonely as his retrospective poems suggest. From accounts of him by his school friends, it appears that he showed no signs of extreme introversion until his late adolescence; and the first part of *Sebastian im Traum* is a vision of childhood that can no more be reduced to factual narrative than any other poem of Trakl's, for all its references to identifiable objects. Yet, on the evidence of the poem, it has even been suggested that Trakl's mother must have been a drug addict, like her son! Narcotics and intoxicants, in Trakl's poetry, are associated with original sin. Drunkenness, traditionally, began after the Flood, when men were so far removed from their first state that life became unbearable without this means of escape. For the same reason, it is with compassion that the father's bearded face looks down at the mother in this poem.

Trakl seems to have been fond of both his parents and at least one of his five brothers and sisters, Margarete, who became a concert pianist and settled in Berlin. Much has been made of his attachment to this sister, for critics of the literal persuasion insist on identifying her with the sister who appears in his poems; but neither the references to incest in Trakl's early work nor the personage of the sister in his later poems permit any biographical deductions. Incest is one of many forms of evil that occur in Trakl's work; and the personage of the sister is a kind of spiritual alter ego, an anima figure, so that in certain poems a brother–sister relationship symbolizes an integration of the self. Trakl used many other legendary or archetypal personages in his poetry – not to write his autobiography, but to compose visionary poems of an unprecedented kind.

Georg Trakl. *Archiv für Kunst und Geschichte, Berlin*

As a boy, Trakl shared Margarete's love of music and played the piano with some skill. At school, on the other hand, he proved less than mediocre. When he failed his examinations in the seventh form, he was unwilling to sit for them again and decided that he was unfit for the professional or academic career originally planned for him. For a time, he received private tuition at home. An Alsatian governess taught him French; and he took this opportunity to read the French poets, especially Baudelaire, Verlaine and Rimbaud. Other influences on his poetry are those of Hölderlin, Mörike and Lenau; and his thought was decisively influenced by Kierkegaard, Dostoevsky and Nietzsche. When, towards the end of his life, he decided to do without books, it was the works of Dostoevsky with which he found it hardest to part.

Already at school Trakl belonged to a literary club. Towards the end of his school years, he grew taciturn, moody and unsociable; he began to speak of suicide, drank immoderately, and drugged himself with chloroform. The career he now chose, that of a dispensing chemist, gave him easy access to more effective drugs for the rest of his life.

From 1905 to 1908, Trakl was trained for this career in his native town. During this time, two of his juvenile plays were publicly performed. The first was something of a *succès de scandale*; the second was an unqualified failure. In 1906, he began to contribute short dramatic sketches and book reviews to a local paper. He left Salzburg in October 1908, to complete his training at the University of Vienna, where he took a two-year course in pharmacy. His hatred of large cities dates from this period. At this time, he worked on a tragedy, *Don Juan*, of which only a fragment remains, and on an extant puppet play on the Bluebeard theme. After his second year in Vienna, during which his father died, Trakl entered on one year's military service as a dispensing chemist attached to the Medical Corps; he was posted to Innsbruck, then back to Vienna, but took the earliest opportunity of being transferred to the Reserve.

In 1912, he considered emigrating to Borneo; but in the same year, he began to write his best work and met his patron, Ludwig von Ficker, in whose periodical *Der Brenner* most of Trakl's later poems first appeared. It was mainly owing to Ficker's friendship and support that Trakl was able to devote the remaining years of his life to the writing of poetry. In January 1913, he accepted a clerical post in Vienna, but returned to Innsbruck after three days' work. Except for a number of other journeys – to Venice, to Lake Garda, various parts of Austria, and Berlin, where he visited his sister Margarete and met the poet Else Lasker-Schüler – and three more abortive attempts to work for his living in Vienna, Trakl moved between Innsbruck and Salzburg till the outbreak of war. In 1913, his first book – a selection of his poems made by Franz Werfel – was published by Kurt Wolff; a second collection appeared in the following year.

By 1913, he had become a confirmed drug addict. In December of that year he almost died of an overdose of veronal; but in spite of this and his alcoholic excesses, his physical strength remained prodigious.

In July 1914, Ludwig von Ficker received a considerable sum of money – 100,000 Austrian crowns – with the request to distribute it as he thought fit among contributors to *Der Brenner*. Trakl and Rilke were the first beneficiaries; but when Herr von Ficker took Trakl to the bank to draw part of the grant, Trakl's good fortune so nauseated him that he had to leave the bank before the formalities had been completed. Long after the event, Ficker revealed the identity of Trakl's and Rilke's patron; he was the philosopher Ludwig Wittgenstein, who gave away most of his inheritance at this time. Later, Wittgenstein wrote to Ficker about Trakl's poetry: 'I don't understand it, but its *tone* delights me. It is the *tone* of true genius.'

'It is such nameless despair to have one's world rent asunder. O my God, what sentence has been passed on me. Tell me that I must have the power to carry on living and pursuing what is true. Tell me that I am not insane. A stony silence has broken in on me. O my friend, how cowed and unhappy I have become.'

November 1913

Late in August 1914, Trakl left Innsbruck for Galicia as a lieutenant attached to the Medical Corps of the Austrian army. After the battle of Grodek, he was put in charge of ninety serious casualties whom – as a mere dispensing chemist hampered by the shortage of medical supplies – he could do almost nothing to help. One of the wounded shot himself through the head in Trakl's presence. Outside the barn where these casualties were housed, a number of deserters had been hanged on trees. It was more than Trakl could bear. He either threatened or attempted suicide, with the result that he was removed to Cracow for observation as a mental case. His last poems, 'Klage' ('Lament') and 'Grodek' were written at this time.

He now feared that he, too, would be executed as a deserter. According to the medical authorities at Cracow, he was under treatment for *dementia praecox* (schizophrenia); but the treatment consisted of being locked up in a cell together with another officer suffering from delirium tremens. During this confinement, Ludwig von Ficker visited Trakl and asked Wittgenstein, who was also serving in Poland, to look after Trakl; but Wittgenstein arrived too late. After a few weeks of anguish, Trakl took an overdose of cocaine, of which he died on 3 or 4 November 1914. He was 27 years of age. It has been suggested that he may have misjudged the dose in his state of acute distress; this was the opinion of his batman, the last person to whom Trakl spoke.

Apart from his juvenilia – poems, plays and book reviews – Trakl's work consists of some 100 poems and prose poems written between 1912 and 1914. The horizontal range of these poems is not wide. It is limited by his extreme introversion and by his peculiar habit of using the same operative words and images throughout his later work. But his introversion must not be mistaken for egocentricity. 'Believe me,' he wrote to a friend, 'it isn't easy for me, and never will be easy for me, to subordinate myself unconditionally to that which my poems render; and I shall have to correct myself again and again, so as to give to truth those things that belong to truth.' His inner experience is objectified in images and in the symbolic extension of those images; his concern, as he says, was with general truths and with the rendering of general truths in a purely poetic manner. For that reason, the melancholy that pervades his work was only a premiss, not the substance, of what he wished to convey; it is as important, but no more important, than the key of a musical composition. It was certainly a limitation of Trakl's that he could compose only in minor keys; but the same could be said of Leopardi and of other lyrical poets whose poetry conveys a distinct mood. Nor should Trakl be assessed in terms of optimism and pessimism, categories that are largely irrelevant to his vision. As Rilke was one of the first to point out, Trakl's work is essentially affirmative; but what it affirms is a spiritual order that may not be immediately perceptible in his poems, filled as they are with images pertaining to the temporal order that he negated.

'Trakl's poetry,' Rilke wrote:

> is to me an object of sublime existence . . . it occurs to me that this whole work has a parallel in the aspiration of a Li-Tai-Pe: in both, falling is the pretext for the most continuous ascension. In the history of the poem, Trakl's books are important contributions to the liberation of the poetic image. They seem to me to have mapped out a new dimension of the spirit and to have disproved that prejudice which judges all poetry only in terms of feeling and content, as if in the direction of lament there were only lament – but here too there is world again.

This tribute is especially important for two reasons: because of Trakl's influence on Rilke's own work, and because Rilke interpreted Trakl's poetry existentially when other critics, less close to Trakl's way of thought, read it as a record of Trakl's morbid states of mind. What Rilke meant by 'world' in the letter cited is what professional Existentialists would call 'being', and he believed that it is the poet's business to affirm whatever aspect of being is manifested to him, whether it be bright or dark. The mood is incidental; what matters is the intensity of the poet's response to the world and his ability to render his perceptions in words and images. Rilke always insisted that praise and lament are not mutually exclusive, but complementary functions; for lament, too, is a kind of affirmation, a way of praising what is lost or unattainable, a way of accepting the limitations of human life or even – in a sense different from that intended by

'Since your visit in hospital I have become twice as depressed. I feel very nearly beyond this world.'
27 October 1914

Blake – of 'catching joy as it flies'. That is why dirges and laments are a traditional form of poetry, though poetry, by the same tradition, is always affirmative. Within the bounds of a Christian orthodoxy that has very little in common with Rilke's private existential creed – but rather more with Trakl's beliefs – the poet's dual function in an imperfect world emerges from George Herbert's lines in 'Bitter-sweet': 'I will complain, yet praise, / I will bewail, approve; /And all my sowre-sweet dayes / I will lament, and love.'

It was Rilke's insight, then, which directed the attention of Trakl's readers away from the categories of optimism and pessimism and towards that 'truth' which Trakl himself thought more important than his own predicament. As the work of so many of Trakl's contemporaries shows, optimism can be just as morbid a symptom as pessimism, because there is a kind of optimism that is a hysterical perversion of the truth; its premisses give it the lie. Trakl, on the other hand, wrote of what he knew; he was true to his premisses, and these premisses were positive enough.

The temporal order that Trakl's poems negate was that of materialism in decay. This is the significance of the decaying household utensils in the first part of *Sebastian im Traum*. To this order, Trakl opposed an existential Christian faith akin to Kierkegaard's and an unreserved compassion akin to that of certain characters in Dostoevsky. All this is implicit in Trakl's poetry, since he rarely stated or defined his beliefs, but translated them into images. Yet all the external evidence supports this interpretation of his beliefs; and, shortly before his death, Trakl handed the following short note to Ludwig von Ficker: '[Your] feeling at moments of death-like existence: all human beings are worthy of love. Awakening, you feel the bitterness of the world: in that you know all your unabsolved guilt; your poems an imperfect penance.' Because poetry is an imperfect penance, Trakl castigated himself to the point of self-destruction.

What Trakl lamented was not the fact or the condition of death, but the difficulty of living in an age of cultural decline and spiritual corruption. The immediate background of Salzburg, an ancient and beautiful city unable to live up to its past, was one element in his melancholy, though it does not account for his own obsession with guilt and death. 'No,' he wrote as early as 1909, 'my own affairs no longer interest me'; and in 1914 – after his breakdown on active service – 'already I feel very nearly beyond this world'. The dead who people his poems – the mythical Elis, for instance – are more vivid, more full of life, than the living. For example, in 'An einen Frühverstorbenen' ('To One who Died Young'), it is the dying friend who smiles, the survivor who becomes obsessed with death and decay. The reason, it appears from other poems, is that those who die young preserve 'the image of man' intact; wherever they appear in Trakl's poems, they are associated with righteousness and with images of the good life; and this, in turn, is associated with an earlier stage of civilization, opposed to modern life in the large cities. Trakl's dead are symbolic of a state of innocence that cannot be identified with youth or childhood, or even with a rustic and pastoral stage of civilization. It is an innocence that precedes original sin. Trakl can, of course, be criticized for his inability to bear the guilt of being alive. Shortly before his death, he said of himself that as yet he was 'only half-born'; and he did not want his birth to be completed.

Most of Trakl's later poems are written in a form of free verse that owes much to the elegies and hymns of Hölderlin. Without in fact imitating the classical hexameter, Trakl suggests its movement by the frequent use of dactyls and spondees (as in the long lines in *Sebastian im Traum*); but in many of his last poems he uses a short line which is also irregular, though more frequently iambic than his longer lines. These last poems are closer to Hölderlin's hymns than to his elegies; and the landscape in these poems is the grand alpine landscape of Innsbruck, as distinct from the more gentle, elegiac landscape of Salzburg and its surroundings. Trakl's adjectives – and especially his colour adjectives – have a function that is partly pictorial, partly emotive (often by means of synesthesia), and partly symbolic. Like all his favourite devices, the colour epithets recur throughout his mature work with a persistency reminiscent of the Wagnerian leitmotiv (and Trakl is known to have gone through a youthful phase of enthusiasm for Wagner's music).

The difficulty of summing up Trakl's work as a whole, and the much greater difficulty of interpreting it as a whole, are two reasons why his work stands out from the German poetry of his time. Trakl's plagiarisms – and especially his self-plagiarisms – lend a deceptive consistency to his work – deceptive, because his poems are essentially ambiguous. His ambiguities derive from the tension between image and symbol, the phenomenon and the idea. Sometimes this tension remains unresolved, so that one cannot tell whether an image is to be taken descriptively or symbolically, an epithet synesthetically or qualitatively. Because of the non-commital character of imagism, it would also be possible to argue that Trakl was an alchemist (as his astrological metaphors confirm!) or a Marxist (because of his vision of capitalism in decay!).

In an age of conflicting creeds and sects, such openness is an advantage. Horizontally, Trakl's range is that of a minor poet, but his vertical range is out of all proportion to it. By 'vertical' here is meant neither profundity nor sublimity, but a dimension related to harmony in music. Trakl's poetry is a series of micro-

Trakl caricatured by Max von Esterle in *Der Brenner*, 1912.
Bildarchiv preußischer Kulturbesitz, Berlin

cosmic variations, poor in melodic invention, rich in harmonic correspondences. Another way of putting it is to say that his work is valid on many 'levels' of meaning. It depends as little as possible on the poet's person, opinions and circumstances. One reason is that Trakl was conscious neither of himself nor of his reader; all his poems had his undivided attention. Of T. S. Eliot's 'three voices of poetry', Trakl had only the first, the voice of the poet in soliloquy; but because it never even occurred to him to cultivate the others, his monologue was strangely quiet and pure.

MICHAEL HAMBURGER

Texts
Walther Killy & Hans Szklenar (eds), *Dichtungen und Briefe* (Otto Müller, Salzburg, 1969). Authoritative collection of poems in 1st vol. and letters in 2nd vol.

Translations
Frank Graziano (ed.), *Georg Trakl* (Carcanet Press, Manchester, 1984). Translations by Michael Hamburger and Christopher Middleton are reproduced with kind permission of the translators.

Secondary sources
Walter Ritzer, *Neue Trakl-Bibliographie* (Salzburg, 1983). Most recent bibliography relating to Trakl, issued as part 12 of Trakl-Studien.
Michael Hamburger, *A Proliferation of Prophets: essays in German literature from Nietzsche to Brecht* (Carcanet, Manchester, 1983). The article on Georg Trakl by Michael Hamburger is an abridged form of chapter seven 'Georg Trakl' which appears by kind permission of the author.

Musik im Mirabell

2. Fassung

Ein Brunnen singt. Die Wolken stehn
Im klaren Blau, die weißen, zarten.
Bedächtig stille Menschen gehn
Am Abend durch den alten Garten.

Der Ahnen Marmor ist ergraut.
Ein Vogelzug streift in die Weiten.
Ein Faun mit toten Augen schaut
Nach Schatten, die ins Dunkel gleiten.

Das Laub fällt rot vom alten Baum
Und kreist herein durchs offne Fenster.
Ein Feuerschein glüht auf im Raum
Und malet trübe Angstgespenster.

Ein weisser Fremdling tritt ins Haus.
Ein Hund stürzt durch verfallene Gänge.
Die Magd löscht eine Lampe aus,
Das Ohr hört nachts Sonatenklänge.

Music in the Mirabel

[Second version]

A fountain sings. White, gentle clouds, aglow,
Hang in pure azure. Slowly, pondering,
And very silent, men and women go
Through the old garden in the evening.

The marble of our forebears has turned grey.
A flight of birds fades off beyond the park.
A faun with his dead eyes looks fixedly
At shadows that glide off into the dark.

From ancient trees the russet foliage falls
And through the open window, circling, drifts.
Firelight that flickers in the room, appals
With many a phantom shape that twists and shifts.

A stranger comes into the house, all white.
Through mouldering passages a mastiff bounds.
Softly a maid puts out the last lamp's light.
At night the ear dwells on sonata sounds.

TRANSLATED BY MICHAEL HAMBURGER

Kindheit

Voll Früchten der Hollunder; ruhig wohnte die Kindheit
In blauer Höhle. Über vergangenen Pfad,
Wo nun bräunlich das wilde Gras saust,
Sinnt das stille Geäst; das Rauschen des Laubs

Ein gleiches, wenn das blaue Wasser im Felsen tönt.
Sanft ist der Amsel Klage. Ein Hirt
Folgt sprachlos der Sonne, die vom herbstlichen Hügel
rollt.

Ein blauer Augenblick ist nur mehr Seele.
Am Waldsaum zeigt sich ein scheues Wild und friedlich
Ruhn im Grund die alten Glocken und finsteren Weiler.

Frömmer kennst du den Sinn der dunklen Jahre,
Kühle und Herbst in einsamen Zimmern;
Und in heiliger Bläue läuten leuchtende Schritte fort.

Leise klirrt ein offenes Fenster; zu Tränen
Rührt der Anblick des verfallenen Friedhofs am Hügel,
Erinnerung an erzählte Legenden; doch manchmal
erhellt sich die Seele,
Wenn sie frohe Menschen denkt, dunkelgoldene
Frühlingstage.

Childhood

Full-berried the elderbush; tranquilly childhood lived
In a blue cave. Over the bygone path
Where now pale brown the wild grasses hiss,
Calm branches ponder; the rustling of leaves

This too, when blue waters sound under the crags.
Gentle the blackbird's plaint. A shepherd
Follows unspeaking the sun that rolls from the
autumn hill.

A blue moment is purely and simply soul.
At the forest edge a shy deer shows itself, at peace
Below in the vale the old bells and sombre hamlets rest.

Now more devout, you know the meaning of the dark
years,
Coolness and autumn in solitary rooms;
And still in holy azure shining footfalls ring.

An open window softly knocks; tears come
At the sight of the decayed graveyard on the hill,
Memory of told legends; yet the soul sometimes brightens
When she thinks of the glad folk, the dark-gold
springtime days.

TRANSLATED BY CHRISTOPHER MIDDLETON

MENSCHHEIT

Menschheit vor Feuerschlünden aufgestellt,
Ein Trommelwirbel, dunkler Krieger Stirnen,
Schritte durch Blutnebel; schwarzes Eisen schellt,
Verzweiflung, Nacht in traurigen Gehirnen:
Hier Evas Schatten, Jagd und rotes Geld.
Gewölk, das Licht durchbricht, das Abendmahl.
Es wohnt in Brot und Wein ein sanftes Schweigen
Und jene sind versammelt zwölf an Zahl.
Nachts schrein im Schlaf sie unter Ölbaumzweigen;
Sankt Thomas taucht die Hand ins Wundenmal.

MANKIND

Round gorges deep with fire arrayed, mankind;
A roll of drums, dark brows of warriors marching;
Footsteps in fog of blood, black metals grind;
Despair, sad night of thought, despair high-arching;
Eve's shadow falls, halloo of hunt, red coin consigned.
Cloud, broken by light, the Supper's end;
This bread, this wine, have silence in their keeping.
Here do the Twelve assembled, numbered, stand;
They cry out under olive trees at night, half-sleeping.
Into the wound Saint Thomas dips his hand.

TRANSLATED BY CHRISTOPHER MIDDLETON

AN DEN KNABEN ELIS

Elis, wenn die Amsel im schwarzen Wald ruft,
Dieses ist dein Untergang.
Deine Lippen trinken die Kühle des blauen Felsenquells.

Laß, wenn deine Stirne leise blutet
Uralte Legenden
Und dunkle Deutung des Vogelflugs.

Du aber gehst mit weichen Schritten in die Nacht,
Die voll purpurner Trauben hängt,
Und du regst die Arme schöner im Blau.

Ein Dornenbusch tönt,
Wo deine mondenen Augen sind.
O, wie lange bist, Elis, du verstorben.

Dein Leib ist eine Hyazinthe,
In die ein Mönch die wächsernen Finger taucht.
Eine schwarze Höhle ist unser Schweigen.

Daraus bisweilen ein sanftes Tier tritt
Und langsam die schweren Lider senkt.
Auf deine Schläfen tropft schwarzer Tau,

Das letzte Gold verfallener Sterne.

TO THE BOY ELIS

Elis, when the ouzel calls in the black wood,
This is your own decline.
Your lips drink in the coolness of the blue
Spring in the rocks.

No more, when softly your forehead bleeds,
Primaeval legends
And dark interpretation of the flight of birds.

But you walk with soft footsteps into the night
Which is laden with purple grapes,
And move your arms more beautifully in the blue.

A thorn-bush sounds
Where your lunar eyes are.
O Elis, how long have you been dead.

Your body is a hyacinth
Into which a monk dips his waxen fingers.
Our silence is a black cavern

From which at times a gentle animal
Steps out and slowly lowers heavy lids.
Upon your temples black dew drips,

The last gold of perished stars.

TRANSLATED BY MICHAEL HAMBURGER

SEBASTIAN IM TRAUM

Für Adolf Loos

1

Mutter trug das Kindlein im weißen Mond,
Im Schatten des Nußbaums, uralten Hollunders,
Trunken vom Safte des Mohns, der Klage der Drossel;
Und stille
Neigte in Mitleid sich über jene ein bärtiges Antlitz

Leise im Dunkel des Fensters; und altes Hausgerät
Der Väter
Lag im Verfall; Liebe und herbstliche Träumerei.

Also dunkel der Tag des Jahrs, traurige Kindheit,
Da der Knabe leise zu kühlen Wassern, silbernen
Fischen hinabstieg,
Ruh und Antlitz;
Da er steinern sich vor rasende Rappen warf,
In grauer Nacht sein Stern über ihn kam;

Oder wenn er an der frierenden Hand der Mutter
Abends über Sankt Peters herbstlichen Friedhof ging,
Ein zarter Leichnam stille im Dunkel der Kammer lag
Und jener die kalten Lider über ihn aufhob.

Er aber war ein kleiner Vogel im kahlen Geäst,
Die Glocke lang im Abendnovember,
Des Vaters Stille, da er im Schlaf die dämmernde
Wendeltreppe hinabstieg.

2

Frieden der Seele. Einsamer Winterabend,
Die dunklen Gestalten der Hirten am alten Weiher;
Kindlein in der Hütte von Stroh; o wie leise
Sank in schwarzem Fieber das Antlitz hin.
Heilige Nacht.

Oder wenn er an der harten Hand des Vaters
Stille den finstern Kalvarienberg hinanstieg
Und in dämmernden Felsennischen
Die blaue Gestalt des Menschen durch seine Legende
ging,
Aus der Wunde unter dem Herzen purpurn das Blut
rann.
O wie leise stand in dunkler Seele das Kreuz auf.

Liebe; da in schwarzen Winkeln der Schnee schmolz,
Ein blaues Lüftchen sich heiter im alten Hollunder fing,
In dem Schattengewölbe des Nußbaums;
Und dem Knaben leise sein rosiger Engel erschien.

SEBASTIAN IN DREAM

For Adolf Loos

1

Mother bore this infant in the white moon,
In the nut tree's shade, in the ancient elder's,
Drunk with the poppy's juice, the thrush's lament;
And mute
With compassion a bearded face bowed down to that
woman.

Quiet in the window's darkness; and ancestral heirlooms,
Old household goods,
Lay rotting there; love and autumnal reverie.

So dark was the day of the year, desolate childhood,
When softly the boy to cool waters, to silver fishes walked
down,
Calm and countenance;
When stony he cast himself down where black horses
raced,
In the grey of the night his star possessed him.

Or holding his mother's icy hand
He walked at nightfall across St Peter's autumnal
churchyard,
While a delicate corpse lay still in the bedroom's gloom
And he raised cold eyelids towards it.

But he was a little bird in leafless boughs,
The churchbell rang in dusking November,
His father's stillness, when asleep he descended the dark
of the turning stair.

2

Peace of the soul. A lonely winter evening.
The dark shapes of shepherds by the ancient pond;
Little child in the hut of straw; O how softly
Into black fever his face sank down.
Holy night.

Or holding his father's horny hand
In silence he walked up Calvary Hill
And in dusky rock recesses

The blue shape of Man would pass through His legend,
Blood ran purple from the wound beneath His heart.
O how softly the Cross rose up in the dark of his soul.

Love; when in black corners the snow was melting,
Gaily a little blue breeze was caught in the ancient elder,
In the nut tree's vault of shade;
And in silence a rosy angel appeared to that boy;

Freude; da in kühlen Zimmern eine Abendsonate
erklang,
Im braunen Holzgebälk
Ein blauer Falter aus des silbernen Puppe kroch.

O die Nähe des Todes. In steinerner Mauer
Neigte sich ein gelbes Haupt, schweigend das Kind,
Da in jenem März der Mond verfiel.

3

Rosige Osterglocke im Grabgewölbe der Nacht
Und die Silberstimmen der Sterne,
Daß in Schauern ein dunkler Wahnsinn von der Stirne
des Schläfers sank.

O wie stille ein Gang den blauen Fluß hinab
Vergessenes sinnend, da im grünen Geäst
Die Drossel ein Fremdes in den Untergang rief.

Oder wenn er an der knöchernen Hand des Greisen
Abends vor die verfallene Mauer der Stadt ging
Und jener in schwarzem Mantel ein rosiges Kindlein
trug,
Im Schatten des Nußbaums der Geist des Bösen
erschien.

Tasten über die grünen Stufen des Sommers. O wie leise
Verfiel der Garten in der braunen Stille des Herbstes,
Duft und Schwermut des alten Hollunders,
Da in Sebastians Schatten die Silberstimme des Engels
erstarb.

Gladness; when in cool rooms a sonata sounded at
nightfall,
Among dark-brown beams
A blue butterfly crept from its silver chrysalis.

O the nearness of death. From the stony wall
A yellow head bowed down, silent that child,
Since in that month the moon decayed.

3

Rose-coloured Easter bell in the burial vault of the night,
And the silver voices of stars,
So that madness, dark and shuddering, ebbed from the
sleeper's brow.

O how quiet to ramble along the blue river's bank,
To ponder forgotten things when in leafy boughs
The thrush's call brought strangeness into a world's
decline.

Or holding an old man's bony hand
In the evening he walked to the crumbling city walls,
And in his black greatcoat carried a rosy child,
In the nut tree's shade the spirit of evil appeared.

Groping his way over the green steps of summer. O how
softly
In autumn's brown stillness the garden decayed,
Scent and sadness of the ancient elder,
When the silver voice of the angel died down in
Sebastian's shadow.

TRANSLATED BY MICHAEL HAMBURGER

KLAGE

Schlaf und Tod, die düstern Adler
Umrauschen nachtlang dieses Haupt:
Des Menschen goldnes Bildnis
Verschlänge die eisige Woge
Der Ewigkeit. An schaurigen Riffen
Zerschellt der purpurne Leib.
Und es klagt die dunkle Stimme
Über dem Meer.
Schwester stürmischer Schwermut
Sieh, ein ängstlicher Kahn versinkt
Unter Sternen,
Dem schweigenden Antlitz der Nacht.

LAMENT

Sleep and death, the dark eagles
Around this head swoop all night long:
Eternity's icy wave
Would swallow the golden image
Of man; against horrible reefs
His purple body is shattered.
And the dark voice laments
Over the sea.
Sister of stormy sadness,
Look, a timorous boat goes down
Under stars,
The silent face of the night.

TRANSLATED BY MICHAEL HAMBURGER

Abendland

4. Fassung

Else Lasker-Schüler in Verehrung

1

Mond, als träte ein Totes
Aus blauer Höhle,
Und es fallen der Blüten
Viele über den Felsenpfad.
Silbern weint ein Krankes
Am Abendweiher,
Auf schwarzem Kahn
Hinüberstarben Liebende.

Oder es läuten die Schritte
Elis' durch den Hain
Den hyazinthenen
Wieder verhallend unter Eichen.
O des Knaben Gestalt
Geformt aus kristallenen Tränen,
Nächtigen Schatten.
Zackige Blitze erhellen die Schläfe
Die immerkühle,
Wenn am grünenden Hügel
Frühlingsgewitter ertönt.

2

So leise sind die grünen Wälder
Unsrer Heimat,
Die kristallne Woge
Hinsterbend an verfallner Mauer
Und wir haben im Schlaf geweint;
Wandern mit zögernden Schritten
An der dornigen Hecke hin
Singende im Abendsommer,
In heiliger Ruh
Des fern verstrahlenden Weinbergs;
Schatten nun im kühlen Schoß
Der Nacht, trauernde Adler.
So leise schließt ein mondener Strahl
Die purpurnen Male der Schwermut.

3

Ihr großen Städte
Steinern aufgebaut
In der Ebene!
So sprachlos folgt
Der Heimatlose
Mit dunkler Stirne dem Wind,

Occident

Fourth version

Dedicated to Else Lasker-Schüler

1

Moon, as if a dead thing
Stepped out of a blue cave,
And many blossoms fall
Across the rocky path.
Silver a sick thing weeps
By the evening pond,
In a black boat
Lovers crossed over to death.

Or the footsteps of Elis
Ring through the grove
The hyacinthine
To fade again under oaks.
O the shape of that boy
Formed out of crystal tears,
Nocturnal shadows.
Jagged lightning illumines his temples
The ever-cool,
When on the verdant hill
Springtime thunder resounds.

2

So quiet are the green woods
Of our homeland,
The crystal wave
That dies against a perished wall
And we have wept in our sleep;
Wander with hesitant steps
Along the thorny hedge
Singers in the evening summer
In holy peace
Of the vineyards distantly gleaming;
Shadows now in the cool lap
Of night, eagles that mourn.
So quietly does a moonbeam close
The purple wounds of sadness.

3

You mighty cities
stone on stone raised up
in the plain!
So quietly
with darkened forehead
the outcast follows the wind,

Kahlen Bäumen am Hügel.
Ihr weithin dämmernden Ströme!
Gewaltig ängstet
Schaurige Abendröte
Im Sturmgewölk.
Ihr sterbenden Völker!
Bleiche Woge
Zerschellend am Strande der Nacht,
Fallende Sterne.

bare trees on the hillside.
You rivers distantly fading!
Gruesome sunset red
is breeding fear
in the thunderclouds.
You dying peoples!
Pallid billow
that breaks on the beaches of Night,
stars that are falling.

TRANSLATED BY MICHAEL HAMBURGER

DIE SCHWERMUT

Gewaltig bist du dunkler Mund
Im Innern, aus Herbstgewölk
Geformte Gestalt,
Goldner Abendstille;
Ein grünlich dämmernder Bergstrom
In zerbrochner Föhren
Schattenbezirk;
Ein Dorf,
Das fromm in braunen Bildern abstirbt.

Da springen die schwarzen Pferde
Auf nebliger Weide.
Ihr Soldaten!
Vom Hügel, wo sterbend die Sonne rollt
Stürzt das lachende Blut –
Unter Eichen
Sprachlos! O grollende Schwermut
Das Heers; ein strahlender Helm
Sank klirrend von purpurner Stirne.

Herbstesnacht so kühle kommt,
Erglänzt mit Sternen
Über zerbrochenem Männergebein
Die stille Mönchin.

DEJECTION

Mighty you are, dark mouth
Within, configuration formed
Of autumn clouds,
Of golden evening stillness;
A greenishly glimmering mountain brook
In the shadow precinct
Of broken pines:
A village
That in brown images piously suffers decay.

There the black horses leap
On a hazy pasture.
You soldiers!
From the hill where dying the sun rolls
Laughing blood roars down –
Under oaks,
Speechless. O the army's
Grim dejection; a bright helmet
Clattering slid from a crimson brow.

Autumn night so coolly comes.
Lights up with stars
Above the broken bones of men
The quiet maiden monk.

TRANSLATED BY MICHAEL HAMBURGER

An Einen Frühverstorbenen

O, der schwarze Engel, der leise aus dem Innern des
Baums trat,
Da wir sanfte Gespielen am Abend waren,
Am Rand des bläulichen Brunnens.
Ruhig war unser Schritt, die runden Augen in der
braunen Kühle des Herbstes,
O, die purpurne Süße der Sterne.

Jener aber ging die steinernen Stufen des Mönchsbergs
hinab,
Ein blaues Lächeln im Antlitz und seltsam verpuppt
In seine stillere Kindheit und starb;
Und im Garten blieb das silberne Antlitz des Freundes
zurück,
Lauschend im Laub oder im alten Gestein.

Seele sang den Tod, die grüne Verwesung des Fleisches
Und es war das Rauschen des Walds,
Die inbrünstige Klage des Wildes.
Immer klangen von dämmernden Türmen die blauen
Glocken des Abends.

Stunde kam, da jener die Schatten in purpurner Sonne
sah,
Die Schatten der Fäulnis in kahlem Geäst;
Abend, da an dämmernder Mauer die Amsel sang,
Der Geist des Frühverstorbenen stille im Zimmer
erschien.

O, das Blut, das aus der Kehle des Tönenden rinnt,
Blaue Blume; O die feurige Träne
Geweint in die Nacht.

Goldene Wolke und Zeit. In einsamer Kammer
Lädst du öfter den Toten zu Gast,
Wandelst in trautem Gespräch unter Ulmen den grünen
Fluß hinab.

To One Who Died Young

O the black angel who softly stepped from the heart of
the tree
When we were gentle playmates in the evening,
By the edge of the pale-blue fountain.
Our step was easy, the round eyes in autumn's brown
coolness,
O the purple sweetness of the stars.

But the other descended the stone steps of the
Mönchsberg,
A blue smile on his face, and strangely ensheathed
In his quieter childhood, and died;
And the silver face of his friend stayed behind in the
garden,
Listening in the leaves or in the ancient stones.

Soul sang of death, the green decay of the flesh,
And it was the murmur of the forest,
The fervid lament of the animals.
Always from dusky towers rang the blue evening bells.

Times came when the other saw shadows in the purple
sun,
The shadows of putrescence in the bare branches;
At evening, when by the dusky wall the blackbird sang,
His ghost quietly appeared there in the room.

O the blood that runs from the throat of the musical one,
Blue flower; O the fiery tear
Wept into the night.

Golden cloud and time. In a lonely room
You ask the dead child to visit you more often,
You walk and talk together under elms by the green
riverside.

Translated by Christopher Middleton

Im Osten

Den wilden Orgeln des Wintersturms
Gleicht der Volkes finstrer Zorn,
Die purpurne Woge der Schlacht,
Entlaubter Sterne.

Mit zerbrochnen Brauen, silbernen Armen
Winkt sterbenden Soldaten die Nacht.
Im Schatten der herbstlichen Esche
Seufzen die Geister der Erschlagenen.

Dornige Wildnis umgürtet die Stadt.
Von blutenden Stufen jagt der Mond
Die erschrockenen Frauen.
Wilde Wölfe brachen durchs Tor.

Eastern Front

The wrath of the people is dark,
Like the wild organ notes of winter storm,
The battle's crimson wave, a naked
Forest of stars.

With ravaged brows, with silver arms
To dying soldiers night comes beckoning.
In the shade of the autumn ash
Ghosts of the fallen are sighing.

Thorny wilderness girdles the town about.
From bloody doorsteps the moon
Chases terrified women.
Wild wolves have poured through the gates.

Translated by Christopher Middleton

Grodek

Am Abend tönen die herbstlichen Wälder
Von tödlichen Waffen, die goldnen Ebenen
Und blauen Seen, darüber die Sonne
Düstrer hinrollt; umfängt die Nacht
Sterbende Krieger, die wilde Klage
Ihrer zerbrochenen Münder.
Doch stille sammelt im Weidengrund
Rotes Gewölk, darin ein zürnender Gott wohnt,
Das vergoßne Blut sich, mondne Kühle;
Alle Straßen münden in Schwarze Verwesung.
Unter goldnem Gezweig der Nacht und Sternen
Es schwankt der Schwester Schatten durch den
schweigenden Hain,
Zu grüßen die Geister der Helden, die blutenden
Häupter;
Und leise tönen im Rohr die dunklen Flöten des
Herbstes.
O stolzere Trauer! ihr ehernen Altäre,
Die heiße Flamme des Geistes nährt heute ein
gewaltiger Schmerz,
Die ungebornen Enkel.

Grodek

At nightfall the autumn woods cry out
With deadly weapons and the golden plains,
The deep blue lakes, above which more darkly
Rolls the sun; the night embraces
Dying warriors, the wild lament
Of their broken mouths.
But quietly there in the willow dell
Red clouds in which an angry god resides,
The shed blood gathers, lunar coolness.
All the roads lead to blackest carrion.
Under golden twigs of the night and stars
The sister's shade now sways through the silent copse
To greet the ghosts of the heroes, the bleeding heads;
And softly the dark flutes of autumn sound in the reeds.
O prouder grief! You brazen altars,
Today a great pain feeds the hot flame of the spirit,
The grandsons yet unborn.

Translated by Michael Hamburger

AUGUST STRAMM 1874–1915

'Germany needs brave soldiers. Nothing else will do. We have to go through with it, however much we condemn the war.'

23 February 1915

August Stramm was, along with Guillaume Apollinaire, among the most innovative poets of the First World War. Treating language like a physical material, he honed down conventional syntax to its bare essentials. Fashioning new words out of old, he created a uniquely expressive poetic medium. Indeed, it has been observed that what James Joyce did on a grand scale for English, Stramm achieved more modestly for German, in a manner which has some affinities with the Imagists. But Stramm was a revolutionary almost in spite of himself. 'Do you remember,' he wrote to his wife on 29 December 1914, 'how I was always dissatisfied with everything that was called art?' This opposition to the outworn modes of German verse led him along a lonely artistic path, until he suddenly found himself at the centre of European modernism in the spring of 1914.

August Stramm was born in Münster, Westphalia, on 29 July 1874. Prevented by his father from studying theology, Stramm entered the post office administration in 1893, where he showed considerable aptitude, advancing to a much-prized position on the transatlantic Bremen/Hamburg–New York run in 1897. After studying various subjects part-time, he gained a doctorate in 1909, and thereupon attained the highest position in the post office administration open to a man of his age. By 1914, he had advanced to the Reichspost ministry. Meanwhile, he had married the popular novelist Else Krafft in 1902, with whom he had two children. They first lived in Bremen, moving to Berlin in 1905.

In these years, Stramm indulged in various artistic pursuits: he was a cellist and a Sunday painter and developed his adolescent love of writing. Between 1902–7, he worked on his *Michael Kohlhaas* drama, based on the celebrated *Novelle* by Kleist. However, it was after gaining his doctorate that Stramm probably began to devote more time to writing, and 'around the year 1912', according to his daughter Inge, 'literature overtook him like a sickness . . . A demon awoke in him.' Plays and poems began to appear in a strange new style that could find no publisher until, in April 1914, Stramm sent some work – probably the two one-act plays *Rudimentär* (*Rudimentary*), *Sancta Susanna* and a few poems – to Herwarth Walden, editor of one of the major Expressionist periodicals, *Der Sturm*.

August Stramm on his final leave, August 1915, Berlin.
Limes Verlag, Wiesbaden

Walden stood at the focal point of the avant-garde movement in Berlin. He was in touch with innumerable international artists, printing, exhibiting and promoting such figures as Kokoschka, Picasso, Vlaminck, Kandinsky, Klee and Marc (killed 1916). A multi-faceted impresario, in the literary world, he was in contact with the founder of Italian Futurism, F. T. Marinetti, and with Apollinaire (q.v.). In 1913, *Der Sturm* published key modernist statements such as Marinetti's 'Futurist Manifesto' and Apollinaire's 'Modern Painting'. For Walden, Cubism, Futurism and Expressionism were essentially the same, and he sought to unite them in his own all-embracing *Sturm-Kunst*. His views on poetics, only fully formulated after his meeting with Stramm, were indebted to Kandinsky's *On the Spiritual in Art*, extracts from which first appeared in *Der Sturm* in 1912; similarly, Walden embraced the literary theories of Arno Holz, which entailed a concentration on the physical medium of language. As Walden put it in 1918 (echoing Kandinsky on painting): 'The material of poetry is the word. The form of poetry is rhythm.' Consequently, he preferred Holz's term *'Wort-Kunst'* ('word-art') to 'poetry'. However, what Walden lacked when Stramm first contacted him in 1914 was a German poet who accorded with his artistic theories and whose work could stand comparison with the international élite who figured in *Der Sturm*.

From their first meeting, a close friendship developed between Stramm and Walden; personally and artistically, they became indispensable to each other, and it can be inferred that Stramm's style now became fully mature through Walden's encouragement. In the next sixteen months, Stramm produced the sixty-two shorter poems and the two extended ones on which his reputation mainly rests. During this period, hardly an issue of *Der Sturm* appeared that did not contain a play by Stramm or a group of his poems.

Between April 1914 and the outbreak of war, Stramm wrote most of the poems published in 1915 as *Du. Liebesgedichte* (*You. Love Poems*). Here, he explores the changing and often tense relationship between the poet's self, the *Ich* (I), and an often undefined *Du* (You). This *Du*, more than a single woman, is extended to include womankind, humanity and God. Thus the 'love' recorded ranges from debased sexuality in 'Freudenhaus' ('House of Pleasures') to the love of God in 'Allmacht' ('Almighty'). Love is seen as essentially ambiguous; or, rather, it cannot be separated from, and always involves its own opposite, strife. Appropriately, the collection begins with a poem that announces this duality: 'Liebeskampf' ('Love-Fight'). Although Stramm celebrates sexuality, as in 'Heimlichkeit' ('Secrecy'), his poems often evoke negative experiences: unfaithfulness ('Untreu'), melancholy ('Schwermut'), despair ('Verzweiflung'). The failure of *Ich* to unite with *Du* – the ultimate separateness of individuality – provides a constant theme.

Yet the very impossibility of complete physical union stimulates a further theme: the quest for metaphysical unity with all Being. While some poems like 'Mondblick' ('Moongaze') aim to capture the concrete particularity of a unique experience, others such as 'Wunder' ('Wonder') or 'Dämmerung' ('Twilight') elevate *Ich* and *Du* into universal principles, and seek to relate and even to unite them totally, in an abstract, metaphysical sphere. Stramm's belief in such mystical unity was nourished by his favourite book, Ralph Waldo Trine's *In Harmony with the Infinite*, a bloodstained copy of which was found on his body when he fell.

Stramm's essential innovation (still too little recognized, even in Germany) was to create a new, non-representational kind of poetry, comparable to the abstract revolution in painting or Schönberg's invention of serial music. The painter Franz Marc's response of 23 October 1915 to Stramm's late play *Geschehen* (*Process*) was wholly appropriate: 'As always, in reading I have musical and painterly (and in this instance *purely cubistic*) ideas . . .' Other Expressionist poets, such as Heym or Trakl (q.v.), created an autonomous world in art, but generally kept to traditional notions of the self, albeit a fragmented one. Stramm forgoes such representationalism; for example, in the poem 'Freudenhaus', he writes: 'Lights are whoring from the windows . . .'. Or he creates a more abstract reality in others such as 'Liebeskampf': 'The wanting stands . . .'

Whereas other poets tended to retain traditional forms and modes, Stramm ruptured the traditional stanza and metrical verse line, sacrificing harmony and flow to achieve a forceful, expressive rhythm. The rhythm and sound largely replace syntax, and act like form and colour in abstract painting to convey an essentially emotive reality. Above all, the texts place greater stress on individual words and roots. The word rather than the sentence acts as the basic vehicle of meaning, which does not emerge discursively, but in bundles of linguistic energy. Evocatively used words convey a host of meanings, and produce a poetry of extreme intensity and concentration.

This richness arises specifically from Stramm's treatment of language as a material, from his refashioning, altering, shortening and recombining of existing linguistic elements. However strange the effects, the method works because Stramm bases his art on accepted German linguistic procedures, and often actually resurrects past forms and meanings. Stramm's favoured devices include the creation of portmanteau words, which telescope two or more words into a single neologism. The most famous is '*schamzerpört*' in 'Freudenhaus', made up of '*die Scham*' (shame; but also having the sense of 'genitals'); '*sich empören*' (to be indignant); and the prefix '*zer-*' (an intensifier which expresses completion, damage or destruction). Only very approximately can the word be rendered into English as 'shamedestraught' (shame + de [from destroyed] + straught [from distraught]). Stramm's compounds suggest a bundle of related meanings which defy exact translation.

No less important a technique is his re-functioning of words. For example, nouns can become verbs: in 'Freudenhaus', the noun '*die Dirne*' (wench, whore) is turned into the verb '*dirnen*' (to whore); while in 'Verzweiflung' ('Despair'), the noun '*der Stein*' becomes the verb '*steinen*' (to [turn into] stone). Such usage revitalizes the poetic language, capturing once and for all some precise shade of meaning, and turning it into a new linguistic reality.

An important set of words are the abstractions formed from verbs such as '*das Wollen*' in 'Liebeskampf' meaning 'the wanting' or '*das Horchen*' in 'Heimlichkeit' meaning 'the harking' and so on. These forms enable an abstract, impersonal mode of expression. Often, it is unclear whether they should be understood as nouns or as verbs in the infinitive. Statements become ambiguous, fluid, dynamic. A series of such words juxtaposed creates that effect of the 'words-in-freedom', *parole in libertá*, advocated by Marinetti. At the start of 'Schwermut' ('Melancholy'), two verbal nouns, '*Schreiten Streben*' (striding, striving), evoke an activity *per se*, without reference to specific agents: the whole of life seems meant. Indeed, though collected as a 'love poem', the ambiguity created by this openness of reference is almost total. The poem 'Schwermut' might refer to the problems which arise between a pair of lovers; but it also evokes the whole life process, from 'striving' to 'dying' and ultimate silence. The condensation of meaning enables a richness of ambiguity second to none.

Stramm's plays, too, became concentrated and brief, distilling situations into a few characteristic and increasingly ambiguous words and gestures. Characters are types like 'He' and 'She', and the surroundings merge into the action: sound, word, gesture and decor blend into a symbolic whole. The first mature plays are complementary opposites: the Symbolistic *Sancta Susanna* (1912–13) portrays a nun who becomes aware of her beauty and sexuality; while the Naturalistic *Rudimentär* (1912–14) shows the first glimmerings of Reason awakening in a Berlin semi-literate. Combining satire of the circumstances with sympathy towards its victims, *Rudimentär* brilliantly portrays the city milieu of the proletariat. With a nice irony, the plot reveals how the central suicide attempt fails because 'He' and 'She' cannot afford to pay for the gas. They behave instinctively, skittishly changing moods with neither reason nor logic. Ultimately, though, 'He' begins to think, rips the newspaper displaying the offending word '*Rudimentär*' from the wall and calls it nonsense: one senses a first insight into the human condition.

Stramm now radicalized his style in such plays as *Erwachen* (*Awakening*; 1914) and *Kräfte* (*Forces*; 1914–15), where the almost monosyllabic '*Telegrammstil*' invests every word with extraordinary resonance. In *Erwachen*, the tempo intensifies, the manner becomes hallucinatory, the style abstract. The plot concerns 'He', 'She' and 'It'. Once again, a specific milieu, this time a bourgeois one, provides the context, and a social fact – an adulterous couple about to be discovered in a hotel bedroom – the starting-point; but the insight, which once again forms the play's focus, now assumes a spiritual character. The irrational action gains added power through the conflict between the protagonist, 'He', and a realistic chorus, the mob; while 'He' stands for anonymous spirituality, 'She' for femininity, the febrile 'Crowd' asserts convention, greed and materialism. As the action approaches its apocalyptic climax which engulfs the whole town, 'She' succumbs to the pull of convention, leaving her younger sister 'It' to recognize the protagonist's quality, and undergo her own awakening. 'He', first condemned as the Devil, proves to be a Nietzschean 'Superman' or an Expressionist 'New Man' – the Architect of the whole town. The awakening self proves to be identical with creation as a whole.

In *Kräfte*, *Rudimentär*'s warring urges of hunger, sexuality and greed become the more abstract 'forces' of love and hate, wanting and refusing, which constantly conflict in the central figure, 'She', who in her inability to accept day and Light succumbs to the negative Night. In a dance of death, the play intimates all six possible binary relationships between the four main characters in terms of love or hate, or both. Because 'She' cannot countenance a *living* unity with her husband and their two friends, they ultimately achieve only negative unity in death.

'Here I am, sitting in a hole in the earth called a dug-out! Great! A candle, stove, chair, table. All modern comforts. The Culture of the 20th century. And up there, it's rattling all the time. Clack! Clack! Scht! Buzz! That's the Ethics of the 20th century. And the worms are crawling out of the mud beside me. That's the Aesthetics of the 20th century.'

25 March 1915

As a captain in the Reserve, Stramm was called up on the outbreak of war, joining the Ersatz Battalion of the newly formed Badener Landwehr-Infanterie-Regiment No. 110 as a company commander. The regiment was active in the Rhineland and the Vosges. From the start, Stramm had few illusions, and never joined in the so-called '*Hurrah-Patriotismus*': 'What will come,' he wrote to Walden on 2 August 1914, 'is inevitable, and that's that.' By 20 August, he was itching for battle, but his attitude quickly changed: 'What can I say? There is so infinitely much death in me death and death.' Glory there was none, but Stramm never renounced duty: 'Murder is duty, is heaven is God. Madness,' he concluded on 6 October. The constant theme of his letters is the horror, the inexpressibility of war: 'Where are words for the experience?'

In January 1915, Stramm became Commander of 9 Company III Battalion in the newly formed Infanterie-Reserve-Regiment No. 272, serving with the 41st Reserve-Corps in the trenches at Chaulnes, near St Quentin. His desperation intensified. 'But there is a horror in me,' he says on 14 February, 'there is horror around me, bubbling, surging around, throttling, ensnaring. There's no way out any more.' In April, the 41st was moved to the Eastern Front for the new offensive. Stramm fought in the crucial break-through at Gorlice, and took part in the almost uninterrupted pursuit of the Russians for some four months, as the front was pushed further and further back to the east. Physically and emotionally exhausted, increasingly, desperately alone as his companions fell around him, Stramm put more and more faith in his mystical ideas: 'Strangely,' he writes on 27 May, 'death and life are one, life is the surface and death the infinite space behind.'

At the time when the German High Command was debating whether or not to call a halt to the eastwards thrust, Stramm fell in action during a particularly unpleasant assault on a Russian position before the Dnepr–Bug Canal on 1 September 1915. He was buried at Horodec the next day.

Although the letters testify to profound inner turmoil, Stramm was a popular officer, and a brave soldier. He was awarded the Iron Cross 2nd Class in spring 1915, and was due to receive the 1st Class when he fell; he was also decorated with the Austrian Militärverdienstkreuz, which brought him a baronetcy. However, his poems tell a different story.

Like no others in German, Stramm's war poems give an immediate impression of the front. By eschewing a self-conscious persona, and treating the poem itself as a reality, Stramm thrusts intense images of the war directly before the reader. Exploiting all his newly perfected techniques, he precisely conveys the exact moments, the various horrors of war: the terror of being under fire in 'Im Feuer', shelling in 'Granaten', hesitation in 'Zagen', the difficult advance in 'Signal', the charge in 'Sturmangriff', combat in 'Haidekampf' or single combat in 'Urtod' ('Primal Death'). But there are also rare moments of beauty, as in the evening atmosphere of 'Abend', when the poet glimpses a higher being, the distant *Du*.

Although Stramm's rigorous, demanding style could never bring him the popular appeal of a Heym or Trakl, he has had a significant influence on German poetry. First, on the *Sturm* poets, including Kurt Heynicke, Otto Nebel and F. R. Behrens. Then, on Dadaism and Kurt Schwitters, who took Stramm as his starting-point. Later, after the Second World War, Stramm became the inspiration for experimental writers such as Gerhard Rühm, but his achievement also prefigures the mature techniques of Paul Celan, while today, several younger writers openly acknowledge his influence. Stramm's place as a modern classic seems assured.

JEREMY ADLER

Texts

René Radrizzani (ed.), *Das Werk* (Limes Verlag, Wiesbaden, 1963). The standard edition of Stramm's works.
René Radrizzani (ed.), *Dramen und Gedichte* (Reclam Verlag, Stuttgart, 1979).
Jeremy Adler (ed.), *Briefe aus dem Krieg* (Arche Verlag, Zurich, 1988).

Translations

'Sancta Susanna. The Song of a May Night' in *Poet Lore* (xxv, No. 6, 1914, pp. 514–22).
'The Bride of the Moor' in *Poet Lore* (xxv, No. 6, 1914, pp. 499–513). Translation of *Die Heidebraut*.
Patrick Bridgwater (trans.), *Twenty-Two Poems* (Brewhouse Press, Wymondham, 1969).
J. M. Ritchie (trans.), *Awakening* in *Seven Expressionist Plays* (Calder & Boyars, London, 1968). Reproduction of the translation of *Erwachen* by generous permission of the translator.

Secondary sources

Karin von Abrams, 'The "Du" of August Stramm's *Liebesgedichte*' in *Forum for Modern Language Studies* (xviii, 1982, pp. 299–312).
Jeremy Adler, 'On the Centenary of August Stramm: An Appreciation of *Geschehen*, *Rudimentär*, *Sancta Susanna* and "Abend" ' in *Publications of the English Goethe Society* (xliv, 1974, pp. 1–40).
Jeremy Adler, '*Urtod*: An Interpretation' in J. D. Adler & J. J. White (eds), *August Stramm: Kritische Essays und unveröffentliches Quellenmaterial aus dem Nachlaß des Dichters* (Erich Schmidt Institute of Germanic Studies, Berlin/London, 1979, pp. 84–97).
Patrick Bridgwater, 'The Sources of Stramm's Originality' in *August Stramm* (op. cit., pp. 31–46).
Patrick Bridgwater, *The German Poets of the First World War* (Croom Helm, London and Sydney, 1985, pp. 38–61).
Christoph Hering, 'The Genesis of an Abstract Poem: A Note on August Stramm' in *Modern Language Notes* (lxxvi, 1961, pp. 43–8).
M. S. Jones, *Der Sturm. A Focus of Expressionism* (Camden House, Columbia, 1984).
C. R. B. Perkins, 'August Stramm's Poetry and Drama: A Reassessment' (dissertation, University of Hull, 1972).
C. R. B. Perkins, 'August Stramm: His Attempts to Revitalize the Language of Poetry' in *New German Studies* (iv, 1976, pp. 141–55).
J. M. Ritchie, *German Expressionist Drama* (Twayne Publishers, Boston, 1976, pp. 53–7).
Richard Sheppard, 'The Poetry of August Stramm: A Suitable Case for Deconstruction', in *Journal of European Studies* (xv, 1985, pp. 261–94).
John White, 'Aspects of Typography and Layout in August Stramm's Poetry' in *August Stramm* (op. cit., pp. 47–68).

AWAKENING

HE
SHE
IT (GIRL)
HOTEL MANAGER
PORTER
MOB

Room in a hotel

Single beds side by side; on the opposite wall double doors; on the back wall between high windows a mirror. Valises and clothing scattered over chairs and bed-side tables.

SHE *in the front bed, sits up and stares into the dark.*

HE [*after some time*]. Why are you awake?

SHE *switches on the light on the bed-side table.*

HE [*takes hold of her arm, tenderly, concerned*]. Why are you awake?

SHE *rubs the sleep from face and hair, turns back the covers and pushes her feet into slippers on the floor.*

HE, *half sitting up, gazes intently at the back of her neck.*

SHE *presses her knees together and places her hands on them, peering round the room.*

HE [*sits up with a jerk, harshly*]. What are you staring at?

SHE *mumbles unintelligibly, gestures round the room with her left hand, flings herself down again, and hides her face in her hands.*

HE [*stares around the room, looks at her, leans over to her, gently*]. Dreams . . . [*His hand caresses her neck.*]

SHE *gives a convulsive start; her hands drop to the bed.*

HE [*reproachfully*]. Child!

SHE [*breathes*]. Don't touch me!

HE [*reassured*]. Darling!

SHE [*horrified*]. Don't touch me!

HE *takes away his hand.*

SHE *shudders.*

HE [*gently*]. What's wrong?

SHE [*cowers away, arms crossed and hands on shoulders, drily, tonelessly*]. I don't know.

HE [*in pyjamas, climbs into slippers, crosses to the door, shaking his head, and switches the overhead light on*]. There you are! [*Rushes about the room swinging his arms.*] Look! Just take a look!

SHE *lifts her head and peers around the room.*

HE [*stops centre between door and window and smiles at her with playful superiority*]. See anything?

SHE [*motionless*]. Yes . . . right there . . .!

HE. There's where *I* am!

SHE [*shudders*]. Yes [*checks carefully and nods*] yes!

HE [*goes up to her tenderly*]. You see.

SHE [*leaps up, wards him off, screams*]. Stop! Stop! Stop there!

HE [*taken aback, returns to the spot reluctantly*]. God!

SHE *scrutinizes him silently.*

HE [*irritated*]. It's stifling here! Let's be reasonable! [*Goes to the window.*]

SHE *goes to stop him, loses interest and wilts, moves forward to the foot of the bed and bends over to look at the spot where he was standing.*

HE [*pulls the curtain and looks back.*] Well? Something there?

SHE *raises her eyes to gaze out the window and gathers her nightdress tighter round her body, shuddering.*

HE [*hand on the window-latch*]. Feeling cold?

SHE. The night is wet.

HE [*stares at her, disconcerted*]. We are safe here! [*Goes over to her and steers her towards the bed.*]

SHE [*pushes him away*]. No! No!

HE. You've had a bad dream.

SHE [*resists weakly*]. I've been asleep.

HE [*sets her down on the bed*]. Then let's go back to sleep.

SHE [*looks around the room, asserting with interest, not fear*]. And there *is* something there!

HE [*impatiently*]. What? What can be?

SHE *gets up and looks curiously at the spot, gives a nod of confirmation.*

HE [*goes back and scrapes with his foot, roughly*]. Where can there be anything?

SHE [*controlled*]. Yes . . . exactly . . . where can there . . .? [*She glances in the mirror and puts her hair into place; stops short in horror.*] And what do I look like? I look like! Oh!

HE [*crossly*]. Leave the mirror alone!

SHE [*presses the palms of her hands against her temples*]. That's not me.

HE [*steps in front of her and blocks out the mirror*]. Who else?

SHE [*repeats after him*]. Yes . . . who . . .?

HE [*explodes*]. God Almighty! [*Controls himself and stamps his foot.*] Nothing!!

SHE [*stares at him horrified*]. Nothing! Nothing!

HE [*controlled*]. You're driving me mad too! Your illusion . . .

SHE [*with feeble resistance*]. Illusion . . . illusion . . .

HE [*seizes her arm roughly and shakes her.*] Be reasonable now.

SHE *screams and retreats from him in horror.*

HE [*lets her go and looks about him in helpless terror*]. What? What?

SHE [*exhausted*]. You are strangling me.

HE [*overstrained, weeps*]. But I . . . I . . . absolutely not a thing . . . I . . . [*Pleading before her with hands clenched fiercely.*]

SHE [*stirs after some time, rubs her wrist, shivers feebly*]. Yes! It is stifling here! Open the window!

HE [*beside himself flings round the room in a rage*]. No! No! No! [*Stops in the middle of the room.*]

SHE [*with feeble firmness*]. Open the window.

HE [*by the window, flings his fists apart as if bursting*

shackles]. All right, damn you! [*Fuming with rage, tears the window latch down with both hands.*] All right!!! [*The window collapses about him, the wall between the windows cracks wide open, the mirror shatters into the room.*]

HE *rigid amid the collapse.*

SHE *horrified.*

HE [*turns the window latch over in his hand, looking at it awe-struck*]. Rotten!

SHE *whimpers.*

HE [*looks across to her hesitantly*]. I didn't mean to do that! Oh!

SHE [*whimpers*]. The mirror.

HE *starts, flings the lever into the debris and rears into wild laughter.*

SHE [*trembling in horror*]. Oh! Oh! You! You! You're terrible! Terrible! You!

Voices, shouts, people running about outside the house. Noises inside.

The dust has dispersed through the great gap in the wall. A star flares in the inky night.

HE *laughs more calmly and reflectively; the laugh ripples away into silence; then stands quite still and looks up at the star.*

SHE [*cowers horrified on the bed, shaking hands clutching the bed-head and listening to approaching sounds at the door, babbles*]. C . . . c . . . coming.

HE [*calm, dreamily*]. See the star.

SHE *babbles unintelligibly.*

HE. Look though! The star!

SHE [*completely dissolved in horror*]. Kn . . . kn . . . knocking.

Violent knocking at the door, shouting, door handle is rattled fiercely.

HE *steps unconcerned further into the gap in the wall and gazes up at the star.*

SHE [*gives a start, hurriedly scrambles over to him, holds him back and babbles*]. You . . . you'll fall! You'll fall!

Heavy banging, rattling at the door; shouts: Hey! Hey there!

SHE [*pulls at him, crawling backwards*]. Listen! Listen will you!

HE *never takes his eyes off the star.*

SHE [*leaps up and shakes him wildly*]. For heaven's sake be . . . *Blows from heavy bar are heard against the door.*

HE *comes to himself, turns to the door and puts his arm round her protectively.*

Running and shouting outside in the street.

The door begins to give under the weight of curses and blows.

SHE *clings to his breast unconscious.*

HE [*carries her across the rubble, looks up at the star, says regretfully*]. Lost in the clouds!

The night turns black.

The door bursts open.

The HOTEL MANAGER *and the* PORTER *force their way in with crowbars, breathing heavily.*

HE *calmly lays her on the bed and tucks her in.*

MANAGER [*wildly threatening*]. You!

PORTER *with upraised crowbar stares dully at the heap of rubble.*

HE *looks up calmly.*

MANAGER [*in front of the pile of rubble, beside himself with rage*]. You're pulling my house down!

HE [*calmly*]. I.

MANAGER [*beside himself*]. You you you! Lie! Lie! Lie!

PORTER [*threatens clumsily*]. Fur chrissake!

HE [*calmly*]. The wall has collapsed.

MANAGER [*beside himself, repeating the words*]. The wall! The wall! The wall! [*Screams wilder and wilder.*] Godal! Godal! Godalmighty! Police! Police! Police! I'll have you arrested! I'll have . . .

PORTER [*joins in*]. Pleece, pleece.

HE [*gives a start, hurriedly*]. But what if I . . . [*Makes a sign*].

MANAGER [*stares at him*]. You you you. [*Gets the meaning and immediately changes tune.*] What?

HE [*calmly*]. Let's discuss this quietly. [*Signs for quiet.*] My wife . . .

MANAGER [*Suddenly all sympathy, puts down the crowbar and rubs his hands together*]. Oh!

PORTER *tugs off his cap in confusion and retreats slowly fiddling with the crowbar.*

MANAGER: We c'n fetch a doctor [*Turns to the* PORTER *who claps on his cap and does an about-turn raring to go.*] 'Kay.

PORTER [*raring to go*]. 'Kay.

HE [*hurriedly*]. No, no no stop! Many thanks! She'll manage all right . . .

Noise and din outside in the street.

Muffled thunder in the distance.

MANAGER [*embarrassed*]. Sure! Sure! [*Looks out.*] Take a look at that mob, willya! [*To porter.*] Get on down! Lock the door! See that scum don't get in!

PORTER [*shifts his cap*]. 'Kay. [*Hurries off in relief.*]

HE *pulls his cashbox out from under his pillow.*

MANAGER [*follows his movements, with fawning servility.*] You can have another room . . . sir . . . sir! [*Peal of thunder.*] That storm.

HE *opens the box which is bursting with gleaming gold coins.*

MANAGER *blinded, gurgles and gulps in confusion, holding out his hands for it greedily.*

HE [*counts a number of gold coins into the manager's hand*]. Is that enough?

MANAGER [*hopping from one leg to the other, stammers in the excitement of his greed*]. Come on. Come on.

HE [*firmly*]. That is enough!

MANAGER [*hesitantly*]. Aw no!

HE [*closes the strong box*]. Yes.

MANAGER [*firmly*]. Naw naw naw [*Seizes the box.*]

HE. You!!

MANAGER. You!!

HE *tries to tear the box free.*

MANAGER [*holds on*]. Get out of my way!

HE. Impudent wretch.

MANAGER [*tugs scornfully*]. Okay young fella, just be quiet will you? Quiet now? Keep your trap shut young fella. [*Tries with all his might to tear the box away.*]

HE. Ha!

MANAGER. I know! I know what's what! [*Meaningfully.*] Your wife.

HE [*furious*]. Swine!

MANAGER [*laughs fiercely*]. Yeh yeh. [*The box gets opened in the tussle; the gold coins roll out into the night.*]

MANAGER [*aghast*]. Oh! Oh! The money!

Rumble of thunder.

MANAGER. Ooh! Ooh! That lovely money! Money! [*Raises his fist against him, who is holding the empty box in perplexity.*] You! You!

Din, screaming and scuffling outside.

MANAGER [*trembling in all his limbs*]. What a pig! What a pig! What a ... [*Hustles to the door.*] Money! All that money! [*Loses coins, picks up, drops more.*] Oooh! [*Makes a frantic rush out into the mounting din outside.*]

HE *shakes the box to make sure it's empty and shakes his head.*

Lightning and loud thunder-clap.

SHE [*roused*]. What was that? What was that?

HE [*calmly mocking*]. Thunder!

SHE [*stares around*]. Where am I?

HE [*as before*]. Here!

SHE [*whimpers and listens*]. Roaring of the river.

HE. Roaring of the rabble.

SHE [*excited*]. That's water! Water! The river! We've crossed the river! Oh! So black! So black in the evening sun.

Wild screams, laughter, din, howls of derision, rattle of hailstones outside.

SHE [*hides in the bed whimpering*]. What's got into the people? What's got into the people?

HE [*calmly, contemptuous*]. My money.

SHE [*horrified*]. Ooh! Put out the light!

HE [*goes calmly to the door and turns off the light*]. Yes.

Lightning, thunder and hail.

The flickering reading lamp lights the bed corner; the rest of the room is in darkness.

SHE [*weeps*]. Oh! If only we were we.

HE [*interrupts rudely*]. What we?

Horrible scream, then sudden silence outside.

HE [*gives a start and peers out, steps back hurriedly*]. We can't stay here. [*Slips into his trousers.*]

Wild screams outside and lamentations: Murder! Murder!

HE [*frantic*]. Look! Get dressed? Get dressed? We must get away! Get away!

SHE [*hurries out of bed*]. Darling, darling. [*Trembling in every limb.*] If they if they if they find us here, if they ... [*Leans against the wall, exhausted.*]

HE [*snatches up her things and throws them to her in the corner*]. Quick, quick! No time.

SHE [*no will left, picks up her clothes – weakly*]. Darling, darling ... [*Lets her head fall back weakly.*]

HE [*urgently pulls on his jacket*]. Please please.

SHE. Darling I'm pregnant! I feel it!

HE *stares at her.*

Banging and shouting on the landing.

HE *hurries to the door to lock it.*

People crowd in at the door screaming.

HE *leaps back into the corner by the bed, which is naturally barricaded off by the heap of rubble, and places himself beside her protectively.*

SHE *by the window, hands supported behind her, stares at the intruders full of horror.*

WORKERS, TRADESMEN *and* YOUTHS *in the doorway are taken aback and fall silent at the sight of the couple, then step in carefully one after the other, peering around lewdly.*

Lightning followed by thunder.

THE CROWD [*moves closer lewdly*]. Wow! Wow! Ooah! Ooah! Oh! Oh! Oh! Take a look at that! Her nightie! Ooah! Shameless hussy! In a nightie! Ooah! [*Lecherous hands lust.*]

Some try to climb over the heap of rubble.

HE *rips open the drawer in the bedside table and pulls out a pistol.*

CONFUSION [*starts back*]. Will ye look at that! The dog! He's going to shoot! Pleece! Pleece! The dog! The dog! The dog! Put it down! [*Surge backwards and forwards, jeering.*] You! You! We'll get you! Kill 'm! The woman! The woman! His woman! His woman!

PEDLAR [*sneaks about*]. What do you know! Well, look at that! Well well! Take a look at that! Strike me dead! Strike me dead! Strike me dead! She's Lumpel's wife! Lumpel's wife! Lumpel the businessman, his wife! His wife! From Bunzel street!

CONFUSION [*shouts*]. From Bunzel street! From Bunzel street! Lumpel! Lumpel! Bunzel! Bunzel street!

PEDLAR [*shouts above the din*]. Yeh yeh yeh! She's Lumpel's wife all right! I'd know her anywhere! His wife!

SHOUTING AND SURGING FORWARD [*held in check by the revolver*]. Bastard! Swine! Women! What a dog! Get Lumpel! Lumpel! Lumpel!

SOME [*hurry away*]. We'll fetch him! We'll fetch him!

BURST OF LAUGHTER. Give him a nice surprise! Give him a nice surprise! Lumpel!

SHE *on the verge of collapse.*

HE *puts an arm round her, holding the pistol at the ready in the other hand.*

EXCITED SHOUTING [*does not dare come closer*]. Will you put that thing down! He'll shoot! He'll kill! It will end in bloodshed! Your life's not safe! Up here! Up here! Pleece! Pleece!

MEN, WOMEN, CHILDREN, YOUTHS [*storm through the doorway amid great din and shouting*]. They're bringing him! They're bringing him! They're coming with him! They got him! They have him! [*Mingled with lewd shouts directed to her.*] Oah! Oah! Oah! [*Frightened retreat as the gun is caught sight of.*] Oh! Oh! Put it down! Put it down!

TWO POLICEMEN *lead in the porter handcuffed, followed by folk and din.*

PORTER [*rushes violently at him*]. That's him! That's him!

POLICEMEN [*stop him*]. Silence! Stop!

CROWD [*screams*]. Grab him! Grab him!

SERGEANT [*enters*]. Silence! Silence here!

All fall silent.

PORTER [*in wild excitement tries to tear himself free and fling himself at him*]. That's him! That's him!

SERGEANT [*seizes him roughly by the scruff of the neck and shakes him*]. Who is?

PORTER [*wildly*]. Him him him him.

SERGEANT [*shakes him*]. Dog! Dog! You've killed the manager. [*Agitation in the crowd.*]

PORTER [*rebels*]. Dog dog dog! Money money money! He has the money the money the money.

CROWD *surge forward in agreement.*

SERGEANT [*calmly to him*]. Put down the gun.

HE lowers the gun.

PORTER [*howls, violently shaken*]. I'm an honest man! I've not hurt a fly! Not a fly! Always have been! Not a fly! What did he what did he chuck the money down for!

CROWD [*agrees*]. If somebody treats money like that! Money! Your own people kill for it! Kill!

SERGEANT *puts his hand roughly over the porter's mouth and looks around threateningly.*

All fall silent.

SERGEANT [*pulls out his notebook, gruffly*]. Who are you?

HE [*calmly, evading*]. Yes.

SERGEANT [*roughly*]. Who are you?

HE *does not answer.*

SERGEANT [*steps closer*]. Put that away!

HE *pushes the gun behind him on to the window sill.*

SERGEANT. For the last time! I'm asking who you are?

HE [*calmly*]. I travel.

CROWD *agitated and murmurs.*

SERGEANT [*flares up*]. For chrissake! [*Controls himself.*] All right! What do you travel with? What in? What for?

HE *does not answer.*

CROWD *becomes increasingly unsettled.*

SERGEANT [*furious*]. Will vou answer me? Will you? Is that your wife?

HE [*cold, incisive*]. Yes.

Thunder and lightning outside.

CROWD [*in shrill revolt*]. That's not true! That's not true! He's lying! He's lying! That's not his wife! That's not his wife! Not his wife! His wife! [*Surges forward threateningly.*]

SERGEANT *keeping them back with outstretched arms.*

HE *picks up the gun again.*

Thunder and lightning.

PROFESSORS, CIVIL SERVANTS, BUSINESSMEN, ARTISANS [*shout in wild confusion and press closer*]. She's my wife! My wife! My wife! She's my wife! My wife! Devil! Devil! My wife! [*The raised pistol time and again pushes back the threatening fists.*]

PEDLAR [*forces through arms flailing and roars above the noise*]. Be quiet! Not mad! Not mad! Just listen! Listen! She's Lumpel's wife! Lumpel the businessman, his wife! From Bunzel street! I know for sure! Bunzel! Lumpel! Lumpel! Bunzel!

SERGEANT. You whore!

CROWD [*catches on*]. Whore! Whore!

PEDLAR [*laughs jeeringly*]. His business is women! He travels in women! Women!

CROWD [*catches on, violently*]. He steals women! Our women! Our women!

BLACKSMITH [*leaps forward*]. He seduced my daughter! He seduced my daughter!

HIS WIFE [*holds him back*]. Joseph! Joseph!

BLACKSMITH. That's what he looked like! That's what he looked like! It was him.

HIS FRIEND [*pulls him away*]. Rubbish!

HIS WIFE [*hanging on to his arm*]. Joseph!

VARIOUS PEOPLE *pull and shove the smith back into the crowd.*

WHORE [*leaps forward, hands on hips, laughs coarsely*]. He's my lover! He's my lover-boy! That's who! You! Baby! You!

SERGEANT [*thrusts her back brutally and roars above the tumult*]. Silence!

Searing flash of lightning followed immediately by deafening peal of thunder.

Deathly silence for a moment, then the women give a screech and cross themselves.

SINGLE VOICES. He's driving us all mad! Nobody knows what he is! He makes the storm! [*Swelling.*] Storm! Storm! His fault! All his! The murder! The murder!

PORTER [*catches on*]. It was him! It was him! It was him! He did the murder! He caused it! I didn't mean to! I didn't mean to! I didn't mean to at all!

CONFUSION. He's the murderer! Murderer! Storm! Storm! Our houses tumble. Our houses collapse! Up! Up! Inside with him! Inside! Prison! Prison! Hard labour! Hang him! Hang him! Arrest him! Arrest him!

The pistol swings in a circle and holds back the frenzy.

SERGEANT [*draws his sabre, foaming at the mouth with rage*]. Put that gun down. You're under arrest! You're under arrest! You're under arrest! In the name of the law law law! Disturbing the peace, the peace! Disturbing the peace of the whole city!

Howl of approval.

SHOUTS [*penetrate*]. We were sitting in the local! Quietly! I've had to leave my drink standing!

PORTER [*through it all*]. I couldn't help myself! I couldn't help myself! I didn't mean to!

ALL [*surge up to him and ebb back*]. Murderer! Murderer! House wrecker! Murderer!

SERGEANT [*flailing blindly with his sabre at the pistol*]. Put it down! Put it down!

PORTER *struggles free and escapes.*

THE POLICEMEN *laboriously follow him, hampered by the throng.*

A female voice gives a long-drawn shriek from the door and paralyses the din.

Glare of fire flickers through the gap in the wall.

WOMAN. Let me through! Let me through! Let me through! Lumpel struck down. Old Lumpel! A stroke! A stroke! Struck him down like a sack of potatoes! Dead! Old Lumpel is dead! The minute we told him! Told him quite quietly! He's dead! [*Goes up to her in mad rage.*] Your husband's dead! Your husband's dead! Your husband.

The glare of fire gets brighter, sparks fly.

SHE *has started up in horror at the woman's screaming, then smiles, puts her arm round his neck and hides her face in his chest.*

WOMAN [*beside herself, in furious indignation*]. She's laughing! She's laughing! She's laughing! She's laughing!

COMMOTION. Something burning! Something burning!

SHOUTS [*outside and at the door*]. Fire! Fire! The lightning!

Alarm bells start to ring.

Klaxons and fire-engines outside.

CONFUSION [*shouts*]. Fire! Fire! The city hall is burning! The market is burning! The street is burning! Everything is burning! Burn! Fire! Fire! [*Flight and dispersal.*]

SERGEANT [*hurries off*]. Have the house surrounded! Have the house surrounded!

WOMAN. Just look! Just look! She doesn't move! Her husband is dead! She doesn't move! Her husband is dead! The devil has her in his clutches! The devil! [*Points in sudden illumination at him.*] He is the devil!

MEN AND WOMEN [*cross themselves*]. The devil! The devil!

WOMEN [*scream outside*]. Our children! Our children! [*More women hurry off.*]

SHE [*listens, giving a sigh of relief, breathes*]. Children!

HE [*holds her tighter*]. *My* child.

CONFUSION. He's set fire to the city! The city! The devil! Devil!

WOMAN. Get the minister! The minister!

VARIOUS. Get him to smoke him out! Smoke him out! Minister! Minister!

INDIVIDUALS *hurry off and bump into the girl.*

GIRL *comes in, holding two children of five and six by the hand.*

GIRL [*looking intimidated, steps forward*]. You, you your husband is dead! Your children.

CHILDREN *look around curiously, cling tight to the girl and cry.*

SHE *struggles free from him and stretches out her arms.*

HE [*holds her with all his might*]. You are lost.

CHILDREN [*see their mother and stretch out their arms shrieking*]. Mother! Mother!

SHE *held fast by him tries with outstretched arms to reach the children.*

HE. Stay stay! [*Holds her, straining every nerve.*]

SHE *pushes him back with wild shriek and collapses clasping the feet of her children.*

HE *stands stupefied and tautly strained.*

GIRL *gapes at him, horrified.*

MOB [*fall on her with a howl of fury*]. There she is! Hooh! Hah! We've got her! Right! Now! Grab her! Hey! This way! [SHE *is pulled to her feet.*] Out with her! Out!

WOMEN [*punch the unconscious woman in the face*]. Filthy bitch! Filthy bitch!

MEN [*push the women back*]. Get away! Get away! We'll have some fun! Some fun! Some fun!

WOMEN. She is a whore! [*Shout into her face.*] Whore! Whore!

MEN. She'll have to be broken in! Let's break her in! [*Trail, drag and push her to the door.*] The town whore! Going to be the town whore! Right away! [*Kick her brutally.*] Hoppla! Hoppla!

THE CHILDREN *hang on to her screaming.*

HE [*has been standing there intent on himself, now leaps with a shout of rage over the barricade of rubble flinging the pistol away, snatches up the centre cross of the window frame and smashes it down among them*]. Let go! Let go! Dogs! Scoundrels!

THE CROWD [*scatters in wild terror*]. The devil! The devil! The devil!

THE CHILDREN *let go their mother in horror and flee screaming.*

THE GIRL *presses herself hard against the wall beside the door and looks at him with enormous staring eyes.*

HE *storms after the crowd, comes back breathing heavily, throws the remains of the smashed window frame away contemptuously; as he looks around it all comes back to him and he bends down to her who is lying in a cringing heap on the floor in the middle of the room.*

HE [*places his hand on her hair, tenderly*]. Darling.

HE *tries to raise her up.*

SHE [*leaps up, twisting and writhing to get away, the palms of her hands extended against him in utmost horror*]. Oh you! Oh you! [*Utters a long-drawn scream.*] Oooooh!!! [*Raging violently hissing.*] You! You! The walls crumble! You!

THE GIRL *presses her fists to her mouth.*

HE [*steps over to her soothing*]. Strong strong!

SHE [*retreats from him to the door and clings to the door-jamb shouting back*]. You here! You! You here!

HE [*leaps after her and seizes her wrist*]. We'll escape we'll escape! We'll get through! Through the turmoil!

SHE [*writhes under his grasp and struggles, beside herself*]. Through! Through! Through! Escape! Escape! Escape! God! Devil! Heaven! Fire! People! You you you.

HE [*holds her*]. Be quiet! Be quiet! Quick!

SHE [*in utmost horror*]. Whore whore whore! Wife wife wife! I will! I will! Will I! Whore whore whore! Not your wife! Never your wife! Your wife! Not [*Tears free and rushes away, drawing out the word in a long scream*] your wiiiiiife!

HE *stands, his empty hands open wide to receive her and stares after her, then turns slowly, head hanging, crushed; clenches his fists in a sudden fit, gnashes his teeth, stamps over to the heaps of rubble, kicks the stones as if they were footballs, laughs with hollow scorn out into the night of flames, his whole body trembling with rage, howling hoarsely.*

A GREAT BELL *strikes, rattles, gives a shrill jarring sound and dies with an almighty crack.*

Din, screaming, lamenting, steadily spreading fierce rain of fire] The church! The church!

HE [*leaps into the gap, props his arms against the walls and roars out with the power of fury*]. Let the river in! Let the river in! Let the river into the streets! Into the gutters! Into the alleys! Let the river in! Open the dam! Open the dam! The devil! The dam!

THE SHOUT [*hurries further and further away into the distance outside*]. The dam! The dam! The dam!

HE [*roars*]. To the right! To the right! That's it! The sluice gates! Yes! Yes! That way! Idiots! That way!

WOMEN AND CHILDREN [*wail*]. Our houses! Our houses!

HE [*roars*]. We'll build them again! Build again! Build them again!

CONFUSED SHOUTS [*outside*]. Build! Build! Rebuild! Rebuild!

HE [*steps back over the rubble and laughs wildly, arms folded, nods in that direction and murmurs*]. Rebuild! Rebuild!

Almighty rushing outside, foaming and hissing.

THE GIRL *pressed hard against the wall stands absorbed in him.*

HE *looks up, groans, sighs and glances around helplessly; his glance takes fright at the* GIRL.

THE EYES *of both stare deep into each other.*

HE. You? You? Who are you? Who you?

THE GIRL [*stammers, confused, trembling*]. I . . . I.

HE *takes a step towards* GIRL.

GIRL *nestles against the wall stretching upwards.*

HE. What do you want here?

GIRL *stands fast staring at him.*

HE [*in front of the* GIRL, *looks into her face, astonished*]. Aren't you? Didn't you bring?

GIRL [*calmly, in an undertone*]. I am the sister.

HE. Sister?

GIRL. Her sister.

HE. Oooooh!! [*Considers* GIRL, *after a while*]. What do you want here? What's the matter with you?

GIRL [*coldly, dispassionately*]. I don't know.

HE. Aren't you afraid?

GIRL *does not answer and stares at him.*

HE. Aren't you afraid? [*Calmly with gentle mockery.*] Heaven fire people! I caused the crime!

GIRL [*calmly*]. I identified you.

HE *snaps upright.*

GIRL. You sir . . . my friend . . . built the church.

HE *stares and nods, folds his arms tight.*

GIRL. The city hall.

HE [*advances one foot*]. You know that?

GIRL [*warmer, livelier*]. The school! The dam!

HE *nods and rocks his body.*

GIRL [*exhausted, breathes*]. I identified! Identified you!

HE [*steps even nearer to her, gently, hesitantly*]. You? You? Sister? GIRL *trembles.*

HE [*hard up against the* GIRL, *whispers hotly*]. Sister?

GIRL *trembles and clings with great effort to the wall.*

HE [*bends over, without touching, his hands clasped tight behind his back*]. You're afraid?

SHE *lays back her head and looks up into his eyes, her whole body trembling.*

The fiery glow outside dies down, distant shouting.

THEIR EYES *locked in each other.*

HE [*giving a sigh of relief*]. She was awakened! Your sister.

SHE *spreads her arms wide against the wall.*

HE [*gently, groping*]. Yes suddenly awakened.

SMOKE *devours the flames, hissing, roaring.*

The shouting comes nearer.

HE. You! You wake up! You! Wake up you! Do you hear! If . . . you . . . awake.

SHE *raises her hand silencing him.*

VOICES OF WOMEN AND CHILDREN [*outside*]. The master builder it was! That was the master builder! [*Rejoicing.*] *Our* master builder master builder master builder.

MEN'S VOICES *mix in, questioning, enquiring.*

HE [*gently seeking bemoaning*]. Others.

WOMEN, CHILDREN, MEN [*call on the landing*]. Master builder. Our master builder! Our master builder!

SHE *gives a start and places herself between him and the door protectively.*

HE *steps between her and the door, smiling, looking over his shoulder to the door.*

SHE [*clasps her hands together and whispers looking up to him*]. Husband!

WOMEN AND CHILDREN [*storm in through the door*]. masterbuil . . . [*The word dies away in fixed stare.*]

A LITTLE BELL *rings for matins.*

THE WOMEN AND CHILDREN *cower down, hands clasped.*

MEN *staring in at the door over their heads, take their caps off and stand mute in silent reverence.*

HE [*strokes her hair and lets his hand rest on her head, gently happy*]. Wife!

The last red glow is extinguished, it grows quite dark outside.

ETHEREAL NIGHT MISTS *waft in through the gap in the wall and dim the room.*

THE STAR *flares up brilliantly.*

HE and SHE *turn round slowly and arm in arm look up to* THE STAR *in close embrace.*

TRANSLATED BY J. M. RITCHIE

Du.
Liebesgedichte

Liebeskampf

Das Wollen steht
Du fliehst und fliehst
Nicht halten
Suchen nicht
Ich
Will
Dich
Nicht!
Das Wollen steht
Und reißt die Wände nieder
Das Wollen steht
Und ebbt die Ströme ab
Das Wollen steht
Und schrumpft die Meilen in sich
Das Wollen steht
Und keucht und keucht
Und keucht
Vor dir!
Vor dir
Und hassen
Vor dir
Und wehren
Vor dir
Und beugen sich
Und
Sinken
Treten
Streicheln
Fluchen
Segnen
Um und um
Die runde runde hetze Welt!
Das Wollen steht!
Geschehn geschieht!
Im gleichen Krampfe
Pressen unsre Hände
Und unsre Tränen
Wellen
Auf
Den gleichen Strom!
Das Wollen steht!
Nicht Du!
Nicht Dich!
Das Wollen steht!
Nicht
Ich!

You.
Love Poems

Love-Fight

The wanting stands
You flee and flee
Not holding
Seeking not
I
Want
You
Not!
The wanting stands
And tears the walls right down
The wanting stands
And ebbs the streams away
The wanting stands
And shrinks the miles to nil
The wanting stands
And pants and pants
And pants
Before you!
Before you
And hating
Before you
And fighting
Before you
And bowing down
And
Sinking
Treading
Stroking
Cursing
Blessing
Round about
The round round hunted world!
The wanting stands!
Process proceeds!
In selfsame cramp
Press our hands
And our tears
Well
Up
The selfsame stream!
The wanting stands!
Not you!
Not thee!
The wanting stands!
Not
I!

Translated by Jeremy Adler

MONDBLICK

An meine Augen spannt der Schein.
Das Schläfern glimmt in deine Kammer
Gelbt hoch hinauf
Und
Schwület mich!
Matt
Bleicht das Bett
Und
Streift die Hüllen
Stülpt frech das Hemd
Verfröstelt
Auf den Mond.
Jetzt
Leuchtest du
Du
Leuchtest leuchtest!
Glast
Blaut die Hand
In glühewehe Leere
Reißt nach den Himmel
Mond und Sterne
Stürzen
Schlagen um mich
Wirbeln
Tasten
Halt Halt Halt!
Und
Zittern aus zu Ruh
Am alten Platz!
In
Deinem Fenster droben
Gähnmüd
Blinzt
Die Nacht!

MOONGAZE

The shine tautens on my eyes.
The drowsiness glimmers to your room
Yellows high up
And
Stifles me!
Weak
Pales the bed
And
Feels the sheets
Pertly grabs the blouse
And freezes
On the moon.
Now
You shine
You
Shine shine!
Glare
Blues the hand
In glowing pain-filled emptiness
Tears at the sky
The moon and stars
Fall down
And beat about me
Whirling
Feeling
Stop stop stop!
And
Tremble to rest
At the old place.
In
Your window high-up-there
Yawning-tired
Blinks
The night.

TRANSLATED BY JEREMY ADLER

VERZWEIFELT

Droben schmettert ein greller Stein
Nacht grant Glas
Die Zeiten stehn
Ich
Steine.
Weit
Glast
Du!

DESPAIR

Above smashes a piercing stone
Night grinds glass
Time stands
I
Stone.
Far
Glaze
You!

TRANSLATED BY JEREMY ADLER

Freudenhaus

Lichte dirnen aus den Fenstern
Die Seuche
Spreitet an der Tür
Und bietet Weiberstöhnen aus!
Frauenseelen schämen grelle Lache!
Mutterschöße gähnen Kindestod!
Ungeborenes
Geistet
Dünstelnd
Durch die Räume!
Scheu
Im Winkel
Schamzerpört
Verkriecht sich
Das Geschlecht!

House of Pleasures

Lights are whoring through the windows!
The sickness
Sprides beside the door
And plies with female groans!
Woman souls are shaming garish laugh!
Mother wombs are yawning children-death!
The unborn
Ghosting
Simmer
Through the rooms!
Shy
In hiding
Shamedestraught
Human sex
Crawls off.

Translated by Jeremy Adler

Heimlichkeit

Das Horchen spricht
Gluten klammen
Schauer schielen
Blut seufzt auf
Dein Knie lehnt still
Die heißen Ströme
Brausen
Heiß
Zu Meere
Und
Unsere Seelen
Rauschen
Ein
In
Sich.

Secrecy

The harking speaks
Fires clamming
Shudders blinking
Blood sighs out
Your knee leans still
The hot streams
Roaring
Hot
To sea
And
Our souls
Rush
In
To
Each.

Translated by Jeremy Adler

Schwermut

Schreiten Streben
Leben sehnt
Schauern Stehen
Blicke suchen
Sterben wächst
Das Kommen
Schreit!
Tief
Stummen
Wir.

Melancholy

Striding striving
Living yearns
Shudders standing
Glances seeking
Dying grows
The coming
Screams!
Deep
Dumb
We.

Translated by Jeremy Adler

Allmacht

Forschen Fragen
Du trägst Antwort
Fliehen Fürchten
Du stehst Mut!
Stank und Unrat
Du breitst Reine
Falsch und Tücke
Du lachst Recht!
Wahn Verzweiflung
Du schmiegst Selig
Tod und Elend
Du wärmst Reich!
Hoch und Abgrund
Du bogst Wege
Hölle Teufel
Du siegst Gott!

Almighty

Seeking searching
You nod answer
Fleeing fearing
You stand brave!
Foul and garbage
You spread pureness
Guile and mischief
You laugh right!
Crazing madness
You feel blissful
Death and sickness
You warm rich!
Peak and abyss
You turn pathways
Hell and devils
You triumph God!

Translated by Jeremy Adler

Wunder

Du steht! Du steht!
Und ich
Und ich
Ich winge
Raumlos zeitlos wäglos
Du steht! Du steht!
Und
Rasen bäret mich
Ich
Bär mich selber!
Du!
Du!
Du bannt die Zeit
Du bogt der Kreis
Du seelt der Geist
Du blickt der Blick
Du
Kreist die Welt
Die Welt
Die Welt!
Ich
Kreis das All!
Und du
Und du
Du
Stehst
Das
Wunder!

Wonder

You stands! You stands!
And I
And I
I wing
Spaceless timeless weightless
You stands! You stands!
And
Rage gives birth
I
Birth my self!
You!
You!
You spells the time
You bends the sphere
You minds the soul
You looks the look
You
Rounds the world
The world
The world!
I
Round the All!
And you
And you
You
Stands
The
Wonder!

Translated by Jeremy Adler

DÄMMERUNG

Hell weckt Dunkel
Dunkel wehrt Schein
Der Raum zersprengt die Räume
Fetzen ertrinken in Einsamkeit!
Die Seele tanzt
Und
Schwingt und schwingt
Und
Bebt im Raum
Du!
Meine Glieder suchen sich
Meine Glieder kosen sich
Meine Glieder
Schwingen sinken sinken ertrinken
In
Unermeßlichkeit
Du!

Hell wehrt Dunkel
Dunkel frißt Schein!
Der Raum ertrinkt in Einsamkeit
Die Seele
Strudelt
Sträubet
Halt!
Meine Glieder
Wirbeln
In
Unermeßlichkeit
Du!

Hell ist Schein!
Einsamkeit schlürft!
Unermeßlichkeit strömt
Zerreißt
Mich
In
Du!
Du!

TWILIGHT

Bright wakes dark
Dark stops shine
Space explodes the spaces
Fragments drown in loneliness!
The spirit dances
And
Swings and swings
And
Quakes in space
You!
My limbs seek self
My limbs caress
My limbs
Swinging sinking sinking drowning
In
Boundlessness
You!

Bright stops dark
Dark eats shine!
Space drowns in loneliness
The spirit
Eddies
Struggles
Halt!
My limbs
Whirling
In
Boundlessness
You!

Bright is shine!
Loneliness drinks deep!
Boundlessness streams
Destroys
Me
In
You!
You!

TRANSLATED BY JEREMY ADLER

TROPFBLUT
GEDICHTE AUS DEM KRIEG

SCHLACHTFELD

Schollenmürbe schläfert ein das Eisen
Blute filzen Sickerflecke
Roste krumen
Fleische schleimen
Saugen brünstet um Zerfallen.
Mordesmorde
Blinzen
Kinderblicke.

BLOOD DROP
POEMS FROM THE WAR

BATTLEFIELD

Lumpish-mellow lulls to sleep the iron
Bleedings filter oozing stains
Rusts crumble
Fleshes slime
Sucking lusts around decay.
Murders' murders
Blinking
Child-like eyes.

TRANSLATED BY JEREMY ADLER

WUNDE

Die Erde blutet unterm Helmkopf
Sterne fallen
Der Weltraum tastet.
Schauder brausen
Wirbeln
Einsamkeiten.
Nebel
Weinen
Ferne
Deinen Blick.

WOUND

The earth bleeds under the helm-head
Stars fall
The cosmos touches.
Horrors roaring
Whirling
Lonelinesses.
The mists
Crying
Distance
Your gaze.

TRANSLATED BY JEREMY ADLER

ABEND

Müde webt
Stumpfen dämmert
Beten lastet
Sonne wundet
Schmeichelt
Du.

EVENING

Weary weaves
Stumping twilights
Prayer burdens
Sunlight wounds
Flatters
You.

TRANSLATED BY JEREMY ADLER

STURMANGRIFF

Aus allen Winkeln gellen Fürchte Wollen
Kreisch
Peitscht
Das Leben
Vor
Sich
Her
Den keuchen Tod
Die Himmel fetzen.
Blinde schlächtert wildum das Entsetzen.

CHARGE

From every corner yelling terror wanting
Shriek
Whips
Life
On
Before
It
Gasping death
The heavens tatter.
Blindly slaughters wild-about the horror.

TRANSLATED BY JEREMY ADLER

SIGNAL

Die Trommel stapft
Das Horn wächst auf
Und
Sterben stemmt
Das Haupt durch flattre Sterben
Sträubt
Gehen Gehen
Sträuben
Geht
Und geht und geht
Und geht und geht
Und geht und geht und geht und geht
Geht
Stapft
Geht.

SIGNAL

The drumbeat plods
The horn climbs up
And
Dying stems
The head through flutter dyings
Struggles
Going going
Struggling
Goes
And goes and goes
And goes and goes
And goes and goes and goes and goes
Goes
Plods
Goes.

TRANSLATED BY JEREMY ADLER

GEFALLEN

Der Himmel flaumt das Auge
Die Erde krallt die Hand
Die Lüfte sumsen
Weinen
Und
Schnüren
Frauenklage
Durch
Das strähne Haar.

FALLEN

The heavens wing the eye
The earth claws the hand
The winds are buzzing
Crying
And
Tying
Women's moaning
Through
The strandy hair.

TRANSLATED BY JEREMY ADLER

URTOD

Raum
Zeit
Raum
Wegen
Regen
Richten
Raum
Zeit
Raum
Dehnen
Einen
Mehren
Raum
Zeit
Raum
Kehren
Wehren
Recken
Raum
Zeit
Raum
Ringen
Werfen
Würgen
Raum
Zeit
Raum
Fallen
Sinken
Stürzen
Raum
Zeit
Raum
Wirbeln
Raum
Zeit
Raum
Wirren
Raum
Zeit
Raum
Flirren
Raum
Zeit
Raum
Irren
Nichts.

PRIMAL DEATH

Space
Time
Space
Waying
Rising
Righting
Space
Time
Space
Stretching
Joining
Swarming
Space
Time
Space
Turning
Spurning
Racking
Space
Time
Space
Wrestling
Throwing
Throttling
Space
Time
Space
Falling
Sinking
Plunging
Space
Time
Space
Whirling
Space
Time
Space
Whirring
Space
Time
Space
Flirring
Space
Time
Space
Erring
Nil.

TRANSLATED BY JEREMY ADLER

IM FEUER

Tode schlurren
Sterben rattert
Einsam
Mauert
Welttiefhohe
Einsamkeiten.

UNDER FIRE

Deaths shuffle
Dying rattles
Lonely
Walls up
World-deep-high
Lonelinesses.

TRANSLATED BY JEREMY ADLER

HAIDEKAMPF

Sonne Halde stampfen keuche Bange
Sonne Halde glimmet stumpfe Wut
Sonne Halde sprenkeln irre Stahle
Sonne Halde flirret faches Blut
Blut
Und
Bluten
Blut
Und
Bluten Bluten
Dumpfen tropft
Und
Dumpfen
Siegt und krustet
Sonne Halde flackt und fleckt und flackert
Sonne Halde blumet knosper Tod.

HEATH COMBAT

Sunshine hillside stamping panting fear
Sunshine hillside glimmers stumping rage
Sunshine hillside sprinkling crazy steel
Sunshine hillside flitting fanning blood
Blood
And
Bleeding
Blood
And
Bleeding bleeding
Dudding drops
And
Dudding
Wins and crusters
Sunshine hillside flares and flakes and flickers
Sunshine hillside budding bloomy death.

TRANSLATED BY JEREMY ADLER

GRANATEN

Das Wissen stockt
Nur Ahnen webt und trügt
Taube täubet schrecke Wunden
Klappen Tappen Wühlen Kreischen
Schrillen Pfeifen Fauchen Schwirren
Splittern Klatschen Knarren Knirschen
Stumpfen Stampfen
Der Himmel tapft
Die Sterne schlacken
Zeit entgraust
Sture weltet blöden Raum.

SHELLS

The knowing stops
Just sensing weaves and tricks
Deafness deadens terror wounds
Banging tapping churning screeching
Shrilling whistling hissing whizzing
Splinting clapping cracking creaking
Stumping stamping
The heavens tamp
Stars dross
Time dishorrors
Stubborn worldens foolish space.

TRANSLATED BY JEREMY ADLER

ZAGEN

Die Himmel hangen
Schatten haschen Wolken
Ängste
Hüpfen
Ducken
Recken
Schaufeln schaufeln
Müde
Stumpf
Versträubt
Die
Gehre
Gruft.

HESITATION

The heavens hanging
Shadows catching clouds
Terrors
Hopping
Ducking
Stretching
Digging digging
Tired
Dull
Desisting
The
Gory
Grave.

TRANSLATED BY JEREMY ADLER

KRIEGGRAB

Stäbe flehen kreuze Arme
Schrift zagt blasses Unbekannt
Blumen frechen
Staube schüchtern.
Flimmer
Tränet
Glast
Vergessen.

WAR GRAVE

Sticks imploring crossing arms
Writing timids pale unknown
Flowers cheek
Dusts shy.
Flickers
Tear
Glare
Oblivion.

TRANSLATED BY JEREMY ADLER

*R*EINHARD *J*OHANNES *S*ORGE 1892–1916

'I suppose it is the imperfection of it all that I feel, and then the longing for our life together breaks through; but soon my soul is soothed and consoled by the conviction that this period has to be, that without it there can be no perfection.'

Sorge on the war

Reinhard Sorge wanted to join the priesthood when the war broke out in 1914. He had already assumed the cognomen 'Johannes' as a sign of his devotion to the prophet John the Baptist. However by October 1915 he had been called up to the Belgian front. On 20 July 1916, at Ablaincourt on the Somme, a grenade exploded, shattering both his thighs, and he died of his wounds. A year later, the day before Christmas Eve, the distinguished theatre producer, Max Reinhardt, mounted the world première of Sorge's first play *Der Bettler* (*The Beggar, A Dramatic Mission*). The play was already six years old, but was a *succès de scandale*, an innovation, changing the course of theatrical history with its revolutionary staging techniques.

Sorge was born in the Berlin suburb of Rixdorf on 29 January 1892 to a Protestant family of Huguenot extraction. The blight of his childhood was his father's mental illness. To escape the oppressive atmosphere at home, Sorge was sent to East Prussia to live with a parson and his family. Here he recovered an inner balance, a sense of purpose which was essentially Christian and which laid the foundations for his future development. The death of his insane father in 1909 prompted his family to move to Jena, where Sorge struck up an acquaintance with the much-honoured German poet Richard Dehmel and absorbed the neo-romantic influences of the day. Sorge's enthusiasm for Nietzsche and the message of his zealous prophet Zarathustra was initially all-embracing, but short-lived. By 1911, Sorge was striking out in a new direction and with a new mission. The result was the story of his development as a writer, *Der Bettler*, written in the last three months of 1911.

While showing the results of his work to friends in Denmark, Sorge made a trip to the popular beach resort of Norderney in northern Germany. There Sorge had a mystical experience which changed his outlook, his life, and the nature of his writings. On the strength of *Der Bettler*, he was awarded the prestigious Kleist Prize of 1912 – an honour which he owed to Richard Dehmel. He used the proceeds to travel to Rome with his newly wed wife Susanne and there he was received into the Roman Catholic Church. All his subsequent dramas were to be centred on fervently religious themes: 'Thenceforth my pen has been and forever will be only Christ's stylus – until my death.'

This was not such an about-turn as it may have seemed to his contemporaries. In a letter of 1913, Sorge explained, 'My soul was always inherently Christian, but I was misled by Nietzsche, entangled in suns and stars. In *Der Bettler*, I invoked the name of God many a time quite unconsciously, and yet thought myself a fervent disciple of Nietzsche, who denies God's very existence.' Sorge's admirers lamented the regressive tendency in his dramatic writing after his conversion, a contrast to the revolutionary form which *Der Bettler* had seemed to initiate.

Although not the first Expressionist play ever performed (Walter Hasenclever's *Der Sohn* of 1914 has this to its credit), *Der Bettler* legitimately lays claim to being the first Expressionist play ever written. Its 'expressionism' lies in its subjective staging techniques as much as in the typical theme of interdependence of Patron–Poet, Father–Son – the problem inherent in biting the hand that feeds one. The central figure, the Poet, does just that in the first scene: he rejects a generous offer of a long-term annuity from a Patron of the arts who is impressed by his talents. The offer is made on the condition that the Poet devotes all his time to perfecting his art. The Poet, on the other hand, wants to implement his experimental dramas on a stage of his own, and dismisses the Patron's offer in favour of an unrealizable dream of a 'communionist' theatre.

This act sets the Poet on a journey of self-discovery, and he proceeds through an obstacle course of temptation in order to find salvation. By saving another soul – that of the Girl – from despair, he appears to succeed. He first steers a course between the temptations of the twin parasites of the theatre – the Prostitutes on the one hand and the Critics on the other. He then destroys through patricide the megalomaniacal and insane delusions of material power nursed by the Father. By shedding the burdens of the material world, the Poet sets out on his mission to prepare for a New World.

It is the form rather than the content which makes *Der Bettler* of major interest. Michael Patterson in his chapter on 'The Theory of Expressionist Theatre' in *The Revolution in German Theatre* describes the staging:

> The play opens with an ingenious inversion: the Poet and Friend converse in front of the closed curtain, behind which voices can be heard. It appears that we, the real audience, are backstage and the voices are those of the imagined audience out front. It is a simple but disorienting trick of stagecraft, whose imaginative spatial reversal is self-consciously

'Look at our people! Their souls have degenerated towards death with the burdens of the night.'
Sorge in a poem to his wife

theatrical. So the audience is alerted to the fact that they are about to see a play and not a 'slice of life'.

When the curtain then draws back, we see a scene reminiscent of the simultaneous staging of the medieval theatre, but with the introduction of a modern dimension – directional spotlighting. The scene is a coffee-house with a raised level to the rear up to which a central flight of steps leads. On the lower level, to the right, are cutomers at their tables, who speak quietly since they are, according to the stage directions, merely 'decoration'. To their left is a more open area, occupied, in turn, by Newspaper-readers, Critics, Prostitutes and Airmen. On the upper level appear the Poet with his Friend and his Patron, and to their right in an alcove sit the Girl and Nurse. Each of these acting areas is picked out in turn by a spotlight, not merely as a theatrical device, but, as Sokel says, as a means of suggesting the mental processes in the mind of the Poet: 'The lighting apparatus behaves like the mind. It drowns in darkness what it wishes to forget and bathes in light what it wishes to recall. Thus the entire stage becomes a universe of [the] mind, and the individual scenes are not replicas of three-dimensional physical reality, but visualized stages of thought.

Moreover, the very quality of lighting is expressive. The alcove in which the Girl sits is lit from a hidden source (Sorge repeats this requirement twice) and the window behind her looks on to a night sky with a shining star and scudding clouds; by contrast, the Prostitutes are lit by the single beam of a spotlight falling diagonally across the stage, and 'their voices contribute to the harsh effect of the naked spotlight'. Lighting here is no longer merely a method of illuminating the stage but is an expressive device to communicate meaning. In other words, it has become an art-form, judged not by verisimilitude but by effectiveness. Sorge's understanding of abstract setting is also impressive. The Poet, by adhering firmly to his principles, has to part with both Patron and Friend, and, speaking of the burdens fate has cast upon him, slowly descends the central staircase to the now deserted lower level. It is a powerful visual image of the artist turning from the exploitation of his art to descend wearily into the wilderness; it is also the first of many expressionistic uses of a flight of steps on stage.

The genius of the 20-year-old Sorge already showed the possibilities of abstract staging, and Reinhardt in 1917, simply by following Sorge's stage directions, was to become the first director to present

'This new drama can only become effective and genuinely fruitful if it's staged.'
The Poet in Der Bettler

a play in a wholly Expressionist style: '*Der Bettler* is performed on an empty stage. There is no pretence, no construction to reduce the space. The light tears out a piece of the great black space, which untouched and limitless, seems to be waiting to be filled: the action takes place here. Or a man stands alone, as a patch of light in front of a black surface. In this darkened space a room is defined by a few pieces of furniture, window and door-frames and free-hanging pictures; a birch in blue light represents a garden. One is a long way from reality. At every moment, reality is sacrificed for inner truth, most boldly and most successfully, I feel, when a starry sky appears over the heads of the lovers in their room without walls or ceiling.'

Other expressionist writers sought to depict spiritual regeneration through some vaguely mystical symbolism (as, for instance, when August Stramm's messiah in *Erwachen* (q.v.) is anointed by a symbolic star). By converting to Roman Catholicism, Sorge had found a stable framework within which he could expound specific, not abstruse ideas. The Catholic religion may have provided him with spiritual fulfilment, yet this was the very cause of his inability to fulfil the expectations of the avant-garde literary world. For the advancement of modern theatre, the Poet with a message proved to be a false prophet.

TIM CROSS

Texts

Hans Gerd Rötzer (ed.), *Werke* (Nuremberg, 1962–7). Complete works in 3 vols. Including plays: *Der Bettler: eine dramatische Sendung* (first published by S. Fischer, Berlin, 1912); *Guntwar: die Schule eines Propheten* (1914); *Metanoeite: drei Mysterien* (1915); *König David* (1916).
The Sorge manuscripts and letters are held at the Deutsche Literaturarchiv, Marbach am Neckar, West Germany.

Secondary sources

R. Samuel and R. H. Thomas, *Expressionism in German Life, Literature and the Theatre 1910–24* (Cambridge, Massachusetts, 1939).
Walter H. Sokel, *The Writer in Extremis* (Stanford University Press, California, 1959). Quoted in text.
Claude Hill and Ralph Ley, *The Drama of German Expressionism – A German–English Bibliography* (University of North Carolina Press, Chapel Hill, 1960). A comprehensive listing of R. J. Sorge's published and unpublished works with an extensive bibliography of reviews and articles on Sorge's output and Susanne Sorge's story of her life with the playwright, *Unser Weg* (J. Kösel, Kempten–Munich, 1927).
Michael Patterson, *The Revolution in German Theatre 1900–33* (Routledge & Kegan Paul, Boston and London, 1981). Passage from 'The Theory of Expressionist Theatre' reproduced with permission of the author.

THE BEGGAR

Act I, Scene 6

As the main lights go down, lights up on the rest of the upstage area; sitting more or less centre stage: THE PATRON, THE OLDER FRIEND *and* THE POET, *eating a meal. A* WAITER *walks to and fro.*

THE POET [*almost as soon as the lights come up*]. You've interpreted the aims I've set myself very clearly from my writing; so I can now talk to you with more hope of a positive outcome than I had before. Though it's hard to explain what I really think about it all. I'm bound to seem immature, I expect, and off-target – if you follow me?

[*short pause*]

My friend's talked to you about my situation – you know the climate I'm forced to work in – And theatres turn my plays down. There's so much that's new in them they're reluctant to take the plunge with a production.

THE PATRON. I totally agree. Unluckily for you, your plays keep getting more curious, more alien, and the upshot is – if I may speak frankly – that you've got less and less chance of being accepted. No one can know for certain of course . . .

THE POET. I'm glad you anticipate the same sort of response as I do – it'll be easier for you to understand the rest of what I say. The sheer impossibility of getting work on – that's what hamstrings me most. Because for me production is vital – the ultimate fulfilment of my own creativity and my responsibility towards Creation.

THE OLDER FRIEND. Remember what I told you – please!

[*short pause*]

THE POET. As you'll appreciate, it can't mean that much to me to see my plays in print – publication is only ever a halfway house, never an end in itself – the end is production. So all I have to ask of you is this: help me establish a theatre of my own.

THE OLDER FRIEND. Talk sense! That's ridiculous!

THE POET. Let me finish. I've given the matter a lot of thought.

THE PATRON. Yes, sir, let him finish . . .

THE OLDER FRIEND. I only want what's best for you. This would never be in your best interests.

THE POET. I've thought it over and looked at it from every angle. I've weighed up all the other possibilities open to me, but I keep coming back to the same conclusion – I must be performed. I see my writing as the foundation, the starting-point of a dramatic renaissance. Just now, you said something of the sort yourself. But this new drama can only be effective and genuinely fruitful if it's staged. My only option is to have a theatre of my own.

THE PATRON. You talk about a New Drama, and if you look at our modern dramatic literature you certainly have a case. What's more, as far as I can see, your plays are so pregnant with meaning it's easy to understand your high opinion of yourself. At all events, I assure you I do appreciate the way you're thinking and why you've reached the decision you have. So if I still suggest a different alternative, it's not because I don't understand but because I have greater insight. And I think your immediate future could turn out very differently. As much as I sympathize with what you're asking, I can see so many risks and problems in putting your plays on, it seems to me we might have to try another way out, and I think I've come up with one.

Reinhard Sorge, *c.* 1914

THE POET. Tell me!

THE PATRON. I think my suggestion is both positive and supportive. I'll provide you with an allowance – generous enough to enable you to live for the next few years just as you choose. More than anything – in my opinion – you need to do a lot of travelling now. You're in danger of becoming sterile unless you seek out new experiences in the world around you. Give it a trial for ten years or so, then we can review the situation. You'll have produced a solid body of work, and reduced the element of risk. What do you say?

THE OLDER FRIEND. Your destiny's in your own hands!

[*short pause*]

THE POET. Sir, I've thought hard about this possibility but rejected it. It isn't the world around me I need in order to create new work. I have to develop my dramatic technique by getting the old work staged. I must be able to test out – in a practical way – the limits of performance, where the boundaries of all drama lie. This is where my writing falls down. Only if I can master these techniques will I be able to cultivate them until they produce mature fruit. The outside world is only of secondary importance to me, and I'll never run the risk of sterility! My vocation demands I follow this path unswervingly, which is why I must say no.

THE PATRON. You don't realize what you're saying, sir! You fail to grasp the overwhelming advantage of my suggestion: the chance to learn your craft in absolute peace and quiet. This is essential to you. Productions would probably do you more harm than good. They'd demand so much of your entire personality you'd not have proper peace and quiet to work in. And it's only in peace and quiet your work can flourish.

THE POET. I will be able to combine writing my plays with putting them on. It's my vocation, so I am capable of it.

THE PATRON. I'm sorry, but you're entering the realms of fantasy. Please let's keep our feet firmly on the ground.

Act II, Scene 1

In front of a curtain.

THE FATHER *in a blue dressing-gown. He is beating a brightly coloured child's drum with an oversize drumstick. We can hear the first drumbeats while the curtain is still shut. Then, as the stage opens up, they become increasingly rapid. Now they follow each other with the speed of a whirlwind.*

THE FATHER [*shouting into the din*]. Get on with you! Go on! Get going! Off you go, boys, off you go! Get on with you! Great, see how they run! Off you go, boys! Off, off, off, off, off! Sounds good! A good sound drum well beaten sounds goods!

[*He breaks off*]

Right – they've gone . . .

[*He looks up*]

Ah-ha, there you are again, Mars, there you are again . . .! And you deserve a kiss, drum, for being such

Ernst Deutsch in the title-role of *The Beggar*, drawn by Ernst Stern from the first production in 1917.
Schiller Nationalmuseum, Marbach

a good boy, and chasing the old frowns away. Here you are . . .

[He kisses the drum]

Urgh! The old frowns. – Over there a fire, over there a coffin-lid and some smoke, over here a louse, over there a toad, over there a heart, over there a heart with a knife sticking in it, over here a bucket of tears, over there a crate of death – and with all this around you're supposed to stay sane. But now I've got the drum – so yah-yah-yah – oh yes, I've got the drum all right. The Good Lord still thinks the world of his architect. It was just lying around up there in the attic all on its own – this drum – when I went to look for the old plans. Ha, ha, ha – the Good Lord still thinks the world of his architect, oh yes, oh yes.

[brief drumbeats]

One, two, three and there's Mars again.

[He blows the sky a kiss]

Good afternoon, Mars, old chap, good afternoon, good old Mars, now I've got the drum!

[suddenly changing tack]

Hey, you . . . what d'you think you're doing! You, you smoke-giant, stop blocking out Mars!

[He starts drumming again]

Get going, go on – go, off you go, off you go! Clear off, can't you! Devil take you . . . off you go! Off you go! Clear off, can't you! Off you go!

[Drumming wildly, he comes DSR, *as if driving someone away. For a little while longer, we can still hear the drum, then silence]*

Act IV, Scene 1

[In front of a curtain]

THE POET. No sleep . . . The stars go out . . . And all the night
Already over – the bells have rung out morning . . .
[pause]
And shout upon shout . . . and burden upon burden . . .
Split many ways, my mind is sorely questioned –
I do not know the answer, for mankind
Makes no response to any of my songs
And offers no hand to my outstretched hand –
[pause]
Down below me glint the harsh green lights
Of the glass-works. The din of morning whirrs
Right up here . . . I am so alone,
I radiate light, but finding no night
To match this light – I shatter on myself . . .
[he addresses the audience]
You! You! Prepare the way for me!
For behold, I storm among you, torches
Burning in my swaying hand. Receive me!
Gather round me! I'm rich in benedictions!
Open wide to me
The gates of madhouses, so that my spark
May yet transform the dreary spider's webs
Of stupid laughter into glowing foliage!
Rejected corpses, break out before me –!
I raise you from your stinking putrefaction,
Glimpsing the star, out through the crust of earth
Into gleaming glory! Thunderous halls, with vaults
Of sombre sky: let the smoke of heavy clouds,
Moulded from the flanks of groaning machinery,
Scatter the sacred blood of my torches!
Open! Open! I want to stretch my images
Into towering gods – an everlasting race –
[He collapses – pause – then he gets up again]
No choice! Boldness is timid here.
My aims burn with the deepest purity:
I want to shoulder the burden of the world
And, singing paeans, carry it to the sun.
[Silence – walking up and down]
But earlier I was dragged by fists – by fists –
Roughly through the rock I'd long avoided.
I can't bear cowardice. The cycle of my circles
Must leave nothing in the other world
It might embody. Never must I weaken –
Not if will-power forces me up mountains.
The time has come. I have a job to do.
Pain's good manure, it seems. I want its fruit.
Even if it dulls the limbs, I'll bear it.
Things take root easily in a wounded heart.
[pause]
Won't day break soon? This torment!
Salvation! Higher! Out of the body's anguish
The soul will freely stretch to do its work –
Twisting ropes of light from stupid questions,
Spinning itself divinity out of longing!
[He kneels down, with his back to the auditorium, his countenance bowed low]

TRANSLATED BY ANTHONY VIVIS

*H*ANS *L*EYBOLD 1892–1914

'Non-writers clear out! The Literati shall not be hand-fed.'

From Revolution

Hans Leybold. *Schiller Nationalmuseum, Marbach*

The year is 1913. In the Munich *bohème*, which generally met in the Café Stephanie, a young man appeared who had declared war on the bourgeois world: Hans Leybold. He rebelled against the inertia of the Wilhelmine era in any way he could. Women and sexuality, military service and war and, not least, writing: for him, all these served to make his life more intense. Leybold's carefree nature, his impertinence and his uncompromising lifestyle attracted the attention of the young Munich literary community, and Klabund, Becher, Huelsenbeck, Emmy Hennings and, above all, Hugo Ball became his friends. For one year, Leybold belonged to the German literary avant-garde, but a life such as the one he led is generally not a long one. Hans Leybold reached the age of 22. He died in 1914, a year in which the death of a single individual was hardly acknowledged.

Leybold, who had so wanted to become a 'real' writer, was soon forgotten. His work is hardly substantial: some thirty commentaries, critiques, essays and reviews, as many poems, some letters and a periodical that he edited, which only lasted five issues. The fact that he is still occasionally remembered is almost entirely due to his close friendship with Hugo Ball. Ball's literary career begins with Expressionism, and Leybold's significance for Ball's development towards Dadaism can scarcely be over-exaggerated. Using the pseudonym 'Ha Hu Baley', the two friends wrote poems which already point in that direction. But Leybold's own work, too, shows that he was not merely a typical exponent of early Expressionism, but also a precursor of Dadaism.

Leybold was born in Frankfurt am Main on 2 April 1892, and like many of his Expressionist writer-colleagues, he came from an upper-middle-class background. Early in his life, the family moved to Hamburg, where he grew up, went to school and took his *Abitur* exam. He volunteered for military service, which he underwent in Itzehoe, and at the end of his obligatory year, he was up for a commission. In the autumn of the same year (1912), Leybold went to Munich to study German language and literature, but after one term, he neglected his studies. Instead, he wrote regularly for Franz Pfemfert's *Aktion*, where most of his work was to appear. In 1913, he edited *Revolution* on his own, whose now-famous manifesto, written by Leybold himself, clearly had Dadaist traits:

> Protect yourselves against responsibilities! Hit out: against old household rubbish! And if some valuable piece gets torn up in the process: what does it matter? You respected people! You well-polished ones! You bigwigs! We ought to stick our tongues out at you! Boys, you'll say. Old men! we'll reply.

After three months, *Revolution* ceased publication. Leybold continued to write for *Die Aktion*, but also for other journals, and concentrated increasingly on poetry. When war broke out, Leybold joined up immediately. He was wounded on the Belgian Front near Namur and, after a stay in a field hospital, returned to his regiment in Itzehoe, where he shot himself on the night of 7/8 September 1914. A few weeks previously, talking to Kurt Hiller, he had said that the hour of death was 'a fantastically interesting thing', and that life was not at all important to him. However, we can only guess at the reasons for his suicide. Did the war make the senselessness of life clear to him? Or could he see no other way out, as he was said to be incurably syphilitic?

Leybold's life itself shows that he was not immune to the philosophical currents of his age. It is above all vitalism that determined his thoughts and actions, and it was this school of thought that moulded his literary work. In his commentaries, he fought the bourgeoisie by attacking its literature. His ideal was Alfred Kerr, his God

'This nation needs to have something on the go all the time. Always the sound of something popping, happening. There is always someone to bewitch. Raise your voices, louder, louder. The end justifies the means.'

Quoted by Hugo Ball in 'Totenrede'

Friedrich Nietzsche. Although not very extensive, Leybold's poetry is remarkable for its variety of forms and themes. Following early works which still show their indebtedness to *Jugendstil*, he wrote poems glorifying the vitalistic temperament and, together with Hugo Ball, verse in the style of van Hoddis or Lichtenstein (q.v.) which grotesquely and disrespectfully describes city life. His last poems are marked by despair and weariness of life, and hint at his approaching death ('End'). However, Leybold's most significant contribution to the development of literary Expressionism was his founding and editing of *Revolution*, which today is counted among the most important Expressionist periodicals.

Hans Leybold died too soon to have had a more lasting influence. Having never published a book, he is nothing more than a classic example of the early Expressionist writer. As such, however, he is almost unparalleled. To use the parlance of the time, Leybold is the 'young poet' *par excellence*, capable of great enthusiasm, but also of profound disgust. And for him, there was very little in between.

ECKHARD FAUL (TRANSLATED BY PHILIP MANN)

Texts
Die Aktion (Franz Pfempfert (ed.), Berlin, 1913/14).
Karl Riha and Franz-Josef Weber (eds), *Hans Leybold* (Postskriptum Verlag, Hanover). The first collection of Leybold's poems, prose pieces and glosses is planned for publication in the series 'Randfiguren der Moderne'.

Secondary source
Hugo Ball, 'Totenrede' (*Die weißen Blätter, vi, April 1915, pp. 523–5).*

NARZISSUS

Ein helles Mädchen spitzt die Kniee, tanzend.
Narzissus sanft vibrierend Küßt ihr blaues Haar.
Zwei gelbe Autos keuchen, fort sich pflanzend,
Und trollen dumpf, geschwächt, zu der Kasinobar,

Es lästern oft Kokotten und Chauffeure.
Doch vor der Taube beugen sie den Nacken tief.
Der Bauch des Universums schwillt aus einem Göhre,
Und Hahn und Pferd verdrehn die Hälse schief.

Es auch geschieht ein ungeheures Tun:
Maria hebt sich von dem Wolkensitze.
Die Zeppeline schreien, Dreatnoughts fliehn.
Ein Grenadier feikt in die Opiumspritze.

Es bleibt kein Hund im Schoße der Madonnen.
Viel Senatoren, Patriarchen jappt das hohe Seil.
Auf Sacco-Ösen schrillen Querpfeif-Wonnen
Der Teufel, die aus Lüften schießen steil.

NARCISSUS

A bright girl, dancing, points her knees.
Narcissus, softly trembling, kisses her blue hair.
Two yellow cars pant while propagating
And, drained and weak, toddle over to the casino bar.

Tarts and chauffeurs often mock.
But give a deep nod before the dove.
The belly of the universe swells out of an urchin,
And cock and horse twist their necks askew.

Monstrous events further come to pass:
Mary arises from her seat in the clouds.
Zeppelins scream, dreadnoughts scuttle.
A grenadier grins into the opium shot.

No dog remains in the lap of the Madonnas.
Many senators and patriarchs gasp at the high wire.
On the hook and eyes of jackets squeal flute-raptures
The devil shooting steeply from the ether.

TRANSLATED BY PHILIP MANN

Ein und kein Frühlingsgedicht

(written with Hugo Ball as Ha Hu Baley)

I

Ein Doppeldecker steigt aus jeder Flasche
Und stößt sich heulend seinen Kopf kaputt.
Der Übermensch verzehrt die Paprikagoulasche,
Zerbröselnd Semmeln, rülpsend in den Kälberschutt.

Den Gästen hängt der Kiefer bis zur Treppe,
Dort hinterlist'ge Fallen tätlich legend.
Aus dem Aburte schlitzt Lolô die Tangoschneppe,
Verpestend mit dem Lockendampf die Absinthgegend.

Denn siehe, ich bin bei euch alle Tage
Und meine schmettergelbe Lusttrompete packt euch an.
Der umgekippten Erektionen Frühlingsklage
Buhlt veilchenblau im Bidet mit dem Schwan.

II

O du mein Hyazinth, die Wade knackte
Und Rolf, der Mops, fraß jäh das Strumpfband auf.
Nach Grammophonen in dem Twosteptakte
Vollzog sich Notdurft Coitus und Lebenslauf.

Der Lampionen blutgeduns'nes Schwirren
Schuf große Monde aus den Wassergläsern.
Ein Schlachtgetöse gab es und ein Klirren
Der Kneifer von Beamten und Verwesern.

Da war auch Dame Wueh in einer Prunkkarosse,
Uns schrak nicht Kino mehr, nicht die Picassofratze.
Wir schluckten Sperma wie Armeegeschosse,
Und fetzten unsren Hausgott Grünekatze.

Wir waren sehr verekelt und verbiestert,
Dem Priapus verschrieben und dem Pan.
Wir rollten von den Dächern, sternverschwistert,
Und glaubten selbst an dieses nicht daran.

(Not) a Spring Poem

I

A double-decker emerges from every bottle
And, howling, bashes its head in.
The Superman eats paprika goulash,
Crumbling bread rolls and belching into the debris of
calves.

The guests' jaws droop down to the stairs,
Brutally laying cunning traps there.
Out of the latrine, Lolo slits the tango-slut
Stinking out the absinthe quarter with the steam from her
curls.

Lo, I am with you alway
And my loud yellow lecher's trumpet grabs you.
Violet-blue, the spring lament of detumescent erections
Courts the swan in the bidet.

II

O my Hyacinth, the calf cracked
And Rolf, the pug, suddenly gobbled up the garter.
Accompanied by gramophones, in two-step beat,
Need, coitus and career were performed.

The blood-swollen buzz of Chinese lanterns
Made huge moons out of water glasses,
There was a hue and cry, and a shattering
Of bureaucrats' and decomposers' pince-nez.

Also present was Lady Wueh in a fine coach;
Cinema no longer shocked us, nor Picasso's grimaces.
We swallowed sperm like army shells
And tore our house-god Greencat to shreds.

We were extremely disgusting and dissolute,
Devotees of Priap and Pan.
We rolled from the roofs, the siblings of stars,
And didn't even believe in that any more.

Translated by Philip Mann

Le Tiers État

(Written with Hugo Ball as Ha Hu Baley)

Zertretene, die sich durch Finsternisse prügeln.
Wir Blutigen! Verworfen dorren unsre Glieder.
Die Nacht legt sich um uns; erlognen Engelsflügeln
gleich fällt sie in schwarze Flüsse; wieder
deckt sie die Wunden zu, wie die Not und Schmerzen.
Wir Durstigen! Kein Quell stillt unsre Brände.
Wir brüten Wut. Es qualmen grau die Kerzen
in unsern Kellern. Verfluchte Sattheit! Unsre Hände
hart geballt. Nur manchmal leuchtet uns der Mond:

gequollenes Symbol des Feisten, der in Villen wohnt.
Der Haß macht schwach! Und stark zugleich. Wozu Gesetz?
Wir beißen uns gequält die Zunge wund.
Belastete: wir sehen auf den tiefsten Grund
des Meers der Zeit. Dort wachsen unsre Zukunftsschätze.

The Third State

Crushed beings that fight their way through shadows.
We bloody ones! Rejected, our limbs wither.
Night wraps itself around us; like false angels' wings
it falls in black streams; once more
it covers up the wounds, the need and the pain.
We thirsty ones! No spring quenches our parched throats.
We breed anger. In our cellars, the candles
smoke greyly. Cursed satiety! Our hands
tightly clenched. Only at times does the moon shine for us:
swollen symbol of the glutton living in his villa.
Hate makes us weak! And yet strong. Why laws?

Tortured, we bite our tongues sore.
Burdened ones: we can see down to the deepest depths
of the sea of time. There, our future treasures grow.

TRANSLATED BY PHILIP MANN

Der Hymnische Fluch

Glutblumen ihr, aus Wolkenbäuchen
im Glanz verstreuten Lichtes laut erblüht,
Stadtbogenlampen. Singend durch die Nebel keuchen
die Hurenlieder. Gelblichgrüner Eiter glüht
um Wunden violetter Zentren. Aus den Gesträuchen

der Fensterrahmen brennt die Nacht.
Glutblumen ihr! So lockt ihr eure gütigen Gewächse
aus Abendkammern; gießet eure Macht
Schönheit-verleihend, bleichend auf sie aus. Die Hexe
Syphilis hockt hinter Pfeilern hoch und lacht.

Gib Licht die ehrerbiet'gen Flügel deines Segens.
O tripple, blaßgeschminkte Dirne; Louis, lauf!
Unermüdlicher Himmel, spritz die Ströme deines Regens.
O ewiger Nebel, halt die stummen Hafenkähne auf!
Schwärzester Mörder: schärf die Spitze deines Degens.

Unstete Weltenbahnen! Rauch, explodiere, heiliger Vesuv!
Ihr ruhbegierigen Lasten! Zerplatzt, ihr blutigen Phantome!
Wutwinde! Überfluss! Und Schönheit, die ich schuf!
Göttlicher Atem, gebietendes Szepter, unverrückbare Atome!
Erzittert! Raset heiss! O, höret Fluch und Ruf!

Verwüstung künde ich und Feuermeere.

The Hymnic Curse

Ye fire-flowers, loudly come to blossom
out of the bellies of clouds in the glare of diffused light,
City gate lanterns. Singing through the fog, the songs of whores
rasp. Yellowish-green pus glows
Around wounds with violet centres. From the undergrowth

of window frames, the night burns.
Ye fire-flowers! Thus you entice your benign growths
Out of evening chambers; pour your power
beauty-giving, bleaching, on to them. The witch
Syphilis crouches behind tall pillars and laughs.

Give light the respectful wings of your blessing.
O step lightly, palely made-up harlot. Louis, run!
Untiring sky, spray the streams of your rain.
O eternal fog, stop the mute harbour barges!
Blackest murderer: sharpen the point of your dagger.

Inconstant orbits! Smoke, explode, holy Vesuvius!

Ye burdens pining for peace and quiet! Burst, ye bloody phantoms!
Winds of fury! Abundance! And beauty that I created!
Divine breath, governing sceptre, immovable atoms!

Tremble! Work yourselves into a frenzy! O hear the curse and the call!
I announce the devastation and seas of fire.

Wildgraue Elefanten zertrampeln eurer Städte
Zedernhain.
Und grellen Feuers Not droht euch. Verwesung, schwere

Seuchen brechen fressend in euch ein!
Zerfall und Fäule! Brandig wilde Heere

Springen Weiber an. Die letzte Lust tobt frech und
dumm.
Sie stieren geil. Aus ihren Schößen brechen Flammen.
Zerstückte Planken krachen. Denkmäler stürzen berstend
um.
Kirchtürme wackeln. Marmorne Prachtpaläste fallen jäh
zusammen.
Tragsäulen splittern. Pylonen beugen sich herab zur
Erde, krumm.

Wild-grey elephants trample your cities' cypress groves
underfoot.
And the peril of glaring fire threatens you.
Decomposition, great
plagues will break in on you, consuming!
Decay and rot! Burning wild armies

Leap at women. Insolent and dumb, the final lust rages.

They stare lewdly. Flames burst out of their loins.
Hacked planks creak. Memorials shatter and collapse.

Church towers teeter. Glorious marble palaces suddenly
implode.
Bearing columns splinter. Pylons bow down to earth,
bent.

TRANSLATED BY PHILIP MANN

WIDMUNG FÜR CHOPIN

(written with Hugo Ball as Ha Hu Baley)

Drei Meere tanzen hochgeschürzt ans Land.
Des Droschkenkutschers Hut durchbohren
Mondesstrahlen.
Als Kehrichtwalze holpert der Verstand,
Wir glänzen durch die Nacht gleich singenden Aalen.

Giraffenhals ragt schräg zum Nordlichthimmel.
Die Mondesratte knüpft ihm bleichen Kragen.
Am Tropenkoller würgt ein Polizistenlümmel.
Bald werden wir ein neues Land erfragen.

Aus unsrem Ohr lustwandeln Eiterströme.
Das Auge rankt sich wüst um das Monokel.
An einem Drahtseil leckt ein schlichter Böhme.
Ein Schwein steht segnend auf dem Marmorsockel.

Zehntausendfarbenschnee, Cocytus, Kinotempel.
Ein Mann greift weibernd nach dem Hosensack.
Auf Eselsrücken brennen handgross Feuerstempel
Und Hähne machen Kopfsprung in den Chapeau claque.

DEDICATED TO CHOPIN

With their skirts rolled up, three seas dance on to land.
Moonbeams bore through the
coachman's hat.
Reason stumbles like a street-sweeper's waltz;
Like singing eels, we shine through the night.

Oblique, a giraffe's neck rises up to the Northern Lights.
The moon-rat buttons up his pale collar.
A police lout chokes of tropical frenzy.
Soon we shall seek out a new land.

Streams of pus trip gaily from our ears.
The vulgar eye creeps around the monocle.
A modest Bohemian licks at a wire rope.
On a marble pedestal stands a benedictory pig.

Snow of ten-thousand-colours. Cocytus. Cinema temples.
Womanizing, a man grasps for his trouser crotch.
Hand-sized brands burn on the backs of donkeys
And cockerels jump head-first into the collapsible top hat.

TRANSLATED BY PHILIP MANN

ENDE

Die Wellen meiner bunten Räusche sind verdampft.
Breit schlagen, schwer und müd
die Ströme meines Lebens über Bänke
von Sand.
Mir schmerzen die Gelenke.
In Mein Gehirn
hat eine maßlos große Faust sich eingekrampft.

END

The waves of my gay drunkenness have subdued.
The currents of my life
lap broad, heavy and tired
over sandbanks.
My joints ache.
In my brain
an infinitely huge fist has wedged itself in.

*A*LFRED *L*ICHTENSTEIN 1889–1914

'Twas quite nice to be a soldier for a year,
But it's nicer to feel free once more.
There's quite enough depravity, pain and fear
In life's remorseless chore.
From 'Abschied', 28 June 1914

Lichtenstein in his student days.

Alfred Lichtenstein was a satirist of his society and of himself. As the son of a factory owner, a Prussian Jew, he was well placed to pass ironic comment on the transparent existence of the bourgeoisie in industrialized city life. He was born in Germany's largest and busiest city, Berlin, on 23 August 1889. As a student he wrote a children's book, *Die Geschichten des Onkel Krause (The Stories of Uncle Krause)*, and a number of poems which found their way into the modernist publications *Der Sturm, Simplicissimus* and *Die Aktion*. Lichtenstein read law at university, but was clearly headed for a self-determined career as a writer: 'I am more interested in theatre and literature. I read Wedekind, Rilke and others. Also Goethe. I do not care for Schiller and George.' The legal manifestation of this literary tendency was his thesis: *The Illegal Performance of Stageworks* (1913). Barely three months out of university, in October 1913, Lichtenstein was entered for the obligatory one year's military service. In August the following year, the 2nd Bavarian Infantry Regiment was called to the Front, and on 24 September 1914, Lichtenstein died of his wounds after the attack on Vermandovillers on the Somme.

Much of Lichtenstein's original work was destroyed in the Second World War. What emerges from his published pieces (collected in 1919 by Karl Lubasch) is a poet of urbane wit, a wistful satirist who showed the city world of streets, playgrounds and coffee houses as stages for the expression of loneliness, prostitution and death. Lichtenstein's poetry, as described by Michael Hamburger in *Reason and Energy*, is 'distinguished by an irony which has the dual purpose of satirizing contemporary civilization and of expressing a *malaise*, a premonition of doom, which was one of the common premisses of all the early Expressionists'. This was first apparent in Lichtenstein's best-known but early poem of 1911 'Die Dämmerung' ('Twilight'), based on Jakob van Hoddis's 'Weltende' ('End of the World').

' "Weltende",' writes Michael Hamburger, 'was the first to appear; and Lichtenstein admitted having used it as a model, though he rightly claimed to have improved on it. Both poems are rhymed and in regular stanza form. What was new about them was that they consisted of nothing more than an arbitrary concatenation of images derived from contemporary life; they presented a picture, but not a realistic one, for the objects described were not such as can be found together in the same place and at the same time. They were a kind of *collage*; but *collage* in poetry is a far less drastic device than *collage* in the graphic arts, since poetry has always been free to assemble its imagery without regard to the unity of space and time. Hoddis could not resist giving the show away in the title of his poem – "End of the World" – an exaggeration all the more blatant because so inappropriate to the ironic understatement of the poem itself. (It says that "most people have a cold", relating this observation to others of a more serious kind – for instance, that "the railway trains are falling off the bridges".) Much of the irony is too crude to be effective as satire; but the poem does express a mood that was soon to become endemic.

'In Lichtenstein's poem, on the other hand, the images are allowed to speak for themselves. His title – "Twilight" – is ambiguous, though one assumes that his twilight is dusk.

'If Lichtenstein's dusk (or dawn) is a cosmic one, he neither says nor implies that it is. He makes no attempt to explain or connect the presence in his poem of the fat boy playing with a pond, the two lame men creeping over a field, the clown putting on his boots, the screaming pram or the cursing dogs. His poem is "expressionistic" because its real purpose is to communicate the poet's own sense of the absurd and the ridiculous; yet, by saying that "the sky looks like the morning after," it relates all the disparate images of modern life to a general sense of vanity, as T. S. Eliot was to do with more subtle skill in *The Waste Land*. Lichtenstein's poem is successful not because it expresses a new mood, but because that mood has found its proper "objective correlative", for all its humour, it is much more disturbing than Hoddis's prognosis of disaster.'

Lichtenstein's use of contrasts is illustrated by his adoption (as his alter-ego) of the hunchbacked poet Kuno Kohn, who expresses poignant, lyrical ideals. He is the central character in most of the Café Klösschen stories and even sets off to war in the second stanza of the war poem 'Romantische Fahrt':

> On top of the wobbliest ammunition cart, like a little toad finely carved in black wood, hands gently clenched, rifle on his back (strapped on loosely), lighted cigar in wry mouth, idle as a monk, keen as a dog – he's holding valerian drops pressed to his heart – looking comically serious, looking crazy in the yellow moonlight, there sits: Kuno.
>
> (Translation by Patrick Bridgwater)

If *Die Aktion* was Lichtenstein's most favoured outlet – in 1913, the poet was honoured with a special issue dedicated to his poems – then the Café des Westens in Berlin was the favoured source of his material. This fashionable literary meeting place, nicknamed 'Café Größenwahn' because of the ambitions harboured by all the *Literaten* who met up there, received another name in Lichtenstein's short stories: Café Klößchen. Lichtenstein deliberately set himself apart from the mainstream of Expressionist poets with his satirizing depiction of Georg Heym as Lisel Lieblichlein's city-dwelling cousin Schulz in the main story. Heym's incessant self-advertisement as a successful lover is mocked by Schulz's distinct failure to win the heart of the naïve Lisel, who is, at least temporarily, won over by the hunchbacked Kuno. The story is littered with references to Heym and the literary scene of the time. Even Heym's death, in a drowning accident on a frozen lake in 1912, is parodied by Schulz's catching the flu by the edge of a pond. A mark of Lichtenstein's success as a humorous writer is that full appreciation of the 'in' references is not a prerequisite to the enjoyment of this story of man's foibles and fallibility. Karl Kraus's journal *Der Fackel* (*The Torch*) becomes Lutz Laus's *Der Dackel* (literally *The Dachshund*, but here *The Scorth)*; the periodical *Der Sturm* becomes *Heiße Helden* (*Hot Heroes*).

The fullest study of Lichtenstein's war poetry is to be found in Patrick Bridgwater's chapter 'Lichtenstein, Ball and Klemm' in *German Poets of the First World War*, in which he highlights the fact that Lichtenstein must have read another German poet apart from Wedekind and Rilke: Heinrich Heine. Lichtenstein's final poem, 'Die Schlacht bei Saarburg' ('The Battle of Saarburg'), says Bridgwater, 'is written in *Heine-Strophen*. As with Heine, there is an alternation of feminine and masculine endings, with only the masculine endings rhyming. There is, therefore, not only the same ambiguity and discord as in Heine, but also the added perspective and depth that comes from the deliberate echo of Lichtenstein's great predecessor. The basic tension in the poem is between poet and reality – that is, war. The poem falls into two distinct halves: the first six lines describe external reality, while the last six are devoted, basically, to the poet's reaction to that overwhelmingly hostile reality. The tension between passive poet-victim and aggressive external event is hammered home in those alternating endings, but inevitably the distinction between the two is blurred, for what matters is how reality is seen by the poet and the effect it has on him.

'Thus the very first line ostensibly describes the world, at dusk, swimming (Lichtenstein says "mouldering") in mist, but from the very fact that he is saying it, and that the line has the feminine ending that denotes victim rather than event, it is clear that it is the poet's sense of reality, even his grip on reality, that is becoming blurred and loosened by the continuous fighting of 18–20 August. The oppressive sense of reality is expressed in the second line: "*Der Abend drückt wie Blei*" ("The evening is heavy as lead"), with the word "*Blei*" standing as a reminder that the poet has been under fire for three days. The third line compares the continuous shellfire to a violent thunder-storm, with the feminine endings suggesting that it becomes a storm in the mind, a brainstorm that reduces the poet to a whimpering, moaning wreck. This reading is reinforced by the ending of the poem.

'The second stanza shows the effect of war on the man-made world and on one individual man. The physical wreckage of ruined villages reflects, echoes and helps to cause the way in which the poet is reduced to mental wreck. The poet lies there, God-forsaken ("My God, why hast Thou forsaken me": the biblical question points to the extent of the poet's desolation), while the incessant, nagging machine-gun fire further aggravates his overwrought condition, bringing him to the point where his grip on reality is loosened. The image in the first half of the last stanza ("*Viel kupferne feindliche Vögelein/Surren um Herz und Hirn*" – "Many copper enemy birds/Whirl about my heart and head") is not just an obvious poeticism, a simile for all the bullets and shells sawing their way through the air, and not just a typical piece of *grotesquerie*; it is also a parodistic echo of Heine, who himself parodies all those *Vögelein* in folk and Romantic poetry; and the childish image also suggests, finally, that the poet's mind has – at least temporarily – gone. It is because he has reached the end of his tether and can take no more that he ends by writing: "*Ich stemme mich steil in das Graue/Und biete dem Tode die Stirn.*" ("I brace myself in the greyness/And face death.") There is nothing else left for him to do but surrender to death, as Lichtenstein did near Vermandovillers (retaken by Wilfred Owen's regiment exactly four years later), just nine days after sending home this poem.'

TIM CROSS

Rückkehr des Dorfjungen

In meiner Jugend war die Welt ein kleiner Teich
Großmutterchen und rotes Dach, Gebrüll
Von Ochsen und ein Busch aus Bäumen.
Und ringsumher die große grüne Wiese.

Wie schön war dieses In-die-Weite-Träumen.
Dies Garnichtssein als helle Luft und Wind
Und Vogelruf und Feenmärchenbuch.
Fern pfiff die fabelhafte Eisenschlange –

Return of the Village Lad

When I was young the world was a little pond
Grandmother and red roof, the lowing
Of oxen and a bush made up of trees.
And all around was the great green meadow.

Lovely it was, this dreaming-into-the-distance,
This being nothing at all but air and wind
And bird-call and fairytale book.
Far off the fabulous iron serpent whistled –

Translated by Michael Hamburger

Die Gummischuhe

Der Dicke dachte:
Am Abend geh ich gern in Gummischuhen,
Auch wenn die Straßen fromm und flecklos sind.
In Gummischuhen bin ich nie ganz nüchtern . . .

Ich halte in der Hand die Zigarette.
Auf schmalen Rhythmen tänzelt meine Seele.
Und alle Zentner meines Leibes tänzeln.

The Galoshes

The fat man thought:
At night I like to walk in my galoshes,
Even through pious and immaculate streets.
I'm not quite sober when I wear galoshes . . .

I hold my cigarette in one gloved hand.
On tightrope rhythms then my soul goes tripping.
And all the hundredweights of my body dance.

Translated by Michael Hamburger

Der Lackschuh

Der Dichter dachte:
Ach was, ich hab den Plunder satt!

Die Dirnen, das Theater und den Stadtmond,
Die Oberhemden, Straßen und Gerüche,
Die Nächte und die Kutscher und die Fenster,
Das Lachen, die Laternen und die Morde –
Den ganzen Dreck hab ich nun wirklich satt,
Beim Teufel!
Mag werden, was da will . . . mir ist es gleich:
Der Lackschuh drückt mich. Und ich zieh ihn aus –

Die Leute mögen sich verwundert wenden.
Nur schade ists um meinen seidnen Strumpf . . .

The Patent Leather Shoe

The poet thought:
Enough. I'm sick of the whole lot!

The whores, the theatre and the city moon,
The streets, the laundered shirtfronts and the smells,
The nights, the coachmen and the curtained windows,
The laughter and the street lamps and the murders –
I am well and truly sick of the whole lot,
To hell with it!
Happen what may . . . it's all the same to me:
This black shoe pinches me. I'll take it off –

Let people turn their heads for all I care.
A pity, though, about my new silk sock . . .

Translated by Michael Hamburger

Aschermittwoch

Gestern noch ging ich gepudert und süchtig
In der vielbunten tönenden Welt.
Heute ist alles schon lange ersoffen.

Hier ist ein Ding.
Dort ist ein Ding.
Etwas sieht so aus.
Etwas sieht anders aus.
Wie leicht pustet einer die ganze
Blühende Erde aus.

Der Himmel ist kalt und blau.
Oder der Mond ist gelb und platt.
Ein Wald hat viele einzelne Bäume.

Ist nichts mehr zum Weinen.
Ist nichts mehr zum Schreien.
Wo bin ich –

Ash Wednesday

Only yesterday powdered and lustful I walked
In this various and resonant world.
Today how long ago the lot was drowned.

Here is a thing.
There is a thing.
Something looks like this.
Something else looks different.
How easily one can blow out
The whole blossoming earth.

The sky is cold and blue.
Or the moon is yellow and flat.
A wood contains many single trees.

Nothing now worth weeping for.
Nothing now worth screaming for.
Where am I –

Translated by Michael Hamburger

Der Morgen

. . . Und alle Straßen liegen glatt und glänzend da.
Nur selten hastet über sie ein fester Mann.
Ein fesches Mädchen haut sich heftig mit Papa.
Ein Bäcker sieht sich mal den schönen Himmel an.

Die tote Sonne hängt an Häusern, breit und dick.
Vier fette Weiber quietschen spitz vor einer Bar.
Ein Droschkenkutscher fällt und bricht sich das Genick.
Und alles ist langweilig hell, gesund und klar.

Ein Herr mit weisen Augen schwebt verrückt, voll Nacht,
Ein siecher Gott . . . in diesem Bild, das er vergaß,
Vielleicht nicht merkte – Murmelt manches. Stirbt. Und
lacht.
Träumt von Gehirnschlag, Paralyse, Knochenfraß.

Morning

. . . And all the streets lie snug there, clean and regular.
Only at times some brawny fellow hurries by.
A very smart young girl fights fiercely with Papa.
A baker, for a change, looks at the lovely sky.

The dead sun hangs on houses, broad as it is thick.
Four bulging women shrilly squeak outside a bar.
The driver of a cab falls down and breaks his neck.
And all is boringly bright, salubrious and clear.

A wise-eyed gentleman floats madly, full of night,
An ailing god . . . within this scene, which he forgot
Or failed to notice – Mutters something. Dies. And
laughs.
Dreams of a cerebral stroke, paralysis, bone-rot.

Translated by Michael Hamburger

Texts
Klaus Kanzog (ed.), *Gesammelte Gedichte* (Arche, Zurich, 1962) and *Gesammelte Prosa* (Arche, Zurich, 1966). Full bibliography in German.

Secondary sources
Michael Hamburger, *A Proliferation of Prophets* (Carcanet, Manchester, 1983). Passage from '1912' reproduced with kind permission of the author.
Patrick Bridgwater, *The German Poets of the First World War* (Croom Helm, London, 1985). Passage and translations from 'Lichtenstein, Ball and Klemm' reproduced by agreement with the publishers and the author.

Café Klösschen

I

Lisel Liblichlein had come to the city from the provinces because she wanted to be an actress. At home she found everything philistine, narrow, stupefying. The gentlemen were silly. The sky, the kissing, the girlfriends, the Sunday afternoons, all had become intolerable. Weeping was what she liked doing best. To her being an actress meant: being intelligent, being free, being happy. How it would be, she didn't know. Whether she had talent, she couldn't tell.

She had a crush on her cousin, Schulz, because he lived in the city and wrote poems. When her cousin wrote her a letter saying he'd had enough of the law and was going to satisfy his desire to be a writer, she told her shocked parents she was fed up with the life of a country bumpkin; she intended to fulfil her ideals by becoming an actress. They tried everything to dissuade her. Without success. She became more determined, menacing. Reluctantly they relented, drove into the city with her, rented her a small room in a large *pension*, and enrolled her at a cheap drama school. They asked cousin Schulz to look after her.

Herr Schulz spent a lot of time with his cousin, Liblichlein. He took her to cabarets; read poems to her; showed her his Bohemian digs; introduced her to the Café Klösschen, a haunt of writers; walked hand in hand with her for hours through the streets at night; touched her body; kissed her. Fräulein Liblichlein was agreeably stunned by all the novelty; though soon realized she had imagined most of it in a rosier light. Right from the start, she found it irritating that the Head of the Drama School, the male students, and the writers who frequented the Café Klösschen – all the men she met regularly – took pleasure in touching her, stroking her hands, pressing their knees against her knee, looking at her suggestively. Even Schulz's touching got on her nerves. So as not to hurt his feelings or seem provincial, she seldom let him know this. But once she slapped his face, hard. They were in his room, he had just explained to her the last lines of his poem, 'Weariness'. They were:

> Evening stands outside my window, man of grey!
> The best thing we can do is go to bed –

Then he had tried to take her blouse off. The slap really dumbfounded Schulz. She must have noticed, he said, almost in tears, that he was in love with her. What was more, he was her cousin. She said she objected to her blouse being undone. And anyway, he had ripped off a button. He said he couldn't stand it any longer. If someone loved a man, she would have to surrender herself. He would try to forget her in the arms of prostitutes. She didn't know how to answer. Groaning, he thought: O God, O God. She sat there beside him, dejected.

For the next few days, he didn't turn up. When he reappeared, he looked pale and grey. His bloodless eyes, reddened and tearful, were clouded by smudgy shadows. His voice was nothing but a sing-song, with an affectedly lugubrious tone. Schulz talked in a despondently wistful way about anguish, whoring, disintegration. About being weary of any joy life could offer. About not being long for this world. He avoided any intimacy, but frequently sighed in pain. Flirted melodramatically with a longing to be dead. Took his girlfriend to tragedies rich in corpses, to gloomy films, to sombre concerts in darkened halls.

Perhaps a week had gone by. A lady had been singing. There was a long, loud crash of applause from the audience. Gottschalk Schulz passionately seized several of Lisel Liblichlein's fingers, laid them good-naturedly on his thigh, and said, 'Isn't it strange how a lady's singing goes straight to one's soul!' Then he started once again to talk, in a pleading, lachrymose way, about love and surrender. Lisel Liblichlein said she found this boring, disgusting. Because she pitied him – and wanted to go up to her room – she eventually told him at the front door she would agree to love if he could do without surrender. Schulz embraced her, blissfully. He stood there a long time, in a trance. He sang, 'O, tears. O, kindness. O, God. O, beauty. O, love. O, love. O, love . . .' He dashed through the streets. Then disappeared into the Café Klösschen.

But Lisel Liblichlein sat in her little room smiling helplessly in the reddish glow of a tallow candle. She couldn't fathom these city-folk; to her they seemed like curious, dangerous animals. She felt abandoned and lonelier than ever. She thought longingly about the innocence of her country life; the windy sky, the ridiculous young gentlemen, the tennis tournaments, the melancholy Sunday afternoons . . . She undid her suspenders, rested her little body on a chair. She was inconsolable.

II

One transparent summer evening the glowing Café Klösschen was enveloped by the city sky, dark blue silk, with a white moon and many small stars lying on it. Somewhere in the background at a tiny table with something on it, Kuno Kohn, the hunchbacked poet, used to sit for hours, lonely and smoking – until his sudden death. People were sitting at the other tables. Between them moved men with yellow and red skulls; women; writers; actors. Shadowy waiters flitted everywhere.

Kuno Kohn wasn't thinking of anything in particular. He was humming to himself: 'A mist has caused such mellow devastation in the world.' Then the poet

Gottschalk Schulz, a law student who had taken great pains to fail every examination he had sat, said good evening. With him came a beautiful young woman. They both sat down at Kohn's table. Schulz and Kohn were contributors to the monthly magazine, *The Scorch*, which the diminutive enthusiast, Lutz Laus, put together to encourage immorality. Schulz explained to Kohn that Laus the Scorcher was about to invent a godless religion on a neo-juridical basis, and wanted to call a meeting, to organize a constituent assembly, in a nearby flea-pit. Kohn listened, shaking his head. The beautiful young woman ate cakes. Kohn said disconsolately, 'Laus is a great, a moving man. But not even a Jesus can make believers of us any more. Every day we sink deeper into the eternal desolation of death. We're hopeless, shattered. Our life will always be senseless play-acting.' Still eating, the young woman looked across blankly with her reddish-brown eyes and cheerful, positive expression. Schulz was lost in dismal thoughts. The young woman said her whole life was play-acting. She couldn't agree it was senseless. In the drama school where she, a sentimental amateur, was preparing for a theatrical career, excellent things were achieved. Herr Kohn was welcome to come and see for himself. Kuno Kohn looked tenderly at the young woman for some time. He thought, 'Such a silly little young woman . . .' But soon he left the café.

Outside, Roland Rufus Müller, the lyric poet, grabbed him by the arm excitedly, and shouted, 'Have you read the article in the *Medical Monthly* by a certain Bruno Bibelbauer, in which he puts my paranoia down to delusions of syphilis?! Everybody looks at me in a special way, I'm famous. My publisher gives me massive advances. But – oh God, I mustn't say it – I'm incurable.' He scurried off into a high-class restaurant.

A horse was hobbling like an old man in front of a carriage. Kohn the hunchback was leaning idly against a Catholic church, reflecting on existence. He said to himself, How ludicrous life is. Here I am leaning against this; at no particular time; in no particular place; uninvolved; unimportant; might just as well, or just as ill, go on walking; to somewhere else. It makes me miserable. In front of him a small, silent prostitute's dog had stopped, and was listening humbly with smouldering eyes.

A sparkling glass bridal coach rattled past. Inside, in a corner, he could see the pale expressionless face of a bridegroom. An empty cab appeared, Kohn followed it. Quietly, he said, 'A seeker without an objective . . . A man without roots . . . A stranger to everyone . . . A man with a terrible longing. What for? – oh, if only one knew.'

The streets were already shimmering in a whitish light by the time he opened the door of the house in which he lived. In his room, he looked silently and in a solemnly disconsolate way at the pictures on a wall of people who were now all dead. He then began to take the clothes off his hump. When he was standing in nothing but underpants, shirt, socks, he muttered, sighing, 'Bit by bit you're losing your mind –'

In bed, his thoughts slowed down. To send him to sleep, the reddish-brown eyes of the young woman from the Café Klösschen suddenly came to him . . .

Over the next few days, these eyes shone remarkably often in his mind. This astonished him. Frightened him. His relations with women were strange. Generally, he had a positive aversion to them, preferring boys. But in certain summer months, when he felt utterly broken and wretched, he often fell in love with a young, childlike woman. As he was usually rejected because of his hump, and sometimes even derided, his memories of these women and girls were appalling. He therefore took special care at these times. Went to prostitutes when he sensed danger.

Lisel Liblichlein had taken him by surprise without even realizing it. It was useless to recall the torments of his fiascos. Useless to imagine Lisel Liblichlein, one of the many delicate creatures who, caught in confusion between marvellous ignorance and a wistful longing for happiness, exist in almost identical form all over the world . . . On a mellow evening full of greenish-yellow lamps, umbrellas and street-filth, a short hunchbacked man was standing apprehensively beside the signboard of a drama school.

III

Sometimes a wind appeared, a venomous, fiery dog. Like sticky, blazing oil, the sun spread over houses, and over streets, and over people. Minute sexless mannikins with spindly legs hopped senselessly around the barred front garden of the Café Klösschen. Inside, Kuno Kohn and Gottschalk Schulz were brawling. Other people happened to be watching. Lisel Liblichlein sat with a grave expression in a corner.

It had all started because Herr Kohn had several times accompanied Fräulein Liblichlein from her drama school to her lodgings. When Schulz found out, he became irrationally jealous. He began running Kohn down. Lisel Liblichlein, who realized what her cousin was up to, defended the hunchback. This annoyed Schulz even more. He made a convincing case for shooting himself. He refrained from doing so, but threatened to shoot her as well. Then she refused to see him any more. Lisel Liblichlein needed someone to whom she could talk freely about the everyday things that mattered to her. After the quarrel with Schulz, some vague instinct made her choose Kohn. Which is why, on the afternoon of the day the brawl took place, she asked to meet him in the Café Klösschen, to talk to him, perhaps about choosing a dress, or interpreting a role, or about some minor incident. Kohn had just arrived, and was about to ask the young woman how he could help, when Gottschalk Schulz stormed in, stood over him with his face swollen and red, and called him an irresponsible seducer of girls. Kohn tried to box Schulz's ears from below. Then they both hit out at each other furiously and in silence. The signboard of the person renting the lavatory, which had said 'My institute is now located here, entrance there', lay shattered on the floor. Suddenly, Schulz's hand stabbed violently at Kohn's hump. The hand was wounded, bleeding, and the hump was also damaged. White as a corpse, Schulz shouted, 'That hump's a danger to life and limb.' Then he got one of the headwaiters to accompany him to a first-aid station. He didn't deign to look at Lisel Liblichlein.

Kohn didn't take much notice of his hurt hump. He sat down at Lisel Liblichlein's table again, ordered lemon tea. She could clearly see more and more blood trickling through his threadbare frock coat. She pointed out the blood on his coat – he was alarmed. She asked if she ought to bandage his wound – he said bitterly that it wouldn't be very agreeable for her to touch a hump. Blushing with compassion, she said that a hump was human – she said he ought to come to her place. The hump needed to be cleaned and cooled. Then she would make him a bandage. He could spend the afternoon with her . . .

With joyful trepidation, Kohn went along with her suggestion. They sat in Lisel Liblichlein's little room till the early hours. Talking about the soul, the hump, love.

From this day on, Schulz the poet was presumed dead. An acquaintance had last seen him one evening standing outside the window of a shoe shop, apparently eyeing every single shoe gloomily. Soon afterwards, *Hot Heroes* – a magazine devoted to Romantic *Décadence* – received a letter by special messenger in which Schulz stated that for psychological reasons he was about to take his own life. Some people considered this information warmed-up self-advertisement. Most people were overjoyed. The press published stirring articles. A Hunt-Schulz's-Corpse-Fund was set up. A factory-owner donated a huge sarcophagus.

Search-parties explored woods and meadows. Stuck long poles in all the lakes. They failed to discover any trace of Schulz. And were about to call the hunt off when they located him, deplorably run down, in a mediocre hotel in a remote suburb. By a windy pond, he had caught a serious dose of influenza, which had confined him to bed for weeks. They bumped into him on the creaking hotel stairs as he, enveloped in lots of blankets and towels, was about to make another suicide attempt. They had no difficulty in dissuading him, and took him back to the city in triumph. The sarcophagus was disposed of. On the proceeds from this and the balance of the Hunt-Schulz's-Corpse-Fund, they organized a Bohemian Fancy Dress Ball.

Gottschalk Schulz sat enthroned in the corner, dressed as Faust, dripping *Weltschmerz*. Dr Berthold Bryler, the man of talent, went as one of the writing fraternity who grow fat. Lutz Laus dolled himself up in pontificals. Spinoza Spass, the grammar-school pupil – and the Klösschen Clown – had thrown a Siegfried costume on and wore his hair in a Goethe-cut. Müller, the lyric poet, was soon lying on the floor as a drunken corpse. Kuno Kohn, who had formally buried the hatchet with Schulz, came as he was. With him came Lisel Liblichlein, wearing a peasant dress. The rest ran hither and thither – as Chinese, chimpanzees, gods, night-watchmen, and men and women of the world – criss-crossing each other and screeching. The whole of the Café Klösschen was there.

Throughout this night full of colours and squeals, Lisel Liblichlein danced with no one but the hunchbacked poet. Many people watched the curious couple, but there was nothing to laugh about. Kohn's hump stabbed at the others' soft bodies as sharply and inconsiderately as the edge of a table. He appeared to enjoy jabbing his hump repeatedly at anyone dancing. He never missed an opportunity to say 'Pardon' in a falsetto, outrageously polite voice, whenever a crazy woman shrieked or a man grunted a curse in mid-rapture. Lisel Liblichlein put one hand under the poet's hump as if it were a handle, and with her other hand pressed Kohn's angular head gently against her breast. Like this, they danced manically for many hours.

Kohn's hump became more and more of a pain to the other people dancing. Some ventured to voice their indignation. The organizers of the Fancy Dress Ball gave Kohn to understand he must desist from dancing. With such a hump, no one should dance. Kohn did not demur. Lisel Liblichlein saw his face go grey.

She led him to an out-of-the-way alcove. Then she said, 'From now on you're more than just a friend to me.' Kuno Kohn did not answer, but he absorbed her compassionate soul into his water-blue troubadour's eyes like a gift. Quivering, she said that without warning she felt such tenderness for him she could not understand it . . . That she never again wanted to let go of his hand . . . That she had never realized a person could feel such bliss . . . Kuno Kohn invited her to call on him the following evening. She readily agreed.

Kuno Kohn and Lisel Liblichlein were probably the first to leave the frenzied Ball. Whispering, they walked through the streets that were as bright as the sky as they shone in the moonlight. The amorous poet cast peculiar shadows, with enormous humps, on the pavement.

As they said goodbye, Lisel Liblichlein brought her head down towards Kohn. She kissed him several times on the mouth. And so Kuno Kohn and Lisel Liblichlein parted . . . He said he was glad she was going to call on him the next evening. She said very quietly: 'I . . . ahh . . . too . . .'

The houses stood on the well-groomed streets as neatly stacked as books on shelves. The moon had scattered light-blue dust on them. A few windows were awake, they twinkled peacefully like lonely people's eyes, all with the same gold-coloured gaze. Kuno Kohn went home deep in thought. His body was leaning forward at a dangerous angle. His hands were clasped tightly at the base of his back. His head was slumped right down. Over everything towered his hump, a peculiar pointed stone. At this hour Kuno Kohn was no longer a human being, he had his own form.

He thought, I want to avoid feeling blissful. Which means: giving up my longing for things beyond fulfilment, my most precious part. Degrading my holy hump – which a benign destiny vouchsafed to me, through which I have experienced existence far, far more profoundly, more wretchedly, more magnificently than people sense – into something burdensome, superficial. I want to develop Lisel Liblichlein's nobler nature. I want to make her utterly miserable . . .

Whilst Kohn the poet was thinking these thoughts, Schulz the poet finally stabbed himself with a vegetable-knife. He had seen Kuno Kohn and Lisel Liblichlein having their intimate talk in the alcove. Had seen them go out together. He attempted to guzzle and gobble his misery away, but to no avail. After eating and drinking for several hours, he was deranged. He sang, 'Death is a grave business . . . Death is no laughing matter . . . Death is an urgent necessity . . .' Then tentatively, hesitantly, he stuck the first knife he could find into his left breast. Blood and bloodstained bits of lettuce flew everywhere. This time his suicide attempt was crowned with success.

IV

Lisel Liblichlein appeared the next evening earlier than arranged. Kuno Kohn opened the door, with a bunch of flowers in his hand. He was obviously delighted, he said he'd scarcely dared hope she would come. She put her arms round his bony body, squeezing him, crushing him tightly against her and said, 'You silly little hunchback . . . I am very fond of you, you know.'

A few simple supper dishes were consumed. She stroked him whenever she liked the taste of something. She said she would like to stay at his lodgings until after midnight. Then she could celebrate the start of her eighteenth birthday with him . . .

The new day emerged from a church clock. The first audible breaths burst into Kohn's overcast room like groaned prayers. The soul of Lisel Liblichlein's young body had become a temple; she had sacrificed herself, painfully but with a moving lack of reluctance, to the hunchbacked priest. Had said, 'Does that make you glad – ?' Lying in a molten trance of dream and emotion, the thin skin of her eyelids enveloped her.

Suddenly, her whole body tingled with horror. Terror tore at her face like claws. Her wide-open, screaming eyes were bending over the hunchback. Tonelessly, Lisel Liblichlein said, 'This – was – bliss –' Kuno Kohn wept.

She said, 'Kuno, Kuno, Kuno, Kuno, Kuno, Kuno . . . What am I going to do with the rest of my life?' Kuno Kohn sighed. He looked into her suffering eyes seriously, good-naturedly. He said, 'Poor Lisel! The feeling of complete helplessness which has overcome you is one I often have. The only consolation is to be disconsolate. If, after feeling disconsolate, you then despair, you ought to make yourself grotesque. Go on living for the sheer fun of it. Try and feel exultant in the knowledge that existence consists of nothing but brutal, nasty jokes.' He wiped sweat from hump and forehead.

Lisel Liblichlein said, 'Why you're making a long speech, I can't imagine. I don't understand what you've said. Taking my bliss away was unloving of you, Kuno.' The words fell like paper.

She said she wanted to leave. Would he please get dressed. The naked hump embarrassed her . . .

Kuno Kohn and Lisel Liblichlein didn't say another word until, outside the front door of the house in which the *pension* was situated, they parted for ever. He looked into her eyes, held her hand, said, 'Farewell –' She quietly said, 'Farewell –'

Kohn took cover in his hump. Ran off, a broken man. Tears smudged his face. He could feel her sad gaze following him. Then he ran round the corner of the next row of houses. He stopped, dried his eyes with a handkerchief, hurried on, weeping.

Like a disease, slimy fog slithered about the blinded city. Street-lamps were marsh-flowers flickering faintly on blackish, smouldering stalks. Objects and creatures had only chilly shadows and blurred movements. Like an ogre, a night-omnibus tottered past Kohn. The poet shouted, 'Now you're completely on your own again.' Then he was met by a tall hunchbacked woman, with long spidery legs, in a spookily translucent skirt. Her upper body was like a ball lying high up on a little table. She looked at him compassionately, enticingly, with an amorous smile, which the fog distorted into an insane grimace. Kohn immediately vanished in the greyness. She moaned, then took herself off.

The lame day limped on. Smashed the remains of the night with its iron crutch. The half extinguished Café Klösschen lay like a glittering fragment in the silent morning. Somewhere in the background sat the last customer. Kuno Kohn had sunk his head in his trembling hump. The gaunt fingers of one hand covered his forehead and face. His whole body gave out a silent scream.

TRANSLATED BY ANTHONY VIVIS

Talking About Legs

I

In the compartment where I was sitting, the gentleman opposite me said, 'Nobody can run you off your feet.'

I said, 'What do you mean?'

The gentleman said, 'You've got no legs.'

I said, 'Is it so obvious?'

The gentleman said, 'Absolutely.'

I took my legs out of my rucksack. I had wrapped them up in tissue paper. And taken them with me as mementos.

The gentleman said, 'What have you got there?'

I said, 'My legs.'

The gentleman said, 'You lift your legs but still can't make any progress.'

I said, 'I'm afraid not.'

After a pause, the gentleman said, 'How do you propose to manage with no legs?'

I said, 'I haven't puzzled that out yet.'

The gentleman said, 'With no legs you can't even kill yourself satisfactorily.'

I said, 'That's a very poor joke.'

The gentleman said, 'Not at all. If you decide to hang yourself, you'll have to hoist yourself on to a window-sill first. And who will turn on the gas for you if you decide to asphyxiate yourself? You can only get hold of a revolver if you secretly send your man out for one. But suppose you misfire? To drown yourself, you'll have to hire a car and get two male nurses to drag you on a stretcher into the river, which will carry you to the far bank.'

I said, 'That's my problem.'

The gentleman said, 'You're wrong there. Ever since you came in, I've been wondering how you could be removed from the face of the earth. Do you think a legless person is an appealing sight? Or has any right to exist? On the contrary, you disturb your fellow human beings' aesthetic sensibilities considerably.'

I said, 'I'm a professor with a chair in ethics and aesthetics at the university. May I introduce myself?'

The gentleman said, 'How would you set about it? Of course you may not introduce yourself in your impossible condition.'

I looked glumly at my stumps.

II

Whereupon the lady opposite said, 'Having no legs must be a very peculiar sensation.'

I said, 'Yes.'

The lady said, 'I wouldn't want to touch a man with no legs.'

I said, 'I'm very clean.'

The lady said, 'I have to overcome an enormous erotic revulsion to talk to you, let alone look at you.'

I said, 'I see.'

The lady said, 'I'm not saying you're a criminal. You may be an intelligent and originally a charming person. But because of your missing legs, with the best will in the world I couldn't possibly have intercourse with you.'

I said, 'One can get used to anything.'

The lady said, 'A legless man gives a woman with normal feelings an indescribable sense of profound disgust. As if you had committed some unspeakable sin.'

I said, 'But I'm innocent. One leg went astray in the commotion when I was inaugurated as a professor. I lost the second when I was concentrating hard on devising that important aesthetic law which revolutionized our discipline.'

The lady said, 'What is this law?'

I said, 'The law is this: All that matters is the structure of the soul and the spirit. If the soul and spirit are noble, one must find a body beautiful, no matter how hunchbacked and deformed it may be.'

The lady ostentatiously lifted her dress and through it revealed, all the way up to the top of her upper thighs, a pair of exquisite, silk-enveloped legs, which protruded from her luxuriant body like boughs in bud.

Meanwhile, the lady finally said, 'You may be right, although one could just as easily claim the opposite. At all events, a person with legs is a considerably different proposition from one without.'

Whereupon she proudly stalked off, leaving me sitting there.

Translated by Anthony Vivis

Max Oppenheim's pen sketch of the poet appeared on the cover of the special 1913 Lichtenstein edition of *Die Aktion*.

Prophezeiung

Einmal kommt – ich habe Zeichen –
Sterbesturm aus fernem Norden.
Überall stinkt es nach Leichen.
Es beginnt das große Morden.

Finster wird der Himmelsklumpen,
Sturmtod hebt die Klauentatzen.
Nieder stürzen alle Lumpen.
Mimen bersten. Mädchen platzen.

Polternd fallen Pferdeställe.
Keine Fliege kann sich retten.
Schöne homosexuelle
Männer kullern aus den Betten.

Rissig werden Häuserwände.
Fische faulen in dem Flusse.
Alles nimmt sein ekles Ende.
Krächzend kippen Omnibusse.

January 1913

Prophecy

Soon there'll come – the signs are fair –
A death-storm from the distant north.
Stink of corpses everywhere,
Mass assassins marching forth.

The clump of sky in dark eclipse,
Storm-death lifts his clawpaws first.
All the scallywags collapse.
Mimics split and virgins burst.

With a crash a stable falls.
Insects vainly duck their heads.
Handsome homosexuals
Tumble rolling from their beds.

Walls in houses crack and bend.
Fishes rot in every burn.
All things reach a sticky end.
Buses, screeching, overturn.

Translated by Michael Hamburger

Die Dämmerung

Ein dicker Junge spielt mit einem Teich.
Der Wind hat sich in einem Baum verfangen.
Der Himmel sieht verbummelt aus und bleich,
Als wäre ihm die Schminke ausgegangen.

Auf lange Krücken schief herabgebückt
Und schwatzend kriechen auf dem Feld zwei Lahme.
Ein blonder Dichter wird vielleicht verrückt.
Ein Pferdchen stolpert über eine Dame.

An einem Fenster klebt ein fetter Mann.
Ein Jüngling will ein weiches Weib besuchen.
Ein grauer Clown zieht sich die Stiefel an.
Ein Kinderwagen schreit und Hunde fluchen.

March 1911

Twilight

A flabby boy is playing with a pond.
The wind has got entangled in a tree.
The sky looks like the morning after, drained
And pale as though its make-up had run out.

Athwart long crutches, bowed and chattering
Across the field a pair of lame men creeps.
A fair-haired poet may be going mad.
Over a lady a small horse trips up.

A man's fat face sticks to a window-pane.
A youngster wants to visit a soft woman.
A greyish clown is putting on his boots.
A pram begins to yell and dogs to curse.

Translated by Michael Hamburger

DOCH KOMMT EIN KRIEG

Doch kommt ein Krieg. Zu lange war schon Frieden.
Dann ist der Spaß vorbei. Trompeten kreischen
Dir tief ins Herz. Und alle Nächte brennen.
Du frierst in Zelten. Dir ist heiß. Du hungerst.

Ertrinkst. Zerknallst. Verblutest. Äcker röcheln.

Kirchtürme stürzen. Fernen sind in Flammen.
Die Winde zucken. Große Städte krachen.
Am Horizont steht der Kanonendonner.
Rings aus den Hügeln steigt ein weißer Dampf
Und dir zu Häupten platzen die Granaten.

9–10 July 1914

SUPPOSE WAR IS COMING

Suppose war is coming. There's been peace for too long.
Then things will get serious. Trumpet calls
Will galvanize you. And nights will be ablaze.
You will freeze in your tent. You'll feel hot all over. You'll go hungry.
Drown. Be blown up. Bleed to death. Fields will rattle to death.
Church-towers will topple. Horizons will be in flames.
Winds will gust. Cities will come crashing down.
The thunder of heavy guns will fill up the horizon.
From the hills all around smoke
Will rise and shells will explode overhead.

PROSE TRANSLATION BY PATRICK BRIDGWATER

ABSCHIED

(Für Peter Scher)

Vorm Sterben mache ich noch mein Gedicht.
Still, Kameraden, stört mich nicht.

Wir ziehn zum Krieg. Der Tod ist unser Kitt.
O, heulte mir doch die Geliebte nit.

Was liegt an mir. Ich gehe gerne ein.
Die Mutter weint. Man muß aus Eisen sein.

Die Sonne fällt zum Horizont hinab.
Bald wirft man mich ins milde Massengrab.

Am Himmel brennt das brave Abendrot.
Vielleicht bin ich in dreizehn Tagen tot.

LEAVING FOR THE FRONT

(To Peter Scher)

Before dying I must just make my poem.
Quiet, comrades, don't disturb me.

We are going off to war. Death is our bond.
Oh, if only my girl-friend would stop howling.

What do I matter? I'm happy to go.
My mother's crying. You need to be made of iron.

The sun is falling down on to the horizon.
Soon they'll be throwing me into a nice mass grave.

In the sky the good old sunset is glowing red.
In thirteen days maybe I'll be dead.

PROSE TRANSLATION BY PATRICK BRIDGWATER

Gebet vor der Schlacht

Inbrünstig singt die Mannschaft, jeder für sich:
Gott, behüte mich vor Unglück,
Vater, Sohn and heilger Geist,
Daß mich nicht Granaten treffen,
Daß die Luder, unsre Feinde,
Mich nicht fangen, nicht erschießen,
Daß ich nicht wie'n Hund verrecke
Für das teure Vaterland.

Sieh, ich möchte gern noch leben,
Kühe melken, Mädchen stopfen
Und den Schuft, den Sepp, verprügeln,
Mich noch manches Mal besaufen
Bis zu meinem selgen Ende.
Sieh, ich bete gut und gerne
Täglich sieben Rosenkränze,
Wenn du, Gott, in deiner Gnade
Meinen Freund, den Huber oder
Meier, tötest, mich verschonst.

Aber muß ich doch dran glauben,
Laß mich nicht zu schwer verwunden.
Schick mir einen leichten Beinschuß,
Eine kleine Armverletzung,
Daß ich als ein Held zurückkehr,
Der etwas erzählen kann.

Prayer before Battle

The men are singing fervently, every man thinking of
himself:
God, protect me from accidents,
Father, Son and Holy Ghost,
Don't let shells hit me,
Don't let those bastards, our enemies,
Catch me or shoot me,
Don't let me snuff it like a dog
For my dear Fatherland.

Look, I'd like to go on living,
Milking cows, stuffing girls
And beating up that blighter Joe,
Getting tight many more times
Before I die like a Christian.
Look, I'll pray well and willingly,
I'll say seven rosaries a day,
If you, God, in your mercy
Will kill my friend Huber, or
Meier, and spare me.

But if I get my lot,
Don't let me be too badly wounded.
Send me a slight leg wound,
A small arm injury,
So that I may return home as a hero
Who has a tale to tell.

Prose Translation by Patrick Bridgwater

Die Schlacht bei Saarburg

Die Erde verschimmelt im Nebel.
Der Abend drückt wie Blei.
Rings reißt elektrisches Krachen
Und wimmernd bricht alles entzwei.

Wie schlechte Lumpen qualmen
Die Dörfer am Horizont.
Ich liege gottverlassen
In der knatternden Schützenfront.

Viel kupferne feindliche Vögelein
Surren um Herz und Hirn.
Ich stemme mich steil in das Graue
Und biete dem Tode die Stirn.

The Battle of Saarburg

The earth is growing mouldy with mist.
The evening is heavy as lead.
Electrical crackling bursts out all round,
And with a whimper everything breaks asunder.

Like old rags
The villages are smouldering on the horizon.
I am lying God-forsaken
In the rattling front-line.

Many copper enemy birds
Whirl around my heart and head.
I brace myself in the greyness
And face death.

Prose Translation by Patrick Bridgwater

ALFRED LEMM 1889–1918

'The international unifying spirit of those who belong, for the most part, to the Jewish population is a blessing in these insane times, and its only weakness is that it only comes about in times like these.'

1917

Very little is known about Alfred Lemm's life. Symptomatic of this is that he wrote under a pseudonym; he was, in fact, born Alfred Lehmann in Berlin on 6 December 1889 and he lived there most of his life as a writer, contributing to such periodicals as the *Neue Rundschau* and the *Vossische Zeitung*. His health had always been poor, and the military duties by which he was burdened during the war only served to worsen his condition. During the great influenza epidemic he died in the autumn of 1918 of a severe lung infection.

During his illness, Lemm found time to write. Most of his short stories and all of his philosophical and critical essays stem from this wartime period; his analysis of the social and cultural difficulties facing the German Jew, *Der Weg der Deutschjuden*, appearing only posthumously. An expressionist novel, *Der fliehende Felician*, was the first fictional work published, in 1917. There followed two volumes of short stories, entitled somewhat misleadingly and uncompromisingly *Mord* (*Murder*), and it is in these that Lemm's satire comes to the fore.

The only other writer with whom Lemm had much in common – and this was uncommon enough – was with a fellow contributor to the *Sturm* periodical, Alfred Lichtenstein (q.v.). His open letter of admiration to Lichtenstein was published in the *Almanach der Neuen Jugend* in 1917: 'You were a saint, because the others wallowed in the mire. You never smirked over into cynicism as those others did, with the pugilistic wit, their athletic but feeble brains with whom you were continually "likened".'

In Lemm's short story 'Weltflucht' ('Fleeing from the World') written in 1914 but only published in the second *Mord* collection, there is a curious episode in a lawyer's office rather reminiscent of Lichtenstein's quirky humour.

> A new gentleman stepped into the waiting-room. When he caught sight of the many office girls, he gave a quick bow in a manner so uncontrolled that, instead of possessing bones in his back, it seemed attached to a hinge. He cried:
>
> 'Oh, oh! All these lovely girls! Go on – show us your breasts!'
>
> Suddenly he seemed annoyed and overtaken by shame and said:
>
> 'I damn well have to pull myself together!'
>
> He sat down by gripping the back of a stool and laboriously lifting his legs on to another. He related – without addressing anyone in particular – that he had sat out three years in gaol, and during this time, the government had secretly extracted his spinal column. Now of course he could not sit properly any more. Regrettably he had only noticed the theft after being released. He could well imagine what the government needed his backbone for – he nodded threateningly several times – but this time they had picked on the wrong man! He would not be robbed! He presented petition after petition in order to retrieve his bones. He had already been to most of the lawyers in town and pressed them unrelentingly to file suit on his behalf.

'Die Hure Salomea' carries these elements of the grotesque and the ironic to an extreme in order to pass comment on the inverted morality prevalent in wartime. It was Lemm's last and longest story.

TIM CROSS

Texts

Der fliehende Felician (Georg Müller, Munich, 1917). An expressionist novel, written 1912/13.
Vom Wesen der wahren Vaterlandsliebe (Heinz Barger, Berlin, 1917). Essay, appearing as part 3 of *Schriften gegen die Zeit*.
Mord (Roland, Munich, 1918). Appeared as vols. I and II of *Die neue Reihe*. Vol. I contains short stories 'Die Hure Salomea'; 'Das Fest der Liebe im Altmännerhaus'; 'Der arme Reinhold'. Vol. II contains short stories 'Der Herr mit der gelben Brille'; 'Radfahrer Behnke oder Wie wird man Mörder?'; 'Der ausländische Professor'; 'Die Schauspielerin, ihre Kammerfrau und Zapkow'; 'Fias Hochzeit'; 'Weltflucht'. All the stories date 1912–17.
Der Weg der Deutschjuden: eine Skizzierung (Der Neue Geist Verlag, Leipzig, 1919). Essay.
Gesammelte Prosa (Thomas Rietzschel (ed.), Brennglas, Assenheim, 1987).

Salomea, the Whore

Salomea, a student of medicine, was sitting in her usual café, which was perched above the main shopping street in the city centre. She used to sleep there all night as well, if she found it too much trouble to stand up. From her window, she could look into the educated class's houses, in which young people sat at handcrafted little tables, smiling as they leafed through the exquisitely gilt-edged, leather-bound volumes of our classical philosophers which kept appearing, week after week, in tasteful deluxe editions. Salomea's oval white head observed attentively what was going on around her, but always, after only a few minutes of listening, a grey veil would come down over her eyes; behind which, listless and distant, she was dead to the world.

From time to time, she used to climb down to the dissecting rooms. Initially, these so shocked her – she had just left grammar school – that she would let out a scream at every visit; she had never realized that one could cut up human thighs so neatly or unthread foreheads. She had chosen this field of study because her guardian – her parents, Sephardic Jews, were dead – insisted that, come what may, she must do something intellectual; and because she hoped it might help her get over the chronic boredom from which she had suffered since first starting school. After one term, she had transferred, as an experiment, to literary history, but after listening to the popular professor of literature giving an eight-hour course of lectures in which he offered strictly scientific proof that the love affair which the Old Master of German Letters had so beautifully immortalized in his poem to Leonore P. had *not* led to sexual gratification, she stayed in medicine, and tolerated the combination of inquisitive horror, cold suffering and the sheer indifference which characterized her approach to this branch of science. None the less, most things gave her the impression of being unalterable. Accordingly, she saw everyone in the street in the naked state, and charted her own lack of sexual desire, her instinctive gestures of revulsion and, whenever she tossed back her head, heard the lobes of her brain slap together.

Occasionally, students would come up to her and hold important meetings at her table. They agreed with their rector on one thing: the removal of the final remaining opposition to their right to register with the 'Official Employment Agency for Incomes over Five Thousand'.

At nearby tables sat the last surviving artists, discussing how a work of art's intellectual remuneration could be expressed in equations of the second degree.

Sometimes, when she opened her eyes, Salomea would suddenly find herself sitting at an empty table.

On Sunday afternoons, when an even stronger smell of cakes wafted up from below, a lot of people used to walk past to see the monument to their national hero – the publisher of the first international democratic newspaper – which had been erected opposite the monument to the old national hero who had steered the country to unification. The colossal monument – the city's new landmark – was clearly visible from where Salomea was sitting. It represented the worthy man at the moment when, on his way to the editorial office, he had thought up the motto 'Truth before everything', which was later printed on the title page of all his journals directly under the rates for advertisements. There, each week, members of every party, even of the erstwhile highly rebellious ones, along with their families, clustered in groups of twos and threes, and under the rapturous smile of the elderly head of state, who used to appear at his window, intoned the hymn: 'He who lets the Lord God rule', thereby expressing the entire nation's mood.

Suddenly, a disturbance pierced the idyll of evenings well wasted in loose living. There was a decidedly greater influx of people pouring towards the city centre. A crowd darkened the pavement under Salomea's café. From the side-streets, a constant stream of people flowed in her direction.

Unheard-of excitement ran through the city. Black swarms burrowed deep into its entrails, driving up against one another.

The jangle of voices rang out more strongly from below. Individual cries could be distinguished. Like a colossal mollusc, the teeming mass coalesced dangerously, leaving large bare patches on the asphalt – then briskly, without warning, dispersed again. Savage gangs wheeled around conspicuous individuals, fighting to get there first. Between them puttered motor-buses, in such a hurry that their back-ends swerved, hurling their drivers off their seats in great arcs.

Metamorphosed, people remained rooted to the street. Cafés and shops stayed open. Lights still burned even during the day, and the neon signs, which people forgot to switch off, hissed like rockets among the tangled surge of bodies. For several days, densely packed crowds stood on one side, yelling: 'Up with . . .! Up with . . .!', while other people, on the opposite side, called out: 'Down with . . .! Down with . . .!' – though no one could tell what anyone was shouting about. Then the clumps of people burst apart again in all directions. On the carriageways, trams raced along at breakneck speed; between them, cars drove recklessly into each other and got locked together.

The mob surged forward with immense force, overturning small carriages and treading perambulators, kiosks and policemen underfoot. Day and night, the echoing roars of the masses floated up. The high arc-lamps screamed in their dreams. Towards morning, you could hear the streets groaning from the strain and the terrifying, incessant pressure; but the day's new excitements were already beginning.

Even by this time, the weak-spirited could take no

more. Genteel ladies turned without any provocation and shouted: 'Where? Where do you mean?' Word had suddenly got round – apparently it had come from people in the know – that a new, sixth continent had been discovered. There had been unmistakable light-signals.

Salomea woke up. She leaned over the windowsill.

In a headlong rush, the unredeemed masses poured, foaming, through the cobbled streets. The infernally concentrated tension shattered house walls, and they came crashing down. Motor-buses' brakes failed, and their drivers sat there helpless while their vehicles drove into the mob on the pavements.

Then people said the President of the United States had done a moonlight flit with the greatest of French tragediennes, and they had died for love of one another.

And then came the Great War.

Salomea climbed down the stairs, and strolled inquisitively through the rejuvenated city. Young people were standing outside the barracks; aglow with oratory and vaunting their physical prowess, they begged the officers, who were calmly scrutinizing them, to let them in. Overwhelmed by gratitude, they could no longer look round at the mothers and sisters who had accompanied them, once they had been given the chance to risk their lives.

On the broad parade-grounds, on which, after decades of the same mechanically reiterated drilling, desolate masses of sand had been pounded down, volunteers busied themselves with the ferocious machinery of war. Fired by holy zeal, they dragged heavy artillery along, and tried their luck with horses which had not been broken in, and which would rear up on their hind legs with three weightless youths hanging on to their halters. Hooves struck young heads. Iron wheels mangled soft bones; with eyes aflame, their companions didn't notice.

In Salomea, something stirred. She became uneasy.

One saw standard bearers at the head of small units, gleaming as they marched through the streets to collect their colours: tall but still pastel-complexioned boys, who had just left cadet school and were taking command for the first time. For sheer pride, they saw nothing beyond their commission, fresh uniform and high collar. They didn't really know if they were giving out the right orders and, under their breath, asked the older soldiers; but their harsh boys' voices did not for one moment mellow into a tone of ringing certainty.

Without warning, Salomea sent her relatives – several families to whom she owed gratitude for having shown her nothing but kindness – letters to say that she was breaking off relations. She threw away several articles of value – some expensive clothes, and books – in her possession, to the amazement of her speechless landlady who, after recovering, sold the items for a substantial sum. Then Salomea suddenly made frantic preparations for a high-altitude mountaineering trip, which she did not, however, undertake. Eventually, she remembered she had studied medicine, and enrolled as a nurse.

The field hospital was under the command of an elderly chief medical officer with white hands and a soft beard. He was in the middle of breakfast: porridge with a few slices of toast.

'The young female colleagues who put their services at the disposal of our institution,' he said, 'do not adopt such a luke-warm, superficial attitude to their duties as they may do in other field hospitals, but devote themselves to their profession with all the strength of their inborn feminine instinct for love.'

The supervisor was an aristocratic woman, a tall, still very young person with a pointed nose and powerful hands. She towered above all the soldiers and called each of them 'my boy'. Every day, in the morning and the evening, she would do her rounds between the soldiers who lay in their beds unable to move their limbs, which were tightly squashed together, stroking their heads and giving them a motherly smile. The soldiers thought: 'If only we could walk by ourselves again!'

The nursing sister under whom Salomea worked had left her fiancé at the outbreak of war, and ever since had only had one thought in her mind – to show the wounded as much kindness as was humanly possible. She hardly ever appeared in the soldiers' ward, but worked herself to a frazzle for them. She left her lunch for stronger colleagues, who were always famished. Already extremely enfeebled, she could only drag herself about with difficulty, and suffered fainting fits. Yet she kept up the same degree of tender, loving self-sacrifice and could only feel annoyed whenever the chief medical officer spoke about her retiring for health reasons.

Then there were also a number of nuns who, without making a sound, flew indefatigably along the corridors day and night in their big, dark, pleated costumes. At the outbreak of war, they had lodged an urgent petition with the king, requesting permission to leave the society of female persons as they intended to establish a third, independent gender; in so doing, they expected their family connections with the top echelons of the Establishment to help them succeed.

Salomea tried to do her work with the same dedication she saw in the nursing sister. She felt warm affection for this gentle, beautiful girl, which she in turn – as far as her hectic existence would allow – reciprocated, until one day Salomea heard an extremely shocked voice behind her:

'For heaven's sake, what's the matter with you? You calmly watch these poor people grimace with pain without going to their assistance!'

Salomea moved her hand, to rip through the thick veil in which she found herself.

'Perhaps you're unwell?' the sister asked indulgently, though anyone observing Salomea's behaviour would, from time to time, notice similar moments, because she was in the habit of giving her contempt free rein. Salomea solemnly swore to herself that she would pull herself together, whatever effort it cost. She tried with all her might to force herself to have normal feelings, and would often secretly pinch herself with her fingernails, to remind herself to feel compassion. But even the soldiers could not summon any affection for this constantly silent girl who never stopped scrutinizing them. Whenever she appeared, they would stop laughing. While sewing some small presents for the soldiers on one of her free nights, the sister said sadly to Salomea:

'People who are incapable of love needn't necessarily be bad people – but they are not suited to this profession.'

Salomea grasped her scrawny hand. She asked the sister to be patient a little longer. It was true, she said, that she could never tell in advance what effect a new environment would have on her. Many things surprised even her. But she did mean to help with the common cause – that she could manage.

Until one morning the supervisor stormed into the ward:

'Last night, a badly wounded patient rang several times, and you didn't even get up! You will leave the field hospital at once!'

Salomea thought about it.

'I certainly heard it,' she said, remembering hard, tormentedly. 'I was reading . . .' She couldn't even explain it to herself. Merely said with a certain defiance:

'Sometimes your mind is on things and sometimes it isn't!'

The well-meaning sister drew back as quickly as possible the hand she had extended in order to say goodbye. Salomea terrified her.

The chief medical officer was halfway through lunch: squabs and hot milk.

'You're gifted, but very heartless. God be with you,' he said.

Salomea sat down in her café again. The disagreeable memory of how badly she had acquitted herself depressed her greatly. She didn't tell anyone about her experiment. Her listlessness, of which she had had unmistakable proof, hit her hard. The question: 'Why couldn't she do what any other normal woman could do with ease?' kept preoccupying her afresh.

Once more, she withdrew behind the curtain of her eyes, and let the bustle of the city drift past her dimly in the distance. Under the thin veneer of her indifference, however, her big white nostrils twitched suspiciously.

One night, cuirassiers rode past the back of the house through a side-alley. Half asleep, she could hear the bottoms going up and down in the saddles, and the dull creaking of the breastplates. She hurried downstairs. The horses' nostrils flared blood-red in the shadows of what few street-lights there were. Their foaming bits were as bright and white as the weapons. Occasionally, a horse would groan, snorting with passion.

Salomea darted up to one of the soldiers, kissed him and dropped down again. Then she leapt up at the next. The horsemen grabbed her round the middle, held her long enough to be kissed, and let her slide down again. Thus she leapt all the way down the long line of clopping horses which, with their wet brown necks gallantly bent, whinnied wildly and meekly allowed Salomea to lean against them – drawing herself up and sinking back down again all night long.

Trains were running one after the other along the iron tracks which traversed the city in all directions like a star. Soldiers were lying in the openings within the carriages, which were decorated with foliage. Every street was full of singing greenery of youth. Boys surged along the embankments. The city roared with the energy of blond youth desperate to see action.

Angrily Salomea thought: 'I don't want to dole out scraps of help any more! If I can't go back to society . . .' She tried to sing along, but she soon let the discordant note she sounded tail off, and such a mouthful of impotent rage rose in her gorge that she had difficulty staying upright.

She felt drawn to the military quarter. Volunteers passed through here from all parts of the country. Young people with sensitive eyes sat on the running-boards and roof-ladders, swinging their legs, cigarettes between their lips. They stood on the platform, stretching their arms into the fresh morning sun after their long journey. Their slender throats were tanned. Nothing but shirts enclosed the noble columns that were their chests, alive muscles flexing under the cloth. Leather puttees, which reinforced the bold outlines of their calves, made them stand boldly, as if they had taken root. Their feet stepped with a light, rocking motion secure in the knowledge that they had, after all, to carry a chest carved out of human flank – even the costliest fabric would compare unfavourably with the material which formed a protective shell for the greatest of glories . . .

Salomea suddenly had a vision, and on her rigidly immobile head, her blue temples, horrified in the extreme, throbbed violently. She saw the young men's bodies in her dissecting-room, clumsily chopped up for autopsy, torn apart and bleeding. The soft, firm muscles had been transmogrified into the stringy, ox-like meat of butcher's shops. Dark brown cavities, refuges for maggots, the stench from coarse, fibrous hollows in rib-cages. Arms, immensely long, with bent stalks of fingers, hung individually on hooks. Eyes as blind as jelly and the colour of pale gums were already drifting in jars – Salomea screamed!

With a feather-light tread, the men climbed to the roofs of the waggons. Shouting jokes down, they went on.

Salomea groaned: 'I don't just want to sit around pleasing myself! I want to be involved!' Almost yelling: 'I'm human, too!'

So many younthful farewells all the time! Old fathers dragged themselves as well as heavy luggage for those moving off, who, though they were uncomprehending, oblivious to any danger, still looked at their mothers indulgently; these, in turn, cast furtive glances at the engine, constantly, repeatedly giving hands yet another squeeze, and asking which way the officer was bound, not knowing who else to turn to.

Along the platform, sounds of joy came towards them. Sitting aloft on pieces of artillery which had been carefully clothed in rich, light-brown leather, and which thrusted their gleaming copper throats diagonally upwards, blond youths with insouciant expressions slowly glided past. With shirts wide open, blue-eyed and clearly aware of what they were risking their necks for, they rode smilingly into battle.

Salomea stood there, unable to free herself from the glances which had clung to her. Atavistic squirms of suffering lay buried beneath her white features. Yet underneath those stony features, passions raced, each one crowding out the next.

'I won't let any chunks be ripped out of your white chests! I'll throw myself in front of the train! I'll sacrifice *myself* . . .' And fiercely accusing: 'They won't stop! No one will listen to me! Already the broad, piercing knives are advancing! Who will help?' She sobbed in such terror that she tottered, desperately toppling forward: 'I won't have it! I'll protect your tender, echoing vaults with my own body! I love you!'

Soft currents poured over her, lifting her mouth open into a painful aperture. Lips protruding, she whimpered, without realizing it, a tormented plea:

'Take me.'

Horseman after horseman hovered past, looking skywards, while everyone who had been left behind bowed low and raised their hats.

Fear of being left behind gave Salomea second wind. The turmoil in her blood increased immensely. She pushed the top part of her body a long way forward, as if she wanted to roll round the earth. With her teeth locked together, she hammered beseechingly with her chin:

'Do something! Do something!'

A voice inside her bellowed: 'Not just you! Me! Me! Me!' She felt pushed on by a swirling feeling.

Then, with a yell of self-release, she distractedly tore off her clothes and ran into the barracks. There, hurling herself at the thirsting bodies with an intensity which made her close her eyes, she found redemption in a thousand arms.

'At last!' she felt, as she gave herself as often as required. 'Oh, you youths,' she said and opened herself wide. She embraced their heads, which rushed up to meet her, and kissed them as if she were kissing an entire nation. She cushioned her two noble breasts, covered with human skin and containing something inexpressible, on white pillows, so that they might not split! – the slightest tear could cause disproportionately terrible damage! The young knights, pregnant with unborn dreams, sank to their knees before her and composed oaths of undying love.

The silent men, who, with hints of blond beard on friendly faces, had marched out to offer their great bodies for the fray, gently took her in their strong hands, thanked her and began to smile. Some of them apologized to her several times. Before long, they were already waiting for her at the entrance. And when she left, songs followed her.

Throughout the soldiers' quarters, 'lights out' was sounded. Blue stars swung through the wide barracks windows. Hovering for ever at the same height, a current of release from the earth's gravity passed through the bare rooms, with their chequered iron camp-beds, like a never-ending sigh.

Salomea hurried from barracks to barracks, spreading out what she had. She failed to understand the crudities of the impure in heart, to whom she was merely a good meal. At first, they shrank from her silk clothes. But then the wooden floors echoed under their stamping hooves as each man competed to help himself first. 'You'll shatter when we grab hold of you,' they laughed. When they grasped Salomea's joints, their hands disappeared. Salomea's slim, nimble body arched back. But only for an instant – then, subsiding, she offered herself indiscriminately. The clumsy ones secretly brought her presents: brightly coloured oleographs of their supreme commanders, or firm hams. Others – to express their great love for her – hit her with their fists, so that her thin arms wept. She was generally known as the 'Jewish whore'.

Salomea would appear without warning, sometimes on one side of the city, sometimes on the opposite side. Sentries everywhere were happy to let her in, knowing full well that their companions would soon come to relieve them and give them a chance to get to the dormitories.

The many male bodies which convulsed before her all night long etched themselves into Salomea's acute mind as bright strokes, and touched her with the tender passion of salvation. The soldiers in the city could talk about nothing but her. Life in the barracks throbbed with a subterranean emotion which superior officers were unable to explain. During the day, the soldiers willingly accomplished the most difficult of tasks because their minds were on the rewards of the night. Delicate city boys handled the heaviest of rifle butts as if they were toys, and those marching into battle sent secret farewells up after her.

Rumours about Salomea found their way out of the barracks to people in the city. A number of women, afraid of illicit interference, complained to the mayor, forcing him to take action.

Hidden in a carriage by some of the soldiers, Salomea travelled out with a departing regiment to the frontiers of the country. This way, she could be close to them up to the last moment before they had to defend themselves.

In the town where the military had their base, fresh supplies of human life and infernal instruments were stockpiled, whence they were hurled into the distantly rumbling, insatiable battle; and whither the used-up, crushed, flattened, ruined remains were vomited back. In the town's exposed brain, untold bundles of intersecting electric wires converged; the harsh, never-ending tick of telegraphed orders dispatched dark clumps of men through the ruins of burn-blackened streets. Between square horses, whipped until they reared up, cars panted, leaping on the cobbles. On the squares, exhausted soldiers crashed to the ground, dropping off, mouths open, between piles of bloodstained kit-bags and rifles clogged with sand, shouting out loud in their sleep to ward off the threatening, unearthly rumbling sound which, as it never broke off, drove the townspeople to attacks of insanity because, however much they barricaded their ears and ran round in circles, they could not escape it anywhere.

Salomea shared herself out with frantic energy. In the dissolution of embraces, she suddenly squirmed in pain, praying:

'Your powerful bodies full of tripes which the waiters toss on to the tables! Your heads balls of clay with silly holes and gashes, your singing souls! Your miraculously coloured skin – skins, let the tanner have them . . .'

'What are you muttering?' asked the soldiers. 'Are you a witch?' and brightly: 'A wonderful witch!'

She saw the young regiments climb out of their trains: from here, they were to be led straight into the line of fire. Like a herd of sensitive-skinned roe deer, fearing surprise from every possible direction, here and there they would suddenly, briskly turn their heads, often shifting on their feet uncertainly. Yet, as if by arrangement, they pretended that the side from which the hollow sound kept nagging did not exist. If eyes met, they smiled past each other. Then the drum snatched back their senses, which had, against regulations, wandered off, drawing all the troops into one unit, so that they, once again quite happy to take their places, marched into the artillery barrage.

With passion in her heart, Salomea gave herself to the youngest soldiers, whose last thoughts before marching off were of their friends; who carried with them in their breast pockets the old, bloodstained pacts they had signed as boys to be unflinchingly brave.

'How white the bodies of many savage warriors are!' smiled Salomea. They opened their eyes wide and let her lead them.

'Just imagine,' they wrote to their parents, 'what a marvellous stroke of good luck we had just before we left! Unfortunately, we can't give you any more details; but we feel as if whole new suns have risen. In the space of an hour, our horizons have broadened immensely. We can hear all kinds of unfamiliar sounds, and can smell smells we never knew existed. We weep at the thought that we might have gone to our deaths without experiencing any of all this. Now we have had an insight into the greatness of reality. Beautiful mother-earth! If we come back, we shall do nothing but sing her praises and try to receive yet more at her hands. A number of us have already fallen. But they weren't aware of having been hit, because they were dreaming about their new experience.'

That ever-menacing 'too late' of the hour to come drove Salomea to fly urgently from one arm to another. The soldiers, aware of the harsh immensity, drank their fill of her and were still in a blissful trance when they went away from her into battle. They smiled at the enemy.

'No one's paying attention!' the officers shouted indignantly.

The soldiers thought: 'We're still under the spell,' shaking their heads.

In the agony of a slow death and intolerable exertions, they longed for Salomea. In the field hospitals, soldiers waking up first thought of her, even before they had realized they were still alive. It was in her that the meek eyes of those who timidly, uncomprehendingly looked at the place where a limb had once been, took refuge.

One day, some companions took her to a lieutenant whose birthday it was. He was sitting alone at his table in his room, surrounded by light. This was the first time he'd spent a birthday away from home, and he'd set out his birthday table just as his mother had always done: a number of candles in a circle on a plate stuck into some sand, with the candle of life in the centre.

Salomea counted the candles. 'Seventeen,' she said, covering him with caresses. 'You're still very young. But what else can I give you?'

He was hostile, making no secret of his contempt. But once she drove her soft hands through his slender, toughened body, he suddenly began to wonder whether it was a deadly sin or a divine miracle that was hanging over him. At this, his long, tender face was filled with terror. He became angry at the person who had aroused these hitherto unknown thoughts in him, and as the pleasantly tumescent flood threatened to engulf him completely, he complained as helplessly and stubbornly as if he were a child. Then, in his first, utterly fresh ardour, as he reached for her body with unpractised movements, she threw herself on top of him.

He would not let go again, was no longer on earth. He wanted to introduce her to his commander-in-chief at once. She was to march at the head of the unit and be awarded the most important decorations. 'Victory will be ours,' he exulted. He let a little of his boundless bliss spill over into her.

One day, sandwiched in the middle of one of the trains set aside for transporting wounded soldiers, which would from time to time drag themselves as slowly as the gasping breath of someone seriously ill, a first-class carriage pulled in under the sieve-like roof of the devastated station. Immediately, a swarm of journalists leapt out, clapping their hands, preening their moustaches, and clicking their cameras.

They were looking for copy to complete a story along the lines of: 'Lighthearted snapshots from the bloodthirsty battle of the nations'. They peered into the carriages which housed the wounded, and took a good look at the open-air eating area, towards which everyone struggled as quickly as humanly possible – hobbling, jumping, swinging their way forward on long crutches. The journalists took pictures of a medical orderly giving a soldier a piggyback ride. They asked some of the older campaigners, 'Well now, young fellow, how long have you been serving your country?' and laid copies of their newspaper, containing their own articles about the theatre of war, on the stretchers of badly wounded soldiers who were carried past still unconscious.

The officer who was showing them round smiled and drew their attention to Salomea.

'At last a subject that'll interest our public!' the reporters shouted, and bore down on Salomea. They had already heard a great deal about her unofficially, they said, and were glad to be able to report to their newspapers about her direct for once. They asked her permission to photograph her surrounded by a group of soldiers, who might hoist her on to their shoulders. She could rest assured, they told her, that far from any hint of suggestiveness they would make sure that the article was totally respectable. Even the most solid family newspapers would be able to publish her photo.

'The public,' one of the journalists said, 'also wants to be given some *cheerful* impressions of the theatre of war now and again, and after all the nervous strain its newspapers put it through nowadays, that's what the public quite properly deserves.'

A second journalist asked her permission to change her Christian name: he intended to write a feature called 'Elsa, the Soldiers' Sweetheart'. The public didn't care for exotic first names. And in any case, biblical names were not at all popular right now.

'The public,' another continued, 'doesn't only want to eat its rations with its reporters, and share their spartan camp-bed – it also wants to follow them in their, how shall we put it, more intimate experiences. Let's not begrudge the public its little weakness – its curiosity, if you like!'

The train was due to continue its journey. The journalists stood in the evening light, leaning against the remains of the station with legs crossed, chatting and toying with their walking-sticks. They were wearing sports trousers and well-tailored casual jackets; and, so it was rumoured, a famous writer was supposed to be among them.

It was only through the family newspapers at home that the authorities learned about Salomea's activities; the military police arrested her and locked her in the local prison.

Salomea did not object to the chance of lying in peace for days on end. She had been suffering attacks of giddiness and sickness recently.

One morning, she was led into a courtroom. She stood in a brightly lit room in front of a body of fierce, distinguished elderly gentlemen.

'Don't come so close,' she heard the judge say, while feeling a grey pince-nez sparkle on her.

A tall young gentleman said as briskly and indifferently as if he were reading a list:

'This is such an open-and-shut case that there is no need for any further evidence. The defendant has practised prostitution on a number of occasions, which the prosecutor's office estimate at 242. In accordance with Regulation 331, Section 4, Chapter 3, Paragraph 1, the defendant must be sentenced to a term of imprisonment not less than . . . at which point I would like to comment that even you, Your Honour' – he took off his wig – 'in this context . . .'

The judge said to Salomea:

'Answer loudly and clearly without using any foreign language.'

No sooner – under the impact of the brisk questions, one following the other, raining down on her like hammer-blows – had Salomea understood enough to know what was at stake, than the whole court suddenly rose to their feet as one, so that they seemed to be invisibly tied together, and announced:

'At a time when every man and woman in the nation has no other thought in their head other than how to serve the land they love, the defendant has abandoned herself to the most shameless debauchery to a degree which considerably exceeds anything previously encountered in this category. At the very same hour that thousands of her brothers were dying heroes' deaths, the defendant's sole object was to satisfy her quite bestial lust. We would have allowed her mitigating circumstances, if she had committed fornication for motives of gain. But without any motive, and with no objective that we, at any rate, could comprehend, to lead the most depraved life of carnal indulgence is not merely immoral, but – if we consider that the defendant has implicated large sections of the population in her activities – amounts to an attitude that is hostile in the extreme to her and our Fatherland; not to mention the suspicion that she was working for a hostile power; which, if we consider the fact that the defendant belongs to the Jewish faith, whose business acumen is, after all, proverbial, cannot be ruled out. For immorality, coupled with behaviour hostile to the Fatherland, the defendant is therefore sentenced to the maximum possible term of 7 years and 8 months imprisonment.'

Whereupon the gentlemen took their leave without giving Salomea, who had by now remembered what she wanted to say, another glance.

In a few days, Salomea was to be packed off to the interior. Since Salomea, who was feeling feebler all the time, was by now suffering from occasional paralysis of the limbs and poor eyesight, she was handed over to one of the trains which was taking wounded back to the homeland. She was locked up in a goods waggon, which was crammed full of seriously injured prisoners and Allies – Russians, Croats, Slovenes and similar nationalities.

A ferociously pungent animal smell – of pus, what used to be human blood, and sweat-drenched clothing – blew towards her out of the brown hollow. From the twilight of grey straw, eyes glinted out of disfigured white faces. In a row, one beside the other, lay packages of human meat which at several points bled afresh and which occasionally, as if inadvertently, moved and whimpered. Powerful Slavic bodies lay in their own excrement, just as the battle had dismembered them. Their extremities, plaster-white stems at the end of which were toes of gigantic proportions stuck on blackened slabs of feet, had difficulty stretching across the thin straw. The yellowy-brown faces gaped in an unwavering bovine stare at their new companion.

On his back in front of Salomea lay a small black-haired Croat. A short shirt of poor quality covered the few remaining parts of his body. His legs were little stumps. He grimaced the whole time, as the little that he could still move squirmed to and fro; already, his tormented features began to change markedly –

Salomea shuffled across to him. On her knees, she collected straw from the sides, laid it gently under his back more and more thickly, until he was softly embedded – and covered him up by giving herself to him. The Croat's face became calm, and in his frugal passion, he forgot his pain. Speechless with gratitude, he looked at her.

How knife-sharp the bony edge of his shins was, when Salomea stroked them! How thin – like arms – his thighs, so that the knee-joints formed curiously thick white knots!

Salomea groped her way forward. Immediately next to stinking clumps, belly-flesh, soft and magnificent, spilled out of gashed uniforms. Beneath the hairy blankets, strong thighs: the lower half of the burned bodies, and heads with no faces: the sexual parts – proudly stood apart from their meeting-point. Despite encrustations of filth and wound, an unbelievably soft blond down blossomed on them.

Salomea embraced a bony body which had been shot to pieces, kissing it:

'This is my body,' kissing his eyes which were blank with fever, 'my gleaming human eyes!' and handed herself to all the mutilated, unfamiliar great bodies. In a feeble ecstasy of love, she pressed herself to them as if she wanted her body to express the men's torments.

'Anguish, anguish has been scattered over you all,' she gasped. 'I want to gather up your anguish.'

From one to another, she crawled through the waggon. The train rumbled on its long, cautious journey. The men – temporarily soothed – now only twitched occasionally. Now and then, Salomea felt the limbs beneath her close stiffly about her, and she detached herself quietly and without horror from the men who had grown cold, whose faces carried her departing beauty away with them.

Weary and limp, Salomea sat down in a corner. Whenever pain overwhelmed the men, she fastened her eyes on them, so that she could bear it. The yellow straw brought a dismal gleam to the twilight. Thus she journeyed amid the groaning and mumbling of the feverish soldiers. Whenever they opened their eyes, she forced herself to give them a kindly smile, which made the dying men happy as, with a glassy stare fixed on the far distance, they looked in her direction. Exhausted, she fell asleep.

All at once, in sudden recognition, the short, filthy Croat lifted up his abandoned hands and, pointing them towards Salomea, slowly crossed them. He now knew: this was his patron saint, the same Saint Anna who in his village church at home sat in the dim wooden niche at the front! She for whom he had so often left his written prayers and little bunches of flowers, and who had always helped him – in the old days when everything was still peaceful, and he drove his oxen-cart cheerily through the farms! On the very day he enlisted, he had brought her a large heart made of gold paper, on both sides of which there were beautiful pictures of sacred events, and two of the most powerful candles money could buy. In return, she had been with him in the war, and had now come down to him, to stroke his legs and show kindness to him in this hour of great, great need. As piously as in the past, he prayed to his Lady of Grace, his lips moving gently.

The other wounded soldiers noticed this and likewise lifted up their powerful hands. She was, after all, *their* patron saint, the one they had each carried with them all through the whole appalling period, in their hearts and in little lockets on their breasts! Without being able to grasp it completely, they stammered unfamiliar sounds. Many names – Olga, Katharina, Sophia – rang out in confusion. The customary formulas of reverence released themselves from their mouths. Those who were unable to raise their hands moved their heads, as often as they could, up and down. Fading, pious glances sank down over Salomea from all sides.

Perhaps – they could see the woman only dimly because they couldn't sit up – perhaps it was Mary, the Mother of God herself, who had appeared to them in that blood-soaked, stinking goods waggon somewhere between terror and pain? Fervently, each in his own language, they praised her, their Blessed Virgin.

Salomea sat on the waggon floor, legs apart, her head leaning against the side. Her clothes were still undone. She had become hollow and hideous. The shape of her breasts was scarcely visible any more. Her thighs were bony. Black furrows cut through her face. Her sensitive hair had become stringy and harsh, as happens to female vagabonds.

The wheels sang, never-ending, in her sleep.

All night long, the wounded soldiers prayed, with lips burning, to the decomposing 'Jewish whore', who, in her dream, had made a gesture of pain.

TRANSLATED BY ANTHONY VIVIS

*P*ETER *B*AUM 1869–1916

'Me down here – it is really fathomless, pointless. If only I could get back to writing again – self-pity O.'
In the trenches, November 1915

Peter Baum. *Stadtarchiv Wuppertal*

The presence of Peter Baum at the front-line in France was an incongruity. Baum was a naturally trusting, naïve and peaceable man, and at 45, serving as a stretcher-bearer on the Western Front he was under more stress than most. The misery induced by the conditions, his resulting insomnia and the ever-mounting deaths about him was put to an abrupt end on 5 June 1916. While digging graves in the late evening after battle, he was fatally wounded by a stray piece of shrapnel. The next morning he died.

Peter Baum was born into a strictly Protestant family of the Rhine valley, in Elberfeld on 30 September 1869. His puritanical upbringing strongly contrasts with the grotesque and inventive tales which form the bulk of his output. His first ventures into the literary world, however, were of a practical nature, although publishing was not an area for which Baum was especially well equipped. He attempted to start up a children's book publishing business on the basis of no experience whatsoever, and his partner then swindled him out of the earnings of the undertaking. Baum's only profit from this disastrous experience was character material for a later novel, *Spuk* (1912), in which his cheating former partner featured as the unappetizing Weitzmann. His forays into academic study in Berlin at the end of the century fared no better.

It was Baum's sister Julie who provided him with the link with the Berlin literary scene that he needed. Julie Baum was a portrait painter of note, and in 1898, one of her sitters was the famous author of *Sappho*, Peter Hille. Peter Baum's contact with Hille led to further introductions. The most influential of these was the poet Else Lasker-Schüler, who was instrumental in persuading Herwarth Walden to accept Baum's writings for the avant-garde *Sturm* periodical.

This was a considerable achievement, for Baum's prose and poetry is in no sense revolutionary or novel. But Walden, having accepted Baum, staunchly defended his choice, even after the latter's death, with characteristic loyalty. Critics in their obituaries of Baum found that he either 'left nothing of permanence behind' or that 'his stories lacked material substance, his poems a formal brilliance'. Walden's response to these critics, who measured a poet's stature by his (lasting) success with the wider reading public, was: 'At any rate, it is preferable to be complete in oneself, than to win acceptance from the press. Peter Baum did not seek this sort of acceptance. But he sought God and dreams.'

The year 1914 saw a change in Baum's work, from employing the lurid and fantastical to the ambiguous use of language, as in *Kammermusik* (*Chamber Music*), a rococo novel. During the war, Baum began the novel *Kyland*, which calls into question the nature of the relationship of race to culture, but the most immediate impact the war had on his writing was in the *Schützengrabenverse* (*Trench Poems*), first published after his death in 1916.

Patrick Bridgwater, in his Epilogue *The German Poets of the First World War*, writes of Baum:

> He was an imaginative writer with a strong sense of the grotesque, which comes across in his war poetry. His plan to write a 'Grabenbuch' in prose came to nothing, but then he knew that it would in any case be unpublishable since it would encourage the Allies. His unpublished letters from the front speak of the progressive demoralization of the German army. A passage from an undated letter, dealing with the *Schützengrabenverse*, speaks of the way in which it is

> possible to smuggle a good deal of one's experiences into unwarlike lines . . . Certainly there is nothing warlike about Peter Baum's verses from the trenches. He is a poet to whom Wilfred Owen's words 'The Poetry is in the Pity' apply. He was, ultimately, more concerned with truth than with poetry, and this sometimes shows in his poetry in the form of archness or gaucheness. In his best work, poetic feeling (Owen's 'Pity') and poetic expression are evenly matched.

To illustrate this, Bridgwater analyses the compatible use of form and subject matter of 'Am Beginn des Krieges stand ein Regenbogen' (1915), which is concerned with the way in which the war has gathered momentum:

Am Beginn des Krieges stand ein Regenbogen.
Vögel schwarz vor grauen Wolken schnitten Kreise.
Silbern glänzten Tauben, wenn auf ihrer runden Reise
Sie durch einen schmalen Streifen Sonne bogen.

Schlacht grenzt hart an Schlacht. Sie himmlisch logen.
Viele Reihn geklaffter Stirnen grausen.

Oft kracht der Granaten Kopf,
Wenn sie schon schwänzelnd leiser sausen.
Immer wachsen der Granaten Wehebogen.

Harrend zwischen Tod und Friedensbogen,
Fester krampfen sie den Lauf, das Heim zu schützen,
Speien auf den Feind, sich wankend stützen,

Über Hügel stürzend, Meereswogen,
Schwanken sie heran, vom Tod magnetisch angezogen.

At the beginning of the war there was a rainbow.
Birds, black, wheeled against grey clouds.
Pigeons shone silver as on their circular journey

They turned through a narrow strip of sunlight.

Battle takes place hard by battle. They lied like troopers.
Row upon row of stoved-in heads fill one with horror.
Shells often explode
As they tumble on beginning to lose velocity.
The shells' pain-bow grows all the time.

Caught between Death and the bow of peace,
They clutch their rifle barrels more firmly, to defend their homeland,
Spitting at the enemy, leaning on one another as they totter,
Tumbling over hills, like waves of the seas,
Staggering on, attracted magnetically by Death.

TRANSLATED BY PATRICK BRIDGWATER

Despite the six-beat trochaic lines, the 14-line poem starts by looking very much like a sonnet. The regular 'abba' rhyme pattern of the quatrain reflects the rainbow of the opening lines and the opening optimistic months of the war; the perfect harmony of the spectrum and of national unity is broken by those black birds of war, harbingers of death, to whose circling, vulture-like movements the trochees point.

The poem proceeds from the image of optimism (even the black birds are offset by the silver dove representing 'peace by Christmas') to the inevitability of death. If the opening quatrain was in some ways ominous (the black birds, those aggressive trochees), this was nothing compared with what should have been the second half of the octave, where things almost immediately begin to go badly wrong. The formal and metrical patterns and the rhyme scheme are all broken: there are five lines instead of four, the 'acdca' rhyme pattern is grotesque, as is the pattern of 55446 accented syllables, which runs directly counter to the rhyme scheme. What started as a sonnet with a difference is being blown apart – a perfectly proper indication of the violence of the war in its post-euphoric period. Much the same points apply to the five lines of what should be the sestet; the 'aeeaa' is surely unparalleled in any peacetime sonnet. If the 'acdca' of the first quintain was odd, the 'aeeaa' of the second is very odd indeed. This is the point. The 'sonnet' is made to reflect its subject matter, the war, in getting right out of control. The war, like the 'sonnet', started 'regularly', but then things started to go wrong. And there is no getting away from the war: the 'sonnet's' end is in its beginning (those 'a' rhymes). Those who are the subject of the violence tearing the poem apart – all the combatants – are caught between death and the mirage of peace; but it is death towards which they are irresistibly drawn, like so many moths towards a light. What makes this violently impressive poem so interesting is the way in which the form of the poem exactly reflects the subject matter.

Both the last poem and another, 'O Deutschland, grosses Muttervolk der Erde', make clear Peter Baum's conviction that the war can only end badly and that Germany needs to change its anachronistic values – 'wandelst dräuend mit dem [Donner-] Wetterschwerte' ('You go around threatening people with your thundering great sword'). The memorable thing in this poem is, however, the reference to 'Tigeraugen, die dich hassumglühn' ('Tigers' eyes glowing with hate all around you'), for here – in expressionistically neologistic form – is the animal imagery in which Peter Baum's view of the war receives its most characteristic and impressive expression.

Baum's fellow contributor to the *Sturm*, August Stramm, was not only worlds apart stylistically, but, in his animal imagery of the war, used a different metaphor, as Patrick Bridgwater explains:

> Peter Baum's message is conveyed through the imagery. He does not use Stramm's hunting vocabulary, which denotes a human (though not humane) activity. He sees the war rather as a fight to the death between wild animals. The imagery of beasts of prey spans the whole collection, recurring in a notable form in the final poem:

Wo Wölfe durch die blanke Schneenacht liefen,
Mit jäherm Hunger war die Nacht geladen:
Luftwildem Heulen. Die Granaten
Und die Schrapnells mit langen Hälsen riefen.
Eiserne Zähne ohne Lippen.
Hungerten heiss nach meinen Rippen.

Früh uns im Schneelichtfieber überschwimmen

Von neuem die vom Tod zerdehnten Stimmen,
Mit gellem Knallen nach uns grimmen.

Where wolves ran through the bright night snow,
The night was full of sudden hunger:
Wild cries filled the air. Long-necked shells
And shrapnel call out.
Iron teeth without lips.
Hotly hungering for my ribs.

In the tension of the snowy light of dawn
We are once again beset by the baying voices of death
Raging towards us with deafening explosions.

TRANSLATED BY PATRICK BRIDGWATER

Now had Baum served on the Eastern Front, the wolves might have been supposed to be real, but as it is, they are identical with Trakl's 'wilde Wölfe' (*homo homini lupus*), although Baum's starting-point is the howling of shells through the air. The shells themselves are animalized (they have long necks and lipless iron teeth), and the whole of 'Wo Wölfe . . .' is dominated by those 'vom Tod zerdehnten Stimmen', of men baying for blood. One can only assume that Baum's work was not understood by the military censor; seen in retrospect, it could hardly be much more clearly 'anti-war'. This is perhaps where poetry has the edge on satire. Satire is always liable to be banned; poetry may get away with it. But Baum does not always leave it to do so, and in another poem, the characteristic imagery is combined with a bitterly clear comment:

Franz Marc (1880-1916): *Der Tiger*, 1912.
Städtische Galerie im Lenbachhaus, Munich

Viele Tiere dräuen, Vielzeller, die Granaten,

Einzeller bohren nur ein kleines Loch.
Zu einem Mythenfest bin ich geladen.
Harpyien suchen tief und schweifen hoch.
Im ganzen mild. Sie könnten furchtbar schaden.

So mancher Arm vermisst den Körper doch,
Den armen Kopf, der eben lenkte noch.
O Sturm, O Ruhm
O Heldentum!
Schön glänzt auf weissem Feld die süsse rote Blum.

Many forms of predator threaten, multicellular, shells;
Unicellular forms only make a little hole.
I am invited to a mythical celebration.
Harpies search high and low.
On the whole they are lenient. They could do terrible damage.
Many an arm is missing its body,
The head which used to direct it.
O Glory, O Honour,
O Heroism!
On a white field the sweet red flower stands out beautifully.

TRANSLATED BY PATRICK BRIDGWATER

Nothing could be clearer, or more apt, or more courageous than the typographically accentuated 'O Sturm, O Ruhm / O Heldentum!': what price 'glory' now? In June 1916, when this harmless, gentle soul died, it was a good question.

TIM CROSS/PATRICK BRIDGWATER

Text Gesammelte Werke (Hans Schlieper (ed.), Ernst Rowohlt, Berlin, 1920).

Secondary source
Patrick Bridgwater, *The German Poets of the First World War* (Croom Helm, London, 1985). Passages and translations from the chapter 'Epilogue' reproduced by kind permission of the publishers and by arrangement with the author.

Leuchtkugeln steigen hoch hinauf,
Nachtweitend Feuerwerk und Lichtgebraus
Zerfallenden Monds. So starr ragst du dahin
Bei deinem Büchsenlauf, wie die erhellten Häuser.

Leuchtkugeln aus gesträubtem Tigerhaar.
Jeder erhellten Regung lauert auf ein Hahn

Bei Späherblick, als blute noch der Tag,
Wo einer noch des anderen Wild,
Mund lag bei Kehle,
Bis man vernahm des andern Orgelton.

Mit aufgerissnen Augen staunst Du auf die Pracht
Des bunten Raubtiers, funkelnd aus der Finsternis.
Bis wieder tief vergräbt mich Nacht und Schneien,
Graugrüne Augen halten wach die wilden Melodeien.

Flares climb high up into the sky,
Fireworks extending the night and the sputtering light
Of a decaying moon. With your gun you stand there rigid
As the houses that are lit up.

Flares of bristling tiger's fur.
A trigger is lying in wait for any movement revealed by light
To watchful eye, as though the day
Were not yet dead in which one man was another's prey,
One man's mouth at another's throat,
Until the organ-cry of death is heard.

With eyes wide open you stare at the brilliance
Of the colourful predator, burning brightly in the night.
Until night and snow conceal me again,
Grey-green eyes keep these wild melodies awake.

TRANSLATED BY PATRICK BRIDGWATER

HERMANN LÖNS 1866–1914

'To me, the noise of battle is like noise in a factory. It fails to excite me, and fills me with loathing.'
War diary, 14 September 1914

It is ironic that the very reason for which Hermann Löns is best remembered in Germany today is the reason why, as a writer, he is now largely discredited. Like Walter Flex (q.v.), Löns was appropriated by the National Socialists in the 1930s as a truly Germanic writer. Löns was seen as the promoter of the racial solidarity of the German peasant. In many ways Löns fitted into the mould made for him. His writings betray an aversion to gypsies, for example, and he revealed xenophobic tendencies throughout his life, composing nationalistic verses against 'Engelland' at the outbreak of the First World War. Yet there is another side to Löns which was deliberately passed over. The short articles and stories he wrote as a journalist in Hanover under the pseudonyms Fritz von der Leine or Ulenspiegel never merited inclusion in the numerous anthologies of his works compiled under the National Socialists. These mischievous examinations of the failings of the big city bureaucracies did not win approval. Instead the intensely folkloristic and rather unwieldy novels like *Der Wehrwolf* and the hunting songs *Ho Rüd'Ho* found favour. But Löns's skill as a master of the short prose form is where his true strength lies. In numerous pieces, notably in 'Heidbrand' ('Fire on the Heath') he depicts with a naturalist's eye for detail poetic impressions of the countryside, and particularly the heath, the Lüneburger Heide, where he grew up.

Hermann Löns was born in the year of Prussia's rise to power, 1866, on 26 August. This was the year of the battle of Königgrätz. He died in the year marking the Prussian kingdom's decline, 1914. In that period, being a near compulsive writer, he produced a substantial body of work which runs to eight volumes. The key asset to his work, his ability to observe with great attention to detail, marked him out as a born naturalist. Nature to Löns was also a form of escape, principally from his bourgeois parents. His over-worked mother and pedantic and intellectually preoccupied father, a high school teacher, had very little time for the child. When the family moved from East Prussia to Lower Saxony and the Lüneburg Heath, the young Hermann Löns turned to the countryside for company. Nature for Löns also provided a refuge from an urban society increasingly consumed in the race towards total industrialization. His first poems, published in a naturalist periodical *Gesellschaft* were critical of this development.

Hermann Löns as a hunter, 1908.
Bildarchiv preußischer Kulturbesitz, Berlin

His career was not that of a zoologist, as he had first intended. After his marriage in 1890 he tried to exploit his writing skills as a journalist. These earlier years as a hack writer were difficult ones, and by 1898 Löns's dissatisfaction was evident. He wrote to a friend: 'To be quite honest, it doesn't matter to me much if I get out of this or not. What have I to gain if, in a state succeeding this one, the little anarchists learn the three lines off by heart: H. Löns, poet, b. 29 August 1866, anarchist in his youth, later reactionary, finally a follower of Nietzsche, and at the end defender of the maxim *omnia* couldn't give a damn [. . .] The prospect of putting my easily, if unwillingly, won gains up – or at least a few hundred worth – in order to secure a form of fame has absolutely no appeal for me whatsoever.' The dissatisfaction with his career strained an already unstable marriage. He divorced his wife, who had little to offer materially or intellectually, and instead married a colleague at the newspaper at which he worked. His output increased as a result of this new-found happiness. From this period stem the novels *Der letzte Hansbur*, *Dahinten in der Heide*, and *Der Wehrwolf*, all written specifically to educate city dwellers

'Days of hardship are behind us; harder ones lie before us. But it is a joy to be alive. What glorious people our nation is made of! The energy and drive the men have! Bismarck was right: I could kiss them. Tomorrow more! We're off again!'
Letter, 20 September 1914

of the rigours of life in the country and to stimulate their feeling for nature and its creatures.

From 1910 Löns had turned freelance, and his best satirical pieces, such as *Lex Heinze* (Heinze's Law) were the result. These two contrasting styles of writing, the humourous and the folkloristic, blend in his appealing animal tales. But the dichotomy was perhaps indicative of his inner turmoil. In 1911 his attraction to his wife's cousin brought the marriage to an end. The stress of the situation is documented in the autobiographical *Das zweite Gesicht*. Löns suffered a nervous breakdown. On recovery he turned to chauvinistic nationalism, and planned a presentient novel showing Germany emerging victorious from a great war which would have revived her native virtues and produced a leader of dynamic personality. But the Great War interrupted these plans. Löns had no military training and was, at 48, not required to serve. Yet the war was another escape, and he took it, volunteering for the infantry in August 1914. 'In 14 days I reckon I will be trained and will then probably be sent to the East. It thrills my heart. For a long time now, I have wished for such an occupation which, apart from tilling the field, is the only one worthy of man.' His misconceptions were twofold. On 26 September he was killed, barely trained, while on patrol, not at the Eastern Front, but at Loivre, near Reims. The farcical saga of how his supposed remains were transferred from an unmarked grave to their final resting place by order of the National Socialists twenty years later, and how their efforts at propaganda misfired, makes a darkly humorous story. It is one the young Löns, as a journalist, might well have relished.

TIM CROSS

Texts

Hermann Löns: Leben und Schaffen (Wilhelm Diemann (ed.), Hesse & Becker, Leipzig, 1923). Complete works in 8 volumes. Contains the fullest available biography, also available in the new edition of 1960.
Ausgewählte Werke (Hans A. Neunzig (ed.), Nymphenburger, Munich, 1986). Contains a broad cross-section of all aspects of Löns' output. Includes 'Heidbrand'.

Secondary sources

Johannes Klein, *Herman Löns heute und einst* (Hameln, Hanover, 1966). An examination of Löns's lyrical style.
Michael Schulte, *Die Hunde beheulen den Tod des Herzogs: der andere Löns* (Düsseldorf, 1981). Concentrates on Löns as a satirist. Contains 'Lex Heinze'.

HEINZE'S LAW

Bright buds are swelling in wood and garden,
The leaves show green in meadow and field,
Nature, the artist of creation,
Shows what her finest skills can yield.
But the North Wind whistles around the blossom,
Snow showers fall on the tender green,
The young corn shrivels, the buds are falling,
And now their flowers will never be seen.
'All we want,' cry the wind and snow,
'Is to kill the vermin that do such harm!'
But in so doing, the snow and wind
Crush the poor flowers without a qualm.
I picked the sad and withered flowers,
Their merriment now all left behind,
I thought of art, I thought of the police,
And Heinze's Law came into my mind . . .

It was on 24 March 19.. that I came back to Hanover from a long trip abroad. I had needed a holiday to recuperate after serving a prison sentence of some length, under the law then in force, for libelling a rascal. As I wanted a good rest, I had read no newspapers all the time I was away, and I knew very little of what had been happening in my beloved Fatherland, particularly Hanöver.

But as early as the spring of 1900 I had suspected that all manner of strange things *would* happen. Someone who knew a lot about nature told me at the time, 'This is going to be a great year for maggots,' and he was right there, because one maggoty notion that came our way was Heinze's Law. And as one maggot doesn't add up to a great year for maggots, we also got Roeren's Law and Stöcker's Law and Ballestrem's Law and Ahlwardt's Law and Oertel's Law and Groeber's Law, and heaven knows how many more laws called after people unable to make their mark in any other way.

I had heard about these laws in railway carriages, on board ship, at hotel dining-tables, on the verandas of lodging-houses, but I thought no more of them. Instead, I got to know the country where I was and its people, tried the local wine and beer, enjoyed the mountains and glaciers, forests and the countryside, the sound of the sea and the surge of the waves, and so I came home to

Germany at last as if to a foreign land.

I had travelled overnight from the Dutch border in a sleeping car, and arrived in Hanover towards morning. As I was about to get out of the train, a man in a costume such as I had never seen before came up to me. He was a very tall man, wearing a blue garment ornamented with silver braid which entirely enveloped him, like a sack. He was clean-shaven, wore a hat like a saucepan, and had a sword slung around his hips. He beckoned to two similarly clad men, and the pair of them forced me back into my compartment, handcuffed me, flung a potato sack over me with a hole cut in it for my head, and then escorted me out through the exit, past the barrier, and into the station building.

There were several people there dressed in the same way, and one of them, whose silver epaulettes particularly caught my eye, told me, 'Sit down!' As I had no idea what they wanted of me I asked the superintendent – for by now I had concluded that these strange figures were policemen – 'I hope you will bear with me, Superintendent, if I ask . . .' But how I jumped when that worthy barked at me, 'I'll have no indecent expressions, if you please! You said "bare". I do beg you to pull yourself together. Don't increase the gravity of your offence, or you'll get three days in the cells!' 'Well, if you're expecting me to . . .' I began again, but once more he shouted at me so violently that I sat down on the bench again, in alarm rather than on purpose. 'Make a note of those two indecent expressions, Suffinski,' the superintendent told his clerk, 'and the prisoner is fined ten marks for improper conduct in persistently offending against morality – make a note of that too.'

Then I was questioned. 'Name?' 'Fritz von der Leine.' 'Came into the world?' 'I was born on . . .' But I got no farther, because the superintendent went crimson with rage and shouted, 'I shall have you locked up in the cells at once if you use such shocking language a third time . . .'

I was baffled. I couldn't make up my mind whether I was the victim of some student prank, or in the clutches of a club of lunatics. 'Yes, I expect you could,' I said, 'but I don't know what I've done wrong. If I've committed some crime I'd rather like to know what it is. I can assure you, sir, I'm not such a fool as to go getting into trouble of my own accord. I've been abroad for some time, Superintendent, and I don't know exactly what things are like here nowadays, so perhaps you'd be kind enough not to have me confined in your cells until I've explained things to you. But first, would you tell me why I'm under arrest?'

The superintendent became more amiable. 'Well, look here, you've just broken the law again, three times. You used filthy language, like "getting into trouble" and "confined", and moreover you said "sir", which is strictly forbidden, being liable to make innocent minds suspect there might be – well, persons who had to be addressed as "madam". I mean' – and here he raised his voice – 'I mean persons of another gender, a most unfortunate thing, hinting at which is strictly prohibited. And moreover again, when questioned you used such indecent expressions as "bare" and "born" and "expecting". But your main crime is arriving in Hanover indecently dressed.'

'But my dear . . . I'm sorry, how am I supposed to address you?'

'Person is the usual mode of address. Nothing suggestive about that,' said the officer kindly. He was definitely feeling sorry for me now.

'Well, my dear person, I'm fully dressed, I'm wearing a jacket, waistcoat, trousers . . .'

'For heaven's sake, do keep quiet! Trousers! Only a judge is allowed to use such disgusting expressions – and then only when the court's *in camera*. That's just what your crime is, you see: by wearing such an article of clothing, thus showing your contempt for all decency in the most impudent way, you've committed a serious breach of Roeren's Law. Don't you see the way we're dressed here? And you've got a moustache too! A mere child could see you're a person of the masculine gender . . . Do *we* wear whiskers?' inquired this obvious veteran of 1870–71 in melancholy tones, sadly stroking his upper lip as a tear ran down his shaven cheek.

'Look here, young person,' he continued, 'I'm sorry for you. You seem to mean well, and I wouldn't like to see you come to grief. I'll fine you only twenty marks. I can't put it any lower. And I'm making an exception for you because I used to enjoy the pieces you wrote in the old days. Now, you watch your step! I'm going to telephone the firm of Goldschmidt to take your measurements for a suit, and then, once you're decently dressed, I'll give you an officer to go about with you for a few days – for a consideration, of course – to help you get some idea of what's what. There's no need to feel awkward about it; nowadays the police keep tabs on almost every decent m– . . . dash it all, I mean every decent person.'

Ten minutes later a young fellow in a grey sack down to his feet turned up. He took my measurements, said they had suitable garments in stock, and soon afterwards sent round a choice of brown, blue, green and black sacks with matching caps. I chose a blue sack, and then the superintendent telephoned for a barber. The poor man practically had a heart attack at the sight of my moustache. Fingers shaking, he snipped off the ends, lathered my face and shaved me. But he surreptitiously popped the ends of my moustache in his pocket.

I looked in the mirror. 'Right, person,' I told the Superintendent, 'and now let's have one of your officers. I don't suppose I'm going to shake the morals of Hanover with my face as smooth as an egg!'

The superintendent smiled, sadly. 'Young person,' he said, 'do be careful! Never speak in a loud voice, and always ask the officer if there's anything improper in what you're planning to say. You've just used the word "egg", thus referring to the natural development of living creatures. If *that* came to the wrong ears, you'd get three weeks in gaol for sure. Now, off you go, and watch your step. You can speak freely to the police officer; he's in the Education Department, and it's not his job to lay charges!'

So the two of us set out. I stopped in surprise when we reached Ernst-August Square, and looked at the monument. I couldn't help laughing at the sight of good King Ernst. He was wearing a long tin shirt reaching right down to the toes of his boots.

As you can imagine, my laughter was very loud. And much as I marvelled at the sight of people dressed in long sacks hurrying over the square, I was even more surprised by the way they all turned to look curiously at me.

'Why are they doing that?' I asked my companion.

'Because you're laughing. People don't laugh nowadays. Laughing's worldly, it's a sign of sensuality, and anyway, what is there to laugh about? Look, I'm a police officer, I earn quite well. But I wish – I know I can speak freely to you – I wish things were back the way they used to be. I took home three hundred marks less in those days, but I got more fun out of life. Such a fine moustache as I had – gone now. All the girls' – here his voice dropped to a whisper – 'they all fancied me. Nowadays they don't give me a glance, or if they do, what good does it do me? Look, there's one now. I mean, where's the fun in it if a scarecrow like that does fancy you?'

I had to agree with him. The slack-faced creature with her figure enveloped in a sack and her golden hair cut mercilessly short was not calculated to make any man's heart beat faster. I was going to walk past, with indifference, when she widened her eyes. Good heavens, I knew her!

'Miss . . .' But I got no farther, because the policeman hissed, 'Ssh!' Of course! I'd said 'Miss'. But she was coming towards me, smiling. 'How good to see you again after all this time,' she said.

'Let's go to a restaurant,' said the policeman. 'We're attracting attention here. Of course, when I'm with you, it's all right for you to walk with' – his voice dropped to a whisper again – 'with a lady, but better safe than sorry.'

So we went to Kröpcke Square. On the way I looked sadly at the girl. I had met her and her parents at a hotel in the mountains two years before. She was just engaged, and the happiest girl in the world. Her fiancé was a young engineer. And what was she now? A shadow of her former self.

'Oh, person,' she said, once we were in a restaurant, 'we didn't read anything about your serving such a long sentence!'

'Long sentence?' said I, surprised. 'Oh, I haven't been in gaol all this time, I've been abroad. What makes you say a thing like that?'

She smiled, and so did the policeman. 'Well, you wouldn't know about that either,' he said. 'Gaol's not so bad these days. Just about everyone's been in gaol. These days, the police keep lists only of those who haven't been to gaol yet – they're under suspicion, the rest aren't dangerous. What did you go to gaol for yourself?' he asked the girl.

'What for? What did all my girlfriends go to jail for? Letting their fiancés kiss them. I only got six months, but Karl – you remember Karl? – he got four years because I was still a minor.'

'What on earth do you mean?' I asked in surprise. 'A minor? But surely – forgive me if this sounds ungallant – but surely you must be twenty by now?'

The policeman smiled. 'Twenty! Didn't you know people don't come of age until thirty these days?'

'Devil take all this nonsense!' I exclaimed. Then I looked at my companion in alarm, but he was smiling. 'Don't worry, it's all right to call on the Devil. In fact, it's approved of. Ever since young Dr Roeren published his paper pointing out that the Lord God created us naked, really devout folk haven't been so sure whether true piety can be reconciled with the worship of God, but on the other hand they think better of the Devil nowadays. On account of the Devil in the form of a serpent tempting Eve to give Adam the apple, so that our first parents' eyes were opened, and they saw that they were naked, and were ashamed. And as he did us such a service, young Dr Roeren's re-interpreting the Bible, showing that the Devil is the really moral character. Mind you, he's just wasting his time, seeing the Devil's in charge already.'

I decided to take a look round the city. If its people were so changed, the city must be too. I didn't meet a single cheerful soul. Not a child laughed, not a baker's boy whistled: all of them, large and small, just shuffled wearily and morosely along the streets in their long sacks. There were guards outside the Court Theatre, men of the 73rd Regiment. They were in uniform: not their old uniforms, though. They wore long uniform sacks instead.

'Why are there soldiers on guard there?' I asked. 'Is the idea to keep modern art away, or what?'

'Oh, there isn't any art these days,' said my companion. 'It's died out. The old plays can't be performed because they have men and women in them, and nobody's writing any more. The theatre's Prison Twenty-five for Persons of the Masculine Gender now.'

Indeed, wherever we looked there were prisons and penitentiaries. The Continental Hotel, the Old and New Local History Museums, the Circus, the Zoological Gardens, the factories, had all been turned into prisons. Almost all the work was done by half the population of the city in these jails, while the other half guarded them. Artists, actors, poets and booksellers had been given life sentences, for fear they might incite the people to rebellion. Several such attempts had in fact been made. There was very nearly a riot in the Klagesmarkt when the police had a long skirt put on the statue of the Goosegirl. The police had some trouble suppressing this insurrection, particularly as the army refused to help them, the commander-in-chief saying, 'The people are quite right to kick up a fuss. Ever since Ballestrem's Law was passed, forbidding even soldiers to wear moustaches and monocles and putting them in uniform sacks, the men have lost their nerve entirely. Those responsible for all this nonsense can deal with the consequences themselves, thank you very much.'

So the policeman told me, adding that all army officers with any gumption had left the Fatherland because they felt quite ill when they set eyes on their men, or looked at themselves in the glass. We happened to be passing the Uhlans' barracks as he was telling me this. A tall fellow in a blue uniform sack was on guard outside. Once upon a time the men on sentry duty there had bright eyes and rosy cheeks, and the nurserymaids would crane their necks to look at them as they pushed their prams past. This doleful youth, with neither moustache nor military bearing, wouldn't have broken any girlish hearts in the year 1900.

'It's a crying shame,' said the policeman, 'what they've done to the really good fellows. My old lieutenant, now, he shot himself. In the old days he had debts of twenty thousand marks, and even that couldn't get him down, but all this constant carping did it. He inherited three big estates, one after another, so all of a sudden he was clear of debt – but what's a person to do with money these days?'

We went on to the French Garden. 'You can still laugh, can't you?' said my companion. 'Well, you'll find something to laugh at in there.'

I could guess what was coming. All the old statues were wearing tin nightshirts. I was getting used to it by now. Suddenly the police officer stopped dead. 'Ssh,' he said, beckoning to me. And as I quietly followed him, I saw another policeman sitting on a bench, with his arm round a girl's neck, giving her a good kiss. All of a sudden he saw us, and turned white as a sheet. But his colleague reassured him, and said we'd keep watch in case anyone came along.

'Nothing else for it these days,' he told me. 'You need a few good friends if you want a word with your girl, or else you risk your job and your livelihood.'

I had had enough of Hanover. I consulted the timetable to find the very next train to South Africa. But then, as we were sitting in the tram, we heard a loud noise from the city. The closer we came, the wilder it sounded, and everyone was racing towards the city centre, where people were throwing special editions of the newspapers out of the windows, and the people in the street were laughing and singing and shouting, 'Hurray, the government in Berlin has fallen! The government's gone to the Devil, the air's clear again.' And strange to say, all the policemen were shouting too, and so were the soldiers, and they all went off to the Palace of Justice where the judges sat sentencing everyone young and healthy to gaol, and the crowd picked up stones and threw them at the windows.

Crash . . . and I woke up, looking stupidly around me. There lay the coffee cup I had knocked off the table while I had that vivid dream. My landlady, alarmed, came into the room.

'Mrs Döllmer,' said I, 'what do *you* think of Heinze's Law?'

'Mercy, what do I think of it, sir? Well, I don't rightly get its drift, I'm sure, but from anything I hear about it, sir, I reckon it's a good thing there's general elections every five years!'

Thus spake Anastasia Döllmer.

TRANSLATED BY ANTHEA BELL

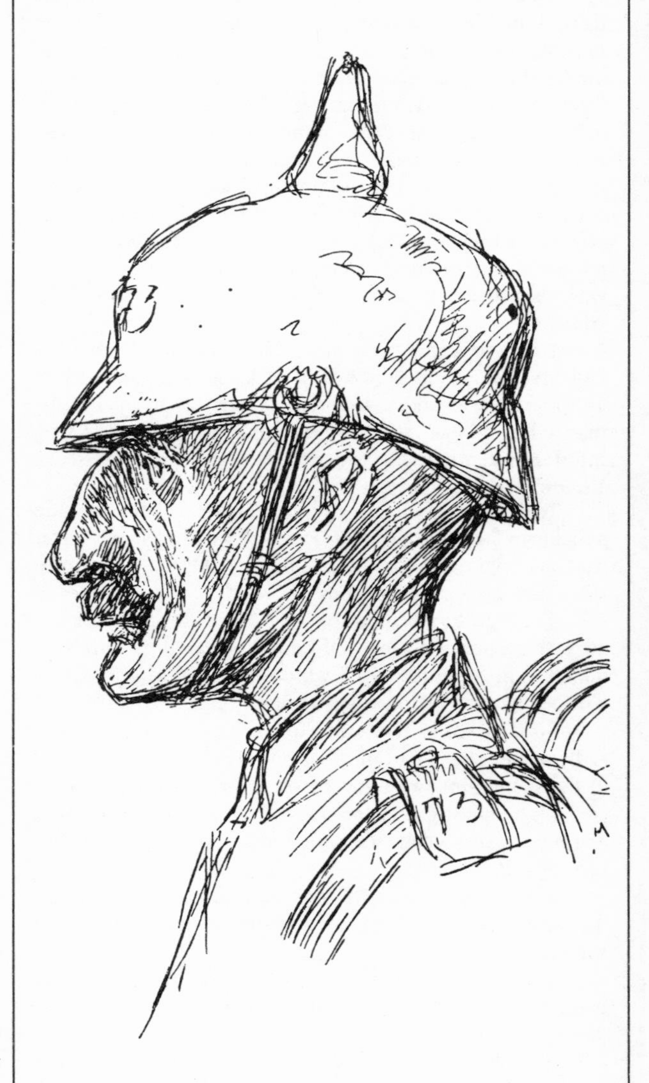

Hermann Löns as a volunteer, 1914.
Bildarchiv preußischer Kulturbesitz, Berlin

Fire on the Heath

The village lies in dark silence. The barn owl swoops soundlessly around the horseheads of the gable ends, a tomcat stalks quietly over the grey road, a bat flutters inaudibly around the oaks. The dogs, after howling at the moon all night, have fallen silent. White mists came surging up from the stream, creeping over the meadows and marsh, hovering above the heath. The moon fought them for quarter of an hour, and then they smothered her.

And now everything around is grey. The road, the meadows, marsh and moorland all lie drowned in grey-white vapour. The birches by the roadside slowly dissolve in it too. A hollow-voiced wind gets up. It shakes the wet birches until they weep cold tears, blows through the rugged pines, making them groan in their sleep, snatches sheets of mist off the tall junipers and leaves them shivering with cold. Then, suddenly, it falls silent as if it had never spoken, mute as if it were not there at all. Only in the coarse grass growing along the path does it rustle faintly, wearily, as if the mist had stifled it as well.

Uneasy silence lies over the heath in its cloak of grey, a silence broken now and then by a breathless sigh, a broken-winded groan, a chilly whisper, as lost, uncertain and indistinct as the grey-white landscape. Up above the grey mists there is a plaintive, anxious whistling, first far away and quiet, then closer, louder, and finally fading hoarsely into the distance again. A thin, alarmed piping rises and then falls. It is the sound of curlews and thrushes migrating. A lament sounds from the thicket, muffled, uneasy. That is the long-eared owl.

A rooster crows in the farmyard on the heath. Another answers it from the village, and then a third. A dog yaps hoarsely like a fox. It wakes the wind again. The wind yawns, stretches, rises from the heather and goes about its daily tasks. First it sweeps the hill clear of mist, then it goes down to the low-lying heath and scours it, pulls the white veils off the meadows, lifts the grey sheets from the marsh, dries all the bushes, clears a pathway for the sun. Up he comes now, blood-red above the black pines, rising from a narrow strip of pale-green sky with a heavy, leaden grey cloud lying over it. Strange, pale-yellow rays fall on the reddish-grey of the heath, making it shine copper, glow russet, tingeing the pallid marshland with verdigris, casting eerie blue light on the pines. Then the leaden cloud sinks lower, covering the strip of sky, leaving only a three-cornered segment of sun glowing red, and at last that too is extinguished. Long grey hours pass. The hollow-voiced wind blows monotonously over the reddish-grey hills, dusts yellow sand over the pink flowers, sighs through the birch trees, whispers in the rushes, moans among the junipers. The sky is a pale, opaque grey, a bleak monotone.

A few small blue butterflies flutter feebly above the heath, the bees fly heavily from flower to flower, there is a moody note in the buzzing of the bumble-bee, the lark's alluring song is melancholy, the crow caws anxiously; there is not an agile lizard nor a nimble beetle to be seen.

But then the wind rises for the third time. It has chased away the ground-mist, dried the trees and bushes, and now it gets to work on the misty clouds above. With a shrill piping it scatters them, driving them north and west and south, hunting them over the hills, over the pine trees, clearing a way for the sun again. The sun breaks through, hot and golden, painting the hillsides rosy red, wrapping the birch trees in springtime green, sprinkling gold on the pines and striking brightness from the sandy paths, cheering the butterflies, livening up the brown bees, luring the lizard out of the heather and the ground beetle from the grey moss, turning the dismal squawk of the crow to a merry cry.

A scent of honey, strong and intoxicating, rises from the countless flowers; innumerable bees hum a noisy chorus, there is a fluttering of little blue wings everywhere, a glitter of golden sparks all along the path, and trilling larksong ripples down to the rose-red ground.

The long, grey hours are followed by short, bright ones: short because they are so beautiful. The hot sun blazes down on the hills, makes the cobwebs on the thin branch of the pine into a web of gold, turns the pebbles in the sand to diamonds, rubies, opals and amethysts, changes the gloomy wood on the edge of the heath to a laughing grove. There is a glittering and a shimmering everywhere, a shining and a glimmering, a sparkle and a glow. The reindeer moss has turned to pure silver, the trunks of the pine trees to bright gold. Pale-blue lights flash up from the distant fishponds, and the moorland sheep have golden fleece.

The merry, light-hearted wind dances uphill, downhill, twists itself a long train of yellow silk from the drifting sand, caresses the ruffled spruces on the hill, the birch trees along the old road, fiddles a tune on a dry stick and whistles a song on the bleached skull of a deer. Then it goes off behind the hill in search of a new toy. It sits down behind the pines, on the dune beyond the marsh, lights its pipe and puffs and puffs. First it raises a small, thin wisp of smoke, then bigger ones, and finally it is puffing out clouds of smoke like baking day on the farm. Nor is the tobacco it smokes of the very best sort: the wind has filled its pipe with turf, rushes, reindeer moss, heather, pine twigs. In all the villages round about, people bringing in the second crop of hay let their scythes and rakes drop, sniff the air, decide it is a foul-smelling mist rising from the marsh, and get back to work. But the sun grows redder and redder, the sky in the east lower and lower, the air thicker and thicker. The haymakers look at each other and shake their heads, wondering why the air is so bright and clear to the west, but so thick and heavy in the east. And all of a sudden there is much hurrying and scurrying, wheels rattle along the road, carts rumble over dusty yellow earth, and the green meadows and fields of red buckwheat are left quiet and empty.

But where the wind sat smoking its pipe, all around the marsh, there is a flurry of white shirtsleeves, a flashing of bright spades. The men stand in long rows, smoke in their faces, smoke beneath their feet, smoke at their backs. In front of them, all is shrouded in thick, blue-white mists, with little red flames breaking out now and then; beside them, black rings on the ground smoulder, then spread with a crackle, red tongues lick at the heather, red sparks shoot across the dry grass. Mattocks come down hard, spades bite crunching into the sand, clods of earth thud dully, the smell of sweat surrounds the men. Now and then they take long, deep gulps from the tankards handed them by the women and children, straighten their aching backs, stretch their tired arms, wipe tired foreheads with blackened hands, and then mattocks strike again, spades crunch, clods of earth thud.

The sun sets, eerily red, as if going to its last repose. The monstrous blue-grey cloud of smoke, shot through with white, stained with brown, now shines golden, blazes fiery red, glows purple. Black, heavy banks of cloud cover the sun, allow it to blaze out once more, then smother it again. It gleams once again above the pines, and then is gone. There is twilight over the heath, a twofold twilight thick with smoke and vapour. The white shirtsleeves are hardly visible now, and there is nothing at all to be seen of the men's sooty, blackened faces. Their arms are failing them, their backs are sore, their knees are weak, but as long as the red flames flicker up, mattocks resound and spades crunch around moorland and marsh.

Deer stand on the heather-grown dunes, in their breeding grounds up in the hills, in hillside thickets, and sniff the stinking fumes rising from the marsh. Hares and black grouse have come here; the fox runs restlessly about. The great fire has taken all their homes. Many animals were smothered by the blue smoke, or the red flames killed them. In the village beyond the marsh, the women, half-grown children and old men stand about the roads in groups, talking of the fire in muted voices. Almost all of them have suffered some kind of damage. One man had peat still outside, the heather another had cut for litter was burnt, yet another has lost all his beehives, and much brushwood and timber has gone. And the worst of it is that if no rain falls, all work in the fields and meadows must stop, perhaps for as long as a week.

Long lines of shadowy figures return to the village, talking quietly, treading heavily in their tall boots. Other figures meet them, going to take their places. A watch must be kept, work must go on all night, for the wind has not died down; it is blowing hard towards the woods between the marsh and the village. The village streets are full of the acrid smoke. Only the village children get any sleep tonight. But towards eleven o'clock, the men at work out on the heath notice that the smoke has stopped stinging their eyes and catching them in the throat; the wind has changed, and is blowing from the west. And there in the west, now and then, a red flash lights up a bank of black storm-clouds. The men work on more cheerfully now, knowing that help is on its way. Around midnight, thunder rumbles behind the moorland hills; a few large drops of rain fall. Then rain comes rushing from the clouds, hissing in the burning heather, in the smouldering marsh, and slowly the smoke dwindles and dies down. In the small hours, the men shoulder their mattocks and spades and walk home, wet through, hands and faces smeared with black, to sleep until daylight shines in at the window. Then they go out to the heath again to dampen down the last places where white smoke still rises from the dying fires. Over four hundred acres have been burnt. As far as the eye can see, all is black and bare. Here and there, in the flat and gloomy waste, rise the ruins of a beekeeper's hives, the black ribs of charred pines, the strange skeleton of a burnt juniper. It will probably be a year before the cotton grass ripples here again and the heather grows; longer than that before pines will grow again. The buckwheat lies wet in the fields, and the rain has washed much of the goodness out of the hay.

But the farmer shrugs his shoulders. Moaning does no good, and the fire on the heath might have been worse.

TRANSLATED BY ANTHEA BELL

*W*ALTER *F*LEX 1887–1917

'I am no longer myself. I used to be. I am now part of the holy horde which sacrifices itself for you – Fatherland.'

1914

'The divine in man perches like a bird in a thornbush; one only has to listen to its song and ignore the thorns.'

1915

Walter Flex's novella *Der Wanderer zwischen beiden Welten* (*A Wanderer between Two Worlds*) has never been out of print since its first publication in 1917, shortly after the author's death. Its posthumous reception was a phenomenon parallel to that of Rupert Brooke in English-speaking countries. This straightforward account of a trench friendship in the first year of the war manages to eschew overt national patriotism in favour of an endorsement of moral well-being, embodied in the young *Wandervogel* Ernst Wurche whom the author encounters on his way to the Eastern Front. Flex reaffirmed this, stating, 'It is not national patriotism that I represent, but demands for the moral good. When I wrote about the perpetuity of the German race and about the deliverance of the world by the Germanic, it had nothing to do with national egotism; rather it is a moral conviction which can be realized as much in the defeat or in the heroic sacrifice of a nation.'

Such a statement was not sufficient to deflect the attentions of the National Socialists in Germany in the years leading up to the Second World War. Flex was paraded as the epitome of German patriotism and as the embodiment of the purity of the German spirit. This exploitation of Flex's popularity has inevitably had a detrimental effect on his reputation as a serious writer. His unremitting glorification of war in the last three years of his life, in works other than *Der Wanderer*, has also contributed to his declining popularity.

Walter Flex was born in Eisenach in Prussia on 6 July 1887, the second of four sons. His father, the high school teacher Dr Rudolf Flex, was a fervent admirer of Chancellor Bismarck, and the four sons were brought up to revere the statesman who had effectively piloted the states of the former Holy Roman Empire towards a unified *Vaterland*. Flex experienced a happy childhood, untroubled by the political tensions of the time. His interest in world affairs was first awakened by the Boer War in Southern Africa and his support for the underdog, the Boer, was unqualified. The 'underdogs' within the German empire were, however, the states in federation with Prussia. The conflict created by the reactionary attempts of the new Chancellor to impose a three-tiered electoral system on all the states which would effectively give lesser voting rights to the growing population of industrial workers did not go unrecognized by the

Woodcut by Walter Dahms, *c.* 1916.
Bildarchiv preußischer Kulturbesitz, Berlin

budding poet. He wrote to a contemporary: 'You write of politics. All I see are the two mighty concerns, farming and industry, fighting each other as conservatives and liberals, but both exploiting the masses with patriotic or idealistic slogans of freedom.'

Walter Flex's first attempt at drama was the tragedy *Demetrius*, about the Tsarist pretender. In his following works for the stage, social problems form the core, as in *Lothar*, *Die Bauernführer*, *Das heilige Blut* and *Der Kanzler Klaus von Bismarck*. These revolve around the premiss that society is necessary. Each individual is like a thread, insignificant, disposable, and only makes sense if he is a thread woven into the fabric of the carpet. Interesting as these plays are in the context in which they were written, it cannot be claimed that Flex was an original writer. As a dramatist he laboured much under the influence of Hebbel. His poetry is the least distinguished

'Privately I am as much a war volunteer on this, as on the first day.'

1917

of his output, and appears more as an exercise towards the prose works such as *Wallenstein* and *Der Wanderer*.

Flex's academic career, however, was a distinguished one, and he followed in his father's footsteps and became a teacher. His first post was as private tutor to the family of his childhood hero Bismarck. A second appointment followed at the house of Baron von Leesen, which was interrupted by the war. Despite weak ligaments in his right hand, Flex volunteered and joined up in Rawitsch, his mother's birthplace, with the 50th Infantry. By September 1914, he was at the front in the Argonne. His poetic outpourings on the war were prolific. Two collections *Sonne und Schild* and *Im Felde Zwischen Tag und Nacht* were produced in the first months of the war. His body, soul and literary talent were placed wholly at the disposal of the war-effort. The 'Christmas Fable for the 50th Regiment' earned him the Order of the Red Eagle with Crown.

It was during officer training in Posen in the first months of 1915 that he met Ernst Wurche, the subject of his novella *Der Wanderer zwischen beiden Welten*. The most immediate bond between the two was their mutual identification with the youth movement, the *Wandervogel*, of which Flex's younger brother Martin, who was to die in 1919 of a lung infection contracted at the front, was a member. In Wurche, Flex thought to identify this new type of German, one who carried in his back pack a copy of the New Testament, a volume of Goethe and Nietzsche's *Thus Spake Zarathustra*; an exemplary German who could set an example to the world with the motto 'To stay pure is to mature'. After Wurche's death, Flex concentrated on a single book, *Wolf Eschenlohr*, which was to depict his own private responses to the war, and deal with the social and religious issues raised by the nature of the conflict: 'Believe me, the best of our men have not died in order that the living die, but that the dead live. Are there not too many dead among our living? Happiness is not the final goal of mankind but his perfection as a corporeal and moral being. That is what the war can help you to be! The victors will be among the dead!' *Wolf Eschenlohr* remained a fragment.

On 16 October 1917 on the island of Ösel, Walter Flex wrote in a letter home,

> Of those comrades who departed for the West hardly one has stayed alive. There were a few great characters among them who I would gladly have met up with again. I can still picture them at the station, waving from the departing train. 'Pity that you can't come with us!' shouted Erichson, the Mecklenburger who with Wurche and me had formed the third leaf of the clover in the command of the 9th company at Augustovo. Now he lies buried before Verdun. Had he guessed that we would shortly be part of the assaults on Tarnopol and Riga, he would probably have stayed with us. Where would I be now, had the telegram [forestalling his transfer to the Western Front] not been dispatched? Coincidence or destiny? I am once more thankful for my balanced faith, which has never been seriously shaken. Do not suppose that I believe myself to be preserved and protected to the prejudice of others – but I have the tranquil, inner knowledge that everything that happens and can happen to me is part of a living development over which nothing dead has any power . . .'

Later that day, a bullet hit Walter Flex and he was killed.

TIM CROSS

Texts

Gesammelte Werke (Beck, Munich, 1925). The collected works include seven plays: *Der Bauernführer*, *Demetrius*, *Der Schwarmgeist*, *Lothar*, *Der Kanzler Klaus von Bismarck*, *Die schwimmende Insel*, *Die evangelische Frauenrevolte*; poems including the war poems *Im Felde zwischen Nacht und Tag*; stories and novellas including *Der Wanderer zwischen beiden Welten* and the unfinished final work *Wolf Eschenlohr*; letters.
Der Wanderer zwischen beiden Welten (Orion-Heimreiter, Kiel, 1986). First published in 1917.

Secondary sources

Konrad Flex, *Walter Flex, ein Lebensbild* (Stuttgart, 1937). A biography by Walter's brother.
Walter Flex, *Aus dem Nachlass: eine Dokumentation* (Fritz Griessbach (ed.), Orion-Heimreiter, Kiel, 1978). An attempt to place Flex's attitudes and writings in the context of the time in which they were expressed. Contains an essay and letters.
The Walter Flex Memorial Museum, operated by the Walter-Flex-Freundekreis, Dietzenbach-Steinberg, West Germany, contains memorabilia, facsimiles and manuscripts.

A Wanderer Between Two Worlds

In memory of my dear friend Ernst Wurche

(abridged version)

A stormy, early spring night was sweeping across the war-torn woods of Lorraine, in which a months-long hail of iron had left every trunk scarred and splintered. As on a hundred previous nights I, a war volunteer on listening-patrol duty, lay in a shell-pocked clearing, gazing through wind-inflamed eyes into the flickering dusk of the stormy night sky, through which searchlights wandered restlessly over German and French positions. The roaring of the night storm rose and fell over my head like breaking waves. Strange voices filled the quivering air. The cutting wind sang and whistled around my steel helmet and the barrel of my rifle, shrill and mournful, and high above the warring armies watchfully facing each other in the darkness I saw a flock of greylag geese heading north, their cries as sharp as razors. The flickering light of descending flares picked out briefly, over and over again, the lumpy outlines of crouching figures who, wrapped like myself in greatcoat and groundsheet, formed a chain of lookouts, nestling in hollows and limepits in front of our wire entanglements. Our Silesian regiment's line of sentries stretched from the Bois des Chevaliers across to the Bois de Vérines, and the migrating army of wild geese swept over us all like ghosts. On a scrap of paper, which in the darkness I could not see, I scribbled down a few intercrossing lines of verse:

Wild geese are winging through the night,
Head northwards, shrilly crying.
Endangered flight, take care, take care!
The world is full of slaughter.

Fly through the stormy, night-filled world,
Grey-armoured, airborne squadrons!
Weapons flash and war cries ring,
Far rolls and seethes contention.

Drive on, speed on, you grey-clad troop,
Drive on, speed swiftly northwards!
When you fly south across the sea,
Who knows where you will find us?

We are like you a grey-clad troop,
And marching for the Kaiser.
Should from our march we not return,
Cry us 'Amen' in autumn!

As I lay writing in the Bois des Chevaliers a twenty-year-old student of theology, a war volunteer like myself, was on listening duty in the Bois de Vérines. At that time we knew nothing of each other's existence. But when, months later, he read these verses in the pages of my war diary, he vividly remembered that night and the wandering army of geese that flew over us. We both watched them with the same thoughts in mind. And in that same hour, from the darkness of the trenches behind us, a runner came to each of us with an order to report at midnight to the regimental orderly room in full marching order. Through our tired, yet singularly alert senses we observed once again, as we descended, the melancholy beauty of the bare grey slopes and hollows, the limestone looking strangely dead and heavy in the moonlight, and the lightless grey solitariness of the wrecked and abandoned stone huts . . .

In the regimental orderly room we learned that we were to be marched off to Germany at dawn with twenty other war volunteers, in order to undergo an officers' training course at the Warthe camp in Posen.

In the early hours of the following day our little squad formed up in the steep village street between the shelled-out church and parsonage with its war graves. A squad of trained butchers, drawn from the troops in the field to serve at home, was to leave the village at the same time as ourselves. As we stood in formation before the parsonage, awaiting our marching orders, a major approached us, calling out as he came, 'Are you the butchers, chaps?', and a chorus of offended and amused voices replied, 'No, sir, we are the officer cadets.' While, with a vexed mutter, the major passed our little grey group to continue his search for the butchers, I suddenly found myself looking into a pair of strikingly fine, light-grey eyes. They belonged to the man beside me, and they were brimming over with delighted laughter. We regarded each other, united in pleasure over one of those harmlessly absurd little incidents of which our life as war volunteers was so full. What pure eyes this youngster has! I thought to myself, and made a note of his name as the regimental clerk called the roll. 'Ernst Wurche.' 'Sir!' Well, I thought, good that you and I are going in the same direction . . .

A few hours later, the slim, handsome young man in the shabby grey tunic was striding like a pilgrim down the mountain from Hâtonchatel to Vigneulles, his pale grey eyes full of sparkle and confident longing. He reminded me of Zarathustra descending from the heights, or Goethe's Wanderer. The sun played with the light dust his and our feet stirred up, and the glistening stone of the mountain road seemed to ring beneath his soles . . .

His gait expressed both will and joy. He was marching from the past into the future, from the years of the apprentice to those of the master. Sinking out of sight behind him were the mountains on which he had drudged with pick and spade, the forests whose weighty trunks he had borne long and far on willing shoulders, the villages whose streets he had kept clean with shovel and dung fork, the trenches in which he had done sentry duty at all hours of the day and night, and the funk-holes and dug-outs in which for so many months he had shared comradeship with manual labourers, factory workers and Polish farmhands. For six months he had worn the grey tunic without buttons or stripes, and had been spared none of the hardest and humblest duties. Now he was marching down from the mountains to become a leader.

In the railway compartment we came into conversation. He was sitting opposite me, and he rummaged in his pack to draw out a pile of much-read books: a little volume of Goethe, *Zarathustra* and a field edition of the New Testament. 'How do those all get on together?' I asked. He looked at me, his clear eyes a little on guard. Then he laughed. 'In the trenches all sorts of alien spirits are forced to rub shoulders. It's the same with books as with people. It doesn't matter how different they are, as long as they're sincere and strong and know how to look after themselves. That's the best kind of comradeship.' I flicked without answering through his collection of Goethe's poems. Another comrade glanced across and said, 'I put that book in my pack too when I left for the front, but what time do we get for reading out here?' 'If there's not much time for reading,' the young student observed, 'you should learn it by heart. This winter I've learnt seventy poems by Goethe. Then I could bring them out as often as I liked.' He spoke freely and easily and without any trace of complacency or schoolmasterliness, but his uninhibited and self-confident manner of talking without embarrassment even of the most essential and intimate things commanded attention. His words were as clear as his eyes, and in each one of his cleanly and openly phrased sentences one felt the kind of person he was.

Our conversation in the railway compartment centred around our tasks in the near future. We were approaching a period of learning. What was to be learnt in the short time available seemed to some a lot, to others little. 'A section commander doesn't have to be a strategist,' one man observed. 'A lieutenant's job is to die in front of his men. You don't need much training for that, if you're a real man.' The speaker seriously meant what he said, and in a few months' time he was himself to demonstrate the truth of his words in Russian Poland; but his clumsy, hot-headed way of making pompous statements, inconsequently and often at the wrong moment, frequently made him a target for mild mockery, for all his honest intentions. And now, too, his words fell like a stone on the light-hearted chatter. Some smiled. But Ernst Wurche deftly picked the stone up, and in his hand it turned to crystal. 'A lieutenant's job is to *live* for his men,' he said, 'and dying in front of them may certainly at some stage be a part of that. Dying first is understood by many, and the *non dolet* with which the Roman woman showed her hesitant husband how good and how easy it is to die is even better applied to an officer and his men. But living for them still remains the finer thing. It is also the more difficult. *Living together* in the trenches was perhaps the best schooling of all, and surely no one will become a proper leader unless he was already one there.'

This at once led to a lively argument over whether it is easy or difficult to influence the thoughts and feelings of the common soldier. A few had fared disastrously with attempts to guide and educate, and had always been treated like strangers among a flock of birds. Much of what was said on one side or the other I have forgotten; it has deservedly faded in the light of a little incident of which the young student told us. 'Big fellows,' he observed with a smile, 'are like children. Scolding and forbidding will achieve little. They have to like you. A game in which one refuses to take part is for them no real game. When eight of us were lying in a dug-out, they would often try to cap each other with dirty jokes. And for a while they thoroughly enjoyed themselves. But there was one, a social democrat from Breslau, with whom I was very friendly. He was always the first to notice I was not joining in. Every time he would then ask me, "Ernstel, are you asleep too?", and both of us knew his mockery was not wholehearted. I would growl something like, "Leave me alone." They knew very well when I wanted nothing to do with them, and they didn't like it. But then it was usually not long before someone told a joke that made me laugh too. After that we had a splendid time.'

The few weeks of training in the Warthe camp added nothing to and took nothing away from the young man's character. He advanced swiftly from corporal to sergeant and then to lieutenant. He mastered his duties smoothly and confidently, and treated the vexations and pettinesses of the peacetime parade ground with nonchalant disdain. On one occasion I myself made a vexed remark, regarding whom or what I no longer recall. He slid his arm through mine, gave me one of his persuasively cheerful glances and quoted from his Goethe:

> 'Wanderer, against such hurt
> You feel the urge to grumble?
> Whirling wind and dried-up dirt,
> Let them twist and tumble!'

And that put an end to it. We wandered out into the Sunday morning and down to the banks of the Warthe, talking of rivers, mountains, forests and clouds . . .

May came, and we moved off for the second time. Where to? Of the few hundred young officers there was none who knew, as the glaring white lights of our lorries sped ahead of us towards the Schlesischer rail terminus in Berlin. The future was filled with mystery and adventure, and out of the darkness of the east, into which the lights of our convoy were cutting, the shadow of Hindenburg grew bigger and bigger . . .

The train steamed through the May night without stopping, as if resolved to reveal neither route nor destination. Just now and again a sign with the name of the station on it flashed by, glaringly illumined by the platform lamps. We were heading east. Hindenburg's shadow grew ever larger. The May morning dawned, cool and cloudlessly sunny, over the lakes of East Prussia. Was Kurland our destination, or was it Poland? As we speculated to and fro, Ernst Wurche continued to point obstinately to those parts of the large ordnance survey map that were coloured deepest blue and palest green. The clear, soft May morning was conjuring up in the *Wandervogel*'s mind enticing dreams of broad, sunny lakes, shady woods and dew-drenched meadows . . .

Gradually our final destination became apparent. We spent a night in Suvalki, and on the following morning our train, consisting now of only a few carriages, began puffing through the endless pine forests of Augustovo towards the front. Part of the railway track was being bombarded by the Russian artillery. We spent several hours at a standstill in open country while the enemy sprayed the rails ahead with shells. Some treetops broke off, as if suddenly struck by lightning. A stretch of the forest was on fire, a hot, blinding red glow eating its way through a dense cloud of smoke from wood and resin. After a while the enemy artillery fell silent, and our train set off again. Pine trees and sand, sand and pine trees slid past with ever increasing speed. Then all of a sudden the whole train was shaken by the crashing roar of a bursting shell, the whistle of whose approach had been drowned by the train's clatter. A grinding of wood and iron. A few jolts, which came through the red cushions like punches from a fist. With a noise like the cracking of a whip a window pane burst from its frame. The carriage tilted violently to the right, rocked, steadied. The shell had struck the embankment beneath the moving train and like a devil's claw torn away the earth under the hot rails. The train had left the track and now lay at a dangerous angle over the steep slope. In the distance, from which the direct hit had no doubt been spotted through field-glasses, a machine-gun hammered: tak-tak-tak-tak-tak . . .

At that moment Ernst Wurche was standing at the window, shaving. The crashing and splintering came in the middle of a razor stroke. He calmly raised the blade from his face, while with his left hand he held himself firm on the luggage rack. We saw our comrades in the other compartments, some of them in shirtsleeves, jumping out of the rocking carriage. A trunk and a sack of washing had fallen on my head and knocked me over. I scrambled to my feet. The train came to rest. I looked at Wurche and had to laugh. He completed the interrupted razor stroke, wiped the remaining lather from his face, then said with serene calm, 'Well, now we'd better disembark.' He allowed nothing to disturb his happy peace of mind, and it was not his way to run in a panic from the barber's shop with soap on his face while there was still time to wipe it off. Composure was one of his favourite words: in it he saw the whole essence of human and manly dignity.

'Disembarking' was in fact not so easy, for all the doors to the outside and to the neighbouring compartments were jammed. 'Then we must do some scaling,' Wurche said, and he climbed out through the broken window. I threw out our luggage and followed by the same route. We piled our trunks up against the steep embankment on the side away from the enemy and stretched ourselves out on the sunlit grass beside them. Two hours later a relief train arrived from Augustovo and brought us, somewhat belatedly, to our destination. Russia had given us her welcome.

The Russian trenches lay at some few hundred metres distance from ours, so that we could move around freely, even in broad daylight, in the woods behind our position. The Russian artillery did indeed spray our trenches now and again with shrapnel and shells, and once a direct hit even blew my dug-out to pieces just as I was opening the door, but all that passed by as swiftly as an April shower, with a single 'whoosh'. It was a game the French played much better, and in general we did not take 'Ivan the Terrible' (as we called the Russians) very seriously. Later we learned to respect them, but for the present we did not allow them to spoil our 'summer holiday in the Augustovo woods'. The myriads of gnats breeding in the woods and marshes bothered us more than the Russians behind their barbed wire.

Only when dusk fell, and the red, blue and multi-coloured blossoms of clover, forget-me-not, arum lily and common pink on the marshy meadow showed pale and colourless in the light of stars and flares, did adventure emerge from the dark woods opposite, like a handsome stag, to gaze at us as we stood and listened at the parapet of our dark trenches. Each night our company sent an officer's patrol into the no-man's-land between us, and we three lieutenants, one each from Mecklenburg, Silesia and Thuringia, shared this duty in turn. Sometimes, when we hoped to make a particularly good catch, two of us would go out with our men, but usually there was just a single leader. Then it was a strange feeling when, standing listening at the parapet, one suddenly heard the crackle of Russian and German rifles or the dull thud of exploding hand grenades. During such hours the strain of waiting, the relief over a safe return, bring human beings as close together as intertwined trees. Of course, nothing much was ever said aloud – just a joke or a handshake when a comrade went out or came back.

Wherever I may be, memories of that first wartime spring in the woods of Augustovo come back to me like soft waves of sunshine. The gentle young friendliness that shone in a pair of bright grey eyes and issued fresh and warm from a living human voice broke like a strong bright light through the window of my soul, casting sunshine on what was stale and heavy, warming what was cool and full of shadow. How clearly, now and forever, when I recall the past, do I hear the quick step of my friend! I see him coming, slender and free, through the door of my bright pinewood hut, and I see a living young hand putting flowers beneath the little picture of my brother, killed in France, with a fresh, heartfelt gesture that nevertheless betrayed something of that faint, yet healthy reluctance of the young to disclose the feelings of the heart. And often it seems as if I might detain the welcome guest and talk with him about the many different experiences of that happy time, in which even the harsh reality of war could dissolve into play and joy. Do you remember, my friend, how we laughed over my first prisoner? In the ditch in front of our trench, where the bodies of more than thirty Russian soldiers killed in the last attack still lay, I came on him during a night patrol. Unsuspectingly, I approached what I took to be a corpse, meaning to take his rifle. However, it was no corpse, but a quick-witted young lad from Moscow who belonged to a Russian patrol that had been hiding from us here in the darkness. We had, without knowing it, cut him off from his comrades, and he was still hoping to elude us by crouching among the corpses, frozen in the same firing position as they. As I was about to grasp his rifle, the 'dead man' suddenly turned it on me, and fright sent me reeling back. Just in time I put my little Mauser pistol to his temple, causing him to throw his weapon away and resignedly to trot back with us. In order that someone else might share something of my fright, I sent him together with his rifle unannounced into the dug-out of the lieutenant of the first platoon. He, the man from Mecklenburg, was sitting contentedly with a bottle before him, but he was not to be shaken. Instead, he raised his full glass towards the awkwardly grinning lad. 'Cheers, Ivan!' And Ivan unfroze and examined the postcards with which our men had decorated the wood panels of our trench. He stopped reflectively before a coloured picture of Hindenburg. 'Ah, Ghindenburgg!' he exclaimed, waving tireless hands around his Russian head to indicate the imaginary dimensions of the fabled field marshal's skull. Questioned by our laughing soldiers about his fellow-countryman, Grand Duke Nicholas, he pressed his head between his hands to indicate a very sick man, and broke out into a fit of coughing that gave a highly distressing picture of the condition of his generalissimo . . .

And do you still remember how under cover of darkness a Russian patrol planted in front of our wire defences a neatly painted placard bearing the words, 'Italiani – also at war'? [Italy had recently declared war on Austria.] And how on the following night our men planted in one of the Russian listening posts, specially cleared for this purpose, a still more neatly painted placard containing our reply: 'Italiani – also a thrashing', which so enraged them that they spent the whole day shooting at it?

Compliance with the godly, steadfastness in the face of human fallibility, these were the qualities that gave Ernst Wurche's character maturity and grace. What he understood by the soul's preparedness he explained on another occasion. 'If the point of human existence is to see beyond human appearances, then war has given us a greater share of life than others. Few have seen as many masks fall as we out here, few have seen so much baseness, cowardice, weakness, self-seeking and vanity as we, and few so much worthiness and silent nobility of soul. We can ask no more of life than that it reveal itself to us: no human being can demand more. Life has given us more than has been given to many. Now let us calmly wait to see whether it still has more to ask of us.'

What pleased him in *Zarathustra* was the uplifting idea that human nature is something to be overcome. His soul was constantly in search of the eternal. Even in matters concerning his country he was not afraid to face the prospect of its transience. Individuals and peoples, he saw them both as transitory and eternal at one and the same time.

His dislike of superficiality could make him at times taciturn, at others eloquent, depending on the circumstances. For that reason he rightly considered a duologue the finest form of conversation, for nothing else provided the opportunity quietly to explore the clear depths without sudden changes of direction. Many a loving and thoughtful word, shaped by young human lips in the still hours of the night, have since become part of my heart's treasure. And none shines more brightly than those with which he once, leaning on the parapet of his trench, concluded a night-time discussion on the spirit of the *Wandervogel*: 'To stay pure and to grow to maturity – that is life's finest and hardest task.'

Gradually the bitter-sweet springtime smell of fallen leaves and sprouting soil had given way to the stifling air of marshes beneath a hot summer sun and a haze over dead waterweed. The thunder of great new struggles rumbled across to us from Galicia. The gigantic limbs of Hindenburg's army, which had seemed locked in an iron sleep, began to stir and stretch, and the endless front resounded to the noise of battle. We were still lying in wait behind our wire defences: all that was now needed was the order to advance.

But before the rising stream of the great battle engulfed us and bore us away in its currents, we were presented with a few clear and happy days, of which the memory shines out of the past like the shimmer of distant, silver-mirrored lakes. At the beginning of July our company was withdrawn from the trenches and sent further back in the woods for a five days' rest in leaf huts and tents. It so happened that my birthday fell in this time, and my friend helped to celebrate it: the weaponless, cloudless sixth of July was a gift in its fullest sense from his fresh heart to mine. As the sun reached its highest point, we left the shadow of the red firs for the meadow on the banks of the Netta. The sun basked in the deep blue of a sky refreshed by a night of thunderstorms and spread a moist glow over the shimmering curves of the river and the shining, steely blue shield of Lake Sajno in the distance. The light trickled through the juicy green of the burgeoning poplars and willows, and over the luxuriant grass of the broad paddocks the air trembled in the breath of the warm soil. On the banks of the Netta we threw off our clothes and bathed. With long strokes we drifted with the current, to swim back against it with the cool water breaking refreshingly over our shoulders, and time and again, from the wooden bridge whose sun-warmed planks burned our soles, we flung ourselves with long leaps into the water. Lying on our backs, we floated peacefully downstream, then ran back on the lukewarm sand of the reedy bank. In the meadow, bright with wild flowers, we allowed sun and wind to dry us, and the soft, shimmering sunbeams poured through air and sand and human bodies alike, filling all that lived with drunken power and relaxing joy.

The thunder of artillery grumbled in the far distance, but the world of battle, from which for a few hours we were set apart, seemed as distant and unreal as a dream. Our weapons lay on the grass beneath our dusty clothes, and we gave them no thought. A large kite circled tirelessly over the wide, shimmering valley of green paddocks and blue water, and it was on the bird, whose slender wings were now moving in wide, majestic beats, now gently hovering, that our eyes rested. Was it this bird of prey that snatched aloft the soul of the young man at my side to sing the praises of God? The young student of theology felt the wings of his soul expand in the knowledge of that eternal power that 'satisfieth thy mouth with good things, making thee young and lusty as an eagle', and lightly and freely he raised himself and his friend upwards over the bright depths of the motley earth. Pale and slender, the young man stood on the blossoming ground, the sun filtered through his lightly outspread fingers, and from the lips that so often poured forth the songs of Goethe the age-old, sacred music of David's psalm streamed over the sun-drenched paradise: 'O Lord, my God, Thou art very great; Thou art clothed with honour and majesty . . . The glory of the Lord shall endure for ever . . . I will sing unto the Lord as long as I live: I will sing praise to my God while I have my being. My Meditation of Him shall be sweet: I will be glad in the Lord.'

Above the noise and the glory of all battles and victories the image of this hour continues to shine within me, in my soul and in my senses, as the strongest impression of my whole life.

But on the evening of that day the same man stood beside me in his grey battledress in a dark hide at the top of a pine-tree with a double crown, from which all day our sentries had been searching the battle ground with field glasses. Playfully he moved his bayonet to and fro to catch the reflection of the red moon in its gleaming steel. Slightly restive, his right hand slid along the blade, testing its sharpness, and eye and hand revelled, as so often, in the Roman shape of the smooth weapon. His head stretched a little forward, he strained to catch a sound through the darkness from the Russian trenches, over which flares were busy rising and falling. From behind the black wooden huts of Obuchavizna there came the red glow of a peat fire, sending black clouds of soot across the torch-bright sky. Huddled in the darkness of the giant pine-tree, we spoke of the battles in which we would shortly be engaged. 'To take part in a genuine charge,' said the young lieutenant beside me, 'that must be a fine experience. Perhaps one will know it only once, but, *all the same*, it must be a fine thing.' And falling silent again, he looked down at the broad steel in his hands. Then all at once he put an arm around my shoulder and waved the sword before my eyes. 'This is *beautiful*, my friend, is it not?' There was something like impatience and hunger in his words, and I could feel how his hot blood was longing for the battles that lay ahead. Thus he remained for a long while without moving, his lips slightly parted, as the moonlight, growing ever brighter, flowed across the broad blade in his pale hands, and he seemed to be watching out for something strange, great and hostile that lay hidden in the darkness.

Do you understand, you who have shared with me this day of which I have been speaking, do you now understand what it means to be a wanderer between two worlds? . . .

In the last days of July we were relieved in the Augustovo trenches by a Landwehr regiment . . . We knew now that the moment had come: we were going into battle.

By the time we marched off, Lieutenant Wurche had received a regimental order transferring him from the ninth to the tenth company. Thus it was that in our first assult on 21 August we did not advance together. The battle of Krasna and Warthi lives on as one of the bloodiest days in the brigade's history. Our battalion took up an extended position behind the bare slopes of Warthi. Ernst Wurche and his men lay in the foremost line. Since his company commander was wounded at the very start of the battle, he had assumed charge of the tenth company in the middle of the attack. His telephonists had laid a line to the rear, and in the middle of the night my friend called me on the field telephone. He asked about each single man in his old unit. I had made a list of the company's losses. In the third squad, too, the day had torn its gaps. He asked me more about each of the wounded than I was able to answer. Of his own experiences he spoke not a word. 'Good luck tomorrow.' 'Good night.' I replaced the receiver. Then I went to the third squad to pass on to the men my friend's greetings. The morning rose palely over trenches and graves . . .

I saw my friend once again beneath the towering roadside cross of Zajle. He had been reconnoitring the road to Posiminicze, which he and a squad of field sentries were to occupy. We talked of the dead in Warthi. I spoke of this man and that whom I had seen fall, after months of tireless work by a leader's fresh and cordial will had moulded him. One leap, one tumble – dead! And for this *single* step so much labour and love. 'Not for this *single* leap,' my friend interrupted me, 'but that he made it with clear and courageous eyes, the eyes of a mortal being. Should that not be enough?'

In this moment I was summoned to the company commander and received orders to take my squad ahead to Dembovy Roq to mount guard over the setting up of a sentry post there. While my men were getting ready I leaped over the trench to shake my friend's hand. 'I'm on picket duty all night in Posiminicze,' he said. 'Won't you come over for an hour or so?' 'Can't be done – I shall be on outpost duty myself.' 'Oh, well – but it's a pity.' I let his hand go and sprang back over the trench. 'Fall in!' I marched off with the advance group, leaving the rest to follow at a short distance. Beneath the tall black cross of Zajle I saw the slim, upright figure of my friend. '*Auf Wiedersehen*!' I called out to him. He stood still beneath the cross and raised a hand to the rim of his helmet . . .

The pickets and outposts were in position, and I and my squad had marched back to the advance post company in Zajle. I was sitting at the table in the living-room of a farm, writing letters home. The company commander was asleep on a pile of straw. The farmer's family lay on a huge wooden bed beneath a patchwork mountain of pillows. In one corner of the room, surrounded by kitbags and rifles, the telephonists crouched around a little stub of light on their switchboard. Now and then the buzzer sounded, a distant quacking voice delivered messages, which the man at the telephone repeated under his breath as he scribbled them down. The overcrowded room was full of stale air. I stood up and opened a window. Pale stars peered hesitantly from the sky. All was still, save for the tread of the sentry outside the house and the occasional sleepy whimper of a small child lying in the Latvian cradle that hung on soot-blackened cords from the ceiling. The night air lapped softly and coolly about my cheeks. There came another buzz from the telephone in the corner. 'Sir –' 'Yes, what is it?' I turned round unsuspectingly. The telephonist was holding the receiver out to me. The buzzer had sounded three long bursts. That had nothing to do with me: it meant that somebody was talking to the battalion. But I took the receiver which the telephonist waved insistently towards me. Why was he looking at me like that? I listened to the call. 'Report from picket post in Posiminicze: Lieutenant Wurche on patrol at Lake Simno severely wounded. Request for ambulance . . .'

There was complete silence in the room. The man at the telephone continued to watch me. I turned away. Thoughts tumbled through my brain. I felt like rushing from the room and running all the way to Posiminicze . . . But I was on outpost duty. And out there my friend was perhaps bleeding to death. I could not leave my post. 'Oh, well – but it's a pity.' His farewell words beneath the cross at Zajle cut suddenly through the stillness. I clenched my teeth. The words kept going through my head, those almost casual, senseless words that mocked me. 'It's a pity . . . It's a pity . . .' And out there my friend was bleeding to death.

I sat and waited. I stood up and walked up and down. The man in the corner followed me with his eyes. I left the room and was alone. From hour to hour I called the tenth company on the field telephone. 'No further report, the men are still out there.' Always the same. And I was sitting hardly an hour's walk away, yet could not hasten to my friend's side. I stood on Zajle's dark street, staring into the blackness of the south-east, and struggled in vain to take a grip on myself.

The window opened. 'Sir!'

I dashed into the room and seized the receiver. 'Lieutenant Flex here.'

'This is the tenth company. Lieutenant Wurche is dead.'

Without replying, I laid the receiver down.

'Call ended,' the telephonist spoke into the mouthpiece. Senseless, it was all so senseless . . . I was standing again under the pallid sky, the houses around me black, threatening blocks. And the hours crept by, one after the other. I waited only for the first glimmer of sunrise, then rushed off in the direction of Posiminicze. The company gave me two hours' leave. I had to be back in time for march-off.

Only when I was standing over his body did I fully realize it: Ernst Wurche was dead. He lay on his grey greatcoat in a bare room, lay before me with a pure, proud face after having made the last and greatest sacrifice of all, and on his young features there lay a sublime and solemn expression of purified acceptance and submission to God's will. But I myself was distraught, with not a clear thought in my head. In front of the house, to the left of the door, I had seen the open grave the outpost soldiers had dug between two linden trees.

Then I spoke with the men who had gone out on patrol with him the previous evening. Ernst's task had been to find out whether the Russians were still occupying the trenches in front of the Simno dam. In its advance the patrol came under shrapnel fire from the enemy. It was impossible for it to reach the reconnaissance target unobserved. The young commander did not withdraw before completing his objective, but he left his men behind. As they waited under cover, he made a final attempt to gain a glimpse into the Russian trenches. Accustomed as commander always to take the major risk on himself, he crept forward alone, metre by metre, and in this way worked himself a further 150 metres forward. The trench was occupied only by a Cossack outpost, but, as he crept forward, the German officer was spotted by one of the Russians, who at once opened fire. A bullet entered his body, shattering the main arteries and leading within a short time to his death. His men recovered him under fire from the fleeing Cossacks. One of them, as they carried him off, asked, 'Is this all right, sir?' He replied, in his usual quiet way, 'Yes, quite all right.' Then he lost consciousness, and died silently, without complaint.

Spring, summer had now given way to autumn. The greylag geese were returning south. Away in the distance their flight rustled over the lonely grave on the silent slopes above Lake Simno . . . I watched the emigrating army as it passed, but not for long. I felt weighed down, as if a heavy hand lay on my shoulders. I went back into the Polish smithy and threw myself down on the straw.
Every night is a lament. The dawning day is besieged by mists, its glory lost. Winter has come, and its frosts make the windows sightless. My soul is as cold as a bare room. The window panes are frozen. No gleam from the familiar world outside comes in to warm me. I sit alone, my friend, behind frozen windows, and stare at your shadow, which is filling the room. And I rail at fate. But the light outside grows brighter. And once again you are beside me, comforting. 'Now let's see if I am not more alive than you! Look, I go to the window and lay my hand on the ice. It melts beneath my fingers. The first ray of sunshine breaks brightly through. I breathe, smiling, on the cold, blind ice: see how it melts! Woods, towns, lakes gaze in, places in which we have wandered, beloved faces gaze in from outside. Will you not call out to them? Were we not always wanderers between two worlds, comrade? Were we not friends because that was what we had in common? Why do you now cling so firmly to the lovely earth, now that it has become my grave, and bear it around with you like a burden and a shackle? You must be as much at home here as there, or you will be that nowhere . . .' Day has taken command, and my heart yields to clarity and faith.

Every night is a lament. In my grey greatcoat I lean on the snow-covered parapet and look up at the pale stars of bleak winter. And my heart rails at fate. 'We have grown old in our deeds and old in our dead. Death was once young and prodigal, but it has become old and greedy.' But my friend has come up beside me, silently, I know not whence, and I do not ask. His arm is linked in mine as in the wood-lined trenches of Augustovo. And he comforts me: 'That is not old age, as you think, but growing maturity. Your deeds and your dead are making you mature and keeping you young. It is life that has become old and greedy, death remains always the same. Do you know nothing of death's eternal youth? It is God's will that aging life should become young again in the eternal youthfulness of death. That is the meaning and the mystery of death. Do you not see it?'

I keep silent. But my heart continues to rail. And he does not withdraw his arm, nor cease to comfort, softly, with a kind, soothing eagerness. 'Mourning is a grave disservice to the dead, my friend. Do you want to make ghosts of your dead, or do you want to grant them the right to live among you? There is no third way for hearts on which God has laid his hand. Do not make ghosts of us, give us the right to live among you! We want to be able to come to you at all hours without disturbing your laughter. Do not condemn us utterly to be solemn, hoary shadows, grant us the fresh bloom of good cheer that lay like a bright shimmer over our youth. Give your dead a home among you, you who are still alive, so that we may be with you in all dark and all happy hours! Do not weep tears for us, making every friend reluctant to speak of us. Give your friends courage to talk freely and to laugh over us. Grant us the place among you we enjoyed while we lived!'

Still I keep silence, but I feel my heart secure in his good hands. And his beloved voice continues to sound and to comfort. 'As wounded trees pour forth sweet and bitter juices, so do poets pour forth their sweet and bitter songs. Poet, God has touched your heart. Sing on!'

'My friend, my friend, my soul reverberates to the sound of yours, like a bell vibrating to the peals of its swaying neighbour!'

In the eastern sky a stream of liquid gold spreads out across the black clouds and the dark earth. A rosy shimmer hovers in the new shoots crowning the birch-trees. A veil of fresh green hangs from treetops far and wide over the black earth. The second springtime of war is beginning. The storm sweeps across the graves in Poland.

A storm blows from the West, the West,
Wind of home, wind of God,
That causes cross and crown to quake,
And finds a grave in Polish lands.
Then wails and wails the western storm:
Woe, son of German soil!
Why held so firm in Poland's earth?
Though German earth shrouds cool and soft,
Thee shrouds it not!

The western storm-wind sings and wails:
Had I strength, had I strength,
Then I would like a nursery maid
Long have stooped down to snatch thee up!
Can not, can not, woe is me!
Had I strength, had I strength,
I would while chasing through the night
Bring you a scrap of homeland soil
To crown your graves!

A storm drives from the East, the East,
Wind of graves, wind of God:
Beloved homeland, be consoled!
We are still sons of thine own soil . . .
From eastern graves the voices sound:
Earth shrouds ever soft.
Earth, from homeland earth new sprung,
We are but homeland earth ourselves.
Be not afraid!

TRANSLATED BY GEOFFREY SKELTON

GASTON DE RUYTER 1895–1918

'This War is the most exciting novel of all.'

Gaston de Ruyter, fighter pilot, 1918.
Musée Royale de l'armée et d'histoire militaire, Brussels

Of all the French-language writers in this anthology, de Ruyter is the one who most acutely exemplifies the problem which its very existence implies. His poetry is uneven in quality. Even by late 19th-century standards, the not-infrequent inconsistencies in its imagery could lay it open to the charge of incoherence. Further, there are sometimes words or phrases whose only function seems to be to fill out a line or complete a rhyme. At other times, the intended imagery seems to have been too complicated to fit clearly into what becomes the strait-jacket of fixed form. There are clichés, and the rhetoric is occasionally uncomfortably old-fashioned.

Set against this are three factors, two biographical and one textual. The biographical factors are simply those of age and circumstance. Born on 23 December 1895 at Huy, halfway between Namur and Liège, de Ruyter was only 18 when war broke out. He was planning to take a degree in commerce, but volunteered for the infantry straightaway. As a result, all of de Ruyter's poetry that we have was written by a young soldier, much of it in the trenches, some of it on leave or behind the lines, but always with the author under threat of imminent death. The miracle is that so many soldiers wrote verse of any coherence at all in such conditions. The less experienced the writer, the more difficult the conditions must have made it to remain vigilant enough to spot the kinds of flaw which do find their way into de Ruyter's poems.

The textual factor arises as a question: are the inconsistencies in imagery necessarily, or only, a sign of inexperience, hurry or lack of talent, or do they in fact betoken an awareness of dualities and paradox in human relations? There are good examples in the fourth and fifth stanzas of the second poem in our selection. Does the girl walk *on* his *peines* ('sorrows', for which the line of shells thrown up by the tide is a metaphor), or does she walk *past* them? In either case, how does the *chaîne* (the line of shells/sorrows) cement or seal their friendship if she is so indifferent to him? And whose sighs are stilled in whose breast? These are just a few of the questions raised by these stanzas, and it is possible to dispute at length whether there is simply lack of clarity here, or an attempt, perhaps only half-successful, to convey the dialectic of self and other. To put it another way: without the lapses in technique in de Ruyter's poetry, would one ever doubt the sophistication of the vision conveyed in the imagery? The technical clumsiness does not hide the ambition to make out of many 'broken' images one complex image in which the tension between contradictions is an essential unifying factor. If all poetry depends on these things, modern poetry tends to highlight them, even to the point of making awareness of them the very thematic stuff of the poem.

Would de Ruyter have become a good modern poet? We do not know: all we have is an often striking vision, an uneven technique and a range of tones and manners, from reworkings in free form of the old delicate conceits of love poetry, through a more sensual vein, to folk ballads. The vision and the range are why de Ruyter figures in the anthology. The uncertainties are inherent in the concept of 'lost voice'.

De Ruyter had a love of physical activity and the outdoors. He founded the first Boy Scout troop in Huy. Gauchez says that he grew up reading adventure stories, and implies that he only seriously developed an urge to write poetry and plays during the war. The plays did not get beyond the planning stage, but the first book of poems is dated May–August 1917, the second September 1917–September 1918. De Ruyter served with distinction in the trenches until March 1918, when he applied to train as a fighter pilot. He was shot down on 7 October 1918, and died in the burning wreckage of his machine.

IAN HIGGINS

Texts
Chansons vieilles sur d'autres airs (Jouve, Paris, 1918).
Chansons ardentes (Jouve, Paris, 1919).

Secondary sources

M. Gauchez, 'Gaston de Ruyter', in *Anthologie des écrivains morts à la guerre* (Malfère, Amiens, 1924 – 6, 5 vols, III).

CHANSONS VIEILLES SUR D'AUTRES AIRS

XIII

Je voudrais que tu viennes vers moi
Les bras chargés de fleurs sauvages,
Je t'attendrai sur l'infini rivage
Parce que j'ai mis en toi
Ma foi.

Veux-tu venir ce soir par le sentier
A l'heure où les étoiles une à une,
S'allument.
J'irai parmi les dunes
Parce que je veux mendier
Ton amitié.

Tes yeux ne pâliront devant la laideur
Profonde de mon âme!
Oh! souviens-toi que tu es femme
Et ne fuis pas devant l'horreur
De la blessure de mon cœur!

Je voudrais que tu viennes vers moi
Et dans tes bras des fleurs sauvages
Et des sourires à ton visage;
Je t'attendrai parce que j'ai foi
En toi.

le 4 août 1917

OLD SONGS TO OTHER TUNES

XIII

I would have you come toward me
Bearing armfuls of wild flowers
While I await you on this endless shore;
For in you I have placed
My trust.

Will you come this evening along the path
At that hour when the stars kindle
One by one?
Then I shall go among the dunes,
A willing suppliant
For your affection.

Your eyes will not lose their lustre
Faced by the sordid squalor of my soul.
You are a woman: oh, remember this
And do not shrink in horror
From my heart's wound.

I would have you come toward me
With wild flowers in your arms
And smiles lighting your face;
And for you I shall wait, sure of my trust
In you.

4 August 1917

TRANSLATED BY D. D. R. OWEN

XV

La vague lassée a déposé
Les frêles coquillages
Que tes pieds nus vont écraser
Tout le long du rivage.

Tu passeras sans comprendre leurs plaintes
Ni saisir leurs émois;
Choses frêles dont la vie est éteinte,
Ils meurent deux fois.

Et pareilles à tant de ces coquilles
Sont les douleurs
Que mon âme souffrante éparpille
Sur les chemins de ton cœur.

Tu passes de même à côté de mes peines
Et ne veux point écouter
Gémir et pleurer la bonne chaîne
Qui scelle nos amitiés.

Va, mon inévitable amie,
Puisque je veux souffrir,
Puisque je veux me lasser de la vie
A taire en ton sein les soupirs!

La vague épuisée a déposé
Les frêles coquillages
Que tes pieds nus vont écraser
Tout le long du rivage.

le 7 août 1917

XV

Wearied of life, the wave has shed
Its burden of frail shells
That lie for your bare feet to crush
Along the reaches of the shore.

Untouched by their laments you will pass on,
Their agitation leaving you unmoved;
Frail objects once alive,
Now suffering a second death.

And like these multitudes of shells
Are all the sorrows
Left scattered by my troubled soul
Along the pathways of your heart.

So you pass by the debris of my cares
And have no wish to hear
The plaintive fretting of these links that bind
Our fond devotion indissolubly.

Walk on, then, my inevitable love,
Since suffering is all I wish:
Wearily to resign my life
Stilling these sighs within your breast!

Its forces spent, the wave has shed
Its burden of frail shells
That lie for your bare feet to crush
Along the reaches of the shore.

7 August 1917

TRANSLATED BY D. D. R. OWEN

Chansons ardentes

'un souffle vient de naître . . .'

Un souffle vient de naître au seuil glauque du soir
Et les arbres penchés tout le long de la route
Ont, malgré la tempête et le vent en déroute,
Frémi de le sentir perdu dans la nuit noire.

Un souffle de confiance et de douce affection
Vient de courir le long des replis de la plaine,
Les cœurs tumultueux ont tremblé dans leur haine,
Un souffle de tendresse a chanté d'illusion.

Pendant que les moulins tournaient au vent du Nord
Et que la mort aussi larguait ses sombres ailes,
Des femmes ont penché leurs corps souples et frêles
Et fermé pour toujours des paupières de morts.

Visions claires d'espoir! Légers fantômes blancs
Venus d'un peu partout vers l'horrible besogne,
Cœurs de femmes, cœurs d'or, penchés à tout instant
Sur des corps moribonds dont les longs râles
grognent;

Oh! gestes de vos mains, sourires de vos yeux,
Légers fantômes bleus au chevet des souffrances,
Ceux qui meurent s'en vont le cœur moins douloureux,
Ceux qui restent sauront saisir votre confiance!

Un souffle vient de naître au seuil de la tempête,
Court et se répercute aux confins de la plaine,
Un souffle d'affection, léger comme l'haleine,
O femmes, vient de vous et passe sur nos têtes!

Hôpital de Hoogstade, 11 novembre 1917

Songs of Passion

'By evening's blue-grey threshold . . .'

By evening's blue-grey threshold stirs a breeze;
And all along the road the bowing trees,
Though gale and tempest have now turned to flight,
Trembled to sense it lost in the dark night:

A breath of trust, tenderly soothing pain,
Has crept about the hollows of the plain.
While raging hearts have quivered in their hate,
A breath of love prompts dreams of happier fate.

As the north wind drove the mills ceaselessly
And death too let its sombre sails turn free,
Frail, lissom women, stooping with bowed head,
Closed for all time the eyelids of the dead.

Ah, hope's bright visions! Spectral wraiths in white,
For your grim work you flock together; then
Your women's, golden, hearts bow day and night
Over long agonies of dying men.

Ah, your hands' gestures and your smiling eyes!
Blue, spectral wraiths beside the beds of pain,
You bring your solace to each man who dies
And reassurance to those who remain!

A breeze has risen in the tempest's train
And steals about the fringes of the plain:
Your breath of tenderness, soft as a sigh,
O women, cools our brows as you pass by!

Hoogstade Hospital, 11 November 1917

Translated by D. D. R. Owen

TRISTE HISTOIRE D'UN MOULIN DE CHEZ NOUS ET DE QUATRE JEUNES FILLES

Moulin caduc, ô mon moulin,
Ce soir, je veux chanter ta vie:
Le souvenir de tes refrains
Berce d'espoir ma nostalgie!

Aux quatre coins du vieux moulin,
Des oiseaux chantaient leurs ramages
Et des moineaux prompts et mutins
Suspendaient même leur tapage.

Aux quatre ailes du vieux moulin,
Les vents ont gémi leurs misères;
Aux quatre coins des gris matins,
Les vents ont soufflé leurs colères.

Aux jours des fêtes de la Vierge,
Après les messes du matin,
Les fillettes brûlaient des cierges
Aux quatre ailes du vieux moulin.

Aux quatre ailes du vieux moulin,
Les jeunes filles du village
Venaient nouer les fleurs sauvages
Ecloses le long des chemins.

Les quatre ailes du vieux moulin,
Tournant à la brise tranquille,
Accompagnaient les vieux refrains
Au son desquels dansaient les filles.

Autour du moulin vermoulu
Brunes et blanches, mes amies,
Vous ne danserez jamais plus
Les cramignons de Wallonie!

Aux quatre ailes du vieux moulin,
Les aigles noirs de Germanie
Ont reposé, les soirs d'orgies,
Leurs carcasses crevant de faim.

Aux quatre ailes du vieux moulin,
Les aigles ont pendu des femmes
Et, quand l'aurore s'en revint,
Le moulin vieux moulait des flammes!

Les quatre ailes du vieux moulin
Ont tourné comme aux jours des fêtes
Et le moulin moulait des mains,
Des corps de vierges et des têtes!

THE SAD HISTORY OF FOUR MAIDS AND OUR VILLAGE MILL

Tumbled mill, beloved mill,
I'll sing your life, tonight:
The memory of your singing still
Cradles hopes of light!

In every corner of the mill
Hung the nests of swallows,
And the timbers echoed to the shrill
Squabbles of the sparrows.

Through the old mill's four great sails
The sighing wind would mourn;
Round every corner angry gales
Whipped up the grey of dawn.

On Lady Day, the girls returning
From mass put off their veils
And set four holy candles burning
On the four great sails.

And the old mill's four great sails
Would turn in lazy furls
Of flower-woven swallowtails
Garlanded by girls.

And the old mill's four great sails
Turned easy in the breeze
To maidens' songs, old village tales
And the dancing in the leas.

Around the wormy-timbered mill
You'll never sing again,
Nut-brown, milk-white girls, nor thrill
To the dances of Ardenne!

To the four great sails of the old mill
There came from Germany
Lusting eagles, came to still
Their black depravity.

From the four great sails of the old mill
They hanged four maids with wire.
The dawning day was grey and chill,
But the mill was milling fire!

And while the four sails of the mill
Still wheeled easy, the stones
Were milling the old mill its fill
Of maidens' skulls and bones!

Les quatre ailes du moulin vieux
Au vent des flammes ont tourné,
Tant qu'elles ont enfin croulé,
Les ailes du vieux moulin pieux!

Aux quatre ailes du vieux moulin,
Des cœurs de vierges sont cloués,
Et nous irons chaque matin
Pleurer au vieux moulin brisé.

Tranchées de Dixmude, le 14 novembre 1917

And the four great sails of the old mill
Turned in the fire's breath,
And they burned and turned until
The mill tumbled in death!

To each great sail of the old mill
Is nailed a maiden's womb:
Each dawn, we'll weep and climb the hill
To the mill, their catacomb.

Dixmude trenches, 14 November 1917

TRANSLATED BY IAN HIGGINS

'DANS LA TIÈDE MOITEUR . . .'

Dans la tiède moiteur et les parfums troublés
Venus avec le soir par la fenêtre ouverte
Et caressant ton corps, ô toi qui déconcertes,
S'élèvent les appels de tes sens éveillés.

Sur le divan de soie où tant de fois à deux
Nous avons oublié tous les bruits de la rue,
Tu t'étais assoupie, enfant, couchée et nue,
La lune tamisant sur toi ses rayons bleus.

J'ai traversé la chambre où dormait ta beauté,
Je me suis prosterné, puis j'ai tendu la bouche,
Appelant ton réveil et le regard farouche,
Aux cils d'or de tes yeux éperdument fixé.

Et puis ton corps sous mon haleine a tressailli,
Un lent regard passant tes paupières mi-closes,
Et comme si j'étais ton esclave et ta chose,
Tu pris ma tête folle en tes bras alanguis.

Nos corps se sont roulés ou crispés ou tordus,
Nos corps jeunes et beaux s'embrasant à leurs jeux;
La lune tamisait sur nous ses rayons bleus
Et tes lèvres mordaient à sang dans mes bras nus!

Tranchées de Dixmude, 28 septembre 1917

'STRANGE SCENTS . . .'

Strange scents, that mingle on the sultry air
Of evening, through the open window steal
And lap your body's dear enigma, where
Your waking senses give forth their appeal.

Upon that silk divan, where we before
Often shut from our minds the city's roar,
Naked you lay as a child drugged by night,
Your body dappled by the moon's blue light.

Your drowsing beauty beckoned my advance
Bowing before you, lips tense with desire
To rouse you and release that untamed glance
Through golden lashes, shot with passion's fire.

Touched by my breath, I saw your body start.
Disclosing a slow glance your eyelids part;
Then, like some plaything captive to your charms,
My dizzy head was in your languid arms.

Our bodies twisted, writhing, all aflame,
Beautiful bodies agile in love's game,
Young bodies dappled by the moon's blue light,
My pale arms bloodied by your mouth's fierce bite.

Dixmude trenches, 28 September 1917

TRANSLATED BY D. D. R. OWEN

GUILLAUME APOLLINAIRE 1880–1918

'You can be a poet in any domain, provided you go forward in a spirit of adventure, seeking new discoveries.'

Wilhelm de Kostrowitzky, alias Guillaume Apollinaire, was born in Rome, probably on 25 August 1880 (although 26 August is stated on his birth certificate), the illegitimate son of Angélique de Kostrowitzky, a young woman of noble Polish blood, and (probably) Francesco Flugi d'Aspermont, an Italian army officer. Guillaume spent his early years in Italy, then in 1888 entered a Catholic boarding school in Monaco before moving to schools in Nice and Cannes, finally leaving at 16 without his *baccalauréat*. His mother (who had herself been expelled from convent school in Rome at the age of 16) had meanwhile changed her name to Olga and seems to have made a precarious living in Monte Carlo until an order was issued banning her from the Casino. In 1899, she moved to Paris with her two sons, and subsequently Guillaume travelled widely around Europe, ranging from Berlin and Prague to London, before settling in Paris, his beloved 'capital of the modern world'.

At 14, Apollinaire was pious, at 16, he was an anarchist, but already at the age of 12, encouraged by a sensitive classics master named Becker, he had started writing poetry. His unconventional origins and status as an illegimate immigrant left him with a deep sense of insecurity, countered by gregarious good humour. Through his writing, he sought to build himself an ambitious identity, deeply rooted in French language and culture, a tradition fervently assimilated, while retaining a cosmopolitan spirit of high adventure. Defender of the immigrant and all minority groups, he peopled his poems and stories with the lonely and the unusual, rootless figures and outcasts. His own growing sense of stability was badly shaken in 1911 by a spell in prison when he was wrongfully arrested after the theft of the *Mona Lisa* and threatened with deportation as an undesirable alien. Only in the war could he finally obtain French nationality. A volunteer wounded in combat, he was refused the Légion d'honneur but was awarded the Croix de guerre ('O cross of heavy torment,' he wrote), a final sign of official acceptance by the adoptive country for which he died.

Apollinaire's two major collections of poetry – *Alcools* (1913) and *Calligrammes* (1918) – lead French verse away from the rarefied beauty of *fin de siècle* Symbolism into an era in which everyday life could seem as astonishing as any heroic legend and so itself provide the matter of art. Blériot realized the dream of Icarus while wireless telegraphy, mass circulation newspapers and high-speed travel fostered a new global consciousness, given voice by Apollinaire. In 'Zone', opening *Alcools*, he announces that grace is now epitomized by a new industrial street, and that his modern muse is the shorthand typist off to work, an assertion which allows him to prove the poetic suitability of a new word, '*sténo-dactylographes*', audaciously rhymed with '*quatre fois par jour y passent*', exemplifying his constant exploitation of the poetic potential he discerned in all registers of language, from the recondite to the idiomatic.

Apollinaire is the finest and most entertaining 20th-century poet of the Seine and of Paris, made pastoral in 'Zone', where the Eiffel Tower is a shepherdess and the honking rush-hour bridges are a flock of bleating sheep. Rising and falling like Icarus, 'Zone' is a peripatetic poem, a 24-hour circle round Paris, a pattern comparable to Joyce's *Ulysses* which later set Homer's *Odyssey* in modern Dublin. Within that chronology however, limits of space and time dissolve as the poem moves back and forth across continents, through one man's life and human history, with seamless transitions and sudden juxtapositions, development by association of words, ideas and images in a controlled stream of consciousness, facilitated by the poet's original and highly influential abolition of punctuation.

Apollinaire's poetry often aspires towards this multi-dimensional simultaneity, perhaps the price of rootlessness but also conferring on poet and reader an aspect of ubiquitous divinity. Similarly, the slide from personal experience towards an apparently recondite literary reference was for Apollinaire a perfectly natural process. His poetry exteriorizes an inner universe where observations and memories mingle on equal terms with disparate images, characters and events gleaned from wide and voracious reading, usually retained because they correspond in some way to his own experience or preoccupations. Life and legends coexist, and the frontier between the known and the possible disappears to create a highly infectious poetic view of reality, enhanced by imagination.

Apollinaire was a modernist for whom Homer and Dante were close contemporaries, so it is typical, but still surprising, that the apparently iconoclastic opening statement of 'Zone' is couched in the form of an alexandrine. Similarly 'La Chanson du Mal-Aimé', a modernist collage of contrasting pieces composed over several years, finds formal unity in the unbroken flow of octosyllabic quintets. Throughout *Alcools* and *Calligrammes*, Apollinaire moves easily between classical versification and extremes of formal experimentation, not hesitating between order and adventure but exploiting all the resources at his disposal. So 'Zone' was composed shortly after 'Le Pont Mirabeau', an immediately accessible short poem of irresistible, hypnotic beauty in the traditional form of a 13th-century spinning song. As a cultural entrepreneur too, Apollinaire promoted and encouraged all new artistic initiatives but never restricted his own creativity to fit the exclusive criteria of Naturism, Unanimism, Futurism or any other avant-garde group. 'Canons are useful only in artillery,' he wrote. 'In art they are mainly restrictions on style as I understand it.'

Marked by the poet's prison days and the subsequent end of a love affair, 'Zone' moves into an increasingly sombre mood, expressing alienation amid inner-city outcasts, a spiritual crisis which comes to a climax in a brutal red sunrise at the hour of guillotine executions. A more lilting strain of autumnal melancholia runs throughout *Alcools*. Indeed, the 'Alcohol' of the title, as an inflammable liquid, implies contradictory elements – fire and water, the vertical flame of creativity, fire engendering the Phoenix, endlessly reborn in its own ashes – while the river symbolizes the fatal downward flow of passing time and lost love. A series of regular and melodic poems, sometimes broken by startling surprises, evoke 'the eternal sound of a river dark and wide', sometimes the Seine, more often the Rhine. Germanic subjects dominate much of *Alcools* as Apollinaire recalls Rhineland folklore, songs and legends, German Jews and travelling entertainers, farmhouses, cemeteries and cafés. These are the poems of a Germanophile. Ludwig II of Bavaria is one of Apollinaire's heroes, and the poet's descriptions of Rhineland landscapes are all uniquely evocative. Steeped in German popular culture, the poems contradict the ungenerous attitude of certain of Apollinaire's newspaper articles on German subjects. The passion in these poems, however, is Apollinaire's unrequited love for Annie Playden, an English girl he met in Germany, and 'La Chanson du Mal-Aimé' is his greatest monument to that affair. But 'La Chanson' ends in Paris, where blazing sunlight gives way to bright evenings that buzz with electricity, energy overflowing through enjambement to prepare the way for a closing quintet in which the poet proclaims himself heir to a timeless Orphic tradition of suffering transposed into music whose beauty can rival the sirens' song. 'No, you shouldn't see sadness in my work,' wrote Apollinaire, 'but life itself, with the constant and conscious voluptuous pleasure of living, discovering, seeing, knowing and finding expression.'

In the pre-war years Apollinaire also established a high reputation as an observant and witty journalist, a short-story writer and France's most authoritative spokesman on contemporary art. *Méditations esthétiques: Les peintres cubistes* (1913) is a collage of material dating back as far as 1905, the year he wrote his first prophetic articles on Picasso, then 24 years old, the artist he consistently placed above all others. Other chapters cover the work of Braque, Gris, Léger, Picabia, Duchamp, Marie Laurencin (including a discussion of Douanier Rousseau and a celebration of women painters since the Renaissance) – an inspired choice by any standards, with further volumes planned for the future. He welcomes the evolution of increasingly non-representational painting since Gauguin and Cézanne, defines cubism and announces the birth of pure abstraction, which, he says, will be to figurative painting as music is to literature. His observations are precise and often daring, as when he proclaims the obsolescence of the archaic hierarchies of subject and materials: 'You can paint with whatever you like, with pipes, with stamps, postcards or playing-cards, candlesticks, bits of waxed cloth, shirt collars, wallpaper, newspaper.' Working with elements from recognizable paintings, Apollinaire transposes the visual into the verbal, responding to an artist's work by reflecting it in equally creative poetic prose. Often his commentary is to the painting as the cubist picture is to its subject, more a conception than a description, appropriate but sometimes oblique, with an autonomous nobility of its own. *Alcools*, *Méditations esthétiques* and the success of his modern arts

'For the poet, a falling handkerchief can be the lever with which he raises a whole universe.'

magazine *Les Soirées de Paris* reinforced Apollinaire's prestige as a prime mover in art and poetry – the painters' poet. He became a powerful unifying spirit amid Parisian rivalries and the major magnetic force for younger poets such as Breton, Soupault, Aragon and Cocteau.

Apollinaire's short stories, published in two collections – *L'Hérésiarque et Cie* (1910) and *Le Poète assassiné* (1916) – again operate in the zone he defined in 1907: 'Placed at the limits of life, on the frontiers of art . . . at the limits of art, on the frontiers of life.' His imagination is always triggered by an actual event or personal experience which is then fictionalized and developed so that, with a twist in every tale, fantasy seems credible and quotidian reality is suddenly infused with unaccountable magic.

Apollinaire's prose masterpiece, according to Picasso, was his erotic novel of 1907, *Les Onze mille verges*. It certainly deserves the same consideration as an important earlier work, *L'Enchanteur pourrissant*. Both are rebel texts, the coded expression of deeply personal obsessions – with, for example, Apollinaire's mother appearing as Angélique in a travesty of the Annunciation and the Assumption in *L'Enchanteur*, reappearing in Chapter 7 of *Les Onze mille verges* as an aristocratic and authoritarian Polish nurse, a lubricious Madonna with an angelic voice. *L'Enchanteur* is a black Christmas, replacing Christ in the manger by Merlin in a tomb, while *Les Onze mille verges* is a voluptuous calvary whose title is a sacrilegious pun, parodying the legend of St Ursula and the 11,000 virgins martyred in Cologne in about the 3rd century AD. To the seminal experiments in simultaneity of *L'Enchanteur*, set in a deep Arthurian forest, correspond the high-speed adventures with transcontinental displacement and cinematic jump-cuts of *Les Onze mille verges*, a change in terms of reference, away from purely literary iconology into the imagery of contemporary experience, city streets and the Orient Express. The bawdy laughter and violent obscenity of *Les Onze mille verges* function as a bold exorcism of boiling anger and frustration which date back to the loss in Germany of Annie Playden, his most obsessive infatuation, and beyond, opening the way for a clear poetic renaissance in 1908, the Phoenix reborn in 'Le Brasier', 'Les Fiançailles' and 'Onirocritique', three of Apollinaire's finest poems.

For André Breton, *Alcools* was 'the greatest collection of French poetry this century' ('Présent des Gaules', an article written in 1955). *Calligrammes* on the other hand, has been the source of a long-running controversy, fuelled largely by the Surrealists' sometimes sceptical reception of Apollinaire's war poetry. These are 'Poems of Peace and War', however, and the sixteen poems of 'Ondes' ('Waves'), the opening section, represent a period of grace between the catharsis of 'Zone' and mobilization. The most striking innovation in 'Ondes' is the appearance of Apollinaire's first picture poems – 'lyrical ideograms' – in which the words spread out in figurative, then abstract designs which combine visibility and readability, the simultaneous, immediate impact of painting with the consecutive quality of poetry as the text is unravelled. A further dimension is contributed by subsequent interplay in the reader's mind between images in the text and the design, the one supporting or contradicting the other, and like the text, the design may itself be ambiguous, suggesting, to take one of the simpler examples, both a heart and an inverted candle flame. Some designs may have cabalistic significance, may suggest male or female principles, emotions such as surprise or doubt, and Apollinaire uses the resources of new printing technology to include snippets of bare reality – postmarks, the design of telegraph wires, noises and other fragments – combined in collages that match ongoing developments in the plastic arts. Apollinaire would develop this technique at the front to evoke a spray of machine-gun fire, the shock of exploding shells and rockets filling the page. In 'Ondes', these and other poems create new forms of cosmopolitan simultaneity and celebrate Parisian street life, while the 'conversation poem' 'Lundi rue Christine' redefines the parameters of poetry by stringing together fragmentary phrases overheard in a busy café, the logical conclusion of a process begun in September 1898, when Apollinaire, on a Monte Carlo terrace, first jotted apparently futile conversations into his diary. Some of the poems transpose the colours and imagery of Delaunay, Chagall and Picasso, while puns and echoes contribute a playful quality, and telegrammatic style and abbreviated syntax produce startling, multi-faceted juxtapositions. Like the Eiffel Tower, modernist emblem of the age, the poet is receiver and transmitter, scanning the airwaves as international signals combine and cut across each other.

The theatre was a constant preoccupation for Apollinaire. *A quelle heure un train partira-t-il pour Paris?* (1914) is a stage version of the 1913 poem 'Le Musicien de Saint-Merry', transposing a text into a visual medium, thereby inverting the process accomplished in *Méditations esthétiques*. This mysterious erotic ceremony re-enacts the rites of Dionysus and primitive African rituals, setting them in the ancient back streets of Paris. The smooth-faced flautist is, in fact, an ambulatory phallus, and the set is filled with Freudian symbols. Apollinaire's stagecraft is powerfully innovatory as bursts of light, slides and perhaps even film interrupt the hypnotic, non-verbal action to create a moving backdrop of high-speed simultaneity, the beginnings of *son et lumière*.

This short protosurrealist play constitutes Apollinaire's most astonishing contribution to the theatre. Unfortunately, planned performances in France and the United States, with music by Alberto Savinio, brother of Giorgio de Chirico, were prevented by the outbreak of war, but the central character would live on as the

> *'Oh God! what a lovely war*
> *With its songs its long leisure hours.'*

faceless figure in Chirico's paintings, directly influenced by this work. The play's obvious narrative link with the Pied Piper legend again demonstrates Apollinaire's interest in German folklore. He revisited Berlin in 1913, and his friendly contacts at that time with Herwarth Walden and young German painters made the sudden unfurling of military banners on both sides in the summer of 1914 appear all the more tragically ironic.

Apollinaire at war believed he was defending France and freedom of expression against an authoritarian invasion (see his poem 'A l'Italie'): the Germans were advancing on Paris. However, he simultaneously strove to save poetry from what he called the 'mechanical rhetoric' of other French poets who 'sing of battles from afar in truly stupid language'. He kept the flame of modernist creativity alive as, throughout the war, he continued his radical experiments in form and subject matter, while the dust from explosions occasionally dried the ink on the page ('It's very handy,' he wrote).

He enlisted in the artillery – having failed to join the Foreign Legion, which was overflowing with volunteers – and, after training, found himself posted to a wood in Champagne, under fire, but several kilometres from the front-line. 'Here it's back to nature. We're living like cowboys in the Far West,' he wrote in a letter of 7 April 1915. In his poetry from that spring, collected in the 'Case d'armons' section of *Calligrammes*, syntax and layout reached their freest and least regimented state, intensifying Apollinaire's aesthetic of surprise, expressing pervasive unpredictability, the spurting adrenalin and libertarian irreverence of gunners in the combat zone. However, throughout the war, Apollinaire also composed many lyrical love poems of great beauty; they increasingly provided a privileged refuge from worsening conditions as the conflict dragged on.

Apollinaire initially enjoyed the relative anonymity afforded by his blue uniform as he fitted into the crowd, for once no longer an outsider in France. True to his interest in minorities, he wrote a powerful poem, 'Les soupirs du servant de Dakar' ('The Sighs of the Gunner from Dakar'), where a black Senegalese soldier, remembering colonial oppression in Africa, reflects that, in the army, he himself has become a white man: 'Je suis soldat français on m'a blanchi du coup' ('I'm a French soldier and so that made me white'). Apollinaire identifies with his subject, a black sheep admitted to the fold. And just as the African questions his strange destiny, so Apollinaire sets a question mark in heavy black type, symbol of his own recurrent unease, at the heart of his most beautiful calligramme, 'La colombe poignardée et le jet d'eau' ('The Bleeding-Heart Dove and the Fountain').

Provocative titles such as 'Fête' and 'Merveille de la guerre' indicate that Apollinaire was amazed by the firework display of night-time artillery battles, a sight for which he had been prepared in the barracks by the account of a wounded eyewitness:

> But at the canteen a pale wounded soldier
> Told of the bombshells' silver splendour

Lines explode at all angles over the page, but this is a fatal beauty, and throughout his war poetry Apollinaire does include the havoc wrought at ground level, as in 'Saillant', just one example, where an aerial torpedo swoops without warning on an unarmed soldier, devastating the landscape. There is laughter, too, but gas regularly seeps into the poetry, and the gas-masks over tears of laughter in 'SP' or the line 'Mais quel fou rire sous le masque' ('But what mad laughter behind the mask') in 'Chant de l'horizon en Champagne' are horribly ambiguous, recalling the ever-present danger of hysteria and insanity preying on the soldier whose inner defences fall. The most notorious lines of all French war poetry are those which open 'L'Adieu du cavalier' ('The Cavalier's Farewell') in *Calligrammes*:

> Oh God! what a lovely war
> With its songs its long leisure hours

But this poem's two quatrains turn on the irony created by the punning progression from 'Ah Dieu' to the later 'Adieu', from the cry of wonder to definitive separation as the soldier on horseback is suddenly killed. Aware of its shock value, Apollinaire scratched the opening line of this same poem on to his soap tin as the caption to a drawing of two gunners facing a bright overhead explosion. The magnificent shellburst is close enough to kill them both.

In November 1915, Apollinaire took up a commission in the infantry. Thenceforth his love letters to Madeleine Pagès, previously a pure domain of reflection and seduction, are invaded by lice and vermin, nameless filth, the walls of trenches built from corpses, the front-line soldiers continually rebuilding collapsing defences – 'Sysiphus with his rock', dreaming only of escape through 'a lucky wound (the loss of an arm)'. Apollinaire's production slowed, but he still composed deeply moving poetry. Blind soldiers lost under the moonlight amid the barbed wire of no-man's-land appear in 'Du coton dans les oreilles' ('Cotton in your Ears'), a long collage poem, and in 'Océan de terre' ('Ocean of Earth'), the ravaged chalklands of Champagne are viewed through streaming eyes (gas again), a desolate nightmare appropriately dedicated to Giorgio de Chirico, in which bombs fall from above, octopus beaks peck at a fragile protective window and fearfully spurted ink forms a long line of unforgettable sorrow: 'Et puis nous sommes tant et tant à être nos propres fossoyeurs' ('And there are oh so many of us digging our own graves').

A splinter of shrapnel pierced Apollinaire's forehead

on 17 March 1916. He survived with a star-shaped scar and, still in uniform but unfit for combat, threw himself back into artistic adventure. Despite prolonged stays in hospital, his last two years, back in Paris, were stunningly productive. His late achievements included fine poems such as 'La Victoire' and 'La Jolie Rousse' for his fiancée, Jacqueline Kolb; *La Bréhatine*, a film script planned to be the first of many; a book on African sculpture; numerous newspaper articles and short stories; a ballet (still unpublished) and *Les Mamelles de Tirésias* (*The Breasts of Tirésias*), a play which reconciles feminism and repopulation in a 'Grand Magic Circus' mixture of theatrical traditions defined as 'surrealist', a term he invented for a type of theatre which would be anti-naturalistic but true to life in its excitement and unpredictability. He compiled his last novel, *La Femme assise* (*The Sitting Woman*), the first page of which contains the first reference in a French novel to Freudian psychoanalysis, while in his important manifesto 'L'Esprit nouveau et les poètes' he reaffirmed his faith in human potential and creativity, even proclaiming that with an inventive and adventurous approach one may be a poet in any domain, a view of life and art which would strongly influence the later surrealist movement.

Countering this optimistic stance, there is an angry libertarian streak running through his work in 1917 – in his poem 'Je suis la vie . . .', for example, where Humanity, torn apart by war, is compared to the divine form of Orpheus, torn apart by the Maenads, to whom Apollinaire now gives another name: 'Et l'on m'a dit qu'Elles s'appelaient "Les Patries!" ' ('And I was told they were called "The Motherlands!" '). Or again in the poem 'Orphée', where he writes:

> Now everything is enormous
> And it seems to me that peacetime
> Will be as monstrous as the war

The vision of a conformist future made in the image of a regimented wartime society now haunts Apollinaire, recurring in newspaper articles, in his preface for *Les Fleurs du mal*, in his allegorical play *Couleur du temps* (*Colour of Time*), where he states that, in war, 'a man counts for nothing', 'a copper coin in the tills of a bank', 'a drop of condensation on the windows of a café': 'He thinks but he is the slave of machines.' The experience of mechanized warfare has shaken Apollinaire's faith in technological progress, and already he fears the totalitarian future of *Brave New World* and *1984*. Furthermore, *Couleur du temps* prophetically warns humanity of its 20th-century capacity for total self-annihilation: at the end of the play, all the male characters destroy each other, ironically fighting over the same ideal.

In 1918, Picasso and Apollinaire were as close as ever, best men at each other's weddings and working on a book together, with new poems by Apollinaire to be illustrated by Picasso. The non-realization of this project, probably to be entitled *Les Oiseaux chantent avec les doigts* (*Birds Sing with Fingertips*), was undoubtedly one of the greatest artistic losses of the war. Weakened by his head wound, his lungs ruined by gas, in November 1918 Apollinaire fell victim to the influenza pandemic and died two days before the Armistice, in his flat above the Boulevard Saint-Germain. From among his last words, a friend recorded: 'Save me doctor! I want to live! I still have so much to say!' His inspirational influence has reached well into the 20th century, and he stands as a major figure in the first rank of European modernism, the greatest French poet of his generation.

PETER READ

Texts
Marcel Adéma et Michel Décaudin (eds), *Oeuvres poétiques* (Gallimard, 'Bibliothèque de la Pléiade', Paris, 1965).
Michel Décaudin (ed.), *Oeuvres en prose*, I (Gallimard, 'Bibliothèque de la Pléiade', Paris, 1977).
Garnet Rees (ed.), *Alcools* (Athlone French Poets, London, 1975). With Introduction and Notes in English.
À quelle heure un train partira-t-il pour Paris? (Bibliothèque artistique et littéraire, Fontfroide, 1982). With a postface by Willard Bohn.
Calligrammes (Gallimard, 'Poésie', Paris, 1974). With a preface by Michel Butor.
M. Décaudin (ed.), *L'Enchanteur pourrissant* suivi de *Les Mamelles de Tirésias* et *Le Couleur du temps* (Gallimard, 'Poésie', Paris, 1972).
M. Décaudin (ed.), *Les Exploits d'un jeune Don Juan* (J'ai lu, Paris, 1987).
M. Décaudin (ed.), *Les Onze mille verges ou les Amours d'un Hospodar* (J'ai lu, Paris, 1976).
Tendre comme le souvenir (Gallimard, Paris, 1952). Letters and poems to Madeleine Pagès.
Most Apollinaire works are currently available in paperback.

English translations
Anne Hyde Greet (trans.), *Calligrammes, poèmes de la paix et de la guerre* (University of California Press, Berkeley/London, 1980). Excellent bilingual edition. Notes by Anne Hyde Greet and S. I. Lockerbie; introduction by S. I. Lockerbie. Reproduced by kind permission of the Regents of the University of California © 1980.
Ron Padgett (trans.), *The Poet Assassinated and Other Stories* (Carcanet, Manchester, 1985).
Samuel Beckett (trans.), *Zone* (Dolmen Press/Calder & Boyars, Dublin/London, 1972). This translation dates from 1950. Some readers may query Beckett's 'So much for poetry this morning' in line 12 of the poem ('That's poetry this morning' would better express Apollinaire's enthusiasm for posters and other modern ephemera), but the translation is otherwise magnificent. Reproduced by generous permission of Samuel Beckett.

Secondary sources
Michel Décaudin, *Guillaume Apollinaire* (Séguier-Vagabondages, Paris, 1986). Contains best available bibliography of works obtainable in France.
Daniel Oster, *Guillaume Apollinaire* (Seghers, Paris, 1975).
Francis Steegmuller, *Apollinaire: Poet among the Painters* (Penguin Books, Harmondsworth, 1986).
Two literary journals are exclusively devoted to Apollinaire studies: *Guillaume Apollinaire*, Paris, Lettres Modernes, nos 1–17, 1962–87 (a continuing series).
Que vlo-ve? Bulletin international des études sur Apollinaire, a quarterly journal, no. 1, January 1973.

A QUELLE HEURE UN TRAIN PARTIRA-T-IL POUR PARIS? (WHAT TIME DOES A TRAIN LEAVE FOR PARIS?)

This 1914 play, published in France only in 1982 after the discovery of the lost manuscript, is here translated for the first time.

Music by Alberto Savinio
Designed and directed by Francis Picabia and Marius de Zayas

THE MUSICIAN WITH NO EYES OR NOSE OR EARS
AS MANY WOMEN AS POSSIBLE
THE EIFFEL TOWER
THE ARC DE TRIOMPHE
NOTRE DAME
A FACTORY CHIMNEY
THE SOVEREIGN
TWO ATTENDANTS
THE SOLDIER
THE POET

Scene 1

A white cloth screen hangs across the stage, near the front. The POET stands to one side, between the front of the stage and the screen. The illuminated screen is crossed by the dark shadows of 'Beings unknown to the Poet but that he at last has the right to salute'. And sure enough, as each figure passes by, the POET raises his hand in a short, jerky, automatic gesture.

A black curtain then falls in front of the screen, hiding even the POET. In complete darkness, a powerful voice shouts through a megaphone:

I sing neither of this world nor of the other planets
I sing of all my own possibilities beyond this world and the planets
I sing the joy of wandering and the pleasure of the wanderer's death.

Scene 2

Against the black curtain, still in place, a strip of white cloth moves horizontally. On it is written the date: 21 May 1913. (The letters are printed in black capitals; the figures are in red.)

The flute of the faceless MUSICIAN is heard far off in the distance. The black curtain is raised. Millions of flies appear, swarming around a column of light. (This level of the set will be placed a little further back than the screen in Scene 1, but not too far from the edge of the stage.)

Then the stage darkens for a moment.

When light returns, the city can be seen, its outline very low, almost at the level of the stage, with rooftops, tall chimneys and smaller ones, smoking. (This part of the set is at the back of the stage.) The background is filled in with trees. The EIFFEL TOWER, the ARC DE TRIOMPHE, NOTRE DAME, a tall FACTORY CHIMNEY. Near the wings to the right of the stage, the outline of a black hand is printed on the wall. This hand points to a nearby sign on which is written: rue Aubry-le-Boucher. THE MUSICIAN WITH NO EYES OR NOSE OR EARS enters from the left, slowly crosses the stage, then goes into the street marked with the sign and disappears (as in lines 11 and 12 of the poem).

The EIFFEL TOWER shoots beams of light into the audience; sounds of the city, car horns; bells ringing; bugles; the crackle of wireless telegraphy, voices shouting phrases such as:

VOICES } When I was a child there were no motor cars
Help . . . it's the sound of an aeroplane
Vive la liberté . . . we'll go to America

Scene 3

A small square. A fountain on the left. In the background, the EIFFEL TOWER, NOTRE DAME, the ARC DE TRIOMPHE and the FACTORY CHIMNEY. Several streets run into the little square, with their names written on signs: rue Aubry-le-Boucher, rue Saint-Martin, rue Simon-le-Franc.

Entering from the right, the MUSICIAN WITH NO EYES OR NOSE OR EARS moves forward slowly, playing the flute. He has no mouth but plays the flute through an opening in his throat into which has been set a rubber or metal ring of the kind used on horses after a tracheotomy. After a short while, he stands still (near the wings, stage right). He continues to play as WOMEN of all sorts approach and little by little gather round him: a headless woman, an armless woman, a blue woman, a red woman, a bald woman, an elegant woman, a little girl, an old lady. Several pretty girls, women with their hair down over their shoulders, naked women (in bodystockings).

When they are all together, the MUSICIAN walks slowly over to the fountain, followed by the WOMEN. The bell rings. The MUSICIAN stops playing and drinks at the fountain. The WOMEN cluster round to see him, to hold him.

Then the MUSICIAN starts playing again and walks back the way he came, followed by the WOMEN.

Other WOMEN appear from several parts of the stage, with arms outstretched and wild eyes. The music fades.

Scene 4

As the music fades, a curtain is lowered at the back of the stage, hiding the buildings. Lights or pictures are projected to express life and all its variety: trains leaving stations – tropical birds and vegetation – the panic and religious life of Equatorial Africa – gentle European rivers – life in bright little towns in central France – freight trains crossing the European night – European city life – and landscapes with factory chimneys.

Then, with music and the projection of pictures, the history of Paris with its ancient processions, crowds of hatmakers, banana sellers and – above all! – soldiers of the Republican Guard. The King passes by, in modern dress: NAPOLEON III with two ATTENDANTS.

Scene 5

A Paris street. Between the middle of the stage and the wings on the right stands the open door of an old house with broken windows, up for sale. The MUSICIAN comes on from the left and enters the house, followed by the WOMEN who before going in announce their names: Ariadne, Pâquerette, Anne, Mia, Simone, Mavise, Colette, Genevieve, Louise, Julie, Armande.

Two men (a SOLDIER and a POET) enter from opposite sides of the stage. They hear the music and the voices of the WOMEN. They stop and wait, surprised, looking frightened.

The music fades. Night falls. The SOLDIER and the POET remain on stage, apparently looking for something. The door of the house is closed. They force it open.

Scene 6

The scene changes and we are once again in the little square with the MUSICIAN standing at his place on the right. The SOLDIER and the POET come out of a door on the left and see him. The automatic SOVEREIGN crosses the stage followed by his ATTENDANTS with handkerchiefs, blowing their noses.

The SOVEREIGN shoots himself with a revolver.

TRANSLATED BY PETER READ

The Countess of Eisenberg

The Count of Eisenberg had loved his first wife dearly.

He had met her in Bonn during his student days there, and had married her after a fairly long engagement. During their honeymoon, after a Norwegian cruise and travels in Italy, the couple had moved into a villa they owned on the banks of the Rhine, at the foot of the Seven Hills.

It was an exquisite spot. From the grounds, full of those silvery pines which are the glory of Rhineland gardens, they could see the river and the legendary hills where Siegfried slew the dragon.

One day, early in the autumn, the Count, called away on a visit to Cologne, had returned sooner than expected.

He opened the gate of the grounds and uttered a terrible oath at the sight which lay before him.

The Countess was seated on a mossy stone bench and a young gardener, with his shirt unbuttoned, was kneeling at her feet.

Mad with jealousy, the Count rushed upon the dumbfounded couple and, without even a glance at his wife, took hold of the young man and threw him over the wall on to the road which ran along the bottom of the property.

The gardener, killed instantly, was found by passers-by. His death, so mysterious in every way, was seen as an act of despair, and this presumed suicide closed the affair.

But it put an end to the Count's marital bliss. He spoke not a word to his wife and cloistered her away like a recluse.

To the servants, nothing betrayed the separation of husband and wife, but the split was deep.

Pride against pride, it was a clash of equals and neither one could forgive the other. The Countess had made no excuses and her contemptuous attitude towards her husband showed that she considered herself blameless and that a discussion would have lifted all shadow of guilt. But her love was dead, while at the same time the Count's passion was deepened by the thought that perhaps he had been unfair, and he suffered the torments of a soul in Hell.

Between love and pride stands brutality, guarantee of their authenticity. The Count spared his wife no indignity. Such a life became intolerable. The Countess resolved to fly far from the man she now found repugnant.

On Easter Monday the following year, the Count had gone out. The Countess, leaning on the wall of the villa, was watching the Rhine and its steamships passing by, carrying groups of girls and students singing songs which echoed back across the water. Along the road came a procession, a line of handsome, ragged gypsies, walking beside their caravans filled with women and children. Some led horses by the bridle, others held the leashes of bears, monkeys or dogs! They begged for charity as they passed and seemed as proud as liberty itself.

There were old men and young, and one of the younger men, wearing golden earrings, stared at the Countess. Her heart beat faster. She let out a sigh. These travelling people and their animals, the strains of zither and cymbalon coming from the caravans, decided her destiny. She raised her hand, then climbed over the wall and fell into the arms of the gypsy with earrings.

'I have nothing,' she said. 'Will you take me as I am and love me all your life?'

Gravely he answered, 'I will. But don't forget that in our language we have one word for Life and Death, one for Yesterday and Tomorrow, one for Love and Hate.'

. . . And, despite all the searches ordered by the Count, the Countess disappeared without a trace.

Forty years passed by. The Count's hair turned white. His true love, run off with the gypsies, had taken his happiness with her.

Since then in his life he had known nothing but failure. In his career, he encountered only setbacks. Responding to family pressure he had decided to get married again, to one of his cousins, whom he did not love, and who died giving birth to a daughter.

The Count then withdrew into his Rhineland villa at the foot of the Seven Hills to devote the rest of his days to bringing up his child.

One morning he had to go to Koblenz, and on his way to the station he met a group of gypsies wending their way along the main road with their caravans and performing animals.

An old gypsy woman approached him, begging for charity. Looking at that old face, deformed and disfigured by life, he was surprised to discover some of the charming features of the first Countess of Eisenberg.

He noticed the resemblance, but did not linger over it, for what connection could there be between an old gypsy woman chewing a hazel twig with catkins, and the Countess, drowned in the Rhine no doubt, her body never recovered, as if the Rhineland dwarfs were keeping her dormant but still alive in a crystal casket, deep in one of their marvellous caverns.

. . . Instead of accepting the coins held out to her by the Count, the gypsy woman drew back her hand. The pfennigs fell down to the dusty ground.

'My name,' cried the old woman, 'is a word which in our language means both Joy and Sorrow. Joy for me but Sorrow for you.'

The Count had continued on his way. He heard these words and found them disturbing. But he was in a hurry and felt cross with himself for paying any attention to the ramblings of a gypsy.

He walked faster, and by the time he climbed into the train for Koblenz, he had forgotten the incident completely.

On his return that evening, he found his villa burned down to the ground. The fire had destroyed it from top to bottom and smoke still rose from the ruins.

Taken by surprise, and to escape the flames, his daughter had thrown herself in panic from a window. She had died instantly.

Among the crowd of onlookers, there was talk of a group of gypsies who had prowled around the house, and an old gypsy woman had been seen amid the flames in the middle of the ruins, dancing wildly and shaking a tambourine.

She had darted away when they tried to catch her and had disappeared into the dark.

1907

TRANSLATED BY PETER READ

L'ADIEU DU CAVALIER

Ah Dieu! que la guerre est jolie
Avec ses chants ses longs loisirs
Cette bague je l'ai polie
Le vent se mêle à vos soupirs

Adieu! voici le boute-selle
Il disparut dans un tournant
Et mourut là-bas tandis qu'elle
Riait au destin surprenant

THE CAVALIER'S FAREWELL

Oh God! what a lovely war
With its songs its long leisure hours
I have polished and polished this ring
The wind with your sighs is mingling

Farewell! the trumpet call is sounding
He disappeared down the winding road
And died far off while she
Laughed at fate's surprises

TRANSLATED BY ANNE HYDE GREET

ZONE

A la fin tu es las de ce monde ancien

Bergère ô tour Eiffel le troupeau des ponts bêle
ce matin

Tu en as assez de vivre dans l'antiquité grecque et
romaine

Ici même les automobiles ont l'air d'être anciennes
La religion seule est restée toute neuve la religion
Est restée simple comme les hangars de Port-Aviation

Seul en Europe tu n'es pas antique ô Christianisme
L'Européen le plus moderne c'est vous Pape Pie X
Et toi que les fenêtres observent la honte te retient
D'entrer dans une église et de t'y confesser
ce matin
Tu lis les prospectus les catalogues les affiches qui
chantent tout haut
Voilà la poésie ce matin et pour la prose il y a
les journaux
Il y a les livraisons à 25 centimes pleines d'aventures
policières
Portraits des grands hommes et mille titres divers
J'ai vu ce matin une jolie rue dont j'ai oublié le nom
Neuve et propre du soleil elle était le clairon
Les directeurs les ouvriers et les belles
sténo-dactylographes
Du lundi matin au samedi soir quatre fois par jour y
passent
Le matin par trois fois la sirène y gémit
Une cloche rageuse y aboie vers midi
Les inscriptions des enseignes et des murailles
Les plaques les avis à la façon des perroquets criaillent
J'aime la grâce de cette rue industrielle
Située à Paris entre la rue Aumont-Thiéville et l'avenue
des Ternes

Voilà la jeune rue et tu n'es encore qu'un petit enfant
Ta mère ne t'habille que de bleu et de blanc
Tu es très pieux et avec le plus ancien de tes camarades
René Dalize
Vous n'aimez rien tant que les pompes de l'Église
Il est neuf heures le gaz est baissé tout bleu vous sortez
du dortoir en cachette
Vous priez toute la nuit dans la chapelle du collège

Tandis qu'éternelle et adorable profondeur améthyste
Tourne à jamais la flamboyante gloire du Christ
C'est le beau lys que tous nous cultivons
C'est la torche aux cheveux roux que n'éteint pas le vent
C'est le fils pâle et vermeil de la douloureuse mère
C'est l'arbre toujours touffu de toutes les prières

ZONE

In the end you are weary of this ancient world

This morning the bridges are bleating Eiffel Tower oh
herd

Weary of living in Roman antiquity and
Greek

Here even the motor-cars look antique
Religion alone has stayed young religion
Has stayed simple like the hangars at Port Aviation

You alone in Europe Christianity are not ancient
The most modern European is you Pope Pius X
And you whom the windows watch shame restrains
From entering a church this morning and confessing your
sins
You read the handbills the catalogues
the singing posters
So much for poetry this morning and the prose is in the
papers
Special editions full of
crimes
Celebrities and other attractions for 25 centimes
This morning I saw a pretty street whose name is gone
Clean and shining clarion of the sun
Where from Monday morning to Saturday evening four
times a day
Directors workers and beautiful shorthand typists go their
way
And thrice in the morning the siren makes its moan
And a bell bays savagely coming up to noon
The inscriptions on walls and signs
The notices and plates squawk parrot-wise
I love the grace of this industrial street
In Paris between the Avenue des Ternes and the Rue
Aumont-Thiéville

There it is the young street and you still but a small child
Your mother always dresses you in blue and white
You are very pious and with René Dalize your oldest
crony
Nothing delights you more than church ceremony
It is nine at night the lowered gas burns blue you steal
away
From the dormitory and all night in the college chapel
pray
While everlastingly the flaming glory of Christ
Wheels in adorable depths of amethyst
It is the fair lily that we all revere
It is the torch burning in the wind its auburn hair
It is the rosepale son of the mother of grief
It is the tree with the world's prayers ever in leaf

C'est la double potence de l'honneur et de l'éternité
C'est l'étoile à six branches
C'est Dieu qui meurt le vendredi et ressuscite le dimanche
C'est le Christ qui monte au ciel mieux que les aviateurs
Il détient le record du monde pour la hauteur

Pupille Christ de l'œil
Vingtième pupille des siècles il sait y faire
Et changé en oiseau ce siècle comme Jésus monte dans l'air
Les diables dans les abîmes lèvent la tête pour le regarder
Ils disent qu'il imite Simon Mage en Judée
Ils crient s'il sait voler qu'on l'appelle voleur
Les anges voltigent autour du joli voltigeur
Icare Énoch Élie Apollonius de Thyane
Flottent autour du premier aéroplane
Ils s'écartent parfois pour laisser passer ceux que transporte la Sainte-Eucharistie
Ces prêtres qui montent éternellement élevant l'hostie
L'avion se pose enfin sans refermer les ailes
Le ciel s'emplit alors de millions d'hirondelles
A tire-d'aile viennent les corbeaux les faucons les hiboux
D'Afrique arrivent les ibis les flamants les marabouts
L'oiseau Roc célébré par les conteurs et les poètes
Plane tenant dans les serres le crâne d'Adam la première tête
L'aigle fond de l'horizon en poussant un grand cri
Et d'Amérique vient le petit colibri
De Chine sont venus les pihis longs et souples
Qui n'ont qu'une seule aile et qui volent par couples
Puis voici la colombe esprit immaculé
Qu'escortent l'oiseau-lyre et le paon ocellé
Le phénix ce bûcher qui soi-même s'engendre
Un instant voile tout de son ardente cendre
Les sirènes laissant les périlleux détroits
Arrivent en chantant bellement toutes trois
Et tous aigle phénix et pihis de la Chine
Fraternisent avec la volante machine

Maintenant tu marches dans Paris tout seul parmi la foule
Des troupeaux d'autobus mugissants près de toi roulent
L'angoisse de l'amour te serre le gosier
Comme si tu ne devais jamais plus être aimé
Si tu vivais dans l'ancien temps tu entrerais dans un monastère
Vous avez honte quand vous vous surprenez à dire une prière
Tu te moques de toi et comme le feu de l'Enfer ton rire pétille
Les étincelles de ton rire dorent le fond de ta vie

C'est un tableau pendu dans un sombre musée
Et quelquefois tu vas le regarder de près

Aujourd'hui tu marches dans Paris les femmes sont ensanglantées

It is of honour and eternity the double beam
It is the six-branched star it is God
Who Friday dies and Sunday rises from the dead
It is Christ who better than airmen wings his flight
Holding the record of the world for height

Pupil Christ of the eye
Twentieth pupil of the centuries it is no novice
And changed into a bird this century soars like Jesus
The devils in the deeps look up and say they see a
Nimitation of Simon Magus in Judea
Craft by name by nature craft they cry
About the pretty flyer the angels fly
Enoch Elijah Apollonius of Tyana hover
With Icarus round the first airworthy ever
For those whom the Eucharist transports they now and then make way
Host-elevating priests ascending endlessly
The aeroplane alights at last with outstretched pinions
Then the sky is filled with swallows in their millions
The rooks come flocking the owls the hawks
Flamingoes from Africa and ibises and storks
The roc bird famed in song and story soars
With Adam's skull the first head in its claws
The eagle stoops screaming from heaven's verge
From America comes the little humming-bird
From China the long and supple
One-winged peehees that fly in couples
Behold the dove spirit without alloy
That ocellate peacock and lyre-bird convoy
The phoenix flame-devoured flame-revived
All with its ardent ash an instant hides
Leaving the perilous straits the sirens three
Divinely singing join the company
And eagle phoenix peehees fraternize
One and all with the machine that flies

Now you walk in Paris alone among the crowd
Herds of bellowing buses hemming you about
Anguish of love parching you within
As though you were never to be loved again
If you lived in olden times you would get you to a cloister
You are ashamed when you catch yourself at a paternoster
You are your own mocker and like hellfire your laughter crackles
Golden on your life's hearth fall the sparks of your laughter
It is a picture in a dark museum hung
And you sometimes go and contemplate it long

Today you walk in Paris the women are blood-red

C'était et je voudrais ne pas m'en souvenir c'était au déclin de la beauté

Entourée de flammes ferventes Notre-Dame m'a regardé à Chartres
Le sang de votre Sacré-Cœur m'a inondé à Montmartre
Je suis malade d'ouïr les paroles bienheureuses
L'amour dont je souffre est une maladie honteuse
Et l'image qui te possède te fait survivre dans l'insomnie et dans l'angoisse
C'est toujours près de toi cette image qui passe
Maintenant tu es au bord de la Méditerranée
Sous les citronniers qui sont en fleur toute l'année
Avec tes amis tu te promènes en barque
L'un est Nissard il y a un Mentonasque et deux Turbiasques
Nous regardons avec effroi les poulpes des profondeurs
Et parmi les algues nagent les poissons images du Sauveur

Tu es dans le jardin d'une auberge aux environs de Prague
Tu te sens tout heureux une rose est sur la table
Et tu observes au lieu d'écrire ton conte en prose
La cétoine qui dort dans le cœur de la rose

Épouvanté tu te vois dessiné dans les agates de Saint-Vit
Tu étais triste à mourir le jour où tu t'y vis
Tu ressembles au Lazare affolé par le jour
Les aiguilles de l'horloge du quartier juif vont à rebours
Et tu recules aussi dans ta vie lentement
En montant au Hradchin et le soir en écoutant
Dans les tavernes chanter des chansons tchèques

Te voici à Marseille au milieu des pastèques

Te voici à Coblence à l'hôtel du Géant

Te voici à Rome assis sous un néflier du Japon

Te voici à Amsterdam avec une jeune fille que tu trouves belle et qui est laide
Elle doit se marier avec un étudiant de Leyde
On y loue des chambres en latin Cubicula locanda
Je m'en souviens j'y ai passé trois jours et autant à Gouda

Tu es à Paris chez le juge d'instruction
Comme un criminel on te met en état d'arrestation

Tu as fait de douloureux et de joyeux voyages
Avant de t'apercevoir du mensonge et de l'âge
Tu as souffert de l'amour à vingt et à trente ans
J'ai vécu comme un fou et j'ai perdu mon temps
Tu n'oses plus regarder tes mains et à tous moments je voudrais sangloter

It was and would I could forget it was at beauty's ebb

From the midst of fervent flames Our Lady beheld me at Chartres
The blood of your Sacred Heart flooded me in Montmartre
I am sick with hearing the words of bliss
The love I endure is like a syphilis
And the image that possesses you and never leaves your side
In anguish and insomnia keeps you alive
Now you are on the Riviera among
The lemon-trees that flower all year long
With your friends you go for a sail on the sea
One is from Nice one from Menton and two from La Turbie
The polypuses in the depths fill us with horror
And in the seaweed fishes swim emblems of the Saviour

You are in an inn-garden near Prague

You feel perfectly happy a rose is on the table
And you observe instead of writing your story in prose
The chafer asleep in the heart of the rose

Appalled you see your image in the agates of Saint Vitus
That day you were fit to die with sadness
You look like Lazarus frantic in the daylight
The hands of the clock in the Jewish quarter go to left from right
And you too live slowly backwards
Climbing up to the Hradchin or listening as night falls
To Czech songs being sung in taverns

Here you are in Marseilles among the water-melons

Here you are in Koblenz at the Giant's Hostelry

Here you are in Rome under a Japanese medlar-tree

Here you are in Amsterdam with an ill-favoured maiden
You find her beautiful she is engaged to a student in Leyden
There they let their rooms in Latin cubicula locanda
I remember I spent three days there and as many in Gouda

You are in Paris with the examining magistrate
They clap you in gaol like a common reprobate

Grievous and joyous voyages you made
Before you knew what falsehood was and age
At twenty you suffered from love and at thirty again
My life was folly and my days in vain
You dare not look at your hands tears haunt my eyes

Sur toi sur celle que j'aime sur tout ce qui t'a
épouvanté

Tu regardes les yeux pleins de larmes ces pauvres
émigrants
Ils croient en Dieu ils prient les femmes allaitent des
enfants
Ils emplissent de leur odeur le hall de la gare Saint-
Lazare
Ils ont foi dans leur étoile comme les rois-mages

Ils espèrent gagner de l'argent dans l'Argentine
Et revenir dans leur pays après avoir fait fortune
Une famille transporte un édredon rouge comme vous
transportez votre cœur
Cet édredon et nos rêves sont aussi irréels
Quelques-uns de ces émigrants restent ici et se logent
Rue des Rosiers ou rue des Écouffes dans des bouges
Je les ai vus souvent le soir ils prennent l'air dans la rue
Et se déplacent rarement comme les pièces aux échecs
Il y a surtout des Juifs leurs femmes portent perruque
Elles restent assises exsangues au fond des boutiques
Tu es debout devant le zinc d'un bar crapuleux
Tu prends un café à deux sous parmi les malheureux

Tu es la nuit dans un grand restaurant
Ces femmes ne sont pas méchantes elles ont des soucis
cependant
Toutes même la plus laide a fait souffrir son amant

Elle est la fille d'un sergent de ville de Jersey

Ses mains que je n'avais pas vues sont dures et gercées

J'ai une pitié immense pour les coutures de son ventre

J'humilie maintenant à une pauvre fille au rire horrible
ma bouche

Tu es seul le matin va venir
Les laitiers font tinter leurs bidons dans les rues

La nuit s'éloigne ainsi qu'une belle Métive
C'est Ferdine la fausse ou Léa l'attentive

Et tu bois cet alcool brûlant comme ta vie
Ta vie que tu bois comme une eau-de-vie
Tu marches vers Auteuil tu veux aller chez toi à pied
Dormir parmi tes fétiches d'Océanie et de Guinée
Ils sont des Christ d'une autre forme et d'une autre
croyance
Ce sont les Christ inférieurs des obscures espérances

Adieu Adieu

Soleil cou coupé

For you for her I love and all the old miseries

Weeping you watch the wretched emigrants

They believe in God they pray the women suckle their
infants
They fill with their smell the station of Saint-Lazare

Like the wise men from the east they have faith in their
star
The hope to prosper in the Argentine
And to come home having made their fortune
A family transports a red eiderdown as you your heart

An eiderdown as unreal as our dreams
Some go no further doss in the stews
Of the Rue des Rosiers or the Rue des Écouffes
Often in the streets I have seen them in the gloaming
Taking the air and like chessmen seldom moving
They are mostly Jews the wives wear wigs and in
The depths of shadowy dens bloodless sit on and on
You stand at the bar of a crapulous café
Drinking coffee at two sous a time in the midst of the
unhappy

It is night you are in a restaurant it is superior
These women are decent enough they have their troubles
however
All even the ugliest ones have made their lovers suffer

She is a Jersey police-constable's daughter

Her hands I had not seen are chapped and hard

The seams of her belly go to my heart

To a poor harlot horribly laughing I humble my mouth

You are alone morning is at hand
In the streets the milkmen rattle their cans

Like a dark beauty night withdraws
Watchful Leah or Ferdine the false

And you drink this alcohol burning like your life
Your life that you drink like spirit of wine
You walk towards Auteuil you want to walk home and
sleep
Among your fetishes from Guinea and the South Seas
Christs of another creed another guise
The lowly Christs of dim expectancies

Adieu Adieu

Sun corseless head

TRANSLATED BY SAMUEL BECKETT

La Colombe Poignardée et le Jet d'Eau

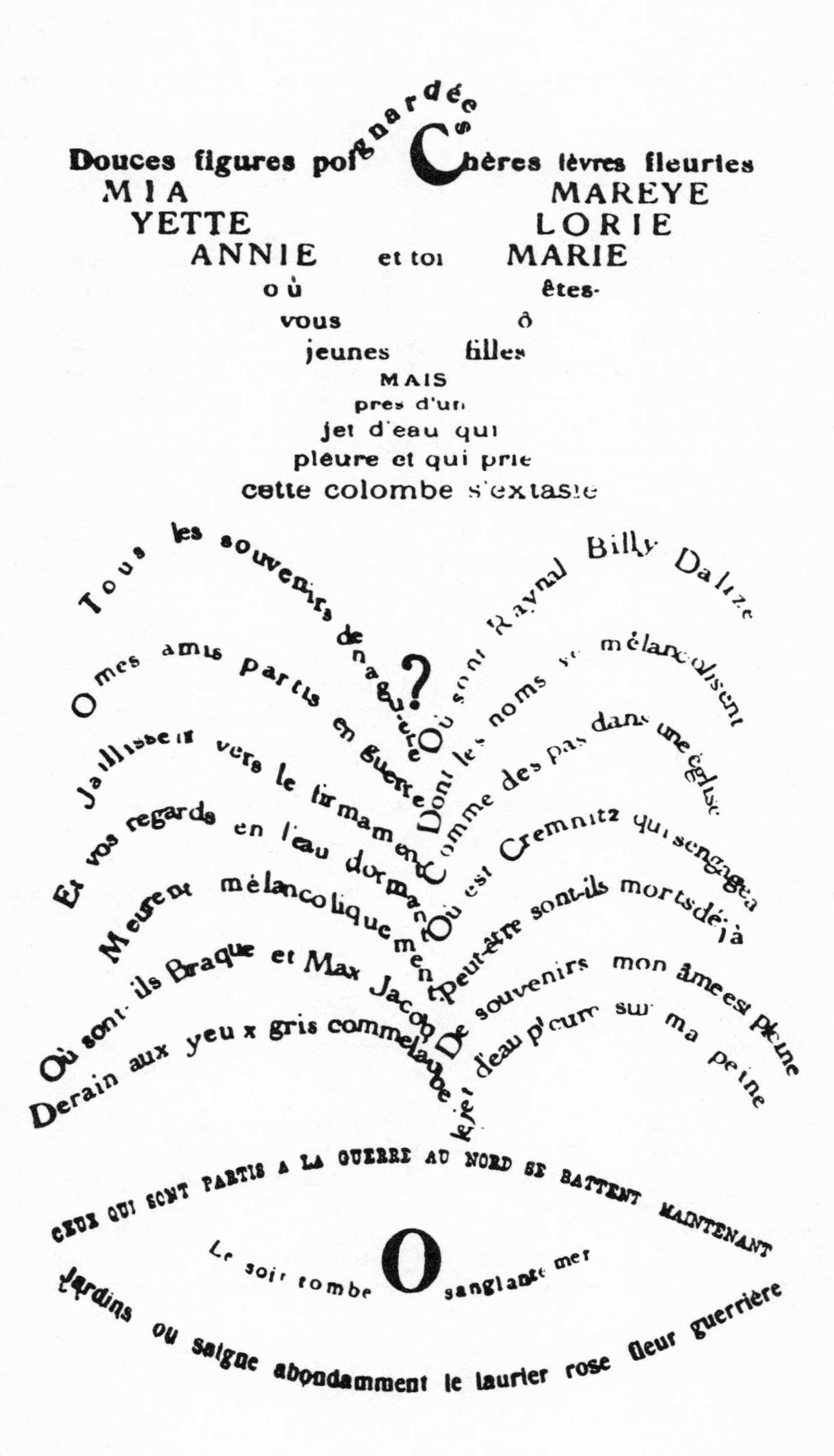

THE BLEEDING-HEART DOVE AND THE FOUNTAIN

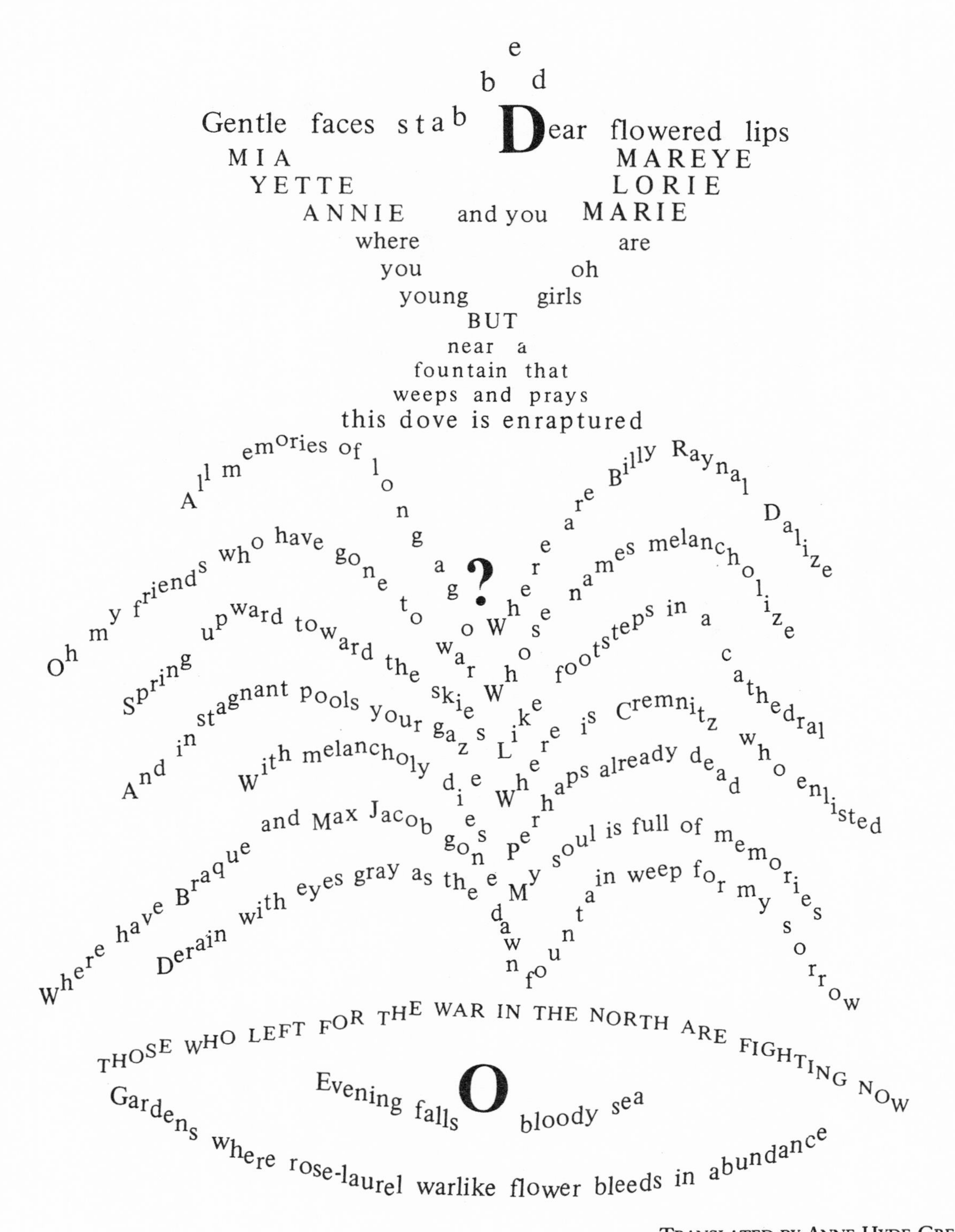

TRANSLATED BY ANNE HYDE GREET

1915	1915
Soldats de Faïence et d'escarboucle ō Amour	Soldiers of porcelain and garnet ō Love

TRANSLATED BY ANNE HYDE GREET

Les Soupirs du Servant de Dakar

C'est dans la cagnat en rondins voilés d'osier
Auprès des canons gris tournés vers le nord
Que je songe au village africain
Où l'on dansait où l'on chantait où l'on faisait l'amour
Et de longs discours
Nobles et joyeux

Je revois mon père qui se battit
Contre les Achantis
Au service des Anglais
Je revois ma sœur au rire en folie
Aux seins durs comme des obus
Et je revois
Ma mère la sorcière qui seule du village
Méprisait le sel
Piler le millet dans un mortier
Je me souviens du si délicat si inquiétant
Fétiche dans l'arbre
Et du double fétiche de la fécondité
Plus tard une tête coupée
Au bord d'un marécage
Ô pâleur de mon ennemi
C'était une tête d'argent
Et dans le marais
C'était la lune qui luisait
C'était donc une tête d'argent
Là-haut c'était la lune qui dansait
C'était donc une tête d'argent
Et moi dans l'antre j'étais invisible
C'était donc une tête de nègre dans la nuit profonde
Similitudes Pâleurs
Et ma sœur
Suivit plus tard un tirailleur
Mort à Arras

Si je voulais savoir mon âge
Il faudrait le demander à l'évêque
Si doux si doux avec ma mère
De beurre de beurre avec ma sœur
C'était dans une petite cabane
Moins sauvage que notre cagnat de canonniers-servants
J'ai connu l'affût au bord des marécages
Où la girafe boit les jambes écartées
J'ai connu l'horreur de l'ennemi qui dévaste
Le Village
Viole les femmes
Emmène les filles
Et les garçons dont la croupe dure sursaute
J'ai porté l'administrateur des semaines
De village en village
En chantonnant

The Sighs of the Gunner from Dakar

In the log dugout hidden by osiers
Near grey cannons turned towards the north
I dream of the African village
Where we danced where we sang and made love
And made long speeches
Noble and joyful

I see again my father who fought
The Ashantis
In the service of the English
I see again my sister with the crazy laugh
With breasts hard as bombshells
And I see again
My mother the witch who alone in the village
Scorned salt
Crushing millet in a mortar
I remember the fetish so delicate so disturbing
In the tree
And the double fetish of fecundity
Later a severed head
Beside a swamp
Oh paleness of my enemy
It was a silver head
And in the marsh
The moon was shining
It was it was a silver head
The moon above was dancing
It was it was a silver head
And I in the cave was invisible
It was it was a Negro head in the dead of night
Resemblances Pallors
And later my sister
Went off with a rifleman
Who was killed at Arras

If I wanted to know my age
I'd have to ask the bishop
So gentle so gentle to my mother
So like butter like butter with my sister
It was in a little hut
Neater than our gunners' dugout
I've known the hiding place at the swamp's edge
Where the giraffe drinks with legs spread apart
I've known the horror of the enemy that plunder
The Village
Rape the women
Lead away the girls
And the boys whose hard rumps quiver
I've carried the administrator for weeks
From village to village
Singing

Et je fus domestique à Paris
Je ne sais pas mon âge
Mais au recrutement
On m'a donné vingt ans
Je suis soldat français on m'a blanchi du coup
Secteur 59 je ne peux pas dire où
Pourquoi donc être blanc est-ce mieux qu'être noir
Pourquoi ne pas danser et discourir
Manger et puis dormir
Et nous tirons sur les ravitaillements boches
Ou sur les fils de fer devant les bobosses
Sous la tempête métallique
Je me souviens d'un lac affreux
Et de couples enchaînés par un atroce amour
Une nuit folle
Une nuit de sorcellerie
Comme cette nuit-ci
Où tant d'affreux regards
Éclatent dans le ciel splendide

And I was a servant in Paris
I don't know my age
But at the recruiting
They wrote down twenty years old
I'm a French soldier and so that made me white
Sector 59 I can't say where
But why is it better to be white than black
Why not dance and make speeches
Eat and then sleep
And we shoot at the Boche supplies
Or at the iron wires in front of the troops
Under the metallic storm
I remember a hideous lake
And couples chained by an atrocious love
A crazy night
A night of sorcery
Like tonight
Where so many horrible eyes
Explode in the brilliant sky

TRANSLATED BY ANNE HYDE GREET

OCÉAN DE TERRE

A G. de Chirico

J'ai bâti une maison au milieu de l'Océan
Ses fenêtres sont les fleuves qui s'écoulent de mes yeux
Des poulpes grouillent partout où se tiennent les murailles
Entendez battre leur triple cœur et leur bec cogner aux vitres
Maison humide
Maison ardente
Saison rapide
Saison qui chante
Les avions pondent des œufs
Attention on va jeter l'ancre
Attention à l'encre que l'on jette
Il serait bon que vous vinssiez du ciel
Le chèvrefeuille du ciel grimpe
Les poulpes terrestres palpitent
Et puis nous sommes tant et tant à être nos propres fossoyeurs
Pâles poulpes des vagues crayeuses ô poulpes aux becs pâles
Autour de la maison il y a cet océan que tu connais
Et qui ne se repose jamais

OCEAN OF EARTH

For G. de Chirico

I have built a house in the middle of the Ocean
Its windows are the rivers flowing from my eyes
Octopuses swarm all over the walls
Listen to their triple heartbeat and their beak knock at the windows
Humid house
Blazing house
Swift season
Singing season
Aeroplanes are laying eggs
Watch out they're going to sink the anchor
Watch out for this ink they're throwing
Oh will you not descend from the sky
The honeysuckle of the sky is climbing
The earthly octopuses quiver
And so many of us are digging our own graves
Pale octopuses of chalky waves oh octopuses with pale beaks
Around the house lies the ocean you know so well
The ocean that is never still

TRANSLATED BY ANNE HYDE GREET

MARC DE LARREGUY DE CIVRIEUX 1895–1916

'At a time when the lies of journalists have perverted so many minds, we do well to remember the profound truth of what Lamartine, the great Champion of Peace, once said – our own national and international Lamartine: "I am a human being *before I am British, French or Russian."'*

Preface, La Muse de sang

Larreguy de Civrieux. *Bibliothèque Nationale, Paris*

All that we know about Marc de Larreguy is gleaned from Romain Rolland's introduction to *La Muse de sang*, Larreguy's own short preface and a few pages written by his father at the end of the book. Marc de Larreguy, born on 27 February 1895 of an old conservative and Catholic family, was at one point a supporter of Action Française, Maurras's royalist movement. When exactly his support for that movement evaporated to make way for his fervent admiration for Lamartine, the great Romantic poet and liberal statesman, is not clear: surely at the latest before the end of 1914, when, according to his father, he was 'dumbfounded' by the suggestion that he should enlist. He did join up, however, and was posted to the front in July 1915.

By the end of the year, he was writing poetry against the war, against censorship and, above all, against the propaganda and chauvinism sustaining the war. This early poetry is, not surprisingly, rather stiffly old-fashioned in style – for example, 'Le drapeau de la révolte' ('The Banner of Revolt'). It is as if an attempted Lamartinian form cannot accommodate the subject matter. Later, the form becomes more supple, sometimes with a successful infusion of folk-song structures, and the language more violent, sarcastic and satirical. Larreguy quickly, almost precociously, developed the ability to mix tone and register for satirical ends. He clearly had the makings of a poet of invective. 'L'épître au perroquet' ('Epistle from a Monkey . . .') is one of two poems in similar vein written by an ugly monkey in the trenches of Argonne to a parrot in Paris. The soldiers are seen as dehumanized by their experiences and thereby, ironically, more truly human than armchair strategists and patriots in Paris.

This poem is a sarcastic attack on Maurice Barrès, with allusions to two books by him: *Sous l'œil des barbares* (*Under the Eye of the Barbarians*; 1888) and *Colette Baudoche* (1909). The first is not actually about the Germans, but the title lends itself to satire; *Colette Baudoche* is about a patriotic French girl in German-occupied Alsace, who refuses to marry a German. The poem's allusion to Bayard (d. 1524), the 'chevalier sans peur et sans reproche', further satirizes Barrès's cult of the dead and the soil, these two things being in his view the essence of *patrie*. Barrès was a right-wing jingoist, a nationalist whose sabre-rattling Germanophobia was given daily space in the *Écho de Paris*. From 1914 to 1918, this newspaper was the archetype of the fervour-whipping, conscience-salving avoidance or ignorance of the facts of military life, which outraged as many soldiers as it reassured civilians. Yet Adrien Bertrand (q.v.), the title of whose novel *L'Appel du sol* has a very Barrésian ring to it, sent a signed copy to Barrès.

Reading Larreguy, Bertrand, Edmond Adam (q.v.) and Gabriel-Tristan Franconi (q.v.) together, with Barrès and Rolland in the background as tutelary deities and bogeymen by turns, gives an idea of some of the components in that complex and tragic reality, the *Union sacrée*. Larreguy's own claim was that his poems captured precisely the true psychology of the soldier at the front. He was killed on 18 November 1916, at Froideterre, by Verdun, but by then, Romain Rolland, who wrote the introduction to *La Muse de sang*, had become, with Lamartine and Louis de Larreguy, 'a third father' to him – Rolland, the pacifist scourge of warmongering statesmen, himself savaged in Adrien Bertrand's 'The Adventures of Town Rat'. Larreguy's father's moving postface, 'Mea culpa', is an act of self-inculpation by a man who had told his son he ought to enlist. Although *La Muse de sang* went to at least four printings shortly after it was published, Marc de Larreguy is quite unknown today.

IAN HIGGINS

Text
La Muse de sang (Librairie du Travail, Paris, 1926).

L'ÉPÎTRE AU PERROQUET

As-tu lu le journal, Jacko, mon vieux Jacko?
Il me semble aujourd'hui t'entendre qui jacasse
– De la façon la plus cocasse –
Tous les 'en-tête' rococos
De la gazette de l'*Echo*:
'Crr . . . Crr . . . on les aurra . . . Crr . . . Rrr . . .
Victoire prroche . . .'
Et tu rêves que tu bamboches
Avec quelques tripes de Boches!
Te voici donc l'"alter ego'
De ton grand maître, l'Hidalgo,
(Toujours 'sans peur et sans reproche')
Qui – 'loin de l'œil des Wisigoths' –
Ecrit, pour tous les bons gogos,
Au nom de Maurice . . . Baudoche!
Crois-le, je suis fier de connaître
Un perroquet aussi savant
Qui peut répéter à son Maître:
'Nous les tenons!' et 'En avant!'
Car nous, les Singes des grands Bois,
Dans notre Argonne, loin des Hommes,
Nous les oublions et nous sommes
Bien plus sauvages qu'autrefois!

'Le hareng toujours se sent dans la caque',
A dit un bipède écrivain:
Vouloir imiter l'homme est ridicule et vain
A moins que l'on ne soit perroquet ou chauvin.
. . . Et j'aime mieux rester:
Ton fidèle
Macaque

EPISTLE FROM A MONKEY IN THE TRENCHES TO A PARROT IN PARIS

Have you read the paper, little Jacko?
I seem to hear you jabbering away
– In the comicallest way –
With all the military rococo
Of the headlines of the *Echo*:
'Crr . . . Over by Christmas . . .
The Hun must pay . . . '
And planning orgies of brioches
With flour milled from bones of Boches!
So there you are, in parrotry
Mirror to your Matamore
(E'er the Captain of necrolatory)
Who, far from eye of Goth and Thor,
For simpleton lays down the law,
And signs the column Maurice Barr . . . atry!
Believe you me, I'm proud to know
So very clever a macaw,
Who imitates his Master's crow
And squawks: 'Stand fast! . . . *Esprrit de corps*!'
– We jungle monkeys never show
Ourselves to men, out in Argonne;
We have forgotten man, and gone
More savage than you've ever known!

'Will out in the flesh what's bred in the bone,'
Might echo any biped hack:
To ape a man is to disgrace your own,
Unless you are a jingoist, a Jacko.
So, warts and all,
I'm faithfully
Macaque

TRANSLATED BY IAN HIGGINS

Les soliloques du soldat

I

Depuis les jours de Charleroi
Et la retraite de la Marne,
J'ai promené partout ma 'carne'
Sans en comprendre le pourquoi . . .

Dans la tranchée ou sous un toit
Par le créneau ou la lucarne,
A cette guerre, je m'acharne,
Sans en comprendre le pourquoi . . .

Quand je demande autour de moi
Quel est le but de ces tueries,
On me répond le mot: 'Patrie!'
Sans en comprendre le pourquoi . . .

Mieux me vaudrait de rester coi,
Et quand viendrait mon agonie,
De m'en aller de cette vie
Sans en comprendre le pourquoi . . .

Février 1916, au front

The Soldier's Soliloquies

I

After the Charleroi affair
And since we waved the Marne goodbye,
I drag my carcase everywhere,
But never know the reason why.

In trench or barn I spend each day,
From fort or attic glimpse the sky,
At this war simply slog away,
But never know the reason why.

I ask, hoping to understand
This slaughter's purpose. The reply
I get is: 'For the Motherland!'
But never know the reason why.

Better for me to just keep mum
And, when it's my own turn to die,
Depart this life for kingdom come,
But never know the reason why.

February 1916, at the front

IV

A ceux pour qui la vie est 'chère' et qui font si bon marché de la vie des 'autres'.

Le civil dit: 'La Vie est chère.'
Moi, je la trouve bon marché,
Car je connais une Bouchère
Dont l'étalage s'est 'gâché':
Une Phrygienne, au bonnet rouge,
Aux lippes fraîches de sang bu,
Au front bestial, aux yeux de gouge,
Qui jette sa viande au rebut!

Vers de monstrueuses Villettes,
Elle se rue aux abattoirs
Et cogne à grands 'coups de boutoirs'
Dessus les hommes qui halètent
Sous les gros poings de ses battoirs!

Elle dépèce, et taille et rogne
Les bras, les jambes, les cerveaux,
Et puis, elle offre sa charogne,
Sous l'étiquette de 'Héros',
Aux rats, aux vers et aux corbeaux!

IV

To those for whom life is 'dear' and who hold the life of 'others' so cheap.

The civvy says: 'How dear is Life!'
I think it's cheap, because I know
A certain cut-rate Butcher's Wife
Whose prices are absurdly low.
She is a Phrygian, red-capped,
Her chops dripping with blood fresh tapped,
Browed like a beast and harlot-eyed,
Tossing unwanted meat aside!

To the vile cattle-mart she goes,
Then straight to slaughter-house she flies
To rain her vicious cleaver-blows
On men, who gasp their anguished cries
As her huge fists above them rise!

Slicing away, she cuts and trims
Flesh from their skulls and all their limbs;
And then this putrid meat she throws
Down on a slab that's marked 'Heroes'
As bait for rats and worms and crows!

Vous dites que la Vie est chère?
Moi, je la trouve bon marché!
Pourquoi laissez-vous se gâcher
Les 'abatis' de la Bouchère?

Mangez! . . . Utilisez les Morts!
Qu'ils servent encore à la Vie
De ceux qui n'ont pas eu remords
De les lancer à la tuerie
Pour protéger leurs propres corps!

Ô bonnes âmes charitables,
Sauvez votre Conscience et, sans peur, récitez,
Avant de vous carrer à table,
Une prière délectable
A la 'nouvelle Trinité'!
Chantez, chantez en chœur le 'Benedicite',
Dans vos festins d'humanité! . . .

Chantez, sanctifiez le divin sacrifice
Et donnez-vous l'absolution
'Au nom du Droit, de la Justice
Et de la Civilisation!!!'

2 septembre 1916 (Robert-Espagne, au repos)

Do you still say, 'How dear is Life'
When it's dirt-cheap (that's my advice)?
Why then accept at knock-down price
That offal from the Butcher's Wife?

Come, eat! Carry the Dead Men in!
They can still serve the Living band
Who've not regarded it a sin
To have them slaughtered out of hand,
So saving their own precious skin!

O souls righteous in charity,
To salve your Consciences chant happily,
Before you settle down to eat,
A prayer, duly mild and sweet,
Addressed to the 'new Trinity'!
In chorus chant the 'Benedicite'
As you feast on humanity! . . .

The sacrifice divine thus glorify
And then your absolution claim:
'For Right and Justice,' be your cry,
'And in Civilization's name!!!'

2 September 1916, Robert-Espagne, behind the front

TRANSLATED BY D. D. R. OWEN

LE DRAPEAU DE LA RÉVOLTE

– Je parle en votre nom, ô Frères ignorés,
Qui n'osez pas clamer votre amère souffrance
Et mourez, sans un mot et sans une espérance,
Pour une humanité aux Chefs déshonorés!

Je parle en votre nom, ô Parents qui pleurez
La mort d'un fils, qui fut pour lui sa délivrance,
Et ne pouvez plus croire, après cette navrance,
En vos Bourreaux menteurs qui vous ont tant leurrés!

Je parle en votre nom, muets amis de la tombe,
Qui sans cesse accroissez l'inutile hécatombe,
Et surgirez de terre au jour de Vérité!

– En votre nom à tous, je m'adresse à la foule
Pour qu'elle arbore enfin, sur l'Univers qui croule,
Le Drapeau de Révolte et de Fraternité!

Mars 1916, au front

THE BANNER OF REVOLT

I call in your name, Brothers in obscurity,
Who fear to shout aloud your grievous sufferings,
But die without a word or hope of better things,
For the dishonoured Leaders of humanity!

I call in your name, Parents weeping bitterly
To mourn a son, for whom death liberation brings:
You can believe no more, smarting from sorrow's stings,
In your false Torturers, who dupe you constantly!

I call in your name, comrades silent in the tomb
As endlessly you swell the senseless hecatomb,
But on the Day of Truth will rise triumphantly!

It is in all your names that I address my call
For people everywhere to raise, as Nations fall,
The Banner of Revolt and of Fraternity!

March 1916, at the front

TRANSLATED BY D. D. R. OWEN

*A*DRIEN *B*ERTRAND 1888–1917

'What will the new year be? . . . Storms will pass over and then return. Nothing will change. History is endless repetition.'

Paris-Midi, *1 January 1914*

How could the enterprising anti-militarist foreign editor of *Paris-Midi* voice (in the quotation above) such seeming fatalism? This same problem is at the heart of Bertrand's novel *L'Appel du sol* (*Call of the Soil*), which won the Goncourt prize for 1916. *L'Appel du sol* follows a group of soldiers from Lorraine to the Marne and beyond. Convincing, moving, sometimes harrowing descriptions of action alternate with discussions of why the soldiers are fighting. Motives are investigated in terms of individuals, individuals in terms of the country, the country in terms, successively, of soil, landscape, language, culture and morality, morality in terms of the group and the divine. Age-old themes, recently rehearsed by Maurice Barrès (e.g. the call of the soil, the dead feeding the earth, etc.), are given fresh credibility by Bertrand's refusal to gloss over suffering, cowardice and the negative face of patriotism as herd instinct. The occasional impression that the central character, Vaissette, in accepting the redemptory virtue and exaltation of resignation and sacrifice, is trying to persuade himself as he speaks, does not weaken the intellectual and emotional challenge of a novel whose narrative and descriptive vividness is matched by masterly changes in mood and atmosphere.

At the end of the novel, Vaissette and his companions are killed. The questions they asked were ones which Bertrand himself was facing in a particular way: wounded early in the war, he was slowly dying. *L'Appel du sol* and the texts of *L'Orage sur le jardin de Candide* (*The Storm over Candide's Garden*) were written by someone lying on his back in a succession of hospital beds. When would he die? And for what?

The 'Carnet de campagne d'un soldat des armées de la République' purports to be the journal of Auguste Rousset, a soldier in the Revolutionary army. He is Bertrand's alter ego. There are clear parallels with 1914, and the same double-edged resignation: exaltation or pessimism? 'History repeats itself,' writes Rousset, just as Bertrand had before the war. The possibility that his characters' unswerving loyalty might serve a tyranny as well as deliver a nation from an invader is one that the dying Bertrand will have been little disposed to dwell on. It is implied in the ambivalent concept of resignation (a crucial factor in morale in the trenches), but is only explicitly raised – and briefly at that – in 'L'Illusion du préfet Mucius', a story based on Tacitus. The idealistic

Adrien Bertrand. *Archives de la Drôme*

Mucius, a Christian and friend of Luke the Evangelist, toys with the idea of preaching the Gospel to the Germani. They for their part, inspired and protected by the goddess Ertha, are marching to punish the Romans for sacrilegiously advancing on to German soil. In the end, 'force is the only language the Germani understand,' and they are defeated in a battle which is a kind of allegory of the Marne.

In 'De la pluie qui surprit Candide en son jardin et d'un entretien qu'il eut avec plusieurs personnages', Candide has been cultivating his garden for 200 years when there is a terrible storm. A number of characters – among them Achilles, Don Quixote, Faust, Mr Pickwick and Vaissette of *L'Appel du sol* – seek shelter in Candide's house. The continuing discussion of the crucial themes of *L'Appel du sol* is here more centrally related to the question of culture. The 'new order' which must come out of the war will involve not only a rediscovery of the Revolutionary ideals of freedom, justice and honour, but a reflowering of culture: the soldiers are dying to preserve the language of Racine and Voltaire from extinction.

'Les Animaux sous la tourmente' is a set of allegorical stories, sometimes reworkings of La Fontaine. To the extent that they take up a classic author, these stories are, like 'De la pluie . . .', evidence in themselves of Bertrand's attempt to define or situate himself in terms of the cultural heritage as well as of the soil, his comrades and political actuality. 'The Adventures of Town Rat' includes reference to several of La Fontaine's fables but also, through one of them ('Le rat qui s'est retiré du monde'), to Romain Rolland, the pacifist author of *Au-dessus de la mêlée* (*Above the Fray*). Rolland's view in this famous, notorious, much-reprinted work is that it would be a crime for the intellectual élite to compromise the integrity of their thought in war. 'The Adventures of Town Rat' are the riposte of a dying soldier who, in the three years given him after he was wounded, confronted with honesty, dignity and considerable talent much of the complexity of this notion of 'integrity of thought'.

Bertrand was born on 4 August 1888. After leaving school, he went to Paris and embarked on a career in journalism, working for, among other papers, *Paris-Midi* and Clemenceau's *L'Homme libre*. He also founded a literary journal, *Les Chimères*, in 1908, edited Verlaine, wrote critical biographies, a paper on the *Zollverein* and light, often song-like poetry in a variety of traditional forms. Everything about him, wrote André Billy, was 'passionate': this seems to have been as true of his anti-militarist socialism as of his love of the Ancients (especially Virgil, Horace and Pindar). Much of his own writing is marked by the Latin tradition, especially in the later verse, but even also in such prose pieces as 'The Adventures of Town Rat'. When war broke out, he was immediately in action in the cavalry. After bringing off several spectacular single-handed exploits, he was wounded in the chest by a shell-fragment in late October 1914. He was moved from hospital to hospital, undergoing numberless operations, knowing he was dying. Feverishly, in addition to the works described above, he wrote a one-act play and a body of verse, classical in form and language, almost Parnassian at times, yet often sensual. He died on 18 November 1917.

IAN HIGGINS

Texts

Les Soirs ardents. Cadences et rythmes (Sansot, Paris, 1908).
La Victoire de Lorraine (Berger-Levrault, Paris, 1917).
Les Jardins de Priape (Dorbon aîné, Paris, n.d. [1915]).
La Conquête de l'Autriche-Hongrie par L'Allemagne. Une nouvelle forme du pangermanisme: le 'Zollverein' (Berger-Levrault, Paris, 1916).
L'Appel du sol (Curandera, Challes-les-Eaux, 1986).
L'Orage sur le jardin de Candide (Calmann-Lévy, Paris, n.d. [1917]). Contains 'De la pluie qui surprit Candide en son jardin et d'un entretien qu'il eut avec divers personnages', 'L'Illusion du préfet Mucius', 'Carnet de campagne d'un soldat des armées de la République, 1792–1795', 'Les Animaux sous la tourmente'.
Le Verger de Cypris (Berger-Levrault, Paris, 1918).
Sonnets sur la Nature (privately printed by R. Dévigné, Paris, 1923).

Secondary sources

R. Dorgelès, *Bleu horizon* (Albin Michel, Paris, 1949).
J. Cruickshank, *Variations on Catastrophe* (Clarendon Press, Oxford, 1982).
M. Tison-Braun, *La Crise de l'humanisme* (Nizet, Paris, 1967, 2 vols).
L. Riegel, *Guerre et littérature* (Klincksieck, Paris, 1978).

The Adventures of Town Rat

'I remembered your invitation,' said Town Rat. 'Do forgive my keeping you waiting for three centuries – one isn't always master of one's time.'

'Better late than never,' replied Country Rat amiably. He was old, and, like all elderly people, he enjoyed talking in aphorisms: a proverb imparts an air of wisdom to the speaker, and wisdom is the ornament of old age; for old age is no longer capable of folly.

Finding that, for some extraordinary reason, butter, cheese, flour and sugar were growing scarce in Paris, Town Rat had left. The threat of shortages had turned his thoughts to his old friend who lived in the country and had once, after visiting him in Paris, invited him to come and rest awhile in his rustic abode. These were troubled times. Food was hard to find. The air was heavy with dread, as if all creation were in the throes of some great and only dimly understood upheaval, destined to spawn a new world.

Town Rat envied Country Rat his happiness and peaceful fields. When storms rage in the ardent hearts of cities and in the breasts of men, we long for the all-pervading tranquillity of soft meadows, propitious rivers and venerable woods.

'Too happy the countryman,' said Town Rat, after Virgil, 'if he only knew his good fortune.'

For city rats are well-read folk. They have not overlooked their education, gnawing away at Latin tomes languishing in libraries, or the ink-stained dictionaries which prove that we did once study classics, or the impassioned love letters which are all that remains of the springtime of youth.

So Town Rat went by easy stages to where Country Rat cherished his household gods. It was an out-of-the-way spot in Champagne, rich in grapes, beet and grain. But his journey was not without its obstacles.

He thought country-dwellers singular folk, their lands all ditches and bristling hillocks.

'I can well understand,' he said, 'that a young rat passing this way in days gone by might have thought himself in the Caucasus or the Apennines!'

But he recognized Country Rat, waiting plump and white-haired at the entrance to his hole, front paws folded across his belly. It was a mild night; the moon shone down on the ploughland, and touched with silver the moustaches and sharp noses of the wily pair.

'You vaunted the peace and quiet of your retreat,' said Town Rat. 'Is this where no one intrudes on your meals?'

'It is indeed,' his friend replied.

He looked embarrassed.

'Would you like dinner?' he asked.

So they set to work, for eating is the only real reason these animals exist. This is what distinguishes them from other creatures, and particularly human beings, some of whom harbour more spiritual concerns.

They ate. Everything lay in profusion, everywhere, between two high walls of earth. Mingled with the mud and straw were the most varied and inviting of scraps. They ate. But what was this? They were not alone! A whole tribe of rats! There were grey rats, there were black rats, some thin and nimble, some fat and clumsy.

'There's room for all,' Country Rat explained, 'the province is so rich.'

'What about storms?' asked Town Rat. 'Do you often have thunderstorms?'

'Thunderstorms?' echoed his companion in surprise.

Town Rat was referring to the continuous thunder he could hear, and the livid, never-ending lightning.

'Don't you worry about that,' replied Country Rat calmly.

He returned eagerly to his meal. But Town Rat could hardly swallow his fear, let alone any food. All these bangs and flashes, all the time. The ground was shuddering in its very depths.

'The earth is in labour,' he thought, 'and it'll be no mouse it brings forth, you can be sure of that!'

'Go on, eat,' urged his companion.

But still Town Rat wondered: 'What is the world giving birth to?'

Now and again there was a sharper bang nearby, and he thought his last moment had come. He was shaking, and sweating all over.

There were men trudging through the ditch. None said a word. Some would stop, or crush a few rats with their boots, but the rest of the rattish clan were quite unmoved by this, for the survivors were so very many that death seemed a trivial affair. Then suddenly, one man stopped and unleashed a thunder more terrible than anything Town Rat had ever heard.

'I'm going mad!' he cried to his friend. 'You throw yourselves under the feet of our enemies, you demand to be massacred, you—'

'Only on condition they pay us back,' replied Country Rat. 'Come and look.'

He led Town Rat through a narrow mole-tunnel to a series of pits packed with the bodies of soldiers. And there, indeed, were hordes of rats, a whole host of rats, swarming among the pitiful corpses, thriving on the martyred, rotting, precious flesh.

Town Rat was thunderstruck. His head was spinning. 'Where are we?' he asked.

'This is War!' replied Country Rat.

But the city-dweller did not understand.

Town Rat arrived back in Paris completely disillusioned with life in the country.

'You've no idea what a thunderstorm is,' he kept saying to himself, 'until you've been out there!'

He was right. No one can imagine what it is to live in a hell like the trenches. The misery of these men cannot be grasped, nor their endless sacrifice understood. It is something utterly beyond us, beyond the capacities of brain or heart. No one can compute the extent of such suffering, for we have no scale by which to measure it. These things do not belong to life. Posterity will be just as incapable as we are of piecing together the fragments of the tragedy. Even the actors will forget what part they played, once they are no longer on stage and breathing the atmosphere, the leaden air of patience and resignation. These realities are alien to us and will ever remain so, like happenings on another planet: the things of this world have nothing in common with the things of war.

Town Rat straight away went and told the Grand Old Rat of the city about his experiences. This was the famous philosopher who had retired from the world and was living in a Dutch cheese. Day and night he meditated, deep in his hole. He spoke little, and so he never said anything silly; and his silence was deemed eloquent and profound. As he grew older, he was beginning to repeat himself. He would say: 'What lovely weather . . . What lovely weather . . .' Whereupon all his admirers – in other words, every rat – would swoon in rapture at the symbolic meanings they saw in his words, just like 20th-century humans listening benightedly to some infantile, incomprehensible play or symphony and dying of wonder-struck boredom.

'I did tell you to stay quietly at home,' said the philosopher.

'It's enough to make a rat think men are mad,' was Town Rat's reply. 'What fools we were to admire their industry and wisdom! They've taken the thunder and lightning and all the forces of nature from the gods, and they're using them to exterminate each other. You should have seen them! There they are, with just a narrow strip of land between them. Then as soon as they see one another they forget the cold and the sun, the mud and the hunger, and all they can think about is killing one another with explosive projectiles.'

The philosopher was interested by this account. Being rather deaf, he had poked his nose out of his hole and was listening intently.

'Cats treat us in like manner,' he said after due meditation.

'Yes,' agreed the traveller, 'but they do it for food, whereas men fight for pleasure.'

The hermit pondered, and then said: 'What can you know about it? Perhaps they are fighting for food as well, without it seeming so. Perhaps, too, it is a way of proving their superiority over other animals, and their divinity; we do not know; the gods reveal themselves to us and to themselves in strange and mysterious ways.'

But Town Rat was getting annoyed. 'You're arguing about things you've never seen and don't know anything about,' he said disrespectfully. 'That's typical of philosophers and academics. But *I* know what's going on! Rats fight cats. They fight men as well, because creatures are always in revolt against the gods. They've even fought the frogs, and the divine Homer himself wasn't too proud to tell the story of that war in 300 lines of epic. The gods on Olympus were neutral at first, but then they came down on the frogs' side; even the crayfish joined in; and that's how we were defeated. But rats have never, ever, fought rats. So why are men fighting men?'

The philosopher said nothing. This was his unfailing reply when at a loss – an attitude which, as we have said, much enhanced his reputation. Finally, he said: 'I have nothing to do with all this. The things of this world are no longer any concern of mine, as I said years ago when a government deputation came seeking my help and advice. I am neutral, like the gods.'

'But the gods aren't neutral,' Town Rat objected forcibly, 'because the gods are men, and I've just told you that they're fighting each other. And I even reminded you that they didn't stay neutral in our great war with the frogs. Staying neutral may confer an air of wisdom, but in the end, it's always a form of cowardice!'

'You are neutral yourself, of course?' the hermit observed.

'I have to be, in the circumstances,' answered Town Rat. 'How could I be anything else, puny rodent that I am? What's happening is quite beyond me. And how could I take sides between two sets of lunatics of the same race – brothers, pointlessly killing each other, for sheer malicious pleasure! But even though I don't know who I want to win, I'm not neutral. I would like us to learn from this, and prepare our people for possible battles with the cats; because I can see that there'll be wars for as long as there's a world. That's my way of not staying neutral.'

The hermit replied, after a silence: 'I am content to cultivate wisdom.'

'The storm is raging,' cried Town Rat.

'I cannot hear it,' said the philosopher, withdrawing into his cheese.

'The rain is beating down on peaceful gardens,' screamed Town Rat.

'Let it rain,' the sage pronounced, 'and seek shelter. *Après nous, le déluge*!'

Beside himself with fury, Town Rat had climbed up to the opening in the Dutch cheese. He shouted in at the Grand Old Rat: 'You are nothing but a self-centred imbecile!'

And he walked away in disgust.

But the hermit, quite unmoved, put his head back out of the window and said: 'I am above the fray!'

TRANSLATED BY IAN HIGGINS

ERNEST PSICHARI 1883–1914

'Our mission in this world is to redeem France by our blood.'

Ernest Psichari was born in Paris on 27 September 1883. He was killed in action on 22 August 1914, a mere three weeks after the outbreak of the First World War. During his lifetime, he was regarded as a promising and important young writer by his literary contemporaries, but over the years his reputation has diminished, for he stands for attitudes and ideals many of which were either destroyed or severely called into question by the events of 1914–18. He reflected the views of a youthful intellectual élite in the early years of the 20th century by his devotion to patriotism and the civilizing mission of France, nationalism and Catholicism, tradition and hierarchy, discipline and austerity. Nevertheless, he remains a historically significant figure to the extent to which he represented these ideals accurately and expressed them vividly and with complete conviction.

Such ideas were not part of Psichari's early upbringing. On the contrary, he was originally nurtured in the tradition of anti-militarism, the rejection of revealed religion, and those rational, sceptical attitudes attributed to his maternal grandfather, Ernest Renan. As a teenager, he was attracted by socialist theory and interested in popular education, and he was associated briefly with the *université populaire* in the Faubourg Saint-Antoine. In 1902, he obtained his *licence-ès-lettres*; this was followed by a period of intense unhappiness due, in part at least, to disappointment in love, and he led a very disorderly existence and came close to suicide.

In November 1903, he began his compulsory military service, mostly in Beauvais and Amiens, and within a year he had decided to enlist as a regular soldier in a colonial regiment. Eventually, in 1906, he received his first overseas posting, taking part in an eighteen-month military expedition to equatorial Africa, a major purpose of which was to explore the area thoroughly (mainly Chad and part of the Congo). Psichari reached the rank of sergeant. On his return to France in 1908, he published an account of his experiences in *Terres de soleil et de sommeil* (*Lands of Sun and Sleep*), attended the artillery school at Versailles, obtained his commission, and set out in 1909 for a new posting in Mauritania in the western Sahara. The purpose on this occasion was the policing of this French colonial territory, and Psichari served with distinction before returning to France in 1912. During this period, he wrote a second book of travel essays, *Les Voix qui crient dans le désert* (*The Voices that Cry in the Desert*), and published his first and best-known novel, *L'Appel des armes* (*The Call to Arms*) in 1913.

Ernest Psichari. *Bibliothèque Nationale, Paris*

Between December 1912 and June 1913, he was in Paris, and was subsequently stationed at the army barracks in Cherbourg before leaving for the war at the beginning of August 1914. Despite his duties, he found time to complete his second and posthumously published novel, *Le Voyage du centurion* (1916). When Psichari fell in battle at Rossignol in Belgium, he was found to be wearing his military medal (awarded for his service in Africa) and a Dominican scapular, and had a rosary of black beads wrapped round his left wrist.

This combination of military and religious objects is, of course, highly significant. It reminds us that Psichari, despite his pacifist and agnostic background, had finally come to regard the army and the Church as the two sources of France's greatness. He wrote of his first spell of military service in Africa: 'I never experienced a greater pleasure in repeating to myself, "I am a French soldier," than during the wonderful hours spent marching under the tropical sun.' Later, six months before his definitive conversion to Catholicism at the end of 1912, he could say: 'All that is beautiful and majestic in our hearts comes to us from Catholicism.' In fact, Psichari had eventually put his faith in the disciplines of the army and the Church because he regarded them as the only institutions capable of maintaining the integrity of venerable traditions and of refusing to compromise with the decadence of the modern world.

In this way, he was an authentic representative of the intellectual élite of the generation of 1914 which had been studied and analysed by Henri Massis and Alfred de Tarde. Using the pseudonym 'Agathon', they published their findings in 1913 under the title, *Les jeunes gens d'aujourd'hui* (*The Young People of Today*). Their inquiry, largely carried out among students between the ages of 18 and 25, showed that a remarkable mutation in ideas and values had been taking place. The main attitudes reported by the inquiry were a desire for action rather than abstract thought, many indications of patriotic enthusiasm, anti-intellectualism (the one feature which disturbed Psichari), readiness to see war as a potential source of national regeneration, and the replacing of scientific rationalism by Christian beliefs.

Psichari – although he enthused in a letter to Massis that this phenomenon represented 'the first symptoms of our moral restoration' – was very conscious of the unusual form of generational conflict which such ideas implied. While the parents of these young men stood for 'progressive' thought – rationalism, internationalism, pacifism and so on – it was the younger generation that expressed 'conservative' thinking with its devotion to tradition in the form of military ideals, nationalist fervour and Catholic convictions. It is this type of conflict which receives fictional expression in *L'Appel des armes*. The novel describes how the young Maurice Vincent, the son of a rationalist, republican schoolmaster who is also anti-militarist, anti-colonialist and anti-clerical, manages to detach himself from these views, joins the army, fights in North Africa and learns to regard army life as a superior school of morals. As the narrator in the novel points out, 'the normal relationship between attitudes was thus reversed, with the father regarding himself as progressive and his offspring, by contrast, playing the role of the older person.'

Like his own fictional hero, Psichari embraced the traditional values represented by the army – and later those enshrined in the Church. He did so all the more enthusiastically because he believed that this was the only way in which intellectual and moral decadence could be overcome. He mainly attributed what he saw as the decadence of the times not to liberal thinking but to various forms of gross materialism being imported from the United States and Germany and wholly at variance with the true genius of France. Decadence had resulted from what he described as 'the gradual and irresistible collapse of traditional values'. In fact, this sense of decadence was widespread during this period: it was strongly expressed by Péguy (q.v.) and Valéry among others, and was not restricted to those associated with the political right. So Psichari turned first to army life, and later to a combination of the army and the Church, in order to identify values which could contribute to the regeneration of France.

Psichari's concept of the professional soldier is expressed most clearly and repeatedly in *L'Appel des armes*, which describes the life of a colonial regiment in the Sahara. It is there that he writes: 'Happy are those young men who, in our days, have led the frugal, simple and chaste life of warriors.' The adjectives used here are in keeping with his doctrine of the army as the secular equivalent of the monastery. He saw the army as providing a serious and austere way of life inspired by a form of mysticism, and the soldier as a kind of secular monk who accepts a hard, disciplined routine in pursuit of certain moral absolutes – honour, duty, obedience and the like – and believes in a 'mysterious destiny'. This view is summed up early in the novel by a major character, Captain Nangès, who believes that, as a soldier, he represents 'a great authority from the past, the only one – along with the Church – to have remained pure, unsullied, uncontaminated by modernity'. A few lines later, we are told that Nangès regards progress as 'a form of Americanism, and Americanism disgusted him'. Another character, Labastière, emphasizes the independent nature of the army, seeing it as a vocation rather than a job or profession, and says that the soldier can only be properly compared to the priest or the scholar. Later in the novel, Nangès characterizes the French colonial officers in terms which are Psichari's own:

> They are plain men, straightforward, upright, serious, and a little sad. Strong, simple, with rather poetic natures, and not modern. A very few had unbridled ambition and were admirable on that account. Others were pleasant, being poets. They were not modern men. One could not fail to pick them out. These men of Africa represented the adventurous, independent character of their race, these 'out-of-date' men possessed distinctive identities.

The purpose of soldiers and armies is to fight wars, and this is something which Psichari acknowledged and accepted in the most positive way. Indeed, he went so far as to say, through the character of Captain Nangès, that 'war is divine'. He added that Nangès 'realized that, in very truth, of all the elements of the divine which remain, war stands out as most clearly marked with a divine seal. And it is both particularly inaccessible in its essence and particularly close to those deep-seated powers which determine our behaviour.' In his letter to his mother two days before his death, Psichari could write: 'We are certainly heading for great victories and I feel less inclined than ever to repent at having desired a war which was necessary for the honour and greatness of France.' It is hardly necessary to add that these 'great victories' which Psichari anticipated were either postponed for some years, or were only achieved at a terrible human cost, precisely because of that unyielding traditionalism of the professional officer which he articulated. The German application of materialist doctrines to warfare, resulting in the concept of the *Materialschlacht*, underlined mercilessly the anachronism of a moral, chivalric doctrine of war.

By this time Psichari's enthusiasm for the military condition and for war was accompanied by deep religious conviction. We have seen that his sense of contemporary decadence encouraged him to turn to Christian values, while his patriotism took a form which demanded belief in the Cross as well as faith in the Sword. He became a Catholic convert in 1913 and was almost certainly about to test his vocation with the Dominican order when war broke out. It is the story of this journey to faith which forms the subject of *Le Voyage du centurion*. The novel takes up again the psychology of the soldier, but this gradually merges into an account of the nature of his Christian conviction and the necessity for it.

Between the ages of 22 and 30, Maxence, the central figure of *Le Voyage du Centurion*, had been aware of the ugliness, lies and general decadence of his society, but was unaware, because of his 'Voltairean' upbringing, of Christian answers to these things. His attitude to contemporary life led him to embrace the austerity and discipline of army life which, though it meant a great deal to him, did not bring him complete satisfaction. However, during his tour of duty in Mauritania, his contact with Islam, his experience of the solitude of the desert, and further meditation on his vocation as a soldier brought him, through a growing sense of a spiritual dimension in life, to ultimate belief in Christianity.

He was impressed by his Berber companions: as the inheritors of ancient Arabic mysticism they were largely indifferent to material wealth and taught him to seek knowledge of certain riches of the spirit. The solitude and silence of the desert affected him in ways recalling the solitude and silence of the cloister. Above all, he interpreted the French tricolour and the colonial regiment which bore it aloft as representing, not the sceptical, sophistical France in which he grew up, but that simple, virtuous, Catholic France that wore 'the helmet of reason and the breastplate of faith'. In this way Maxence's patriotism (and that of Psichari) embraces both the army and the Church. To be proud of France is to be proud not only of her military history but of her status as the eldest daughter of the Church. Loyalty to France must involve loyalty to Christ.

Psichari's distinctive blend of military pride and Christian faith is implied by the title of this second novel. It refers to Christ's miraculous healing of the centurion's servant and his comment on the soldier's belief: 'I have not found so great faith, no, not in Israel' (Matthew 8:10). Psichari interprets this as implying that Christ chose a soldier as the subject of this remark in order to suggest that the glory and discipline of the Christian life has its earthly counterpart in the glory and discipline of the military condition. And Psichari adds that a centurion is singled out among those at the foot of the Cross who see the crucified Christ, and who exclaims with conviction: 'Truly this was the Son of God' (Matthew 27:54).

There is little point in speculating on how Psichari's military and religious ideas might have changed had he survived to witness the succeeding four years of mechanized slaughter and tragic human waste in France and Belgium. Nevertheless, it must be acknowledged that the very values which nourished his enthusiasm for war in 1914 were the same values which were either thoroughly discredited or seriously challenged by 1918.

JOHN CRUICKSHANK

Texts

Œuvres complètes (Conrad, Paris, 1948). Contains all Psichari's published prose works, arranged in order of composition, together with much of his collected correspondence in 3 volumes. Vol. i: *Carnets de route* (first published 1948), *Terres de soleil et de sommeil* (1908); Vol. ii: *L'Appel des armes* (1913), *Les Voix qui crient dans le désert* (1920); Vol. iii: *Le Voyage du centurion* (1916), *Lettres du centurion* (1933).

Secondary sources

Henriette Psichari, *Ernest Psichari, mon frère* (Plon, Paris, 1933).
Wallace Fowlie, *Ernest Psichari* (Longmans & Green, New York/Toronto, 1939).
A.-M. Goichon, *Ernest Psichari d'après des documents inédits* (Conrad, Paris, 1946).
Avriel Goldberger, ' "Le Grand Ernest" and *The Call to Arms*: Ernest Psichari (1883–1914)' in *Visions of a New Hero* (Lettres Modernes, Paris, 1965, pp. 137–44).
Alec G. Hargreaves, *The colonial experience in French fiction: a study of Pierre Loti, Ernest Psichari and Pierre Mille* (Macmillan, London, 1981). Contains a chapter on Psichari 'Absolution'; also a fuller bibliography.
John Cruickshank, *Variations on Catastrophe* (Clarendon Press, Oxford, 1982).

L'Appel des armes

At about that time, a conversation took place at the home of Timothée Nangès which illustrates quite well the ground which Maurice Vincent had covered at a stroke, in just one stride, a single leap. A description of the feelings of a number of officers will enable us to sketch out the terrain and to measure the complex operations accomplished spontaneously by the soldierly Vincent quite naturally, almost without realizing it.

We will therefore report exactly what was said that evening in Nangès's home, since it is far more important for our purposes than the discussions that Vincent had with his father, which appeared to have strained their mutual affection to no useful purpose. We will see in due course that, for once in his life, this young man had succeeded in simply listening to his own self, his own heart, and he had thereby gained more knowledge of his country's destiny than all those others wasting their youthful energies in polite talk.

It is perhaps to be regretted that Nangès did not take part in this conversation. He was no theorist, and in particular there were certain lines of thought that he believed should have no place in a soldier's head. He was nevertheless entirely in agreement with his lieutenant, Labastière.

A young lieutenant in the colonial infantry, known as 'The Marine', was just back from active service in Africa, where he had acquitted himself well. But instead of recounting his exploits, he preferred to spurn war, despite the fact that it was what he excelled in.

'What do you mean?' said Labastière. 'I don't understand. Isn't war your ideal?'

The Marine explained:

'It would certainly suit me personally to wage war, and I don't think I'm better at anything else. But if we raise the discussion to a higher level and leave aside for a moment my purely selfish point of view in order to consider the interest of our country, in that case, no, I have no right to desire war, I mean a major war, war on an epic scale.'

Labastière blinked, then looked his comrade in the eye and replied:

'What you have just said is important, my friend. But it makes one wonder what we are doing in the army. For when all's said and done, every Frenchman will do his duty in time of war. I mean *every* Frenchman – even those who claim at present that they won't, who may in the event prove more zealous than anyone else. So the duty of waging war is not a criterion by which to measure us. Our duty starts on a higher plane and is more far-reaching. I'd go even further and say that our duty is qualitatively different from that of a simple patriot, a worthy member of the electorate. An officer isn't simply one notch higher in the scale of patriotism than an ordinary citizen. That's a commonly held view, but it's incorrect. He is patriotic in a different way, and the difference is so great that we run the risk of confusion if we use the same word about two things which are as different as these are from each other. It isn't an absolute difference or a difference of origin that divides the two types of patriotism. It isn't a difference of intensity somewhere between minimum and maximum. It isn't a quantitative difference. It is a qualitative difference. And having said that, we then have to see whether our role lies in that particular and unique quality, unmeasurable on any conventional scale, or whether, on the contrary, our place is to be assigned to us by the State, in which case our only ambition should be to act as faithful, dedicated servants of the State. I ask you, my friend, would you agree that a man of learning, for example, should be a servant of the State – and what would you say of a man of learning for whom knowledge was not the ultimate ideal? Observe here too that the respect in which a man of learning holds scientific knowledge is not simply a point higher in the scale of respect than that which we might feel, granted that we are more inclined to put science in its rightful place. And what would you say about a priest without charity?'

'Excuse me,' said the Marine. 'Like the man of learning and the priest, I have my own particular role, which is to learn the art of war. I have a goal, which is to prepare for war. The day we are attacked – or the day (sadder in my view) when we attack – I want to be able to serve with all my strength, with all my mind, with all my heart ... But you must understand, Labastière, that whatever it may cost me personally, as a member of the French nation, as a citizen – in a word, as a French human being – I cannot wish a war upon us, with all the woes that it will inevitably bring in its train.'

Nangès's guests had gathered round. Their cigars were being left to go out. All felt ashamed at being unaccustomed to thinking about these things.

'You can tell me all over again about the horrors of war,' said Labastière, 'but you still won't convince me. What you believe is full of common sense and wisdom. But I don't regard it as something we can take to ourselves and act upon. Observe that I am not condemning your belief as such, simply the use you want to put it to. Whatever you may preach, the army cannot be equated with the nation. The moral code applicable to the nation cannot be applied to the army. The principles which are valid for the one do not hold for the other. The army has its own ethic, its own laws, its own spiritual principle. And this is neither the ethic nor the spiritual principle of the nation. What we have is two completely different scales of value, and you cannot put one above the other without committing an error.'

'Hold on!' cried the Marine. 'Let me stop you there, comrade, for you must agree that the nation is above the army, and therefore that, if the army doesn't have the same principles as the nation, its principles must be rejected, its ethic must be rejected if it goes against the nation's ethic.'

Many of Nangès's friends could not understand what Labastière had been saying, for Labastière liked to reflect on his condition and thought that everyone else had reached the same point as himself in their inner development. He went on to explain his concept of the military condition:

'The army's principles are necessary in a nation, even though they often run counter to the principles of that nation. In a moment, I'll even go so far as to say that the only utility of that corps, of that mechanism which we call the army, lies in its independence, in the fact that it operates alone, that it functions under its own steam, and it is precisely by its independent workings that the army contributes a useful principle to the life of the nation. You cannot change the fact that we have a spiritual principle, one that belongs to us alone, one that cannot be changed for any other. You cannot change the fact that ours is something more than an occupation or profession as those words are normally understood. Viewed in this light, when you look at society as a whole, virtually the only people with whom you can compare us are priests and men of learning.'

'What you are saying, Labastière,' interjected the Marine, 'is that we are the hand as the priest is the heart and the man of learning the head of one and the same body. It's true that we have there the "three realms of man". But the hand, the heart and the head, each is nothing on its own. And the hand in particular is no more than an instrument which must obey. Let me for my part see an element of beauty in our allotted role, that of self-sacrifice, complete resignation to being a means, not an end.'

He spoke softly. His fine words were matched by his splendid military record which all of them knew about. But Labastière replied in a hard, distant voice:

'We are more than that. We are no more than a means for the country, but we are an end in ourselves. And this is very important both for us and for others. It's very important for everyone. I believe it is necessary, my friend, that there should exist a certain number of men called "soldiers" whose ideal is fighting, who love to do battle, not necessarily to win, but simply because they enjoy fighting, just as hunters enjoy the hunt, not the quarry. As Pascal says, "They do not realize that it is the hunt, not the prize, that they seek." If an officer is simply a man who does his duty – his professional duty – in time of war, that's quite a lot, it's true, but it's a lot less than will satisfy me. The condition of being an officer carries with it an additional set of principles. It involves a number of doctrines, an independent body of doctrines which are not for the use of everyone, *ad usum universi*, just as the man of learning and the priest have a kind of professional ethic, a moral doctrine inherent in their condition – in a word, special moral obligations beyond those of a purely professional, material or worldly nature. Our role, without which we lose our *raison d'être* and cease to have any meaning, is to maintain a military ideal, not, it should be noted, a national military ideal, but, if I can put it this way, a military military [*sic*] ideal. We must do that come what may, even if it involves injustice, iniquitous violence, or ruin. For our ethic goes far beyond the requirements of everyday common-or-garden morality. If you like, what it amounts to is that in time of war, the army is there to wage war, and in time of peace, it is there so that there are soldiers.'

'Only conquerors are systematic in life, have principles and formulas of application which work in every case. And that is why soldiers regard art with horror. It has no real strength and cannot accommodate algebraic signs. Soldiers, by contrast, are armed for life and solitude.'

from Les Voix qui crient dans le désert

Like those of certain preachers, his words hit his audience without convincing them. An officer fresh out from military school a few months earlier spoke for the young people present:

'Your words are very subtle, Labastière. But you are not taking sufficiently into account the way in which our duties depend on present circumstances. Had I been born under the First Empire, I'm sure I would share all your ideas. Being in fact a humble soldier of the Third Republic, with my eyes fixed firmly on France above all else, when I ask myself what future I most wish my country to have, I come pretty close to sharing our comrade's ideal: namely, universal peace. Devil take it, we cannot simply close our eyes to the terrible consequences of war. We would be going against a century of enlightenment. Of course, that won't stop me – as long as war is necessary, and that will no doubt be the case for a long time to come – from preparing myself for it to the best of my ability. I hope to do my duty like everyone else, and to enjoy the additional satisfaction of being a more useful, a more essential cog, at a higher point in the scale of utility, as you would say, than my other compatriots.'

'I need something different from you, comrade,' said Labastière. 'I also want you to maintain an ideal which is waning, and of which we are the last representatives. I think the people need this idea to be maintained. I don't claim that every citizen agrees with what I want to do. We shouldn't aim to convert people or to engage in propaganda. On the contrary, in an exactly parallel way it would be senseless to want every Frenchman to adopt the spiritual principle of the man of learning or of the priest. But think carefully about this, my friend. The day we forget our beautifully crazy ideas, we will lose practically all our value, and the people as a whole will suffer from our own particular decline. I want you to be a zealous priest, and not just a conscientious one.'

'I must protest. I am indeed zealous . . .'

'Yes, you enjoy learning the art of war. You put your all into it, very zealously. You enjoy studying war. But you condemn those who want to wage war. You like everything about the job apart from one thing: its ultimate goal. You set out the premisses quite happily, but you are terrified by the logical conclusion, so fearful, indeed so unimaginable is the idea of force, the idea of using and dominating by force.'

'Beware, Labastière,' said the Marine. 'Without realizing it, you are leading us into an apology for Caesarism.'

'I don't know what a Caesarist soldier is any more than I know what a republican or a non-republican soldier is. But I *am* trying to find out what a soldier is, and I feel surer of my own position than you can of yours. How lamentable this job must seem to you at its roots, buffeted as you are between the dreams of the past and the realities of the present! How heavily it must weigh upon you when, in your own heart of hearts, you measure the goal which is put to you against your modern conscience; how demoralizing those moments must be for you! You must feel like one of those sentenced to hard labour, who, it is said, spend their days pushing a wheel round and round for no reason, exhausting themselves to no practical purpose . . .'

Timothée Nangès broke in with a good-natured conclusion:

'Perhaps you are going too far, Labastière,' he said. 'The fact is that you two gentlemen represent two types of soldier which have always and will always exist. But what is the good of philosophizing? The admirable thing about our condition is that theorists have no place in it. Napoleon himself said as much. As you know, he didn't like theorists. We stand at the limit which will always be the breaking point of philosophers and moralists, philanthropists, public health inspectors, orators and politicians. I'm afraid they are all prone to undergo the same unfortunate experience as that which befell a minister who came to visit us some time ago. I'd like to tell you the story, for it has an inner meaning which I'm sure you'll understand. This eminent servant of the State had come to a dead halt in the middle of the barracks in front of a fountain spouting unfiltered water. Horror of horrors! Soldiers might drink the water. In fact, they certainly were already drinking it. Gentlemen, they were drinking unfiltered water! Public health was all the rage at the time. The poor fellow couldn't get over it. He made it clear that he was unhappy about the situation and attempted to show the officers around him that the artillery soldiers stationed in the barracks were certainly drinking contaminated water, and as an old NCO happened to be on hand, he appealed to him to bear out his point: "You, for example, Sergeant," he said, "I am sure you drink this water!" But, unruffled, the sergeant replied in a rough, phlegmatic tone: "Excuse me, Minister, but I never drink water!" The effect was stunning. This man was one of our oldest NCOs, as well as one of the best, and you could tell from his voice that he was telling the truth! All the modern concern with public health, the work of so many committees and sub-committees, the virtuous and zealous efforts of so many servants of the State, had collapsed in ruins when faced with this little bit of military reality, this good fellow drinking his litre of wine instead of the water that flowed in the fountain. Gentlemen, don't you agree that this is worth all your theories? . . .'

Next day, Nangès saw Maurice Vincent in the barracks. He was pleased by the look of the young corporal. Vincent had changed. Nangès had been watching him for some days now, and found him more resolute than previously, more settled in his occupation, more decided. The fact was that the few hours Vincent had spent in Crécy with his schoolteacher father had done more for his personal confidence than any speech that Nangès might have made. In a word, he was more of a soldier now. He had found his feet, and was settling into his new life.

Thinking back on the previous evening's conversation, it occurred to Nangès that if his NCO had found the right answer to the public-health fanatic, Maurice Vincent's look alone would be enough to see off a philosopher. Just think, that young man had been brought up to be a zealous humanitarian, valuing peace. He had been born at a time of enormous defeatism, huge disloyalty, and terrible losses, amid what was indisputably the steady weakening of old strengths and values. He could have made a decent, respectable citizen, a young man of virtue, a thoroughly average young person, 'modern' and sensible as everyone should properly be – he could have been all those things; instead, some words from an army captain about Africa, the knowledge that people sometimes shoot guns in earnest – not as a joke – had been sufficient to secure his engagement, and in just a few months, this young man had been taught everything a soldier needs to know, everything Nangès himself knew – namely, how to take and give orders. It was an exhilarating adventure, a new departure. This young Frenchman could be seen to be emerging as a kind of symbol, exemplifying a historic fact. This young Frenchman was becoming the very embodiment of France.

People had got used to cursing war. Rousseau had taught us about brotherly love, the Revolution had taught us that peoples should be free and that military conquest is iniquitous. It was all very idyllic. Yet a mere artillery lieutenant was still enough to conjure up the *grande armée.* These extraordinary paradoxes go together. The case of Maurice Vincent enables us to understand how Bonaparte was able to find the tools he needed and, conversely, the epic of the First Empire teaches us why and how Maurice Vincent is still possible in France.

TRANSLATED BY ALEC G. HARGREAVES

Extract from a letter written by Ernest Psichari to his mother on 20 August 1914, two days before his death.

My dearest Mother,
I am writing this letter in the hope that it may get through to you, but with no clear idea of when or whether it will reach you at all. We will have to put up with not hearing from each other for a while, but we shall gladly accept this small privation, like the others which the campaign will bring. I too have received no letter from you since leaving Cherbourg; this comes as no surprise, and I am confident that you and Corrie and all our loved ones are well. My only concern is that you should not worry too much about your sons, whose good fortune it will be to see through the recovery of our beloved France. The fate of our beloved infantryman [Psichari's brother Michael] is a matter of constant concern to me; the war will be harder for him than for me, and that is surely unjust.

As for us, everything has gone well so far. I cannot give you any details of what we have been up to until now, but you will be glad to know that I am feeling very well, that my command, however modest it may be, is giving me the greatest satisfaction, and that I am surrounded by a band of hale and hearty men who are extremely proud to be marching against the enemy and very determined to give a good account of themselves. I am under an excellent captain just back from active service in Morocco, with whom I am getting on very well. What I mean is that everyone is getting on well with each other at present, but he and I have a particularly good rapport.

We hear only vague news about the war, but what we hear fills us with joy and confidence. We are certainly heading for great victories, and I feel less inclined than ever to repent at having desired a war, which was necessary for the honour and greatness of France. It has come at the time and in the manner that we required. Let Providence remain with us in this great and magnificent adventure!

TRANSLATED BY ALEC G. HARGREAVES

Psichari on the African campaign.

*E*DMOND *A*DAM 1889–1918

'Nothing (not even if it is French) is worthy of unqualified praise.'
Open letter to Paul Magnette, in Les Cahiers idéalistes, *August–September 1918*

Very little is known of Edmond Adam. He was born on 4 September 1889 in Libourne, and, after a studious youth, he qualified in civil engineering in Paris and embarked on a career as a roads engineer in Bordeaux in 1910. The war broke out just before he was due to finish his national service; he volunteered for the front and was on active service from December 1914 onwards. He died on 24 August 1918 at La Veuve, of shrapnel wounds sustained on a reconnaissance mission three days earlier between Courmelois and Thuisy. While unconscious in hospital, he was awarded the Légion d'honneur.

Adam's first publications were in *Les Humbles*, edited by Maurice Wullens. This was a literary magazine fiercely opposed to what it saw as the senseless and immoral butchery of the war, and it repeatedly fell foul of the censor. One whole issue, on the pacifist Romain Rolland, was censored, and the journal was even banned for some months in 1917–18. To publish in *Les Humbles* was to dissent from the war. As it happens, Adam's first contribution, in May 1918, was nothing to do with the war, but was rather a kind of stylistic exercise in exoticism. 'Kacidas mauresques' are three Divan-type love poems, reminiscent also of Gide's *Les Nourritures terrestres*; a measure of Adam's skill is that they do read disconcertingly like translations.

The next issue of *Les Humbles*, however, contained – or rather, was supposed to have contained – much more provocative material by Adam. Under the heading 'Poèmes des tranchées', there were to have been four poems. The first three were in German, and were censored in their entirety; the fourth, 'Coqs de combat' ('Gamecocks'), had lines 83–102 and 109–128 cut out. The poems in German were printed after the war, in the magazine *Soi-même*: two are gently comic love poems, the third a whimsical Heinean mock-heroic sonnet on getting shaved, and intrinsically, they are instances of Adam's remarkable virtuosity, wit and taste for experiment. In content, then, the German poems were not remotely inflammatory; to the censor, however, their being in German was a provocative gesture, as Adam doubtless well knew. As a result, *Les Humbles* was violently criticized, in the standard chauvinist language of the time, as a 'Germano-defeatist' publication. One of these critics was Paul Magnette, to whom Adam addressed the vigorous open letter from which the quotation above is taken.

'Coqs de combat' is much more scandalous. According to Dorgelès, it was written in two nights, on the Somme, and captures exactly the true mood of the *poilu*, a mixture of 'chirpy good humour, grandeur, anger and resignation'. Is the element of resignation related to the escapism of, say, 'Kacidas mauresques' or 'Nisita' (of which more below)? If so, it is in a different mode: there is no escaping the anger.

A more clearly ambivalent escapism is found in Adam's mock (and approximate) late-medieval texts. He wrote letters in this manner, and also a number of poems, one of which was a humorous *rondeau* addressed to the censor who had cut the poems in German. This appeared in the July 1918 issue of *Les Humbles* – with the last three lines censored! Meanwhile, in the June issue of *Soi-même*, another journal which had regular censorship trouble, there appeared 'Rondeau' and, in the July–August issue, 'Supplicque' ('Peticion'). It is extraordinary that 'Rondeau' in particular should have been allowed to appear intact; perhaps it was read by a different censor from the one who perused *Les Humbles*. At all events, this poem is an interesting anticipation of what French Resistance writers in the Second World War called 'contraband' poetry – that is, a text which on the surface is unexceptionable, but smuggles through a message for the alert reader. Here, the facetious affectation of late-medieval language only thinly veils a message close to that of 'Coqs de combat'.

The variety of styles in Adam's writing suggests an undoctrinaire readiness to experiment. 'Nisita ou Les amours d'Eurydès', written in 1917, is different again from the texts already mentioned. In something like the manner of Pierre Louÿs, it purports to be the translation of a set of ancient Greek texts found among some ruins. An exercise in 'decadent' writing, it recounts the wooing and wedding of a chaste virgin, and the disillusion and regret which follow her eventual infidelity. It is actually more like harem literature than Greek, with a touch of the Song of Songs thrown in. It is very sensual, more suggestive than explicit, and shows a taste for fantasy as well as a gift for pastiche and a mastery of a wide variety of tones. It ends abruptly with a piece entitled 'Antidote': '. . . Do not believe a word of this mendacious story. The adventures in this bizarre account are nothing but the playful fantasy of a *poilu* who, during the war, did all he could to think about something else.'

Alongside 'Nisita' and the poems, Adam wrote an essay on verse, 'Le Néostiche et le verbe intégral'. A letter to his friends shows him sitting up at night in the trench, working hard to complete this in June 1918. Based on a comprehensive reading of contemporary works on phonetics, rhythm and accentuation, the essay argues for an eclectic verse-form, dictated by expressive need, and ranging from interjection to melody, from prose to verse. This is an extreme application of late 19th-century theories of free verse, and looks forward to a mixture of registers and subject matter as well as of prosodies. 'Nisita' and 'Coqs de combat' give just a hint of what this mixture might have become.

IAN HIGGINS

Texts

'Kacidas mauresques', in *Les Humbles*, May 1918.
'Rondeau' ('Cil qui pourra . . .'), in *Soi-même*, 15 June 1918.
'Coqs de combat' (censored version), in *Les Humbles*, June 1918.
'Rondeau' ('Ou mien censeur . . .', censored version), in *Les Humbles*, July 1918.
'Supplicque', in *Soi-même*, July–August 1918.
'Sonnet à m'amye cruelle', 'Rondeau' ('Ou mien censeur . . .', uncensored version), 'Scheuen', 'Krieg und Liebe', 'Geschaerfter Stahl', in *Soi-même*, 15 December 1918 (a special issue on Adam). The last three pieces are the German poems censored in *Les Humbles*, June 1918; there are French translations of all three, the first two by Adam.
'Le Néostiche et le verbe intégral: Essai sur les tendances poétiques contemporaines', in *Les Humbles*, January 1919.
'Nisita ou Les amours d'Eurydès: Palimpseste d'un Hellène ignoré', in *Les Humbles*, August–September 1925.
'Coqs de combat' (uncensored version), in *Anthologie des écrivains morts à la guerre* (5 vols, Malfère, Amiens 1924–6, ii). There is also a short piece on Adam by M. Lebarbier.

Secondary sources

M. Wullens, 'Edmond Adam', in *Les Humbles*, December 1918.
R. Dorgelès, *Bleu horizon* (Albin Michel, Paris, 1949).
The special issue of *Soi-même* (15 December 1918) contains material on Adam as well as by him.
See also *Les Cahiers idéalistes*, August–September 1918, for the Adam–Magnette–Wullens correspondence.

RONDEAU

A trop puissants et trop félons messires tant François que Germains de nostre siècle qui, gardant cul mollement fourré en leur curule, crachent sus nous moult belles et sophisticques parolles, ce pendant que laissent périr povres et honestes compaignons, leurs subjects, par maschines horrificques, infectes fumées et aultres diabolicques inventions de novelle industrie.

Cil qui pourra mieulx que moi dire
De nostre eage grand martyre,
Laschetez de nostre raison,
Et plours en chascune maison,
Que desjà résonne sa lyre.

Lors, qu'il crye treshaut son ire
– Si n'est vaine ceste oraison –
Contre coulpables grands messires,
    Cil qui pourra.

Si n'a paour de pendaison,
Géhenne ou aultre rançon,
Qu'il donne à Diable, qui n'a pire,
Toutes maschines à occire,
Et die à chascun sa chanson,
    Cil qui pourra.

RONDEAU

To those too myghty and too wicked lordes of our tyme, Frenshe and Germaine alyke, who, so snugly ensconced in their seates of staite, spuwe upon us their fine sophistic speache, the whyle they leave their poore honest companyons, their subjects, to perish by monstrous engynes, putred fumes and other diabolyk new fangled invencyons.

He who can tell better than I
Of our dayes the dyre miserie
And of the craven schemes insane
That floode with teares ilk man's demeine,
O let his lyre resound on hyghe.

So let him reise his wrathfull crye
– Should this my plea be not in vaine –
'Gainst grand lordes who rule guiltily,
    He who can tell.

Let him, shewing them fyne disdayne
For torture, noose or other paine,
Ban to the Devyl's armorie
Warre's engynes built for butcherie
And syng to all his bolde refrayn,
    He who can tell.

TRANSLATED BY D. D. R. OWEN

Coqs de combat

En rampant je sors de mon trou,
de ma tranchée noire, où la boue
nous enlise.
Je rampe en allongeant le cou
et sans oser lever la tête.
Mon sang bout, et bat mes tempes.
Je rampe
et mes hommes me suivent
en rampant
dans la boue,
et s'accrochent aux fils de fer
qui grincent et les écorchent
de leurs dents croches,
et leur baïonnette cliquette.

Tacatacatac . . . dzzitt! dzzitt! . . .
On se fait plat . . . Tacatac . . . dzzitt!! . . .
On voudrait s'aplatir davantage.
'Ils nous ont vus . . . – Ils nous ont entendus!'
Pointu comme une baïonnette,
un frisson nous glace le dos . . .
Mon poing crispé serre mon revolver.
Et je relève un peu la tête.
Mon front est moite et mon corps sue.

Mais ils ne tirent plus.
Nous avançons péniblement,
en rampant . . . Chut!!
Nom de Dieu, faites doucement!
Attention à vos baïonnettes.
Eh bien, là-bas, avancez donc!
Clac! . . . jjjhhvv . . .
Une fusée décrit sa trajectoire,
et vient s'épanouir en éblouissement
sur nos têtes prosternées.

Tacatac! . . . Ils ne nous voient pas,
mais: tacatacatacatac! . . . et: dzzitt! dzzitt! dzzitt!
Cochons de Boches!
Puis la nuit se refait, plus noire,
et nous gagnons un trou d'obus,
pour respirer un peu.

*

Ta koum! . . . Ta koum! . . .
que c'est sinistre!
Dzzitt! dzzitt! . . . Tacatac! tac!
Mais nom de Dieu, cochon de Boche,
vas-tu longtemps nous embêter
avec ta mitrailleuse?
Je sais bien: tu nous vois ramper
vers toi.

Gamecocks

I come crawling out of my hole,
my black trench, where the mud
sucks us back.
Neck stretched out I crawl,
not daring to raise my head,
temples hot with thudding blood.
I crawl,
and after me my men
come crawling
through the mud,
until they catch in the wire
and it screeches, and skins them
with hatchet fangs,
and clashes on their bayonets.

Rat-at-at . . . zing! zing!
Lie flat . . . Rat-at-at . . . zing!
If we could only flatten further.
'They've seen us . . . They've heard us!'
Sharp as a bayonet-point,
a shudder chills our spines . . .
My clenched fist clutches my revolver.
And I do just raise my head,
brow and body sweat-soaked.

But they've stopped firing.
We struggle further forward,
crawling . . . Shh!!
For Christ's sake make less noise!
Careful with your bayonets.
You over there, come on!
Crack! . . . Shhwhizz . . .
A flare comes climbing to its zenith
and opens out, a blinding flower
over our cringing heads.

Rat-at-at! . . . We can't be seen,
but: rat-at-at-at-at! . . . and: zing! zing! zing!
Boche bastards!
Then blacker night returns,
and we can find a shell-hole
and breathe again.

*

Ker-rack! . . . Ker-rack! . . .
this is horrible!
Zing! . . . Rat-at-at!
For God's sake, you Boche bastard,
how long's it going on for,
this machine gun?
Yes, I know: you can see us crawling
towards you.

Alors, à travers ton créneau,
tu dégorges ta gueuse de mécanique.
Tu voudrais bien nous amocher . . .
Si tu nous entendais hurler, Sauvage,
comme tu gueulerais: 'Komm, Fritz!
Hör' die Franzosen singen!'
Tacatacatac! . . . Tac! . . . Tac! . . .
Mais enfin que t'avons-nous fait?
Nous sommes dans nos fils de fer,
à nous;
nous allons les couper, faire une brèche!
Demain, quand nous serons chez toi,
pendant le coup de main,
défends-toi, nom d'un chien,
tire sur nous: mais pas ce soir!
Laisse-nous préparer notre affaire.

Tac! . . . Dzzitt! . . . dzzitt! . . . dzzitt! . . .
Eh! tire donc après tout,
sale brute!
On t'as mis là pour ça. Tire, tire!
Tu fais ton métier, nous le nôtre.
Ta koum!
On s'en fout, va,
tu peux tirer:
tu tires au hasard, sans nous voir,
dans le noir qui nous cache.
C'est pour rien que ta gueuse crache.

*

Je ne t'en veux pas trop, tu sais.
Voilà quatre ans que tu fais ce boulot
derrière ton créneau . . .
Ben, nous, voilà quatre ans aussi que l'on travaille
à tricoter ces grandes mailles de réseaux,
et les couper, la veille des attaques,
pour passer à travers et te chasser
de tes tranchées.

Tu vois, on est voisins
d'atelier, presque copains.
On turbine pour deux maisons rivales.
Bah! peut-être qu'elles se valent;
on n'en sait rien!
Mon patron m'a dit que le tien
était une crapule, un gueux, une canaille,
un rien qui vaille, un assassin!
Mais ton patron
t'a peut-être dit ça du mien . . .

Bref, on se bat comme des chiens,
comme des coqs
dont les maîtres s'acharnent
à jouer l'un contre l'autre
une partie où ils s'enragent.
L'un, à la fin, sera ruiné;

So, from behind your parapet,
you're pumping out your mechanical pig.
Wouldn't you just love to smash us . . .
If you heard us scream, you savage,
wouldn't you just yell: 'Komm, Fritz!
Hör' die Franzosen singen!'
Rat-at-at! . . . Rat-at-at! . . .
But what have we done to you?
We're in the middle of our wire,
our wire;
we're going to cut a way right through!
Tomorrow, when we've reached you,
and the raid's on, hell,
defend yourself then,
shoot then – but not tonight!
Just leave us be, we've work to do.

Rat-at! . . . zing! . . .
All right, you dirty animal,
go on, shoot!
That's what you're there for. Fire away!
You're doing your job, like us.
Ker-rack!
We don't give a damn,
shoot all you like –
you can't see us, you're firing blind
at the night we're hidden in.
Your pig is spitting in the wind.

*

I don't really mind, you know.
That's four years now you've been on this job
behind your parapet . . .
And, well, we've been at work for four years, too,
knitting great meshes of entanglement,
then cutting fresh tracks through them, ready
to attack next day and flush you
from your trenches.

Look – your works gates
are next to mine, we're almost mates.
We're flogging ourselves for rival firms,
as bad as each other, perhaps –
we can't be sure!
My boss has told me yours
is a villainous, treacherous, murderous,
good-for-nothing swine!
But yours, perhaps,
has said the same of mine.

Anyhow, we're scrapping like dogs,
like gamecocks
with masters relentlessly
and furiously betting one another
and themselves into frenzy:
when it's over, one'll be ruined,

l'autre ne sera pas plus riche.
Et leurs coqs se seront plumés,
déchirés et déchiquetés,
saignés, tués . . .

*

Tac! tac! tac! tac!
Assez, mon vieux!
Tu es plus bête que ces coqs.
Dzzitt! . . . Dzzitt! . . .
Mais, malheureux, que tu es bête!
Tac! tac! . . . c'est révoltant, à la fin.
Mon maître a raison,
tu n'es qu'une brute.
Tu vas peut-être me tuer.
J'ai des enfants et une femme . . .
Tac! Mon vieux, je me vengerai.
Et je t'embrocherai, demain, devant ta mitrailleuse!
Et si tu as une femme,
tant pis pour elle,
et tant pis pour tes enfants!
Moi aussi, je suis une brute,
quand on me pousse à bout.

*

Et nous ferons comme ces coqs courageux
qui, une fois lancés l'un contre l'autre,
bravement, héroïquement,
combattent sans merci,
et crèvent tous les deux, le soir, de leurs blessures,
aux bravos de la galerie émerveillée
pour la gloire, mais pour la ruine aussi,
hélas!
de leurs maîtres impardonnables.

14 mai 1918

and the other no better off.
And their birds will have slashed each other
to shreds, feathers and flesh,
and bled to death . . .

*

Rat-at! Rat-at!
That'll do, old son!
You're stupider than those cocks.
Zing! . . . Zing! . . .
You imbecile! You really are so stupid!
Rat-at! . . . – all right, it's atrocious!
My master's right,
you're just an animal.
Perhaps you're going to kill me.
I've got children and a wife . . .
Rat-at! Old son, you'll pay for this.
I'm going to skewer you tomorrow, right by your Spandau!
And if you've a wife,
that's just too bad,
and too bad for your children!
I'm an animal as well,
when I'm pushed too far.

*

And we'll do as brave gamecocks do, when
they're thrown into the pit at one another,
and unflinchingly, heroically
and ruthlessly fight,
till they drop and die at nightfall of their wounds,
roared on and clapped by an ecstatic crowd,
for the glory, but the ruin too,
alas,
of unpardonable masters.

14 May 1918

Translated by Ian Higgins

SUPPLICQUE

A chief qui poinct n'entend de mon cœur triste peine.

Ces jours que sommes en repos,
Qu'à la guerre, un temps, est accalmie,
Laisse-moi, chief, si t'en supplie,
Accourir par davant ma mie,
Et lui conter guallanz propos.

Je fay serment, si m'en convies,
Ne lui rien dire de nos maulx,
Ne parler poignarts, ne bourreaulx;
Ains – feust même par menterie –
De nostre sort lui faire envie.

Lors, seichiant plours par tendres mots,
Diray adieu aux yeulx si beaulx,
Et reviendrai, l'âme guarie,
Pour long temps de mélancholie,
Deffendre ma doulce Patrie.

Las! peines et larmes à flots
Enflent mon cueur à l'agonie.
Par fer mourray ou par sanglots . . .
Ne fais, Chief, que je perde vie,
Las, sans avoir reveu ma mie!

PETICION

To a captayn who comprehends naught of my hertte's bane.

Whyle we enjoy tranquillitie
And from warre's storm some briefe reprieve,
I prithee, Captayn, graunt me leve
To haste to my love's side and weave
Swete speaches spyced with gallantrie.

Then, an you urge me, I'll not tell
One worde, I vowe, of this our hell,
Prate of poniards or butcherie,
But, stooping to mendacitie,
Of our lot rouse her jelousie.

To drye her teares I'll bylle and coo,
Then to those fayre eyes bid adieu
And, from my soul all sadnes banned
For many a daye, resume my stande
To warde my cherished Mother Lande.

Such teares I shedde and woes I feele
My hertte, alas, must berste in twayne.
These sobbes shall slay me, if not steele . . .
Ah, Captayn, let my life remayne
Tyl I have seen my love agayne!

TRANSLATED BY D. D. R. OWEN

Albert Weisgerber (1878-1915): Homecoming from the Field.
Stadt St Ingbert

GABRIEL-TRISTAN FRANCONI 1887–1918

'The fate of a slave, to remain earthbound, when you can live and die in the sweet sky.'
'Les Départs des enfants d'aujourd'hui', c. *1908*

How to fly? Images of upward movement, physical action, departure and running free are common in this writer's poetry. When Franconi, born on 17 May 1887 in Paris, where he spent most of his life, enlisted at the start of the war, he was drafted into the artillery, but this was too passive a role for him, and he got himself transferred to the infantry. He was wounded in 1916 and, after discharge from hospital, applied for the air arm. They turned him down, so he tried tanks. They turned him down as well, and it was only after strenuous protests that he managed to avoid being sent back into the artillery: if he could not fly an aeroplane or drive a tank, he wanted the infantry, to be 'nearer the action'. Franconi really does seem to have been the kind of *poilu* that the propaganda shouted about and so few of them were, with a lust for battle, a taste for killing Germans, and extraordinary bravery. He was mentioned many times in dispatches before his death and was decorated four times.

In so far as he is known today, it is by scholars, as the author of *Un Tel de l'armée française* (1918). There is no plot to this novel; rather, it is more a set of short stories or vignettes. Each chapter is a separate episode or description: a trench, a patrol, a leave, an attack and so on. In most chapters, events are seen through the eyes of Un Tel, a name that translates as something like 'So-and-So' – a kind of Everyman or Thomas Atkins of the French army. Un Tel is Franconi's spokesman, and passes energetic judgement on whatever he sees. Fiercely brave, beloved of his men, he is impatient with feather-bed civilians, and determined that, after the war, they should not deprive returning heroes of their due. Un Tel, also like Franconi, was irritated by what he saw as the pretentiousness and emptiness of modern art and literature. More disturbing, perhaps, is his anger at what he sees as the debilitating presence in French society of Jews and foreigners.

Despite this, the book is often funny, often strident, occasionally straining a bit hard to be 'literary'. It is uncompromisingly realistic, often vivid, always passionate. Sometimes Un Tel is not the focus of attention, as in the extraordinary evocation of a reconnaissance flight, 'Shot Down', but it is hard not to see the pilot here as a persona of Franconi the poet, dreaming of 'living and dying in the sweet sky'. Was Franconi the would-be flyer the same as Franconi the film-enthusiast? What his art occasionally lacks in writerly qualities it makes up for with an acrobatic, laconic vision. This is very clear in the economy and saccadic structure of 'Shot Down', and it is also true of his poetry. The form is traditional, the writing not always free of prosodic padding, yet one often finds oneself reacting in terms of cinematic shots and cuts (more often, it is true, in the longer poems). Some of Franconi's best pieces are ironic short sketches of contemporary Parisian types.

Franconi is a mystery. The artist might have made a film director rather than a writer; the ideologue perhaps exhibits, as Holger Klein has argued, a disturbing proto-fascism alongside his heroism. As it is, we are left with a relatively small body of poems, an irreplaceable account of the French soldier's war, and a short satirical work, *Bisbur au Démocratic-Palace*, in which Franconi recounts his experience of hospital in 1916.

He was killed by a shell at Sauvillers wood on 23 July 1918.

IAN HIGGINS

Texts
Bisbur au Democratic-Palace (Edition de *La Grimace*, Paris, 1917).
Un Tel de l'armée française (Payot, Paris, 1918).
Poèmes (La Renaissance du Livre, Paris, n.d. [1921]). Contains a preface by F. Divoire.

Secondary sources
R. Dorgelès, *Bleu horizon* (Albin Michel, Paris, 1949).
J. Cruickshank, *Variations on Catastrophe* (Clarendon Press, Oxford, 1982).
H. Klein (ed.), *The First World War in Fiction* (Macmillan, London, 1978).

Shot Down

The lieutenant pilot's machine skimmed across the turf away from the camouflaged sheds of the airfield. In seconds, he was off the ground. The propeller was flinging a gale into his face, the engine beating with a steady roar. A little Japanese doll on a string, a mascot given him by a dancer, seemed to stare into space in horror.

The sky was stormy, barred with clouds and alive with shells. His aeroplane shook with explosions, as it probed the light to find a way. He had to fly through artillery barrages and over the enemy lines, braving the dreaded machine guns to detect where they lurked in their hidden nests.

Steering by instinct, the pilot was thinking back to his games-playing youth. He pictured the vigour and the grace and harmony of sport, and how his sweethearts would anxiously wait for his safe return home after a game. Burned-out villages and flattened woods, the vast cemeteries and wasted countryside were flashing dizzyingly past. Tiny, heroic groups were moving across the roads, a miniature host in sky-blue making ready to die!

The attack would be launched very soon, and the aeroplane flying ahead like some beautiful bird was preparing the way for the advancing waves.

Riding his mount of wood and steel and metal panels, the pilot enjoyed a sense of utter self-mastery as he calmly examined every fold in the terrain, every watercourse, any disturbed or trodden earth – anything that betrayed the presence of men. Sometimes a shell-burst plumed the sky, as if the enemy were wanting to present an honoured visitor with a bouquet of light.

The engine started bellowing like a dragon of the apocalypse, its metal flanks juddering irritatedly. An arrow of birds fled in alarm from this marauder at large in the skies.

The aeroplane was over the French lines.

All the earth churned up for war, the hidden weapons, the whole mechanical contrivance of fire and destruction, was a pitiful sight from above. Could human beings really be so stupid as to think those little piles of soil afforded any protection? From the air, they were just mud pies, practically invisible in the all-enveloping haze.

The pilot was trying to pin-point where the enemy trenches were dug. The essential question was whether the infantry could storm them. He turned the engine off, to catch any sounds coming up from the ravine.

Suddenly, a gigantic shadow hid the earth from view. A pungent smell of explosive caught his throat. Invisible guns were throwing up a barrier of shells across his path of light. He was all but rocked out of the cockpit by the blast, and as his machine was thrown about, he had an unpleasant sensation that it was breaking up under him.

A thin splinter of iron pierced the engine, there was a spurt of flame, and in a maelstrom of torn fabric, fire and molten metal, its wings broken, the bird hit the bottom of the ravine.

In the distance, the infantry saw a globe of light fall out of the sky.

The dead pilot lay crushed in the wreckage of his machine. And so the scout who lit the way for our troops, the young lieutenant with broken body and outflung arms, waits in vain to be relieved. May a glorious and triumphant attack carry his comrades to where he lies!

How many dead, mingled with the deathless earth, or lying as bones on the ground like a clamour for help, are waiting like him to be avenged? Will those who did not fight, those who lived a life of pleasure, hear the voices of the dead from no-man's-land?

Their voices do carry, on the winter wind. Surely, when dawn comes and the civilian wakes in his warm bed, ready to enjoy another day, he can hear icy fingers at his window? If he opened his door to the passing wind, perhaps he would understand the vast lament of all those soldiers who have not been relieved, and never will be. Will we see the ghosts of heroes rise against the cities, coming back to haunt the banquets and spill the fine wines of ladykiller tipplers down their paramours' breasts?

Beware, you bright young things of the sportsfield, you daredevil home-front leaders of fashion, you languid tangoers in hideaway bars! Beware, lest the pilots who died for their country return one night to join in the dancing!

Translated by Ian Higgins

La Petite Individualiste

Le corps souple et l'esprit nerveux comme une lame,
Son amour qu'elle donne à de beaux déclassés
Est un dévergondage insolent. Elle a l'âme
En rumeur, il y gronde un idéal blessé.

Des érudits voyous elle est la sœur tragique;
Muse des petits bars où l'alcool est brûlant,
On la voit partager la misère énergique
De pâles Juifs proscrits de leurs pays sanglants.

Elle aime, au Luxembourg, vivement deviser;
Menue, elle s'anime, ivre de mots blasés.
Son poing léger menace au lointain Bakounine.

Ingénue elle oublie outre les vils tourments,
Que par des soirs troublés, ses délicats amants
Pour des assassinats ont dressé leurs mains fines.

Été 1913, Laon

The Little Individualist

She's lissom, with a quivering knife-blade mind,
And the love she gives handsome outsiders she'll
Flaunt brazen-bold. She's a soul that's alive
With a muttering, rumouring, injured ideal.

In rough brandy bars she's the tragic muse;
A sister to erudite thugs, she shares
The busy misery of sallow Jews
Forbidden the blood-soaked lands that are theirs.

She loves to discuss in the Luxembourg Gardens,
Dizzy with throwaway mots, and terribly ardent.
To threaten Bakunin with featherweight fist she thrills.

She naïvely forgets, aside from scandalous tortures,
The nights of riot when her fastidious courtiers
Have raised their delicate hands to kill.

Summer 1913, Laon

Translated by Ian Higgins

The Old Soldier

Seeing how the old soldier's stories were received, Un Tel tried to guess what kind of respect and affection he would eventually be shown himself by the youngsters he had fought for, youngsters lucky enough to have been born in a country which was calm, prosperous and feared.

The old soldier certainly commanded something less than profound respect. Scruffy of manner, florid of face, juicy of voice, he did look oddly like a tramp. He was a pedlar and rag-and-bone man, and he picked up cigarette-ends. He was an example of that scrofulous aristocrat, the Paris vagrant. Passers-by always think they know him from somewhere, because they are so used to seeing him on the same street corner, heedless of the dust and the wind and rain, as picturesque a part of the scene as the newsstand and the trees.

Lodging in doss-houses and hostels where destitutes sleep ten to a garret floor, the old soldier was an habitué of the soup-kitchen, and perfectly content with such rudimentary comforts and unassuming conviviality. He enjoyed simply roaming the streets, gravely expatiating on economic problems with men who had come down in the world and yet still, sometimes, maintained a kind of elegance under their tatters.

Living off peelings and slops, swept along in the street-crowd's excitement, the beggars of Paris lead adventurous lives. They are a society apart, a kind of colourful, independent Estate which will perhaps one day stage its own revolution and seize power.

An old idea of Un Tel's was that, as the Fourth Estate of syndicalism declined, we would witness the rise of a Fifth Estate in which the vagabond would reign supreme. Why should the old soldier, for all his pustules, not have his turn as fortune's darling and become a master? For he had never accepted servitude.

The old soldier, who was quite unaware of this rosy future in store for the down-and-out, considered himself relatively happy. It was twenty years since he had slept in a bed. In summer, in the country, he slept in the trees. It mattered not at all if he was covered in crow droppings. Gently rocked by the wind like a sailor up a mast, he would recall good times he had had, when farmers, for a jest, invited him to their wedding celebrations and he got a drink from the bride's glass, a delicious Anjou wine worth thirty francs a bottle. Autumn would find him back near Notre Dame, for he was fond of the Place Maubeuge. He did occasionally do modest jobs, like selling pamphlets, but he never managed to earn enough to put by. He did not in any case particularly care to save, holding that poverty was his profession.

There were moments when the old soldier assumed

a seriousness of bearing which he otherwise seemed to have forgotten. These were the moving occasions when he talked about his war experiences. He was a forestry warden in 1870 and, fearing neither death nor capture, he carried dispatches through the enemy lines. How many times had he told this story? Un Tel was saddened to think of the irony and indifference which used to greet it. Before the war, youngsters were inclined to dismiss accounts of what France had suffered in 1870 and how her steadfastness and courage had earned the enemy's admiration, as the ramblings of old men in their dotage.

Yet this beggar they laughed at had been a soldier fighting to defend French soil. Would it be the same for the soldiers in the Great War? Might it one day happen that a gunner or a fusilier who had fought on the Yser or at Verdun would be laughed to scorn by a generation that did not care? It was a painful question, and one that it was impossible not to ask oneself when in the presence of this old man, obstinately refusing to die or forget the honour and suffering of long ago.

However, the wheel of fortune has turned now, and they do listen to the old soldier. In dives where men on sick-leave make free with the girls, he raises his voice, not wanting the soldiers of 1914 to accuse him of never having served. He bangs a gnarled stick on the greasy table, rattling the bottles and glasses. His eyes flash, his voice is a bugle sounding the charge. The matronly woman who runs the dive has no need to call for silence now. Soldiers, wastrels and tarts alike are all reverently listening to these reminiscences from a past that is inseparably bound up with our tempestuous present. Un Tel marvels at the logic and harmony of our unfolding history, and thinks to glimpse the endless procession of all the wars in which beggars have had to die in affirmation of our strength and urge to live.

The voice of the race is so very simple! It says:

'It was terrible in 1870, too. I saw long supply trains at a standstill, full of provisions going mouldy that were meant for Mac Mahon's heroic army. What did for us was Bazaine's cowardly surrender of Sedan, just when Mac Mahon was holding out a lifeline. I used to cross the German lines at night with dispatches, and I recovered the paybooks from our comrades' bodies. Poor kids, the surprise was so complete they hadn't even had time to defend themselves. There was a dixie full of potatoes right by them, they'd been about to eat. There were no sentries, no outposts, nothing – they'd all been killed. I saw all these things! The brutes came looking for me in my house – I had a house, covered in ivy. They turned the whole place upside down, from cellar to attic. But they didn't get me.

'When it started, I wondered if it would be like 1870. Then there was the Marne. You're plucky lads. So were we, but we were betrayed.'

Hearing the voice of the past, this witness to past valour, Un Tel is embittered by the old ex-serviceman's miserable fate. It makes him more determined still, when he returns from the war, to take steps to ensure that fortune smiles more kindly on the men who saved their country from thraldom. Those who know no gratitude or have grown rich on the war will learn to dread the sight of young veterans who have lost everything in this enormous conflict, returning to swell and organize the ranks of the vagabond army of the Fifth Estate and endow it with unconquerable militancy and strength.

TRANSLATED BY IAN HIGGINS

LA MORT DU VANDALE

Un obus éclatant à l'autel déserté
Le sang de la rosace a giclé sur les dalles;
L'église paysanne où se croisent les balles
Martyre auguste et calme offre son corps divin
Au soudard exalté par les ferments du vin;
Et les coqs du village ont cessé de chanter.

Un reître épouvanté, loin de ceux qu'il adore,
Expire au seuil troué de l'église en priant
Le dieu d'amour dont il profana la chaumière;
Dans l'abside ont sifflé des obus flamboyants.
Les yeux bleus du Germain sont morts à la lumière,
Mais le coq orgueilleux du clocher chante encore.

THE VANDAL'S DEATH

A shell has burst at the abandoned altar
And splashed rosace blood from porch to crypt;
The martyr country church lies bullet-whipped,
Offering her body in holy dignity
To a brutish wine-excited soldiery;
And in the village, cock-crow's heard no more.

A frightened savage, far from the ones he loves,
Dies at the forced door of the church, in prayer
To the god of love whose hearth he defiled;
In the sanctuary, shells have whizzed and flared.
The Teuton's blue eyes have died to the light,
But the steeple cock still proudly crows above.

TRANSLATED BY IAN HIGGINS

JEAN-MARC BERNARD 1881–1915

'This "reintroduction of the whimsical" . . . does seem to correspond to the general contemporary movement towards a French renascence.'
'Les poètes fantaisistes', Œuvres

Jean-Marc Bernard was born on 4 December 1881, at Valence, and was exempted from national service on health grounds. After three years as a bank clerk, he worked in bookshops, first in Valence, then in Reims. Back in Valence, he founded the 'critical, nationalist and classical' literary magazine, *Les Guêpes*; thirty-four issues appeared, between January 1909 and November 1912.

In his critical writing, Bernard is one of the leading apologists for the neo-classical reaction in France against Symbolism (synonymous with 'anarchy') and free verse. While not advocating imitation of 17th-century masters such as Racine and Boileau, he argues seriously that a renewed classicism (synonymous with 'order') is essential, and that only restoring the monarchy will create the right conditions for this renewal. Classicism for Bernard means 'necessarily adopting a method of thinking and working capable of sustaining, channelling and universalizing our personalities and instincts'.

His earliest poetry, *La Mort de Narcisse* (*The Death of Narcissus*; 1904), is a vaguely deliquescent eclogue, for the most part in classical alexandrines but dabbling (the first and last such case in Bernard) in free verse at the end. *Quelques essais* (*Some Essays*; 1910) again uses a variety of classical forms, and the subjects are often taken from antiquity. *Sub Tegmine Fagi* (*Under a Spreading Beech*; 1913) contains his best poetry, that which allows him to be classed as one of the *poètes fantaisistes* ('whimsicalists'; Francis Carco, to whom 'Après-dînée' is dedicated, was another). Sometimes elegiac, sometimes sensual, sometimes witty or humorous, this poetry never takes itself too seriously. Whereas, in Bernard's earlier work, his classicism frequently results in rather stodgy verse, in this volume it takes the form of an often ironic awareness, a refusal to let oneself by taken in by either fate, other people or one's own emotions. Writers he considers to take themselves too seriously, such as Mallarmé and Henri de Régnier, are the object of excellent pastiches. In *Sub Tegmine Fagi*, Bernard readily identifies his own position by reference to the cultural tradition: Virgil ('sub tegmine fagi', 'et nos cedamus amori'), Beaumarchais ('tout finit par des chansons'), Mallarmé again ('aimai-je un rêve').

It is intriguing to wonder for a moment what French poetry might have been without the war. Perhaps an extended *belle époque* would have allowed neo-classicism as practised by Bernard and the *fantaisistes* to occupy a significant area of the cultural map. Certainly, Bernard's epicureanism (in the best sense of the word) and his discreet, sometimes playful, restraint find distant echoes, *mutatis mutandis*, in later poets as different as Char, Guillevic and Ponge. As it is, the association of neo-classicism with a real or imaginary socio-cultural establishment must surely have prevented writers like Bernard surviving the onslaught of Dada and Surrealism.

According to Pierre Richard, Bernard returned to Catholicism well before the war, and might have become a great Christian poet. This view does not completely accord with most of the published work, although the distressed cry 'De profundis' rings like that of a believer. According to Bernard, this poem was written in a temporary mood of discouragement; he was already planning a counter-weight, 'Dies irae', just before he was killed.

All but two of the poems below are from *Sub Tegmine Fagi*. The exceptions are 'Nos clochers' and 'De profundis', which were not published in Bernard's lifetime. 'Nos clochers' is dedicated to Maurice Barrès, the anti-Republican politician, journalist and writer, who had published a polemical work entitled *La Grande pitié des églises de France* following the separation of Church and State in 1905. It is worth comparing with 'La Mort du vandale' by G.-T. Franconi, another admirer of Barrès. 'Et nos cedamus amori' is a set of ten poems, too long to reproduce in full; the poems chosen exemplify the variety in mood and style of the whole.

Alongside his poetry and criticism, Bernard published in 1912 a large, aggressively royalist anthology ('the Republic has never inspired such magnificent poetry'). He also edited a selection from Charles d'Orléans, the medieval poet, and wrote a book on François Villon, with translations into modern French, which was published posthumously.

When war broke out, Bernard immediately joined up, and was posted to the front in April 1915. On 9 July 1915, he volunteered to take rations to the front line at Souchez. On the way, he was blown to pieces by a shell.

IAN HIGGINS

Texts
Pages politiques des poètes français (Nouvelle Librairie Nationale, Paris, 1912).
Charles d'Orléans: Rondeaux choisis (Sansot, Paris, 1913).
François Villon: Sa vie, son œuvre (Larousse, Paris, 1918).
Œuvres, suivies des *Reliquiae de Raoul Monier* (Le Divan, Paris, 1923, 2 vols).

Secondary sources
P. Richard, *Jean-Marc Bernard, Dauphinois* (Galerie Drômoise, Valence, 1926).
M. Décaudin, *Les Poètes fantaisistes* (Seghers, Paris, 1982).

ET NOS CEDAMUS AMORI

Pour S. V.

I

C'est encore un printemps qui vient sur cette route;
Dans les airs, les oiseaux l'accompagnent, joyeux.
Mais vous, je vous retrouve en proie au sombre doute,
    Des larmes plein les yeux.

Que votre âme pourtant ne soit plus abîmée
Dans les tristes erreurs qui la faisaient mourir;
Laissez, avec la terre aujourd'hui ranimée,
    Un autre amour fleurir.

II

Que l'aube est froide après une nuit d'insomnie!
Beau souvenir d'amour, ah! pourquoi me blesser?
Sans doute, avec le jour, qu'ils vont enfin cesser
Mes soupirs, mes regrets et ma peine infinie . . .

Mais voici s'élever, sous les treilles épaisses,
Le râle continu des pigeons palpitants,
Et j'évoque aussitôt son image et j'entends
Son lent gémissement sous mes lentes caresses.

*

VIII

Ton épaule sort demi-nue
De ta chemise qui descend;
Elle est fraîche, ronde et charnue:
C'est un délice attendrissant.

ET NOS CEDAMUS AMORI

For S.V.

I

Spring struts up the road with a swing
In its step; and the birds are all singing.
But you, at the rendezvous, in winter mood
    Sombrely brooding.

Earth's coming awake, and nothing's amiss
That's alive. High time to allay
Your doubts, allow new love to live, dismiss
    Your sad dismay.

II

How can remembered love, so joyful,
Hurt so much? Will day heal
My suffering? After a sleepless night
Dawn rises, but rises chill.

I hear the doves, their throat-cries throbbing
Under the vines. Then plain and clear
I see her, hear again beside me
The dove-cry, the love-cry – as if she were here.

*

VIII

Your shoulder (as the slip
Slips) is bared to my lips,
Luscious, carnal, fresh,
Caressable flesh.

Mais, plus que ton corps, je désire
Ta bouche offerte dans la nuit.
De mes lèvres je la respire,
Je la savoure comme un fruit.

Gardons nos bouches accolées,
Laisse ta langue entre mes dents.
Tes belles tresses déroulées
Rafraîchissent mes doigts brûlants.

Je retiens mon souffle et j'épie
– Aux lueurs qu'entre les rideaux
Laisse passer la lune amie –
Ton front farouche et tes yeux clos.

Soudain, je sens tes nerfs se tendre;
Tes yeux se cernent brusquement.
Oh! la jouissance d'entendre
Ton râle et ton gémissement!

IX

Ô corps tant caressé, d'autres mains que les miennes,
Ce soir, s'alanguissent sur toi.
Oublieux, je le crains, des caresses anciennes,
Tu frémis d'un pareil émoi.

Je n'aurai point pour toi de jalouse colère:
Je saurai contenir mon cœur;
Car je redoute, ô mon amour, de te déplaire
En découvrant trop ma douleur.

Tu ne sais repousser l'attrait d'une caresse;
Toujours tu cèdes au désir.
Il faut, à ta chair tiède et souple, la paresse
Qui suit l'étreinte et le plaisir.

Vois: je suis calme, et je souris au doux sourire
Offert à ton nouvel amant;
Mais cependant, parfois encore, je soupire . . .
Et je suis triste infiniment.

X

C'est le calme des dimanches,
Jardin, sous tes marronniers.
Voici sauter dans les branches
Les moineaux et les verdiers.

De ce coin de la terrasse
Où, triste, tu viens t'asseoir,
Vois-en un, d'une aile lasse,
Qui s'élève dans le soir.

But most of all your mouth
Offered in the night, sweet
As the scent and taste of fruit
After long drouth,

Mouths moulding each other,
Let your tongue slither
Round mine. Long hair unpinned
Is cool to the hand.

By the moon's furtive light
Peering through chinks of curtain,
I see your shy wild frown,
Your eyes shut tight.

Sudden your sinews stiffen,
Your eyes grow dark as night;
O the delight of hearing
The sounds of your delight!

IX

So much caressed when all your nights were mine,
Caressed tonight by other hands than mine,
You soon forget the old emotion,
But thrill to an identical sensation.

I'll not speak anger at your lechery,
Or eat my heart out at your treachery;
I could not bear, love, your vexation
If all my jealous grief made full confession.

You can't resist desire, you can't forego
The least caress, or utter the word 'No';
Your body, yielding, warm and supple,
Loves nothing better than to kiss and couple.

You smile at the new lover in your arms;
My smile replies; I promise you I'm calm,
Though sad at times; I don't complain,
Except – grief is my one friend that remains.

X

The garden's dressed in green
And in its Sunday calm;
Among the chestnut trees
The sparrows swarm.

You sadly come to watch
The approach of night;
See one bird spread its wings
In hesitant flight,

Mais bientôt le ciel l'enivre:
Il monte d'un vol plus sûr;
Et tu ne peux plus le suivre
Dans le vide de l'azur.

Ah! pauvre insensé qui pleures,
Puisse-t-il te rappeler
Qu'il ne faut que bien peu d'heures
A l'amour pour s'envoler!

*

Te voici donc qui t'envoles,
Bel oiseau, mon pauvre amour!
Et mes plus douces paroles
Ne te gardent pas un jour.

Je murmure: Aimai-je un rêve!
(On dirait du Mallarmé.)
Dans cette aventure brève
Ai-je seulement aimé?

Allons! soyons philosophe!
Mettons-nous à l'œuvre pour
Faire une petite strophe
De tout cet immense amour.

Mais quelle misère, en somme,
Qu'en nos cœurs nous maudissons,
D'observer, poètes, comme
Tout finit par des chansons!

Then gaining courage, soaring
To join the sky's kermesse,
And soon is lost to sight
In emptiness:

Few minutes to the hour, few hours
To fill a day;
It takes few days for love
To fly away.

*

Sparrow, my ragged love,
You're fled, you're gone.
Sweet words don't count,
There's nothing to be done.

It's hateful how it comes
Always to grief.
My God, was this 'true love'?
It was so brief.

Resign yourself; philosophize;
Don't curse.
Compress eternal love
Into a verse.

It was a dream I loved
(Pure Shakespeare!). Time
Ends everything in rhyme,
In nursery rhyme.

TRANSLATED BY GRAHAM DUNSTAN MARTIN

NOS CLOCHERS

À Maurice Barrès

Clochers aigus, vous seuls donnez
Leur accent à nos paysages
Qu'ont façonnés,

Lentement, à travers les âges,
L'azur, un fleuve, ces feuillages
Et les humains.

Vous détruits – éteinte la flamme! –
Nos bois, nos rives, nos chemins
Seraient sans âme.

OUR CHURCH SPIRES

To Maurice Barrès

Sharp bell-spires, you alone have power to give
Its intonation to our countryside
Attuned to life

Through gradual centuries by hedge and grove,
Blue sky and river and the careful pride
Of human love.

If you were once destroyed – the flame gone cold! –
Then it would be for forest, ford and field
Death of the soul.

TRANSLATED BY GRAHAM DUNSTAN MARTIN

Après-dînée

À Francis Carco, en souvenir du 9 août 1909

Par les fentes du contrevent
Je regardais vers la tonnelle,
Où tu m'attendais en rêvant
Quelque brève chanson nouvelle.

J'apercevais près du rosier
Un coin de table avec des verres,
Et ton large fauteuil d'osier
Sous les glycines et les lierres.

Mais, accablé par la torpeur
De l'immobile après-dînée,
Tu laissais la tête, ô dormeur,
Sur tes deux paumes inclinée.

Or, tandis qu'au fond de l'enclos
Tu somnolais avec paresse,
Moi, dans l'ombre des volets clos,
Je déshabillais ma maîtresse.

After the Meal

To Francis Carco in commemoration of 9 August 1909

Peeping through shutters from an upstairs room,
These fragments of the garden I can view –
A tablecloth, azaleas in bloom,
Wine glasses, the geranium, and you

Ensconced in comfort in your wicker chair,
Waiting under the ivy by the rose;
And we'd agreed that I should meet you there,
Distil some poem from the summer's prose.

We've eaten well, drunk well enough to drown.
You're knocked out by the drowsy heat. Too long
I've kept you waiting in the sun. That song
Will not be written now. Your head goes down,

You doze upon your folded arms, replete.
So, while you snore in sunstruck idleness,
I in the bedroom – shaded, cool, discreet –
Embrace my mistress and remove her dress.

Translated by Graham Dunstan Martin

De Profundis

Du plus profond de la tranchée,
Nous élevons les mains vers vous,
Seigneur! ayez pitié de nous
Et de notre âme desséchée!

Car plus encore que notre chair,
Notre âme est lasse et sans courage.
Sur nous s'est abattu l'orage
Des eaux, de la flamme et du fer.

Vous nous voyez couverts de boue,
Déchirés, hâves et rendus . . .
Mais nos cœurs, les avez-vous vus?
Et faut-il, mon Dieu, qu'on l'avoue?

Nous sommes si privés d'espoir,
La paix est toujours si lointaine,
Que parfois nous savons à peine
Où se trouve notre devoir.

Eclairez-nous dans ce marasme,
Réconfortez-nous, et chassez
L'angoisse des cœurs harassés;
Ah! rendez-nous l'enthousiasme!

Mais aux Morts, qui tous ont été
Couchés dans la glaise ou le sable,
Donnez le repos ineffable,
Seigneur! ils l'ont bien mérité!

De Profundis

The trenches, Lord, are stark and deep,
We raise our hands towards you.
The steps out of the dark are dark and steep,
Have mercy on our souls!

Exhaustion of the spirit is worse
Than of the body. On our heads
A hurricane of death and pain has burst,
Flame, iron rain and flood.

You see us ragged, caked with mud,
Haggard, disheartened, weary.
But have you seen our naked souls, O God?
Shall we confess the worst?

Peace is intangible as prayer
And every day more distant.
This quagmire where we crouch is named Despair;
Faint is the lamp of duty.

Give us some heart, some light, console
Us in this mire, this pit of Hell,
And heal the soldier's agony of soul.
Restore our resolution.

But those who suffered in the trenches' mud
And in this mud lie buried,
Clothed in their sacramental blood –
Grant them the peace they merit.

TRANSLATED BY GRAHAM DUNSTAN MARTIN

*C*HARLES *P*ÉGUY 1873–1914

'Entering into a text means collaborating with its author, and this sort of reading is an act which is common to the reader and to the author. When this takes place, the text fulfils its destiny.'

from Clio II

'It is better to have a war for justice than peace in injustice.'

L'Argent Suite, *1913*

Péguy was born in Orléans on 7 January 1873, and died in action at Villeroy on 5 September 1914 on the first day of the Battle of the Marne, serving as a reserve lieutenant in the 276th Infantry Regiment, 6th Army. Two weeks later, thanks to numerous obituaries and tributes from distinguished pens, beginning with that of Barrès (*L'Echo de Paris*, 17 September), Péguy attained fame, something that had eluded him all his life, and in due course, he became a symbol and a legend, even abroad.

'His design,' wrote Edmund Gosse (*Edinburgh Review*, January–April 1916), 'was to carry out in the 20th century the sacred labour of Jeanne d'Arc.' John Middleton Murry, remarkably sensitive to one of Péguy's obsessions – namely, that his was a defeated generation which would be forgotten because it had no dead bodies to present to history – wrote: 'It has been the tragic, yet the beautiful destiny of Péguy's generation that it should bring forward its dead in hecatombs that History herself cannot number' (*Quarterly Review*, January 1918). The editor of the German revolutionary periodical *Die Aktion* (24 October 1914) – where, prior to the war, Ernst Stadler (q.v.) had published translations of Péguy's work – saw things differently. After having paid tribute to him as one of the most powerful moral forces in European literature, Franz Pfemfert wrote: 'Charles Péguy lived for humanity and he died for the grotesque conception of national honour held by the worst of his compatriots.' The cover of this edition of *Die Aktion* carried a haunting drawing of a sad Péguy, victim of 1914, which in no way conveys the poet's mood in this farewell to a friend: 'I go as a soldier of the Republic in the cause of disarmament and the last of all wars.'

During the interwar period, Péguy was largely forgotten until he re-emerged during the Second World War as a figurehead for both Vichy France and the Resistance. It was in protest against such annexations that Romain Rolland, a friend and collaborator of Péguy, wrote his two-volume biographical study of the writer, published in 1944. Rolland admitted, however, that given the diversity of Péguy's friends, each of whom might be familiar with one facet of his complex personality, distortions were not surprising. Perhaps this is the price the founder of the *Cahiers de la quinzaine* had to pay for gathering around him 'a perfectly free association of men who all believe in something'. However, there remains, Rolland remarked, the work itself; a close study of it should produce a reasonable synthesis.

Lieutenant Péguy (seated, right) during the military manœuvres of 1913.
Centre Charles Péguy, Orleans

In France, Péguy has been much studied since, but he remains a controversial figure. Perhaps this is, after all, how it should be, for he himself was not afraid of controversy and even contradiction. He did not care much for unifications: 'I feel no need to unify the world. The more I see of it, the more I discover that free men and free events are varied.'

At first glance, Péguy's life and work lend themselves to a justifiable 'before and after' approach which highlights moments of crisis and change. The first obvious such break occurred in 1897 when Péguy abandoned his studies for the pressing realities of the outside world. It was a momentous decision to take for this son of the people, the first in a long line of illiterate peasants and semi-literate small artisans (his grandmother could neither read nor write, and his mother had left school at the age of 10), whom the Republic's enlightened educational policy enabled to receive a full-time education, and even to enter the most prestigious of academic establishments, the École Normale Supérieure (1894). Instead of becoming '*un monsieur professeur*' as his mother had hoped, the working-class lad rejected what he described as '*le monde bourgeois*': 'Good Republicans imagined that democracy consisted of the sons of the people becoming, by a series of competitive examinations and eliminations, a ruling aristocracy.' Moreover, in the classroom he had already encountered the 'modern world' ruled by the metaphysics of progress and oblivious of the outbreaks of barbarism. One example of the latter was the Dreyfus Affair and the cries of 'Death to the Jews!', to which Republican politicians replied that the 'Jewish Question' did not exist because, in the best of all possible Republics, there were only Republicans. From this, Péguy drew important lessons, later endlessly widened and deepened. The other important discovery that Péguy the student made unexpectedly in the Parisian slums was economic misery. This, too, was to remain an unforgettable experience for a boy who had known poverty but not such destitution.

To his youth (1894–1900) belong his active political involvement (socialism, the Dreyfus Affair, defence of the Republic) and his left-wing creative writing (*De la Cité socialiste*, *Jeanne d'Arc*, *La Cité harmonieuse*). Once he had founded his review in 1900 – the *Cahiers de la quinzaine* – he settled down (if 'settling down' is the right term for so alert and anguished a mind) to being a critical observer of political and intellectual life, the self-appointed conscience of men of action, especially of friends and former *dreyfusards* suspected of deviating from what he believed to have been commonly held ideals, of turning '*mystique*' into '*politique*', to use one of his favourite and untranslatable later expressions. Until his departure for the Front in August 1914, he fought all his battles from the iconoclastic 'city' of the *Cahiers* which, as one *habitué* put it, was constantly echoing with the sound of broken glass, of broken friendships and of smashed idols. As for Péguy's contributions to the first few series of the review, they are numerous, varied and, as we now realize, unusually perceptive, but they consist largely of polemics or prefaces to and comments on other people's works, which often acted as pretexts for his own texts.

Until, that is, the Tangier crisis of 1905 – when Kaiser Wilhelm II visited the Moroccan capital and pledged Germany's support for that country's independence, as a ploy to decrease France's control and break up the Anglo-French *entente*. This inspired what is arguably the first typical Péguy *cahier*: 'Notre Patrie' ('Our Nation', October 1905). Stylistically, it is one of the tidiest examples of his explorations round a central theme, with the help of seemingly irrelevant but carefully thought-out digressions and contrasts, unusual images and *rapprochements*, apparent repetitions which do not quite repeat. And here we have a major 'before and after', clearly expressed by Péguy himself at the end of 'Notre Patrie': on that grey but illuminating morning when France seemed to be under threat of German invasion, 'A new period had begun in the history of my own life, in the history of this country, and surely in the history of the world.'

Two more works with the theme of war ('Les Suppliants parallèles' and 'Louis de Gonzague', December 1905), as well as two posthumously published sequels to 'Notre Patrie' close the eventful year of 1905. Henceforth the threat of war would be a constant preoccupation. The theme was frequently accompanied by reflections on the mortality of peoples and civilizations. Like Valéry's Hamlet picking up the skulls after the upheaval of 1914 and concluding 'We civilizations now know that we are mortal,' so Péguy, a decade earlier, listed the victims of modern persecution and massacre and called on the 'professional optimists', those who still lived in an imaginary world of progress, to take note that

> entire civilizations have died, in the old and the new worlds. Absolutely, entirely and totally died . . . Man could easily accept the fact that he grows old, that he passes, that he disappears, since such is his nature, such is his lot; if only he had the consolation that generations pass but humanity remains. Unfortunately, we no longer have that consolation . . .

The tragic and global perspective in which he perceived the impending war, as part of an 'enormous belly of barbarism' which had already devoured American Indians, Christian Armenians, Russian Jews, African tribes and which now threatened to crush the fragile free nations of Europe, that perspective alone gives his call to arms an unusual resonance. It was better understood in July 1939, when the most sombre sequel to 'Notre Patrie' was published for the first time, than by Péguy's contemporaries. They were generally divided, with the Nationalist Right trying to annex him and the Republican Left, for long embarrassed by the attacks of the *enfant terrible*, happy to let him go. 'Notre Jeunesse' ('Our Youth', 1910) was Péguy's reply to both, but to no avail. From that point onwards, a legendary 'before and after' developed – Péguy the socialist versus Péguy the nationalist – which lies well outside the 'shock' to his innermost being that he had received in 1905.

For the last four or so years of his life, Péguy was hailed by the young as a master of the nationalist revival. No doubt this earthy peasant struck a new and invigorating note in a field occupied by royalist intellectuals (the Action Française) and professors of energy (e.g. Barrès). Ernest Psichari dedicated *L'Appel des armes* (1913; q.v.) to 'our *maître* Charles Péguy . . . in whom relives the soul of France'. However, by then master and disciple had already gone their separate ways. Even at its most bellicose – in *L'Argent suite* (1913), for example, where he calls for pacifist voices such as Jaurès's to be silenced – Péguy's nationalism remains firmly anchored in revolutionary tradition. His conception of France was that of Hugo and Zola: the country whose mission, whose *mystique*, was to bring freedom. This is why Péguy's freedom-loving God loves the French.

From a spiritual and artistic point of view, Péguy's *annus mirabilis* was 1910, the year of the first of his three 'mystery' verse plays, *Le Mystère de la charité de Jeanne d'Arc* (*The Mystery of the Charity of Joan of Arc*), itself a proclamation of his return to faith some two years earlier; or perhaps it should be called his *rediscovery* of belief, since Péguy was opposed to the description of his spiritual journey as a 'return' or, even more inappropriate, a 'conversion'. With the exception of a few regular verses in the first drama he wrote about Joan of Arc in 1897, he had not written any poetry. And now suddenly, at the age of 40, he found himself in a state of creative frenzy, feverishly composing in three and a half years a life-time's work, an astonishing corpus of poetry in both its quantity and quality of techniques. The latter include the *vers libre* (used in the first three 'mysteries'), regular and irregular sonnets and 1400 quatrains. In these last, published posthumously as *Ballade du Coeur* (*Ballad of the Heart*), more than a glimpse can be caught of the great emotional crisis unleashed in body and soul by his love for Blanche Raphael; passion, too, the poet discovered at 40. The final, monumental *Eve*, an epic in 8000 alexandrines, was envisaged as a Divine Comedy but, as one might expect, without Hell. To give an idea of Péguy's extraordinary creative energies in the last years of his life: *Eve* was completed in six months (June–December 1913), and this in addition to other writings and the usual editorial tasks and financial worries. The latter were as intense as ever, for it seems that *Eve* was the last straw even for the small band of hitherto faithful subscribers.

From both a technical and inspirational point of view, the three mysteries are outstanding achievements both in Péguy's poetry and in French religious poetry as a whole.

The Joan mystery of 1910 inevitably invites comparison with the Joan drama of 1897. Indeed, in order to demonstrate that the rediscovery of belief was a matter of deepening and not a conversion, Péguy first had the original idea of writing an extended commentary on the youthful drama, the latter to be reproduced word for word without any deletions. One can only regret that he had to abandon the project, although this was understandable enough: the additions appended to the first two acts of the 1897 play alone filled a volume of 230 pages, and the original trilogy had a total of 24 acts! The Joan mystery as published in 1910 consists of commentaries incorporated into two of the dialogues of the original play: the opening conversation between Joan and her friend Hauviette, and the confrontation of Joan and Madame Gervaise which followed. These dialogues are each preceded by Joan's monologues, which did not figure in the play of 1897 and which are a measure of the depth of despair of Joan as a Christian.

The Joan of 1910, like the Joan of 1897, wishes to save better than Christ, and this is still the crux of the debate between her and the nun Madame Gervaise, who represents orthodox faith and theology, but now Joan also questions some fundamentals; to begin with, the whole purpose of the Crucifixion. Given that evil still exists, has it all been in vain? This is the formidable subject of her first monologue.

Joan's friend Hauviette remains the same earthy, commonsense peasant, but is considerably more articulate than in 1897. In her critical appreciation of Joan, we have Péguy's Bergsonian portrait of his Pascalian alter ego: an insatiable soul, consumed by 'a fever of sadness' and feeling the sufferings of others more than the sufferer himself, seeing only suffering and almost looking for evil, perpetually anguished at the thought of the future and of eternal damnation. Hauviette is an earthy sort of Bergsonian. She actually quotes the words discussed at great length in the Bergson *Cahier* – 'Sufficient unto the day is the evil thereof' – and she proceeds to give an endearing peasant explanation of what this means: one prays at certain times of the day just as one eats at certain times of the day. Six days of the week are reserved for work and Sunday for God. There is a time for everything. The present is the present, and the future must not be forced into it.

The down-to-earth wisdom of a Hauviette has no effect on Joan. Left alone, she resumes the subject of her monologue: has the Crucifixion been in vain?

The longest and most remarkable additions were made to the dialogue between Joan and the nun, and here we move away from Christ's long absence from the earth to his eternal absence from Hell. The debate is still the same as in 1897, but it has a new width and depth because the protagonists have developed. Madame Gervaise now understands how Joan in her immense pity for man blasphemes against the divine, isolates herself from ordinary humanity and finally exposes herself to all the varieties of pride. She warns Joan against pride and despair. They can lead towards God and man, but also away from them.

Joan, too, has developed. Her sense of vocation has given her some bold certainties against which the nun with her slightly mechanical theology battles in vain. 'Orléans, in the country of the Loire': with these words, Joan abruptly concludes the discussion on damnation. And on this cryptic note of temporal success ends a drama of intense spiritual despair.

Pencil drawing of Péguy in 1894 by Léon Deshairs.
Centre Charles Péguy, Orleans

Incorporated in this battle between a serene saint accepting what is and basing her certainties on texts, and an angry saint concerned with what might be and posing certainties of the heart, we have something altogether new: a recitative of the Passion and a *pietà*. It is *sung*, so to speak, by an inspired young nun who gradually retreats and lets the suffering Christ and Mary tell their own stories in free indirect speech.

Again and again in this complete but unchronological history of Christ's life evoked by Madame Gervaise, Mary and Christ Himself, we come back to the blood and sweat, the hands and feet pierced by nails, the burning throat, the physical pain. In the moving *pietà*, we see Mary – her eyes swollen, eyelids bruised, eyelashes stuck together, swallowing back tears – grow old and ugly, a stupefied, hideous and very touching *Mater Dolorosa* who tries to understand how it all happened as she walks and weeps, and who only succeeds in remembering without comprehending. She is the eternal mother. Similarly, Pilate is the harmless and indifferent senior civil servant concerned with order, and the crowds are the crowds of always: watching an execution and taking pity on the relatives of the condemned. 'Péguy re-presents the past,' as André Gide aptly remarked. This is how Péguy intended to develop his mysteries, a genre comparable with the tragedy of the ancients, he thought, or with French classical tragedy.

Stylistically speaking, the Passion and the *pietà* provide the most original part of the Joan mystery, a marvellous example of Péguy's 'incomparable musical prose' – his own 'modest' comment on his skilful manipulation of *vers libre* – which was perfected in the two mysteries that followed.

In *Le Porche du mystère de la deuxième vertu* (*Porch of the Mystery of the Second Virtue*) and *Le Mystère des Saints Innocents* (*Mystery of the Holy Innocents*), we move to Heaven. The speaker is God, a kindly paterfamilias who uses simple language and homely images. The familiarity of language, which gave offence at the time, is one of the hallmarks of Péguy's religious poetry. Another is what one might call the poet's theological imagination. He questions and says things which have not been questioned or said before. This is particularly true of his God the Father, a delightfully original creation which probably owes much to Péguy's desire to link Judaism and Christianity (at least, *his* view of Christianity) and thus somehow associate his Jewish friends with, or even involve them in, his spiritual adventure. Hence God's admission that He, representing justice, and the Virgin Mary, representing mercy, do not always agree. But both adore children who in their doctrinal innocence, best seen when they are sleepy and oblivious of learned differences, confuse in their prayers 'Our Father' and 'Hail Mary'. God the Father is gradually coming to understand His Son's Passion and, through Him, the human condition. Joan's despair about the meaning of the Crucifixion is in part answered. On a more psychological level, a remedy to Joan's permanent state of anguish and despair is suggested in the beautiful hymns God offers to His creations Night, Sleep and Hope, His allies in managing man, that monster of anguish. At the time Péguy was composing these hymns, he was such a monster. He exorcised his anguish in the act of writing, not in favour of idle dreams but a difficult act of confidence in God and time.

Péguy's Catholicism is as personal and as unorthodox as his socialism and it aroused much criticism in official circles. There was even a rumour, especially in view of his defence of Bergson, that his works might join the latter's on the Index Librorum Prohibitorium. The last *Cahier* and last polemic ('La Note conjointe', August 1914), interrupted by mobilization, ends with a discussion on that very subject. One cannot help remembering that Péguy founded the *Cahiers* as a reaction against the socialist 'Index', the censorship imposed at the 1899 Socialist Congress. Eternal Index. Eternal fear of freedom.

Eternal excommunication from the city.

Underlying all the breaks, explosions and 'crises' in Péguy's life is a remarkable continuity of thought which derives from a fundamental anarchist temperament. His anarchism was fervently city or society orientated, for it is only within a free society that man can develop his full intellectual and artistic potential. Péguy's libertarian socialism involved three critiques, all of which add up to a formidable – and often prophetic – critique of the modern world, the world of 'politique': a socialist critique of capitalism, a liberal critique of socialism and a philosophical critique of the metaphysics of progress. What Péguy was attacking in the last was the deification of the historian who explains, orders and predicts everything in the name of laws taken to be inexorable. In such a world, belief, freedom of choice, explosions, revolutions, even action become irrelevant. More tragically, this kind of progressive evolution accepts (as did Ernest Renan in his philosophy of history, and Péguy liked to quote Renan on the subject) that civilizations, like individuals, are born, develop and then die, succeeded by others who will follow the same pattern. The 'death of humanities', which haunted Péguy like a recurring nightmare, becomes acceptable as a natural development, a fact of life on a par with the victory of the strong over the weak. This, to Péguy, was the formidable barbarism of the modern world.

NELLY WILSON

Texts

Œuvres Complètes (N.R.F., Paris, 1916–55). Incomplete; thematic arrangement in 20 vols.
Œuvres Poétiques Complètes (Pléiade, Paris, 1941).
La Ballade du Cœur (Julie Sabiani (ed.), Klincksieck, 1973). A previously unpublished poem.
Œuvres en Prose (Pléiade, Paris, 2 vols). Works of 1898–1908 published 1959 in 1st vol. Works of 1909–14 published 1957 in 2nd vol.
Péguy tel qu'on ignore (Jean Bastaire (ed.), Gallimard/Idées, Paris, 1973).
A scholarly new, 4-vol Pléiade edition which promises to be complete and which will bring together and properly situate the hitherto scattered posthumous publications, is in process of preparation. The first 2 vols (*Prose 1897–1909*) appeared 1987 and 1988 respectively. Vol. 1 comprises the first complete collection of Péguy's pre-*Cahiers* writings, with the exception of the 1897 Joan of Arc drama which will join the poetry in vol 4.
The Mystery of the Charity of Joan of Art (Carcanet, Manchester 1986). Adapted version by Jean-Paul Lucet in a translation by Jeffrey Wainwright. Extracts reproduced with permission.
The Amitié Charles Péguy is based at the Centre Charles Péguy, Orleans, which has a collection of books, periodicals, correspondence and theses.

Secondary sources

J. Delaporte, *Connaissance de Péguy* (Plon, Paris, 1944, 2 vols).
A. Dru, *Temporal and Eternal* (Harvill Press, 1958). Translations of 'The Republic' and 'The Dreyfus Affair' reproduced by kind permission of Collins Harvill.
A. and J. Green, *Basic Verities* (Kegan Paul, 1943); *Men and Saints* (Kegan Paul, 1947). The translations of the poems 'Night', 'Hope', ' "Our Father" and "Hail Mary" ' and 'Blessed are Those' reproduced by kind permission of Associated Book Publishers (UK) Ltd and Pantheon Books, a division of Random House Inc.
Geoffrey Hill, *The Mystery of the Charity of Charles Péguy* (A. Deutsch, London, 1983). A poetic analysis of the writer's impact.
J. Isaac, *Expériences de ma vie, Péguy* (Calmann-Lévy, Paris, 1959).
Pierre Manent, 'Charles Péguy: between political faith and Faith', in *Rediscoveries* (J. A. Hall (ed.), Clarendon Press, Oxford, 1986). The translation of 'Réponse brève à Jaurès' reproduced by kind permission of Oxford University Press.
Pansy Pakenham, *The Holy Innocents and other Poems* (Collins Harvill, London, 1956). Translations used by kind permission.
Romain Rolland, *Péguy* (A. Michel, Paris, 1944, 2 vols).
F. Laichter, *Péguy et ses Cahiers de la Quinzaine* (Sciences de l'homme, Paris, 1985). A meticulous examination, from the original Czech.
Marjorie Villiers, *Charles Péguy, a study in integrity* (Collins, London, 1965). Translations reproduced with permission.
Nelly Jussem-Wilson, *Charles Péguy* (Bowes and Bowes, London, 1965). Translations from this study are used in the introductory article.

THE REPUBLIC: *MYSTIQUE AND POLITIQUE*

(from 'Notre Jeunesse')

The Third Republic was Péguy's great contemporary. They grew up together and, gradually, apart, but all the same it remained one of his two loves (the other being Joan of Arc). The polemics behind the piece that follows are quite complex. Suffice it to say that Péguy was defending, inter alia, the republican ideal (mystique) *against attacks by anti-republican forces (e.g. Action Française). The distinction between* mystique *(purity, ideal but also the city) and* politique *(money, bourgeois competition, political manoeuvring and divisiveness) is a vital concept developed throughout his writing. It is seen here in a largely political and philosophical context.*

We are the last generation with a republican *mystique*. And our Dreyfus Affair will have been the last operation of the republican *mystique*.

We are the last. Almost the ones after the last. Immediately after us begins the world we call, which we have called, which we shall not cease calling, the modern world. The world that tries to be clever. The world of the intelligent, of the advanced, of those who know, who do not have to be shown a thing twice, who have nothing more to learn. The world of those who are not had by fools. Like us. *That is to say*: the world of those who believe in nothing, not even in atheism, who devote themselves, who sacrifice themselves to nothing. *More precisely*: the world of those without a *mystique*. And who boast of it. Let no one make a mistake, and no one, consequently, rejoice over it, on either side. The *de-republicanization* of France is essentially the same movement as the *de-christianization* of France. Both together are one and the same movement, a profound *de-mystification*. It is one and the same movement which makes people no longer believe in the Republic and no longer believe in God, no longer want to lead a republican life, and no longer want to lead a Christian life, they have had enough of it, and one might almost say that they no longer believe in idols, and that they no longer want to believe in idols, and that they no longer want to believe in the true God. The *same* incredulity, *one single* incredulity, strikes at the idols and at God, strikes at the false gods and the true God, the old God and the new gods, the ancient gods and the God of the Christians. One and the same sterility withers the city and Christendom. The political city and the Christian city. The city of man and the City of God. That is the specific sterility of modern times.

We are extremely badly placed. We are in fact situated at a critical point, a distinguishing point, a dividing line. We are placed between the generations which had the republican *mystique* and those which have not got it, between those who still have it and those who no longer have it. So no one believes us. On either side. *Neutri*, neither the ones nor the others. The old republicans do not want to believe that there are no more young republicans. The young do not want to believe that there were old republicans.

I am horrified when I see, when I discover, that the older men among us do not want to see what is self-evident, and which only has to be seen to be believed: the extent to which the young have become estranged from everything related to republican thought and its *mystique*. This is seen, above all, naturally, in the fact that thoughts, which were thoughts to us, have become, for them, ideas, in the fact that what was to us an instinct, a race, thoughts, have become for them *propositions*, from the fact that what was to us organic, has become for them a matter of logic.

Today we prove and demonstrate the Republic. When it was alive no one proved it.

One lived it. When a *régime* is demonstrated, easily, comfortably, victoriously, that means it is hollow, done for.

When a *régime* is a thesis among others (among so many others) it is down and out. A *régime* which is standing, which is alive, is not a thesis.

'What does it matter?' say the professionals, the politicians. 'What does it matter to us? What can it matter to us? We have excellent administrators. So what can it matter to us? It works well. We are not, it is true, republicans any longer, but we do know how to govern. Indeed we know how to govern far better than when we were republicans,' they say. 'Or rather when we were republicans we had no idea at all how to govern. And now,' they modestly add, 'now we are beginning to know, just a little. Look at the elections. They are good. They are always good. And they will be better still. All the better because it is we who make them. And because we are beginning to know how to make them. The Right lost a million votes. We could just as easily have made them lose fifty and a half million. But we are moderate. The Government makes the elections; the elections make the Government. You get your money back. The government makes the electors, and the electors make the government. The government makes the Deputies. The Deputies make the government. The country pays. And everyone consents. It is not a vicious circle as you might suppose. It is not at all vicious. It is a circle, and nothing more, a perfect circle, a closed circle. All circles are closed. Otherwise, they would not be circles.

'We therefore turn towards the young, we turn to

another side, and we can only say: "Take care. You treat us as old fogies. That's quite all right. But take care. When you talk airily, when you treat the Republic lightly, you do not only risk being unjust (which is not perhaps very important, at least so you say, in your system, but risk what in your system *is* serious), you risk something much worse, you risk being stupid. You forget, you fail to recognize that there is a republican *mystique*; but ignoring it and failing to recognize it will not prevent its having existed.

Men have died for liberty as men have died for the Faith. The elections, nowadays, seem to you a grotesque formality, uniformly false and bogus in every respect. You have the right to say so. But men have lived, men without number, heroes, martyrs and I would even say saints – and when I say *saints* perhaps I know what I am saying – men have lived, numberless men, heroically, like saints, and have suffered and died, a whole people lived in order that the last of fools today should have the right to accomplish that bogus formality. It was a laborious and fearful birth. It was not always grotesquely funny. And all around us other peoples, whole races, are labouring in the same agonizing birth, working and struggling for that contemptible formality. The elections nowadays are ridiculous. But there was a time, my dear Variot, a heroic time, when the sick and the dying had themselves carried on their chairs in order *to deposit their ballot in the urn*. To deposit one's ballot in the urn; to you, today, the expression is pure comedy. It was prepared by a century of heroism. Not by literary heroism, that costs nothing. But by a century of incontestable heroism, of the most authentic quality. And, I should add, typically French.

It is not precisely what our founders foresaw. But our founders did not manage all that well. And then one cannot go on founding indefinitely. It would be tiring. The proof that it is lasting, that it stands up to it, is that it has gone on for forty years. There is no reason why it should not go on for "forty centuries". The first forty years are the worst. It's the first forty years that count. Afterwards, one gets used to it. A country, a *régime* does not need you, it does not need mystics, a *mystique*, or its *mystique*. That would only embarrass it. For such a long journey. It needs a sound *politique*, which means a good government policy.'

They are mistaken. The politicians are mistaken. From the summit of the Republic forty centuries (of the future) do not look down upon them. If the republic has worked for the last forty years, it is because everything has worked for the last forty years. If the republic is solid in France, it is not because the republic is solid in France, it's because everything is solid everywhere. In modern history, though not in all history, there are great waves of crises, usually going out from France (1789-1815, 1830, 1848), which shake everything from one end of the world to the other. And then there are longer or shorter periods of calm, periods of flat calm which pacify everything for a shorter or longer time. There are *epochs* and there are *periods*. We are in a period. If the republic has settled down it is not because it is the republic (this Republic), and not through any merit of its own, but because it is, because we are, in a period. The duration of the Republic no more proves the lasting quality of the Republic than the duration of the neighbouring Monarchies proves the lasting quality of Monarchy. They belong to the same age. That is all it proves. For what is lasting in the republic is *la durée*, duration. It is not the *régime* which is lasting, but time. The tranquillity of a certain period of history.

'The elections are ridiculous. But the heroism and the holiness with which one obtains contemptible results, temporally contemptible, are the greatest and most sacred things in the world. The most beautiful. You reproach us with the temporal degradation of the results. Look at yourselves. Look at your own results. You are always talking about republican degradation. But isn't the degradation of a *mystique* into a *politique* the common law? You talk of the decay of the Republic, that is to say of the collapse of the republican *mystique* into a republican *politique*. Have there not been, are there not other degradations? Everything begins as a *mystique* and ends as a *politique*. Everything begins with *la mystique*, in mysticism, with its own *mystique*, and everything ends in politics, in *la politique*, in a policy. The important point is not that such and such a *politique* should triumph over another such, and that one should succeed. The whole point (what matters), the essential thing, is that *in each order*, *in each system*, THE *MYSTIQUE* SHOULD NOT BE DEVOURED BY THE *POLITIQUE* TO WHICH IT GAVE BIRTH.'

People are always talking of the degradation of republicanism. When one sees what the clerical *politique* has made of the Christian *mystique*, why be astonished at what the radical policy has made of the republican *mystique*? When one sees what the clerks have, in general, made of the saints, why be surprised at what our parliamentarians have made of heroes? When one sees what the reactionaries have, by and large, made of sanctity, why be astonished at what the revolutionaries have made of heroism?

TRANSLATED BY A. DRU

The Dreyfus Affair

(from 'Notre Jeunesse')

The Dreyfus affair was Péguy's chosen event, his entry into political life. Few people since have explained its significance in the same depth. Here, he is trying to demonstrate that his dreyfusism was not opposed to either Christian or republican mystique. *On the contrary: it could well be, though it need not be the case, that Péguy is Christianizing his dreyfusism, although at the time he was a self-proclaimed atheist.*

There was a singular virtue in the Affair, perhaps an eternal virtue. I mean a singular power. And we can see this clearly today now that it is all over. It was not an illusion of our youth. First of all, it should be noted that it possessed a very singular virtue. In two senses. A singular power of virtue, as long as it remained a *mystique*. A singular power of malice as soon as it entered the field of politics.

One should say, with all due solemnity, that the Dreyfus Affair was a crisis in three histories, each of them outstanding. It was a crisis in the history of Israel. A crisis, obviously, in the history of France. And above all, it was a supreme crisis, as appears more and more distinctly, in the history of Christianity. And perhaps in several others. And thus, by a unique election, it was a triple crisis. Of triple eminence. A culmination. As for me, if I am able to continue the studies which we have begun on the situation accorded to history and to sociology in the general philosophy of the modern world, following the method we always observe, of never writing anything except what we have experienced ourselves, we shall certainly take that great crisis as an example of what a crisis is, an event with its own, eminent, price.

There is no doubt whatsoever, as far as we are concerned, the Dreyfusist *mystique* was not only a particular instance of the Christian *mystique*, but an outstanding example, an acceleration, a crisis, a temporal crisis, a sort of transition, which I should describe as necessary. Why deny it, now that we are twelve or fifteen years distant from our youth, and that we at last see clear in our hearts? Our Dreyfusism was a religion; I use the word in the most exact and literal sense, a religious impulse, a religious crisis, and I should even advise anyone who wanted to consider, study and know a religious movement in modern times, to take that unique example, so clearly defined, so full of character. I would add that for us, that religious movement was essentially Christian, Christian in origin, growing from a Christian stem, deriving from an ancient source. To that we can now bear witness. The Justice and the Truth which we have loved so much, to which we gave everything, our youth, to which we gave ourselves completely during the whole of our youth, were not an abstract, conceptual Justice and Truth, they were not a dead justice and a dead truth, the justice and truth found in books and libraries, a notional, intellectual justice and truth, the justice and truth of the intellectual party; they were organic, Christian, in no sense modern, they were eternal and not temporal only, they were Justice and Truth, a living Justice and a living Truth. And of all the feelings which impelled us, in fear and trembling, into that unique crisis, we can now admit that of all the passions that drove us into that seething, boiling tumult, into that furnace, there was at the heart of them one virtue, and that virtue was charity. And I do not want to re-open an old quarrel, an argument that has become historical, historic; nevertheless, among our enemies, our enemies of those days, I can see a great deal of intelligence, a great deal of lucidity and even much shrewdness and sharpness, but what strikes me most is certainly a certain lack of charity.

What may have deceived people is that all the political forces of the Church were against Dreyfusism. But the political forces of the Church have always been against its *mystique*. Particularly against the Christian *mystique*. That is the supreme illustration of the general rule laid down above.

One might even say that the Dreyfus Affair was a *perfect example* of a religious movement, of the beginning or origin of a religion, a rare case and perhaps a unique one.

In fact, the Dreyfusist *mystique* was, for us, essentially a crisis in the French *mystique*. For us, and through us, the Affair was very definitely in the direct French line. Just as for us and through us, it was in the Christian line. We ourselves were situated very exactly in the French line, just as we had been in the Christian line. We were in it in our character as Frenchmen, just as we were in it in our character as Christians.

We deployed the French virtues, the French qualities, the virtues of the race: a lucid courage, speed, good humour, firmness, constancy and an obstinate courage, but of a decent, well-behaved kind: fanatical, and at the same time measured; passionate but full of sense; a cheerful sadness typical of the French; a deliberate purpose; a resolution at once cold and heated; a constant freedom and intelligence; docility in face of the event and at the same time a perpetual revolt against it; an organic incapacity to consent to injustice. A supple, subtle blade. The point well sharpened. More simply, we were heroes. More precisely, French heroes.

We were heroes. One must say it quite simply, for I really do not think anyone will say it for us. And here, very exactly, is how and why we were heroes. In the world in which we moved, where we were completing our years of apprenticeship, in all the circles in which we moved and worked, the question which was asked, during those two or three years of the rising curve, was never whether Dreyfus was *in reality* innocent (or guilty). The question was whether one could have the courage to recognize and to declare his innocence. To proclaim his innocence. Whether one had the double courage. First of all, the first courage, the outward, crude courage, difficult enough in itself, the social courage to proclaim him innocent publicly, to testify publicly to him. To bet on it, to risk everything, to *put* everything one had on him, all one's miserable gains, the little man's money, the money of the poor; to put time, life and career on him; health, the heartbreak of family feuds, the quarrels with one's nearest friends, the averted gaze, the silent or violent reprobation; the isolation, the quarantine; friendships of twenty years' standing broken, which meant, for us, friendships that had always been. The whole of social life. One's whole life in fact, everything. Secondly, the second courage, more difficult still, the inward courage, the secret courage, to admit to oneself in oneself that he was innocent. To give up one's peace of mind for the sake of that man.

Not only the peace of the city, the peace of one's home. The peace of one's family and household. But the peace of one's heart.

To the supreme good, the only good.

The courage to enter the kingdom of an incurable unrest for the sake of this man.

And of a bitterness that would never be cured.

Our adversaries will never know, they could not know what we have sacrificed for him, or how that sacrifice came from the heart. We sacrificed our whole life to him, for that affair marked us for life. Our enemies will never know how few we were, we who overturned and changed the country, they will never guess the conditions in which we were fighting, what precarious, miserable, ungrateful conditions we were in. And in consequence the extent to which, in order to win, since after all we did win, we had to deploy and reveal and rediscover in ourselves, in our race, the oldest and most precious qualities of the race. The very technique of heroism, and notably of military heroism. One must not boggle over words. The *discipline* of the *anarchists*, for example, was admirable. It cannot have escaped the notice of any perceptive onlooker that the military virtues were on our side. In us, and not in the General Staff of the Army. We were, once more, that handful of Frenchmen under a crushing fire, breaking through sheer masses, carrying the assault, carrying the position.

Not only were we heroes, but the Dreyfus Affair can only be explained by the need for heroism which periodically seizes this people, this race, by that need for heroism which then seizes a whole generation of us. The same is true of these great movements, these great ordeals, as of those other great ordeals, wars. Or rather there is only one sort of temporal ordeal for a people, and that is war and those other great ordeals are, in fact, wars. In all those ordeals it is the inward force, the violence of the eruption which constitutes the thing, the historical matter, rather than the matter which constitutes and imposes the ordeal. When a great war or a great revolution breaks out, it is because a great people, a great race, needs to break out; because it has had enough, particularly enough peace. It always means that a great mass feels and experiences a violent need, a mysterious need for a great movement . . . . A mysterious need for a sort of historical fecundity. The mysterious need to inscribe great events and historic events in eternal history.

In reality, the true position of those opposed to us was not of saying or thinking Dreyfus guilty, but of thinking and saying that whether he was innocent or guilty, one did not disturb, overthrow, or compromise, that one did not risk, for one man's sake, the life and salvation of a whole people. Meaning of course: the *temporal* salvation, *salut temporel*. Now our Christian *mystique* was merged so perfectly, so exactly with our patriotic *mystique*, that what must be recognized, and what I shall say, what I shall put into my confessions, is that *the point of view we adopted was none other than The Eternal Salvation of France*. What, in fact, did we say? Everything was against us, wisdom and law, human wisdom that is, and human law. What we did was in the order of madness and the order of sanctity, which have so many things in common, so many secret understandings, with human wisdom and the human eye. We went against wisdom, against the law. That is what I mean. What did we say in effect? The others said: 'A people, a whole people is a great assemblage of interests, of the most legitimate rights. The most sacred rights. Thousands, millions of lives depend upon them, in the present, in the past, in the future, hundreds of millions of lives. Rights that are legitimate, sacred and incalculable.

'And the first duty of a people is not to risk the whole thing, not to endanger itself for the sake of one man, whoever he may be, however legitimate his interests and his rights. One does not sacrifice a city, a city is not lost, for one citizen. That was the language of wisdom and civic duty, of ancient wisdom. It was the language of reason. From that point of view it was clear that Dreyfus had to devote himself to France: not only for the peace of France, but for the safety and salvation of France, which we endangered. And if he would not sacrifice himself it would, if need be, be done for him.' And we, what did we say? We said that a single injustice, a single crime, a single illegality, particularly if it were officially confirmed, particularly if it were universally, legally, nationally condoned, a single crime is enough to make a breach in the social compact, in the social contract, a single forfeit, a single dishonour is enough to dishonour a people. It becomes a source of infection, a poison that corrupts the whole body. What we defend is not only our honour. Not only the honour of a whole people, in the present, but the historical honour of our whole race, the honour of our forefathers and children. And the more past we have, the more memory (the more, as you say, responsibility we have), then the more we have to defend. The more past there is behind us, the more we must defend it. *'Je rendrai mon sang pur comme je l'ai reçu.'* That was the Cornelian impulse, the old Cornelian rule of honour. And the rule and the honour and the impulse of Christianity. A single stain stains a whole family. And a whole people. A people cannot rest on an injury suffered, on a crime as solemnly and definitely accepted. The honour of a people is all of a piece.

What does all this mean, unless one doesn't know a word of French, except that our adversaries were speaking the language of the *raison d'état*, which is not only the language of political and parliamentary reason, of contemptible political and parliamentary interests, but the very respectable language of continuity, of the temporal continuity of the race, *of the temporal salvation of the people and the race?* They aimed at nothing less. And we, by a profoundly Christian movement, a profoundly revolutionary and traditionally Christian impulse and effort, following one of the deepest Christian traditions, one of the most vital and central, and in line with the axis of Christianity, at its very heart, we aimed at no less than raising ourselves, I do not say to the conception, but to the passion, to the care of the eternal salvation, *le salut éternel*, of this people; we achieved an existence full of care and preoccupation, full of mortal anguish and anxiety for the eternal salvation of our race. Deep down within us we were the men of eternal salvation, and our adversaries were the men of temporal salvation. That was the real division in the Dreyfus Affair. Deep down within us we were determined that France should not fall into a state of mortal sin. Christian doctrine, alone in the whole world, in the modern world, in any world, deliberately counts death at nought, at zero, in terms of the price of eternal death, and the risk of temporal death as nothing compared with the price of sin, mortal sin, eternal death.

TRANSLATED BY A. DRU

THE THREAT OF WAR: PATCHES OF FREEDOM

An extract from the first sequel to 'Notre Patrie', written in 1905 and published for the first time in July 1939 in the Nouvelle Revue Française. *It was subsequently published in 'Par ce demi-clair matin'* (1952). *Péguy's 'nationalism' was not confined to France.*

The free and cultured peoples, the liberal and liberty-loving nations, that is, the peoples who have some culture . . . how little culture, how little liberty I know as well as anyone else, but who have at least a little culture, a little freedom . . . France, England, Italy (the north), some parts of America, some bits of Belgium and of Switzerland . . . on the map of the world they occupy a small space, a few patches, they are miserably precarious, narrow in width and restricted in depth, a thin fragile skin . . . This free humanity, more or less free, this small part, the only part, which has some degree of liberty, this little fragment which floats, but which, rocking as it does, could founder, is the world's only hope . . . these patches of culture and of freedom, which some parts of humanity have painfully acquired and conquered, are incessantly threatened by the enormous waves of barbarism. Barbarism arising almost everywhere, arising in almost all the other peoples, and in these peoples too, in these chosen people, these people chosen by some kind of self-election; dumb barbarism rising out of these very peoples and only asking to sink the flotsam and the monuments of culture . . . We are the heirs and administrators accountable and responsible for an estate that is continually threatened.

TRANSLATED BY MARJORIE VILLIERS

ON HABIT AND GRACE

(from 'La Note conjointe', 1914)

For Péguy, the relationship between sin and grace was a close one.

The worst distresses . . . weaknesses, turpitudes, crimes, sins even, are often so many cracks in the armour . . . through which grace can reach man. It is only against the inorganic cuirass of habit that all blades break . . . Great criminals have been saved by . . . the articulation of their crimes [but] one has never seen the deeply habit-ridden soul saved by the articulation of habit, because in habit there is no articulation . . . No amount of water will go through a stuff which has been made waterproof; it is not a question of quantity but of contact . . . There is no point of entry for the liquid.

Not all souls are penetrable . . . This explains the astonishing victories of grace in the souls of great sinners and the impotence of grace in the souls of decent people, the most decent people, those who have no cracks in their armour. Those who are never wounded, whose moral skin is intact and makes a faultless leather jerkin. At no point do they offer grace the opening of an appalling wound, an unforgettable distress, an invisible regret, *un point de suture éternellement mal-joint*, a mortal anxiety . . . a wound eternally unhealed. They do not offer grace that door of entry which sin leaves open . . . even God's charity cannot succour those who are unwounded.

TRANSLATED BY MARJORIE VILLIERS

SOCIALISM, THE CHURCH AND THE MODERN WORLD

(from 'Notre Jeunesse')

Our Socialism – was not in the least anti-French, not in the least antipatriotic, not in the least *anti*national. It was essentially and strictly, exactly *inter*national. Theoretically it was not in the least antinationalistic. It was exactly internationalistic. Far from reducing, far from obliterating the people, it on the contrary exalted and purified it. Far from weakening or reducing, far from obliterating the nation, it on the contrary exalted and purified it. Our theory, on the contrary, was, and still is, that contrarily, what obliterates the nation and the people is the bourgeoisie, bourgeois-ism, bourgeois capitalism, capitalistic and bourgeois sabotage. One must indeed think that there was nothing in common between the socialism of those days, our socialism, and that which we know today under that name. Here again, politics have done their work, and nowhere as much as in this case have politics undone, denatured mysticism.

For the philosopher, for every man who philosophizes, our socialism was, and was no less than a religion of temporal salvation. And even today, it is no less than this. We sought for no less than the temporal salvation of humanity by the purification of the working world, by the purification of work and of the world of work, by the restoration of work and of the dignity of work, by a purification, by an organic molecular repair of the working world, and through it of the whole economic, industrial world. – By the restoration of industrial morality, by the purification of the industrial workroom, we hoped for no less, we sought no less than the temporal salvation of humanity. Only those will laugh who do not wish to realize that Christianity itself, which is the religion of eternal salvation, is stuck in this mire, in the mire of rotten economic, industrial morality; those who do not wish to realize that Christianity itself will not emerge from it, will not be drawn out of it, save through an economic, industrial revolution; and lastly that there is no place of perdition better made, better ordered, and better provided with tools, so to speak; that there is no more fitting tool of perdition than the modern work-room.

All the difficulties of the Church come from this, all her real, deep difficulties, all the difficulties with the people come from the fact that in spite of a few so-called charities for workmen, under the cloak of a few so-called charities for workmen and of a few so-called Catholic workmen, the work-room is closed to the Church and that she is closed to the work-room. Because she too, undergoing a modernization, has become in the modern world, almost entirely the religion of the rich; and thus, if I may say so, she is no longer socially the communion of the faithful. All the weakness, and perhaps one should say the growing weakness of the Church in the modern world, comes from the fact that what remains today of the Christian world socially, is profoundly lacking in charity. It, this same weakness of the Church, does not come – as people think – from the fact that Science has established so-called invincible systems, that Science has discovered, has found arguments and supposedly victorious reasonings against Religion. Arguments are not in the least lacking. It is charity that is lacking. All these reasonings, all these systems, all the pseudo-scientific arguments would be as nothing, would be of little weight, if there were an ounce of charity. All these intellectual attitudes would have short shrift if Christianity had remained what it was, a communion, if Christianity had remained what it was, a religion of the heart. This is one of the reasons why modern people understand nothing of true, real Christianity, of the true, real history of Christianity and what Christendom really was.

The Church is nothing of what she was and she has become all that is most contrary to herself, all that is most contrary to her institution. And she will not reopen the door of the work-room and she will not be open once more to the people, unless she too, she like the rest of the world, unless she too pays the price of an economic revolution – a social revolution, an industrial revolution, in short, a temporal revolution for eternal salvation. Such is, eternally, temporally, the mysterious subjection of the eternal itself to the temporal. Such is properly the inscription of the eternal itself in the temporal. Economic expenses, social expenses, industrial expenses, temporal expenses must be met. Nothing can evade it, not even the eternal, not even the spiritual, not even the inner life.

TRANSLATED BY ANN AND JULIAN GREEN

The Value of a Parcel of Earth

(from *A nos amis, à nos abonnés,* 1909)

Our antipatriots will experience in the carnal and even in the mystical temporal system, in any temporal system, that a body, a temporal flesh is needed as a material support, to become the support, the matter of an idea. This, precisely in the very political and social order, in the historical order, is the problem of relations between body and spirit. As, in natural creation we naturally do not know spirit without bodily support (as a rule, there is no memory not supported by some matter), we do not know spirit which is not, to a certain extent, incorporate and incarnate (and this, in fact, is possibly the only rather serious definition which can be given of natural creation). Again, we naturally cannot conceive of an idea, pertaining to the political or social spirit, I would even dare to say the religious spirit – which has been able to appear without a certain *corpus* – without a prop or stay, without a mechanism, without the support of a people, without matter – in a word, without fatherland. The philosopher had to have the Greek city. The prophet had to have the race and people of Israel. The saint had to have the Christian people and certain Occidental peoples, at least to make a start . . . Our positivists will learn metaphysics as our pacifists will learn war. Our positivists will learn metaphysics by the firing of rifles. And that mutually, for I mean firing and being fired at. They will learn even psychology. They will learn the relation between a people's body and a people's spirit. Our antimilitarists will learn war and they will wage it very well. Our antipatriots will learn the price of a carnal fatherland, of a city, of a race, of a communion – be it a communion of the flesh – and, to support a revolution, the value of a parcel of earth.

Translated by Ann and Julian Green

Joan's Lament

(Extract from *Le Mystère de la Charité de Jeanne d'Arc*)

After having recited the traditional Our Father, Joan takes up some salient points to express her despair at the continued existence of evil, to the point of questioning the purpose of the Crucifixion. These sombre reflections, the darkest of his Christian poetry, mark, paradoxically, Péguy's public proclamation of his return to faith.

Notre Père, notre Père qui êtes aux cieux, de combien il s'en faut que votre nom soit sanctifié; de combien il s'en faut que votre règne arrive.

Notre Père, notre Père qui êtes aux cieux, de combien il s'en faut que votre volonté soit faite; de combien il s'en faut que nous ayons notre pain de chaque jour.

De combien il s'en faut que nous pardonnions nos offenses; et que nous ne succombions pas à la tentation; et que nous soyons délivrés du mal. Ainsi soit-il.

Ô mon Dieu si on voyait seulement le commencement de votre règne. Si on voyait seulement se lever le soleil de votre règne. Mais rien, jamais rien. Vous nous avez envoyé votre Fils, que vous aimiez tant, votre Fils est venu, et il est mort, et rien, jamais rien. Quatorze siècles, quatorze siècles de chrétienté ont passé depuis le rachat de nos âmes, et rien ne coule sur la face de la terre, qu'un flot d'ingratitude et de perdition.

On dirait, mon Dieu, pardonnez-moi, on dirait que votre règne s'en va. Jamais on n'a tant blasphémé votre nom. Jamais on n'a tant méprisé votre volonté. Jamais on n'a tant désobéi. Jamais notre pain ne nous a tant manqué; et s'il n'y avait que le pain du corps qui nous manquait, le

Our Father, our Father which art in heaven, how long must it be before your name is 'hallowed', how long before your kingdom does come.

Our Father, our Father which art in heaven, how long before your will is done; how long before we do have our daily bread.

How long before we forgive the trespasses against us; and are not led into temptation; and are delivered from evil. Amen.

O my Lord, if only we could see the coming of your kingdom. If only we could see the sun start to come up on your kingdom. But there isn't anything, there's never anything. You sent us your Son, that you loved so much, your Son came, and he died and there isn't anything; there's never anything. Fourteen centuries of Christendom have gone by since he bought back our souls for us, and nothing flows across the earth, only ingratitude, a wave that sweeps souls away.

Anybody would say, Lord, forgive me, anybody would say that your kingdom is gone for good. Never has there been so much blasphemy of your name. Never has there been so much sneering at your will. Never has there been so much disobeying. Never have we lacked for bread pain de maïs, le pain de seigle et de blé; mais un autre pain nous manque; le pain de la nourriture de nos âmes; et nous sommes affamés d'une autre faim; de la seule faim qui laisse dans le ventre un creux impérissable.

so much; and lacked not only that bread for the body, corn, rye, wheat, but lacked as well another sort of bread; the bread that feeds souls; and we are hungry with a different hunger; with the only hunger that leaves the stomach scooped out for ever.

Jamais il n'a été fait tant d'offenses; et jamais tant d'offenses ne sont mortes impardonnées. Jamais le chrétien n'a fait tant d'offenses au chrétien, et jamais à vous, mon Dieu, jamais l'homme ne vous a fait tant d'offenses. Et jamais tant d'offenses n'est morte impardonnée. Sera-t-il dit que vous nous aurez envoyé en vain votre fils?

Never has your creature trespassed so much; and never have so many trespasses gone unpardoned into death. Never have Christians trespassed so much against Christians, and never so much against you, Lord, never have people trespassed so much against you. And never have so many trespasses gone unforgiven into death. Will they say that you sent your Son in vain?

Mon Dieu, délivrez-nous du mal, délivrez-nous du mal. Nous sommes des bons chrétiens, vous savez que nous sommes des bons chrétiens. Alors comment que ça se fait que tant de bons chrétiens ne fassent pas une bonne chrétienté.

Il y a des saintes, il y a de la sainteté, et jamais le règne du royaume de la perdition n'avait autant dominé sur la face de la terre. Il nous faudrait peut-être quelque chose de nouveau, quelque chose qu'on n'aurait encore jamais vu. Mais qui oserait dire qu'il puisse encore y avoir du nouveau après quatorze siècles de chrétienté.

My Lord, deliver us from evil, deliver us from evil. We are good Christians, you know we are good Christians. Then how is it that so many good Christians don't make Christendom good?

There are saints, there is saintliness, yet never has the rule of that kingdom which steals away souls lorded it so much over the face of the earth. Perhaps we need something new, something never seen yet. But who is there will dare say there could be something new in Christendom after fourteen centuries.

ADAPTED BY JEAN-PAUL LUCET

TRANSLATED BY JEFFREY WAINWRIGHT

ON FREEDOM

(from 'Réponse brève à Jaurès', 1900)

Free art – a reply to Jaurès who had spoken of 'socialist art'.

It would be dangerous if we let it be believed that we have a socialist conception of art. We have a human conception of art. The social revolution will bring about the liberation of art. It will give us a free art, but not a socialist art . . . We demand that scholars and artists, as scholars and artists, should be in the city, should be independent from the city. We demand that science, art and philosophy be left unsocialized, just because the socialization of the major means of production and exchange, or rather of the labour indispensable to guarantee the bodily life of the city, will have given to that city the leisure and the space not to have to socialize what does not appertain to it, but appertains to mankind itself.

TRANSLATED BY PIERRE MANENT

Golgotha Witnessed by Mary

(extract from *Le Mystère de la Charité de Jeanne d'Arc*)

This is the first of many depictions of Golgotha and of the Passion. Here it is seen as part of Mary's experience and grief, that of any mother who not only sees her son put to death but does not understand the reason. A moving and realistically portrayed Mater Dolorosa *who is also a peasant woman.*

Technically, it is Péguy's first and highly successful attempt at the flowing vers libre.

Depuis trois jours elle errait, elle suivait.
Elle suivait le cortège.
Elle suivait les évènements.
Elle suivait comme à un enterrement.
Elle suivait comme une suivante.
Comme une servante.

Comme une pleureuse des Romains.
Des enterrements romains.
Comme si ça avait été son métier.
De pleurer.
Elle suivait comme une pauvre femme.
Déjà comme une habituée.
Elle suivait comme une pauvresse.
Comme une mendiante.
Eux qui n'avaient jamais rien demandé à personne.
A présent elle demandait la charité.
Sans en avoir l'air, sans même le savoir elle demandait la charité de la pitié.

Elle suivait. Elle pleurait.
Les femmes ne savent que pleurer.
On la voyait partout.
Dans le cortège mais un peu en dehors du cortège.
Sous les portiques, sous les arcades.
Dans les rues.
Dans les cours et les arrière-cours.
Et elle était montée aussi sur le Calvaire.
Elle aussi elle avait gravi le Calvaire.
Elle aussi elle avait monté, monté.
Dans la cohue, un peu en arrière.
Monté au Golgotha.
Sur le Golgotha.
Sur le faîte.
Jusqu'au faîte.
Où il était maintenant crucifié.
Cloué des quatre membres.
Comme un oiseau de nuit sur la porte d'une grange.
Lui le Roi de Lumière.
Au lieu appelé Golgotha.
C'est-à-dire la place du Crâne.

Ce qu'il y a de curieux c'est que tout le monde la respectait.
Les gens respectent beaucoup les parents des condamnés.

For three days she wandered about, she followed.
She followed the procession.
She followed the events.
She followed as at a funeral.
She followed like an attendant.
Like a servant.

Like a weeper hired by the Romans.
For Roman funerals.
As if that were her trade.
To weep.
She followed like a poor woman.
Already like one who is used to it.
She followed like a pauper.
Like a beggar.
One of those who had never asked anything of anybody.
Now she was asking for charity.
Without seeming to, without even knowing it, she was asking for the charity of pity.

She followed. She wept.
Women know nothing but weeping.
That could be seen everywhere then.
In the procession, but a bit outside the procession.
Under porches, under arcades.
In the streets.
In courtyards and backyards.
As she climbed Calvary as well.
She also scaled Calvary.
She also climbed, climbed.
Among the crowd, a bit to the back.
Climbed to Golgotha.
To the top of Golgotha.
To its top ridge.
Right to the very top.
Where now he was crucified.
Nailed by his four limbs.
Like an owl on a barn door.
The King of Light.
In that place called Golgotha.
The place of the Skull.

What is so curious is that everybody respected her.
People have a lot of respect for the parents of the condemned.

Elle suivait, elle pleurait, elle ne comprenait pas très bien.
Mais elle comprenait très bien que le gouvernement était contre son garçon.
Ce qui est une mauvaise affaire.
Que le gouvernement était pour le mettre à mort.
Toujours une mauvaise affaire.
Et qui ne pouvait pas bien finir.

*

Non seulement elle pleurait pour aujourd'hui et pour demain.
Et pour toute sa vie à venir.
Mais elle pleurait aussi pour son passé.
Pour les jours où elle avait été heureuse dans son passé.
L'innocente.
Pour effacer ses jours de bonheur.
Ses anciens jours de bonheur.
Parce que ces jours l'avaient trompée, ces jours l'avaient trahie.
Ces jours où elle aurait dû pleurer d'avance.
Par provision.
Il faudrait toujours pleurer par provision.
En avance des jours à venir.
Des malheurs à venir.

Elle aurait dû prendre ses précautions.
Prévoir.
Il faudrait toujours prendre ses précautions.

Si elle avait su.

ADAPTED BY JEAN-PAUL LUCET

She followed, she wept, she didn't understand it all very well.
But she understood very well that the government was against her boy.
Which is a bad business.
That the government was for putting him to death.
Always a bad business.
And one which could not come to a good end.

*

Not only did she weep for today and tomorrow.
And for all her life to come.
But she wept also for her past.
For the days when she had been happy in the past.
A simple woman.
She wept to rub out her days of happiness.
Her old days of happiness.
Because those days had tricked her, those days had betrayed her.
Those days when she ought to have been weeping ahead.
Making some provision.
It's always as well to do some weeping in advance.
To provide for what's to come.
Any misery to come.

She should have put something by.
Looked to the future.
You should always put something by.

If she had known.

TRANSLATED BY JEFFREY WAINWRIGHT

La Liberté de l'homme

The Liberty of Man

(from *Le Mystère des Saints Innocents*)

God's conception of freedom for man excludes the kind of determinism or predestination which was anathema to Péguy. It lays stress on man's freedom of choice; without it, God feels belittled. 'Choice and belief' formed Péguy's spiritual motto.

Dieu parle

Telle est la difficulté, elle est grande.
Et telle la duplicité même, la double face du problème.

D'une part il faut qu'ils fassent leur salut eux-mêmes.
C'est la règle.
Et elle est formelle. Autrement ce ne serait pas intéressant. Ils ne seraient pas des hommes.
Or je veux qu'ils soient virils, qu'ils soient des hommes et qu'ils gagnent eux-mêmes
Leurs éperons de chevaliers.
D'autre part il ne faut pas qu'ils boivent un mauvais coup
Ayant fait un plongeon dans l'ingratitude du péché.
Tel est le mystère de la liberté de l'homme, dit Dieu,
Et de mon gouvernement envers lui et envers sa liberté.
Si je le soutiens trop, il n'est plus libre
Et si je ne le soutiens pas assez, j'expose son salut:
Deux biens en un sens presque également précieux.
Car ce salut a un prix infini.

Mais qu'est-ce qu'un salut qui ne serait pas libre
Comment serait-il qualifié.
Nous voulons que ce salut soit acquis par lui-même.
Par lui-même l'homme. Soit procuré par lui-même.
Vienne en un sens de lui-même. Tel est le secret,
Tel est le mystère de la liberté de l'homme.
Tel est le prix que nous mettons à la liberté de l'homme:
Parce que moi-même je suis libre, dit Dieu, et que j'ai créé l'homme à mon image et à ma ressemblance.

Tel est le mystère, tel est le secret, tel est le prix
De toute liberté.
Cette liberté de cette créature est le plus beau reflet qu'il y ait dans le monde
De la Liberté du Créateur. C'est pour cela que nous y attachons,
Que nous y mettons un prix propre.
Un salut qui ne serait pas libre, qui ne serait pas, qui ne viendrait pas d'un homme libre ne nous dirait plus rien. Qu'est-ce que ce serait.
Qu'est-ce que ça voudrait dire.
Quel intérêt un tel salut présenterait-il.
Une béatitude d'esclaves, un salut d'esclaves, une béatitude serve, en quoi voulez-vous que ça m'intéresse. Aime-t-on à être aimé par des esclaves.

God speaks

Such is the difficulty, it is great.
And such the very duplicity, the double face of the problem.
On the one hand they must achieve salvation themselves.
That is the rule
And it is strict. Otherwise it would not be interesting.
They would not be men.
Well, I want them to be virile, to be men and to win
Their spurs of knighthood themselves.
On the other hand they must not be allowed to swallow a nasty mouthful
Having dived into the thanklessness of sin.
This is the mystery of the liberty of man, God says,
And of my management of him and of his liberty.
If I support him too much, I endanger his liberty
If I do not support him enough, I endanger his salvation:
Two goods, in a sense, almost equally precious.
For this salvation has an infinite price.

But what would salvation be if it were not free.
How could it be described.
We want him to gain this salvation by himself.
By himself, by man. Procured by himself.
That it should come, in a sense, from himself. Such is the secret,
Such is the mystery of the liberty of man:
Such is the price we put on the liberty of man.
Because I, myself, am free, God says, and because I have created man in my image and in my likeness.
Such is the mystery, such is the secret, such is the price
Of all liberty.
This liberty of the creature is the most beautiful reflection that exists in the world
Of the Liberty of the Creator. That is why we attach to it,

That we put on it a proper price.
A salvation which was not free, which was not, which did not come from a free man would mean nothing to us.
What would it be.
What would it mean.
What interest could be found in such a salvation.
A beatitude of slaves, a salvation for slaves, a servile beatitude, how do you expect that to interest me.
Does one love to be loved by slaves.

Translated by Pansy Pakenham

LA NUIT

NIGHT

(from *Le Porche du mystère de la deuxième vertu*)

Together with the hymn to Sleep, the celebration of Night is regarded as one of Péguy's finest poems, one of those in which he says what has never been said before. Night not only means renewal for man but also for God, who recalls the anguished Night of His Son's death and the peace of the following night.

Dieu parle

Ô nuit, ô ma fille la Nuit, toi qui sais te taire, ô ma fille au beau manteau.
Toi qui verses le repos et l'oubli. Toi qui verses le baume, et le silence, et l'ombre
Ô ma Nuit étoilée je t'ai créée la première.
Toi qui endors, toi qui ensevelis déjà dans une Ombre éternelle
Toutes mes créatures
Les plus inquiètes, le cheval fougueux, la fourmi laborieuse,
Et l'homme ce monstre d'inquiétude.
Nuit qui réussis à endormir l'homme
Ce puits d'inquiétude.
A lui seul plus inquiet que toute la création ensemble.
L'homme, ce puits d'inquiétude.
Comme tu endors l'eau du puits.
Ô ma nuit à la grande robe
Qui prends les enfants et la jeune Espérance
Dans le pli de ta robe
Mais les hommes ne se laissent pas faire.
Ô ma belle nuit je t'ai créée la première.
Et presque avant la première
Silencieuse aux longs voiles
Toi par qui descend sur terre un avant goût
Toi qui répands de tes mains, toi qui verses sur terre
Une première paix
Avant-coureur de la paix éternelle.
Un premier repos
Avant-coureur du repos éternel.
Un premier baume, si frais, une première béatitude
Avant-coureur de la béatitude éternelle.
Toi qui apaises, toi qui embaumes, toi qui consoles
Toi qui bandes les blessures et les membres meurtris.
Toi qui endors les coeurs, toi qui endors les corps
Les coeurs endoloris, les corps endoloris,
Courbaturés,
Les membres rompus, les reins brisés

De fatigue, de soucis, des inquiétudes
Mortelles,
Des peines,
Toi qui verses le baume aux gorges déchirées d'amertume
Si frais
Ô ma fille au grand coeur je t'ai créée la première
Presque avant la première, ma fille au sein immense

God speaks

O night, o my daughter Night, you who know how to hold your peace, o my daughter of the beautiful mantle,
You who shed rest and oblivion, you who shed balm, and silence, and darkness,
O my starry Night, I created you first.
You who put to sleep, you who, already, in an eternal Darkness bury
All my creatures,
The most restless, the spirited horse, the hard-working ant,
And man, that monster of restlessness,
Night, you who succeed in putting to sleep man,
That well of restlessness,
More restless in himself than all creation put together,
Man, that well of restlessness,
Just as you put to sleep the water in the well.
O my night of the long robe,
You who gather children and young Hope
In the folds of your robe,
But men won't allow themselves to be treated thus.
O my beautiful night, I created you first,
And almost before that,
Silent one of the long veils,
You by whom there comes down on earth a foretaste,
You who spread with your hands, you who shed on earth
A first peace,
Forerunner of eternal peace,
A first rest,
Forerunner of eternal rest,
A first balm, so cool, a first beatitude,
Forerunner of eternal beatitude,
You who soothe, you who smell sweet, you who comfort,
You who dress wounds and bruised limbs,
You who put hearts to sleep, you who put bodies to sleep,
Aching hearts, aching bodies,
Bodies all stiff.
Limbs overwhelmed with fatigue, backs broken with weariness,
With tiredness, with cares, with restlessness,
Mortal restlessness,
With troubles,
You who shed balm on throats rent by bitterness,
Such a cool balm,
O my daughter of the great heart, I created you first,
Almost before the first, my daughter of the limitless bosom,

Et je savais bien ce que je faisais.
Je savais peut-être ce que je faisais.
Toi qui couches l'enfant au bras de sa mère
L'enfant tout éclairé d'une ombre de sommeil
Tout riant en dedans, tout riant secret d'une confiance en sa mère.
Et en moi,
Tout riant secret d'un pli des lèvres sérieux
Toi qui couches l'enfant tout en dedans gonflé, débordant d'innocence
Et de confiance
Au bras de sa mère.
Toi qui couchais l'enfant Jésus tous les soirs
Au bras de la Très Sainte et de l'Immaculée.
Toi qui es la soeur tourière de l'espérance.
Ô ma fille entre toutes première. Toi qui réussis même,

Toi qui réussis quelquefois
Toi qui couches l'homme au bras de ma Providence
Maternelle
Ô ma fille *étincelante et sombre* je te salue
Toi qui répares, toi qui nourris, toi qui reposes
Ô silence de l'ombre
Un tel silence régnait avant la création de l'inquiétude.
Avant le commencement du règne de l'inquiétude.
Un tel silence régnera, mais un silence de lumière
Quand toute cette inquiétude sera consommée,
Quand toute cette inquiétude sera épuisée.
Quand ils auront tiré toute l'eau du puits.
Après la consommation, après l'épuisement de toute cette inquiétude
D'homme.
Ainsi ma fille tu es ancienne et tu es en retard
Car dans ce règne d'inquiétude tu rappelles, tu commémores, tu rétablis presque,
Tu fais presque recommencer la Quiétude antérieure
Quand mon esprit planait sur les eaux.
Mais aussi ma fille étoilée, ma fille au manteau sombre, tu es très en avance, tu es très précoce.
Car tu annonces, car tu représentes, car tu fais presque commencer d'avance tous les soirs
Ma grande Quiétude de lumière
Éternelle.
Nuit tu es sainte, Nuit tu es grande, Nuit tu es belle.

Nuit au grand manteau.
Nuit je t'aime et je te salue et je te glorifie et tu es ma grande fille et ma créature.
Ô belle nuit, nuit au grand manteau, ma fille au manteau étoilé
Tu me rappelles, à moi-même tu me rappelles ce grand silence qu'il y avait
Avant que j'eusse ouvert les écluses d'ingratitude.
Et tu m'annonces, à moi-même tu m'annonces ce grand silence qu'il y aura
Quand je les aurai fermées.
Ô douce, ô grande, ô sainte, ô belle nuit, peut-être la plus

And well I knew what I was doing,
Perchance I knew what I was about;
You who lay the child in his mother's arms,
The child suffused with light by a shadow of sleep,
All laughter within himself, secretly laughing because of his confidence in his mother
And in me,
Secretly laughing with a serious pucker of his lips,
You who lay the child that is replete and overflowing with innocence
And confidence,
In his mother's arms.
You who lay the child Jesus every evening
In the arms of the Very Holy and Immaculate one,
You who are the portress of Hope,
O my daughter, first among all, you who succeed even, in this,
You who sometimes succeed, in this,
You who lay man in the arms of my Providence,
My maternal Providence,
O my *dark and gleaming* daughter, I greet you,
You who restore, you who nourish, you who rest,
O silence of darkness,
Such a silence reigned before the creation of unrest,
Before the beginning of the reign of unrest,
Such a silence will reign, but it will be a silence of light,
When all that unrest is brought to an end,
When all that unrest is exhausted,
When they have drawn all the water from the well,
After the end, after the exhaustion of all that unrest
Of man.
Thus, daughter, you are ancient and you are late,
For in this reign of unrest, you call to mind, you commemorate, you almost establish anew,
You almost cause to begin again the former Quietude
When my spirit moved upon the face of the waters.
But also, my starry daughter, daughter of the dark mantle, you are very much ahead of time, you are very precocious.
For you announce, for you represent, you almost cause to begin, ahead of time, every evening,
My great Quietude of light,
Of eternal light.
Night, you are holy, Night, you are great, Night, you are beautiful,
Night of the great mantle.
Night, I love you and greet you, and I glorify you, and you are my big daughter and my creature.
O beautiful night, night of the great mantle, daughter of the starry mantle,
You remind me, even me, you remind me of that great silence there was
Before I had opened up the floodgates of ingratitude,
And you announce to me, even me, you announce the great silence there will be
When I will have closed them.
O sweet, O great, O holy, O beautiful night, perhaps the

sainte de mes filles, nuit à la grande robe, à la robe étoilée
Tu me rappelles ce grand silence qu'il y avait dans le monde
Avant le commencement du règne de l'homme.
Tu m'annonces ce grand silence qu'il y aura
Après la fin du règne de l'homme, quand j'aurai repris mon sceptre.
Et j'y pense quelquefois d'avance, car cet homme fait vraiment beaucoup de bruit.
Mais surtout, Nuit, tu me rappelles cette nuit.
Et je me la rappellerai éternellement.
La neuvième heure avait sonné. C'était dans le pays de mon peuple d'Israël.
Tout était consommé. Cette énorme aventure.
Depuis la sixième heure il y avait eu des ténèbres sur tout le pays, jusqu'à la neuvième heure.
Tout était consommé. Ne parlons plus de cela. Ça me fait mal.
Cette incroyable descente de mon Fils parmi les hommes.
Chez les hommes.
Pour ce qu'ils en ont fait.
Ces trente ans qu'il fut charpentier chez les hommes.

Ces trois ans qu'il fut une sorte de prédicateur chez les hommes.
Un prêtre.
Ces trois jours où il fut une victime chez les hommes.

Parmi les hommes.
Ces trois nuits où il fut un mort chez les hommes.

Parmi les hommes morts.
Ces siècles et ces siècles où il est une hostie chez les hommes.
Tout était consommé, cette incroyable aventure
Par laquelle, moi, Dieu, j'ai les bras liés pour mon éternité.
Cette aventure par laquelle mon Fils m'a lié les bras.
Pour éternellement liant les bras de ma justice, pour éternellement déliant les bras de ma miséricorde.
Et contre ma justice inventant une justice même.
Une justice d'amour. Une justice d'Espérance. Tout était consommé.
Ce qu'il fallait. Comme il avait fallu. Comme mes prophètes l'avaient annoncé. Le voile du temple s'était déchiré en deux, depuis le haut jusqu'en bas.
La terre avait tremblé; des rochers s'étaient fendus.
Des sépulcres s'étaient ouverts, et plusieurs corps des saints qui étaient morts étaient ressuscités.
Et environ la neuvième heure mon Fils avait poussé
Le cri qui ne s'effacera point. Tout était consommé. Les soldats s'en étaient retournés dans leurs casernes.
Riant et plaisantant parce que c'était un service de fini.
Un tour de garde qu'ils ne prendraient plus.
Seul un centenier demeurait, et quelques hommes.
Un tout petit poste pour garder ce gibet sans importance.

holiest of my daughters, night of the long robe, of the starry robe,
You remind me of that great silence there was in the world
Before the beginning of the reign of man.
You announce to me that great silence there will be
After the end of the reign of man, when I will have resumed my sceptre.
And at times I think of it beforehand, for that man really makes a lot of noise.
But specially, Night, you remind me of that night,
And I shall remember it eternally:
The ninth hour had struck. It was in the land of my people Israel.
All was over. That enormous adventure.
From the sixth hour, there had been darkness over all the land until the ninth hour.
All was over. Let us not mention it any more. It hurts me.

That unbelievable coming down of my son among men,
In the midst of men,
When you think what they made of it,
Those thirty years during which he was a carpenter among men,
Those three years during which he was a kind of preacher among men,
A priest.
Those three days during which he was a victim among men,
In the midst of men,
Those three nights during which he was a dead man among men,
In the midst of dead men,
Those centuries and centuries when he is a host among men.
All was over, that unbelievable adventure
By which I, God, have tied my arms for my eternity,

That adventure by which my Son tied my arms,
For eternally tying the arms of my justice, for eternally untying the arms of my mercy,
And against my justice inventing a new justice,
A justice of love, a justice of Hope. All was over.

That which was necessary. In the way that was necessary. In the way my prophets had announced it. The veil of the temple was rent in twain from top to bottom;
The earth did quake; the rocks rent;
The graves were opened; and many of the bodies of the saints which slept arose.
And about the ninth hour, my Son uttered
The cry that will never be still. All was over. The soldiers returned to their barracks,
Laughing and joking because that duty was over,
One more guard duty they would not have to stand.
Only one centurion remained, with a few men,
A very small post to guard that unimportant gallows,

La potence où mon Fils pendait.
Seules quelques femmes étaient demeurées.
La Mère était là.
Et peut-être aussi quelques disciples, et encore on n'en est pas bien sûr.
Or tout homme a le droit d'ensevelir son Fils.
Tout homme sur terre, s'il a ce grand malheur
De ne pas être mort avant son fils. Et moi seul, moi Dieu,
Les bras liés par cette aventure,
Moi seul à cette minute père après tant de pères,
Moi seul je ne pouvais pas ensevelir mon Fils.
C'est alors, ô nuit, que tu vins.
Ô ma fille chère entre toutes et je le vois encore et je verrai cela dans mon éternité
C'est alors ô Nuit que tu vins et dans un grand linceul tu ensevelis
Le Centenier et ses hommes romains,
La Vierge et les saintes femmes,
Et cette montagne, et cette vallée, sur qui le soir descendait,
Et mon peuple d'Israël et les pécheurs et ensemble celui qui mourait, qui était mort pour eux

Et les hommes de Joseph d'Arimathée qui déjà s'approchaient

Portant le linceul blanc.

The gallows on which my Son was hanged.
A few women only had remained.
The Mother was there.
And perhaps a few disciples too, and even so, one is not sure of that.
Now every man has the right to bury his son,
Every man on earth, if he has had that great misfortune
Not to have died before his son. And I alone, I, God,
Arms tied by that adventure,
I alone, at that moment, father after so many fathers,
I alone could not bury my son.
It was then, O night, that you came,
O my daughter, beloved among all, and I still see it, and I shall see that in my eternity.
It was then, O Night, that you came, and in a great shroud you buried
The centurion and his Romans,
The Virgin and the holy women,
And that mountain, and that valley on which evening was descending,
And my people Israel and the sinners, and together him who was dying, who had died for them,

And the men of Joseph of Arimathea who already were approaching,

Bearing the white shroud.

TRANSLATED BY ANN AND JULIAN GREEN

NOTRE PÈRE ET JE VOUS SALVE, MARIE

A CHILD'S PRAYERS

(from *Le Mystère des Saints Innocents*)

The place of the Old Testament in relation to the New Testament receives lengthy treatment in this Mystère, *in a variety of unusual images all of which, however, ultimately propose a quite traditional interpretation. In one variation of this theme, as here, sleepy children are used, oblivious of any dogmas they might have learned, to bring Justice (Old Testament) and Mercy (New Testament) together. Note the delightful idea of God and Mary disagreeing: harmonious Celestial City?*

Dieu parle

J'ai vu les plus grands saints, dit Dieu. Eh bien je vous le dis
Je n'ai jamais rien vu de si drôle et par conséquent je ne connais rien de si beau dans le monde
Que cet enfant qui s'endort en faisant sa prière
(Que ce petit être qui s'endort de confiance)
Et qui mélange son *Notre Père* avec son *Je vous salue Marie*.
Rien n'est aussi beau et c'est même un point
Où la Sainte Vierge est de mon avis –
Et je peux bien dire que c'est le seul point où nous soyons du même avis. Car généralement nous sommes d'un avis contraire.
Parce qu'elle est pour la miséricorde.
Et moi il faut bien que je sois pour la justice.

God speaks

I have seen the greatest saints, says God. But I tell you

I have never seen anything so funny and I therefore know of nothing so beautiful in the world
As that child going to sleep while he says his prayers
(As that little creature going to sleep in all confidence)
And getting his *Our Father* mixed up with his *Hail, Mary*.

Nothing is so beautiful and it is even one point
On which the Blessed Virgin agrees with me –
And I can even say it is the only point on which we agree. Because as a rule we disagree,

She being for mercy,
Whereas I, of course, have to be for justice.

TRANSLATED BY ANN AND JULIAN GREEN

L'ESPÉRANCE

(from *Le Mystère des Saints Innocents*)

The following two short extracts are from a lengthy development in which Faith, Hope and Charity are embodied in a variety of people and things. Hope is evidently the favourite virtue, and Péguy likes to picture it as a perky little girl. His picture of children as symbols of purity, innocence and spontaneity is quite traditional.

Je suis, dit Dieu, Maître des Trois Vertus.

La Foi est une épouse fidèle.
La Charité est une mère ardente.
Mais l'espérance est une toute petite fille.

Je suis, dit Dieu, le Maître des Vertus.

La Foi est celle qui tient bon dans les siècles des siècles.

La Charité est celle qui se donne dans les siècles des siècles.
Mais ma petite espérance est celle
qui se lève tous les matins.

Je suis, dit Dieu, le Seigneur des Vertus.

La Foi est celle qui est tendue dans les siècles des siècles.

La Charité est celle qui se détend dans les siècles des siècles.
Mais ma petite espérance
est celle qui tous les matins
nous donne le bonjour.

*

Je suis, dit Dieu, le Seigneur des Vertus.
La Foi est la lampe du sanctuaire
Qui brûle éternellement.
La Charité est ce grand beau feu de bois
Que vous allumez dans votre cheminée
Pour que mes enfants les pauvres viennent s'y chauffer dans les soirs d'hiver.
Et autour de la Foi je vois tous mes fidèles
Ensemble agenouillés dans le même geste et dans la même voix
De la même prière.
Et autour de la Charité je vois tous mes pauvres
Assis en rond autour de ce feu
Et tendant leurs paumes à la chaleur du foyer.
Mais mon espérance est la fleur et le fruit et la feuille et la branche
Et le rameau et le bourgeon et le germe et le bouton.
Et elle est le bourgeon et le bouton de la fleur
De l'éternité même.

HOPE

I am, says God, Master of the Three Virtues.

Faith is a faithful wife.
Charity is an ardent mother.
But hope is a tiny girl.

I am, says God, the Master of Virtues.

Faith is she who remains steadfast for centuries and centuries.
Charity is she who gives herself for centuries and centuries.
But my little hope is she
Who rises every morning.

I am, says God, the Lord of Virtues.

Faith is she who remains tense for centuries and centuries.
Charity is she who unbends for centuries and centuries.

But my little hope
is she who every morning
wishes us good day.

*

I am, says God, the Lord of Virtues.
Faith is the sanctuary lamp
That burns for ever.
Charity is that big, beautiful log fire
That you light in your hearth
So that my children the poor may come and warm themselves before it on winter evenings.
And all around Faith, I see all my faithful
Kneeling together in the same attitude, and with one voice
Uttering the same prayer.
And around Charity, I see all my poor
Sitting in a circle around that fire
And holding out their palms to the heat of the hearth.
But my hope is the bloom, and the fruit, and the leaf, and the limb,
And the twig, and the shoot, and the seed, and the bud.
Hope is the shoot, and the bud of the bloom
Of eternity itself.

TRANSLATED BY ANN AND JULIAN GREEN

HEUREUX CEUX

(from *Eve*)

Heureux ceux qui sont morts pour la terre charnelle,
Mais pourvu que ce fût dans une juste guerre.
Heureux ceux qui sont morts pour quatre coins de terre.
Heureux ceux qui sont morts d'une mort solennelle.

Heureux ceux qui sont morts dans les grandes batailles,
Couchés dessus le sol à la face de Dieu.
Heureux ceux qui sont morts sur un dernier haut lieu,
Parmi tout l'appareil des grandes funérailles.

Heureux ceux qui sont morts pour des cités charnelles.
Car elles sont le corps de la cité de Dieu.
Heureux ceux qui sont morts pour leur âtre et leur feu,
Et les pauvres honneurs des maisons paternelles.

Car elles sont l'image et le commencement
Et le corps et l'essai de la maison de Dieu.
Heureux ceux qui sont morts dans cet embrassement,
Dans l'étreinte d'honneur et le terrestre aveu.

Car cet aveu d'honneur est le commencement
Et le premier essai d'un éternel aveu.
Heureux ceux qui sont morts dans cet écrasement,
Dans l'accomplissement de ce terrestre voeu.

Car ce voeu de la terre est le commencement
Et le premier essai d'une fidélité.
Heureux ceux qui sont morts dans ce couronnement
Et cette obéissance et cette humilité.

Heureux ceux qui sont morts, car ils sont retournés
Dans la première argile et la première terre.
Heureux ceux qui sont morts dans une juste guerre.
Heureux les épis mûrs et les blés moissonnés.

BLESSED ARE THOSE

Blessed are those who died for carnal earth
Provided it was in a just war.
Blessed are those who died for a plot of ground.
Blessed are those who died a solemn death.

Blessed are those who died in great battles.
Stretched out on the ground in the face of God.
Blessed are those who died on a final high place,
Amid all the pomp of grandiose funerals.

Blessed are those who died for carnal cities.
For they are the body of the city of God.
Blessed are those who died for their hearth and their fire,
And the lowly honours of their father's house.

For such is the image and such the beginning
The body and shadow of the house of God.
Blessed are those who died in that embrace,
In honour's clasp and earth's avowal.

For honour's clasp is the beginning
And the first draught of eternal avowal.
Blessed are those who died in this crushing down,
In the accomplishment of this earthly vow.

For earth's vow is the beginning
And the first draught of faithfulness.
Blessed are those who died in that coronation,
In that obedience and that humility.

Blessed are those who died, for they have returned
Into primeval clay and primeval earth.
Blessed are those who died in a just war.
Blessed is the wheat that is ripe and the wheat that is
gathered in sheaves.

TRANSLATED BY ANN AND JULIAN GREEN

JEAN-PIERRE CALLOC'H 1888–1917

'The war has been a good thing for Brittany. Bretons are no longer ashamed of their origins, but hold their heads high. Their pride in their race lay dormant in the grave of the last Breton rebel, but the voice of the guns has roused it from its slumber.'
War diary, in Ar en deulin

The bard 'Bleimor'. *Kantvlead Bleimor*

Jean-Pierre Calloc'h was born on the island of Groix, south-west of Quimper, on 24 July 1888. He was educated at Catholic schools on the island and, from 1900, at Vannes. Studious, and a devout Christian, he was devoted to Breton renascence as much as to the Church. He wanted to be a missionary, but he was debarred from priesthood by a ruling which excluded people from families with a record, however slight, of mental illness. This exclusion caused him great distress, but in any case, he had quickly to become the family breadwinner, his father, a fisherman, having been lost at sea in 1902. A series of supervisory posts in schools in Paris and Reims was interrupted only by national service at Vitré from 1909 to 1911, during which period his passionate commitment to Brittany found expression in teaching illiterate Breton servicemen to read and write, and in a study of Breton language and culture. After national service, he studied for a degree in French literature at Paris and at the same time pursued research into a history of Groix. He never completed this work.

Calloc'h's first writings were in French, but from around 1905 he wrote in Breton, often under the pseudonym 'Bleimor' (literally 'sea-wolf' – that is, 'sea-dog'). A convinced regionalist, he initially predicted a vigorous separatist movement if the 'putrefying, stinking Latin regime' of the French Republic did not soon collapse. 'I am not the least bit French,' he used to say, but by the time he did national service, he had decided against separatism. When war broke out, he was preparing a Breton language course to be taught outside school hours, since it was against the law to speak or learn Breton in schools. ('Spitting, and speaking Breton, prohibited,' read a notorious public notice.)

When the war came, Calloc'h, like so many others, saw it as a defence of civilization and Christianity, and immediately volunteered for the front. Only Ireland and Brittany, he writes in one poem, still help Christ carry the cross: in the fight to reinvigorate Christianity, the Celtic peoples are in the van. In addition, now readily fighting for France, under the French flag, he saw the war as the great chance to affirm the national identity of Brittany and resurrect its language and culture.

His pre-war poetry is either devotional, militantly Catholic or militantly Breton. These three strands are often spun into one. Calloc'h himself selected what he thought was the best of his work, and gave the manuscript, along with his own French translations of most of the poems, to a friend. If he were killed, it was to be published, under the title *Ar en deulin* (*Kneeling*). (The book by L. Paulaux contains further texts, including two short stories revealing a touch of humour one would not have suspected from the author of *Ar en deulin*.)

The poem 'Veni, Spiritus Sancte!' is, then, thematically typical. In form, it is less so. While Calloc'h's evident masters are the Old Testament prophets and the Psalmist, his metrical variety usually excludes extended lines of free verse of this kind. Even his 'Miserere' contrasts in this respect with Claudel's reworking of the same psalm. But 'Veni, Spiritus Sancte!' does suggest that there may have been, in Calloc'h, a Breton Claudel about to emerge. At any rate, this poem, like many of Claudel's, is thoroughly oratorical – part prayer, part sermon, part call to arms. It needs, not just to be read aloud, but to be declaimed. Perhaps Urban II sounded something like this at Clermont. Such was Calloc'h's militant fervour ('For God and Brittany' was his motto) that his enthusiasm for the war might even have survived the miseries of 1917. He was a terrible foe in attack, wielding a sailor's axe of the kind formerly used in boarding enemy ships. He was killed by a shell, outside his dug-out, on 10 April 1917.

IAN HIGGINS

A note on the translation. 'Veni, Spiritus Sancte!' has in essence been translated from Calloc'h's French text, itself his translation from the Breton. Where the Breton and the French diverge, I have tried to follow the Breton. However, I would have been quite unable to do this without the help of Dr H. Ll. Humphreys, of the University College of Wales, Lampeter, and I thank him very warmly for his indispensable advice.

IAN HIGGINS

Text
Ar en deulin/A genoux (Edition Kendalc'h, 1963).

Secondary sources
L. Palaux, *Un Barde breton: Jean-Pierre Calloc'h 'Bleimor'* (Librairie Le Goaziou, Quimper, 1926).
G. Le Bras, *Jean-Pierre Calloc'h Bleimor* (Les Presses bretonnes, Saint-Brieuc, 1967).
Y. Le Gallo and J. Balcou (eds), *Histoire littéraire et culturelle de la Bretagne* (Champion, Paris, 1987, 3 vols, iii).

DEIT, SPERED-SANTÉL

Kan doné-mad d'er blé neùé

I

Nag en nandeg-kant-pearzegved blé goudé Ganedigeh er Hrist ér hreu;
Èl penn er Peur én un taol doh fenestr er bediz, diroll geté er horolleu;
Èl en tèr gomz ar er vangoér, é amzér koén-meur Baltazar;
Èl ul loér a ganv hag a lorh, dallet peb héol d'hé splanndér gouéù,
A-uz de zremmùéleu didalvé er Gatell Europ,

Dremm-goèd er Brezél!
Hag er Stérenn vlaoahuz e gilas én hé raog er stéred oll, gwintet betag sol en nozieu;
Hag el labourieu ha chomel, de hortoz devé en Obér-Meur;
Hag en dud ha stagein o deulagad ar en tachenneu lahereh en em lidé énné er Hevrin divent, er Road uzanian,
En Overenn e zo en tan hé béleg, er hanol hé orgléz dispar, hag e hrér mab-dén ag hé Aberh . . .

VENI, SANCTE SPIRITUS!

A song of welcome for the new year

I

Now in the one thousand nine hundred and fourteenth year after Christ was born in the stable;
Like the Poor Man's face all at once against the windows of the worldly rich at their wild dancing;
Like the three words on the wall, when Belshazzar made his great feast;
Like a moon of grief and terror, blinding each day's sun with its savage splendour,
Over every contemptible horizon of the Strumpet Europe,
The blood-face of War!
And before that terrible Star every star fell back, cast into the depths of night;
And all works ceased, until the Great Work should be wrought;
And men fixed their eyes on fields of carnage, the place of celebration of a great Mystery, a transcendental Sacrifice,
The Mass whose celebrant is Fire, its unexampled music the gun, the Mass whose Victim they call the son of man.

II

Èl kanerion en Doéré-mad, e ya dré Vreiz a zor de zor, de houél benniget Nedeleg,

(E koun ag en Éled e gemennas er peuh d'en dud, é noz ketañ en Oed kristén),

Klasket em-es mem breudér hénoah, de lavared dehé heteu er barh.

Ha dén n'em-es kavet ér gér . . .

Gouli é tiér kun Keltia; meid un oéled bennag, aman hag ahont, lahet en tan énnoñ gwerso,

E wélér diragtoñ mouézi peur é houélar, ha bugalé vihan e hra chonjeu, e hra chonjeu . . .

O men Doué, pé bosenn 'zo bet ar er vro-man?

Kelt Alban-Ihùel, 'men éh ous? Na té, Kelt Iwerhon? Men éh ous 'ta, Kelt a Gembré? O Kelt a Vreiz, men goèd, émen éh ous?

Gouli int, tiér kun Keltia! Pe saùé héol en hañù ar er flangenn, er oazed 'zo oeit kuit ged o gléaniér . . .

II

Like those who sing the Good News through all Brittany, from door to door, at the blessed feast of Christmas,

(Remembering the angels proclaiming peace to all men in that first night of Christianity),

I have looked for my brothers tonight, to give them greetings from the bard,

And found no one in their homes . . .

The gentle homes of Celts are empty, save for some, here and there, where the fire died long ago,

And by the dead fire poor women weep, and little children dream, and dream . . .

O my Lord God, what plague has passed over this land?

Where are you, Celt of mountain Scotland? And you, Celt of Ireland? Celt of Wales, where are you? And you, my own blood, Celt of Brittany, where are you?

Empty, the gentle homes of Celts! As the summer sun was rising over the valley, the men left, taking their swords . . .

III

Goéfieu e oent én amzér gent: breman o-des fuzulienneu,

Fuzulienneu ha kanolieu, e skop er marù, med er gléaniér e zo ataù er gléanier,

Ha kemmadenn erbed n'en-des dégaset en oedeu é kalon milliget er German.

Lamm peurbadel er German ar er Gornog, più e harzo dohtoñ, ma ne saù ket er Helt en taol-man?

Er Helt e zo bet getoñ en orbid gourdadel: ur ganenn doh é héneu, oeit é.

You, you! Keltia e zo Keltia bepred: 'ma hé faotred ar en harzeu.

Béh d'er German, breudér karet! Ho touareu é e ziùennet.

Er Gornog e zo dem. Ni bieu er Gornog. Mar fall d'er German hé saotrein, klopenn er German e feutim.

Diùennet on-es er Gornog doh en oll vagadeu.

Harzeu Galia zo ur véred d'en Disevénidi, kardellet on douar d'o helaneu.

Disevénad hiriù, er German é arré. Béh d'er German, pe fall dehoñ!

Béh de loskour on ilizieu, de éntanour Moliah Reims,

Iliz er Rouané nevedet, e oé ken mad pédein énni, édan askell klodeu er Frans.

Araog, Kelt mad! ha tenn, ha sko! Kouéh mar kouéhes: eid er vro é!
Med sko, sko, sko! o breur, sko!

III

Once, they carried lances; now they have rifles,

Rifles and guns spewing death, but a sword is still a sword,

And the ages have wrought no change in the accursed German heart.

Who shall resist the endless westward German surge, if the Celt does not rise and stand against the German now?

The Celt has done as his fathers did: with song on his lips, he has marched.

Therefore raise a cheer! For Celts are still Celts: our young men are at the frontier.

Fall upon the German, beloved brethren! the lands you defend are your lands.

The West is ours. The West belongs to us. If the German would defile the West, then let us split the German's skull.

We have defended the West against every horde.

The marchlands of Gaul are a graveyard to Barbarians; our soil is rich with their corpses.

The Barbarian today is once again the German! Fall upon the German, since he would have it so!

Fall upon the Burner of churches, the one who burned the Wonder of Reims,

Church of anointed kings, where it was so sweet to pray under the wing of French glories.

Forward, good Celt! and shoot, and thrust and strike! Fall if you fall: it is for our country! But thrust and strike, thrust and strike, O my brother, thrust and strike!

Heb éhan, heb diskuih, heb trué, tan dehoñ! Lah ha tag, pen dé red! o breur, lah!

Bes er freill hag e val, er garreg hag e flastr, er gurun e freuz, er mor e veuh:

Bes er Hadour!

Dalh koun é oé ha gourdadeu kaored divent, e gréné Germania dirag sell o lagad.

Dalh koun é ma genous inour ha Houenn: des éndro, des éndro tréh!

Kanenneu gaer e saùo er barh ar er ré-hleù, ken e drido eskern er Gelted koh é yeindér o béieu!

Without rest, without cease, without mercy, thrust and strike! Kill and strangle, since you must! O my brother, kill!

Be the flail that thrashes, the rock that crushes, the lightning that destroys, the sea that drowns:

Be the Warrior!

Remember the matchless deeds of your fathers, remember that the German trembled under the gaze of their eyes.

Remember that you bear the honour of your Race: return, then, and return conqueror!

The bard will make brave songs for the brave, Celtic songs to stir the bones of the ancients in their cold graves!

IV

Ne gouskan mui. Ur vouéh e zo, én noz-gouiañù, doh men gerùel, ur vouéh iskiz;

Ur vouéh gréñù, ur vouéh garù ha duah de gemennein: en dud yaouank e blij dehé ur vouéh èlsé;

(Ha nen dé ket mouéh ur verh é, na mouéh er horrigézed-hont, e réd dré er mor keltieg);

Ur vouéh ha ne hell dén chomel disent ohti; hudadenn er Brézel ar en harzeu.

Sentein e hrin. Kent pell é vin ged mem breudér, kadour de heul er gaderion;

Kent pell é vin él lahadeg . . . Peh arouéieu zo ar me zal? Ha gwéloud e hrin ha zevé, bléad neùé?

Ha petra vern? Abred pé devéhad, a pe sono en eur de vond devad en Tad, leùén éh in. Jézuz oér dihuz on mammeu.

Revées benniget, bléad neùé, nag é vehé, é touéh ha dri-hant pemp dé ha tri-uigent, men dé devéhañ!

Revées benniget! Rag estroh eid kant vlé en-des treménet ar er vro-man heb n'o-doud anaùet meid kounnar Doué, ha té, arvest e hri E drugaréieu.

Gwéloud e hri distro er hrédenneu harluet, en tréh é tarneijal arré édan plégeu banniél er Frans, hag er Vro adsaùet de virùikén;

Gwéloud e hri mem Breiz dihaod 'benn en devé, hag hé yéh inouret, èl pe oé béù hé marhegion eid hé diùenn.

Bléad neùé, bléad brezél! Revées benniget nag é tégasehes én ha vantell, a-gevred ged en neùé-hañù eid er Bed, er marù eidon.

Petra é marù unan, pé kant, pé marù kant mil? arlerh ma vo béù ha kloduz er vro, arlerh ma kendalho er houenn . . .

A pe varùin, laret er pédenneu, ha béiet mé, èl me zadeu, troeit me zal doh en énebour;

Ha ne houlennet tra eidon ged men Dasprénour, meid el léh devéhañ én É Varaouéz . . .

IV

It is long since I slept. There is a voice, in the winter's night, calling to me, a strange voice;

A strong voice, and harsh, a voice accustomed to command: such a voice rings agreeably in young men's ears;

(And it is no woman's voice, nor the siren voice that haunts the Celtic sea);

A voice that none can disobey: War howling at the frontiers.

I will obey. Soon I shall be with my brothers, a soldier following soldiers.

Soon I shall be among the slaughter . . . What signs are on my brow? New year, shall I see your end?

But it is of no account! Sooner, or later, when the hour to approach the Father strikes, I shall go with gladness. Jesus is the Comforter of our mothers.

Be blessed, new year, even if, among your three hundred and sixty-five days, there should be my last!

Be blessed! For more than one hundred years have passed over this land, knowing only the anger of God, but you shall witness His mercies.

You shall see banished beliefs returning, the wings of victory spread again, under the beating flag of France, and our country exalted for evermore;

You shall see my Brittany free at last, and her language held in honour, as it was when her knights were alive to defend her.

New year, year of war! Be blessed, even should you bring, wrapped in the folds of your cloak, alongside springtime for the world, death for me.

What is the death of one man, or one hundred, the death of one hundred thousand men, if our country only lives, if the race still lives . . .

When I die, say the prayers and bury me like my fathers, my face set towards the enemy,

And ask nothing for me of my Redeemer, except the last place in His Paradise . . .

V

Me wél! . . . Me wél!

Strill Doué ar gein en Déneleh. Er glen hag er morieu e zo ru ged er goèd.

Goèd ar gornog, goèd ar greiznoz; goèd é kreisté hag é retér: honneh e zo ur bénijenn, ahoel!

Jed ha béhed breman, Europ, doh gleur-iùern en tanieu-goall: skopet ha-poé ar Zremm douéel me Hrist é kroéz ha chetu deit eur er Hasti.

Eur el lahadeg hag el lorh; eur er gurun hag en tarh dareu: eur reihted Doué!

O goalh o-do er bléad-man, er blei, er vran hag et preñùed: marhad-mad é er hig kristén!

Er blé-man é vo braù en had; évet en-des en douar goèd mab-dén . . .

Na p'ha-pehé karet, Europ, ne vehé ket dégouéhet genous ur darvoud èl hennan;

P'ha-pehé karet évad ged doujans É Oèd-Éañ, goéd deg broad ne vehé ket bet red dit en éved;

P'ha-pehé karet deulinein dirag kelan douéel er Halvar, hag azeulein, ne vehé ket hiziù, Europ, Europ, kement a gelaneu . . .

Glahar, glahar! n'en-des mui meid gobeu ged klehiér en Douar: me wél enan er gaderion lahet é tarneijal uz d'en dachenn, hanval doh er fru ar ur mor . . .

VI

Ur gampouézenn. Kelaneu ar er gampouézenn, mil ha mil e zo anehé. Ha 'n é saù 'mesk er helaneu, èl gwéharall Ezékiel harluet, er barh peur, Spered, Ho kalùa.

Deit, Spered Santel!

Diouganet é bet Ho tonedigeh d'Unan ha ne lar ket geùiér: en Hani e zougas É Boén en É unan, hag e varùas dianzaùet, étré divréh kaled ur groéz.

Deit, Spered Santel!

Meur a unan, a-houdeùeh, en-des, o Spered, Ho korteit; ha dré ne hellent mui harz ged en hirêh o-doé Deoh doned, abred é mant oeit d'o béieu.

Deit, Spered Santel!

Ha hiriù, a! hiriù! meur a unan arré e ouél Deoh hag Ho klask, é téoélded ur bed kollet dehoñ é Zoué.

Deit, Spered Santel!

O! Ho klod ne houlennam ket en arvestein én é greisté; med, èl ma hras Doué de Voïz evid en Douar-Grateit, gwéled a bell, un eur, dremm er bed adneùéiet Deoh, ha merùel.

Deit, Spered Santel!

Ha ne hellim 'ta birùikén diazéein ar Ho peuh un oéled? Hag én anér é vo bepred é saùim tiér ha kérieu, e zei hanal er Brezél d'o diskar?

V

What do I see! I see

God's scourge on the shoulders of Humanity. The earth and the seas are red with blood.

Blood over the west, blood over the north; blood in the south and the east: here is penitence indeed!

Now weigh your sin, Europe, by the hell-glow of the fires: you spat in the face of my Christ on His cross, and now the hour of Reckoning has struck.

The hour of carnage and terror; the hour of thunder and lightning and tears; the hour of God's judgement!

They shall have their fill this year, the wolf, the crow and the worm: Christian flesh is cheap!

This year's corn will be good: the earth has drunk of human blood . . .

Ah, Europe! had you but wished it, this fate would not have been yours;

Had you but respectfully and gladly drunk His Blood, you would not now be choking on the blood of ten nations;

Had you but gladly and adoringly knelt before the body of God on Calvary, you would not now, Europe, O Europe, be so filled with bodies . . .

Grief, grief! The bells of the Earth only toll for deaths now: I see the souls of dead warriors across the battlefield like spindrift over a sea . . .

VI

A plain. Bodies on the plain, thousands and more thousands. And, standing among the bodies, like Ezekiel in his exile once, the poor bard calls out to you, Spirit.

Come, Holy Spirit!

Your coming has been prophesied by One who spoke no falsehood, by Him who bore His suffering alone, and died denied, between the unbending branches of a cross.

Come, Holy Spirit!

Many are those, since then, who have longed for Your coming, O Spirit! and when their longing would no more be denied, gone early to their graves.

Come, Holy Spirit!

And today, yes! still today! there are those who weep for You in the darkness, in a world which has lost its God.

Come, Holy Spirit!

Oh! we do not ask to contemplate Your glory in its noon, but only, as God granted Moses to glimpse the Promised Land, to glimpse from afar, for one hour, the face of a world made new by You, and then to die.

Come, Holy Spirit!

For shall it never be given to us to build hearth and home on the foundation of Your peace? Shall it always be vain, our building of houses and cities, shall the breath of War always blast them?

Deit, Spered Santel!

Penaoz e vo dem-ni béùein, ma nen det ket d'or hennerhad? Koh é mab-dén, ha yein er glen 'dan é gorv peur.

Deit, Spered Santel!

Tad er beurion, Gouleu er haloneu! Dihuzour, o Dihuzour-dreist, é truegeh er brezél-man n'en-des bet biskoah par dehoñ, Ho aspédein e hram: deit devadom ged er blé neùé!

VII

Goud e hran é teet. Goud e hran é oh é tond, me gred é kevrin er Glahar.

'Gwilvoud erbed heb poén', e gelenn er vuhé d'er barh. Hag er barh d'er vuhé: 'Poén erbed heb gwilvoud. N'en-des ankén erbed difréh, èlsé 'ma el Lézenn.'

'A-houdé m'en-des en Ankén kavet ur Pried, Henneh hag e zo bet lakeit hag adlakeit é kroéz d'er hantvedeu.'

Red é d'er gran merùel eid ma tei er hellid. Kelaneu mem breudér e wélan èl gran én douar: ar o ludu é kellido fréh moliahuz . . .

Hanval doh ur roué gouéù en em hronn a voug eid merùel, héol devéhañ er bléad-hont zo oeit de guh én ul linsél a oèd . . .

Arhoah é vo kaer ar er Bed!

Hag èl er voéz é gwilvoud a pe wél dremm er mab ganet dehi, dirag kened en Héol neùé en Douar nendo mui koun ag é ankén.

Pariz, genver 1915

Come, Holy Spirit!

How shall we live, if not made strong by You? Old is the son of man, and cold the earth under his poor body.

Come, Holy Spirit!

Father of the Poor, Light of our hearts! Comforter, O most excellent Comforter, in the misery of this war, whose like men have never seen, we beseech You: come to us with the new year!

VII

I know that You will come. I know that You are near. I believe in the mystery of Grief.

'There is no birth without pain' is life's teaching to the bard. And the bard's to life: 'No pain without a birth. There is no sorrow that is barren, for such is the Law;

And has been, since Sorrow found a wedded Husband, Him whom the centuries have crucified, and crucified.'

The seed must die if it is to spring up and thrive. I see the bodies of my brothers like seeds in the earth: on their ashes wonderful fruit shall thrive . . .

Like a barbarian king who wraps himself in crimson before lying down to die, the year's last sun has sunk in a shroud of blood . . .

Tomorrow the sun will shine on the World!

And like the woman in labour when she sees the face of the child born to her, when it sees the beauty of the new Day the Earth shall not remember its sorrow.

Paris, January 1915

TRANSLATED BY IAN HIGGINS

*L*UCIEN *R*OLMER 1880–1916

'Poets are born in a state of grace . . . Nascuntur.'
L'Eloge de la Grâce, *1913*

Real poets are born, not made, says Rolmer. Rolmer was born Louis Jean-Marie Ignace ('Luigi' to his family) Roux in Marseille on 31 July 1880. He was educated at a Jesuit school, and left steeped in the Ancients, with whom he felt a Latin affinity. He was, however, more a 'Romantic deist' (according to Jean Desthieux) than a Christian. He went to Paris to study law, but lived for literature. He was full of projects, and an inspiring colleague.

Those who knew him speak of his own extraordinary ability to improvise, both verbally and at the piano. Edmond Jaloux, indeed, draws attention to Rolmer's failure to concentrate on and control his verbal facility, and sees this as the one weakness in his work. Desthieux, however, says that his manuscripts were always very heavily corrected. If there is a weakness here, it is only really apparent in *Maïvine* and some of his literary criticism. His poetry is generally light, sure-footed, sometimes melancholy, sometimes witty or satirical, usually conveying a fervid love of life, always traditional in form. After two early books of slight verse, he published *Chants perdus* (*Lost Songs*) in 1907 and *Le second volume des Chants perdus* in 1911; his subsequent poetry was collected together with these in one posthumous volume. However, although Rolmer saw himself as a poet above all (a view shared by most of his friends), it is as a novelist that he is most likely to lay claim to our attention today.

Rolmer's first, short, novel, *Madame Fornoul et ses héritiers* (*Madame Fornoul and Her Heirs*), is a ferocious account of the vulture-like gathering of Madame Fornoul's relations round her death-bed. The novel is written with verve and humour and, considering it is a first novel, surprising economy. Underlying the account of the characters' unctuous rapaciousness is the theme of freedom: Madame Fornoul is paralysed and cannot speak, yet her very helplessness has the family dancing like puppets. The final irony is that, after her death and all their machinations, there turns out to have been no money to leave. The reader, too, has fallen for the illusion, swept along on the narrator's words, dancing to his tune.

The second novel, *L'Hôtel de Sainte-Agnès et des célibataires* (*The St Agnes and Bachelor Hotel*), is a farce set in a hotel run by a devout lady, Mlle Agneau, who will only take unmarried guests. Naturally, some of them are priests. The permutations of liaisons between the characters become increasingly hilarious, until everything suddenly lurches into a sombre ending. Right from the

start, the foundation of Mlle Agneau's devoutness has been open to question, and now satire gives way to her soberly described emotional collapse. The only way of saving the reputations of the clergymen involved is to have her committed to an asylum, which happens on the very day the Senate ratifies the separation of Church and State (1905).

Rolmer's third novel, *Maïvine*, is different in manner from all the others, more reminiscent of a Symbolist opera than a novel. In long, cumulative tirades, by turns dithyrambic and threnodic, it expresses the hero's yearning for the perfect love which would let him accede to oneness. He meets Maïvine (Marie + Divine + Maïa), and the novel follows the struggle between the call of the flesh and the call of the will. Hegel and Villiers de l'Isle-Adam are in the background here; and given the linguistic inventiveness which Rolmer shows in his other novels, especially his fourth, one cannot help thinking of Julien Gracq and a novelistic branch of Surrealism which Rolmer might have helped develop. (Looking forward to what literature would be like after the war, he did foresee a period of febrile excitement, followed by twenty-five years of 'psychosis' and then a strange new classicism: an interesting adumbration of, say, Dada, Surrealism, Ponge and the New Novel.)

Rolmer's fourth and last novel is *Les Amours ennemies* (*Inimical Loves*), which is by far his best work. It is also the most complex. The questions of identity, authenticity and freedom, so frequent (often wearyingly so) in the literature of this century, are interwoven with those of geographical and biological determinism, racism and Europeanism, in a wholly original and refreshing narrative, which is consistently funny, often moving, sometimes dramatic, always thought-provoking, but never cumbersome or didactic. The despotic, loud-voiced, womanizing Marquis de Trévalas, a big fish in a small Provençal pond, anti-Republican, unabashable, egocentric, linguistic swashbuckler, tries to rape his son Bruno's foster-mother, Virginie. When she resists, he pushes her into a mountain stream and she drowns. He becomes legal guardian to her son Just, who grows up alongside Bruno. Each of the boys sees the other as a kind of inverted *doppelgänger*, to be feared, resented, courted and emulated all at once, and both are in love with Germaine Loucquets-Damenthe.

Just comes into an inheritance and the Marquis takes him to Paris to sort out his affairs. It is on this trip that the Marquis sees Ella Jassy, who plays the cello in a women's orchestra at Le Bluff, a big department store. A waitress tells him the cellist's name, and that she is Jewish, and when the concert has finished, he sets off in an unsuccessful attempt to woo her. Eventually Bruno goes to Paris and unwittingly meets Ella. They fall in love and live together. Germaine comes to Paris and seduces first Bruno, and then the sinister Just, who tells Ella of Bruno's lapse. In a plot of increasing complexity, which just keeps melodrama at bay, the multiple calls of the blood, the soil and the will lead eventually to an ending whose relative 'happiness', if real, is palpably fragile. On the evidence of this novel, there was in Rolmer a talent one might have got by mixing one part Gide to one part Sartre to two parts Marcel Aymé. Such a writer would be irresistibly readable. Perhaps not in poetry, but certainly in the novel (and conceivably in the theatre), a major talent was lost in Rolmer.

And an eccentric one. Alongside his novels and poetry, Rolmer was an energetic critic. Vigorously, almost embarrassingly conservative in taste, he founded a literary review, *La Flora* (1912–15), in which he castigated all that he saw as ugly and contrary to Latin gracefulness – that is, such poets as Verhaeren or Romains, and painters such as the Cubists. He was even suspicious of the then current revival of interest in Celtic history and culture. He argued against schools and theories, and for spontaneity. His concept of grace in art is close to that of inspiration: if not divine, it is certainly a 'gift'. So, for example, Apollinaire is 'unquestionably' a 'talented writer', but his poetry is of 'questionable' quality because he is too 'theoretical and erudite'. Rolmer's criticism, most of which was collected in *L'Eloge de la Grâce*, is voraciously wide-ranging, and equally immoderate in praise and in blame.

Although he had never done national service, Rolmer volunteered when war broke out. He was so physically delicate that he was often exhausted, and one of his officers said it was unforgivable to have let himself be drafted into the infantry. Asked whether artists would gain anything from their experience of the trenches, Rolmer thought not: 'The artists have disappeared, and their sole aim now is to be good soldiers, and painfully to defend not the moral heritage, but the heritage of France.' The war was a war of 'national revenge, a difficult revenge to take, a cure':

> We're fighting and suffering so that young men coming after us might have pride. Apart from poets and artists, I don't think there's enough pride in French people. What a burden of remorse, never to have had any pride! A war is useful to people suffering remorse; we artists had no remorse – we had hopes! But now, all our heroism and all the heroism we've seen won't have been in vain. All these shining examples will save a lot of people a lot of humiliation. We hope!

In the trenches, he felt like a root, proud to be steeped in the soil of France: 'I want to live, but above all I want France to live and impose her Republican will on these feudal Germanies – and I'm suffering willingly for our France and willingly for future freedom.' Rolmer was pleased to have 'done [his] duty', and was afraid lest, after a two-month spell in hospital, he should be invalided out of the front line. On 28 February 1916, a month after coming out of hospital, he was in the fighting for Douaumont, near Verdun. His trench was overwhelmed. Most of his comrades were killed. One, made prisoner, watched as Rolmer was seized and struggled to break free. An enemy officer put a revolver to his head and blew his brains on to the snow.

IAN HIGGINS

Texts

L'Inconstance (Moullot fils, Marseille, 1900). Published under the name Luigi Roux.
Thamirys (Raybaud, Marseille, 1901). Published under the name Luigi Roux.
Madame Fornoul et ses héritiers (Mercure de France, Paris, 1905).
L'Hôtel de Sainte-Agnès et des célibataires (Ollendorff, Paris, 1907).
Maïvine (Auctoris Opèra, Marseille, 1909).
Les Amours ennemies (Figuière, Paris, 1912).
L'Eloge de la Grâce (Figuière, Paris, 1913).
Chants perdus (Edition de *La Flora*, Paris, 1938).

Secondary sources

J. Desthieux, *La Statue du poète Lucien Rolmer* (A l'Office bibliographique, Paris, 1930).
Cahiers Lucien Rolmer. Four numbers published in Paris, in 1934, 1935, 1936 and 1948; they contain pieces by and about Rolmer, and letters by him.

INIMICAL LOVES

The first of these extracts from Les Amours ennemies *is an account of M. de Trévalas's pursuit of Ella after the concert. In the second, back home in Provence, he regales his social circle with what the reader discovers is a fictitious account of the episode.*

Monsieur de Trévalas had quickly caught up with Ella Jassy. First he overtook her, then he walked behind her. In the darkness and bustle of the street, his eyes strained only for her, he heard nothing but her presence.

The cellist had the figure of a lyre: passers-by, as they saw her coming, looked at her in surprise and her own beauty floated above her like a spirit, a breath or a song.

At the corner of the boulevard, she took the turning into a broad, empty street, disturbed only by the shouts of a few schoolchildren.

'For an artist,' the Marquis thought to himself, 'my little Jewess is very self-possessed. She does not turn round, nor does she stop. Good Lord, can she perhaps be respectable? No, that is impossible, Jewesses are never respectable, especially musicians! and anyway, if she were, she would not venture out alone at nightfall into the streets. It stands to reason.'

What he longed to do was to pounce upon her, without any warning, without any introduction, to bring her down like an antelope; he longed to carry her off like a turtledove, to ravish her trembling but yielding body and to make her cry out in his arms.

The shadows and the lamplight flickered over her figure, hiding then revealing it by turns. How elegant and shapely nature had made her, how the outline of her form was music to the eyes!

M. de Trévalas took off his hat, and leaned on his cane. His knees were giving way. The tempest of love was whirling in his head; the wind blew all around.

Then a calm descended on him as it had on the street. The predator saw a gleam ahead, desire struck like lightning. The Marquis caught up with Ella Jassy under a gas lamp.

'Mademoiselle, Mademoiselle, Mademoiselle,' he began in his booming voice.

The string-player stopped and considered the stranger. He seemed to tower over her, bursting with self-confidence, superb in his glossy fur coat. She saw the high-coloured cheeks, the flaring nostrils, the greying beard and the crimson evening tie.

'Monsieur?'

Such was the ardour of the man of breeding that his teeth began to chatter. The gas light was ebbing away like his soul. The schoolchildren jostled him as they chased past. The wind swooped down and moaned.

'Mademoiselle, Mademoiselle,' M. de Trévalas repeated, with a bow.

His features stiffened in a grimace: he coughed and put a hand to his lips.

'I thought for a moment you had rendered me speechless,' he murmured. 'Well, Mademoiselle, if you would allow me to walk alongside you for a few moments, I shall put my request to you. Did you notice me at the concert?'

Mlle Jassy lifted the veil of her fur toque. This delicious child was strong-minded; this daughter of the east loved white roads and long clear vistas like those of her homeland. She held herself firmly erect and her great blue eyes shone out of her sun-kissed face.

'Monsieur, let me first make something plain: if you wish to speak to me about my music, I am ready to listen; if, on the other hand, you were about to propose anything improper or incompatible with the situation of a young lady, it is, believe me, fruitless to continue.'

An inexplicable dread, a mysterious fear gripped her breast; her voice was trembling like her heart.

The Marquis smiled and waved an airy hand:

'Oh so serious, so soon! Goodness me, Mademoiselle, calm yourself. I will speak first and then we shall see . . .' And without giving her time to open her mouth: 'I have guessed your name and your surname. I imagine that you are about 20 years old, that you are Jewish, and I am sure that you lead an independent life.'

The young foreigner lost some of her fear. A smile lit up her lips. Her words softened along with her features.

'Monsieur, my grandmother was a harpist in Cairo, but she also practised palmistry, and when she took the trouble to go down to the terrace of her old house in Gama-El-Akmar to read the hands of the Maltese, the Bulgarians and the Arabs who consulted her, she could tell them in a few words so much about themselves that the foreigners fell down before her and called her by the names of their divinities.'

The colour of her voice, at once dark and light, was like the transparency of her skin. Listening to it, so hesitant, so full of life, so fragile, one might fancy one could see the vibration of her soul, like a wave stirred by perpetual trembling.

'Mademoiselle, you entrance me,' M. de Trévalas replied. 'I address you in the most banal of terms, and you repay me with irony! Well, so be it, if I may continue to address you. Do you wish me to come straight to the point? Very well. That is my only desire, that is all I seek – my secret and fragrant aim! I should like to make love to you, I adore you, and beg you to take me home with you immediately!'

The cellist was walking away without a word; the Marquis took her by the arm.

'Mademoiselle, Mademoiselle, if you refuse, I shall carry you off ! I am Monsieur Bertrand de Trévalas. Shall I show you my card? I live in Saxivaire-en-Provence, I have about 30,000 francs a year. If you will not take me to your home, I shall take you to mine! Oh Mademoiselle, am I so ugly? What do you want from life, to run away from me like this?'

'Let me go, Monsieur, I beg you,' pleaded Mlle Jassy, trying to pull her hand away.

The Marquis became transported:

'Can you breathe this odious night air around us, Mademoiselle? Neither you, as I can tell by your skin, nor I, as I can tell by the fever in my blood, can ever be at home here. Have you ever been to Provence? The curve of the coastline, the bare and magnificent hills, the warm and passionate air, the rugged rocks, the nights, the sun, the dense trees in the deep valleys! I am leaving tomorrow. Come with me! You could live there, you could live . . . as happy as one of the Hesperides. Here in Paris, everything is of base metal, but there the sun turns everything to bronze! There, the landscape is full of fire, here the skies are leaden! There, the air is fragrant with lavender and frivolous with the heartbeats of dancing tambourines, while here minuets freeze on the lips! There, every fountain gushes living water, but here even the rain falls as poison. Here, all hope lies buried, there, oh, there is – immortality! Ah, Mademoiselle, am I hurting you? Leave your hands in mine to warm them through your gloves! There, I should worship you like an idol. Are you not doomed to unhappiness by staying here?'

'Monsieur, I have asked nothing of you. Why do you make such grim prophecies?'

'Very well, I will be indiscreet. How do you live in Paris, Mademoiselle?'

'Good heavens, what a question! How do you imagine I live? By my music of course. My fees from Le Bluff would be enough, but I also give a few lessons . . .'

'Your music? But one cannot make a living from music. Music is a charming accomplishment, no more. Le Bluff indeed! Bluff is the word for it, Mademoiselle!'

'Oh, Monsieur, do not talk nonsense. When you are by the sea, at home where you live, does the Mediterranean (I have seen it, you know!) does the Mediterranean seem like a millpond to you?'

'Mademoiselle, you do not understand me.'

'Monsieur, you do not understand me.'

'I have never fallen in love with an ordinary woman. If I love you, it must therefore be because you are worthy of it. Only trust me and I will be your lover. You shall be my little songbird, my chaffinch. I will spoil you and cherish you. As soon as I saw you, I wanted to have you, like a thirsty man when he sees water. Are you really so full of prejudice? Perhaps you still are. If so, stifle such feelings, you will never regret it! Ah, in my heart I feel such burning curiosity, it is eating me up! Such a delicious wild creature. When I touch you, I feel I am melting away.'

'Monsieur, that is immaterial. Your feelings are of no consequence to me. Keep them to yourself and let me go.'

'I seek only your own good.'

'You seek only *your* own good. And you accost a young woman, a foreigner, thinking "She will be easy prey!" Very noble, very charming, I'm sure. You are too intrigued not to start play-acting, you know the art of beguiling women, you are used to conquests, I imagine, and I am prepared to excuse you, but this time you will have to beat a retreat.'

'Really, Mademoiselle, am I so ancient? Try me, I assure you . . .'

'Oh, Monsieur, I have no intention of inquiring about your age. And in any case, you are as presumptuous as a young man!'

'Ha! Yes, well said! Upon my word, you really do appeal to me!'

A few drops of rain began to fall. M. de Trévalas let go of his prisoner's hand. She shook herself all over, like a bird in the cold.

Underneath the gas lamp, with the veil thrown back from her face, her hair blowing from her temples in the wind, her eyes shone like pure pools where her soul floated, and seemed to utter a lament.

The Marquis stepped back and looked her up and down.

'What is this? You are not running away now, Mademoiselle. Ha! Ha! What was the point of all the protests, if now you are hypnotized like a lark in front of a mirror!'

'You are mistaken, Monsieur. Like all women of my race, I hold the family sacred. I was thinking of your daughter, if you have one. It saddened me. I was feeling sorry for you!'

'Sorry for me! Ho! that is not the particular feeling I would like to arouse in your fascinating and delicious little person. If I had a daughter like you, Mademoiselle, make no mistake, I would make love to her!'

The street fell quiet. The rain held the wind in its meshes, the silence lapped against the edges of the moist air. Trévalas's voice itself seemed to come from under water.

Mlle Jassy had stifled into a sigh the cry of indignation that came burning to her lips. She took a step. The Marquis sprang in front of her.

The young woman took shelter in a doorway. She looked at M. de Trévalas with scorn.

'Do not go before I have finished, please, Mademoiselle. Before you make up your mind, you should know with whom you are dealing and you will not dare to refuse when you know what kind of man I am! When I look at you, my head explodes, my blood boils, I desire your musician's body! I shall not let any obstacle prevent me from . . . from lying beside you, on your bed! Ah, you did not know, did you, Mademoiselle, that I am capable of anything!'

The Marquis brandished his cane: the sulphurous light of his pupils flashed.

'Did you notice me at the concert?' he repeated,

lowering his voice in exasperation. 'Did you see the rather thickset, dark-skinned young man with me? He is my ward. Twenty years ago, his mother rebuffed me as you are doing. I crushed her in my arms – ha! She spat in my face – ha! She scratched me here – you can still see the scars from her five fingers – she tore at me like a lioness. Well, I flung her into a mountain stream!'

The predator's laughing teeth bit into his fleshless lip.

'Believe me, the waters that swallowed up Virginie also quenched any need I had of a woman that day, and for two whole weeks I was as penitent as a drowned rat! What do you say to that, Mademoiselle?'

'That if I believed in Beelzebub, I would think he stood before me. But I am not afraid of you. I wish to go. Are you going to let me pass or not?'

'Oh, we *are* in a hurry now. Going so soon?'

'Yes, if you will step aside.'

'If you have the courage, you mean. In any case, you will soon be back.'

She replied, in spite of herself:

'Be back?'

'Yes, of course. I order you to. Go home, have dinner, think over what I have said, take your time. It is now twenty minutes past six. At nine o'clock, Satan though I may be, I shall be waiting for you in the café I noticed opposite Le Bluff in the Boulevard Richard-Wagner. *Au revoir* then, Mademoiselle, I am quite confident in taking but a temporary farewell, which I can see annoys you. Not goodbye but *au revoir*! Think it over, take your time, my pretty little Jewess. Let us not argue about it now, do not trouble to reply for the moment. Till we meet again . . .'

An evening like this was like night-time in Hades! Some factory girls going past laughed like young ghosts, at the sarcastic tone of the Marquis. Gazelle-like, Ella Jassy slipped away.

'*Au revoir*,' M. de Trévalas called after her.

'Well,' began the Marquis, addressing Madame Usseins, 'you must imagine that this beautiful Jewess had a profile like a cameo, blue eyes like living pools, the elegance of a Lady Milner, and the most sweetly turned of waists. I noticed her in the music room at The Bluff and I sat through two whole hours of classical music, which I detest, for love of that elegance, that waist, those eyes and that profile. On the way out, I lay in wait for the dusky maiden and tackled her in a nearby street.

' "Mademoiselle, you are wondrously beautiful."

' "Monsieur, you are extraordinarily importunate." '

M. de Trévalas raised his bony face with its great aquiline nose and cast his cruel gaze round the room.

All the guests sat listening to the Marquis. Mme Lydie Usseins inclined towards him her childlike face and moist lips. The engineer with the expressionless features had taken a seat some distance from his wife, and was following with his lips every word of M. de Trévalas's story, which was also being received with rapt attention by M. Loucquets-Damenthe. Neither the mayor's wife, nor Mme Ennuyé, neither the notary nor Mme Gardous, neither M. Borelly, M. de Pourponia, nor M. and Mme du Clos, the owners of the Château de Favary, could take their eyes off the Marquis. Near the door, Bruno listened with half an ear as he sat daydreaming in the little Louis XV armchair purchased by his father at The Bluff, the store in question.

'That was how our conversation began,' the booming voice went on.

'Deciding to be as insolent as my Jewess, I replied:

' "Mademoiselle, I am a man who speaks his mind and hang the consequences, when it is called for. I have decided to go to bed with you!"

' "Monsieur, are you out of your mind?"

' "What do you mean?"

' "Have you looked at me?"

'What vulgarity! I couldn't believe my ears. I thought she was alluding to her youth.

' "How old are you then?"

' "Twenty."

' "You are a virgin?"

' "Do you doubt it?"

'This way of answering me with questions infuriated me more than I can express. I insisted that she take me home with her. She refused point blank. I threatened her. She mocked me.

'Since it was pouring with rain, I let her run away, and followed her in a cab.

'The rain was cascading down. My heroine, her head protected by an umbrella, had lifted her skirts to the knee and I was lost in adoration of her trim, shapely calves as they twinkled in and out, and of a pair of ankles as delicate as a gazelle's.

'As we went up the street, the water came streaming down to meet us. The cab horse stumbled at every step. I looked out of the window at the water running down the pavement, and from inside my cab I cursed the weather and I cursed love! I did not dare call out to my dusky maiden.

'At last she entered, a doorway; seconds later, I stopped my driver, a few yards up the street.

'I ran through the rain to the door my little Jewess had entered, and saw her crossing the courtyard. An old woman came to meet me.

' "I'm sorry, Monsieur," she began mumbling, "but the apartment was let this morning. The gentleman paid a deposit as well as a little seasonal offering . . . Monsieur will understand."

' "What gentleman and what apartment?" I replied. "You are mistaken, my good woman. Here you are, here's a New Year present, although the year is already a month old. Tell me the name of the young lady who just came in."

' "The pretty, dark girl? That's Mademoiselle Ella Jassy, a musician."

'She had hardly finished speaking when a motor car came roaring through the hailstorm, to pull up at the pavement.

'A man with a gold pince-nez and a hooked nose dashed into the corridor and bumped into the old woman.

' "Madame Jassy?" he cried in a squeaky voice.

' "Across the yard, ground floor!"

'The vulpine person was already there. I threw up my arms in frustration, and the concierge looked at me with her red-rimmed eyes, her apron shaking with laughter. I resigned myself.

' "I will wait," I said, leaning my elbow on the bannister.

'A little girl brought me a chair from the lodge. I sat there in the cold draught. There were traces of mud on the stairs. The flagstones gleamed with damp footmarks. I can still see every detail of that little porch.

'The evening grew dark, as if there would be no moon that night.

'A quarter of an hour passed. For all I know, it was a quarter of a century. The rain had stopped. The old woman had lit the gas lamp. No, the lamps were already lit in the stairwell and the porch. No matter. I do not remember exactly. But I did have time to watch arriving in succession the businessman from the first floor, the schoolboy from the second, with his satchel full of books, the blonde lady from the third floor, the mathematician from the fourth, the policeman, and finally the photographer (complete with scolding mistress) from the fifth – when, at last, I saw Ella Jassy's visitor emerge from the building at the rear. He departed as rapidly as he had come, and I could hear the whine of his motor car far into the distance.

'And then, without so much as a by-your-leave, another long-nosed individual pushed past me, and had disappeared into my little Jewess's lodgings before I could recover from my astonishment. I scolded myself. Anger welled up in a wave inside me. Hang it, I *was* going to visit her! Then we would see. I was just walking across the courtyard, through the flickering shadows, when the second fellow came out of the musician's door and brushed past me without a glance, in as much of a hurry as the first. This time, the coast was clear, if I may so express myself, and I could not longer hesitate. I rang the bell.

'The door clicked slightly, and I had to push it open. I entered an antechamber illuminated by a red nightlight and hung with Turkish tapestries. Nine dusky-skinned children, of between about two and nine years of age – nine little blackamoors, I should say – all clamoured at once in their strange barbaric accents: "Waat the jaantlemaan waant?"

'Twittering like tropical birds, they led me to the exotic draperies of an immense room, and there, I saw Ella Jassy, now wearing a peignoir that matched the colours of the wall-hangings. She lay reading on a sofa of blue and yellow satin, while at her side slumbered two more little blackamoors, mere babies about ten months old, like little monkeys, twins no doubt; her dusky hand rocked their cradle.

'On seeing me, the maid of Jerusalem rose. I thought that a light sprang up with her, so great were the rays that her dark beauty emitted like the blaze from a burning coal. Her great eyes repelled me with their blast.

' "You, here!" she cried, like an actress in a melodrama. "No Monsieur, no, no, no!"

'With an imperious finger she pointed to the door of this salon, which was more like a conservatory than a ghetto, so many flowers were there standing in ewers, so many plants in Oriental vases.

'Without heeding her and pretending not to see her gesture, I strode towards her.

' "You are play-acting!" I cried. "I may be as lustful as Pantaloon, but I am no miser. And I do not care for Grand Guignol. I have come here to see Olympia or Atalide. Lie down on the sofa. It is warm in here. Take off your robe. Weep and wail, I shall do the rest. I shall give you in return whatever you most desire. O my dear Aïda, my Egyptian princess, I shall possess you!"

' "How can you think of it," cried Ella Jassy in indignation. "Did I not tell you that I am a virgin!"

' "I am not easily mocked!" I replied, "What about the two men I have seen leaving here?"

' "So, you have been spying on me? Well, Monsieur, let me tell you that, like me, those two men are Zionists. May I not receive Jews, my compatriots, in this place?"

'The nine Hebrew children surrounded me with white-flashing eyes and sidelong glances. I could hear the little monkeys waking up in their cradle.

' "What is that to me?" I asked.

' "I am a virgin, Monsieur."

'I pointed to the little blackamoors.

' "And all these children?"

' "They are mine!"

'Good God! This time, I burst out laughing. Was she mad, or was I?

'She enfolded me in the aura of her eyes as blue as the east, as distant as the sky.

' "You do not understand me," she cried. "I am a virgin to Frenchmen, to Aryans. I am a virgin as far as you and any other Christians are concerned."

' "Ah you are, are you?" '

'I fell upon the odalisque, I struck her, I beat her like Ménabréa beating his mule, while the dusky infants set up a howling like a troop of monkeys.

'Hearing the sound, a harpy appeared from the depths of the kitchen, showing her talons.

'The little blackamoors hung about my arms. I shook them off and beat a retreat. One of them had nevertheless managed to bite me – here on this finger! Rage and fury possessed me. Uttering oaths and blasphemies, I left the room. All Paradise thundered with me! Ella Jassy caught up with me in the antechamber, under the red night light, and in a changed voice, beguiling and coaxing, she murmured:

' "Stay, since you have beaten me. I beseech you, I beseech you. I have brought eleven little Israelites into the world. Would you like the twelfth to be a little Christian?"

'Ha! ha! ha!'

Monsieur de Trévalas fell into a fit of coughing. His sulphurous eyes flashed and he threw back his head like a cock crowing.

His guests were overcome with admiration.

'Such things could only happen to you,' the Baron du Clos clucked ecstatically. 'It is quite unheard of. I should never have had such luck!'

'Admirable, admirable, admirable!' chimed in M. Loucquets-Damenthe, his eyes blinking away behind the lenses of his pince-nez.

But Emma du Clos had not missed any of her husband's words:

'Will you hold your tongue!' she exclaimed, turning indignantly on the traitor. 'Why in heaven's name wish to have "such luck"? Oh, God in heaven, oh, Holy Virgin, with such a wicked father, how can Jean-Pierre fail to have wicked instincts?'

'Trévalas, you really are unique, absolutely unique,' repeated M. de Pourponia, rolling his cinnamon eyes.

'All the same, the story is a bit risqué,' and Mme Ennuyé, not without regret, concealed a laugh behind her handkerchief.

'I thought I would die laughing,' twittered Mme Lydie Usseins, her Japanese eyes brimming with tears. 'Oh, nobody could make up a story like that!'

'What a man, what a man,' the curator of La Méjane announced didactically to the engineer. 'What a way with words, what gestures, what fire, what character!'

'What do you think of that story?' Mme Gardous asked her husband.

'Er . . . What about you, Blanche?' sniffed the lawyer, shaking his crinkly locks.

'The more I think about it, the less I can believe that she could have had eleven children by the time she was twenty!'

The Marquis had overheard: he bent down toward this plump and freckled woman in her too-tight bodice:

'But I assure you dear lady, it is absolutely as true as I am standing here. Jewesses, like Arab women, bear children from the age of ten or twelve. Besides, during the only too rare moments I had the pleasure of spending with her later, Ella Jassy told me that she had given birth to three sets of twins.'

'Did she play much music for you?' inquired Lydie Usseins, perhaps a little too innocently.

'Now and then. She is – did I not say – a cellist at the afternoon concerts at The Bluff.'

And M. de Trévalas added, fixing his cruel eyes upon M. de Pourponia and M. Loucquets-Damenthe:

'Let us not forget that I was drawn into telling you my story by our conversation just now about determinism. In this instance, there was resistance, I broke it. The rebel became a slave. I triumphed. My will prevailed.'

TRANSLATED BY SIÂN REYNOLDS

*L*OUIS *P*ERGAUD 1882–1915

'A pox on "Latin purity": I'm a Celt.'
Preface, La Guerre des boutons

In the short preface to *La Guerre des boutons* (*The War of the Buttons*), Pergaud the countryman, the nonconformist, the unprecedented chronicler of animal life, declares his irritation with an emasculated age whose veneration for Classical virtues is often sheer neurosis, and his intention to write a Gaulish, bawdy, epic, Rabelaisian novel in which vulgarity gets back its original sense and has its rightful place. This novel is also redolent of Franche-Comté, the province in the east where all Pergaud's works are set. Pergaud himself was a Franc-Comtois, born on 22 January 1882 at Belmont, in the Doubs. His father was a village schoolmaster, and, after training at the École Normale at Besançon, Louis followed him into primary school teaching. Jealous of his freedom, he found the discipline at training college irksome, and several times fell foul of the college authorities. National service in 1902–3 did nothing to cure him of his anti-militarism. He became the schoolmaster at Landresse, about fifteen miles from Besançon, in 1905 – the moment of the separation of Church and State in France. The predominantly Catholic villagers of Landresse were hostile to their local teacher, by definition a servant of the Republic, and who never went to Mass. Feeling cut off in an alien environment, tired of constantly battling against suspicion, ill-feeling, innuendo and accusation, Pergaud resigned his post and went to Paris to work in an office. At work all day, writing all night, he found this way of life no more congenial, and returned to teaching in the suburbs of Paris.

His first published works were unexceptional poems, but his love for, and intimate knowledge of, the countryside of Franche-Comté were finding startlingly original expression in short stories whose main protagonists were animals. The *Mercure de France*, at that time France's most prestigious literary magazine, published two of these, and then, in 1910, a whole collection in book form, under the title *De Goupil à Margot*. A combination of realism and vivid, almost dream-like imagination, these stories are never sentimental and never didactic. However, in many of them, human beings do play a part, and the reader cannot avoid reflecting not only on the amoral cruelty and beauty of the animal world, but also on the animality of human beings and the morality of their relations both with animals and with one another. *De Goupil à Margot* won the Goncourt prize, in competition with, among others, Apollinaire.

At around this time, Pergaud was moving back into

Pergaud in July 1913. *Les Amis de Louis Pergaud, Paris*

Paris, to a clerical job at the Préfecture. Though the literary man of the moment, he was fiercely independent of coteries and -isms, and remained very much a country person in Paris. A further volume of what, for want of a better word, we may call animal stories, *La Revanche du corbeau* (*The Vengeance of the Crows*), appeared in 1911, and a novel about one of the earlier animal characters, *Le Roman de Miraut*, in 1913. Following this, Pergaud wrote several more stories in this vein, just as powerful as the first ones; these were published posthumously.

Meanwhile, however, he had published in 1912 *La Guerre des boutons*. Like all the animal stories, this is set in rural Franche-Comté. It is like a cross between *Bevis*, Richmal Crompton, *Clochemerle* and Rabelais, with perhaps a touch of *The Lord of the Flies* as well. According to Pergaud, it is based on his own childhood, but it certainly also draws on his experiences as a schoolteacher and on reminiscences of his in-laws. It is the story of the colourful, inventive, cunning, naïve and merciless battles which take place after school between the 10-to-13-year-old schoolboys of two rival villages. Warriors unfortunate enough to be taken prisoner are stripped of anything that holds their clothes together – buttons, garters, shoelaces and so on – and are sent back to their village in that sorry state. Interlarded with the battle scenes are equally funny schoolroom episodes, in which the master's vigilance is regularly deceived. When the grown-ups have finally found out what is going on and put a stop to the war, the novel ends with one of the boys saying of his elders and betters: 'To think when we're grown up we might be as stupid as them.' A series of short stories, *Les Rustiques*, set in the same area and often involving the same characters, was published posthumously.

Pergaud's work has always been popular, especially *De Goupil à Margot* and *La Guerre des boutons*; the latter has been published in over thirty editions in France, and there have been a number of adaptations for radio and cinema. The reader of *La Guerre des boutons* has mixed feelings: laughter, exultation at victory over the little bigots of the neighbouring village, unease at the streak of cruelty and bloodlust and the native cunning that feeds them. The reader of the animal stories also has mixed feelings, but, as long as the human connection is not made, there is no morality involved. It is impossible, however, not to be disturbed by *La Guerre des boutons* as much as one is amused by it, and impossible not to reflect with anguish on the irony of its anti-militarist author having been killed in war. On the night of 7/8 April 1915, Pergaud led an attack to try to capture Marchéville, in Lorraine. He was caught in the German wire and wounded in the foot. He was taken behind the German lines with the other French wounded, and given medical treatment. On the morning of 8 April, the French artillery opened fire. The French wounded were killed where they lay.

IAN HIGGINS

Texts

Œuvres complètes (Mercure de France, Paris, 1987).
E. Chatot (ed.), *Louis Pergaud: Correspondance 1901–1915* (Mercure de France, Paris, 1955).
D. English (trans.), *Tales of the Untamed* [*De Goupil à Margot*] (Eveleigh Nash, London, 1911).
C. W. Sykes (trans.), *The Vengeance of the Crows* [a selection of animal stories] (John Hamilton, London, 1930).
Stanley and Eleanor Hochman (trans.), *The War of the Buttons* (Walter & Co., New York, 1968).

Secondary sources

H. Frossard, *Louis Pergaud* (L'Amitié par le Livre, Labergement, 1982).
The Association des Amis de Louis Pergaud has, since 1965, published an annual *Bulletin*, rich in biographical, bibliographical and critical material. The Association's address is: 178, rue de la Convention, 75015 Paris.

A TERRIBLE ESCAPE

(extract from *De Goupil à Margot*)

Darkness lay thick about. Nothing disturbed the continuous dripping of the thaw. A sudden metallic snap cut a swathe of silence, then a scream from beyond the living world seemed to spring from the void, spilling into space like a cataract of horror, bursting the floodgates of the night . . . The wild creature was trapped.

Born the spring before last from a casual mating, Fuseline, the little stone marten, with her grey-brown coat and snow-white shirtfront, had set out that day as usual from the edge of the beechwood, where she had taken up winter quarters in the hollow fork of an ancient pear tree overgrown with moss.

Since the snow had driven the migrating birds south in wedge-shaped skeins, her food supply had quickly dwindled, and to satisfy her unquenchable thirst for blood, she, like her sisters in rapine, had been obliged to leave the deserted woodlands and hunt for her daily ration nearer the village.

She had taken to coming every evening, more wary or less adventurous than her former companions who had long since made themselves lairs in the roomy eaves of tumbledown shingle roofs.

The time was long past when, with the help of the harvest moon, she would climb into oak saplings to surprise in their sleep recently arrived blackbirds with their broods of fledglings; now the woods held only a few long-standing residents whose wariness could never be outwitted, making surprise attacks out of the question.

One night, sliding her slender body first through a broken window pane patched up with paper, then through the catflap in a door, or the hole in a wall where a beam had once been, she had managed to slip into some farmer's hayloft, and then, dropping through the trapdoor into the manger, had found her way into the warm cowshed where the chickens were roosting.

Light-footed, she had leapt up on to the perch where they slept in a row, with their feet tucked under them; and had drunk the blood of every bird in turn.

With a quick bite near the ear, she severed each bird's carotid artery and, as the warm blood gushed out, sucked it voluptuously, pinning down the poor stupid creature meanwhile with cat-sharp claws, before throwing it aside, limp, drained, and still warm, in its final death throes.

Drunkenly disdaining the flesh after the draught of blood, delirious with joy, her fur matted, her white front spattered, her belly swollen, she had returned to her wood, careless of the footprints left behind to give her away.

But what had happened in the space of time – so short, it seemed – that it had taken to digest her banquet of blood?

Now the houses were all barricaded like fortresses; behind their walls growled huge dogs with powerful jaws; on moonlit nights watchful men would loom like giants from shadowy doorways, shattering the darkness with a flash of red lightning and a thunderclap, the shotgun blast that scattered any four-legged prowlers drawn by hunger towards the village.

Now nocturnal hunts were spent in fruitless and monotonous wandering along garden walls, through holes in orchard hedges or on the gables of shingled roofs.

How many days had this wretched existence lasted! Then one night, by the pale glow of a star shining between two clouds, like a ray of light from the doorway of some cottage in the sky, she had yielded to the irresistible invitation of a hole in the wall. She had padded along beside a pile of dried-out pea-sticks, grey stripes on the snow, and then at the end, as if these half-rotten branches had been signposts providentially pointing the way, she had found, almost camouflaged by the whiteness of the snow, a large new-laid egg, which she had greedily devoured. The next night, she found another, and so it had been for several nights in a row, for now she came every evening in search of this, her only food. The remaining hours of darkness would be worn away in fruitless searching, and the belated dawn of these wintry mornings always found her, curled up, lithe and prudent, in the hollow fork of her woodland retreat.

Night had fallen once more, a night bringing thaw, the sky livid and heavy with clouds; slabs of snow saturated with water hung dripping from the tall trees like the linen of some giant washing-day, or crashed to the ground with a muffled thud like peaches bursting where they fell; rivulets of water trickled everywhere; the earth seemed to have been taken under some mysterious and mighty wing, bringer of warm air and sounds of stirring, and over everything hung a kind of anguish as if something was being born or dying.

At the dark mouth of the pear-tree fork, the little white shirtfront had appeared like a silent snowfall from a higher branch, and picking her way slowly, Fuseline came to the ground.

Hurry, hurry, it has been such a long day and her stomach is empty. She trots along the familiar path that brings her here each night. The pointed tips of her curved paws, flexed by powerful sinews, scarcely touch the grey slush of melted snow and damp earth; her long bushy tail swings lightly from side to side; she cuts across deserted paths making dark stripes in the snowy evening; she pads along past rough stone garden walls and black hedges iced with overhanging layers of snow, like giant water-clocks from which the dying season seems to be dripping away; the pulse of hope beats strongly in the little creature's veins and her craving for the long-awaited food increases.

Here is the hole in the wall and here are the decayed pea-sticks across which someone has left, as if by an oversight, those thick wooden planks, providing the only pathway, a narrow bridge leading to the egg, its whiteness standing out tonight against the earth, now bare of the snow of previous days. Now she sees it, now she is sure of her meal, and something inside her beats faster and more strongly. Another few bounds and she will be cracking open the fragile eggshell – off she goes! As she dashes forward, suddenly, the prompt jaws of the trap snap fiercely shut, seizing in their terrible bite the daring little paw, holding it fast in a relentless grip.

In the unspeakable pain of the capture, her cry bursts out, shearing through the calm night in terror, while all around furtive rustles, muffled bumps and snapping twigs signal the hasty retreat of any other wild creature nearby.

The terrible agony of the broken paw, the torn flesh, the lacerated skin, makes her stiffen in a desperate attempt to tear herself free from the hold of the trap. But what can straining muscles do against the implacable strength of those jaws of steel?

In vain she makes as if to bite them – but her teeth recoil from the cold and pitiless metal that would only break them, and as with every desperate exertion that fails, the pain that had prompted it escapes in a moan.

In the distance, a gunshot rings out. Then she understands what the trap means: the man will be coming to finish her off and she will be able neither to flee nor to defend herself. Driven by pain from the biting grip and panic and the approaching danger, she hurls herself from side to side in the convulsions of despair.

The trap remains unmoved, fixed to the ground. The little head is flung back as the undamaged front paw stiffens and stamps the earth with rage, while the back legs brace themselves like coiled springs.

The taut-stretched haunches pull backwards, sideways, forwards – nothing moves, nothing gives way. A great chain runs from a ring in the wall to the jaws of the trap now tearing deeply into her flesh. Drops of blood ooze from the wound and she licks them slowly. Then, as if abandoning the struggle after her exhausting spasms of activity, she seems at one moment to give up, to forget herself, to fall into a lethargy from pain or weariness, the next she is up again, pulsating with extraordinary vigour, throbbing, starting and screaming with all her might as she strives to break or undo the clasp that holds her tight.

But all to no avail, and time is passing, and the man may be coming. Before long, over there, behind the white shoulder of the snow-covered mountain, day will be breaking; a neighbouring rooster announces it with his rusty crowing and wakes the oxen, who rattle their halters in the silent darkness.

She must escape, escape at all costs. And with a convulsion more violent than before, the bones of the paw break under the steel bite. One more effort: she flings herself to one side, and now the tips of the broken bones pierce the skin like sharp needles, the upper part of the leg near her chest is almost free. All her energy is condensed into this one aim. Her bloodshot eyes shine like rubies, froth flecks her lips, her fur is matted and stained; but her flesh and skin are still ropes binding her to the murderous trap. The danger is coming ever closer, the cocks are crowing, the man is about to appear.

Then in a paroxysm of pain and terror, quivering under the relentless lash of instinct, she hurls herself at the broken paw, and with quick bites, she gnaws, severs, cuts and saws through the throbbing, bleeding flesh. At last. One sinew still holds: stiffening her back, bracing her haunches, she snaps it like a bloody thread.

The man will not catch her now.

And Fuseline, without even a backward glance of farewell at the red, jagged stump, left behind as proof of her invincible love of freedom and life, limps away, blind with suffering – but free after all – into the morning mist.

TRANSLATED BY SIÂN REYNOLDS

THE CLINCHER

(extract from *Les Rustiques*)

Pugface and the friends referred to in this story are all characters from La Guerre des boutons. *The dialogue is richly franc-comtois. It is difficult to translate dialect convincingly, and the solution adopted here is a transposition into a completely different idiom. This has necessitated a further transposition: while Pergaud's narrator is obviously a local, he writes in an educated, literary style; but the idiom chosen for the translation requires dialogue and narrative to be more of a piece, tonally speaking, than they are in the French. The translation/transposition below does, however, leave the affectionate good humour of the original intact.*

Young Pugface, just 12 years old, had been sent on a confidential mission; and boy, was he proud.

That morning, he's mooching about the kitchen, shuffling his clogs on the stone floor to make a clatter, and waiting, none too keen, for it to be time for school, when his Pa comes in from the cowshed and yells at him, just at the very moment that Pug's pocket handkerchief is creeping over a handful of hazelnuts, skilfully sneaked from the bag where his Ma keeps them.

'What in hell's name you up to, son?'

'What me, Pa? Nuthin', Pa.'

His old man's piercing eyes are going straight through him, and making him feel pretty uncomfortable in case he's searched – on account of he can always expect a good leathering if he gets caught thieving in the house – so he sure is surprised when the old man quits questioning him and tells him instead:

'Get your boots on, and quick about it!'

Pug's arm being ready and twitching to come up and meet the box on the ears that goes before a hiding, he is good and struck dumb to hear this.

'What for, Pa?' he manages after a few seconds, still wary, but keeping his wits about him.

'Because you're going to take our nanny goat up to Ole Gosey's billy.'

'Take the goat?'

'Yep!'

'Holy shit!'

'What in hell is it now?' says his Pa. 'Don' his Lordship feel like it? Maybe I should get the bishop to come an' ask him nicely?'

'No, Pa, no, Pa, you got me wrong: I mean, I'd be real glad to do it. And don't you worry Pa, Blanchette, she won' come back without she's got her forty cents worth!'

'I don' want none of your lip, Mister Snotty-nose. First off, you goin' to keep your mouth shut, an' if you breathe a word to Legrand or the rest of your little gang, jes' you wait and see what you get!'

'What, me? I never telled any of 'em nuthin',' says Pug with big eyes. 'Why would I go and tell 'em anythin'?'

'Well you jes' keep it that way. Now get going, an' shift your ass, why don't you.'

Pug has no ambition to wait and be told twice along these lines, and he's in such a hurry to tie his boots, he even breaks both his laces. He keeps quiet about it though, and fixes one by tying the ends together, and finds a piece of string to replace the other.

Two minutes later, cotton kerchief round his neck, army beret rammed down on his mop of hair, he's standing to attention, calm and composed, waiting for the old man's marching orders.

'Now get this straight,' his Pa lectures him, 'this here's the forty cents for Ole Gosey. Don' you go losin' it, and if I hear you been dawdlin' on the way, darn me if I won't get my stick to your hide. You go up the back way now.'

Pugface takes the four coins in his left hand, and with the other he grabs the rope round Blanchette's neck. The nanny goat, she's bleating and her little tail's wagging away, and she's anxious to be off. Happy as Larry, off goes Pug, through the wood and up the path on to the hill, holding himself in with might and main, to keep himself from bawling out his favourite song:

Roll me o-over
In the clo-over

'Oh, ain't it jes' prime,' says he to himself. 'A morning's school missed and blamed if I know the twelve times table! An' all them weights an' measures 'n stuff, why they're so b . . . bamboozlin'! I jes' bet Legrand gets hisself kep' in after school. An' Quiffy, an' Fats. But me, I'm gonna have some fun with ole man Gosey's billy goat. Meh-heh-heh-heh! He don' half get excited when he sees the nanny coming! Ain't they jes' going' to be staggered when I tell 'em what he gets up to! Our Pa, he don' want me to tell a soul, he don' want me to breathe a word; well, I'm a-goin' to tell the lot of 'em, so there!'

And he's so pleased with himself, that he takes one deep breath and fair sings out at the top of his piercing voice:

Roll me o-over,
In the clo—

But this joyful caterwauling, Blanchette she ain't expecting it at all; and she's so scared, she gives a start and leaps forward, sending her guardian head over heels, till he lands up flat on his back, plumb in the middle of a bramble-patch.

Pug is about to start cussing with rage, only he thinks first of his goat, and soon as he's up, he makes a grab for the rope. Once it's safe in his hand, he hauls Blanchette right back to the scene of the crime and ties her up good and strong to the first tree stump he lays eyes on.

'Why you crazy, no-good creature you! You plaguey goat! Jes' you wait, you gonna get the worst hiding' of your life, you ole bag of bones! . . . Jiminy cricket! the money! I've been an' dropped the money! Oh Jeez, my forty cents, where's it gone?'

And a cold sweat breaks out down his back. Because what if he don't find the money? How's he going to face that mean ole skinflint Gosey without the right price, because he don't do you no favours in that direction, not him! But then, how can he go back home without he's finished what he set out to do?

'I jes' gotta find it! Ain't nobody else gonna help me,' he decides, and still rubbing his ribs, he stakes out the patch he reckons is the most promising for searching operations, and he gets right down to it and fast.

'Well, it sure is my lucky day!' he sings out cheerfully after a few minutes, because he's found one of the coins.

The other three, they're going to show up any minute, no doubt about that.

And sure enough, some more careful searching and here's another coin, wedged between two tree roots, so he grabs that one too, fast as he can.

Now his blood is up, and he's grubbing about everywhere, while Blanchette, she's getting mighty impatient, and she's bleating away, piteous and longing like.

'Bleat away, ole girl!' mutters Pugface. 'That'll learn you!'

But try as he will, poking into every hole, prodding the ground inch by inch, turning over every leaf and every twig, never another coin can he find, and a quarter hour later, he's sitting crying, as desolate and sad as can be, by the side of his goat.

'What'm I gonna do? Holy Moses, what'm I gonna do?'

He's so mad at Blanchette, he itches to give her a thrashing, but that ain't going to help him any, so he just falls to cussing hard as he can to relieve his feelings.

And that's where he still is, his brow creased deep with the most miserable frown you ever saw, only now after cussing Him so hard, he's asking the Good Lord to send a miracle, when in the distance there appears the figure of Father Martin from the next parish, coming over to eat dinner with the priest in the village.

Pugface thinks his prayers have been answered and he sends a quick 'Thank you' up aloft.

Tears streaming down his cheeks, and calling on all the holy saints in heaven, he looks a mighty pathetic sight when the traveller, touched by this picture of despair, finally comes up to him.

'Why whatever is the matter, my child?'

And in a few jerky words, hiccuping and sniffing back the tears, Pug sobs out his story:

'I ain't got no more'n twenty cents and I cain't go to Ole Gosey like that, an' if I go home, our Pa he won' half tan my hide!'

'It does seem to be a mighty bothersome situation,' says the priest, nodding his head.

'If only I jes' had the other twenty cents,' Pug hints, in his most miserable voice.

But Father Martin, he don't seem to be able to take the hint; all the same, he don't want to leave this young member of his colleague's flock wallowing as it were in the waters of tribulation; so he gives him some words of comfort and encouragement.

'Why, don't take on so, my boy. Mr Gosey is a good-hearted fellow. He will surely understand the misfortune that has befallen you, and he will be satisfied with the twenty cents you have left.'

'Oh no he won't, Father!' protests Pugface, who's been around a bit, and knows that everything in this world has its price.

'Oh yes, he will, son.'

'I'm tellin' you he won't.'

'And I'm telling you he will!'

'You're a believer, Father, and you believe that?' says the boy.

And then, racking his brains, he comes out with it, the real clincher, the reason that's going to make the priest change his mind, because when you think about it, there ain't no answer to it:

'Looky, Father, would *you* do it for twenty cents?'

TRANSLATED BY SIÂN REYNOLDS

ANDRÉ LAFON 1883–1915

'It is not happiness I ask of God; or rather, it is, but happiness in Him and through Him – that is, His presence in every sorrow and every joy. May He show me the way at last: I will follow it, even if it be too narrow for two to walk together; if only it leads to Him!'

Quoted in François Mauriac,
'La Vie et la mort d'un poète'

There appears to be no doubt among those who knew Lafon that he was unusually devout, some say saintly.

François Mauriac, who was a close friend and published 'La Vie et la mort d'un poète' as a tribute to him in 1924, suggests that Lafon might eventually have entered a monastery. Born on 17 April 1883, he was brought up a devout Catholic. He turned from his faith for a while, but reconverted in 1910, after his uncle's suicide. He worked as a supervisor in a succession of schools, first at Blaye, on the Gironde, and then in Paris.

Much, but not all, of Lafon's writing reflects his faith, not unalloyed with doubt and anguish. However, his first published work – *Poèmes provinciaux* (1910) – does not have a predominantly Christian theme. These are short studies of provincial towns, gardens or people, the people often observed in their rooms and houses. Many scenes are described from a child's or adolescent's point of view, but there is often also a sense of coming age and death. The overall tone is of a kind of Parnassian quietism. The verse is sometimes awkward, but Lafon shows an undoubted ability to capture atmosphere economically.

La Maison pauvre (*The Poor House*; 1911) is more varied in theme and technically more accomplished. It is structured as a whole, to convey the struggle between a momentarily forgotten or abandoned yearning for God and an unspecified love. The identity and even the sex of the beloved are left vague, and the affair comes to represent the temptation of the flesh in general. The 'maison pauvre' is a symbol of a dwelling where physical desire is unknown, in which the individual might find spiritual nourishment. There is a gradual movement through the volume towards meditation, but Lafon depicts a troubled mind as convincingly as he does the sometimes mysterious or eccentric details of domestic and social life. He occasionally excels in the creation of chiaroscuro atmosphere: Mauriac is perhaps right to see in him a poet rather than a novelist, and we would be right to join Mauriac in regretting the loss of that poet.

André Lafon. *Bibliothèque Municipale de Bordeaux*

The two novels do, however, share much in common with the poetry. They exhibit the same tension between a longing for spirituality and an evident pleasure in the things of the concrete world. *L'Elève Gilles* (*Jean Gilles, Schoolboy*; 1912), Lafon's best-known work, is largely autobiographical. (This was, incidentally, the first work to be awarded the Grand Prix de littérature by the Académie française). It covers one year in the life of Gilles, starting when he is 10. He is sent first to stay with his aunt, where he spends Christmas, and then to boarding-school. The reason for this only gradually becomes clear: his father is mentally unstable and eventually, so it is implied with a discretion (or an inhibition?) typical of Lafon, commits suicide. This suicide is modelled on that of Lafon's uncle, an episode which contributed to the spiritual crisis expressed in *La Maison pauvre*.

The central themes of *L'Elève Gilles* are solitude, friendship, loyalty and betrayal. There is little plot, more a creation of atmosphere and a compelling expression of childhood needs and fears. Aside from the vivid and economical evocation of boyhood and the concrete setting, the reason why the book has retained its popularity (never a best-seller, but regularly reprinted) is surely its straightforwardness. If it has any symbolic or didactic intention, this is very discreetly buried in the texture of setting and mood. It would certainly not be inconsistent with Lafon's own spiritual yearnings to see references to Eden and spiritual exile in Gilles's love of his aunt's garden and his fear of a hostile world beyond the gate, and in the almost dream-like glimpse of the lady in the garden next to the school. There is, however, no need to interpret the novel this way. Be that as it may, it is interesting to compare the brief episode of the lady and the garden with the lost *domaine* in Alain-Fournier's *Le Grand Meaulnes*, published the following year.

Lafon's other novel, *La Maison sur la rive* (*The Riverside House*), is the diary of a devout young girl, Lucile Hervaux. The anti-clerical majority on the town council are refusing to grant funds for the urgently needed restoration of the church. Lucile, after much heart-searching and a brief but violent attraction to a boy she had known as a child, agrees to marry the son of a local landowner, both because the father will pay for restoring the church and because it will save her own father's vineyards. With absolute submission to her duty, she accepts from God the husband He has chosen for her. The novel is excessively edifying, heavily symbolic, slow-moving and written in an obsolescent, 'silver' style. It is as ponderous as *L'Elève Gilles* is light, although the writing in the latter is in fact just as Augustan. One is left certain that, in *La Maison sur la rive*, Lafon was working out his own spiritual crisis of 1910, but one is also left wondering why he should try to do this through the persona of a girl.

When war broke out, this physically frail man, of devout humility and generosity of spirit, felt it his duty to enlist. Pronounced unfit for active service, he was at first a medical orderly, tending French and German wounded at Blaye. Eventually, after repeated requests, he succeeded in having himself transferred to a fighting unit. He fell ill with scarlet fever at Saint-Ciers-sur-Gironde before seeing action, and died in the military hospital at Bordeaux on 5 May 1915.

IAN HIGGINS

Texts

Poèmes (Edition du Temps Présent, Paris, 1913). Contains *Poèmes provinciaux* and *La Maison pauvre*.
L'Elève Gilles (Hôtel de Ville, Blaye, 1987).
La Maison sur la rive (Perrin, Paris, 1914).
Lady Dorothea Davidson (trans.), *Jean Gilles, Schoolboy* (G. Bell & Sons, London, 1914).

Secondary sources

François Mauriac, 'La Vie et la mort d'un poète', in *Œuvres complètes* (Grasset: chez Fayard, Paris, 1950–6, 12 vols, IV).
M. Suffran, '*Sur une Génération perdue*' (Samie, Bordeaux, 1966).

JEAN GILLES, SCHOOLBOY

In this extract Gilles is at his aunt's house on Christmas Eve.

Snow fell several days running, and kept me a prisoner in the house. I spent the time with my nose glued to the window, staring at the whitening fields, and the few straggling houses that resembled ships riding at anchor in calm waters. Some passages of Bible history read aloud by my aunt led me to fancy myself a denizen of the Ark, stranded, but endowed by the hand of an unknown friend with the necessary provisions.

Christmas Eve was a day of soft haze, whose misty touch turned all things to shadows. Scampering about the garden that morning, I felt like a dweller in the depths of a blue sea which the sun failed to penetrate. About noon, however, it shone for a few minutes, but hastily retired, leaving behind it a faint light which grew feebler every hour. Towards four o'clock I was standing in the kitchen, watching Segonde knead a huge wheaten cake, when I happened to glance out of the window; to my surprise, the garden seemed suddenly to have burst into blossom. I made an exclamation, and Segonde, without removing her hands from the dough, turned her head to look in the direction I was pointing. I seized my chance, snatched up my cap, and ran out. The increased chilliness of the twilight had congealed the fog on the branches and twigs and endowed them with a shining efflorescence. I tore along the paths, delighting in the ermine draperies of the box-hedges; the trees were more thickly powdered with blossom than peach espaliers in spring; the shrubs were all crystallized, and their pendent leaves resembled the petals of flowers. In the meadow I found every blade of grass encased in rime. Beyond lay a mysterious domain whence the naked boughs of the trees rose like smoke. It was fairyland. I almost expected to witness the advent of a procession of angels. The half-light failed suddenly, the fog darkened to purple, and I turned towards the house which now showed, sketchily outlined, at the end of the garden; the firelight shone through the kitchen casement, and I ran joyfully home.

'Well! and where are those flowers?' smiled Segonde.

I held out my wet hands, still bathed in hoar-frost, in a mute gesture, and threw myself down before the fire to dry my shoes.

I was enchanted at the prospect of going to Midnight Mass, a treat I had never hitherto been allowed. We dined later than usual, to shorten the time of waiting. Afterwards we gathered by the fire in the little sitting-room. Segonde, in a low chair, prepared meal for the fowls; my aunt, seated by the lamp, read aloud occasional passages from a book of Meditations. Dinner had been as frugal as usual. The splendid turkey, whose execution I had witnessed that morning, and the cakes and sweets I had watched in the making, were reserved for the next day. 'The Holy Child is not born yet,' my aunt observed chidingly, when I grumbled at our uninteresting dessert of dried almonds and medlars; 'at this moment, Joseph and Mary are seeking where they may lay their heads; the inns are full of travellers, and no man can be found willing to give up his place at the table or under the roof-tree . . .' I thought of the fog outside, and the long, lonely road: 'What a welcome we should offer them,' I said to myself, 'if they would only come and knock at the door tonight!' A huge log had been brought in. At six o'clock it was laid on a thick bed of ashes. I took up a position whence I could gaze at my ease into its blazing depths; golden palaces sprang up, only to crumble gently and make way for further splendours; by blowing on certain spots, one could evoke long tongues of flame, which crossed each other with a crackling sound, and vanished. Segonde placed a few grains of maize on the embers; presently they burst into the semblance of little white flowerets, which I was allowed to eat. We were so accustomed to going to bed early that, in our fear of falling asleep over our prayers at Midnight Mass, we had all partaken of a specially strong brew of black coffee; so I was not troubled with drowsiness. One of the passages my aunt read aloud from her book mentioned 'ravening wolves'. In the silence that followed, Segonde said to me, 'I saw some wolves once, one Christmas Eve, when I was walking back from the town. Their eyes shone like fireflies through the bushes.'

'What did you do?' I asked.

'I shrieked out, *"Wolves!"*, made the sign of the Cross, and ran away so fast that I dropped one of my shoes, and arrived at home hopping on one foot. My word, I was scared!'

'What would you do now if it happened again?'

She shook her head.

'It couldn't. There are no more wolves in the country. That was in the old days, before they cut down the woods to plant vineyards.'

She proceeded to describe those days, before the advent of steamboats and railways, when a carrier's cart formed the only link with the market town. Her father had gone there on foot the two or three times in his life that he had had business to transact; he was once attacked by robbers in a wood he was crossing. Segonde herself had never quitted the countryside.

The time passed rapidly, and the sound of the carriage rolling into the courtyard took us quite by surprise. Justin came into the house by way of the wood-room, swinging his lantern. He informed us the night was mild, but we shivered a little in anticipation of the chill outer air, after the warmth of the room. We wrapped ourselves up, banked up the fire, put out the lamp, and with Justin lighting our steps, went down to the omnibus. I had carefully contrived to place myself between my aunt and Segonde, but just as we reached the darkest of the unoccupied rooms, the latter remembered something she had left behind, and turned to feel her way back, leaving me to close the procession. I grasped my aunt's cloak so tightly that she guessed my feelings and, opening its folds, drew me close to her side and folded me within. Segonde joined us at the entrance of the courtyard; a white muslin veil hung over her arm. I asked whether she was going to be married. 'Just that,' she replied smiling, and climbed into the omnibus after us. The fog was thick. The lanterns only made a splash of yellow in the opaque obscurity. The coachman drove slowly. Every now and then we passed a dim silhouette on the roadside; Justin called out a greeting, the foot-passenger answered, and was speedily swallowed up in the darkness. The odour of the charcoal foot-warmers we carried for use in the church, created a stifling atmosphere. I became frightfully sleepy. I tried to count the poplars as we passed them; I thought of the song my mother lulled me to sleep with, and endeavoured to recall the words and fit them to the rhythmic squeak of the carriage wheels. I was aroused by the sound of voices, the sudden stoppage of the carriage, and a blast of cold air coming in at the open door. We had nearly run over an old woman, and Segonde was urging her to come inside.

'D'you mean to say, Mariette,' she was remonstrating, 'that at your age you are struggling to Midnight Mass? Surely your bed would be a more suitable place for you.'

'Well, well, one can't just live like an animal,' the old creature panted; and blowing out her lantern, added: 'Saves the light, anyway . . . to say nothing of my legs,' and cackled harshly. We drove on. The sound of bells penetrated to our hearing; the foot-passengers increased in number, and gradually the solemnity of the moment which could thus people the empty roads, and fill the air with sound at this unwonted hour, penetrated my being. The horrible rattling of the window-panes made us aware that we had reached the cobblestones of the town, and presently we drew up at the church door.

The service was commencing. The church was brilliantly lighted, and vibrated with sound. I recognized the words of a hymn we often sang at home –

Venez, divin Messie,
Sauvez nos jours infortunés;
Venez, Source de vie
Venez . . .

We found seats with difficulty. The building was crammed, and the people not much inclined to disturb themselves. At last I found myself wedged in by the side of a small girl, who was putting her whole soul into shrieking in a shrill voice the words of the hymn –

Pour nous livrer la guerre,
Tous les enfers sont déchaînés;
Descendez sur la terre . . .

The organ and the voices ceased. The priest intoned. I must have fallen asleep with my head on my aunt's shoulder and dreamed of my mother, for the recollection of her is mingled in my memory with this Mass, though I know her to have been far away. I seem to recall her arms holding me close, and her soft breath on my forehead, as her beloved voice chanted, close to my ear—

Les anges, dans nos campagnes
Ont entonné l'hymne des cieux . . .

I was brought back to reality by the bustle around me. My aunt, after folding her gloves and laying them, with her purse and missal, on her *prie-Dieu*, rose to join the throng moving slowly up the nave towards the altar-rails. I then saw that before following her mistress, Segonde had thrown the white muslin veil she had brought with her over her head. All the women of her class and the working women had thus draped themselves in white to receive the sacred Host. The column of people struggled forward, inch by inch. Those returning from the Holy Table crept down the side aisles, their hands reverently joined, and their faces concealed by the flowing veils. When they reached their places, they fell upon their knees and immersed themselves in prayerful meditation. Meanwhile, the organ made soft music. The little girl beside me stared awestruck at the lights and flowers on the altar. My aunt returned to her place with serene countenance and fingers interlaced. Segonde followed, her head, beneath its muslin folds, bent reverently over her joined hands. Both were instantly absorbed in prayer.

At the conclusion of the service, the congregation was beginning to melt away with a sign of the Cross and a slight genuflection, when the organist struck up a prelude, and the triumphant sound of the final hymn of joy burst out simultaneously from those hundreds of throats, to the shuffling accompaniment of many feet.

Il est né, le divin Enfant,
Jouez hautbois, résonnez musettes . . .

The people sang with all their hearts, and the harmony, proceeding as from one mouth and one voice, must assuredly have soared straight to the Great White Throne, and returning thence, flooded the quiet fields and roads slumbering in the winter moonlight . . .

TRANSLATED BY LADY THEODORA DAVIDSON

JULES LEROUX 1880–1915

'If you can tell of happy days and days of tears, for those who cannot speak; if you can make those people dream and smile, then I shall call you poet.'
The Muse, in La Muse noire

Jules Leroux. *Musée de la Chartreuse, Douai*

Jules Leroux may be said to have dedicated his work to the poor, the underprivileged, the inarticulate. He himself knew hardship from boyhood.

He was born on 11 December 1880 at Villers-Semeuse, near Mézières (Ardennes). When his father, a carpenter on the railways, died, there were problems about the will and the family was left destitute: Mme Leroux became a housemaid and the two sons went to work straight away. However, the local schoolmaster, aware of Jules's intelligence and talent, took him under his wing and prepared him for the Ecole Normale at Charleville, to which he went in 1897 to train as a primary teacher. As a student, and after he had started teaching, Leroux did a variety of jobs during vacations, often as a farmhand or a navvy. In 1905, he went back to college, this time to Saint-Cloud, to train for secondary teaching. By the time he was 26, he was himself a lecturer in literature at the teacher training college in Douai. Among his students were Maurice Wullens, who later edited *Les Humbles* and published Edmond Adam (q.v.). Leroux was a popular colleague and lecturer, despite his reserved manner, and was respected for his commitment and intellectual honesty. In Douai, he also lectured on art history at the Ecole Municipale des Beaux-Arts, and contributed to the popularization of art by publishing low-priced books on painting. He organized his time so that he could work at his poetry and novels between nine at night and one in the morning.

Leroux's first publications were short volumes of poetry, derivative (with hints of Baudelaire, Verlaine and Henri de Régnier), rather sentimental, full of references to the Ancients and, for the most part, very traditional prosodically. This early poetry is well-wrought verse by a well-read writer, but one feels that Leroux has still not found his voice. *La Muse noire* (*The Black Muse*) is a big change of direction, towards the 'social poetry' pioneered by Verhaeren. These poems are, indeed, influenced by the latter's diction and brand of free verse, and they accord better than the earlier poetry with what we know of Leroux and with his novels. They express sympathy with the victims of the industrial revolution – including the natural world – and imply a militant determination to improve their lot. The poems combine rhyme and repetition to produce great dynamism. This is a poetry of accumulation, of overstatement, matching the arrogant excessiveness of industrialization: the imagery and sympathies expressed are sometimes uncomfortably well-worn, but this is counterbalanced by the sometimes awesome splendour Leroux discerns in industry and its battle with nature.

In his novels, as in *La Muse noire*, Leroux's art may to some extent be called painterly. This collector, art critic and friend of painters excelled in the visual set-piece. Like the poetry, too, the novels have the poverty-stricken urban or peasant world as their setting. *Une Fille de rien* is about a kind of Emma Bovary figure who leaves her husband for a soldier; their money soon runs out, and her lover drags her into misery and prostitution – only an unexpected inheritance saves her. *Le Pain et le blé* (*The Bread and the Wheat*; 1922) would appear to be considerably autobiographical. The grit and hard work of the central character, Paul, triumph over the scheming avarice of his relations and neighbours to rescue his widowed mother from poverty. The novel is a kind of patchwork of character studies, the narrative emerging almost incidentally, and one striking feature is the success with which Leroux captures the child's vision of the adult world. There are vivid descriptions of the skills deployed and the effort expended in country trades, including agricultural work, and sometimes an extraordinary empathy with the physical labours of farm animals. The author's radical, even socialist sympathies are not hidden, but not thrust in the reader's face either. Paul can no longer say the Lord's Prayer, because being *given* one's daily bread is a middle-class luxury – the rest have to earn it. Alongside the social implications runs a dramatic, touching and plausible love story.

There were clearly the makings of a politically committed peasant novelist in Leroux, perhaps a cross between Giono, Bosco and Dabit, but with some of Nizan's fire as well. He himself dreamed of a Balzacian series of novels set in the Ardennes and having characters in common. However, the only other novel he had time to write was *Léon Chatry, instituteur* (*Léon Chatry, Schoolteacher*; 1913), his best-known work and several times reprinted. This is set in 1900, and is clearly autobiographical: the story of Léon's struggle to become a schoolteacher and pay off his mother's debts. The dominant tone is affectionate and indulgent, and sometimes tinged with the sentimentality from which the other novels are also not entirely free. Like *Le Pain et le blé*, the novel consists to a great extent of set-piece descriptions and episodes. Leroux does, however, introduce steel into the story in Léon's continuing proud refusal to compromise his principles and kow-tow to the mayor, a political bigot. (A combative pride and sense of honour is typical of Leroux's heroes.)

The novel is very much of its age in as much as it focuses on the conflict between Republican and Catholic or monarchist politics. Léon, as the state-employed primary teacher, is the butt of right-wing polemic, and he has a violent confrontation with the author of a newspaper attack on him. Leroux excels in narrating conflict, whether the lovers' feud in *Le Pain et le blé* or Léon's fight. He also has a good ear for dialogue and a gift for satirical writing, both very apparent in *Léon Chatry*. Another side of Leroux's art is the chuckle-rousing vignette, already found in *Le Pain et le blé* but much more abundant here.

Leroux volunteered at the outbreak of war. He disappeared in action at Neuville-Saint-Vaast on 14 June 1915.

IAN HIGGINS

Texts
Les Franges du rêve (Edition du *Beffroi*, Roubaix, 1908).
L'Aube sur Béthanie (Edition du *Beffroi*, Roubaix, 1908).
La Brume dorée (Sansot, Paris, 1910).
Une Fille de rien (Figuière, Paris, 1911).
A propos d'un tableau de l'Eglise Notre-Dame de Douai (Lefèvre, Lille, 1911).
La Muse noire (Figuière, Paris, 1911).
La Vie et l'œuvre de Jehan Bellegambe, peintre excellent (Goulois, Douai, 1911).
Léon Chatry, instituteur (Manufacture, Lyon, 1985).
Jehan de Bologne (Goulois, Douai, 1913).
Le Pain et le blé (L'Amitié par le Livre, Saint-Vaast-la-Hougue, 1947).

Secondary sources
F. Leprette, *Jules Leroux*, in *Les Humbles*, February 1922 (constitutes the whole issue).
A special issue of *Les Primaires* (August 1921) was devoted to Leroux.

LÉON CHATRY, SCHOOLTEACHER

These extracts centre on Monsieur Rambourg, the village schoolmaster to whom Léon has been appointed assistant for his first post. M. Rambourg is a genial giant out of school, and a tartar in it. He is of limited intelligence, not very cultured and engagingly vain. The villagers love him (once they have left school). The first passage tells of Léon's first morning, before school starts; M. Rambourg is speaking. The second comes a little further on and gives an idea of M. Rambourg in class.

'First of all, you must have discipline – discipline above all. You're giving a lesson, so you insist on folded arms and straight feet. Anyone who unfolds his arms: twenty lines. If a foot moves: twenty lines. A boy doesn't put his hand up to answer: twenty lines. Don't tolerate any excuses or complaints. If anyone doesn't like it, send him to me. I'll soon have him dancing to your tune, and without any music, either.

'Inspect them before they go into class. Anyone with dirty hands or clogs – to the wash house. There's water and polish, and give them twenty lines apiece.

'Get them into lines before they go in; and they go in singing. It's very easy. Rap the table once with a ruler – that's the signal to start singing. They always sing the same song, so you just have to wait till they reach the end. When they've got to their places, five more raps on the table. Rap one, they stop singing. Rap two, each boy places his right hand on the back of his chair. Rap three, he stands at the table. Rap four, he sits down. Rap five, he folds his arms and looks at the teacher. To get them back outside, reverse the order. Twenty lines to anyone who gets it wrong. If they're not all together, make them do it again and keep them all back after school.

'You have seventy-two boys, divided into four groups. From 8.00 to 8.15, five or six boys selected by you will recite one of the pieces listed on the wall by the blackboard. The boy reciting stands up with his hands behind his back, or he gets twenty lines. After 8.15, the four groups have different work, so you follow the timetable exactly. Here it is. As you see, the first group write out, in their exercise books, the grammar they've learned at home. You just say: "Group One: grammar!"

'You immediately set the other groups working in the same way. After a day or two you'll have them thoroughly drilled and doing everything instantly and soundlessly.

'Your teaching methods are your own affair. We all have our methods. You'll find the books in this cupboard. You know the syllabus. You've done teaching practice at college, so I won't interfere in class at all. I'll simply give you these three rules of pedagogy:

A good teacher never lets anything go.
A good teacher never sits down.

A good teacher's classroom is as orderly as his living-room.

'Now go and have your breakfast.'

When Léon came back at a quarter to eight, he looked apprehensively at the groups of boys talking in the yard, hands in pockets, satchels on backs. M. Rambourg was standing stock-still in the covered playground, reading a letter and correcting the spelling mistakes with a red pencil.

'One of my old pupils,' he told his assistant heatedly, slashing the letter with angry red lines, 'one of the best I had last year, and he has the cheek to make spelling mistakes when he writes to me! He doesn't even deign to cross his *t*s any more!' . . .

M. Rambourg was a fearsome taskmaster and a stickler for accuracy. He waved his arms about and shouted, like a man in a tavern brawl. The boys had neither thought nor time for making paper darts or counting their marbles.

'I have my eye on you all!' he would thunder. 'I can see you all at once, even the ones who think they're hidden behind their friends! I can see some boys who aren't listening! . . .'

Wide-eyed, bolt upright, the whole class strove so hard to look like models of attentiveness, they were all so afraid of not following when their teacher was explaining something, that their minds became an inspissated fog.

Whenever a boy was thrown by an unexpected question, the headmaster brought an obedient, craven smile to the lips of his charges with the invariable pun:

'You're off form, get on it!'

Slowly, with a sigh of resignation, the boy stood up on his form.

'Say seven times: "I am a nincompoop".'

The boy tearfully repeated 'I am a nincompoop' seven times, his tormentor counting each one. Then M. Rambourg would look him up and down for a few seconds, before saying:

'Sit down, nonentity.'

The pitiful child would quickly sit back down at his table, scarlet with shame.

The words and the number of times they were to be repeated varied, and the headmaster's imagination was inexhaustible. Twice, five times, often seven, a voice would be heard vouchsafing, in a painful monotone:

'Henceforth I shall walk on all fours!'

'Blessed are the simple in mind.'

'I am as dense as the day is long.'

'Aures habent et non audient.'

'I am a buffoon.'

'I will be the death of my parents.'

'I am as vapid as a thrice-peeled turnip.'

'I do not deserve the air I breathe.'

'I am as intelligent as the back end of a goods train.'

When he thought a boy had given a truly ridiculous answer, M. Rambourg would go and stand in front of him, fold his arms and give him a withering glare. Then he would suddenly turn towards the others, who were sitting cringing in fear of being asked the same question, and, extending an arm like a gibbet over their heads, roar the terrible command:

'Everyone laugh!'

Instantly, with nobody budging an inch and every eye glued to the teacher, they gave a tremendous 'Ha, ha, ha' which could be heard as far away as the church square.

Sometimes he thought he would try the avuncular approach. He called the boy who did not understand up to him and explained the problem again, affectionately tapping him on the cheek:

'Do you understand, Tibert?'

Tibert, his head spinning, hurriedly said a tremulous 'Yes.'

'Repeat it.'

The answer failed to come.

In self-imposed penitence, M. Rambourg went through it all again, but the affectionate taps turned gradually into slaps.

'Now do you understand?'

This time, Tibert, with thoughts only of getting back to his table as fast as he could, abandoned all self-respect and shook his head.

'Ah! First you say "Yes", then you say "No" . . . You're blowing hot and cold!'

And slap across face made way for box on ear.

He turned to the rest of the petrified children:

'It's no use showing you boys kindness, it's a complete waste of time!'

Then he took his watch out:

'Tibert, you have cost each of us three minutes. There are forty of us here. Forty times three?'

'A hundred and twenty,' said Tibert, eager to redeem himself.

'One hundred and twenty minutes. Right . . . How many hours?'

'Two hours,' said Tibert in triumph.

'Then you shall stay behind for two hours after school.'

And sometimes he said to his deputy:

'The pupil has to see his punishment as the logical consequence of his mistake. We're punishing them, not passing sentence.'

Every Saturday, the head inspected the exercise books. One by one, the boys took their books to his desk, and the dreaded red pencil immediately swooped. Agitatedly awaiting their turn, they turned the pages without a sound, hunting for uncrossed *t*s and licking bits of india rubber which they used to rub at the blots. When their names were called, they tiptoed up (anxious to show they were aware of the respect one should show for the labours of others), opened their exercise books and endeavoured to stand out of M. Rambourg's reach. But M. Rambourg instructed them to turn the pages, which they did with apprehensive sidelong looks in his direction. With timid movements of hand or head, or strangulated monosyllables, they tried to justify themselves in advance when they saw their teacher's eyes widen or his moustache meet his eyebrows in a terrifying scowl:

'Woirin, you miscreant! Write out the conjugation of "to work like a roadmender" ten times.'

'Saunois! Repeat after me: I smear and smudge . . .'

'I smear and smudge . . .'

'With a besom of birch . . .'

'With a besom of birch . . .'

'Full of filth.'

'Full of filth.'

And Saunois gets a smack across his cheek, but doesn't dare rub it or cry, and two pages are ripped out and tossed away, then another, and the book skims the ducking heads as it flies to the back of the room!

Wednesday was the day the oldest boys dreaded. M. Rambourg censured and mocked and slapped them into cowed submission.

'You have to pull them down a peg from time to time,' he said to Léon one day during break, 'or they'll think they know it all when they've got their leaving certificate.'

He told him about the crass mistakes his top class had made. The boys themselves were not playing; they were sitting flopped down in one corner of the playground, happy to be able to draw breath for once. M. Rambourg read Léon the dictation, discussing the difficulties. Léon smiled dutifully, and in some embarrassment, because very often he himself would not have been able to solve the brain-teasers the headmaster inflicted on his pupils in spelling and arithmetic. Not daring to admit his ignorance, he agreed that exercises like these developed intelligence and subtlety of mind. When, somewhat pusillanimously, he objected that they were perhaps a little hard for 12- or 13-year-olds, M. Rambourg triumphantly savoured his own superiority.

The boys were indeed stumped by the kind of problem which involved measuring a field with a chain which is too long or too short, or working out how long it takes a greyhound to catch a fox with a sixty-stride start, or how many seconds it takes two railway trains to pass each other.

'In all my time at Bourimont, not one boy, not a single one, has been able to solve this problem without help from me: "A father is five times older than his son. He married at 24 and that was long enough ago for the son to be 24 himself. How old are the father and the son?" – Not one! In fifteen years!'

And yet the boys knew the answer. There were not ten people in Bourimont who did not, although none of them could remember the ingenious way it was arrived at. In fact, they would celebrate public holidays by putting the question to their guests or people from neighbouring villages. Since nobody ever got it right, they had their sons explain how it was done, and the sons glowed with pride.

TRANSLATED BY IAN HIGGINS

ALAIN-FOURNIER 1886–1914

'I don't know exactly where *God is in this war because none of us can solve the riddle of existence, but I know that I'll be shot down only when He wants, how He wants and where He wants.'*
From a conversation with Pierre Maury, 1914

Sub-lieutenant Fournier in military training, 1909.
(Association des Amis d'Alain Fournier, Viroflay)

'Alain-Fournier' was the *nom de plume* of Henri Alban Fournier who was born on 3 October 1886 in La Chapelle-d'Angillon, a small village due north of Bourges, in the Cher *département* of France. His parents were country schoolteachers, and his earliest formal education took place in the school they administered between them at Epineuil-le-Fleuriel, another small and remote village in the extreme south of that same *département*. Like many other ambitious parents in the French teaching profession, the Fourniers set their sights on the École Normale Supérieure (ENS) in Paris, one of the State's most prestigious *grandes écoles*, entry to which is secured through a fiercely competitive open examination normally undertaken at the age of 18 or 19. With that still-distant end in view, Fournier was dispatched to Paris as a boarder at the Lycée Voltaire in October 1898.

His early academic results encouraged hopes that the ENS would not prove beyond him, but in September 1901, apparently at his own insistence, Fournier transferred to the *lycée* in Brest which specialized in preparing entrants for the naval officers' entrance examination. The reasons for this abrupt change of direction remain obscure: Cher is the most land-locked of all French *départements* and there were no naval antecedents in either branch of his parents' families, although one of the earliest photographs from the family album reveals the 14-year-old Fournier decidedly dapper in a smart sailor suit. He had a good school record at Brest, passing the first part of the *baccalauréat* and winning the prize for the best all-round performance of his year, but in December 1902, he decided to leave the *lycée* as suddenly as he had resolved to go there. His parents, unfailingly compliant, acquiesced, and from January to July 1903, he studied at the *lycée* in Bourges which, in 1937, was renamed the Lycée Alain-Fournier. In his final weeks there, he passed the second part of the *baccalauréat*.

In October 1903, he resumed in earnest his studies for the École Normale Supérieure entrance examination. He enrolled as a boarder at Lakanal, a fashionable *lycée* in the southern suburbs of Paris, much favoured by the French well-to-do and pupils from overseas. Here, Fournier made a number of crucial encounters, the most important of which was with a fellow-pupil, Jacques Rivière, son of a medical professor at the University of Bordeaux. Jacques had an acutely analytical mind and a passionate love of literature and music. He was later to marry Fournier's sister, Isabelle (born in 1889) and, in 1919, became director of *La Nouvelle Revue Française*, one of the most distinguished of all 20th-century literary journals.

Fournier and Rivière immersed themselves in the cultural life of contemporary Paris which, in the years immediately preceding the First World War, was arguably the world's artistic capital. From January 1904 onwards, they became devotees of Debussy's opera *Pelléas et Mélisande* and of César Franck, Fauré and Dukas. They never missed a contemporary art exhibition, their particular idols – and, subsequently, personal friends – being Maurice Denis and André Lhote (*see illustration*). They devoured all the modern poetry and fiction they could lay hands on, often as soon as it was published, and their perceptive comments on all of this, expressed in the many letters they wrote to one another during the period 1905–14, provides a correspondence particularly rich in value to the cultural historian.

It is also rich in human interest because, in their letters, they frankly discuss their emotional and spiritual problems together with their plans and ambitions for life. From those letters and from notes unpublished in his lifetime, we can construct the story of another of the decisive encounters of Fournier's schooldays. On 1 June 1905, emerging from an art exhibition at the Grand Palais beside the Seine, Fournier saw a fair-haired young lady and an elderly companion going down the steps just ahead of him. Instantly captivated, he followed them on to a *bateau-mouche*, across the Seine, and along the Left Bank until they entered a large house in the Boulevard Saint-Germain. Here he returned to keep vigil until 11 June, Whitsunday, when the young lady emerged alone and he was able to engage her in conversation. He learned that her name was Yvonne de Quièvrecourt, that her father was a high official in the French Admiralty, that she was on holiday in Paris and lived in Toulon. At the end of the brief encounter, she asked him not to follow her further and walked away. His immediate response was to race back to Lakanal and, on the pages of a school exercise-book, record, while they were still fresh, his impressions of the meeting. Shortly afterwards, while working in London for two months to improve his English as a translating-clerk for the Sanderson Wallpaper Company in Chiswick, he transposed those impressions into the most accomplished of his youthful poems 'À travers les étés . . .'; they were later to provide the model for the meeting between Meaulnes and Yvonne de Galais at *la fête étrange*.

Seminal though all these experiences were, they proved a serious distraction from the academic matter in hand: to pass the entrance examination to the Ecole Normale. Rivière made his attempt in July 1905 and failed, though, as a consolation, he was awarded a university scholarship at Bordeaux. Fournier failed more comprehensively *and* on two occasions: first in July 1906, and then in July 1907, at the ripe age of nearly 21. The day after the second result was announced, he called at the house in the Boulevard Saint-Germain where he had followed Yvonne de Quièvrecourt. He was told that she had been married since October 1906. It seems somehow

> *'Neither philosophy nor art nor literature is worth the years of life lost studying it.'*
> *Letter to Jacques Rivière, 1906*

appropriate that, while she was now both as fair and as remote as his beloved Mélisande (with whom he had associated her from the very outset), her husband, a doctor, was in the French navy, the career to which Fournier had once been so powerfully attracted and which remained forever out of reach.

In the event, he joined the army, on 2 October 1907, when he began his two years of compulsory military service. He was initially enlisted into the 23rd Regiment of Dragoons but, on 10 November 1907, was transferred into the 104th Regiment of Infantry. In his letters to parents and friends, he regularly complained about the harshness of the conditions and the loutishness of many of his companions, but his army career was by no means an unmitigated disaster. He was physically tough, an outstanding gymnast at school and subsequently, and the route-marches and life under canvas on manoeuvres proved an effective antidote to the long months of cerebral torment in the schoolroom. ('The great relief and the brutal physical life I'm going to enjoy for the next two years will sweep away every trace of any emotional difficulties.') He saw at first hand rural regions of central and southern France which, on the evidence of the vivid *reportage* in his letters, he came to appreciate. He proved a thoroughly competent soldier, being promoted to corporal in April 1908 and to second lieutenant in April 1909 when he was posted to the 88th Infantry Regiment based in Mirande, in the far south, within sight of the Pyrenees. Here he underwent a religious crisis after visiting nearby Lourdes and failed yet another State examination – on this occasion, the *licence* (or degree) in English.

Throughout his army career, he periodically returned to the ambition he had first formulated as a schoolboy: to become a fulltime writer. Like many a would-be young writer and, at the same time, voracious reader, it took him quite a while to discover what he really wanted to say and how best to say it. While he readily responded to the heady cultural atmosphere of Paris, he was always loyal to his rural background. His earliest writings, strongly influenced by the rustic poetry of Francis Jammes (1868–1938) and Émile Verhaeren (1855–1916), are poems in free-verse form, evoking the sights and sounds of his country past. Details of this sort also dominate the few fragments that have survived of *Les Gens du Domaine*, the first attempts he made to write a novel, in the summer of 1905.

Memories of his childhood and of the brief encounter with Yvonne de Quièvrecourt also feature prominently in the first piece ever published under the name Alain-Fournier: 'Le Corps de la femme', which appeared on Christmas Day 1907 in *La Grande Revue*.

Completed just before he was called up, it can be seen as a farewell to youthful innocence. It argues that the female body is most alluring when it is clothed, and seeks to substantiate this with a series of vignettes depicting young mothers tending their children. It provides a stark contrast to the piece he wrote just over a year later, 'La Femme empoisonnée', in which the central figure is a prostitute, disfigured by disease picked up from and passed on to the soldiers of the local garrison.

When time permitted, he continued to seek a solution to the still unsolved problem of finding an appropriate form for the novel he was determined to write. In the summer of 1908, it was to have been called *Le Pays sans nom*, and the few unconnected episodes which have survived – all prose-poems – suggest that the nameless country in question was to have been an amalgam of the land of heart's desire and the 'other landscape' which visionaries sometimes perceive just beyond the scenery of everyday.

On 25 September 1909, Fournier was demobilized, just four days after he had learned from a private inquiry agency that Yvonne de Quièvrecourt (now Brochet) was the mother of a child. This news, following soon after the marriage of his sister to Rivière and his acutely painful religious uncertainties, plunged him into deep despair. The consequences can be seen in the next plan he devised for his novel, now to be entitled *Le Jour de Noces*, in which the hero, Meaulnes, is unexpectedly reunited with the beloved he thought he had lost, marries her, then promptly deserts her on their wedding day to enter holy orders.

Back in Paris and living with his parents (who had secured transfers from the Cher *département* in order to teach in the capital), Fournier secured employment as a literary gossip-columnist with the review *Paris-Journal*. This enabled him to read widely and to meet the good and the great of the Paris cultural scene. For a while in 1910 he acted as the private French language tutor to T. S. Eliot, then a philosophy student in Paris. He became particularly friendly with two writers with country backgrounds similar to his own: Marguerite Audoux, author of the near-autobiographical novel *Marie-Claire*, and Charles Péguy (q.v.). Together with Péguy, Rivière, Giraudoux and the publisher Gaston Gallimard, he regularly played rugby – and some tennis – for the group La Jeunesse Littéraire. Between February 1910 and April 1912, he had an affair with a young milliner, Jeanne Bruneau, in which tenderness and concern regularly alternated with anger and recrimination. Part of Fournier wanted to remain pure and to serve his *princesse lointaine* as her *chevalier sans peur et sans reproche*; the other part, rarely able to resist sexual temptation, led him into a number of affairs which seem mainly to have increased his self-disgust. The conflict is all too apparent in the definitive version of his novel, *Le Grand Meaulnes*, finally completed in December 1912, serialized in *La Nouvelle Revue Française* between July and November 1913, and published in book form in October 1913. Often described as an escapist romance, it in fact expresses a deal of remorse and guilt, the central male characters embodying, as Fournier himself said, what he would like to have been and what he actually was.

'There's a wonderful book to be written about this war, if God will help me.'
Letter to Simone Casimir-Perier, September 1914

In April 1912, through the agency of Péguy, Fournier became secretary to Claude Casimir-Perier, son of a former President of the Republic and himself an aspiring politician. In the following May, after a fortnight's military service at Mirande, Fournier once again met Yvonne de Quièvrecourt at the naval port of Rochefort, where her husband, by now a doctor of high distinction, was currently stationed. Conversation was frank but inevitably strained, the more so after Fournier handed her a copy of a love-letter he had written to her sixteen months previously. A desultory correspondence resulted, in the course of which Yvonne suggested a number of stylistic amendments to the text of *Le Grand Meaulnes*, but the second meeting finally confirmed that his cause was hopeless. On 29 May 1913, after attending the stormy première of Stravinsky's *Le Sacre du printemps*, Fournier spent the night with Casimir-Perier's wife Simone, who was then one of the most powerful actresses on the Paris stage. Their affair, punctuated with the same periods of euphoria and storm as the relationship with Jeanne Bruneau, ended only with Fournier's death: 'I know now, my love, where to find happiness, the free and joyful life, the fortunate isle, but the whole war stands between it and me.'

After the publication of *Le Grand Meaulnes*, Fournier began work on a novel, *Colombe Blanchet*, and a play, *La Maison dans le forêt*, neither of which was very far advanced when general mobilization was decreed in France on 1 August 1914. Fournier joined his unit, by now the 288th Infantry Regiment, at its base at Mirande ('Many of my former soldiers are still under my command. They kept saying this morning: "*Mon Lieutenant*, how good it is to be back with you again." ') and on 9 August, it set off for the Front. The letters and cards he sent home all expressed the conviction that his country's cause was just, and they presaged the approaching battle. He was in action from 1 September onward in the still developing Battle of the Marne. On 22 September, he was ordered to lead his platoon from the hamlet of Vaux-les-Palaneix into Saint-Rémy wood. His immediate superior, a half-crazed captain, insisted that they locate and kill as many Germans as possible. The objective to which he assigned them turned out to be an ambulance station behind the German lines. The platoon was promptly caught in intense cross-fire, and one of the few survivors afterwards claimed that Fournier fell early on, shot through the head. A young lieutenant set out next day to recover the body, the spot being marked by a sword implanted in the earth with Fournier's *képi* hung on the pommel. The German fire was so intense that this mission was abandoned. His body was never found, and he was posted as 'missing presumed killed in action'.

'Portrait' was the last of several stories Fournier completed before *Le Grand Meaulnes* and must have been inspired by a newspaper cutting, found among Fournier's papers, published in Brest on 8 May 1911. This tells of the suicide of a young naval ensign, Yves Pony, who shot himself through the head in a hotel lavatory. Pony had been a fellow-pupil of Fournier's during his brief stay as a boarder in the *lycée* at Brest in 1901–2, and it is generally accepted that, in renaming him Davy, Fournier was paying tribute to one of the favourite novels of his childhood, *David Copperfield*.

A rather more important role is played in the story by another of Fournier's favourite books: Eugène Fromentin's classic love story *Dominique* (1863). The narrator, Dominique de Bray, falls in love, while still a schoolboy, with the cousin of a schoolfriend, Madeleine d'Orsel. The episode quoted by Fournier conveys the feelings of these two central characters at an early stage. Madeleine learns of Dominique's adoration for her only after she is married, and she then falls in love with him. His response is to agree never to see her again, to learn to accept second best and to immerse himself in a full and useful life.

One of Dominique's friends, Olivier, tries to shoot himself but succeeds only in disfiguring himself. This may or may not have provided a model for the unfortunate Pony, but it would certainly seem to have inspired the episode in *Le Grand Meaulnes* when Frantz de Galais tries to blow his brains out but succeeds only in wounding himself in the forehead. These are not the only features in 'Portrait' which prefigure *Le Grand Meaulnes*: most prominent among these is the visit to Barnum's Circus, where outlandish scenes and characters follow each other in quick succession, and the vision of the beautiful girl seen in the distance with her back to the viewer. Noteworthy also is the 'message', expressed by both of the principal female characters in *Le Grand Meaulnes*, that the romantic approach to life can – and normally does – lead to disaster.

'Portrait' was first published in *La Nouvelle Revue Française* on 1 September 1911. It was immediately warmly praised by Alexis Leger (the poet later to be known as Saint-John Perse) and by Péguy, who declared: 'You'll go far, Fournier, and you'll remember that I was the one who told you so . . .'

ROBERT GIBSON

Texts

Le Grand Meaulnes & *Miracles* (Alain Rivière and Daniel Leuwers (eds), Garnier, Paris, 1986). Includes a very full bibliography.

Lettres à sa famille (Fayard, Paris, 1986).

Lettres au Petit B. (Fayard, Paris, 1986).

Correspondance d'Alain-Fournier et Jacques Rivière (Gallimard, Paris, 2 vols, 1948).

The Lost Domain (trans. Frank Davison, Oxford University Press, 1959 and Penguin, London, 1985).

Secondary sources

David Arkell, *Alain-Fournier – a brief life* (Carcanet, Manchester, 1986).

Robert Gibson, *Alain-Fournier and Le Grand Meaulnes* (Grant & Cutler, London, 1986).

Les Amis de Jacques Rivière et Alain-Fournier, 31 rue Arthur Petit, F-78220 Viroflay, France.

Portrait

We know what it is to feel regret, remorse and contrition even when we've done no wrong or done anything with which to reproach ourselves. We know what it is to feel sinful without having sinned. And we know that these feelings are all-powerful and quite indelible.

Charles Péguy

His name was Davy.

I met him when I was 15, at the *lycée* in Brest where, over a period of ten months, I was studying for the naval college entrance examination. He must have been the son of a fisherman or a sailor. Whenever we went out walking, he used to wear, as we all did, an overcoat that was too small for him. But out of the sleeves of his protruded two enormous hands that were all heavy and swollen.

There was nothing special about him.

Looking at his little head, his short neck and teenager's body, you couldn't have guessed how remarkably strong he was. Even his ugliness was unremarkable. He had pinched features, protruding lips like a fish's and nondescript hair which he'd keep smoothing down with his hand whenever he became confused . . .

I spent a long time in his company before I really noticed him. When I arrived at the *lycée*, he was already one of the old hands. He used to go round with a group which I wasn't tempted to join. There were ten or so naval apprentices from the *Brittany*, coarse and sullen, interested only in going into odd corners for a furtive smoke. They were in the habit of addressing each other only by their nicknames: 'Nanny-goat', 'Coachman' (which they said in English), 'Catskin' . . . When I spoke to him for the first time, I politely called him Davy: 'I say, Davy, if you don't mind . . .' He looked me over with a glum expression, then rubbing the decidedly unsightly skin of his face, he announced: 'Nobody calls me Davy. My name's "Catskin".' At which, he turned to the boy beside him and went off into an artificially hearty laugh.

I avoided talked to him for ages. Every so often, I'd see him with his group, performing feats of strength or aiming to cuff all and sundry with those big, flabby hands of his, which made everybody hoot with laughter. He seemed to enjoy being poor. I rather resented the fact that he wasn't more miserable about it. And I spent my break-periods with some of the brighter day-boys who used to ply me with questions about Paris and the theatres there . . .

Round about May, Davy, who was swotting hard for the exams, came equal top with me for a Latin or French translation. I can't remember which. This brought us closer together. Sometimes, during prep, he'd come over to compare his rough copy with mine and we'd have a little chat. He wasn't at all self-satisfied, as I'd come to

Alain-Fournier in a drawing by André Lhote.
Archiv für Kunst und Geschichte, Berlin

believe. Like the rest of us, he had the burning desire to become a naval officer one day, but he wasn't optimistic about his chances. Indeed, I've never met a young person who was more pessimistic than he was. He spoke about himself with utter contempt. And if ever I praised him about anything, he'd respond by shaking his head and breathing out heavily through his nose . . . And yet there were occasions when he'd relax completely and behave in a way that was at one and the same time gentle and clumsy. He'd do his best to be pleasant and friendly. He'd come out with absurd little sayings that made him quite ridiculous.

Now that I know what later became of Davy, I find it impossible to recapture even the odd snatch of our conversations. All we ever used to talk about were exams and prep. It would never have occurred to me to talk to him about anything else. And yet, from those summer months of 1901, I've retained two or three memories which, as I now set them down, make me feel upset and uneasy . . .

Very early each morning, we'd go down into the playground where we'd be allowed a short break before lessons got under way. It was a small paved yard with walls all around it. At that early hour, it still hadn't been touched by the sun's rays. We were enveloped in cold and gloom. But if we looked up to the neighbouring roof of the Hôtel des Postes, we could see the telephone wires shining blue and red and gold in the rising sun and all vibrating with the singing of hundreds of little birds.

Nobody shouted out. Nobody played around. Some of them used to smoke a cigarette which they'd first cup in their hand and then conceal in their pocket as they paced up and down under the roof of the school shed. The other boys used to huddle together up against a blocked-off doorway, in a sort of cavity which was formed between the doorway and the place where the playground suddenly sloped steeply downwards to bring it on a level with the street outside. You'd sit down with your legs dangling, either on the rim of the cavity or perched on the iron bars which sealed off the former doorway. You couldn't see out into the street but now and then, as you pressed up against the shutters, you could hear close beside you – so very close – the footsteps of someone going away into the distance . . .

As for us, our heads were heavy, our stomachs were empty, we were all running a temperature . . . Just occasionally, someone would snap out of the general torpor and there'd be a scuffle or a flurry of blows. 'Nanny-goat' would bawl at 'Catskin'. Someone would snigger. Someone's book or beret would be sent flying across the playground and the whole pack would scuttle after it . . . Then, one by one, they'd saunter back and take their seats again.

It was on one of these mornings, towards the end of break, that I discovered, in an anthology, a page from *Dominique*:

> The prize-giving ceremony was held in what had once been a chapel. It had been out of use for ages and it was reopened and decorated just once a year, specially for this occasion. This chapel was situated on the far side of the main quadrangle of the college. To get to it, you had to pass between the twin row of lime-trees, the over-arching greenery of which introduced the one note of brightness into the cold promenade. From some distance away, I saw Madeleine make her entrance, accompanied by some young ladies of her social set in their light summer dresses, under their open sunshades which were dappled with sunlight and shadow. A fine dust raised by the swirling movement of their dresses hovered round them like a faint cloud, and the effect of the heat was such that, from the tips of the branches which were even then turning to gold, leaves and fully grown blossom came fluttering down and settled on the long muslin scarf which Madeleine had arranged around her neck . . .

And so on till I got to this section which I now quote from memory:

> And when my aunt gave me a kiss, then handed her my laurel coronet and invited her to congratulate me, Madeleine completely lost her composure. I'm not entirely sure what words she used to express her pleasure and pay me the routine compliments. Her hand was trembling slightly. What I think she tried to say was:
>
> 'I'm very proud, my dear Dominique' or 'You've done very well.'
>
> In her eyes, which conveyed great distress, there were tears of – what could it have been? – personal involvement? Pity? Or merely the spontaneous reaction of a shy young lady? Who can tell? I've often tried to explain it and I've never been able to.

As I read this passage, I felt as though a long, fine needle was being driven into my adolescent heart . . . I couldn't bear to keep it to myself. I got up. I walked up and down for a few moments, holding the page open, and I caught sight of Davy, standing quite still, propped against the playground wall. He had his hands pushed right down to the bottom of the pockets of his big, blue greatcoat, and he seemed to be shivering in the icy shadows. I said to him: 'Here, read this.' He stood there, reading slowly. When he'd finished, he looked up. His face didn't register the admiration I'd been expecting, but some indefinite and unbearable embarrassment. He put on an artificial smile, placed a hand on my shoulder and gently began to shake me. He said: 'It had to happen – and now it has!'

Am I imagining all this? Are my memories being coloured by my knowledge of what happened later? I have the impression that about this time, Davy began to behave slightly differently. Sometimes he'd leave his former cronies and worm his way into the day-boys' group to find out what we were talking about. I noticed that he'd take on prep which wasn't really part of the exam. At the end of our French lessons, we had to take it in turns to read aloud. The naval apprentices, who were quite different in this respect from the day-boys, despised this activity. But one day, Davy made an effort to read posh. The teacher did all he could to encourage him, but the result was total disaster. He made a point of reciting in a 'natural' voice. In the event, this meant that he read out the dialogues of Corneille as though they were an ordinary conversation. He swallowed the mute 'e's with such speed and so much difficulty that he'd run out of breath before the end of the line . . . That evening, out in the playground, surrounded by his usual cronies, he suddenly started to imitate his breathless recitation, then went off into peals of laughter, distributing kicks and punches in all directions.

Some time after that, at the beginning of July, Barnum's Circus came to town. On one of our free mornings, I was wandering through one of the lonely suburbs when I ran into Davy. He was as much at a loose end as I was, and he suggested that we went down to the Place du Vieux-Port where they were in the final stages of setting up the American circus.

The square which, in normal times, would have been

strewn with broken glass and odd stones like any stretch of waste ground, was now alive with the most extraordinary activity. Exotic characters went gliding between the square-shaped tents and shot us a sideways glance. Employees went silently about all manner of mysterious tasks. From vast marquees over on the far side, every so often there would come a tremendous clatter like plates being clashed together.

Closer at hand, in the shade of the trees, stood some drowsy camels. A long streak of a character, dressed in cotton, was doing his best to stir them into life, and he gave them a brief lecture in English which Davy and I were able to understand. Over on the higher part of the square, an elephant was pushing a tree trunk. Now in sunshine and then in shadow, two men wearing strange loin-cloths egged it on by endlessly repeating the same guttural and incomprehensible word.

It was getting on for eleven o'clock when, regretfully, we set off back towards the town, following the line of the big white and grey tents which looked like a long wall bathed in sunshine. I was beginning to feel thirsty, the sort of thirst you feel in the morning which you know won't be quenched with wine but which makes you want to sit in the shade and watch a stream go flowing by. I was going to ask Davy if he was thirsty too when, all of a sudden, a waft of summer breeze lifted up the corner of a tent-flap and revealed a corner of the camp-site. We both peered through inquisitively . . . Between the tents, we could see a sort of inner courtyard which, to my eye, seemed vast. Over at the far side, sitting in the shade with her back towards us, a girl was reading. She might well have been a bareback rider. Her hair curled down on to her delicate neck. She was lying back in her chair and didn't see us. She seemed so far away from us, in a garden that looked so cool, so peaceful, so lovely, that it was as though we were looking at her through a telescope.

I turned towards my companion and smiled at him. He stared hard at me for a moment and raised a hand as if to say: 'Don't make a sound . . .' Then, with great deliberation, he put the tent-flap back in place, and we both stole silently away.

Soon after that, I left Brest *lycée*. As I sift through my memories, I can find only one more of Davy: one evening, the evening of 14 July that same year. The celebrations ended with a procession of townspeople carrying blazing Chinese lanterns and singing bawdy songs. At eleven o'clock, Davy and I decided to turn in. Along the deserted road to the *lycée*, some lanterns were still alight. Somewhere, far away, there must have surely been a marvellous summer's night. We came face to face with a prostitute of our age who we'd somehow got to know. She said proudly: 'Know something? I was picked up by two officers!'

With a sort of unsteady, angry laugh, Davy retorted:

'Is that so? Well, if I ever get to be an officer, I shan't be chasing after *your* sort.'

And he looked at me, sure that I'd approve, as if to say, 'We know, don't we, the sort of ladies *we'll* be courting . . .'

It's been years now since I last saw Davy, and I know now that I'll never see him again. All I've got to remember him by are two old postcards which I couldn't be bothered to answer and this cutting from a newspaper:

> A naval ensign, François Davy, aged 24, one of the crew of the cruiser *X*, shot himself in the mouth this morning with a service revolver. Heartbroken after being thrown out by the father of his sweetheart, he wrote a despairing letter to his brother, locked himself in a room he'd rented at Brest, and tried to shoot himself.
>
> The bullet passed through his skull.
>
> He is in critical condition in the Naval Hospital.

Who would have imagined that Davy could ever have done such a thing! Everyone is baffled. He'd done so well. He was so proud. He'd said: 'Now I've passed, I don't give a damn for anybody.' His younger brother wanted to follow in his footsteps. His parents would ask his advice about everything they did.

Now he's dying, inside a closed room. It's midday. There's nothing more the doctors can do. A sailor walks down the empty corridor spreading it with sawdust.

His story is in all the newspapers. It was a perfectly straightforward, entirely honourable story. He wanted to marry this girl. *He'd met her*, so they say, *when he was on leave where her parents live*. I can well imagine that walk when he met her for the first time. Towards the end of the morning, in Brittany, all rainy and romantic, the girl looking down from a balcony or smiling as she vanished from view in the garden between the dripping trees . . . Ah, as soon as you saw that first smile, my brother, I know the great despair which filled your heart.

And so he went on his way, wearing his casual uniform, his cane in his hand, whistling a little tune . . . He suddenly felt dreadfully clumsy and stupid and ugly. He remembered *Dominique*. He remembered that morning when we glimpsed that American girl in the circus clearing. This time, he was all alone, he'd lost his bearings down that difficult road, in that land of romance to which I'd so thoughtlessly pointed the way. I wasn't there beside him to encourage him, to lead him by the hand down that treacherous track. When he got back home, he thought of writing to me. Then he remembered those postcards that had gone unanswered. So he decided he wouldn't say anything to anybody . . .

TRANSLATED BY ROBERT GIBSON

JEAN DE LA VILLE DE MIRMONT 1886–1914

'I really think there's something divine about war, despite its horror. It's immortal, like cholera and the plague. This will perhaps be the last – and the most terrible – great war of the modern age.'
Letter to his parents, 6 August 1914

Jean de La Ville de Mirmont in naval uniform, 1907.

Jean de La Ville was born in Bordeaux on 2 December 1886, of a line of sailors and scholars. Serious illness kept him from the naval career he originally intended. Much of his writing expresses a longing for travel and the exotic, coupled with an awareness that the one big mistake would be to arrive. This restless spirit was at the same time deeply attached to his mother. Like the petrels in his story of the same name, he was near-sighted: did he feel, as they perhaps do, that a world out of focus was at once alien and banal, a world out of reach and a prison cell? Be that as it may, his writing is often self-mockingly ironic, as if he were wary of lapsing into the clichés of Romantic-Symbolist exile- or escape-literature.

After taking a degree in French literature and studying law for a year, he did national service and then decided to stay on as a regular, but a bad fall led to his discharge as unfit for military service. Eventually, in 1909, he went to Paris to pursue a literary career, the other dream which had accompanied that of a life in the navy or the army, and it was here that he met François Mauriac again. They had been students together, but their friendship only dates from 1909. Mauriac speaks of La Ville's enthusiasm, the high standards he demanded of himself, the generous encouragement he gave others. Mauriac saw in him a dreamer who was not afraid of life, a young man with a streak of melancholy but who was a marvellous playmate for small children. It is certainly easy to see the man Mauriac describes building gang huts and playing games as the poet of *L'Horizon chimérique* (*Illusory Horizons*).

In 1911, La Ville got a job as legal officer in the Préfecture. It was in Paris that he wrote most of the poems of *L'Horizon chimérique*, published posthumously. These poems are variations on the theme of exile and longing, sometimes nostalgic, sometimes tragic, often comic, and some (the first four in our selection) were set to music by Fauré (Op. 118). It is no surprise that the restless, ocean-tossed ships and shore-bound dreams should have commended themselves to this composer, but Jean de La Ville did not always take himself as seriously as the music may suggest.

Nevertheless, his short novel, *Les Dimanches de Jean Dézert* (*The Sundays of Jean Dézert*), may be seen as a tragic obverse of the poems. In this work, irony lends a kind of bitter grandeur to the understated desolation of Jean Dézert, truly a 'man without qualities', who is somewhere halfway between Flaubert's Frédéric Moreau and Camus's outsider; Pooter is a distant relative, too. Jean Dézert is a clerk in the Ministry for Encouragement to Good (Equipment Section), and decides to commit suicide (but on a Sunday, so that he doesn't miss work) because his imagination is not strong enough to cope with reality. In the end, after a day's comic and touching procrastination, he decides that there is not actually any point in suicide, because he is indistinguishable from anyone in the crowd and incapable of dying completely. Jean de La Ville also wrote a number of short stories (*Contes*, published posthumously), similarly bitter-sweet and similarly understated. 'The Petrels' and 'A Conversation with the Devil' illustrate well the mixture of vivid imagination and stylistic sobriety which inform his writing. (The epigraph to 'The Petrels' is from one of the poems of *L'Horizon chimérique*.)

Although unfit for active service, Jean de La Ville de Mirmont volunteered immediately war broke out, but it was only after being repeatedly turned down that he finally managed to enlist. It has been suggested that here at last was the great adventure he had been longing for. Certainly, the prelude to war 'interested' him, and he was keen to witness and, if possible, take part in a war which was probably going to 'set the whole of Europe on fire'. His *Lettres de guerre* develop movingly from initial enthusiasm for the defence of Civilization and a conviction that the enemy was the entire German people, through a growing irritation with chauvinistic brainwashing and the flagrancy of what would now be called the 'disinformation' peddled through the French press (so much more heavily censored than the British, he said), to an eventual admiration, at the front, for the heroism and humanity often shown by the enemy.

Mentioned in dispatches on 2 November 1914, he was buried by a landmine at Verneuil on the 28th. He was still alive when his comrades dug him out, but his spine was broken and he died soon afterwards. One version says that he died saying 'Maman', the other that he never regained consciousness.

IAN HIGGINS

Texts
L'Horizon chimérique suivi de *Les Dimanches de Jean Dézert* et *Contes* (Grasset, Paris, 1929).
L'Horizon chimérique (R. Picquot, Bordeaux, 1947).
Les Dimanches de Jean Dézert (Editions d'Aujourd'hui, Paris, 1976).
Lettres de guerre (Imprimeries Gounouilhou, Bordeaux, 1917).

Secondary sources
Vie de Jean de La Ville de Mirmont, par Sa Mère ('La Cause', Paris, 1935).
M. Suffran, *Jean de La Ville de Mirmont* (Seghers, Paris, 1968). Contains *L'Horizon chimérique*, some previously unpublished poems and a short selection of prose texts.

L'HORIZON CHIMÉRIQUE

V

Vaisseaux, nous vous aurons aimés en pure perte;
Le dernier de vous tous est parti sur la mer.
Le couchant emporta tant de voiles ouvertes
Que ce port et mon cœur sont à jamais déserts.

La mer vous a rendus à votre destinée,
Au-delà du rivage où s'arrêtent nos pas.
Nous ne pouvions garder vos âmes enchaînées;
Il vous faut des lointains que je ne connais pas.

Je suis de ceux dont les désirs sont sur la terre.
Le souffle qui vous grise emplit mon cœur d'effroi,
Mais votre appel, au fond des soirs, me désespère,
Car j'ai de grands départs inassouvis en moi.

XI

Diane, Séléné, lune de beau métal,
Qui reflètes vers nous, par ta face déserte,
Dans l'immortel ennui du calme sidéral,
Le regret d'un soleil dont nous pleurons la perte,

ILLUSORY HORIZONS

V

Tall ships, our love of you is loss complete,
The sea has taken you; the wind of evening
Filled all your sails with sunset, leaving
Both heart and harbour desolate.

You are all gone to seek out fate's design.
My steps lead merely to the water's edge.
You craved horizons beyond mine;
Why chain you to the anchorage?

Landward I turn: that's where my longings bide.
Yet still you call me from the other side
Of twilight, set me grieving
For great adventures never tried.

TRANSLATED BY GRAHAM DUNSTAN MARTIN

XI

Diana of bright metal, Goddess-Moon
Shining upon us out of tranquil space,
The everlasting starry wilderness –
You reflect our sorrow for the absent sun,

Ô lune, je t'en veux de ta limpidité
Injurieuse au trouble vain des pauvres âmes,
Et mon cœur, toujours las et toujours agité,
Aspire vers la paix de ta nocturne flamme.

So luminous and lucid, so unlike
The dark disturbance of the human soul –
I hate such cold dispassion, yet extol
Your flame of silence offered in the night.

TRANSLATED BY GRAHAM DUNSTAN MARTIN

XIII

La mer est infinie et mes rêves sont fous.
La mer chante au soleil en battant les falaises
Et mes rêves légers ne se sentent plus d'aise
De danser sur la mer comme des oiseaux soûls.

Le vaste mouvement des vagues les emporte,
La brise les agite et les roule en ses plis;
Jouant dans le sillage, ils feront une escorte
Aux vaisseaux que mon cœur dans leur fuite a suivis.

Ivres d'air et de sel et brûlés par l'écume
De la mer qui console et qui lave des pleurs,
Ils connaîtront le large et sa bonne amertume;
Les goélands perdus les prendront pour des leurs.

XIII

The sea is infinite and strange my dreams:
Seas surge in myriad sparks of light, and beat
Against the dark cliffs; but my reveries
No longer dance like birds across the deep,

The rolling seas carry my dreams away:
The wind enfolds them, whirls them into night;
They form an escort, playing in the wake
Of ships my heart has followed in their flight.

Drunk with air and salt, burned by the waves
Which wash salt tears away, consoled by foam,
My dreams will know the deep's kind bitterness;
Lost gulls will recognize them for their own.

TRANSLATED BY HUGH MORISON

XIV

Je me suis embarqué sur un vaisseau qui danse
Et roule bord sur bord et tangue et se balance.
Mes pieds ont oublié la terre et ses chemins;
Les vagues souples m'ont appris d'autres cadences
Plus belles que le rythme las des chants humains.

A vivre parmi vous, hélas! avais-je une âme?
Mes frères, j'ai souffert sur tous vos continents.
Je ne veux que la mer, je ne veux que le vent
Pour me bercer, comme un enfant, au creux des lames.

Hors du port qui n'est plus qu'une image effacée,
Les larmes du départ ne brûlent plus mes yeux.
Je ne me souviens pas de mes derniers adieux . . .
Ô ma peine, ma peine, où vous ai-je laissée?

Voilà! Je suis parti plus loin que les Antilles,
Vers des pays nouveaux, lumineux et subtils.
Je n'emporte avec moi, pour toute pacotille,
Que mon cœur . . . Mais les sauvages, en voudront-ils?

XIV

I've taken passage on a full-rigged ship
That heels, keels, plays pitch and toss from port
To starboard. Gone is the steadiness of paths;
The supple waves have rhythms that surpass
The tired verses sung by human lips.

On *terra firma*'s endless continents,
My soul was from its proper home exiled.
My longing is the sea, the wind to lull
Me in the breakers' cradle like a child.

Time's mist obliterates the distant port,
Tears of farewell no longer sting my eyes,
I cannot recollect those last goodbyes . . .
All my regrets are emptied overboard.

To lands inscrutable I'm long departed,
Beyond the East, beyond the Isles of Spice;
My only cargo is my heart for barter . . .
But will the savages think it worth the price?

TRANSLATED BY GRAHAM DUNSTAN MARTIN

THE PETRELS

Believing only in what can't be done,
We have taken as our target
The blood-red disc of the sun!

The first thing that has to be said is that petrels are shortsighted birds. To this congenital infirmity may be attributed their uncertain flight and their shy, yet incautious, behaviour. The fact that their very habitat is blurred and unsatisfactorily lit may perhaps explain (although not excuse) the incongruous adventure into which they so senselessly rushed one day.

It might have been seven in the evening. The petrels were sitting on the warm sand of a lonely beach, along the line of foam which the tide leaves, before turning, to mark the territory it imagines it has conquered. A man out after gulls with his dog would have taken them, from a distance, for a row of white stones among the flotsam. A few jellyfish still caught the light here and there; a pool reflected a cloud; a ship seemed motionless on the horizon.

Finally, like a great blinding moon, the sun (it shines for everyone, alas) was making ready to fall into the water in front of all the usual promenaders of the coast, watching for the last green ray.

But the petrels knew how much deeper the night is for them than for other birds, and they were filled with sadness. One of them stood, stretched its neck skyward and voiced a brief lament. Hearing the signal, the others silently flapped their wings, still on the ground, as if to blow the dark away. This was an ancient custom, a relic from superstitious times, like a religion they no longer believed in. The ritual over, the petrels should have been thinking, as they did every evening, about settling on one leg and going off to sleep, forgetting the day just done in the certainty of another, just the same, tomorrow. Not one, not even among the oldest, was wise enough to set the example. They could not take their eyes off the sun, which was taking an eternity over all the elaborate ceremonial prescribed for its setting.

Suddenly, like the restlessness which sometimes drives whole tribes to migrate, an irrational urge set them running, every one, clumsily down the beach to the sea. Then every wing opened, and they all took flight, unsteadily over the first few waves, but soon in a perfect triangle, and through the air they sped, wings beating the rhythm of a sailors' song, straight for the last dazzling signs of light; over the inshore line of reefs that rise and sink with each slow heave of the sea; past a small fishing boat returning to port, barely heeling in the wind, one side red, the other dusk-black. All along the coast, one by one, the lighthouses were blinking into life.

At first, the petrels skimmed along on wings which long ago, 'like those of all sea-birds', took on the shape of the waves. Herds of white horses from the open sea galloped frantically beneath them. A gull, soaring high, wheeled unconcernedly against the sky before flying off, uncomprehending. Porpoises leapt from the water in hopeful imitation of Arion's dolphins, and followed the birds for a while, trying to guess what quarry could be tempting them so far or what danger could be causing them such fright. But (as has often been regretted) the petrels never met the cormorant of good counsel, who would have told them in his wisdom: 'You short-sighted birds, how little you know the world! Go back home and go to sleep! A sun once gone is never caught.'

They flew up to the furthest reaches of space, so high that the Ocean looks curved and at peace. Up there, in the night, the western horizon still has a pallor which marks it apart from every other. They flew through the gathering dark in a white gust of wings and cries. It is even said that they accidentally holed a cloud which had lost its fellows and was waiting till daylight to resume its trek across the seas. But soon they found themselves locked into a hemisphere of unbroken night, tinged only by the frosty geometry of far-distant stars. They had to sing louder then, to sustain their faith, for there was no longer the slightest trace of light to guide it.

Some, exhausted at last, would suddenly fold their wings and plummet headlong from the flock. Beads of blood dripped from beaks and blew in a spray in the wind. Every bird was buffeted and rumpled, and it is said that it snowed feathers on the sea that night. Nothing could dash the headstrong hope of that ignorant, dim-witted breed.

Those few who apparently survived the adventure have never been able to understand how they could have been chasing the sun since it set and still have it come up behind them. And so, today, the reputation of the petrel is firmly established.

Often, on a stormy night, they will crash head-first into the dazzle of a lighthouse.

TRANSLATED BY IAN HIGGINS

Jeux

I

Ô mes moulins à vent, ô mes vaisseaux à voiles,
Qu'est-ce que l'on a fait de vos âmes de toile?
Que reste-t-il de vous, hors ces tristes pontons,
Mes frégates, mes avisos et mes corvettes?
A quel souffle divin, vieux moulins, vous voit-on
Tourner comme ici-bas dans le ciel où vous êtes?

On a tué bien trop de choses que j'aimais,
Desquelles c'est fini, maintenant, à jamais.
Le 'mare ignotum' des vieilles mappemondes
Hante encore mon esprit à travers tous les temps.
Je songe à des marins sur les mers du levant
Qui voguaient sans savoir que la terre était ronde.

Je regrette des paysages de coteaux
Aux fleuves traversés par des ponts à dos d'âne.
La route poudroyait, comme disait sœur Anne;
Les moulins agitaient leurs quatre bras égaux.
Qu'est-ce que l'on a fait de vos âmes de toiles,
Ô mes moulins à vent, ô mes vaisseaux à voiles?

Trifles

I

O windmills, windjammers with mast and sail,
What have they done with all your canvas souls?
What's left of you but these few rotting hulls,
My frigates, schooners, cutters and corvettes?
Is there for mills some cornland of the blest
Where they turn still to a seraphic breath?

Too many favourite things have been destroyed,
Ransacked by ruinous time, spoiled or despoiled;
The *mare ignotum* of the ancient charts
Across lost centuries still haunts my heart.
I dream of seamen to the Levant bound
Who sailed not knowing that the world was round.

Gone the old countryside of dales and farms,
And windmills gesturing with four sail-cloth arms;
Gone Bluebeard's tower from which you saw the road
With horsemen riding in a dusty cloud;
What have they done with all your canvas souls,
O windmills, windjammers with mast and sail?

TRANSLATED BY GRAHAM DUNSTAN MARTIN

IV

Lorsque je t'ai connue aux Îles de la Sonde,
Ton sourire, ma sœur, était noir de bétel . . .
Depuis, deux ou trois fois, j'ai fait le tour du monde,
Et je me suis guéri de tout amour mortel.

Matelot jovial aux mouvements pleins d'aise,
Et très fier, je portais, d'un torse avantageux,
La vareuse gros bleu de la marine anglaise.
Enfant, ta passion fut un terrible jeu.

Quand je resonge encore aux nuits de Malaisie,
Je pardonne à ton cœur ardent qui me brava,
Car pourrais-je oublier de quelle fantaisie
Tu grisas mon ennui sous le ciel de Java,

Jusqu'à l'instant fatal où mon rival mulâtre
Me frappa dans le dos, un soir, avec son kriss?
Mais le Seigneur plaça, dans ma vie idolâtre,
Un Chinois converti qui me parla du Christ.

C'est lui qui m'a conduit, par des chemins austères,
A mériter ma place au nombre des élus
En semant le bon grain parmi toute la terre
Comme simple soldat dans l'Armée du Salut.

IV

'Twas from the Isles of Spice you hailed,
My beauty, with your betel-blackened smiles,
Since then three times around the world I've sailed
And have become immune to female wiles.

So proud to be a jolly sailor-boy,
I dressed my muscular and manly form
In blue – the British naval uniform.
My child, your eyes were passionate and coy.

O hot Malayan nights I still regret!
O Java sky that set my heart's pulse racing!
I can forgive but never shall forget
The ardours of our passionate embracing,

Until that evening when my half-breed rival
Took up his sinuous kris and with it scored
My skin. Now God bless the arrival
Of the Chinaman who led me to the Lord

Upon the holy paths of abnegation
(To him are due my everlasting thanks)
To scatter the good seed through all creation,
A private in Salvation Army ranks.

TRANSLATED BY GRAHAM DUNSTAN MARTIN

VII

Vous pouvez lire, au tome trois de mes *Mémoires*,
Comment, pendant quinze ans captif chez les Papous,
J'eus pour maître un monarque exigeant après boire
Qu'au son des instruments on lui cherchât ses poux.

Mais j'omis à dessein, en narrant cette histoire,
Plusieurs détails touchant l'Infante Laïtou,
Fille royale au sein d'ébène, aux dents d'ivoire,
Dont la grâce rendit mon servage plus doux.

Depuis que les échos des Nouvelles-Hébrides
Qui répétaient les cris de nos amours hybrides,
Terrifiant, la nuit, les marins naufragés,

S'éteignirent au creux des rivages sonores,
Laïtou, Laïtou, te souvient-il encore
Du seul de tes amants que tu n'aies point mangé?

VII

In Volume 3 of my *Memoirs* you may read
How, held a captive by the Papuans,
The King, my drunken Master, often made
Me search his lice out to the sound of drums.

But in the telling, somehow I forgot
To give you full details of the Royal Princess:
Laïtou's graces made my service sweet
Hunting for lice between her ebon breasts.

Often, a shipwrecked soul with terror froze
Hearing the echoes of our mixed caress
Among the dunes of the New Hebrides,
The sounding shores our mattress and our sheet:

Often I ask, do you recall, Princess,
The only lover whom you did not eat?

TRANSLATED BY HUGH MORISON

A CONVERSATION WITH THE DEVIL

Given our present state of civilization, it seems hard to imagine the Devil as anything other than a black monster with fiery eye and cloven hoof, concealing the horns of a goat under a red hat and a hairy tail in a pair of breeches.

Yet there are superstitious tribes in central Africa who, if the missionaries are to be believed, revere him almost as much as we do, but describe him as white. The Shintoists of Japan, for their part, are quite convinced that this worthy appears in the guise of a fox, while, by a strange coincidence, the Maldive islanders sacrifice cocks and chickens to him.

In fact, all these beliefs are equally mistaken. The Devil is a poor insignificant-looking chap, rather like a schoolteacher or a highways official. One could even wish him a little more dignified, or at least more in tune with the political trends of recent decades.

The first time I met him was, naturally, in Paris. It was about eleven at night, and he was drinking black coffee at a bar on the Quai de la Tournelle. We were both a little drunk. I can, however, remember that the café gramophone was playing an American negro banjo tune. The Prince of Darkness challenged me first to a game of three-dice 'ace-hole', so called because only the ones count. I refused, aware that the bounder was notorious in a number of clubs and seaside casinos. He then invited me very courteously to walk with him along the river until the first stroke of midnight, which is when he goes on duty. We went a short way in silence. Soon, however, as I had only to expect, he tried out a few temptations on me, with a view to acquiring my immortal soul on favourable terms.

'Would you like to be invisible?' he murmured insinuatingly, in the tone of voice Parisians use when selling transparencies to British tourists outside Notre Dame. 'Simply take the heart from a bat or a black hen or, better still, a 15-month-old frog, and carry it under your right arm. More effective is to steal a black cat, buy a new pot, a mirror, an agate, a steel, tinder and charcoal . . .'

I was in no mood to listen to a recitation from the *Kabbalah Unveiled* or *The Key of Solomon*, which I grew out of years ago.

'It seems to me,' I replied, 'that in our age of social and economic progress your skills are rather behind the times. Mademoiselle Irma (who was after all reading tea leaves near Réaumur–Sébastopol metro station when she became my first mistress) knew just as much about it as you do. Why, she once secured me a private conversation with General Boulanger just by turning a mahogany-veneer table. I was hoping for exemption from national service at the time.'

'My art is eternal, my son,' the Devil replied, 'and its precepts are ever sound. But I perceive that, while sceptical and coarsened by the spirit of the age, you are not an uneducated man. I would be inclined to put you down as an intellectual.'

I was flattered by my companion's words, which led

me to suppose that this time he was seeking to tempt me into the sin of pride.

'If you want us to remain friends,' I said at length, 'do give up trying to outmanoeuvre me. You want my soul, do you? Very well, then, you shall have it at face value. So please refrain from nudging me every time we walk past one of these scarlet temptresses forced by poverty to number among your clients. I ask only one thing in exchange for what you want: find something to divert me. You see, Devil, I'm as bored as any man on this earth can be. The Slough of Despond, that's where I am. I've even lost interest in the crimes of passion in the daily papers – the murderers always get caught, anyway. Manille, piquet, skittles – none of these things have any secrets for me. My transcendental yearnings are hardly going to be satisfied by the cycling results, or the benefits of Swedish gymnastics. I would like you to show me something I could get excited about, if only for ten minutes. Why not an aurora borealis, here and now, behind the wine market! Unleash unheard-of calamities; have the bells of Notre Dame ring out on their own, or the Eiffel Tower take off into the sky like a rocket. Let the two giraffes out of the Jardin des Plantes, then waken the dead in Père-Lachaise and lead them by age and rank in orderly procession through the boulevards to the Place de la Concorde. At least give us a volcano in Montmartre and a geyser in the Luxembourg Gardens. If you do that, I'll renounce all claim to eternal life in Abraham's bosom. But something unexpected! We've been dying, all of us, for want of the unexpected, ever since we came down from the trees!'

'My son,' came the Devil's indulgent reply, 'do remember that there are over three million people living in Paris and the suburbs. If I were to grant your wish for things supernatural, I would immediately be faced with two-and-a-half million religious conversions. (That's assuming, of course, that 500,000 or so of the feeble-minded would die of fright on the spot.) Think what it would mean for my books: an enormous debit, and just your one paltry soul to set against it; not much of a transaction, all things considered . . . However, since you will not be denied, turn and look.'

So saying, the Devil vanished, quite unexpectedly leaving not the slightest whiff of sulphur.

I did as I was bid, and my legs gave way under me as I saw the most stupendous sight. There were— there were *two moons* in the sky. Two moons, two identical moons were rising above the horizon, side by side.

This, it will readily be agreed, was altogether too much for one summer's night, which was quite poetic enough as it was. I was thinking what a splendid excuse this unprecedented event would be for not going to the office in the morning, when something suddenly struck me. One of the two moons was showing exactly midnight. It was in fact the illuminated clock on the Gare de Lyon.

That is how, one intoxicated evening, I sold my soul for a timepiece.

TRANSLATED BY IAN HIGGINS

Louis Codet 1876–1914

'I think Novelty should be one of the Muses.'
Louis, in Louis l'Indulgent

It is really Codet himself who is Louis in *Louis l'Indulgent*. 'With principles like yours,' says his friend Albert, 'you're going to go through life like a butterfly.' What little is known of Codet's life does indeed show him to have some of the characteristics of the protagonists of his novels – always on the move, never settling for long in either his emotional or his material life. It would take a net to catch this butterfly, but he has a wary eye for nets and entanglements, and he is quick on the take-off.

Codet was born on 8 October 1876 in Perpignan. He studied there first, then in Paris, and completed a doctorate in law (of all things) in 1903. A private income enabled him to travel – to Majorca, to Scandinavia, often to London. He was an accomplished watercolourist (one cannot imagine him painting in oils). He was elected to Parliament in 1909, as the member for Haute-Vienne, but he lost his seat the following year. (He had made one speech, on public libraries, but he had also published a novel set in Montmartre, and his constituents are said not to have found the idea to their taste!) He was a keen sportsman, and one of the first Frenchmen to climb Mont Blanc. He wrote above all for pleasure, and apart from texts in magazines, only *La Rose du jardin*, a collection of stories, and *La petite Chiquette* (1908), the novel set in Montmartre, were published in his lifetime.

Codet's art, even in his novels, is the art of the vignette. He is a genuinely original writer. The style itself is light and precise, in the manner of great classics such as La Fontaine, Voltaire (who was his great great-uncle!) and Montesquieu, all of whom, if we are to believe the evidence of *Louis l'Indulgent*, were writers he much admired. Classical limpidity and contemporary slang sit easily side by side. Especially in *La petite Chiquette* and *La Fortune de Bécot* (*The Fortunes of Bécot*; 1921), there is a sometimes whimsical, sometimes ironic, often gently humorous understatement which reveals the paradox of a new kind of 'sweet sickness': these are characters who are hungry for experience, jealous of their independence, and yet hurt by their own unwillingness, or inability, to commit themselves emotionally to another person. There is potential anguish under the playfulness, both in *La petite Chiquette*, the entertaining and moving account of a short-lived affair in bohemian Paris, and in *La Fortune de Bécot*, which is like an equally ambivalent episode from a *Bildungsroman*.

There is no such anguish in *César Caspéran* (1918), however. This is a long short story, a sketch of the

Louis Codet. *Musée Louis Codet, Perpignan*

eccentric and engaging Caspéran, who ends up as curator of a museum in Gascony which has nothing but four soup plates and a view of the Pyrenees from the top floor. *Louis l'Indulgent*, written in 1900 but published posthumously, is really a prototype of *La petite Chiquette*, and throws into relief the easy mastery of style and structure which makes the latter work so impressive. The light, ironical *Poèmes et chansons* express in free verse the same sensibility as the fiction.

The word 'light' should not be taken as a synonym for 'slight'. Codet the writer is as difficult to dissect as Codet the butterfly evidently was to net. This is partly because the novels are easy-paced, nuanced analyses of feelings which most novelists would dispatch in a chapter. Codet's selective eye for (sometimes quirky) detail also makes its contribution to this leisurely elaboration of character and atmosphere. He is hard to anthologize for similar reasons: each novel is really an episode recounted circumstantially, and any extract is bound to be inconclusive.

La Fortune de Bécot is in some ways like a comic version of *Le Rouge et le noir*. Gilles Tixador, otherwise known as Bécot, is the engaging, 20-year-old, tennis-playing life and soul of any party. If bored, irritated or in a tricky situation, he is wont to turn and jump out through the window, even of a first-floor room. This disconcerting habit neatly typifies Codet's heroes, who are all, at least metaphorically, jumpers-out of windows. Bécot is spending the summer near Vernet with his godmother, Madame Bouillon-Lamothe, and he is infatuated with a young widow summering at Vernet, Georgette Borelli. He does have a mistress, a music-hall actress called La Prairie, but it is Georgette he loves. He resolves to seduce her, but events conspire against him and his nerve keeps failing him. His naïve courting of Georgette scandalizes polite society in Vernet, but she tolerantly indulges him. He gets rather drunk one evening at the Casino, which leads to some embarrassment for Georgette; she gently scolds him, and he feels rebuffed. Meanwhile, there is to be a fancy-dress ball at the Casino, to which Bécot intends to go as a confectioner's kitchen-boy (he has already borrowed a genuine jacket from a local confectioner). The chapter in which Bécot goes to the ball (and has adventures away from it) exemplifies what one might call the 'incredible quicksilveriness of being' typical of Codet's main characters: learning to recognize their own feelings is something they are decidedly not good at, and that is where the threat of anguish lies. After this episode and further ups and downs, Georgette eventually gives herself to Bécot. With an idyll on the horizon, he breaks the relationship off and chooses instead, weeping salt tears, to join the army.

Louis Codet left for the war on the second day of hostilities, and on 4 November 1914, he was wounded in the neck by shell-splinters by the bridge at Stenstraate in Belgium. He was thought to have recovered, but succumbed to an aneurysm on 27 December. He was honoured posthumously with the Croix de guerre and the Légion d'honneur.

IAN HIGGINS

Texts

La Rose du jardin (Fasquelle, Paris, 1907).
La petite Chiquette (Editions Rencontre, Lausanne, 1961).
César Caspéran (Gallimard, Paris, 1952).
La Fortune de Bécot (Gallimard, Paris, 1933).
Louis l'Indulgent (Gallimard, Paris, 1925).
Poèmes et chansons (Gallimard, Paris, 1926).
Images de Majorque (Les Artisans imprimeurs, Paris, 1925).
Lettres à deux amis (Les Marges, Paris, 1927).
Poèmes en prose (La Petite Ourse, Lausanne, 1953).
Anthony Bower (trans.), *The Fortunes of Bécot* (Weidenfeld & Nicolson, London, 1954). Has an introduction by Thérèse Mayer.

THE FORTUNES OF BÉCOT

Chapter 12

In which we hear the story of a kitchen-boy's cap, a glass of whisky and a love letter. And the reader is warned, gratis, that Bécot once more jumps out of a window.

'*. . . D'Artagnan already imagined himself (so fast do dreams progress on the wings of imagination) being accosted by a messenger from the young woman, who would give him a note arranging a meeting, or a golden chain or a diamond. We have already said that young cavaliers felt no shame in accepting gifts from their king; let us add that in those days of easy morals, they felt no more shame as regards their mistresses . . . One made one's way with the help of women without blushing about it. Those who had nothing but their beauty gave their beauty; whence, no doubt, the proverb: "the most beautiful girl in the world can only give what she has got . . ."*'

When he came to the end of this sentence, Bécot stopped reading. 'In those days, ladies must have been very like my godmother,' he mused. 'I can just picture her in a court intrigue . . .'

He snapped the book shut, got up and stretched. Oh, to be a musketeer! . . . He would have loved to have lived in those days and been a musketeer! To have 'made his way' with the help of women: a rascally life, and a lot of fun!

He went to the window and stared absently at the evening shadows, spreading caressingly over the mountains. Near the house could be heard the enchanting sound of a watering-can.

'I was reading for a long time,' thought Bécot.

He stood quite still, head tilted to one side, deep in meditation.

Back to examining his feelings, he found to his amazement that his attitude had changed yet again. He felt hard and powerful and filled with an unfamiliar desire. It was the desire for revenge. Yes, real revenge!

'So she snubbed me! She couldn't have been more unpleasant! Well, I've been a coward long enough! I've whined for long enough! You're not leading *me* by the nose, Georgette, I promise you! . . . You won't drag *me* captive behind your chariot!'

'Gosh, what about the ball?' he said to himself. 'I'd forgotten all about it!'

And so he had. The fancy-dress ball that night! He had forgotten his visit to Monsieur Bernadague and his kitchen-boy's costume. And what about his hat!

Yes, he would go to the ball. He would go, and he would dance.

'Hatred's a fine feeling!' he concluded. 'It's satisfying, it's vigorous and it's masculine!'

Filled with this grim thought, he left his room and went looking through the house for his godmother.

As it happened, Madame Bouillon-Lamothe was in her linen-room at that very moment. Dressed in a pale green dressing-gown, her ample figure bulging all over the stool she was sitting on (in sooth rather like an enormous frog), she was watching Toinon, the maid, arranging sheets in the huge airing-cupboards, their shelves still lined with old flowered paper.

'You want me to make you a what? . . . A kitchen-boy's cap for tonight? . . . For tonight, child, you can't be serious! You are the most terrible slave-driver,' she exclaimed, when Bécot had explained what he needed.

Bécot coaxed her as best he could, and started looking himself for the piece of calico he needed. He got in the way, and Toinon made such a fuss that his godmother pushed him out of the room.

He went, however, entirely satisfied, for he knew Mme Bouillon-Lamothe very well: she was a woman of great resource and nothing ever defeated her. 'Give me an egg and I'll make a meal fit for a king,' she would say when she was in a good mood.

And indeed the cap was cut, sewn, tried on and ready by dinner-time. It stood proud on Bécot's head and he came to table wearing it. He was back in his usual high spirits now that he felt himself sustained by hatred.

Bécot announced that he would put on his costume at a friend's house, and he set off for Vernet, parcel under arm, at the first stroke of nine.

He avoided showing himself in the main street and walked along the stream. He was going to call on his mistress, La Prairie. He was sure he would find her in, because she did not perform at the Casino in the evenings. He had a key to her room in any case.

He listened at the door for a moment. Hearing a strange voice, he knocked discreetly. La Prairie opened the door.

In the room, sitting at the table, was a fat woman with black hair and a flat nose, loosely clad in a voluminous peignoir of flame-coloured silk, and busily polishing her nails. She turned her head to see who it was, then picked up her cigarette and drew deeply.

Bécot recognized her: it was Rose Raymond, the singer from the Capitole who lived in the same house as La Prairie.

The table was covered with old hats, unpicked ready for restyling, and little silver and ivory toilet articles. A bottle of Italian aperitif stood among a pile of crumpled artificial flowers.

'Mademoiselle,' said Bécot with airy gallantry, 'please accept my homage and admiration. Ah! your nightingale likes *china*!' he added, catching sight of a drop of the dark aperitif in a wine glass at the singer's elbow.

'Why the big eyes, Sonny Jim?' asked Rose Raymond. 'Look at me: do I look as if I live on water like cress?' She laughed at her joke and her big white bosom heaved gently beneath the poppy-coloured silk. Her skin was enticing. She would have been quite good-looking had it not been for her short neck and squashed nose.

'She's quite a card, isn't she?' said La Prairie by way of explanation, although, far from being put out by Rose's familiarity, Bécot was actually rather amused.

They toasted each other on the spot, in *china*. Then Bécot took off his jacket and started putting on his costume. Rose Raymond polished his nails for him. Then she offered to curl his hair, telling him to take a candle and come to her room for the curling-tongs. But La Prairie intervened:

'You've everything you need in here,' she said curtly.

'Holy Virgin! I'm not going to steal your RRRomeo!' exclaimed the diva with comic theatricality.

When Bécot was all decked out, powdered, curled, slightly rouged, in his cap and his real kitchen-boy's white jacket, the two women walked round him admiringly.

'Isn't he pretty?' exclaimed Rose Raymond. 'Whatever you do, do go inside if it rains! A couple of drops and a pretty boy like you just melts away!'

Bécot gave her a playful push and then kissed her. He kissed La Prairie too; and went his way, whistling.

Fencing had been erected in the park, round the Casino, so that people could dance in the open without being bothered by townsfolk. The chestnuts and pines were decorated with orange balloons.

Pierrots and Pierrettes, white monks, Ophelias, white satin dominoes, Mlle Campon as a village bride, the beautiful American as a snow fairy, her head covered in snowflakes and dripping with diamonds, were all on the dance-floor when Bécot arrived. He was entranced: the white-clad crowd mingled, laughed, skipped, formed little circles, all up and down the flower-covered steps of the illuminated Casino. From time to time, a golden rocket rose in the distance, and when the music stopped, the sound of fountains could be plainly heard.

He wanted to have some fun, and he was not in form. But he wanted to prance and dance in front of Georgette . . .

He did not know if she had come. He still had not seen her, and did not dare ask.

What should he do? Have a drink. Of course.

He perched on a stool, put his elbows on the bar. His cap was too hot and he took it off. He called the barman and asked for a bottle of whisky and a big glass.

He filled the glass three-quarters full and took a swig.

Then he turned round, and saw Georgette.

She was standing a few feet away, on her own. She was watching him, and said:

'Monsieur Tixador! Surely you're not going to drink all that?'

She was wearing a silver net on her hair, and her exquisite breasts were covered with a network of shining pearls.

Bécot, lipsticked and rouged, with his little turned-up moustache and his poodle-curled hair, Bécot, still holding the bottle of whisky, frowned and replied in tones of the greatest composure:

'Me, Madame Borelli? Not drink all that, and as much of the rest as I want? . . . Why ever not? . . .' And he downed two more swigs.

Georgette gave a little shrug. Then, when the barman had gone, she said softly: 'Oh Bécot! . . .' And went away. Bécot followed her with his eyes.

For a second, he longed to run after her, to seize her hand or her dress . . . kneel down before her . . . carry her off in his arms . . . He had a vivid picture of himself sliding over the polished floor in pursuit of her. Madness, yes!

Then he sat down again and slowly finished his neat whisky.

He left the bar and, turning away from the bandstand, went and leaned dreamily against the fencing, away from the dancers in their white masks.

Not far from Bécot, two women were leaning on the other side of the fence watching the dancing. One was wearing the Catalan head-dress and a red scarf. The other, who was considerably older, was dressed in black, her head covered with a widow's pleated black veil.

Bécot suddenly heard one of them saying: 'This confectioner must be deaf, my dear! Hey! kitchen-boy! The milk's boiling over – you'll get a beating!'

Bécot realized they must have been talking to him, and turned round. 'Well now!' he exclaimed. 'I'd upset every saucepan in the place to get a spanking from a pretty girl like you!'

The two women laughed prettily, turning their heads and hiding their mouths with their hands.

Bécot went up to them. He knew them both. The younger one was little Madame Xambo, one of the prettiest girls in Vernet, whose husband kept a shop.

'You do look handsome in that costume, Monsieur Tixador!'

'Ah, a compliment,' said Bécot. 'That deserves a kiss!'

She warded him off and then playfully snatched his hat.

Bécot jumped the fence. She was running away. He set off in pursuit.

She ran squealing down a narrow path, pitch dark beneath a curtain of pine branches. All that could be seen of her was her round head-dress, like a pale moon. Bécot caught her when she ran into a clump of trees, completely out of breath. He took her in his arms. He could feel her heart beating, like a bird's. He gently kissed her cheek and then her lips, slightly rough but very fresh. And the delicious scent from the bending, prickly black branches of the pines and cedars mingled exquisitely with the warm perfume of her body.

'Let me go!' she exclaimed. 'My aunt's waiting for me! That's my aunt with me!'

'What about tomorrow, then?' Bécot asked. 'What time shall we meet tomorrow?'

She broke free and ran off without answering. This time Bécot did not follow.

He noticed a bench, a little way off in the moonlight, and went and sat down.

'Well, well,' he thought, 'Madame Xambo! Little Madame Xambo fancies me and I never knew! Lucky old me! . . . Well, we'll try and make her happy – it'll enlarge her husband's stock of horns . . . And I don't mean antelope horns either, Monsieur Xambo!'

From the bench he was sitting on, the young man could see, framed by black cedars, the coloured lights of the Casino and the dancers, gently moving, like white dolls. Occasionally, a Bengal light blazed weirdly, and the red or green smoke magically outlined some huge tree which looked as if it had been surprised in its sleep.

Bécot was in fine fettle now. The big glass of whisky had done him a power of good. 'You have to drink,' he mused. 'That was the first discovery the Ancients made. Clever chaps, our ancestors.'

Suddenly he saw a child silhouetted on the lawn in front of him. The child came up and said, in the brusque Catalan way:

'Monsieur Gilles, there's a note for you!'

Bécot recognized him by his voice: a young ball-boy from the tennis club.

In some surprise, Bécot picked up a white envelope the young messenger had left on the bench.

An envelope . . . What was in it? A love letter, no doubt. An assignation from Madame Xambo for tomorrow . . . Things were happening fast!

He felt in his pocket for a box of matches to read the letter, but he could not find any.

He was about to get up when he saw another silhouette, or rather two, appearing through the trees: two women in filmy mantillas.

They came closer, and suddenly the rich, well-rounded tones of Rose Raymond's voice could be heard saying: 'My goodness, it *is* our little kitchen-boy. I said it was! . . . What are you doing stuck on that bench like a butterfly with a pin through it?'

'Are you all right, Bécot?' asked La Prairie. 'We came to watch you dancing.'

Bécot got up. His head started spinning and he laughed. Strong stuff, whisky!

Then suddenly, completely unexpectedly, an idea came into his head.

'I'm hungry, girls,' he said. 'And bored by this ball. Let's go and have some supper.'

'Heavens! You're hungry?' said La Prairie. 'What have you been up to? Have you been unfaithful to me?'

Bécot found this very funny. He laughed out loud.

'I think, old girl, that your young man has gone and got himself stewed,' opined the singer from Toulouse in mock-dramatic tones.

Bécot took off his cap, and with a deep bow in true musketeer style, said to her:

'Mademoiselle, you are a fine person, which is why I felt on such good terms with you so quickly. You have a beautiful white bosom, which puts me strangely in mind of the pleasures of babyhood, and that makes me like you still more. La Prairie, darling, don't get cross, there's no need to be jealous! Everything turns out all right in the end, as my cousin Hubert de Lomagne always says; everything turns out very well, when there are three of you, and you're all in the same bed . . .'

Rose Raymond laughed: 'You're full of bright ideas!' she said.

'Mademoiselle, we shall go back and sup together. My mistress here, who usually answers to the sweet name La Prairie, invites us both. There are always ample provisions to be found at her home, and a few flagons of excellent wine which she adroitly purloins from a local hostelry. Onward, my beauties! . . .'

And Bécot slipped between the two friends and took each by the arm. He stumbled and pretended to be completely drunk. The two women supported him good-humouredly.

In this manner, they walked back through the park and arrived at La Prairie's room, but not before Bécot had made as if to fall on every step of the staircase and prompted a series of shrieks from his mistress.

They entered the room. Bécot lit the lamp and all the candles, cleared the table and opened all the cupboards. He took the largest towel, to use as a tablecloth. Then, having unearthed four eggs, he entreated La Prairie to make a rum omelette.

La Prairie, who had a little gas stove in her bathroom, made ready to do his bidding.

Meanwhile, Bécot moved restlessly round the room, missing no opportunity to give Rose Raymond a stroke or a little pinch. She resisted, in the approved manner.

'Come on, stop it, you silly boy!' she protested, 'I've got nothing in my pockets! No. I mean it, stop it, you're scratching my breast. I'll call your girl-friend! Now keep your distance, Mister Persistent! Don't you know I'm a mother? Really not? I have a little girl, who calls me Mummy . . . It would be too, too wicked of you to lead me astray!'

'You're disgusting! You're worse than a couple of dogs!' La Prairie shouted through to them.

Eventually, Bécot grew tired and settled in a big armchair – the only one in the room – and pulling Rose Raymond towards him:

'Unbutton my jacket, beautiful,' he said, 'my little kitchen-boy's jacket; it's much too tight . . .'

Laughing, she unbuttoned the jacket.

'Take my trousers off!' Bécot continued languidly.

At these words, La Prairie strode back into the room. Her forced laughter showed how much she appreciated the joke. But Bécot could sense that she did not dare get too angry, for fear of losing the esteem of a singer from the Capitole in Toulouse.

She seized Rose by the arm and pulled her into the bathroom.

Bécot, who really was drunk by now, started undressing noiselessly.

'Imagine the look on their faces when they come back in!' he thought wickedly.

So it was half naked he was when he suddenly remembered the note the little boy in the park had given him. He still had not read it.

'Where in the name of the blessed Gilles, my patron saint, have I put my love letter?'

He found it in a pocket.

'If it's little Madame Xambo giving me a rendezvous for tomorrow, that's perfect! What a handful!' He went over to one of the candles, tore open the envelope, which bore no address, and read these pencilled words:

Bécot, come to my house at half-past nine tomorrow. I want to see you. We shall be alone. G.

Georgette! . . .

Bécot was completely stunned, and stood motionless for several seconds, his mind a blank. Then, with a slow, gentle gesture, he lifted the letter to his lips:

'You want to see me, Georgette! . . . You want to see me tomorrow morning! . . . We shall be alone!'

By now Bécot was thrilling with anticipation and joy. He cast fearful glances round the room, like an animal caught in a trap.

He was suddenly completely sober.

One of the women called through: 'What are you up to, Bécot? Are you asleep? You've gone very quiet!'

He did not answer. He was thinking.

'I've got time to escape!'

He was still in his shirt. He hurriedly pulled his trousers back on, left his socks off and laced his espadrilles on his bare feet. Then he went over to the window, which was fortunately half open, and opened it wide without a sound.

The window was on the second floor, but it gave on to a little balcony. The branches of a nearby tree looked close enough to jump to. The light from the room lit the tree sufficiently. Bécot knew the tree in any case, having often worked out how to climb down it.

He climbed over the balcony and launched himself into space like a trapeze artist. He had no difficulty catching hold of the branch he had aimed for.

A few seconds later the young man found himself down on the path by the stream. The only damage was a bit of skin off one hand.

Leaning against this friendly tree, Bécot started laughing silently. What a sight the women would be when they came back solemnly bearing the omelette on a platter and instead of Bécot found only his socks!

Suddenly he realized they could see him if they happened to lean out of the window. He slipped into the shadows and went quickly on his way.

He followed the stream and crossed the bridge . . .

It was a marvellous feeling, walking home beneath the stars.

TRANSLATED BY ANTHONY BOWER
EDITED BY IAN HIGGINS

ALBERT-PAUL GRANIER 1888–1917

'Hate! Hate! How the word hurts! Hate, we have to hate! Hatred unto ecstasy!'
'Haïr', in Les Coqs et les vautours

About Granier virtually nothing is known, beyond what Fauré-Fremiet tells us. To judge from 'Haïr' ('Hate'; 1914), he was certainly no revanchist. He was born in Le Croisic, near Saint-Nazaire, on 3 September 1888, and trained as a solicitor at Nantes. He was a keen sportsman and a devotee of all the arts, but his biggest love was poetry.

Les Coqs et les vautours consists of poems written between 1914 and 1916, all but two of them war poems. Virtually all are in free verse, often of the kind practised by Verhaeren. One of them, 'L'exode', is indeed dedicated to Verhaeren, and this and some others are in a few respects reminiscent, in content as well as in expression, of *Les Campagnes hallucinées* and *Les Villes tentaculaires* in particular. Sometimes, too, there is a grisly Laforguian comedy in the pierrot-soldiers' plight. This is not, however, primarily derivative poetry. Even in the more Verhaerenian poems, the vision is an individual one, a revolted fascination with the gamut of aesthetic qualities of the war. If *Les Coqs et les vautours*, his citations and his Légion d'honneur are any indication, invasion and destruction turned Granier into a regretful, but completely committed, participant in the war. In one poem, 'La Fièvre' ('Fever'), he voices the dream of a peaceful death in bed, with soothing nurses all around, but rejects it at last with a wish to die in battle, in the 'great Epic', with a lump of steel in his chest.

Granier went into the artillery at the outbreak of war. Some of his best poems express the eerie beauty of the guns and mortars, both in action and on the move along the roads. His style is least convincing and individual, as with most writers about the war before about 1930, when he attempts to convey the sheer unimaginable scale of the carnage, destruction and noise. The grotesque mode works best – this is seen to some extent in 'L'incendie' ('The Fire') – and loaded silence would seem easier to capture, as in 'Nocturne' and 'Le Ballon'. These last two poems show an art of restraint, almost understatement, in which Granier promised to become as accomplished as in the *con brio* deployment of rhythms, alliterations and imagery on a grand scale.

Granier's arresting vision and often successful manipulation of certain types of free verse are accompanied by an occasional readiness to experiment linguistically: his rare use of 'escarboucle' is perhaps a symptom of this, and the coined compound 'sourd-roulant' occurs in 'Les tambours' both as an adjective and as a transitive participle. After the war, one of the things the Surrealists were to do was to use a kind of parataxis in imagery to compensate for the relative difficulty the French language has in achieving the compression which comes so naturally to English in compounds: the works of Gerard Manley Hopkins and Dylan Thomas are simply extreme realizations of a tendency inherent in the language. Now in Granier, there is at times a dream-like coherence in the wildly mixed metaphors which is similar to that found in some Surrealists. This, allied to his still tentative experiments in grammar, only makes one regret all the more bitterly the loss of a possibly major voice.

That loss occurred in the air. In 1916, Granier became an artillery observer in aircraft. His plane was hit by a shell on 17 August 1917, near Verdun. Nothing was found of machine or men.

IAN HIGGINS

Text
Les Coqs et les vautours (Jouve, Paris, 1917).

Secondary source
P. Fauré-Fremiet, 'Albert-Paul Granier' in *Anthologie des écrivains morts à la guerre* (Malfère, Amiens, 1924–6, 5 vols, iii).

Le Ballon

Le ballon gris descend sur l'horizon des bois,
le ballon descend, comme un astre néfaste
qui a fini sa parabole courbe,
et qui s'enlise dans la mer.

Le ballon gris, chargé de regards fourbes,
plonge insensiblement dans la forêt.

Et les bouleaux blancs qui m'abritent
– pauvres tiges sacrifiées en pleine force –
les bouleaux nés sur le sol de France,
liés et jetés là comme des fagots
avec des chênes et des charmes,
les bouleaux blancs hérissent leur légère écorce,
comme des chiens qui sont en colère . . .

Observatoire de . . ., 1915

The Balloon

The grey balloon floats down to the forest horizon,
the balloon floats down – like a planet of doom,
its trajectory ended,
sinking into the sea.

The grey balloon, heavy with inquisitive treachery,
slips imperceptibly beneath the trees.

And the white birches which shield me,
– such slender stems, martyred in their prime –
the birches, born on the soil of France,
bundled and dumped like faggots
along with aspen and oak,
the white birches ruffle their feathery bark
into hackles of anger.

Look-out post at . . ., 1915

Translated by Ian Higgins

Nocturne

Les canons se sont tus, bâillonnés de brouillard,
dans la nuit d'hiver qui abolit l'espace,
et un calme, plein de menace
comme un cri de hibou sur des remparts,
flotte au cœur multiple du silence.

Les sentinelles, à l'affût,
tendent leurs muscles dans l'attente
énervante de l'inconnu.

Avec un bruit de linge humide,
quelques fusils, dans la vallée,
à coups sourds claquent soudain,
incertains d'ombres devinées
et de frôlements dans le vide . . .

Et l'on dirait, ce soir,
comme dans les nuits légendaires
de Bretagne, que d'infernales lavandières,
agenouillées au bord d'invisibles lavoirs,
dans le fleuve épais battent des suaires . . .

Observatoire de . . . sur la Meuse, 1915

Nocturne

The guns have fallen silent, gagged with fog,
in the winter's night that cancels space,
and a calm full of menace,
like the screech of owls over castle walls,
hangs in the many-hearted silence.

Sentries, peering out,
tense every muscle, edgily
awaiting the unexpected.

A thwack like wet cloth
sounds from the valley –
sudden muffled rifle-shots
unsure of guessed-at shadows
and the rustling emptiness.

This is a night
like the nights in Breton legend
when hell-hag washerwomen
kneel invisible at riverside stones,
beating shrouds in the thick water.

Look-out post at . . . on the Meuse, 1915

Translated by Ian Higgins

L'INCENDIE

Un obus est tombé dans la grange,
avec un fracas formidable,
comme l'écroulement de séculaires espérances,

et le feu a surgi de l'obus, comme un diable
hors de sa boîte minuscule.

Par la grand'porte à claire-voie,
je vois le feu sourdre sournoisement
dans la paille et le foin des récoltes dernières,
puis, avec des murmures de joie,
danser en flammèches claires
une sarabande légère . . .

Le feu sait que tout est pour lui dans la maison,
aussi explore-t-il pas à pas son nouveau domaine,
grimpe aux poutres et aux chevrons,
puis se laisse glisser du haut des tas de foin
comme font les enfants pendant la fenaison.

Le feu gambade et siffle de joie,
ondule, flue, et se déploie,
et casse les vitres des fenêtres
pour regarder un peu dehors:
Le feu veloute de cramoisi
les vieilles poutres vermoulues,
crève les sacs dont le blé ruisselle
en cascade d'or et de rubis,
et pousse à travers les tuiles du toit
en chevelure escarbouclée;

Le feu regarde par la haute claire-voie
de la porte, et caresse les barreaux de bois
qu'il enlumine d'écarlate.
Le feu s'en donne à cœur joie;
nul ne vient plus troubler ses jeux
et l'agacer de la pointe des jets,
sous lesquels il rageait
comme un fauve sous la cravache.
Le feu danse à grands cris dans la grange embrasée.

Puis, quand il s'est lassé
de cascader par les étages,
– cambrioleur tranquille – il escalade
le toit oblique dont il casse les tuiles,
et, comme un enfant coléreux,
à qui, soudain, son jeu
devient hostile,
casse la porte qui se désarticule,
défonce le toit qui s'engloutit,
et saute sur la maison voisine:

THE FIRE

Down into the barn
a shell came crashing
like the hopes of all the years collapsing,

and fire sprang out of the shell, like a jack
from its tiny box.

Through the great slatted door
I see the fire rise and sneak
among the season's gathered straw and hay,
then, chattering in glee,
dance in sparks across the floor
a light fantastic reel . . .

The fire knows it has the run of the place:
and prospecting, it paces out its new demesne,
climbing the beams and eaves,
then sliding back down on the heaps of straw
like a haymaking child left to play.

The fire skips and whistles with glee,
ripples, flows, unfolds and spreads
and breaks the window-panes
to take a peep outside:
The fire mellows the wormy timbers
with velvet crimson,
splits open the sacks of grain
that tip cascades of gold and ruby,
and bushing up between the tiles
red-heads the roof;

The fire nuzzles through the slats to look
and flatters the wood, illuminating every fret
with gaudy scarlet.
Fire's cutting loose in glee;
there's no one now to spoil its sport
and torment it with the hose-play
it used to seethe to,
big cat to the tamer's whip.
Fire's dancing and whooping through the blazing barn.

Then, when it's had enough
rumbustious ladder-tumbling,
it swarms unruffled-burglar-like
up over the roof, breaks the tiles
and, like a child
in a tantrum, that suddenly
takes against its game,
it twists off the breaking door,
punches in the roof and brings it down,
and jumps on to the house behind:

Curieusement, par les lucarnes
il regarde et passe ses longs bras en tentacules,
et, tout à coup, a le désir aigu
d'y fureter et d'y jouer encore,
et d'y danser à perdre haleine,
comme un ivrogne dans un cabaret . . .

Le feu, beau comme un beau monstre,
que nul ne peut caresser,
tourne et tourne dans le village,
comme un tigre dans sa cage . . .

Keur-la-Grande, 1914

Inquisitively, through the skylights,
it looks inside, snake-necks about inside,
and suddenly it's itching
to poke and pry and play again,
and dance itself breathless,
like a drunk in a pub . . .

Fire, a monster of beauty,
beautiful, unstrokeable,
possesses the village
as a tiger paces its cage . . .

Keur-la-Grande, 1914

TRANSLATED BY IAN HIGGINS

MUSIQUE

La neige duvetait l'espace comme un songe . . .

Au carrefour, la fontaine était figée . . .

Et, alors que je passais
près de la source immobile,
glissèrent sur mon âme blanche,
fluides dans la neige papillonnante,
des accords légers et délicats,
comme des échos d'harmonica,
des accords aériens,
comme des murmures de séraphins,
comme des violes miraculeuses d'anges.

Au coin du carrefour, dans une grange,
un homme
appuyait doucement sa joue au violon
et caressait les cordes chantantes
des crins tendus de l'archet blanc.

C'était une musique merveilleuse,
délicieusement svelte et gracieuse,
avec des doubles cordes et des arpèges,
et qui s'évaporait, parmi la neige,
– la neige blanche et mate –
en un miroitement de moire en arc-en-ciel:
La musique m'emmitouflait de songerie,
m'auréolait de sortilège,
m'épanouissait dans l'irréel,
comme si je voyais quelque fée
qui, avec de belles mains de neige,
aurait jonglé avec des perles,
des cristaux et des pierreries,
ou comme si quelqu'un avait capturé
un poisson fabuleux, mordoré de nacre,

MUSIC

Snow was filling space with a dream of down . . .

At the crossroads, the fountain was frozen . . .

And as I was walking
past the stricken water,
over my snow-blank soul
there stole delicate light harmonies,
fluid through the mothy whiteness,
like echoes of harmonicas,
harmonies of the aether,
like whispering cherubim,
like a miracle of angel flutes.

By the crossroads, in a barn,
a man,
cheek gently leaning to the violin,
was stroking melody from gut
with the pliable, taut, white bow.

This music was marvellous music,
exquisite in slenderness and grace,
with runs, arpeggios and double chords,
breathing its soul among the snow,
– the dry white snow –
in shimmering rainbows of shot silk:
The music had wrapped me round in dream,
a halo of enchantment,
full flower of fulfilment,
as if I could see, beyond vision,
a lovely sylph with hands of snow
juggling with pearls,
crystals and precious stones,
or an iridescent sequined fish
lured from fable,

dont les écailles chatoyantes
et irisées comme des prismes
se fussent éparpillées, impondérables
en éclaboussement diamantaire . . .

Le canon, là-bas,
a défoncé le soir profond
avec un bruit de cataclysme,
comme si des cyclones
avaient heurté en route des typhons . . .

La neige, lente et persuasive,
apaisa de douceur dormante
le bondissement dur des échos affolés,
et la musique merveilleuse
reprit son frêle échafaudement de reflets,
sa trame d'impalpable vertige,
comme une fontaine lumineuse,
si fragile, sur le cristal mobile de sa tige . . .

Et je demeurai là, sous la neige silencieuse,
comme un enfant
qui écoute un conte de Noël.

Rupt-devant-Saint-Mihiel, 1914

with glistening
prismatic skin
scattering impalpable
diamond-splashes through the air . . .

Gunfire, cataclysmically,
smashed from somewhere
through the evening,
like tornadoes cannoning
off hurricanes.

The slow, persuasive, sleepy snow
was a soothing gentleness
to the percussive panic-stricken leap of echoes,
and the marvellous music
resumed its fragile paradigm of watered light,
a swaying weave of ecstasy,
like some luminous fountain,
so frail, on the wavering crystal of its stem . . .

And I stood there, in the quiet snow,
like a child
listening to stories on Christmas Eve.

Rupt-devant-Saint-Mihiel, 1914

TRANSLATED BY IAN HIGGINS

SCIPIO SLATAPER 1888–1915

'Set your eyes on humanity; not the individual man.'

Scipio Slataper was born in Trieste on 14 July 1888, to an Italian mother and a father of Slavonic origin. The family was of only modest means, but the author's childhood seems to have been happily inspirational, to judge by what he later wrote. He grew up fit and strong, but in adolescence suffered a bout of nervous exhaustion as a result of which he was sent to convalesce in the rocky uplands of the Carso, north of Trieste. It was a highly charged encounter with the natural world in one of its more awesome manifestations, and the experience marked his whole life. The salubrious but romantic landscape was to be zestfully exploited as a theatre for self-exploration, commitment to youthful ideals and the assumption of heroic poses.

Circumstances in Trieste around 1900 inevitably presented any budding intellectual with a number of problems to resolve, in view of the political and cultural ambiguities and the economic links with Austria which characterized the city. Slavonic, German and Italian mythologies all fired the imagination of Slataper in his boyhood; Garibaldi and Oberdan were his particular heroes. As a young man striving to define his moral values and political directions, he remained subject to the differing cultural influences at work in the Trieste of the 1882 Triple Alliance. Because of this, and a reluctance to form any precise political allegiance, his attitudes to major questions of the time – such as Irredentism and Socialism – fluctuate or seem unfocused.

In 1908, he enrolled at the University of Florence, where he was to graduate in 1912 with a thesis on Ibsen which was published posthumously. He was reading widely in contemporary Italian and German literature and, soon after arriving in Florence, joined Prezzolini and the other young intellectuals who had just begun to produce the influential literary review *La Voce*.

Having graduated and married in 1912, he left Florence to work, first, in Vienna and then in Hamburg. At the outbreak of war, he returned to Italy and began to argue, in the columns of *Il Resto del Carlino* (Bologna), in favour of Italian intervention. By June 1915, he had voluntarily enlisted, taking the precaution of using an assumed name, since he was still officially an Austrian subject, and was on his way to the front:

Scipio Slataper. *Marzorati, Milan*

> Never as in the deathly silence, when the trench is sleeping and 10 metres beyond lies an ambush of darkness and foliage, does one feel the presence of war. War is not in the explosion of grenades or a fusillade nor in hand-to-hand combat. War is not in what, from far off, one believes to be its terrible reality and which, close at hand, turns out to be a poor thing and makes little impression; it is – as Tolstoy realized – to be found in that curious space beyond one's trench, where there is silence and calm and where the corn is ripening to no purpose. It is that sense of certain death which lies 'beyond', there where the sun still shines on the age-old roads and the peasants' houses.

However, it was there, among the trenches and barbed wire on Mount Podgora, that he was shot and killed on 3 December 1915.

Slataper first appeared in print on 26 January 1905 when he was 17. 'The Tyranny of School Regulations', published in *Il Lavoratore*, was an attack on the Austrian education system and its deleterious influence on the youth of Trieste. The year 1907 saw a number of publications in the form of drama, verse, literary criticism and short stories, most notably 'Il Freno' ('The Brake') which came out in *Il Palvese* (25 August).

As an undergraduate in Florence, he began to publish in *La Voce*, beginning with the outspoken 'Letters from Trieste', which appeared between February and April 1909. The first of these was the inflammatory 'Trieste Has No Cultural Traditions' (11 February) which may have cost him his study grant. In 1910, he edited two numbers of *La Voce* (nos. 52 and 53) devoted to Irredentism. In the same year, he published 'Snow on Mount Secchieta', a lyrical piece so well received that it later found its way into the prose poem *Il mio Carso*, as well as numerous articles of literary criticism along with translations, notably of Friedrich Hebbel. Until 1912, most of his work was for *La Voce*, but he did write for other journals and newspapers and, in 1914–15 was a regular contributor to *Il Resto del Carlino*.

Entering the 20th century in the shadow of that great literary triad – Carducci, Pascoli and D'Annunzio – Italy was to experience a period of cultural unrest within which, in an atmosphere of impending upheaval, movements as diverse as Crepuscularism and Futurism could co-exist. For those associated with *La Voce*, and particularly the 'moralists' such as Boine, Jahier and Slataper, it was axiomatic that literature should address the major social issues of contemporary life. To his diary in 1909, Slataper confided that 'art is universal and necessary for it transfixes what continues to be created within us. No social function is more important.' This goes some way to explain the insistence with which Slataper strives to clarify his ambivalent attitude to his native city. From the high ground of the Carso, Trieste is castigated initially as a cultural backwater where complacency, bourgeois self-interest and hypocrisy prevail: 'No one trusts anyone, though all greet each other,' as he puts it at the end of the first section of *Il mio Carso*. Later, the city, or at least its industrious and colourful port, is celebrated as a society fit for any free spirit and worthy of the greatest sacrifice.

Il mio Carso, composed between 1910 and 1912, has been described as a prose poem, a diary, a fragmented masterpiece. But the book does have a degree of tonal unity and can be read as a coherent spiritual portrait. The aspirations of adolescence are expressed in a sustained flight of lyricism, but at the same time, there is a movement or dramatic development in the account which leads from a completely egocentric position to one of recognition of the social world and a desire for integration in it. It is the poetic and intensely subjective account of youth's last chapter.

More a collection of evocative tableaux than a narrative of events, *Il mio Carso* nevertheless has some chronological order as reflected in its division into three parts. The first concerns infancy, adolescence and the discovery of the magical Carso landscape. The second relates the descent from the mountain into the city and society. The third deals with the experience of grief and confusion, finally resolved with the active commitment of the individual to the social and cultural self-determination of Trieste.

Although he was later to express dissatisfaction with the book, Slataper took pride in its vigour and freshness of tone and a certain 'barbarous' quality which, like Carducci before him, he believed would be culturally regenerative. The writing is lean, spare and direct even in its pantheistic vitality, carefully eschewing that richness of effect typical of D'Annunzio, with whom comparisons are inevitably made, and showing a preference for brevity of phrasing, parataxis, exclamation and the sounds of spoken language.

Slataper determined to concentrate poetic effect into simpler structures where the individual word counted for more. His recourse to bold rhetorical devices such as hypallage and the use of dialect words amid a generally erudite vocabulary were all consonant with the aspirations of 20th-century Italian lyricism, and they confer upon this novel, despite its limitations, the importance which is due to any work which is original and forward-looking in its time. The drama of the individual or outsider, which was to be developed to such an extreme form twenty years later by Pavese, emerges here with an intensity that sets Slataper apart from his contemporaries. In the selection from his work which follows, one discerns the progress of an idealistic young patriot from contemplative to active involvement in society as the time approaches for his symbolic mountain fastness of the Carso to become the historic killing-ground upon which Italy's claim to Trieste will be vindicated.

MARK M. GRIMSHAW

Texts

Opera Completa (G. Stuparich (ed.), Mondadori, Milan). The complete works were published in the following volumes: *Epistolario* (1950); *Appunti et note di diario* (1953); *Scritti politici* (1954); *Scritti letterari e critici* (1956); *Alle tre amiche* (1958); *Il mio Carso* (1958).

Secondary sources

V. Vettori, 'Scipio Slataper' (in *Autori Vari, I contemporanei*, vol 2, Marzorati, Milan, 1963).

A. M. Mutterle, *Scipio Slataper* (Mursia, Milan, 1965). Contains an exhaustive bibliography.

G. Baroni, G. A. Peritore and D. Frigessi, 'Scipio Slataper' (in *Autori Vari*, Novecento 2, Marzorati, Milan, 1979).

Il Mio Carso

I'd like to tell you: I was born in the Carso, in a hovel with a thatched roof blackened by smoke and by the rain. There was a mangy dog hoarsely barking, two geese with their bellies caked in mud, a hoe, a spade, a dung-heap virtually without straw from which, when it rained, rivulets of dark brown juice came forth.

I'd like to tell you: I was born in Croatia in the great oak forest. In the winter, everything was white with snow, the door could only be opened a crack, and in the night, I could hear the wolves howl. Mother would bind rags round my swollen red hands, and I would rush to crouch against the hearth, whimpering because of the cold.

I would like to tell you: I was born on the Moravian plains, and I used to run like a hare down the long furrows, driving the jackdaws up in croaking flocks. I would throw myself flat on the ground, uproot a beetroot and gnaw at it with the earth still on it. Then I came here; I've tried to become domesticated. I've learned Italian, I've chosen my friends among the most cultivated young people – but soon I must return to my own country because here I don't fit in at all.

I would like to deceive you, but you wouldn't believe me. You are clever and shrewd. You would understand at once that I'm a poor Italian attempting to barbarize his solitary preoccupations. It's better that I confess to being your brother, even if sometimes I gaze at you as if far away in a dream and feel shy when faced with your culture and your skill in argument. Perhaps I'm afraid of you. Little by little, your objections cage me in as I listen to you, unconcerned and content and unaware that you are savouring your own intelligence and skill, and then I blush and remain silent at the end of the table and my thoughts wander to the consolation of the great trees open to the wind. I think avidly of the sun on the hills and liberty in full bloom; of my real friends who love me and recognize me in a handshake, in calm and cordial laughter. These are sound and good-hearted people.

I think of my dim and distant origins, of my ancestors ploughing the endless field with a ploughshare drawn by four great dappled horses, or clad in heavy leather aprons as they bent over the burners and the molten glass; of my enterprising grandfather who came down to Trieste when they proclaimed it a free port; of the big, pale-green house where I was born and where, hardened by suffering, our grandmother lives.

I saw the whole Abyssinian campaign on a big map that Father pinned up in our bedroom. He would explain, with a copy of *Il Piccolo* in his hand, where the Italians were advancing. Down at the bottom, on horseback, with black faces and feather head-dresses were Menelik and Ras Alula, and I would puncture their noses with the pins of the little marker-flags. I was very happy that the Italians were winning. I believe I prayed for them.

At that time, I believed in God and I used to pray every evening: 'Our Father who art in heaven', and then I would shut my eyes tight and stay as still as still could be, thinking only of that person that I wanted God to love. That was praying and I prayed for my beautiful Italy, that had a big battleship, the *Duilio*, which was the most powerful in the world. Our homeland was over there across the water. Not here, where Mother used to close the Persian blinds the evening before the Emperor's birthday, because our windows would not be lit up and we were afraid that stones might be thrown.

But Italy will win and will come to liberate us. Italy is immensely strong. You just don't know what the word *bersagliere* meant to me.

I was known to the land on which I slept through my deep nights and the wide sky resounding to my victorious cry as, plunging down with the waters through broken riverbeds or rattling down the hills in a whirling landslide of dust and earth, I would check my step to snatch up the little sky-blue flower.

I ran with the wind, expanding towards the valley, joyfully leaping over low walls and juniper scrub, whistling by, shot from a sling. Bolt from a crossbow glancing from trunk to branch; from tree stumps and earth, I would bound back in fury and roar through the forest like a river excavating its bed and, angrily stripping away the last foliage in my path, plunge out of the trees, my hair spiky with twigs and leaves, my face all scratched but my soul unfurling, fresh as the white flight of doves rising in alarm at my harsh, impulsive cries.

And panting for breath I would throw myself headlong into the river to slake the thirst of my skin, to fill my throat, nostrils and eyes with water, choking on great gulps of it, plunging my mouth below the surface, wide open like a pike. I would swim against the current, with each stroke clutching at the whirlpools that splashed foaming against my body, sinking my teeth into the bright wave as one might bite on a blade of grass when walking in the mountains. And the wave would buffet me and carry me down, rolling me over and over in the current, knocking me against the bottom, flinging me back into the sunlight, dragging me for a while against the steep banks among roots and stones at which I'd clutch in vain. Then I'd let myself sink to the bottom and haul myself over the rocks to make my way back upstream exhausted.

The sun on my body dripping with water! Hot sun on naked flesh plunged in the rough heather, thyme and mint among the buzzing of golden bees!

And in mid-month, in the hour when the moon emerges from the distant thicket and makes her way among the clouds, glowing white like a field of jonquils in the depths of the wood, I felt myself abandoned to a sweet and mysterious diffusion as if fluttering gently in some infinite dream.

In my city, they were demonstrating in favour of an Italian university in Trieste. They were walking, arms linked, eight by eight; they were shouting: 'We want the Italian university in Trieste!' and scraping their feet to annoy the police. So I took my place in the front lines of the column, and I scraped my feet like the others. That's the way we followed the Aqueduct down.

Suddenly, the first row stopped and took a step backwards. From down by the Café Chiozza, the gendarmes were marching against us, broadly deployed in two rows, bayonets fixed. They were marching as on the parade-ground, stiff-legged with long strides, expressionless. Each one of us felt that no obstacle on earth could stop them. They had to advance until the Emperor should say: 'Halt!' Behind those gendarmes was the whole of the Austro-Hungarian empire. There was that power which had held the world in its grip. There was the will of a vast monarchy stretching from Poland to Greece, from Russia to Italy. There was Charles V and Bismarck. Each one of us felt this, and they all took to their heels panicking, white with fear, pushing and jostling, losing sticks and hats.

I stood there marvelling at the soldiers. They were marching straight ahead without smiling or laughing. For them, these people in flight were no different from the compact column which had been marching for the Italian university. I stayed to watch them and was arrested.

A gendarme took me by the left wrist and off we went. It was a very strange business. He continued walking with that step of his and I tried to imitate it. People passing ran their eyes over me with a look that felt like drops of cold water down my spine, making me shudder so that the gendarme thought: *The bloke's scared.* Or maybe he had no thoughts at all but just carried on walking with that step. I remember vividly how a young man, passing, put out his gloved right hand to twirl the right extremity of his moustache and then the left to twirl the left. I had turned my head to watch him so that, as the gendarme went on, I felt myself pulled forward. A woman with a fine boa averted her eyes, but I saw that she was laughing. Why am I letting myself be led along by this imbecile?

He has big yellow and black epaulettes. Why not let him lead me along? I don't know where we're going, but I don't need to know. He's leading the way, he turns this way and that, at every step my feet are placed parallel to his. The bayonet is shining bright as can be. Is your rifle loaded?

Why does he not answer me? A butcher's boy, to avoid going round it, leaps over the promenade bench, and his apron, with its old bloodstains, puffs up, flutters and slaps. As soon as we get past, he looks at us and yells: 'Let the gendarme have it!' And off he runs.

I can see the artery pulsating distinctly in the neck of this imbecile. And my hands are very long and the pulp upon them is like bone and there's nobody around. Alboin . . . But I'm worth more than Alboin. I'm worth more than Bismarck. Imperceptibly, I squeeze my thumb between my fingers and make my hand a narrower extension of my wrist. Slowly, I slide through his fingers made loose by the cold. Meanwhile, I'm talking: 'No fun this life of yours! Of course, I can see you're only doing your duty. How many hours' service do you have? Eight? Without a break? And up there on the Carso in every kind of weather, even at night.' In my throat, I can hear the fresh music of words learned from my beautiful Venetian grandmother: 'Right or wrong, succeed or fail, keep yourself well clear of gaol.' I look the gendarme in the eye, I wrench my hand free and off I go. Long live freedom! I'm an Italian.

He didn't even chase me. And I, after 200 metres of furious running, I was disappointed to see him standing there in the distance, undecided. Then he resumed his rhythmic march, *toc tac*, in the opposite direction.

Toc tac, I imagine him getting closer, coming up behind me, with his hand falling on my shoulder. I shot into a doorway: in the doorkeeper's lodge, I see a bald head ringed with a crown of fine hair like that of a baby, someone bent over a lady's shoe. I go back out; I pull my beret down more firmly on my head, wrap my cloak around me and I walk, stamping down hard on the paving stones as if, between them and my heavy boots, there were something that had to be mastered.

Then I ran as far as the sea.

In the sea, I washed my face and my hands. I drank the salt water of our Adriatic. Far away in the sunset, the Italian Alps were red and gold like dolomites. On the sailing boats up from Romagna, the tricolour was fluttering bravely and the stoves on board were steaming for the polenta. This sea of ours! Free and content, I breathed deep as one might after a fervent prayer.

But soon I noticed that people were staring at me. My hob-nailed boots were covered in dust and my behaviour was odd. I didn't look anything like those immaculate people who were strolling up and down the waterfront without going anywhere. People out to look and be looked at. The young men had long flared coats with a deep vent at the back like that in a servant's jacket, and walking-sticks which, whether stout or slender, were made to look like freshly peeled branches. The young ladies were accompanied by their father or mother, and they wore little boots as shiny as the back of a beetle. Their boots were distinctly brighter and more limpid than their eyes. They too looked at me with an aloof air, but when I looked at them, they averted their eyes. They cannot sustain a man's gaze.

Now in all this to-ing and fro-ing, the young men were skilfully managing not to jostle the young women but to brush against them, though gently enough for no one to be able to say 'Watch yourself!' In general, everyone was smiling and bowing and raising their hats every five yards. I was watching all this in amazement, and I plunged in among them, bewildered by so much shuffling of feet and whispering in all that aimless moving about.

I drifted slowly along the city streets, transported by that leisurely flow. It's difficult to walk among idle people. The man in front of you stops without warning, a woman comes out of a shop, looking back to thank the assistant who had just disengaged her puffed sleeve from the shop-door handle, some other man insists on walking behind a particular young lady. In the end, sick of the effort of avoiding people, I dug my hands into my pockets and walked straight on, making the studs in my boots crunch on the pavement.

At Puntofranco at 6.00 a.m., cold and with eyes glazed for lack of sleep, the pilot on duty salutes the guard with the keys who opens up the equipment store. The great brown and black oxen slowly haul the empty wagons into place by the steamships which berthed last night; and when the wagons are in place, at ten minutes past six, the dockers spread through the hangars. Each has a pipe and a piece of bread in his pocket. A ganger gets up on a loading platform. More than 200 men crowd around him, all holding up their work-cards and shouting to be taken on. The ganger rapidly selects and snatches up as many cards as he needs and goes off with the hired men behind him. The others fall quiet and then spread out through the hangars again. A few minutes before 6.30, the mechanic in his dark blue smock climbs the ladder into the crane and turns on the water pressure; and finally, last to arrive, come the carts, piled with long ladders, bouncing and clattering. The sun washes over the horizon, orange on the straight grey lines of the warehouses. The clear light of the sun is upon the sea and the city. Along her shores, Trieste awakens, full of movement and colours.

Our great steamships weigh anchor, bound for Salonika and Bombay. And tomorrow the trains will thunder over the iron bridge across the Moldau and, with the River Elbe, drive into Germany.

And we too will obey our law. Uncertain and nostalgic travellers driven on by desires and memories for what will never be ours anywhere. Where did we come from? Our homeland is far away, our nest all broken up, but love will stir us to return to our native city of Trieste and we'll start from here.

We love Trieste for the restless soul she gave us. She takes us away from our little sorrows and makes us her own, makes us brothers of all those who have to fight for a homeland. She has reared us for struggle and for duty. And if from these plants out of Africa and Asia ranged in her warehouses, if from her Stock Exchange where the financial foundation of the new wealth, from Turkey to Puerto Rico, is calmly relayed via telegraph, if from the life-force in her, if from her troubled and fractured soul a new will is made manifest in the world, Trieste is blessed for having let us live without peace or glory. We love you and bless you because we are happy even to die in your fire. We will go out into the world suffering with you. Because we love the new life which awaits us. It is an ordeal of strength and pain. We must suffer and remain silent. We must endure solitude in foreign cities where one envies even the carter who is cursing in a language understood by all around him and, in the evening, passing sadly among unknown faces who don't dream we exist, we raise our eyes on high, above the impenetrable houses, trembling with tears and glory. We must suffer the limitations of our slender human possibilities, incapable of stemming a sister's tears or helping back to his feet a companion who has flung himself down in despair and can only ask 'Why?' Ah, brothers, how fine it would be if we were sure of ourselves and proud and could rejoice in our intelligence, plundering the wide, abundant fields with the strength of youth, and know and command and possess! But we, taut with pride, consumed by shame, offer you our hand, and we beg you to be just towards us as we seek to be just towards you. For we love you, brothers, and hope that you will love us. Our wish is to love and work.

TRANSLATED BY MARK M. GRIMSHAW

*R*ENATO *S*ERRA 1884–1915

'How different war looks and feels when you're in the midst of it. You fight. But it becomes like life itself. It's all there is: not a passion any more nor a hope. Like life, rather sad and resigned, it wears a tired face, seamed and worn, similar to our own.'
From Serra's diary, 7 July 1915

Renato Serra, 1908. *Biblioteca Malatestiana, Cesena*

Renato Serra was born at Cesena in Romagna on 5 December 1884 and, after a brilliant school career, enrolled at the University of Bologna in 1900. There he studied under Carducci and graduated in 1904 with a thesis on the *Trionfi* of Petrarch. During the next two years, he was occupied with his military service, training as an infantry officer. In 1907, he began a series of publications in the literary review *La Romagna* with an article on Rudyard Kipling, and the following summer brought the first of several meetings with the celebrated literary critic Benedetto Croce. In 1909, Serra was nominated director of the Malatestian library in Cesena. The month of August 1910 was spent in military manoeuvres in the mountains near Belluno, and in December, he published an article in *La Voce* on Carducci and Croce, the two major influences upon literary criticism in the early 1900s.

In his tranquil, provincial environment, reading and scholarly research now occupied much of Serra's life. However, not all of it was so innocently spent, as the attempt made upon his life by a jealous husband in 1911 would indicate. Unlucky in love by his own report, Serra might have expected compensation at the gaming-table, but as a certain percentage of his published work was produced to pay off gambling debts, we can take it that little was found there.

Contacts between Serra and the young literary set in Florence were selective and cautious on his part, but in 1911, he began to correspond with the budding critic Giuseppe De Robertis, future editor of *La Voce*, who was to become his friend and disciple. In the summer of 1912, Serra published 'Departure of a Group of Soldiers for Libya', memorable for its reflections on history, and in October he was promoted to the rank of lieutenant. In 1914, he was called up for further military service but, switching between the sword and the pen, still managed in the same year to publish 'Letters', an admirable, panoramic survey of contemporary Italian literature. As the war approached, however, it became harder, psychologically, to work. Compare these two observations, both from 1914: 'Work . . . is the only thing which allows us to retain something of life which otherwise slips away easily and evenly like water through our fingers' (letter, 30 May, to De Robertis) and 'Unproductiveness, born out of a sense of shame and consumed in impassioned idleness, that's my situation' (letter, 15 October, to Carlo Linati).

In April 1915, as the Italian forces mobilized, he was dispatched to the North-east Front. He had only just completed *Esame di Concienza di un Letterato* ('Self-examination of a Man of Letters'), the piece for which he is best remembered, and it was published in *La Voce* on 30 April. Three months later, on 20 August, he died in action on Mount Podgora, which overlooks the river Isonzo. He met his death after rising from the trenches at suicidal risk to his own person (according to his soldiers) to advance against the enemy positions. A medal for valour was later awarded to him posthumously.

Apart from periodic military activity and a passion for sport, Serra seems to have made of his whole life a disquisition upon literature, aware as he did so of the danger of living by proxy, and lamenting, at the ripe age of 25, the sacrifice of his youth.

An extremely literate childhood had predisposed him to benefit from the tutelage of Carducci, that numinous manifestation of the Italian tradition and a critic of exemplary philological rigour. In company as stimulating as that of Carducci and, later, Croce, some twenty years his senior, Serra rapidly developed a very high degree of sophistication in literary analysis but, from the beginning, gave signs of a problematic relationship with this activity. Consuming and comprehending a work of literature by application of every critical resource seemed as natural as breathing to him, but committing himself to print with formal value judgements, in the name of whatever objective criteria, was contemplated only with the greatest reluctance. This seems to have been the case even from the time of his undergraduate thesis on Petrarch, which, though deeply pondered, had to be hurriedly written down to meet its deadline. Again the problems of formulating a coherent judgement were made explicit in the article on Rudyard Kipling published in 1907: though a relatively youthful work, the piece suffers from being too intense a scrutiny. The stories and Kipling himself are approached on a variety of levels with an overprovision of critical instruments. There is clearly a fascination with Kipling's India, the military ethic, the colour, the 'divine bestiality' of a world where human values relate to action and courage, but Serra finds it difficult to do more than pass this on to his Italian readers via a multitude of impressions and frequent recourse to the text itself. Excessive admiration seems to cheat the young critic of his autonomy, and he fails to define or characterize his subject. It is difficult in the end not to feel that Serra, whose knowledge of English was slight, overrated the intellectual depth of Kipling's work.

In 1908, he undertook to produce for *La Romagna* a series of profiles of writers of his native region, the most prominent of which was Pascoli, a poet whose work centred on the objects and situations of the natural world. This type of writing was essentially more congenial to Serra than the cultivated 'literariness' of even masters such as Carducci. Rhetorical, obsessive and labyrinthine, the essay on Pascoli is typical of Serra's multi-angular approach, aiming to reveal the human identity beyond the pages and concealing formal judgement behind a lyrical prose-reading of the *oeuvre*. Literary criticism is even at some risk of confusion with autobiography in the 1914 piece 'In Thanks for a Ballad by Paul Fort'.

These writings and others on Machiavelli, Carducci, D'Annunzio and so on constituted for the literary élite of the time a fascinating alternative to the solid, methodological work of Croce. Serra is more interesting today, however, for the questions he raises with regard to the role of the writer in a divided society. The problem arises in 'For a Catalogue' (1910), but comes to the fore in 'Departure of a Group of Soldiers for Libya' (1912) as well as in 'Self-examination of a Man of Letters' (1915), the most celebrated of Serra's writings and that which has most to say to us across the intervening years.

The soldiers departing for Libya from Serra's birthplace leave behind them, in the writer's eyewitness account, a Cesena where the justifiable anxiety of the few is drowned by rhetoric and euphoria. Scathing and pessimistic as to whether any sense is to be made of things, the introspective intellectual was nevertheless stirred by the prospect of action and the spectacle of men merging in a common purpose which offered them a refuge from the uncertainties of the individual personality.

'See it all; all the works, the letters, the people, the events of their lives, the maliciousness of their contemporaries; and don't pass judgement ever; that's for blockheads with no sense of shame – but understand – feel the quality *of the spirit, of the thought and of the style.'*

1907

Among young intellectuals writing in *La Voce*, there was growing support for Italian intervention when the time came for war. With the exception of De Robertis, however, these were people whom Serra treated warily, viewing *La Voce* under Prezzolini as primarily a vehicle for permanent, anarchic protest. Serra was, by comparison, a traditionalist and conservative. He shared with Carducci and Croce a faith in the absolute value of the literary text, but not Carducci's faith in history and civilized values nor Croce's faith in systematic, objective analysis.

The 'Self-examination' was written between 20–25 March 1915 and published in *La Voce* on 30 April. Among other things, it is an attempt *in extremis* to get some purchase on life. He makes the choice at a simple, existential level to quit his tormented isolation and entrust his person to the conscripted throng. As he says towards the conclusion, 'The present is enough; I neither wish to see nor live beyond this hour of passion.' Serra comes to the war ideologically unprepared but convinced that, between inertia and action within the human fraternity, the latter is to be preferred. It would have been offensive anyhow to try and devise some justification for the slaughter then beginning. So what was this passionate bibliophile doing in the trenches? 'Will you tell me that this, too, is literature?' he muses wryly. 'Very well, I won't deny it.'

MARK M. GRIMSHAW

Texts

Scritti (G. De Robertis and A. Grilli (eds), Le Monnier, Florence, 1958, 2 vols).

Scritti letterari, morali e politici; saggi e articoli dal 1900 al 1915 (M. Isnenghi (ed.), Einaudi, Torino, 1974).

Le lettere (M. Biondi (ed.), Classici della società italiana 1, Loganesi, Milan, 1974).

Secondary sources

Giovanni Pacchiano, *Renato Serra* (Il castoro 39, La Nuova Italia, Florence, 1970).

Sandro Briosi, *Renato Serra* (Civilatà letteraria del Novenceto, Profili no. 15, Mursia, 1968).

Ezio Raimondi, *Il lettore di provincia, Renato Serra* (Quaderni di letteratura e d'arte 22, Le Monnier, Florence, 1964).

Self-examination of a Man of Letters

War is a fact like so many others in this world, just one fact, though an immense one, alongside the others, which have been or are to be. It adds nothing, it takes nothing away. It doesn't change a single thing in the world. Not even literature.

... Literature doesn't change. It may suffer interruptions or pauses, but as a spiritual achievement, as a need and intimate awareness of life, it remains at that point to which the work of the latest generations brought it, and whatever survives of it will resume from that point, continue from there. It is idle to expect transformations or renewals to be brought about by war, which is something quite unrelated; just as it is pointless to hope that writers will return changed, improved or inspired by war. War may take them as men, in the most elementary and simple sense. But, as for the rest, each remains what he was. Each returns – of those who do return – to the work he left behind – tired perhaps, affected, drained, as if emerging from a flood, but with the spirit, the manners, the abilities and qualities he had before.

... One would wish that, between companions of an hour and of a passion, something in common might remain for ever. But that is impossible. Everyone must go back to his own path, to his own past and to his own sins.

To return to our theme: war does not change anything. It doesn't improve, it doesn't redeem and it doesn't erase by itself. It can work no miracles. It cannot pay debts, it cannot wash away sins in this world of ours, which no longer believes in a divine grace.

One's heart finds it hard to admit this. We should like those who have toiled, suffered and resisted for a cause, which must always be holy, when one can undergo suffering for its sake, to come out of the trial as from a sacred font: purer, every one of them. And they that died, at least these we should like to see exalted, sanctified, without blemish and without guilt.

But, no. Neither sacrifice nor death can add anything to a life, to a work, to a heritage. The work which a man has done remains what it is. We should be lacking in that respect which is due to him and his work if, in valuing it, we brought to bear some extraneous criterion, some vote of sympathy or rather of pity. That would be an affront to one who has laboured seriously, to one who died to accomplish his duty.

... What is there, on this tired earth, that will have changed, when it has drunk in the blood of so great a slaughter: when the dead and wounded, the tortured and the abandoned, shall sleep together beneath the ground, while the grass above will have become tender, bright and new, all silent and luxuriant in the spring sun which returns unchanged?

I am not prophesying; I am merely looking at things as they are.

I am gazing at this earth, which has now the faded tints of winter; one can almost see the silence exhaling in the form of a bluish vapour from the ruins of this world, lost in the frigid oblivion of empty spaces. The motionless clouds rest on the summits of the mountains, stacked and squeezed together, and under the vacant sky, I can feel nothing but the weariness of the old white and worn roads lying in the midst of a sombre plain. I see no traces of mankind. The houses are small and scattered like debris; a dull, opaque greenness has merged the furrows and paths into the monotony of the field; there is neither voice nor sound, unless it be that of the lowering sky or of the rising fog, whose sluggish waves are as lifeless as cold ashes.

And yet life does persist, clinging to these ruins, inlaid in these furrows, concealed in these seams, indestructible. One cannot see mankind, nor hear its ant-like swarming: it is a multitude of little beings lost in the squalor of the earth, who have been there so long that they have become part and parcel of the earth.

Centuries have followed upon centuries, and these herds of men have remained among the same mountains, among the same valleys: each in its own place, but with an endless turmoil and ferment, which has however kept within the same boundaries. Peoples, nations and races have been encamped for almost 2000 years amid the folds of this hardened crust. Fluxes and refluxes, sudden overflows and conquests, have from time to time submerged boundaries, swept whole regions, overturned, destroyed and changed: but how little, and for how short a time!

The traces of movements and transits have been worn away in the confused treading of our roads, and all around, in the fields, in the furrows, among the stones, life has continued the same as ever; it has always sprung up again from its hidden seeds, with that sameness of form, of language and of mysterious links which, within a definite yet indefinable circuit, makes of so many distinct little beings an individual whole: a race, which renews throughout 100 different generations the shape of skulls which lie buried and unknown beneath the strata of the ageless earth, and perpetuates accents and unwritten laws.

What is a war, amid these innumerable and tenacious creatures which continue to dig each one its own furrow, to tread each one its own path, to produce offspring upon the very ground which covers the dead; which when interrupted, begin again, and when driven away, return?

The war has brought in its wake devastation and confusion: but millions of men are unaware of it. Individuals have fallen or fled; but life has remained, irreducible in its primitive and instinctive animality, for which the course of the sun and of the seasons is of more importance than all wars: passing commotions, dull blows, which mingle with all the remaining fatal travail and suffering of existence.

And after 100, after 1000 years, war beats once again on its return against the same dikes, and brings back to the same outlets the same human groups that had previously been driven or drawn from their abodes.

This is the same human tide which overflowed beyond the Rhine and into Flanders, which flooded the Germanic and Sarmatic plains and broke at the mountain passes.

The fields of battle are the same, and the roads to them are the same.

It is true that this time a mighty, irresistible wave appears to have stirred up the most ancient strata of the humanity which is encamped in the regions of Europe: it is not a local adventure or disturbance, but a movement of entire peoples torn from their roots.

During the first days of the war, an indefinable impression was rife, that the time of the great floods, by which one race may take the place of another, had returned. Europe had not seen the like for nearly 2000 years; and it was the barbarians of old, the masses of the newer peoples, who began to move again from the places in which they had finally settled when the tide they constituted had fallen back; for during the whole of this interval, partial movements and disturbances had not shifted them for any length of time.

Nor is it likely that they will be shifted even this time. Probably we shall not even see those partial conquests of the kind which fail to destroy the down-trodden vitality of a race, which gradually rises again like trampled grass and envelops, permeates and absorbs the foreign element, as occurred to the Germanic element which, having overflown into western and southern Europe, remained there when the invasions were over and was absorbed by our Latin countries.

One can already hear the opposing tides clashing and then flowing back from their line of impact, which is still unchanged. And in the end, everything will return more or less to its place. The war will have disposed of a situation which already existed; it will not have created a new one.

. . . This Italy of ours exists, is alive, pursues her course. If she does not answer the call today, she will tomorrow perhaps, in fifty years or in a hundred and she will still be in time. What importance do years have for a people?

The sea, the mountains, this theatre of history does not change: Italy has time. There are no failures or losses for a people with the vitality and the spirit of this one, even if no part is taken in the war.

This may be a little hard to admit. It goes against the grain with some to have to acknowledge in the end that all these splendid people that we have around and who seem to have the fate of our country in their hands – parliament, press, professors, Giolitti, that excellent man, and diplomats, priests, socialists, even better – will not have done a lot of harm, just as they were not able to do much good; and that the anger felt towards them was as excessive as the scorn was irrelevant. The destiny of Italy was not in their hands. We will have nothing to avenge. That quiver of shame and anger which we thought to carry locked in our heart until the moment came to express it, ends almost in a smile. And this, too, is a sad thing, something wasted, but just one thing among many. And all these things are as nothing if I think of what is wasted every minute, while I am speaking, while I am thinking, while I am writing: blood and pain and distress of men caught up in this great maelstrom of war, a whirlpool consumed in its own violence. What is the significance of the results, the claims with regard to territory or borders, the indemnification, the agreements and the final liquidation, however full and complete, compared to this?

Let us believe, for a moment, that the oppressed will be avenged and the oppressors humbled, that the final result will be full justice and the greatest possible good on earth. But there is no good that compensates for the tear shed in vain, the lament of the wounded left abandoned, the pain of the tortured of whom there is no news, the blood and human carnage which serves no purpose. The good of the others, those who remain, does not make up for the irreparable harm, sustained for all eternity.

Then again what sort of good are we talking about? Even those exiles who await the end as the fulfilment of a prophecy and the advent of heaven upon earth know that the dream is in vain.

Perhaps the benefit of war, as of all things, is in itself: a sacrifice that one makes, a duty one discharges. One learns to suffer, to resist, to be content with little, to live a worthier life with a more real fraternal spirit, a more religious simplicity. This goes for both individuals and nations: until they forget the lesson . . .

. . . But let us go forward! Behind me, those that follow are all brothers, even if I do not see them or know them well.

I am satisfied with what we have in common, which is stronger than all that divides us. I am satisfied with the road which we shall have to tread together, which will bear us all equally; and there will be but one step, one breath, one cadence, one destiny for us all. After the first miles of our marching, all differences will have fallen, drop by drop, like the sweat from our downward-cast faces, amid the dragging of heavy feet and the growing heaviness of our breathing; and then there will be only tired men who grow dejected, but gather new strength and proceed, without murmuring and without becoming enthusiastic, for it is so natural to do what one has to do. There is no time for remembering the past or for thinking a great deal when we are moving shoulder to shoulder and there are so many things to be done, or rather, one thing only between us all.

Let us move together: one after the other, up the paths between the mountains, which smell of broom and mint. We file upwards like ants upon a wall, and finally, we cautiously peep over the mountain ridge in the silence of the morning. Or let us move together in the evening along great wide roads, soft with dust, which muffle and multiply the tramping of feet in the darkness, while above there gleams the faint, silvery-green thread of the new moon, right up in between the small, white, virgin stars of April; when if one halts, one can feel on one's neck the warm breath of the column closing up behind. Or, at night, let us sleep together a sleep that is buried in the depths of the black, frozen sky; and later, feel in our sleep the mournful weeping of the morning dew, as subtle as the flaw in a crystal; and then: up, for the day is already breaking. So: marching and halting together, resting and rising together, toiling and remaining silent together; lines and lines of men, who follow the same track, tread the same soil, a dear, hard, solid and eternal soil, firm under our feet and good for our bodies. And then there are all the other things of which one does not speak, because one must be there to understand them, and then one feels them, and in a manner which makes words useless.

Down there in the city, they are still talking about party politics, bickering factions, people who cannot agree, people who would be afraid, who would refuse or come reluctantly. There could be something true in all that, as long as one stays among those streets, among those houses.

But I live in another place. In that Italy which seemed deaf to me and empty when I simply looked upon it, but which now I feel to be full of men like myself, gripped by my anxiety and setting out with me upon this road, able to support each other, to live and to die together, without even knowing why, should the time come.

Perhaps it will never come. We have been waiting so long and it never came! What is there more certain for me to believe in today than this desire which grows stronger and stronger within me?

I don't know and I don't care. My very being vibrates with hopes to which I abandon myself without question, and I know that I am not alone. All the apprehension, the agitation, the quarrelling, the background noise make up a confused murmur in which I hear the voice of my hope. And this is all the certainty that I now need.

No further assurances are necessary about a future which doesn't concern me. The present is enough; I neither wish to see nor live beyond this hour of passion. No matter how it finishes, this hour belongs to me and I will not give up one minute of a wait which is mine. Will you tell me that this, too, is literature? Very well, I won't deny it. Why should I disappoint you? Today I am content.

TRANSLATED BY MARK M. GRIMSHAW

*J*ERZY ŻUŁAWSKI 1874–1915

'And you will go...To fight for a Poland that's ours, that is free.'

From 'To My Sons'

This Polish poet, novelist, dramatist and art critic was born on 14 July 1874 in Lipowiec (present-day Rzeszow county). His father Kazimierz had been a participant in the January Uprising of 1863. Jerzy Żuławski was educated at secondary (grammar) schools in Limanowa, Bochnia and Kraków, and studied at the polytechnic in Zurich before transferring to the philosophy department in Berne where, in 1889, he was awarded a doctorate for his thesis on Spinoza entitled: 'Das Problem der Kausalitat bei Spinoza' ('The Problem of Causation in Spinoza'). On returning to Poland, he taught at secondary schools in Jaslo and Kraków. In 1910, he moved to a villa in Zakopane where the poets Kazimierz Tetmajer, Jan Kasprowicz and Leopold Staff were frequent guests. He became involved in the nationalist and neo-romantic literary and artistic movement 'Young Poland' in Kraków and published his works in *Życie*, *Młodość*, *Krytyka* and the Warsaw-based *Strumień*, as well as *Chimera* and the Lvov *Słowo Polskie*. He travelled extensively in Germany, Switzerland, Italy and France, and was an enthusiastic and very good mountaineer, one of the founders of the Tatra Volunteer Mountain Rescue Service in southern Poland. At the outbreak of the First World War, he joined the Legions in order to take part in the battle for his country's independence. This is how his son Juliusz Żuławski recorded the event:

> And then one day, after a brief absence, father came home wearing a Legion uniform. The Damascene sword which had served my grandfather Kazimierz in 1863 had disappeared from the library wall and was now shining on the sword-belt at my father's side. (A quarter of a century later, I was to wear it when I was an officer during the September campaign of 1939.) From then on, my father appeared rarely; all that remained from that last period was a pile of cards sent to my mother by the field post, and to us boys, too, in which he gave details of the marches he'd been on in the saddle – through Jędrzejów, Pincz, Chmielnik, Opatów, Ozarów, Sandomierz, Tarnobrzeg and then Piotrków again – and he suggested we ask Mother to show us where they all were 'on the large map hanging in the dining-room'. The last time I saw his tall, military figure was in Zakopane in the spring of 1915.

Jerzy Żuławski. *Polish Academy of Sciences*

Initially, Żuławski's Legion service was in the Rifles, but later he moved to the Army Department. He was an officer on the staff of the High Command of the Legions, and he edited the Legion publication *Do Broni* (*To Arms*). During a journey to the front from Piotrków, he was caught up in the typhus epidemic and died in the field hospital for infectious diseases in Dębnica on 9 August 1915.

Jerzy Żuławski's debut as a poet was in 1895 when he published a collection called *Na strunach duszy* (*On the Strings of the Soul*). Written during the 'Young Poland' period, his work did not show any divergence from the literary conventions of the time. In his early poems, one can see clearly the influence of the French Parnassians, although there are also traces of the Positivist tradition. Literary critics refer to the intellectual and erudite qualities of his verse, and his contemporaries (P. Chmielowski, J. Lorentowicz, Wilhelm Feldman) went so far as to accuse him of over-indulgent intellectualism. It is generally accepted that the characteristic feature of all of Żuławski's verse is his search for transcendental values; yet, although he wrote poems on eschatological themes, he also wrote verse about the Tatra mountains. Connections with the philosophical ideas of Schopenhauer, Nietzsche and Bergson (i.e. dynamism, aspiring to strength) are obvious in Żuławski's poetry, particularly in his predilection for verbs expressing movement, speed, momentum, and in his kinetic metaphors such as 'an orgy of lightning-flashes', 'deluges of lights', 'a hurricane of voices'. In this period, he resorts frequently to solar symbolism, and to symbols from the Old Testament and classical literature. The heroes of his works are balladeers, sages and prophets.

Between 1897 and 1904, Żuławski published further collections of verse: *Intermezzo*, *Stance o pieśni* (*Songs for Stanca*, 1897), *Poezje II* (1902), *Z domu niewoli* (*From the House of Enslavement*; 1904). Żuławski, who in his intellectualized works combined elements typical of both modernist and traditional poetry, was not well understood by his contemporaries. However, he was also a soldier-poet, and in 1914, he published in the *Viennese Polish Courier* one of his last patriotic lyrics, probably the best known of his poems, called 'To My Sons'. In order to put Żuławski's patriotic verses in their proper context within Polish poetry of the First World War, a few words about the literature of those years are necessary.

Polish war poetry of 1914–18 cannot be regarded as a single, consistent phenomenon since there are many different, though partly contiguous, strands running through it. Of these, one can pick out the populist works, such as the verse of J. Mączko, J. A. Teslar or E. Słoński, which were published in the civilian and military press; the more high-brow works that were published mainly in book form and written by poets with an established reputation (e.g. Staff, Ostrowska); and the mass of verse and songs written in the trenches. These last can be regarded as a kind of soldier's folklore – for example, the creation and social importance of Boleslaw Wieniawa-Dlugoszewski's songs. The drive to independence which arose in 1914 meant that poets who were dealing with subjects of battle and freedom were often overly inclined to return to the literary conventions of the Romantic period. Quite often Żuławski did the same, using as early as his volume *Z domu niewoli* almost the entire catalogue of independence symbols and tropes: spring announcing the rebirth of the nation, a call to arms, an eagle preparing to fly, a resurrected Christ, a phoenix rising from the ashes and so on. To song, which he identified with independence poetry, he ascribed the role of advocate for a nation's action: song, he wrote, 'must be like a powerful bell which wakes the dead and rallies the living' (*Stance o pieśni*). Sometimes, however, the real subject of the poem was expressed in modernist conventions – as, for example, in the sonnet cycle *Warszawa*.

Żuławski's patriotic poetry was just one of many strands in his writing, which combined the work of a patriot and a modernist artist. These two aspects could be found most strikingly in his aesthetic theories.

He was also a highly versatile writer. He wrote plays using historical and contemporary subjects – *Eros and Psyche* (1904); *Wianek mirtowy* (*A Myrtle Wreath*, 1903); *Gra* (*The Game*, 1906) – and translated Richepin, Nietzsche and parts of the Bible. As a poet, he was forgotten by succeeding generations, and nowadays he is best remembered as the author of the words of the song 'To My Sons' (with music by Stanislaw Ekiert) and of the science fiction trilogy *Na srebrnym globie* (*On the Silver Globe*, 1903–10), which earned him the sobriquet of the 'Polish Wells'.

The trilogy takes its name from the first of the three novels. Part I takes the form of the memoirs of the surviving member of an expedition to the moon by five human heroes of various nationalities; and it records the rise of their descendants, the Selenites, a race of dwarfs whose nostalgia for the planet of their forefathers leads them to believe in the coming of a messianic champion. The second part *Zwycięzca* (*The Champion*) tells of the arrival of the humanoid Marek, who lands on the moon in a spaceship and is identified as the 'Champion' by the lunar dwarfs. The Champion enjoys some initial success, liberating the Selenites from their oppressors, the aboriginal Sherns. However, he ultimately proves incapable of fulfilling the high hopes placed in him and perishes, tortured by the Selenites in circumstances recalling the Passion of Christ. Part III – *Stara Ziemia* (*The Old Earth*) – relates the adventures on Earth of two dwarfs, Materet and Professor Roda, who have hijacked Marek's craft. Their reactions to their new environment are depicted with humour and imagination, but the main element in the narrative is the author's vision of Europe in the 27th century. Here he expressed his conviction that the only true progress for humanity lies in spiritual, not material development.

TRANSLATED BY JACEK LASKOWSKI
from material provided by the
Polish Academy of Sciences, Warsaw
and Harry Leeming

Texts

Z domu niewoli ([*From the House of Enslavement*] Warsaw, 1902). Patriotic verse.

Na srebrnym globie ([*On the Silver Globe*] Warsaw, 1903-11). Science-fiction trilogy.

Eros i Psyche (Warsaw, 1904). Zulawski's most successful work for the stage.

Poezje (Warsaw, 1908, iv). Verse which reflects the philosophical influence of Schopenhauer, Nietzsche and Indian mysticism.

Secondary Sources

Literatura Polska. przewodnik encykopedyczmy (Polskie Wydawnictwo Naukowe, Warsaw, 1984-5, ii, 6).

Julian Krzyzanowski, *Dzieje literatury polskiej* (Warsaw, 1987).

Do Moich Synow

Synkowie moi, poszedłem w bój,
Jako wasz dziadek a ojciec mój –
Jak ojca ojciec i ojca dziad,
Co z legionami przemierzył świat,
Szukajac drogi przez krew i blizny
Do naszej wolnej Ojczyzny.

Synkowie moi, da nam to Bóg,
Ze spadna wreszcię kajdany z nóg
I nim wy meskich dojdziecie sił,
Jawa sie stanie, co dziadek śnił,
Szcześciem zakwitnie krwia wieków źyzny
Łan naszej wolnej Ojczyzny!

Synkowie moi, lecz gdyby Pan
Nie dał zejść zorzy z krwi naszych ran,
To jeszcze w waszej piersi jest krew
Na nowy świetej Wolności siew:
I wy pójdziecie, pomni spuścizny,
Na bój dla naszej Ojczyzny.

To My Sons

I went to the battle, dear sons of mine,
Like my father went, and his father went,
And his father's father, the world content
To cross with the legions hoping, in time,
Through the blood and the wounds a path he'd see
To a Poland that's ours, a Poland that's free.

Let's pray to God, dear sons of mine,
That the shackles binding our legs disappear,
And before you reach your grandfather's years
His dream to waking truth will incline
And the ages of blood which nourished the leas
Will make them blossom in a Poland that's free.

But if the good Lord, dear sons of mine,
Has not let the dew come from blood that we spilled,
Then your hearts contain enough blood still
To give holy Freedom a new harvest time,
And you will go, your birthright's trustees,
To fight for a Poland that's ours, that is free.

Translated by Jacek Laskowski

Stara ziemia

From the third book of the science-fiction trilogy The Old Planet. *It is the 27th century. A race of lunar dwarves has developed from the first earth settlers on the moon. The unexpected re-appearance of a fully grown man, freshly arrived from earth who they call 'The Champion', prompts the dwarves to investigate their planetary neighbour more closely. They hijack the earthling's spacecraft back to the 'Old Earth' . . .*

Chapter 3

After regaining consciousness, Mataret was for some time unable to understand the recent happenings and his present whereabouts. He rubbed his eyes now and again, uncertain whether he was in fact plunged in impenetrable gloom or whether his eyelids were stuck together. Realizing he was in the spacecraft which had flown down to earth from the moon, he tried without success to switch on the electric light. It took him a long time to locate the button as the interior of the craft was in a rare state of chaos. When he did find it, he pressed in vain. Obviously there was something wrong with the circuit. They were left in pitch darkness.

In the gloom, he began to call his companion's name: 'Roda! Roda!' For a long time, there was no reply, until at last he heard a groan, which at least informed him that the master was still alive. He groped his way in the direction of the voice. It was not easy for him to find his bearings. During the whole of the journey, the craft had turned under the gravitational pull, first of the moon and then of the earth, but they had always had the floor at their feet. Now Mataret noticed that he was crawling along the concave wall of the shell.

He found Roda and shook him by the arm.

'Are you alive?'

'Just about.'

'Are you hurt?'

'I can't say. I feel dizzy. My whole body aches. And I feel a weight, a terrible weight . . .'

Mataret knew what he meant. Any movement demanded the most strenuous exertion.

'What has happened?' he asked.

'I don't know.'

'We were getting quite close to the earth. I could see it spinning . . . Where are we now?'

'I've no idea. Maybe we flew over and past it! Yes, that's it! We missed the earth and now we're heading out into space with her shadow behind us!'

'But why do you think the craft has tilted like this? We're walking along the wall.'

'Wall or ceiling – who cares? It's all the same. We've had it. It's only a matter of time.'

Mataret said nothing but felt the Professor must be right. He lay stretched out on his back and closed his eyes, succumbing to the weariness which slowly overcame him like a portent of approaching death.

However, he did not fall asleep. In a semi-conscious delirium, he saw again the moon's broad plains and the town by the Warm Pools on the sea coast .

He rubbed his eyes. In fact, someone *was* calling him.

'Yes, Roda?'

'Were you asleep?'

'No, I'm not asleep. The Champion . . .'

'To hell with the Champion. I've been calling you for half an hour. Come on, open up those goggles!'

'It's light!'

'Yes it is. And getting lighter. What is it?'

Mataret sat up and craned his neck, looking up at the porthole, now above him, where a patch of grey was slowly brightening against the dark background.

'It's daylight,' he whispered.

'I don't understand,' said Roda. 'Our days and nights come so quickly, in a single moment . . .'

Now the light grew suddenly brighter and a dry rustle reached their ears, the first sound from outside since their departure from the moon.

'We must have landed!' Mataret exclaimed.

'What are you so happy about?'

The question fell on deaf ears. Battling against the abnormal weight of his own body, Mataret clambered up towards the window, over which clouds of sand seemed to be moving, sometimes becoming so dense that the inside of the craft was again left in pitch blackness. The observer could make no sense of this at all. Suddenly he blinked his eyes as a blinding flash of light caught them. The sand disappeared and the dazzling light of the sun fell on the porthole. The hiss of the wind rushing over the earth's surface could be clearly heard.

When he opened his eyes again he had a clear view through the window of a dark-blue sky, coloured by the atmosphere, not at all like the black curtain of interstellar space through which they had travelled.

'So here we are on the earth,' Mataret repeated confidently and began to loosen the screws which had kept them secure in their long confinement.

He did not find it easy. Everything seemed to be extremely heavy and his own limbs feeble and lazy, tiring so easily that he had to break off every minute for a rest. When eventually the last screws dropped with a clatter to the floor, the fresh air came straight through the porthole into his face and gave him such a shock that he lost his footing. Exhausted by his efforts and intoxicated by the fresh air, he was for the moment too weak to clamber out.

He regained his balance only after a long rest. Then, gripping the window frame with both hands, he lifted first his head out and then his whole body. Roda squeezed out after him, poking his big tousled head out of the craft.

There was a long silence as they looked around.

'Well, and didn't I tell you there's no life on earth?' Roda inquired at last.

Before them and around them, as far as the eye could see, was a vast expanse of yellow sand, humped like the waves of the sea but scorched by the merciless glare of the sun. In landing on the earth, their craft had driven into an enormous dune but the now-slackening desert wind had disinterred them.

Mataret gave no answer. He stared around with wide-open eyes, trying to make sense of his jumbled impressions. All around was silent, dead, still; he could hardly believe this was the planet he had seen only a short time before, violently spinning at his feet . . . He rubbed his eyes and marshalled his scattered thoughts, unsure whether he was still asleep or just recovering from some mysterious hallucination.

Occasionally he had a bout of nervous dread without understanding the cause. His whole body would then shudder from head to toe, as in tormented frustration he uttered a silent prayer that the whole expedition, the journey and the earth landing might prove to be nothing but a figment of his imagination . . . He tried to gain control of himself, to think rationally.

At last, he felt the pangs of hunger. He went back to the spacecraft and recovered the remainder of their food and water supply.

'Come on, have something to eat,' he told Roda.

That worthy shrugged his shoulders.

'I really don't see why I should bother to eat, just to prolong my life by a couple of hours.'

All the same, he attacked their stores so greedily Mataret had to remind him they should be rationing their supplies.

'What's the point?' growled Roda. 'I'm feeling hungry so I'll eat what there is. Then I'll go and hang myself on the beak of that blasted space-kite.'

Mataret ignored these grumblings. He filled a sack with the rest of the food and brought from the craft various easily detachable small articles which might prove useful later. Eventually, when he had packed it all up, he tried to swing the bundle over his shoulder. He immediately realized he had overestimated his own strength and failed to take account of the sixfold increase in weight in his new surroundings. He was now forced to jettison everything that was not absolutely essential. He split the rest into two bundles.

'Here, take this!' he told Roda, handing one to him. 'And now let's go!'

'Go where?'

'We'll see. Just follow your nose.'

'The whole idea's completely futile. What does it matter whether I die here or somewhere else in this barren wilderness?'

'Remember when we saw this planet spinning beneath us. I then saw land and sea. I saw greenery. Maybe we can reach some habitable spot.'

Grumpy and unhappy, Roda shouldered his burden and followed Mataret's lead. Choosing an easterly direction, they made off, feet sinking in the sand at every step. Exhausted by the heat and by the terrestrial air, too rich for their lunar lungs, they were most oppressed by the sheer weight of their own bodies, which, puny and diminutive, now seemed as heavy as lead. They halted at frequent intervals, wiping the hot sweat from their brows.

During these breaks, Roda adduced every observable detail as yet further evidence for his theory that the earth was uninhabited and uninhabitable.

'Just give it a moment's thought,' he argued. 'The force of gravity is so oppressive that no living creature could sustain it for any length of time.'

'But what if the earth people were bigger and stronger than us? Like the Champion, say!'

'Don't talk rubbish! If people here were bigger, they'd weigh more. They wouldn't be able to move.'

'But what if . . .'

'Don't interrupt when I'm speaking!' The Professor was affronted. 'This isn't a free-for-all. I'm simply passing on to you the fruits of my long experience. If you listen, you might learn something.'

This brought no response from Mataret who merely shrugged his shoulders, picked up his burden and moved off again. The Professor followed him, constantly asserting, though short of breath, the accuracy of his predictions.

'It's all over. We'll die here. Like stray dogs,' he went on. 'I tell you, there's not a single living creature here.'

'So that means we're the first,' Mataret broke in. 'We should plant a flag and claim the whole planet.'

'A fat lot of good you'll get out of it! Nothing but sand. And that water we thought we saw. If it was water and not a mirage.'

Meanwhile Mataret had stopped. He was staring ahead, fascinated by something that had caught his eye.

'Do you see what I see?' He pointed with outstretched hand.

'Well, what is it?'

'I've no idea. Let's have a closer look.'

About fifty paces further on, they reached harder, stony ground and now had a clear view of a line crossing the path they had taken and running out to infinity in either direction. Coming closer, they saw the iron rail, hoisted clear of the ground on metal trestles, which bisected the desert wilderness from horizon to horizon, as far as the eye could see.

'What can it be?' Roda wondered in an awed whisper.

'There must be some life here after all,' Mataret declared. 'This strange contraption must be the work of human hands.'

'Oh no! You're wrong there! It's just possible there may be some life here after all, but there are no human beings on this planet! Just think it over, it stands to reason . . . Why on earth would *Homo sapiens* make such a useless object . . . Why waste so much iron? There's no sense in it!'

'But you do agree now that the earth's inhabited?'

'Well, yes, only who lives here? Some race of creatures . . .'

They examined the mysterious iron bar intently. Suddenly it began to hum and the hum grew louder until . . .

They both drew back terror-stricken. A colossal glittering juggernaut with a flat snout roared past along the rail at such a tremendous speed that it was far away in the distance before they recovered. They watched in fear and trembling, not even daring to speculate what this could have been.

It was Mataret who eventually broke the long silence, gazing fearfully into the distance where the apparition had disappeared.

'A terrestrial beast, I suppose . . .'

'Well, that's all we needed,' muttered Roda, 'if that monster's an example of the local fauna. It must have been a good hundred yards long, I'd say. Shot past like a bullet. Did you get a glimpse of its legs?'

'No, I didn't. It was the eyes I noticed, all along its body from head to tail, and they looked like windows . . . Also I got the impression it had wheels. Maybe it wasn't a monster at all, but some sort of transport.'

'Oh, use your brains, man! How could any vehicle go at that speed with nothing at all to pull it?'

'Well, tell me who pulled our craft through space?' Mataret butted in. 'Maybe they have something similar here.'

'No, that can't be. Nothing could run along such a smooth single rail. It would simply topple over.'

Stealthily they crept along under the trestles, looking up at the rail suspiciously as they followed the track. They felt complete strangers on this planet, the original cradle of humanity according to a lunar legend they had both long decried. For them, this was a desolate wasteland.

Roda, who tired more quickly than his companion, was now stopping every minute and complaining bitterly of the intolerable heat which, while not approaching the moon's midday temperature, seemed more oppressive in the denser atmosphere of earth. Moreover, nothing in that immense expanse of yellow sand offered them any shade. Only far ahead in the distance loomed the weird shapes of towering cliffs, white in the sun's blinding light and, in among them, something like enormous ragged plumes on tall, slightly bent columns.

They were making for those cliffs, calling on their last reserves of strength in the hope that they might find there some cool shelter from the heat, when suddenly their attention was caught by dark shadows moving swiftly over the sand. It was Roda who first looked round to see, silhouetted against the sunlight, a flock of gigantic birds with broad white wings and flattened tails. Mataret noticed that some which were flying low had wheels, not feet. They sped swiftly through the air without moving their outstretched wings. It was difficult to determine where body ended and head began. In place of a beak, there was something that spun round so rapidly the eye could make out nothing but a dim blur.

They soon vanished in the same direction as the first gleaming monster.

'Everything here's so horrible,' whispered Roda through lips numb with fright.

Mataret did not reply. While watching the birds, he had been struck by the position of the sun low down in the sky. Suffused with a crimson glow it was sinking behind a yellowish haze.

'How long is it since we left our kite?' he asked after a moment's reflection.

'You're asking me . . . Four maybe, or possibly five, six hours . . .'

'And the sun was then overhead?'

'Yes.'

Mataret pointed westward.

'Well, it's going down now. It just doesn't make sense. Could it have crossed the sky so quickly?'

At first, the master too was puzzled by this strange mystery. In terror and consternation, he gazed at the globe which had apparently gone berserk, traversing half the firmament in six hours, whereas on the moon it would have taken a few dozen. But soon his wide mouth creased in a beaming smile.

'My dear Mataret,' he chuckled, 'do you really remember nothing I taught you back at the Truthseekers' Guild?'

The bald student waited in silence for some further explanation.

'Now look here,' Roda continued, 'earth days are short and last only twenty-four moon hours, so . . .'

'Of course, of course.'

In spite of this reassurance, they both watched with some disquiet as the sun seemed to move visibly.

'It can only be another hour till nightfall,' Mataret's voice dropped to a whisper.

'Damn!' The teacher now himself forgot his lesson of a moment before. 'Damn, damn, damn! Three hundred and fifty hours of unbroken frost and gloom! What on earth are we going to do? We should never have left the vehicle . . .'

This time, it was Mataret who first regained his poise.

'One earth day – twenty-four hours. One earth night – twelve hours more or less!'

'Of course, of course!' Roda chimed in. 'It's strange all the same,' he went on, after a short pause. 'Very strange. Anyway, one thing's certain: we're in for a chilly night. I don't know whether we should expect snow. On the moon, snowfalls come some twenty or thirty hours after sunset. Here it should be day by then.'

'Maybe the snow comes sooner here.'

During this discussion, they kept on the move. The heat was now less intense and they had become used to the increased weight of their bodies so that their progress was brisker than before.

Soon they were approaching the cliffs. Now they found a hard stone surface under the sand and even a feeble yellow blade of grass appeared in the odd crack.

They stopped to examine these botanical specimens carefully, trying to determine on this slender evidence what the more luxuriant flora might look like, if indeed any such existed.

The sun had set and the two moonmen had reached the cliffs in their search for a place to spend the night when, in the rapidly gathering dusk, they caught sight of a gigantic stone figure, half human, half animal. Of all the creatures in their experience, this monster's body reminded them most of a dog, the only quadruped still familiar to the Selenites. However, this was more rounded, more muscular, and its upright neck supported a human head.

'There must be intelligent creatures like us or the Sherns down here, too,' Mataret suggested after a moment of dumbstruck wonder. 'Otherwise they couldn't make such things from stone.'

'What if this is a statue of one of them?' Roda added, staring at the motionless hulk.

Scared and depressed beyond words, they discovered a hiding-place – a cleft in the rock – as far as possible from that portentous figure, and took what precautions they could against the coming night's frost. The eastern sky now began to glow with a gradually spreading, soft, golden light. The bright stars were dimmed as eventually an orange disc emerged, enormous, luminous.

This was as strange and incomprehensible as anything they had experienced in what had been the shortest day of their lives. Meanwhile, the sphere, like a balloon full of light, rose ever higher, appearing to gain in lustre as it shrank in size. The darkness yielded to a gentle silver pallor which glimmered on sand and rock, and even seemed to bring the horrendous stone monster to life.

'That star! What can it be?'

The master racked his brains but in the end shook his head, admitting defeat.

'Beats me. It's not one I recognize,' he said, gazing at the moon, from which he had taken off only a few hours previously.

But Mataret suddenly remembered the view he had had from the porthole as they shot into space. At close range, the image had been both larger and fainter, but there was a certain resemblance . . .

'It's the moon!' he cried.

'Our moon . . .'

With grim, heartrending nostalgia they contemplated their lost homeland, calmly gliding across the sky.

TRANSLATED BY HARRY LEEMING

*F*RANTIŠEK *G*ELLNER 1881–1914

'I want to get drunk again, I want to get drunk again, I want to get drunk again on champagne!!!'
(The Joys of Life, V)

František Gellner, Czech artist, poet, short-story writer and dramatist, published his first poem, in an established periodical, at the age of fifteen. In 1900 he was sent by his Jewish shopkeeper father to Vienna to study technology, but devoted himself instead to the superior life of bordellos and drink. In 1901 he was transferred from Vienna to the Příbram (Bohemia) School of Mining Technology, which enabled him to join the Prague radical clique of writers. He did his military service from 1904 to 1905 and then travelled to Munich to study painting. Dissatisfied by Munich, he went to Paris, where he remained until 1908, moving in bohemian anarchist circles and contributing caricatures to French satirical periodicals like *Cri de Paris* and *Rire*. After a brief spell back in Bohemia and a year studying art in Dresden, he returned to Paris for nearly two years. Then in 1911 he went to Brno (Moravia) and, for the first time, took a steady job, on the editorial board of the leading paper, *Lidové noviny*. He was called up in August 1914 and was sent almost immediately to the Galician Front. His regiment declared him missing on 13 September. No evidence has ever been provided to substantiate rumours which circulated after the war that he had escaped into a monastery; Gellner was an anticlerical atheist.

His first two collections of poetry, *Après nous le déluge* (1901) and *The Joys of Life* (1903), consisted of iconoclastic lyric verse, often with pronounced epic elements. His poems are frequently compared with those of Jehan Rictus, but often they come close in tone to the early verse of Arthur Symons and even to the gloomy jokes of the leading Czech Decadent, Karel Hlaváček. His poems often read like *chansons*, but he does no more to *épater les bourgeois* than other, more conservative Decadents except in his language, where he often tries to imitate the language of the streets. Both collections demonstrate a jolly *je m'en foutisme*, but with an undertone of profound melancholy. (His mocking caricatures nearly always contain a darkly rabbinical mentor in their heavy lines.) He was, he wrote, as unlucky with his brawls as he was with his whores; in both cases he invariably ended up as an outpatient at some hospital or other. Gellner satirized sentimentality, but could not conceal his own tendency to sentimentalize. Regularly his Decadent, hedonist pursuit of destructive sensuality moved towards a Vitalist striving for some creative, nature-bound existence. His anarchism always appeared a little studied, though his desire to see all hidebound, reactionary institutions destroyed was as ardently sincere as might be expected. In *The Joys of Life* he included Jews among those institutions, partly because of their exalted positions in industry, partly because of their political opportunism. He attacked institutions, while at the same time feeling hurt by them: 'They all lied to me . . . journals, poets, scholars; men lied to me; women lied to me; most of all women' (*The Joys of Life*, XXX). The conception of the whole of society as a lie again echoed Decadent writing. Behind the sarcasm of his first two collections lay a strong wish to find gullibility justified.

František Gellner.

New Poems, his third collection, written between 1904 and 1913, was published posthumously in 1919. While he remained an anti-authoritarian satirist his sarcasm had diminished, and the occasionally elegaic mood was new. His ironic perception of self was more open, no longer necessarily clothed in *je m'en foutisme*. *The Joys of Life* ends with a line in which romantic willows address the poet: 'Friend, brother, come here and hang yourself'; while 'News in Brief' in *New Poems* tells of a woman who tries to commit suicide, but is rescued by the authorities and compelled to return to the poverty and cold she had decided to abandon. In *New Poems* Gellner often wrote as if his conscience were troubling him because he had failed to live up to his anarchist aspirations. The long mock ballad, 'A Moral Tale about a Good Boy and a Bad Boy', relates the stories of two classmates. Giles is a goody-goody at school, comfortably enjoys life and ends up a senior law court official with a charming wife, well-behaved children, no debts, and eating the roast goose he loves as often as he likes. Jimmy perpetually fails exams at school, manages three days in a seminary, then reads all manner of subjects at various Austrian institutions; soon after he is called up for military service, he deserts and joins the Foreign Legion. After adventures in Haiti, North America, Australia and China, he dies with a bullet in his skull in Paraguay.

The talent for the grotesque manifest in Gellner's verse was equally evident in his prose, even though, on the surface, his prose did not have the avant-garde qualities of his verse. He published only one collection of short stories, *Into the Mountains and Other Tales*, which appeared when he was already at the front, perhaps already dead. These stories combined the traditional nineteenth-century comic tale with something which approached Dadaism, their satire directed mainly at petty-bourgeois values, but also at all forms of sexual relationships. In one story a particularly gross and uneducated rich Czech peasant sits in a Munich nightclub commentating on and salivating over the delectable figure of a *chanteuse* who turns out to be a transvestite. The story itself is, presumably coincidentally, strongly reminiscent of the Bulgarian satirist Aleko Konstantinov's *Bai Ganyo* (1895). At the end of Gellner's story, the peasant has fallen into a drunken sleep in a Linz café: 'It was not until an hour later that I noticed my comrade had his thumb submerged in the cocoa he had ordered. I carefully pulled it out of its steaming bath. The flesh had already begun to peel off the bone. I bandaged his suffering extremity with my handkerchief and took him to the nearest hospital.' Such grotesque scenes abound in Gellner's tales. Although the comic and the quaint predominate, one notices how many suicides and near-suicides occur. The collection does contain one serious story written in the fashion of Pater's *Imaginary Portraits*; it concerns the suicide of the republican Marcus Porcius Cato, as he is being besieged by Caesar.

Apart from *New Poems*, which Gellner had compiled himself, three other complete works were published posthumously; a long poem *Don Juan* (1924), a play, *The Haven of Marriage* (1928), and a long story, *A Nomadic People* (1928).

ROBERT B. PYNSENT

Texts

Radosti života [The Joys of Life] (Prague, 1903).

Cesta do hor a jiné provídky (Pardubice & Jihlava, Prague, 1914). Contains 'Sports a zdraví' ['Sport and Health'].

Secondary sources

Milan Kundera, *Básnê* (Prague, 1957). Contains an introduction to a selection of Gellner's verse.

Rudolf Havel et al., *Slovník ceskýeh spisovatelû* (Prague, 1964).

Radosti Života

I

A nastává mi, tuším, vážná jízda.
Před sebou samým v dálku utíkám.
Mé srdce, to si bezstarostně hvízdá,
a rozum ptá se nudně kudy kam.

Bud sbohem, podunajská metropole,
ulice křivé, jež jste patřily
na mne, jak ztrácím klobouky a hole,
za tmy se domů klátě opilý.

Na Prater jistě stěží zapomenu,
kde hýříval jsem často za noci.
Za večeři tam koupí člověk ženu
s nádavkem venerických nemocí.

Hotely vždycky budou žít v mé touze
s portýry zdvořilými u vrátek,
s pokoji pro dva s jedním ložem pouze
a s legiony drobných zvířátek.

Na policii budu myslit v světě,
jíž osoba má spáti nedala,
která v mém opuštěném kabinetě
spisy a třaskaviny hledala.

A s šantány se těžce loučit budu,
v nichž večer chudý sbor své písně pěl,
i s kavárnami. Mám tak rád jich nudu.
Dvě mladá léta jsem v nich prodřepěl.

XIV

Drobky pod stůl hází nám osud,
ostatní vše je nicota.
Alkohol ještě je! Holky jsou posud!
Jsou ještě radosti života!

Žena jak žena. V života vraku
konečně jedno vše bude ti.
Jedna ubíjí něhou svých zraků,
druhá jedem svých objetí.

Šetřiti léty, jež nemají ceny,
v tom velká moudrost nevězí.
Dobré je opium, alkohol, ženy,
schází-li schopnost k askezi.

The Joys of Life

I

I have to go, there's simply nothing for it.
I've got somehow to leave myself behind.
My heart sings on, it's never really bothered.
But what can still a boring, anxious, mind?

O fare ye well, fair city on the Danube,
O streets that hitherto have on me gazed,
Counting all the hats and canes I've squandered
As I staggered nightly homewards in a haze.

I surely cannot now forget the Prater,
Where many a night I've lived the life of ease
And in exchange for dinner got a tart, who
Repaid me with venereal disease.

Hotels are something else I'll always treasure:
Commissionaires so unctuously polite,
And double rooms with single beds for pleasure
And many a pertinacious parasite.

A special place reserved in my affection
Is for the police I gave such trouble to;
They spent long hours on fatuous detection
Of non-existent bombs, and papers too.

And music-halls I'll always love – their floor-shows
With rotten singers singing rotten songs –
And dreary coffee-houses even more so:
It's there my teenage vagrancy belongs.

XIV

Destiny drops us the crumbs from its table;
All else is really naught.
Booze we've still got, and girls, to enable
The joys of life to be sought.

Woman . . . What woman? It makes little odds
Once life is a matter of crutches.
One uses her charms to finish you off,
Another her venomous clutches.

Conserving those years whose value is nil
Is rather a dull sort of fetishism.
There's opium, alcohol, women still
For those disinclined to asceticism.

Askety vycházeti vidím
z téhož jak já na svět názoru,
stejně jak oni nenávidím
rozumy dobráckých pastorů.

Jsem smutný mládenec, rouhavý cynik,
v rozpuku mládí zhořkl mi svět,
v ovzduší krčem a v zápachu klinik
vypučel písně mé jedový květ.

Děkuju bohu a děkuju čertu
za plaché chvíle prchavý dar.
Života číši jsem naklonil ke rtu,
piju z ní smutek a bolest a zmar.

Ascetics and I, though, do see eye to eye
On some things that life tries to teach us.
For instance, we share a hearty dislike
Of well-meaning but meddlesome preachers.

I'm a miserable case, a blaspheming cynic,
Whose young world turned sour all too soon.
Born of foul stinking air in tavern and clinic,
My song's but a poisonous bloom.

I thank the good Lord and I thank the deuce
For this moment no man can detain.
My lips have touched the cup of life's truth –
And sorrow, frustration and pain.

TRANSLATED BY DAVID SHORT

SPORT AND HEALTH

I feel terribly soppy today.

The moment I got up I looked at the calendar on the wall and I saw that today's motto was, 'Don't despair, just work.' At the same time I learnt what day of the week it was and the exact date. Then I realized that today is once more the anniversary of the heart-rending demise of our unforgettable friend, of that illustrious devotee of sport, Otakar Kuželka.

Realizing this so upset me that I went straight back to bed and there I surrendered myself to pious memories of a dear friend who, although he was years younger than I, was still in a way my mentor, the man who made me decide sport was a good thing, at least intellectually speaking, though, unfortunately, in the world of material reality unforeseen obstacles were laid across the way of his noble endeavour.

Naturally, in the days when I was a child and young man, sports education was entirely neglected. Where I grew up, hiking consisted only of fathers and mothers walking with their offspring for pleasure for three-quarters of an hour on Sunday afternoons. Then we children gathered wild strawberries in the woods or played forfeits or blindman's buff, while our mothers ate sponge-cake and our fathers fortified themselves for the walk back with six-kreutzer beer, which inflated them like young clover.

At grammar school we did not have physical training, even as an optional subject. I cannot definitely say how that was possible. But, as far as I know, the cause of that shameful situation was the stadholder, then Count, now Prince, Thun who banned exercising in the Sokol patriotic gymnastic club buildings. As a result, in schools which did not have their own gymnasiums, the physical training of pupils was forgotten.

I should be doing myself an injustice if I did not mention at this point that I did once make an honourable attempt to compensate for the failings of grammar-school education. I did have the firmest intention of strengthening my biceps and I even once wanted to buy myself some barbells.

I decided to take the advice of a highly recommended physician who was a not infrequent guest in the house I lived in. As a young man, this excellent fellow had taken part in the 1866 Austro-Prussian war when he had sustained a head wound; since that time he had lived

modestly off the thirty-guilder pension the state had to pay him till the belated end of his years.

This experienced old man's first question was why I needed muscles. 'Do you want to be a blacksmith or an expert in dance-hall brawls?' That put the kybosh on my honest intentions. Now I regret it. If that old quack had not objected, I could have devoted myself to politics.

There is, of course, an enormous difference between physical training and sport. The aim of physical training is somehow contained in itself, whereas sport has nobler goals – the establishing of records. Physical training is, if I might be so bold as to put it like this, a mere entrance-hall to sport, and a very dark and dingy entrance-hall at that.

I first got to know Otakar Kuželka at a sporting event, and so my first experience of the man who was to be my friend and mentor was at the height of his endeavour. It was at a swimming tournament. Kuželka managed to swim round a lake three times in 2 hours, 18 minutes and 33.5 seconds, after which he turned blue and lay unconscious on the bank. At that time I was sharing a flat with a medic, who had been trying to pass his final exams for a good twenty years, and so I had picked up a certain amount of medical knowledge. I helped bring the half-dead Kuželka back to life with artificial respiration. I almost dislocated his right arm, but we finally managed to resuscitate him.

To show his gratitude Otakar Kuželka was so kind as to offer to teach me to ride a bicycle. I should have gone a long way in this practical branch of sport if roads had been built differently in Austria-Hungary: I mean, if the middle of the road had been the deepest part of the road and not the highest. It stands to reason that if the camber inclines both to the left and to the right, an irrational machine like a bicycle will always incline to the left or right ditch.

I do not wish to bore you by enumerating the exact number of bent spokes, broken handlebars, smashed bells, grazed knees and elbows and torn trousers, since it is generally known that the beginner's life is not a happy one.

Later we used to go on pleasant trips along the banks of the river which had, unfortunately, been regulated by large dykes. It happened once that we were pushed right into the dyke by two hauliers' wagons avoiding a collision with a motor car, which had unhappy consequences for the further development of my love for sport. I ended up on the dyke with my head smashed in, and with my bicycle in the river. I had no trouble in overcoming my physical injuries, but my sporting ambitions were dead.

There was, however, one more occasion in my life when I discovered that sport was particularly useful and beneficial. When I was in the sixth form I was called up for military service in spite of the fact that I had pointed out my bad eyesight, my feeble physique and my nervous disposition. On the other hand, when my friend Otakar Kuželka showed the recruiting officers his wonderfully developed athletic body, the regimental M.O. took an immediate liking to him and discovered he had a dicky heart and varicose veins. Otakar left the recruiting office with a certificate that he was permanently unfit for military service.

My friend's success drove me to buy a blue and white striped vest so that I could join the Měcholupy Sports and Football Club, of which Otakar Kuželka was a member of long standing. An unfortunate accident, however, prevented my friend from nominating me as a member, as he had sworn he would. In a match between Měcholupy and Birmingham, one of the Englishmen broke Otakar Kuželka's shin. He was taken off to hospital and had to stay there for four weeks. I still have my vest and use it when I go swimming at Komín.

As I have just said, within a month Otakar's fracture was healed. Two months later he still limped a little, but later he only had twitches in the ankle. And, thank God, that does not matter in winter sports like sledging.

I very willingly accepted my friend's invitation to go and watch the way the better, fitter classes enjoyed the cold.

The sledge path was a track of ice in the snow beside

the fringe of the woods. It was wonderful to see the sledges with one, two or three riders whisking down the hill and doing little jumps at every bump in the path. Many of them tipped over and their riders were flung on to the ice; subsequent sledges rode over them and then went flying themselves. In one of these accidents someone's boot flew straight into Otakar Kuželka's face. But that was not so bad; it was worse for those sledgers who ran off the path into the wood and crashed against birches. Ambulancemen had to take them away.

For someone not directly involved, this all made a most interesting spectacle. In my initial enthusiasm I agreed to Otakar Kuželka's suggestion that we should go into the mountains together. Since in those days there was inflation, like today, I was left to my own devices as far as getting mountaineering kit together was concerned, and so it took some good time before I could fulfil our agreement.

It was not that I did not have the will. I bought myself a piggy-bank and in the first few days of the month I put a considerable sum of money into it. Apart from that I obtained a post-office savings book and diligently pasted ten-heller stamps into it. But, because of the bad harvest in South America, in the last few days of the month the general financial situation became so desperate that I was compelled to empty my polypod bank and write a special request to the directorate of the Austrian Post Office Savings Bank for the withdrawal of my deposits when they had amounted to the sum of two crowns, fifty hellers.

So Otakar Kuželka went into the mountains by himself. To this day I cannot actually remember what sport he pursued there. All I know is that one day, in some hut or other, he got into the wrong bed and came to know his future spouse, who was very good at skiing.

Soon after his descent from the mountains Otakar Kuželka got married and within a time which could also be called a record his wife gave birth to a son.

Since both parents were sports enthusiasts they did their best to bring up their child in their image, as a man sound in body, sound in mind. When he was two years old they used to put him under the pump in the winter so that he would be tough. As a result of that, the left side of the child's body became paralysed. Apart from that, the child became dumb. Thanks be to God that the Almighty soon took the boy away.

As soon as enough snow had fallen the couple would go off skiing together. Kuželka was somewhat clumsy in comparison with his fleet-of-foot spouse and so one day it came to pass that he lost her. He spent two days looking for her, but in vain. On the third day, however, he did find her, lying in a snowdrift.

She was taken away on a stretcher and after a great deal of effort on the part of several doctors she regained consciousness. Her nose and the fingers on her right hand had been so thoroughly frozen, however, that there was nothing for it but to amputate them. Which is what happened.

Once his spouse had lost her charming little nose Otakar lost all interest in marital sporting endeavours, as a result of which there was domestic conflict.

It was thanks to these family differences that Otakar Kuželka at long last did me the honour of paying a visit.

He had a waterproof linen knapsack on his back, studded boots on his feet, a green hat adorned with a chamois tail on his head and a six-foot staff in his hand. Thus decked out, he invited me to join him in climbing an icecap.

I turned down his invitation with the inept excuse that I had to write two letters. My friend gave me a pitying look and said, 'Do you call that life? Aren't you ashamed of just sitting here rotting? Is it manly behaviour to spend all one's leisure by the fireside?'

'Come on,' I answered, 'now that we have cold summers, a fellow is glad to have the chance to warm himself by the fire at least in winter.'

Otakar Kuželka saw no reason to deem me worthy of his instructions or enthusiasm and so he left with the clear intention of climbing the icecap by himself. But his stars had something else planned for him.

Kuželka's mother-in-law was waiting for him at the station. She did not utter a word, but she followed her son-in-law to the ticket office and bought a ticket to the same place as he. She got into the same carriage as he and got out at the same station as he.

Shivers ran down Otakar Kuželka's spine. He did not even stop at the pub for a fortifying dram. He went straight to the most difficult face of the mountain and started climbing. When he looked round, he went weak at the knees. He saw his mother-in-law thirty yards behind him.

To this day, it has not been explained how that tragedy up there on the icecap came about. On the third day Kuželka's mother-in-law returned down into the valley, bringing the news that her son-in-law had plunged into a six-thousand-foot chasm.

Three rescue parties were sent to find him. The first was smothered by an avalanche. The second got lost in the mountains and two of its members committed suicide. Finally, the third brought back to the valley Kuželka's right leg which had got caught on a cliff as he was falling.

One can only despair at life on this earth when the healthiest and most promising human beings perish, while useless riff raff calmly continue living like vegetables. Oh, what hopes disappeared in the grave with you, Otakar Kuželka! What a wonderful hunk of humanity you would have represented if you had remained alive! But this is what happens with everything beautiful in the world. It is rather like the mare the farmer tried to teach not to want to eat. When she was on the brink of perfection and was being given only a single straw to eat every day, she suddenly died.

The gods envy their creatures' greatness.

TRANSLATED BY ROBERT B. PYNSENT

*M*ILOŠ *M*ARTEN 1883–1917

'From time to time barbarians come and stir the smooth surface of art with the waves of primal instincts, the wild undercurrents of the ego.'
Style and Stylization

Miloš Marten.

Miloš Marten was born of upper-middle-class parents in 1883 and went to grammar school in his native Brno (Moravia); he was first published when he was fifteen. While still a law student at Prague University he established himself as an art and literary critic in the Decadent and Symbolist circle around the periodical *Moderní revue*. He became a close friend of the French writer Paul Claudel (whom he labelled a 'mystic Naturalist'), when the latter was French Consul in Prague. From about 1908 he tried to turn away from Decadence, but his attempts at a 'strong' neo-Classical form of writing remained firmly marked by Decadent style and ideology. He was called up in 1915 and was eventually sent to the Russian Front, where he was wounded. He died as a result of his wounds on 23 July 1917 in Přepeče near Turnau in northern Bohemia.

Marten was more important for the development of Czech literature as a critic than as a writer of fiction. Indeed, his assessment of three writers from Romanticism to the turn of the century in his collection of essays, *A Chord* (1916), established a Modernist account of mainstream Czech literature which still has at least an indirect impact on scholarship. His other main works of criticism and theory are *Style and Stylization* (1906) and *A Book of the Strong* (1910). In his criticism and his fiction he manifested a distilled influence of Schopenhauer, Baudelaire, Nietzsche, Barbey d'Aurevilly, Huysmans and Wilde. Since subject-matter is limited, all development in the plastic arts and literature is brought about by stylization. In true art, content and form are the same thing; the artist reshapes and re-evaluates his subject-matter by style, and style is form. One may not discuss just the style of a work of art any more than one may discuss just the form. Content disappears in form, just as form becomes part of content. Here Marten was following Pater's conception that all art aspires to music, where 'it is impossible to distinguish the form from the substance or matter, the subject from the expression'. According to Marten, all art is necessarily subjective: great art constitutes a synthesis between the most and least subjective, but the 'excited' ego is always perceptibly pulsating in works where this synthesis has been attained. True art is inviolable: it cannot be argued against, proved or disproved like a scientific theory. It contains infinite possible nuances and so can never be delimited or defined. In *Style and Stylization* Marten proclaimed a radical hedonism which looked forward to much Czech avant-garde writing of the 1920s: 'Living is art . . . and the will to stylize life is one of those instincts which are only rarely awakened and fully developed, but are the most valuable . . . There are artists of life . . . artists of deed, artists of love, artists of sensual enjoyment, artists of orgasm; they stylize life, render up sacrifices to its forms in the cult of orgasm and death.'

Marten criticized *fin de siècle* theorists for having claimed to have liberated the artist as individual from conventions and regulations and to have enabled him to be original. That had resulted in originality's becoming a cult, an end in itself, and thus a barren path. The artist should develop 'strength', not originality; in art that strength 'is identical with the desire for that perfection whose name is beauty' (*A Book of the Strong*). The *fin de siècle*, he averred, had consisted in a 'guerilla warfare of ideas'. He had himself been too much under the influence of the Decadents who had cultivated 'an art of despairing pathos, manic passion, febrile sensuality, an ideology of catastrophism and a conception of beauty as Gehenna'.

Marten was critical of conventional views of Czech history. In his dialogue *Looking down on to the City* (1917), he rejected the general notion that the Counter-Reformation had been a period of decay and darkness for the Bohemian Lands. Elsewhere he claimed that what the Bohemia of his day lacked was style. The Slavs in general suffered from an excess of primitive, despairing compassion and an inveterate desire to torment their consciences.

In his fiction Marten tried to develop a psychology of mental and physical violence; his stories constitute almost static pictures which aggressively reject moral judgment. When movement is introduced it is violent, often melodramatic, and his characters are generally rigidly drawn *fin de siècle* types. Thus Egon in *Cycle of Death and Delight* (1907) is 'paralysed by ceaseless self-analysis'; the demonic artist Roman in *Predators* (1913) conceives of the sexual act as the essence of art, and his works are 'visions of pain and evil, sensual pleasure and terror'. As far as Czech literature is concerned, *Cycle* is innovative in its detailed, convincing depiction of erotic stress. As a whole the collection is pervaded by what Marten himself later rejected, a sadomasochistic aesthete's pretended worship of death, 'not as punishment or defeat but as the last, wild, glorious scream of a being sacrificed to insatiable longing'. Death fuses with orgasm: it becomes a 'godhead; every vein in one's body, every drop of blood calls out, quivering with sensual pleasure.' In *Cortigiana* (1911), the end of which follows, sexual desire is directly linked with the plague as it is, for example, in Hofmannsthal's *Marshal de Bassompierre's Experience* or Mann's *Death in Venice*, and, before that in two stories by the leading Czech writer of the last third of the 19th century, Julius Zeyer, a writer Marten considered exemplary. In *Cortigiana* womanhood uses the plague to avenge itself on manhood. In both *Cycle* and *Cortigiana* Marten exploits the idea of crime (particularly murder) as aesthetic and sensuous delight (cf. de Quincey, Barbey d'Aurevilly, Wilde and, again, Zeyer). In *Predators* Roman declares that 'crime is the final meaning of freedom'. All this would be in order if Marten had had the anarchist leanings of 1890s Czech Decadents, but he did not.

The reader's problem with Marten's fiction is that because the characters express Decadent views or behave like Decadents, one is inclined to imagine the author to be as much of a Decadent as his creations. That is probably not the case. Decadent characterizations and Decadent purple passages are, so speak, etched into Marten's pages with a precision which reminds one of a forensic pathologist. Almost all Marten's descriptions and analyses of sin, evil, the existential sense of the *néant*, of the power of the unconscious or of frenetic erotic desire have more in common with a baroque ice-house than with the hot-house plants of the European Decadence.

ROBERT B. PYNSENT

Text
Cortigiana (Prague, 1911).

Secondary sources
Rudolf Havel, *Slovník ceskýeh spisovatelů* (Prague, 1964).
Pierre Moreau (ed.), *Cahiers Paul Claudel, ix* (Prague, Paris, 1971).

CORTIGIANA

Isotta was horrified by her own calmness at the knowledge that she had the plague. She had the oppressive feeling that she was already dead in the living sarcophagus of her body, which was in itself dying a different, new death.

A vision of the hideousness in which the hot flower of her beauty was to perish revealed itself to her like some wraith.

She turned towards the looking-glass. With an urgent, almost instinctive movement, she tore off the enamelled gold belt which secured her tunic to her body. The brocade slowly flowed down to her ankles. Naked, suffused with the white glow of her complexion, she stood gazing at her reflection, opalescent in the pale silver of the looking-glass.

An immense melancholy overcame her. Not because she was to die, but because she was beautiful and her beauty had to perish with her. She sensed that she had never before seen herself thus. She felt a desire to touch every contour of the thrilling, fragile object which was Isotta, to kiss and inhale the pallid cloud whose delicate texture was furnished by the hot tinting of the sun. She unclasped the gold snakes at her brow and trembled in ecstasy under the intoxicating surge of her hair which asperged her throat, insinuated itself around her breasts and spilt down over her back to her thighs.

Life purled in her blood with such desire, such heat, such frenetic sweetness that she pressed her hands to her breasts as if in indignation, as if she wanted to stem the flow which should have issued from them.

Now she saw herself as a child, a thirteen-year-old Beatrice poring over neo-Platonic manuscripts. She had feverish thoughts of those sumptuous flowers of love which had not blossomed for her. The chimeric virginity of her heart within the depraved beauty of her body oppressed her, and she would have liked to pour out that virginity on someone's feet like spikenard and then dry those feet with her hair.

And she was overwhelmed with a sense of cold futility.

She heard voices in the corridor outside her room. Someone was giving a mocking response to urgings she could not hear. An elderly woman's head appeared through the curtain and then disappeared, pushed away by some vigorous hand.

A young Antinous-headed man entered, with the limbs of a Greek god under white satin embroidered with lions. His animal beauty was combined with signs of insatiable hedonism to form a seductive harmony of graceful depravity and luxuriant strength. She could sense in him unexpected perversions of tenderness into crime, of gentleness into predatory ebullition.

'They wanted to stop me coming in,' he said with a

laugh, but suddenly he stopped; suddenly he was shackled by the sensuous magnetism of the pale nakedness before him which was irradiating an immaterial atmosphere, a bemusing current of sensual desire.

As Isotta was quickly reaching for her tunic, he uttered the quiet plea, 'Wait . . .'

Isotta's eyes darkened. The sensual idolatry contained in that plea renewed the desire in her blood which she had been trying to suppress. She would hear the dangerous, whisperingly salacious inveighing voice echoing within her. Just once more I must reach out for pleasure and drain it, infused as it is with the almighty pervasive scent of death! I must not give death anything but the bitter, empty rind of my beauty and life, which has been tempered by the crimson gold of my beauty's blood!

She was sitting on her bed. Phoebus's head was lying in her lap as if overburdened by youth and beauty. Dark thoughts inflamed the young man's mind.

'There's something different about you today,' the young man said. 'I've never seen tenderness in your face before – that tenderness which one sees in the eyes of women who love. Your hands have lost their coldness . . . And I do know you don't love me. Perhaps you are hiding some young man of classical beauty in your house and perhaps you grant him all the passion you deny us. But, please, let me drink at least a reflection of that beauty. I promise I shall forget reality; I shall pretend to myself that I am that divine lover . . . an Apollo or Adonis with glowing hair and marble limbs, which you kiss as ardently as we kiss you . . .'

Bathed in sweet corruption, she wondered at this boy who had so little regard for the artifice of love and was so easily satisfied by the mere reality of sensual satisfaction. She was grateful for his cynicism. In this, the last hour of her beauty, with the stigmata of destruction which it contained, a man who showed a heart overflowing with passion might have penetrated the diamantine cloister of her soul – perhaps he would have ignited that flame of love, without which she would have to die. She would have given herself up to an elevated madness, trembled with desire for his life and, having torn herself out of his embrace, she would have died happy, thanking the stars for the happy escape of her real self.

This man, however, was no more than a beautiful goblet in which life was for the last time offering her its sinful sweetness, and she could freely break this goblet when she had finished drinking . . . Wouldn't giving these hungry lips a mortal kiss, fruit with a hidden poison, serve as that last cry of desperate, cruel laughter by which she would have her revenge on life for its falsity? That mental intoxication devolving from our capacity to offer death – when all our days had been one creeping death of the purest essence of our being!

And her lips fastened themselves so passionately to the boy's that they became suffused with blood.

'You're bleeding!'

Instead of answering, the white serpents of her arms wound around his neck. A trembling, fiery cloud quivered beneath his lips and his lips imprisoned it and etched themselves into it; his senses became obscured and vertiginous delight penetrated his heart.

The hot, white night opened like a fruit bursting with sweetness.

Isotta was cooling her brow on the marble balustrade in the twilight of the loggia.

So the last mad impulse of desire had been severed from her; all that remained was to follow the corrosive fire which was burning into her . . .

A wild No was howling in her brain.

She had no desire to fight a vain battle against the power which was taking her over. But she longed to find revenge in resistance, to be a sacrifice, but not a prey to her fate. To die as she had lived . . .

With weird laughter she began to recite a sentence from some book she had read, in the way a child reels off the homework it has learned by heart: 'When the walls of Nineveh did fall and a mighty fire overtook the city, Sardanapalus had a great fire built in the courtyard of his palace and he mounted that fire and had himself burnt with all his women and slaves and all his treasures.'

Had not she perhaps been given the power likewise to die in the midst of a miraculous, monstrous orgy of death? She too had fire, a fire which she could swell into a conflagration in which all the treasures and people of her realm could be consumed. What a funeral pyre her body was, her body imbued with arcane flames which burnt quicker and more surely than any crimson tongues of pitch torches!

She called. The old woman appeared to receive instructions.

'I want a sedan-chair!'

'To go to the Palazzo Vergellesi?'

'Yes,' said Isotta.

In the pale light which spread like the gleam of thousands of metal looking-glasses infinitely reflecting the dislocated ice of the moon, the city looked like a mysterious mirage of towers and palazzi, arcades and gardens.

In the banqueting hall Isotta was met by shouting. She was standing in the midst of an orgy, on to which mists of drunkenness were descending. The affected music of lutes, lyres and flutes was almost smothered by the din of voices. Upturned bowls were spilling fruits on to the tables; gold and silver vessels lay on the floor; the air was heavy with the exudations of wine and oil. The bare shoulders of the women shone out from brocade and samite bodices with an irritant, phosphorescent sheen.

The men gathered round the courtesan. She handed out sweet words and smiles and shrouded them in long, bacchantic gazes. They understood her feverishness to be a burning suffusion of sensual delight in which the waves of intoxication concentrated as in a whirlpool – and those waves surged in their veins.

'I feel happy,' she said. 'My memory is conjuring up for me the tastes of the lips of each one of you here.

'I used to mock you, Gherardo, that you besieged women's breasts like fortresses. Don't say anything. Your coarse grappling makes us feel like princesses raped by barbarians. And you, Tullio, you're as gentle as a child and as depraved as a woman. And Sandro is unable to forget the perverse delights he knew in Byzantium . . .'

The chimerical force of sin spread around this woman. She told every one of them of his hidden passion, his concealed vice, as if she were showing up their secret beings in a grotesque hall of mirrors. They started to be overcome by an amalgam of panic, desire and shame; they were both excited and humiliated by the words she was using to play with the serpents of sensuality in their blood.

Suddenly someone shouted out, 'Let her choose a bridegroom for tonight, someone who will kiss the love of all of us on to her lips.'

That was a custom Isotta had once introduced into Bacchanalia in Rome. To the contempt she made her lovers feel, she added torment, so that they suffered under the futility of their desire and the abstract jealousy which developed from the hope which they had lost. And they accepted this refined mental torture as if it were a new sensual pleasure in the orgasmic inferno they had found by knowing her!

'Choose a partner for tonight,' they shouted, 'someone to represent all of us!'

Isotta rose from her chair. 'A partner, you say? So be it. I choose – all of you. Do you hear what I say? All of you. Every single one of you will be Isotta's bridegroom tonight. Make sure the sun does not rise too early! Don't forget nights are briefer than desires! And may no one believe in tomorrow . . .!'

The men formed a solid circle around her: 'Let's celebrate the great feast of Aphrodite!'

Sandro knelt blasphemously before her and proffered a gilt crystal goblet of topaz wine.

Slowly Isotta rent the silk covering her breasts; she bent down and dipped her amber nipples in the wine.

All the men, transfixed by this immodest ceremony, brought their goblets to the courtesan so that she would dip her nipples into the wine with the same calm, brash movement of her breasts, which had become two torpid, cold, cruel moons in the sensuous night which had bewitched their minds.

As if they had imbued some pure sin from her body which clung to their lips, they approached her blinded by dreams of unknown, extreme, barbarian orgasms.

Isotta began to become oblivious of the excitement which was gradually burning up her body, of the chilly mucus which adhered to her skin like the touch of moist snakes. She felt only the demonic power which she irradiated and which scalded the men's hearts; and she revealed the men to Death, who had flowed into the hall in a crimson cloud of intoxication. She imagined herself not living but dying through innumerable lives of love, that she was opening herself to pour forth some terrible sweetness fermented in her veins, surging into her lips, inundating her eyes with the dark joy of killing. She expended great willpower in refraining from uttering the words of the blasphemous prayer which, at that moment, came to her lips . . .

She looked round once more as if she wanted to ascertain the extent of the manic desire inscribed in the eyes of the men who were longing to devour her.

Finally she took up the agate ball whose function was to cool the palms of men's hands, and, having placed it in Sandro's hand – *as a mark of election* – she started slowly mounting the staircase adumbrated at the furthest end of the banqueting hall.

TRANSLATED BY ROBERT B. PYNSENT

FERENC BÉKÁSSY 1893–1915

'It is not actual life, but the prospect of variety, that makes me want to live.'

On the horror of dying young

The only known portrait of Ferenc Békássy. *Claire Hertelendy*

Born into an old, aristocratic Hungarian family at Kiszsennye (County Vas) on 7 April 1893, Ferenc István Dénes Gyula Békássy was educated in England. He was one of six of the Békássy children to receive an English schooling and went to Bedales in 1905 with his younger brother John, who later settled in England and married into the Wedgwood family of Barlaston. Ferenc Békássy read history at King's College, Cambridge taking a BA in 1914: 'The aim of education is to create, by means of circumstance, men and women independent of circumstance.' At King's he befriended John Maynard Keynes (who visited Békássy in Hungary in the summer of 1913) and became a member of the exclusive debating society known as The Apostles. Békássy possessed a keenly analytical mind, but was aware of the dangers inherent in developing one of his talents at the expense of others:

> There are those whose character is not so far developed as their mind; these are the breakers of values.
> But those whose minds are less developed than their characters; these are the conservers of values.
> And he alone, in whom mind and character are one, is the Creator of new Values.

Békássy does not seem to have been overawed by his Cambridge experience. As an outsider, he seems to have acquired a refreshing view of the academic scene: 'A doctor for nervous diseases gains more and more insight into human character, yet the more he knows, the more wrong is his judgment of it, for the less he is able to consider anything in it that is not morbid. You Cambridge knowers of men! This is how you have insight.'

When the major European powers mobilized their armies, Békássy, with Keynes's help, avoided internment, returned home and volunteered for military service. In analysing his fear of dying young, Békássy wrote:

> It is not actual life, but the prospect of variety, that makes me want to live. Everything in me is just beginning to develop its nature; my every future instant is to be different from this one. When all my qualities are static and my whole being determinate, even though I may be still quite active, I shall not prefer life to death, or only because I do not like breaking habits and putting a stop to old relations with people.

As lieutenant of a Hussar regiment he fell at Dobronoutz in Bukovina on 25 June 1915. Only at the insistence of Keynes was a plaque to Békássy's memory secured in King's College Chapel. Although in the same side-chapel as his fellow-students who fought with the Allies, his name is carved into the stone wall to one side of the main plaque. 'These Cambridge people have little to do with me; they merely know more or less what I am like.'

Though only 22 when he died, Békássy left behind two volumes of poetry, one of prose, and one of literary criticism, letters to J. M. Keynes, Noel Olivier, James Strachey and J. T. Sheppard as well as a great deal of poetry in English, a selection of which appeared in 1925 from the Hogarth Press of Leonard and Virginia Woolf. In his Preface to this, F. L. Lucas wrote of the 'unique and fascinating thing about him: his gift for being outside and inside himself almost at the same time', and, indeed, in some of his aphorisms we can glimpse the unique double perspective that must have acquired an excruciating dimension when he found himself on the opposite side to his fellow-students in the war. In an anguished article the greatest Hungarian critic of the century, Mihály Babits, mourned Békássy's loss and berated himself for an over-magisterial response to the teenager's Hungarian poems when Békássy first sent them to him from Cambridge. He found in them a unique welding of the voice of Shelley and Keats with that of the Hungarian classical poets Arany and Vörösmarty, and thought they would have given Hungarian lyrical poetry a much-needed impetus: 'had he lived, Békássy could have become a very great Hungarian poet.' Nevertheless, none of his work has ever been reprinted, and the selection here from *Adriatica* are a necessarily pale, English shadow of promise unfulfilled.

PETER SHERWOOD

'To have strong and definite preferences, and paint a waterfall because there is some one thing you like about waterfalls; but to try to paint it as it is – that is, to paint its general character, not this one thing only – because you also respect waterfalls; this balance of fancy and contemplation, of subjectivity and workmanship, is admirable in an artist or a historian.' *On Hiroshige*

Texts
Elmerült szigetek (Budapest, 1915). Poems.
Hátrahagyott irásai: Fantáziák és gondolatok (*Posthumous writings: Thoughts and Fancies*; Budapest, 1916). 2 vols. Essays & letters.
Írókról és irodalomról (On Writers and Writing; Budapest, 1918).
Adriatica and other Poems (The Hogarth Press, London, 1925). Békássy's English poems, with a preface by F. L. Lucas.

Secondary sources
Mihály Babits, 'B. F. huszárönkéntes: elesett az északi harctéren, 1915. június', *Irodalmi problémák* (Budapest, 1917, pp. 267–77, 285).
Lásló Cs. Szabó, 'Egy kisértet föltámadása', *Uj Látóhatár* (1961, pp. 83–6).
George Gömöri, 'Ferenc Békássy's letters to John Maynard Keynes', *The New Hungarian Quarterly* (Budapest, Autumn 1980, vol. xxi, 79, pp. 59–70).

1914

He went without fears, went gaily, since go he must,
And drilled and sweated and sang, and rode in the heat
 and dust
Of the summer; his fellows were round him, as eager as
 he,
While over the world the gloomy days of the war dragged
 heavily.

He fell without a murmur in the noise of battle; found
 rest
'Midst the roar of hooves on the grass, a bullet struck
 through his breast.
Perhaps he drowsily lay; for him alone it was still,
And the blood ran out of his body, it had taken so little to
 kill.

So many thousand lay round him, it would need a poet,
 maybe,
Or a woman, or one of his kindred, to remember that
 none were as he;
It would need the mother he followed, or the girl he went
 beside
When he walked the paths of summer in the flush of his
 gladness and pride,

To know that he was not a unit, a pawn whose place can
 be filled;
Not blood, but the beautiful years of his coming life have
 been spilled,
The days that should have followed, a house and a home,
 maybe,
For a thousand may love and marry and nest, but so shall
 not he.

When the fires are alight in the meadow, the stars in the
 sky,
And the young moon drives its cattle, the clouds graze
 silently,
When the cowherds answer each other and their horns
 sound loud and clear,
A thousand will hear them, but he, who alone
 understood, will not hear.

His pale poor body is weak, his heart is still, and a dream
His longing, his hope, his sadness. He dies, his full years
 seem
Drooping palely around, they pass with his breath
Softly, as dreams have an end – it is not a violent death.

My days and the world's pass dully, our times are ill;
For men with labour are born, and men, without wishing
 it, kill.
Shadow and sunshine, twist a crown of thorns for my
 head!
Mourn, O my sisters! singly, for a hundred thousand
 dead.

GÉZA GYÓNI 1884–1917

'What madness gave you the right to play
With my life, with my God-given life?'
From 'Caesar, I will not go', 1912

Géza Gyóni. *Petőfi Irodalmi Múseum, Budapest*

Born in Gyón (now part of Dabas, south of Budapest) on 25 June 1884 into a distinguished and crusading Lutheran family, Géza Áchim took the pen-name Gyóni (literally 'from Gyón') after the village of his birth. Intended by his pastor father for the Lutheran ministry, the over-sensitive Gyóni was nevertheless drawn to journalism and the arts, especially poetry: he contributed articles and poems to the provincial Hungarian press from 1903 onwards, and had his first slim volume, *Versek* (*Poems*), published privately in Pressburg (Pozsony, now Bratislava, Czechoslovakia) in 1904. Despite conventional themes – 'Song of the Cotton Dress', 'Autumn', 'Dreams', 'Stanzas of Sorrow' – these show the grasp of traditional poetic forms with the neat turns of phrase that always characterize his work.

In the same year, a somewhat mysterious suicide attempt put paid to his theological career, so his enrolment (at his father's behest) for a diploma in administration in Budapest followed in 1906. This served only to deepen his involvement with the lively café-journalism and the poets of the Hungarian capital. At first, he had mixed feelings about the latter, as shown in his poem addressed to Endre Ady, certainly the greatest Hungarian poet of the time, written in 1908 (the year of the founding of *Nyugat* [*West*], the leading Hungarian literary journal until the Second World War), and published in Gyóni's second collection *Szomorú szemmel* (*With Sorrowful Eyes*) in 1909:

'What a lot of little moons
You drag out of obscurity
O tired comet;
All think themselves
Brave blazing flames
When they kindle a small light
From your blazing tail.'

Nevertheless, he was considerably influenced by Ady's broader and deeper themes and very varied forms, as shown by the poems written between 1909 and 1914, and published as *Élet szeretője* (*Lover of Life*) in 1917. What had turned the languorous man with the sorrowful eyes into a lover of life was the physical and mental suffering he endured in the Balkans. Called up in November 1907, he took part in the war-fever manoeuvres of the Austro-Hungarian army and helped break rocks and build a railway line in Bosnia, until the 'exercise' was called off in April 1909. These experiences are memorably described in his letters. They also gave birth to his great pacifist poem 'Cézar, én nem megyek' ('Caesar, I will not go') written in 1912, when his regiment was again summoned to Bosnia for some months. Putting contemporary words into historical mouths was the traditional way of getting round the censors:

. . . And as for your crown,
That, O Caesar, defend on your own,

Praetorian Guards may quickly send
This stubborn head to smash or bend;
But an animal to the abbatoir – no,
No, O Caesar, – I will not go.

When war finally came, Gyóni with many others at first believed the monarchy's claim of a 'plot against us' and the necessity, therefore, of fighting a 'defensive' war. Some writers even saw this as a continuation of the old wars of independence, as if the Hungarians were repaying the Tsar for his crucial assistance to the Austrian Emperor in 1849. Gyóni's first, still elated, poems from the Polish Front recall the 16th-century Hungarian poet Bálint Balassi's soldiers' songs of the marches, written during the campaigns against the Turks. These 20th-century poems of Gyóni's, collected in *Lengyel mezőkön, tábortűz mellett* (*By the Campfire on Polish Prairies*; 1914), but flown individually out of Przemyśl, where he and more than 100,000 of his fellows were eventually besieged, were exploited by the conservative lobby of Jenő Rákosi in their campaign against the anti-war Ady, but as the siege wore on, the poet's tone changed: 'Csak egy éjszakára' ('Just for One Night'; dated November 1914, in the same volume), widely translated and even set to music, became one of the best-known anti-war poems of the time.

Following the Russians' capture of the fortress in March 1915, Corporal Gyóni was fortunate to be made orderly to his younger brother Mihály, a professional soldier, in the prisoners' transport – via Kiev, Moscow, Alatyr, Petropavlovsk and Omsk – to the POW camp at Krasnoyarsk in Siberia. Here, the presence of his brother, access to books and the relative peace of the officers' quarters made it possible for him to write some of his finest poetry, published in *Levelek a kálváriáról és más költemények* (*Letters from Calvary and Other Poems*; Budapest, 1916), and the posthumous *Rabságban* (*In Prison*; Budapest, 1919). News of how his poems had been exploited during the war came as a bitter blow:

In haughty Hungary
How cheap is one's song!
I've not yet returned,
Not asked for shelter to stay
And already they'd turn me away.

'Gőgös Hunniában' ('In Haughty Hungary')

And he wrote a remarkable poem on the Russian Revolution:

I fall on my knees before your sacred face,
The embittered son of a distant, sorrowful people

*

Now you waken, fresh and young,
Revolution
And dance along the world smelling of blood

'Utolsó tánc' ('Last Dance'), 22 March 1917

With the death of his brother Mihály on 8 June 1917, the last thread tying him to the seemingly endless limbo of the POW camp was snapped. Géza Gyóni had a breakdown and died on his 33rd birthday, 25 June 1917. As he wrote on the nine-month journey to Siberia:

'A Hungarian bard's is my fate:
To carry across the world
My bloodied, crusading Magyarhood
Like a pilgrim with a picture of Christ.

'Magyar bárd sorsa' ('A Hungarian Bard's Fate')

PETER SHERWOOD

Texts
Csak egy éjszakára (Sándor Z. Szalai (ed.), Szépirodalmi könyvkiadó, Budapest, 1984). A new edition of the complete poems, first collected in this form in 1959. Gyóni's complete poems originally went into four editions edited by his brother-in-law Ferenc Gyóni (né Szolár) *Összes versei* (Budapest, 1941, 1942, 1943) with a supplementary *Ismeretlen versei* [*Unknown Poems*] in 1943.
Lengyel mezőkön, tábortűz mellet [*By the Campfire on Polish Prairies*] was reprinted inside Przemýsl in 1914 several times, the total number published reaching some 10,000 and it went into five editions in Hungary between 1915 – 21. It was translated into German as *Auf polnischen Fluren, am Lagerfeuer, Przemysler Gedichte* (Dresden, 1915).

Translations
Watson Kirkconnell (ed.), *The Magyar Muse: an anthology of Hungarian Poetry* (Kanadai Magyar Ujság Press, Budapest, 1933). Watson Kirkconnell's translation: 'Just for One Night'.

CSAK EGY ÉJSZAKÁRA . . .

Csak egy éjszakára küldjétek el őket:
A pártoskodókat, a vitézkedőket.
Csak egy éjszakára:
Akik fent hirdetik, hogy – mi nem felejtünk,
Mikor a halálgép muzsikál felettünk;
Mikor láthatatlan magja kél a ködnek,
S gyilkos ólom-fecskék szanaszét röpködnek.

FOR JUST ONE NIGHT

Send them along for just one bloody night –
Your zealous heroes spoiling for a fight.
For just one bloody night:
Their former boasts within our memories ring
As rending shells of shrapnel scream and sing,
As mists of strangling poison slowly rise,
And leaden swallows swoop across the skies.

Csak egy éjszakára küldjétek el őket:
Gerendatöréskor szálka-keresőket.
Csak egy éjszakára:
Mikor siketitőn bőgni kezd a gránát,
S úgy nyög a véres föld, mintha gyomrát vágnák;
Robbanó golyónak mikor fénye támad,
S véres vize kicsap a vén Visztulának.

Csak egy éjszakára küldjétek el őket:
Az uzsoragarast fogukhoz verőket.
Csak egy éjszakára:
Mikor gránát-vulkán izzó közepén
Úgy forog a férfi, mint a falevél;
S mire földre omlik, ó, iszonyú omlás –
Szép piros vitézből csak fekete csontváz.

Csak egy éjszakára küldjétek el őket:
A hitetleneket s az üzérkedőket.
Csak egy éjszakára:
Mikor a pokolnak égő torka tárul,
S vér csurog a földön, vér csurog a fáról,
Mikor a rongy sátor nyöszörög z szélben,
S haló honvéd sóhajt: fiam . . . feleségem . . .

Csak egy éjszakára küldjétek el őket:
Hosszú csahos nyelvvel hazaszeretőket.
Csak egy éjszakára:
Vakító csillagnak mikor támad fénye,
Lássák meg arcuk a San folyó tükrébe',
Amikor magyar vért gőzölve hömpölyget,
Hogy sirva sikoltsák: Istenem, ne többet.

Küldjétek el őket csak egy éjszakára,
Hogy emlékezzenek az anyjuk kínjára.
Csak egy éjszakára:
Hogy bújnának össze megrémülve, fázva;
Hogy fetrengne mind-mind, hogy meakulpázna;
Hogy tépné az ingét, hogy verné a mellét,
Hogy kiáltná bőgve: Krisztusom, mi kell még!?

Krisztusom, mi kell még!? Véreim, mit adjak
Árjáért a vérnek, csak én megmaradjak!?
Hogy esküdne mind-mind,
S hitetlen gőgjében, akit sosem ismert,
Hogy hivná a Krisztust, hogy hivná az Istent:
Magyar vérem ellen soha-soha többet!
– Csak egy éjszakára küldjétek el őket.

Send them along for just one bloody night –
Your men of gross, gargantuan appetite.
For just one bloody night:
When thundering cannon start their ravishment,
And red earth groans with belly gouged and rent,
And bursting bullets break in glittering hate,
And ancient Vistula flows red in spate.

Send them along for just one bloody night –
The money-sucking leech, the parasite.
For just one bloody night:
When shell-volcanoes' fire the mud upheaves
And flings torn bodies eddying like leaves.
To crumbling earth the crisping corpses thresh,
Mere blacken'd heaps of bones instead of flesh.

Send them along for just one bloody night –
The unbeliever and the uncontrite.
For just one bloody night:
When hell's hot jaws in paroxysm expand
And vomit blood and horror on the land.
In tatter'd tents, the wounded pass from life,
And sigh across the wind: 'My son . . . my wife . . .'

Send them along for just one bloody night –
The patriots of the tongue, of speech and spite,
For just one bloody night:
That, as the blinding star-shells leap the dark,
And cheeks reflect the terror of their spark,
And reeking mists are made of Magyar gore,
They may scream out in tears: 'My God, no more!'

Send them along for just one bloody night –
That they may call their mothers in their fright.
For just one bloody night:
That they may cower low in fear and cold
And grovelling gasp, their guilt so manifold;
That they may rend their clothes, and beat their breasts,
And cry: 'My Christ, what are thy dread behests?

My Christ, what dost thou ask?' My blood demands
That they shall vow to cleanse their greedy hands
Which now oppress these lands:
That brazen infidels who blindly trod
May trust in Christ and put their faith in God,
And never more the Magyar nation blight.
– Send them along for just one bloody night!

TRANSLATED BY WATSON KIRKCONNELL

*D*IMCHO *D*EBELYANOV 1887–1916

'Oh, my work was aimless work and fruitless dream was my dream!'

From 'With muted strings'

Dimcho Debelyanov's literary career spans only a single decade – he began publishing poetry in 1906 and he was killed in 1916 – and even his first book of poems appeared posthumously, but he is still one of the best Bulgarian poets. And this is only one of the many paradoxes of his life and work. He was born in a well-to-do family, and yet he spent all his life in poverty. He is the most lyrical Bulgarian poet, but his gentle and sensitive soul was hidden behind a robust and burly, typically Balkan exterior. Quite unknown and unrecognized during his lifetime, after his death he became so popular that even those who did not know him referred tenderly to him by his first name. And finally the paradox of his death: another name instead of his was wrongly entered in the list of those going on a leave of absence; and also, although he was killed in a major battle before the eyes of a multitude of people, the accounts of his death are quite contradictory.

He was born on 28 March 1887 in Koprivshtitsa, Bulgaria, where he spent the happiest part of his life. After the death of his father nine years later, Dimcho, his mother and his three sisters moved to Plovdiv where his elder brother was working as a telegraphist. His school years in Plovdiv were among the saddest of his life and he often referred to Plovdiv as 'a sorrowful city'. But he was no happier in Sofia, where the family moved in 1904.

After he finished school in Sofia in 1906, he found a job as a junior clerk in the Central Meterological Station. In 1909, he left, hoping he would never again work in an office. For the next three years, he was employed as a freelance journalist, a newspaper reporter, a proofreader, an editor, a translator from French and Russian, a stenographer at the National Assembly and so on, not infrequently doing two or three jobs simultaneously to make ends meet and, at the same time, managing to enrol as a law and literature student at the University of Sofia.

In 1912, he joined the army and took part in the first Balkan war. In the summer of 1914, he was once again compelled to take an office job (which he detested) until January 1916, when he was sent to the front. He was killed on 2 October 1916, at the age of 29, during the battle against Irish troops between the villages of Dolno and Gorno Karadjovo.

When Debelyanov began publishing his first poems, Bulgarian literature was at a crossroads. On the one hand, the mainstream was still characterized by its reliance on national folklore traditions, an eagerness for self-knowledge and the attempts to educate the people through the idealization of the glorious past and the faithful presentation of the reality at that time. This was the tradition initiated by Paissy, Petko Slaveikov, Karavelov and Botev, and it was epitomized in the work of Ivan Vazov – the greatest living Bulgarian writer of that era.

On the other hand, by the beginning of the 20th century there were a number of Bulgarian writers who were not only well-read in foreign literature and influenced by foreign writers but who were also doing their best to put an end to what they considered to be the 'backward provincialism' of Bulgarian literature. The dominant figure in this tendency was the poet Pencho Slaveikov, the son of the older writer of the same name, an erudite man of letters and a formidable personality.

And it was under the influence of Pencho Slaveikov that Debelyanov wrote his first poems, which began to appear in the autumn of 1906 in an obscure literary magazine which would have been completely forgotten except for the fact that this poet took his first steps in it.

Debelyanov's early poetry was derivative and imitative, but very soon he found his own voice and within a few years he became a poet with distinct individuality. There were three major influences on his development as a poet: the works of the Bulgarian poets Slaveikov and Yavorov and the works of the Symbolist poets. And yet, although traces of these influences are to be found even in some of his later poems, he was so gifted and talented that he quickly shook off all external influences and began to be influential in his own right.

The poems 'Poet', 'Foreboding', 'Medal', 'A Hero's Dream' and two short love poems are fairly representative of his overall work. 'Poet' reveals the peculiar position of the poet who rejects worldly success, apparently craved by all others: who seeks joy without knowing where to find it; who laughs in the presence of others but weeps when alone; who pursues the vague shadows borne by his inspiration and is offered fame instead of the bread he really needs. It is a straightforward expression of a motif, familiar from the Symbolist poetry – the fate of the poet alienated from his society – and it is recurring in Debelyanov's poetry.

'Foreboding' is even more typical of Debelyanov because it is essentially confessional (his favourite form), and both its mood and tone reveal the gloomy melancholy of the poet. Moreover, it is the only one of the six which contains unmistakable Symbolist elements. The fruitless quest for love, the indescribable fatigue, the craving for rest and the preoccupation with death are frequent motifs in his poetry.

The theme of death is also dominant in practically all his war poems, and 'A Hero's Dream' is no exception. So is the romantic concept of a hero's death. At the same time, the idealized sense of duty and heroic death in this poem makes it somewhat different from his other war poems where death, waste and the absurdity and senselessness of war are prevalent as motifs.

'Medal' illustrates well the special qualities of his humorous and satiric verse, while the two short poems reveal his skill as a major lyrical poet. Thus, it is possible to see both the range and the dominant qualities of his poetry. And this is very important because, coupled with his unique way of expressing clearly vague feelings and emotions, his technical innovations and the unrivalled musicality of his verse, the versatility of Debelyanov's poetry is also one of his chief merits.

G. D. PAPANTCHEV

Texts
Dimcho Debelyanov: Complete Works (Sofia, 1983). Vol. 1 contains collected poems. Vol. 2 contains prose pieces and letters.

ПОЕТ

Оттам, де целий свят отива,
той, рано стигнал, се завръща,
пред туй, що другите упива,
лице с презрение отвръща.

Уж търси радост, пък – къде е?
Да го попиташ, сам не знае,
пред хорските очи се смее,
а сам пред себе си ридае.

На час по триж се вдъхновява;
разправя се със сенки бегли;
наместо хляб му дават слава
и за това той славно тегли!

THE POET

From what the entire world is fêting
he flees, by other visions drawn;
from what the crowd finds fascinating
he turns his face away with scorn.

He would seek joy – but where to find it?
You ask him: he has no replies.
Cheerful in front of others, blinded
by tears when he's alone he cries.

Just now and then some inspiration:
with shadows to converse he tries.
Not bread, but fame and reputation –
but oh, that fame exacts a price!

TRANSLATED BY EWALD OSERS

ПРЕДЧУВСТВИЕ

Изнизват се години след години.
Аз все напред и все напред летя,
И в адский зной на тъжните пустини
преследвам призрака на любовта.

Венец челото ми не украсява –
Оттам на струйки кървав пот се лей,
Ужасна мъка взорът замъглява,
Че за почивка моят дух копней.

О иде час на ужас и тревога,
Възпрян на бездните край тъмни бряг –
Ръце ще да отпусна в изнемога
И с грозен вик ще литна в черний мрак.

FOREBODING

Year follows year, how quickly now they run!
I'm flying forward, forward: high above
the melancholy wasteland burns the sun
as I pursue the phantasm of love.

No laurel chaplet on my forehead rests
but bloody sweat is trickling down my cheeks;
my eyes are veiled by pain as if by mists
but blissful rest is all my spirit seeks.

Alarm and terror fill me: it's the hour
when to the cliff-edge I am holding tight –
but then my fingers lose all strength and power
and screaming I am hurled into black night.

TRANSLATED BY EWALD OSERS

СЪНЯТ НА ГЕРОЯ

Врагът отстъпи, млькнаха гърмежи,
димът вечерний ветрец разпиле,
очите морни сладък сън замрежи
и пак утихна бойното поле.

И той залряма в миг и засънува,
на свойта пушка наклонил глава,
и стори му се, майка си че чува,
че му нашепва сладостни слова:

– Не бой се, сине мой, от враговете,
макар и в боя ти да паднеш пръв –
за отмъщенье роден край зове те
пет века ръсен със невинна кръв.

Ако загинеш – загини достоен,
ако се върнеш, знай, че цял народ
ще слави вечно своя верен воин,
за него сложил своя млад живот!

Тя пак замлъкна. Той простря десница
да я прегърна – но за миг откри
очи – в небето грееше денница
и сипваха се румени зари.

Тръбите пак тревога затръбиха...
И стана бодър, и в ужасний бой
падна на устни със усмивка тиха,
тъй както пада всеки смел герой.

A HERO'S DREAM

The enemy's retreated and the noise
and smoke of battle's drifted over the hill.
Sleep and relief descend on weary eyes
and now once more the battlefield lies still.

And he, too, shuts his eyes and falls asleep,
his rifle butt supporting head and limb,
and thinks he hears his mother in the deep
enfolding silence whispering to him:

– Fear not the foe, my son, fear not his challenge,
even though in battle you may soon be killed:
your native land expects you to avenge
five hundred years of blood guiltlessly spilled.

If you're to die, die like a man, my son;
if you return, then know that the whole nation
will honour you for all that you have done,
staking your young life without hesitation.

Then she fell silent. He reached out and tried
to embrace her – then he saw, as he was waking,
the morning star still hanging in the sky
as on the horizon the new day was breaking.

The trumpets sounded the alarm. And while
fighting the battle with disdain of death
he fell, on his young lips a quiet smile:
a gallant hero to his final breath.

TRANSLATED BY EWALD OSERS

ОРДЕН

Когато някой мъдър цар
след тежък труд потърси мир
и умори се да мъдрува,
събира той разкошен пир
и в най-големия му жар
решава да се пошегува.

Корона кривнал настрана,
с усмивка хитра на уста,
на своя златен трон се качва,
и сред гробовна тишина –
той, горд от тая висота –
великолепно се изхрачва.

И всички храчката следят –
(те виждали са неведнъж
историята вечно съща), –
че щом се лепне въз ликът
на някой тлъст държавен мъж,
тя в златен орден се превръща.

MEDAL

When bored or tired of dispensing
the wisdoms of his special brains,
a king decides to take a rest
and forget the burdens of his reign,
he has his men prepare a feast
for courtiers, noblemen and priests.

When the gaieties reach their height,
the king gets up from his royal place,
and with a wily smile on his face,
he spits with all his regal might
in the direction of his guests,
but no one present feels distressed.

The festive hall is filled with tension
and each eye follows with attention
the course of the majestic spit,
to see whose lucky face the spit will hit,
for they know (it's a custom old)
that it will turn into a medal of gold.

TRANSLATED BY PETER TEMPEST

Debelyanov (*arrowed*) at the front.

*M*ILUTIN *B*OJIĆ 1892–1917

'Youth is our god, and passion our strength.'

Milutin Bojić was born on 7 May 1892 in Belgrade where he went to school and attended university. The years of his boyhood were crucial times for the Serbs at the beginning of the 20th century, and he was a student during the deeply traumatic Balkan wars of 1911–13. The atmosphere of his formative years was one of patriotic fervour with which he himself was carried along: one of his early works, the patriotic epic poem *Cain* (1915), was confiscated and burned by the invading Bulgarians. At the beginning of the Great War, he was a military censor in the southern town of Niš, and he subsequently experienced at first hand the disastrous defeat of the Serbian army and its harrowing retreat through the mountains of Albania to the Adriatic in the autumn and winter of 1915. In 1916, he reached Corfu and later went with the army to Salonika, where he died of tuberculosis in the military hospital on 8 November 1917, at the age of 25.

Only a small part of Bojić's writing was published during his lifetime: his first poetry came out in 1914, but he is best known for his collection, *Pesme bola i ponosa (Poems of Pain and Pride)*, published in Salonika in 1917. The poems are an authentic personal reflection of his country's bitter defeat and humiliation, despite heroic resistance to the invader. Bojić sees the cataclysm as yet another episode in the long history of suffering and oppression inflicted on the Serbs, but apart from their sad and elegiac tone, his poems are not without hope for the future. Many of them were learned by heart by Serbian soldiers on the Salonika Front in the latter part of the war and their impact, though less immediate, was similar to that of the British war poets of the same generation.

BERNARD JOHNSON

Milutin Bojić. *Vojina M. Diordjevića*

Texts

Pesme bola i ponosa (Salonika, 1917).
Pesme i drame (Belgrade, 1927).

Secondary sources

B. Lazarević, *M. Bojić* (1914).
M. Pavlović, *M. Bojić* (1962).
Mihailo Đorđević, *Anthology of Serbian Poetry: the Golden Age* (Philosophical Library, New York, 1984). Translations 'The Legend of Woman' and 'The Kiss' reproduced with permission.

BAJKA O ŽENI

Ljubičastom parom diše Zemlja sana,
Modri su čempresi sagli glave tužno,
Vrh mrtvoga mora krikne koja vrana,
U zlatnome bakru tone sunce južno.

Usijan se pesak beli i preliva,
Zadrev u nebesa red planina spava,
Na crvenom žalu slet ždralova sniva,
Roj mušica doršće iznad rečnih stava.

Vruć, zapahnut mirom i muzikom boja,
Sa dosadom Čovek svu tu raskoš motri,
Leži sirov, krvav, pun dlake i znoja,
I traži u suncu da svoj odgled smotri.

Zrelost jednog dana prazna mu je sena,
Nejasnih oblika jedno Novo čeka,
Skup raskoši, sunca, nestalno k'o pena.
– I odjednom on se strašću zacereka.

Sa jelovih gora slazila je Žena.

THE LEGEND OF WOMAN

Sleepy Earth breathed its purple vapours,
Blue evergreens lowered their heads,
Over dead seas, crows were flying sadly,
The southern sun was melting in golden bronze.

The burning sand glared and shimmered,
Tearing the skies, tall mountains slept,
On the red beach, dreamed a flock of cranes,
Flies were dancing over the river.

Hot, drowsy, in the music of peace and colours,
Bored, Man watched this luxury,
He lay, bloody, a mess of hair and sweat,
And tried to see himself in the sunny rays.

The ripe hour of the day was empty,
Man waited for a New Form,
A thing lush, sunny, like sea foam.
Suddenly he laughed with throaty passion.

Down evergreen slopes came the Woman.

TRANSLATED BY MIHAILO ĐORĐEVIĆ

Albert Weisgerber (1878-1915): *Mother Earth* (1914). *Staatsgalerie moderner Kunst, Munich*

Poljubac

Mi smo deca sreće i života zrela,
Naša čudna ljubav do niskosti naga,
Mrzi legendarnih noći čeda svela:
Za nju mladost Bog je, a strast joj je snaga.

. . . Januar fijuče u sutonskoj studi,
Bičevana reka modri se i peni.
Jauk golih grana mrtve iz sna budi:
Kikoće se vreme u večitoj smeni.

Sve tutnji u snazi napregnute volje,
Krši se i pišti i seva i para,
Razjaren se orkan s nebesima kolje,
Polusmrznut Neptun s Adom razgovara.

Opijeni mržnjom, opkoljeni vriskom,
Pripijene usne do krvi smo grizli,
Moćna su nam rebra drhtala pod stiskom
Prstiju, što medj njih neznano su sklizli.

Taj poljubac duše pio nam je do dna,
I hiljade šara, vrelih k'o strast lavlja,
Igrahu k'o oči dva pantera srodna,
Dok nebesa siva bivahu sve plavlja.

Plašljivih fauna, videh, jure čete
Upivši u mene sav svoj pogled zečji,
Pevajući psalme neke vere svete,
Koje gušio je njihov pogled dečji.

Vekovima tako kikoću se oni,
Splet njihov nevidljiv vaseljenom ide
I, tek kad u nama zvuk srca zazvoni,
Njihove se čete oživljene vide.

Mi smo deca sreće i života zrela,
Naša čudna ljubav do niskosti naga,
Mrzi legendarnih noći čeda svela;
Za nju mladost Bog je, a strast joj je snaga.

The Kiss

We were born to be happy, to love life fully,
Our love is bizarre, naked and coarse,
And we hate those born for frozen nights:
Youth is our god, and passion our strength.

. . . January storms howl through frozen eventide,
And whip the river into ice-blue froth,
While moaning trees arouse the dead:
Bitter is the laughter of vanishing time.

The world is a clash of conflicting wills,
Bellows and screams, thunders and death.
While rabid gales tear the skies apart,
Frozen tides duel with burning hell!

Intoxicated with hatred, surrounded by screams,
In a sensual kiss our bleeding lips are glued,
And strong ribs strain under the pressure
Of unconscious fingers that grip them with passion.

In that kiss we exchange our burning souls.
Myriads of embers and glowing cinders
Dance and flash as the eyes of tigers,
While grey skies are turning pale blue.

Then I see flocks of scared fauns dashing,
Starting like rabbits with terrified eyes,
Chanting psalms of an unknown religion
Buried deep in their childlike gaze.

For centuries already they've snickered like that.
Unseen their rabble swarms the universe
For to see them we need our hearts to bleed
And echo their fear and thus bring them to life.

We were born to be happy, to love life fully,
Our love is bizarre, naked and coarse,
And we hate those born for frozen nights;
Youth is our god, and passion our strength.

Translated by Mihailo Đorđević

Bez uzvika

Ni čudnog ni novog za nas nema više,
Sve su zemlje nama i drage i srodne;
Sred sjaja, i vrh nas kad se bure sviše,
Besmo mirni, kao usred zemlje rodne.

Otadžbina naša sa patnje je znana,
Lutajući mi je nosimo u sebi;
Ona je u krvi naših večnih rana,
I, kušam te, sudbo, takvu je pogrebi!

Zato nama nisu okeani strani,
Ni grobovi starih umrlih stoleća;
Mirni smo na gozbi u svetskoj dvorani
I kad nebrat pije miris našeg cveća.

Mi, kao litija, lutamo s trubama
Od kuta do kuta, od grada do grada,
Čas sami, čas s decom, stadom i ljubama,
Noseći stegove i vlasti i pada.

Ponavljamo skalu što poznasmo rano,
Skalom sudbe kojom drugi jedva mili;
Zato nama danas ništa nije strano,
Čini nam se, svuda već smo jednom bili.

I kad razgrnemo pepelišta snova,
Stari će se dani uz reć da pomenu:
Slušaćemo vatru i veselost njenu,
Ko domaćin što se vratio iz lova

S pesmom s kojom jutros y planinu krenu.

1917

Without Complaint

Nothing more for us is new or strange,
All lands to us are dear and kindred:
In the bright sun, beneath the wild storms' rage,
We were as calm as in our native land.

Within us through our wanderings we bear
Our homeland and its sufferings' renown;
And now, I beg you, Fate, lay her to rest,
Stained with the blood of our eternal wounds!

And so for us the oceans are not strange,
Nor yet the graves of centuries long dead;
Calmly we sit at table in the world's great hall
While still the foe drinks in our flowers' scent.

With trumpets like a solemn church parade,
Alone, or with our children, wives and herds,
We wander on from place to place, from town to town,
Bearing the banners of our greatness and our fall.

The scale we learned of old we now play out once more,
The scale of fate with others less than kind;
And so for us today nothing is strange,
It seems we passed through everywhere before.

And when we stir anew the ashes of our hearth,
And tell again the tales of olden days:
We'll listen to the fire, hear its mirth,
Just as the master, homewards from the hunt
Carries upon his lips the self-same song

With which he left that morning for the mountain.

1917

Translated by Bernard Johnson

VLADISLAV PETKOVIĆ-DIS 1880–1917

'Am I the expression of the corruption of my age?'
From 'Fate'

Vladislav Petković-Dis was born in the Serbian village of Zablaće in 1880. He worked as a schoolteacher before coming to Belgrade in the early 1900s, where he published his first poems in 1903. In what has come to be seen as the golden age of Serbian poetry, Dis was a representative of the non-traditionalist, modernist current, and he became co-editor of the journal *Književna nedelja* (*Literary Weekly*) in 1905 with his friend and fellow-Symbolist Sima Pandurović. Together with Milan Rakić, the three made up the group of so-called 'poets of pessimism', drawing their inspiration from the then current European *fin-de-siècle* 'decadent' movement in poetry as typified by Baudelaire, Verlaine and Edgar Allan Poe.

Individual poems such as 'Plave misli' ('Blue Thoughts'), 'Možda spava' ('Perhaps She Only Sleeps') and 'Tamnica' ('Prison') established Dis's reputation as a skilful poet with an instinctive feel for the music of his language. However, this was a time when the main stream of Serbian poetry was traditionalist or 'Parnassian', and Dis's gloomy, metaphysical poetry, with its pessimistic approach, seemed out of tune with the era of general hope and optimism. His collection of poems *Utopljene duše* (*Drowned Souls*; 1911) aroused the anger of the influential critic Jovan Skerlić who, in his famous attack on the poet, accused him of 'great and various imitation' and also of lack of patriotism. This latter charge was more than refuted in Dis's collection *Mi čekamo cara* (*We Wait for an Emperor*; 1913), although modern critics generally consider these poems to be weaker and more dated than his earlier work.

From the Bohemian café life of Belgrade, Dis went to serve as a war correspondent attached to the Serbian High Command during the Balkan wars in 1912. In 1915, as a refugee, he followed the defeated Serbian army on its retreat through Albania, and was then evacuated to France where he lived in exile until 1917. Like many of his contemporaries, he contracted tuberculosis as a result of the hardships and rigours of wartime life.

On his way back to Greece to rejoin his fellow countrymen in May 1917, he was drowned in the Ionian Sea off Corfu when a German submarine torpedoed the boat in which he was sailing.

Dis never finished his schooling, and his work, first as a temporary primary teacher and later as a minor Customs official left his further education very much in his own hands. His only contact with the European mainstream of poetry seems to have been through Sima Pandurović, who was a graduate in philosophy and generally well read. For this reason, it is all the more surprising that his poetry should have been so much in accord with the themes and preoccupations of the French Symbolist movement, and perhaps even more so with the Russian decadents – Bryusov, Balmont, Gippius and Merezhkovsky – who seemed to carry the French current still further. These Russian Symbolist poets were characterized by their belief in their special gift and role as mystics and seers, interpreters of signs and portents, and prophets of coming cataclysmic change; it was as if they were attuned to some special wavelength which gave them access to the mysteries of time and the absolute.

Like them, but apparently quite independently, Dis was a true poet of visions and dreams: as a visionary he sensed, more clearly than his contemporaries in what for the Serbs was a decade of confidence and optimism, the fragile fabric of his time and the omens of impending catastrophe, and also the implications of his own role as a poet. In the famous line from the poem 'Fate', he says: 'Am I the expression of the corruption of my age?', and in the poem 'Secret', published shortly before the war: 'That sense of dread that rises in me . . . Or do I take that sense of dread to mean, for my unhappy people, the shattering of all their dreams?'

Yet the visionary nature of much of Dis's poetry is centred on himself and contains an overwhelming preoccupation with death – from a sense of loss of a loved one in 'Perhaps She Only Sleeps', through a vision of death as a complete negation of all being, as in 'Nirvana', to a strange presentiment of his own death in 'Drowned Souls'. (The sea is a recurring element in his poetry, and in a letter to a friend [June 1916], he speaks of a dream in which he struggles with great waves of water.)

Generally accepted as Dis's finest work, 'Prison' (1910), is a metaphysical poem combining the poet's sense of sadness at the loss of some finer state of being, half-remembered only in dreams, with his perception of life as a preparation for the greater reality and beauty of death – again at one with the universe. As before, Petković-Dis's view of life and death as a continuous process of existence shows a clear affinity to that of the Russian decadents, whose philosophy in turn owes much to elements of Eastern mysticism and Buddhism.

By no means fully appreciated in his time, Petković-Dis was to prove an important influence for several outstanding modernist poets of the immediate post-war generation, particularly Crnjanski, Tin Ujević and Momčilo Nastasijević. And in the decade of poetry which marked the first years of this century, his reputation now places him alongside those great names of Serbian poetry who were his contemporaries such as Dučić and Šantić.

BERNARD JOHNSON

Texts
Utoplijene duše [*Drowned Souls*] (Belgrade, 1911).
Mićekamo cara [*We wait for an Emperor*] (Belgrade, 1913).

JUTARNJA IDILA

† Mihailu Petkovicú, mome bratu

Imao sam i ja veselih časova,
Nije meni uvek bilo kao sada;
Imao sam i ja sate bez bolova,
Osmejaka vedrih i radosti, mada

To je davno bilo . . . Na grudi sam ruke
Prekrstio svoje. Gledam kako tama,
Nećujno i tiho, ne praveći zvuke,
Po zidu se penje u čudnim slikama:

Ko ljubavna čeznja, kao tuga znana
Preko mrtve drage, preko groba lednog;
I nasuprot tami iz ranijih dana,
Javlja mi se slika srećnog jutra jednog.

Ustao sam rano, preko običaja;
Otvorio prozor. Izgledaše kao
U prirodi da je bilo okršaja
Nekog groznog, strašnog. Vazduh mokar pao.

Neba nigde nema. Možda je propalo.
Elementi strasti negde se još bore.
Možda je i sunce ropstva nam dopalo.
Znam, tog jutra zemlji nije bilo zore.

MORNING IDYLL

on the death of my brother, Mihailo Petković

I too have had my happy moments,
Things were not always such as now;
I too had hours free from pain,
With tranquil smiles, and joy, although

That was so long ago . . . I crossed my hands
Upon my breast. I watch the darkness
Noiselessly and silent, giving off no sounds,
Climbing along the wall, tracing strange pictures:

Like lover's yearning, like familiar sadness
Over a loved one dead, over an icy grave;
Against the darkness, from my earlier days,
There comes an image of a happy morning.

I rose up early, quite against my custom;
Opened the window. It seemed as if outside
Some fearful, awesome battle had been joined
In nature. Moist air fell.

Nowhere the sky. It could have disappeared.
Somewhere the elements of passion still fight on.
Perhaps the sun itself came down to us in slavery.
I only know that day the earth put on no dawn.

Oblaci se sivi uplašeno nagli
Ispred moga oka, i kao da mole
Za pomoć, spasenje njima, kiši, magli,
Od nečije ruke što ih tera dole.

Naglo odoh k njima. Tamo videh kako
Zalaze sva bića, i propast ih nosi;
Videh da se gasi i svetlost i pako,
Neku mutnu utvar da maše i kosi.

U trenutku jednom ne znam šta se desi . . .
Kada se probudih, udarahu zvona,
Uz očajni ropac umirahu gresi,
Kupljeni životom: to mre vasiona.

Zemlja, njeno vreme. Umirahu boje,
C njima duše ljudi i grobovi njini;
Sazrevahu zvezde, al da ih opoje
Ne ostaše niko, ni noć u crnini.

I nesta planeta i životu traga;
Izumire i smrt. Više nema ljudi;
Sa mene se poče da otkida snaga,
Svi udovi, redom, i pogled što bludi.

Minu sve što beše, htede biti ikad.
Tama se uvuče u ideju snova:
Raskosnije smrti nisam gledo nikad.
Imao sam i ja veselih časova.

Fearful the greying clouds bent low
Before my eyes, as if entreating
For help, for rain and mist's salvation,
Against some hand that drove them down.

I started off towards them. There I saw
All beings disappearing, borne by the abyss;
I saw the light extinguished, yet made out
some vague and phantom shape scything and reaping.

And for a moment then I know not what took place . . .
When I awoke, it was to tolling bells,
Death rattled in the throat of dying sins,
Redeemed by life: the universe's death,

The earth, its time. Colours were dying,
With them the souls of men and all their graves;
The stars were ripening, but none now was left
To sing their requiem, nor night to put on blackness.

The planet and all trace of life was gone:
And even death was dying. No more people:
My strength began to fade away,
Each limb in sequence, and my wandering gaze.

All things that ever were or would be passed.
The darkness slipped back into dreams' idea:
I never saw more sumptuous death revealed.
I too have had my happy moments.

TRANSLATED BY BERNARD JOHNSON

NIRVANA

Noćas su me pohodili mrtvi,
Nova groblja i vekovi stari;
Prilazili k meni kao žrtvi,
Kao boji prolaznosti stvari.

Noćas su me pohodila mora,
Sva usahla, bez vala i pene,
Mrtav vetar duvao je s gora,
Trudio se svemir da pokrene.

Noćas me je pohodila sreća
Mrtvih duša i san mrtve ruže,
Noćas bila sva mrtva proleća:
I mirisi mrtvi svuda kruže.

Noćas ljubav dolazila k meni,
Mrtva ljubav iz sviju vremena,
Zaljubljeni, smrću zagrljeni,
Pod poljupcem mrtvih uspomena.

I sve što je postojalo ikad,
Svoju senku sve što imađaše,
Sve sto vise javiti se nikad,
Nikad nece – k meni dohođaše.

Tu su bili umrli oblaci,
Mrtvo vreme s istorijom dana,
Tu su bili poginuli zraci:
Sve selenu pritisnu nirvana.

I nirvana imala je tada
Pogled koji nema ljudsko oko:
Bez oblika, bez sreće, bez jada,
Pogled mrtav i prazan duboko.

I taj pogled, ko kam da je neki,
Padao je na mene i snove,
Na budućnost, na prostor daleki,
Na ideje i sve misli nove.

Noćas su me pohodili mrtvi,
Nova groblja i vekovi stari;
Prilazili k meni kao žrtvi,
Kao boja prolaznosti stvari.

NIRVANA

Last night the dead paid me a visit,
New graveyards and old centuries;
Came here to me as if I were a victim,
The colour of the transience of things.

Last night the seas paid me a visit,
Their waters all dried up, no waves or foam,
A dead wind blowing from the mountain heights
Struggled to set the universe in motion.

The fortune of dead souls paid me a visit,
Last night, and a dead rose's dream,
And all the times of spring were dead last night,
And everywhere around dead odours teemed.

Last night love came here to me,
The long dead love of all the ages,
Lovers entwined in death's embrace
Under the kisses of dead memories.

And everything that ever was,
All things that ever cast a shadow.
And everything that never more will be,
Never exist – all came to me.

Here too were clouds that long since died,
Dead time with all the history of days,
Here too came all the perished rays of light;
Nirvana spread through all the universe.

And in Nirvana's eyes was seen,
A gaze unlike all human eyes:
No shape, no joyousness, no grief,
A gaze of death, a depth of emptiness.

A gaze that seemed as if a stone
Had fallen over me and on my dreams,
Upon the future, on the distant space,
Upon all thoughts and new ideas.

Last night the dead paid me a visit,
New graveyards and old centuries,
Came here to me as if I were a victim,
The colour of the transience of things.

TRANSLATED BY BERNARD JOHNSON

*F*RANC *M*ASELJ-*P*ODLIMBARSKI 1852–1917

'As for freedom in Bosnia, things are looking better now than ever; laws are like the strings of a violin: they can be tightened, they can be loosened. What happens will depend on circumstances . . .'
Vilar in Gospodin Franjo

Among the victims of the First World War, albeit in exceptional circumstances, was the Slovene writer Franc Maselj, born on 23 November 1852, near Limbarska Gora on the road between Ljubljana and Celje in what is now north-western Yugoslavia. He took his pen-name 'Podlimbarski' from his birthplace. Because of a youthful indiscretion, he had to interrupt his secondary education and he was never able to realize his ambition to become a historian. He began writing while still quite young and published his first sonnets and sketches when he was 20; he also had plans for theatrical works. Circumstances often forced him to abandon literature temporarily and he was able to devote himself more whole-heartedly to writing only in his later years.

Of his years service as a captain in the army in various parts of the Austrian Empire, the most decisive for his literary output were those he spent in occupied Bosnia. Here he gathered material for several of his works, notably his most ambitious and memorable novel, *Gospodin Franjo* (*Master Frank*).

In the 1880s he published a number of stories, particularly in the *Ljubljanski Zvon*, the most renowned Slovene literary monthly of the time. Some of these early works were sketches of life in Bosnia. A little later he began to write full-scale novels. In 1895, he published an autobiographical novel, *Mountain Streams* and the catastrophe which struck Ljubljana in the same year provided him with material for his *Story of an Earthquake*, which came out in 1903. He drew on his army service for his *Moravian Sketches*, but it was to his impressions of life in Bosnia that Podlimbarski returned for *From an old Notebook* (1908).

Franc Maselj-Podlimbarski's most celebrated work is his large-scale novel *Gospodin Franjo*, which, characteristically, includes both a great deal of autobiographical detail and also a severely critical analysis of conditions in Bosnia which, together with Hercegovina, was occupied by Austria under the terms of the Congress of Berlin of 1878. The author makes no attempt here to conceal his commitment to Pan-slavic and Yugoslav aspirations and openly condemns the policies of the Austrian occupiers. Personal reminiscences and imaginative elements merge, as Podlimbarski relates in fifty chapters the experiences of the Slovene engineer, Franjo Vilar, in occupied Bosnia from the summer of 1881 to the spring the following year.

Shortly after completing his studies, Vilar, an officer in the reserves, is recalled for service with the occupying forces. Having since returned to civilian life, he is hoping to make a useful contribution to the economic development of the country he had last seen in the winter of 1878. He is engaged to help develop the timber trade and he does what he can to improve the conditions of the lumberjacks who are continually exploited and poorly paid. Although Vilar appreciates the reasons for the Bosnian insurrection, he abhors the methods of those who take to banditry. One such is a monk of the Serbian Orthodox Church, Jovica Milošević. In addition, the story of Vilar's affection for the monk's younger sister, Danica, and their eventual marriage is one of the strands of the narrative, but not the main one. Despite censorship, Podlimbarski sought to discuss as openly as possible the political solutions to the 'Bosnian Question'. As Professor Anton Slodnjak, an eminent historian of Slovene literature says, *Gospodin Franjo* is 'a genuine novel of social and political protest' in which the author 'exposes the oppression of the Bosnian people by the occupying authorities and their hangers-on and the energetic resistance of the Orthodox Serbs in the first decade after the occupation of Bosnia and Hercegovina.'

On its publication in 1913, the novel met with a favourable reception. While some critics found its content more impressive than its style, there was general agreement that this was a work of importance and topicality. A reviewer in *Ljubljanski Zvon* saw in the book a 'real treasure', a serious and honest work which offered a solution to many problems relating to history and national psyche. The great Slovene poet Oton Župančič published a particularly favourable review in the journal *Slovan*, of which he was then editor. This novel, he claimed, came into being not because the author had the urge to write, but because he had something to say. It was a sincere account of the activities of a representative of Slovene culture in Bosnia. The topicality of the novel was reinforced by the fact that, the following year, the shots which set the tinder alight on 28 June and flared into the conflagration of the First World War were fired by a Bosnian revolutionary.

With the outbreak of the war, Podlimbarski's fortunes took a turn for the worse. His novel was confiscated and the Slovenska Matica (Slovene Literary Society) which had published it was forced to close down. The author was summoned to face a court martial, accused of high treason and stripped of his officer's rank. He was confined in June 1916 and, his health broken, died in exile in September 1917. The satire on war entitled *St Valentine and the Pilgrim*, which he was writing during his exile, remained unfinished. The ban on *Gospodin Franjo* was rescinded only after the war when his mortal remains were brought home to Slovenia, where he was buried with full honours as a national martyr. Some years later, there appeared a collected edition of his works, in which *Gospodin Franjo* held pride of place.

DUŠAN MORAVEC
TRANSLATED BY HARRY LEEMING

Text
Zbrani spisi [*Collected Works*] (J. Šlebinger (ed.), Ljublijana, 1923–31, vols 1, 2, 4).

GOSPODIN FRANJO

It is the spring of 1882. The Bosnian insurrection has been suppressed by the occupying Austrians. Franjo Vilar is imprisoned after being suspected of being in league with the monk-turned-bandit-chief, Jovica Milošević.

Through his window Vilar looked out at the prison yard where Meglić the gaoler held sway. He saw the path along which, in those troubled times, a weekly batch of Bosnian captives was marched off to face the firing squad, sentenced for the possession of arms or for providing the insurgents with food and shelter. The offices of the military tribunal were on the ground floor of the station building and immediately below his own place of confinement was a spacious office used for the interrogation of suspects and witnesses. When there were too many, interrogation took place and sentence was pronounced in the large yard behind the station building, separated from the prison garden by a high wall. Vilar looked down on the yard again and at the unhappy victims of summary justice. How calmly these poor wretches accepted their fate! He was afraid he might glimpse among them the noble head of Danica's brother, Jovica, who had accepted without complaint a stressful life, in whose countenance fate had etched lines of strength and grim determination, a man cast by destiny as teacher and prophet, who willingly shouldered the martyr's cross and grasped with pride the torch of liberty. Although there were indeed many bandits among the ranks of the captive insurgents, he had not counted Danica's brother among them. He had not spotted him among those who had gone to their death.

Lisinski, the military judge, had sided with Vilar's enemies, those who maintained that stubborn characters be ruled with a rod of iron. But he was not yet ready to recommend a verdict, for some aspects of Vilar's case were still obscure. As the supreme legal authority and the custodian of martial law in the Tuzla district, the brigadier was much concerned with the case of the engineer. He had already decided to exercise clemency at the appropriate moment because of Vilar's expert work on the 'General's Bridge'. He called the engineer to his office, where, as prudence dictated, he gave him a most frosty reception.

'You are accused of illegal contacts with the bandits,' he said, his features taking on an expression of grim menace. 'In the course of the investigation, it has become clear that you have been conniving at their activities in every way. The workers had the insolence to praise the Sultan, but you made no attempt to make them keep their mouths shut. You were standing on the brink of a precipice and you lost your footing. In these hard times we must all pull together, we are all in the same camp. Anyone who is not with us is against us.'

'I never realized, General, how easily a man can become a traitor,' said Vilar with simple candour.

The general wagged a warning finger in Vilar's face. 'We can't have any rapid changes, any leaps in the dark here. I too would like to see order restored in the country, but everything points to the likelihood of having to wait until this generation which has seen the occupation has passed on.'

'More likely it will take two generations,' added the brigade adjutant who attended the general on all his official duties. As previously when interrogated by Lisinski, Vilar refuted all charges completely. He spoke convincingly, guilelessly, with the ardour and vehemence of youth. While rejecting all accusations of treachery, he did not flounder in excessive protestations of loyalty. The harsh treatment of the Bosnians had bred liberal ideas in the engineer's mind, and he now gave full vent to his feelings.

'Pigheadedness, incredible pigheadedness,' von Merks whispered in the general's ear.

'I don't care what you do with me, but I have right on my side,' Vilar said and, with this, concluded his defence.

The severe expression on the general's face softened a little. He gazed at the earnest enthusiast and said, 'All this just goes to show you are one of these radicals who imagine that things will soon change for the better if they're continually moaning about everything under the sun. Why aren't you satisfied with the improvements you've already got for your men? They are materially better off and you have your spiritual satisfaction.'

'When I met these unfortunate people, I was so sorry for them I took up their case. That is the extent of my crime. If it had not been for this unfortunate revolt, for this sudden outburst of universal indignation, I would have restored order in the lumberjacks' camp and won the approval of the Bosnian government. That was my resolute hope. As for the revolt, I had no hand in it all. I have an unblemished record with not a hint of treachery against me. General, you have arrested an innocent man, but I will make no effort to escape my fate; I will not flinch, I can take whatever punishment I am given.'

The general was incensed by these words; he waved his hand as a sign that he was fed up with the whole affair. A moment later he bowed perfunctorily, and the engineer was led back to his place of confinement.

'The fellow's a raving lunatic,' the general said, sitting at his office desk and rummaging through his papers. 'Really, the way these young chaps flare up, like putting a torch to a bundle of straw. Cato or Brutus, that's the role they see themselves in.'

'It was a Bosnian powder keg he put his torch to,' adding, as was von Merks's wont, his own gloss to the other's statement.

The general was deep in thought. 'The man isn't dangerous, he just can't see sense. He says the Bosnians are poor wretches. It's not poverty but great expectations that make men unhappy. Even so, personally I would prefer a policy of gentle persuasion. But I have my orders to apply the emergency regulations and put down this revolt.'

'Why don't they just give up? If only they would take on our culture unconditionally, if only they would accept our ways, then they'd see – ah well!' Von Merks shuffled his papers.

The general wondered somewhat at the sort of marvels the Bosnians might see if they accepted the Austrian way. 'Once we start philosophizing, we'll discover contradictions on all sides,' he said and so concluded the discussion.

Vilar was treated as Jovica had been six months previously: he was to be held as a dangerous subversive till things improved; he would then be released. The general delivered his verdict and Vilar was thereafter forgotten.

When spring came, he was still confined to his cramped quarters. Resigned to his situation, Vilar spent much of the time deep in thought, chiefly pondering official policy and human malevolence. Until recently, his heart had been impervious to hate; now a dull, baleful depression clouded his innermost soul. He paced about the room clenching his fists, gritting his teeth and muttering to himself. If a man's thoughts could be read as actions, the general and his adjutant would have sentenced him on the spot. Blind and obdurate, the law itself breeds criminals. Life now seemed to present a dismal prospect. Previously, he had been irritated by the investigation and had either repeated his pleas of innocence or devised new arguments; now he was left alone without a living soul to take the slightest interest in him. An orderly brought his food from the cook-house and tidied up his miserable quarters. Apart from this he had no human contact. As time passed in his tranquil solitude, his memories of Danica provided him with happier moments. Some day, in the end, they would have to release him; then, free as a bird, he would escape to the woman he loved; together they would start a new life. Jovica also was often in his thoughts. Was he still alive? Had he secured a hide-out? Was he continuing the struggle in his native Hercegovina or had he joined his sister in flight? Vilar thought long and often about that remarkable man. And the day arrived when he heard the bandit's name mentioned in the yard below.

One morning early in April, he was still drowsing on his bunk, when he was wakened by the rattle of chains and a great uproar. He leapt up and looked through the window to see what was going on in the yard. Five Bosnians under a heavily armed guard, securely fettered, weary and utterly exhausted, were lined up by the wall. An army clerk was laying out with pompous ritual the paraphernalia of his trade. Behind him stood the members of the court-martial, a sort of military jury. The adjutant appeared with a sheaf of papers under his arm. The general followed, accompanied by his aide. The proceedings were brief and perfunctory, in accordance with a law dating from medieval times.

Vilar's heart beat faster. He could hardly hear a word through the closed window. He stared at the impassive faces of the accused, stoic and unmoved by the major's harangue, like a resentful church congregation hearing a preacher cataloguing their sins. The adjutant read from a document, then said something to the prisoners and interrogated the witnesses. When he had done, the members of the court-martial started to consult in whispers, then drew their swords as a sign that they had reached agreement. The adjutant again addressed the accused and announced the verdict. At this, their self-control broke down. They rattled their chains. Vilar had been expecting an explosion of anger, a fit of blind rage. Quietly he opened his window. He saw and heard three of the felons raise their manacled hands and one by one raise their voices in protest.

'Three of us did fire at the police but the other two never even had guns to shoot with. I swear by the living God: they are both innocent as babes in arms!'

'They had no weapons. Shoot us but let them go!'

'For God's sake, don't murder innocent men!'

Vilar saw that the three wrongdoers were only concerned about the fate of the two who had been wrongly condemned.

The prosecutor's bleary eyes sought the general's advice. With a contemptuous wave of the hand, he gave the order: 'The sentence stands. Execute all five of them!'

Vilar was stunned by the sheer brutality of the sentence. Numb, in a state of shock, he would have moved away from the window but was held there by another spectacle.

They had now brought to the place a grey-haired man wearing an Albanian cap and bent so low that Vilar could not see his face. Shaken by a racking cough, the prisoner pressed his manacled hands against his chest. His eyes were fixed on the ground, as if seeking a pit, where he might find the rest he craved.

'What can this poor old man be accused of?' Vilar wondered, leaning out of the window and staring down at the yard. From the brief charge read out by the adjutant he realized that the prisoner was Pero Mušić from Pilić, owner of the inn in Oskova valley. He was accused of providing a bandit chief, Jovica Milošević, with food and shelter – an offence punishable under martial law by death.

The prosecutor himself seemed to feel sorry for the old man. He was clearly and deliberately framing his questions in such a way that a simple affirmative would have secured the prisoner's release.

'Now look here Mušić, you had no idea it was Jovica Milošević, the bandit chief, on his way back from Hercegovina with his companions?' he said loudly.

'Of course I knew, of course I knew. Even the kids knew,' Pero the innkeeper replied in a weak voice.

'But you didn't know that harbouring a bandit is by law punishable with the death penalty?'

'Of course I knew. But Our Lord says: Feed the hungry!'

Here the general lost his temper. 'Yes, you know everything and maybe that's to your credit; but you needn't think you can get away with everything,' he roared. 'Enough of this! You deserve to die with the rest of them. Shoot the lot!'

Again the members of the court conferred in whispers, then pronounced the sentence demanded. Vilar's hair stood on end, his face felt numb. 'Poor bastard, you moved east from Hercegovina only to meet a violent death,' he thought. It was like a living nightmare.

At this point, Pero raised his head and dully contemplated the faces of his judges, as if to see whether these were men made in the image of God. Then he fixed his eyes on the sunlight flooding the wall of the station building. Perhaps, with death only moments away, he felt in his soul the deep wave of sympathy from the open window. He noticed Master Frank and recognized him.

'Our dear Master Frank, how are you keeping?' he called in a feeble voice.

Vilar did not answer his question. He was too preoccupied with the condemned man's fate to have any thought for his own. All the same, he felt he must speak a few words of comfort to this doomed acquaintance, now only a few steps from death.

'Hold your head high, my friend, and don't despair!' he shouted.

The general and his entourage glanced up angrily at the window.

'God's will be done!' the old man replied. Meglić the gaoler standing beside him, gave him a poke in the ribs.

'A dog barks till someone shuts it up,' Mušić protested, again racked by a violent fit of coughing.

'Well, you haven't got long and that's for sure!' the other growled, with a grin at the general and the major.

'May your victims' tears scald your cheeks when your turn comes.' And after speaking these, his last words, Mušić dropped his head.

An Orthodox and a Muslim priest approached the condemned men.

The procession left the yard.

'Oh, to get away from here, from this place of death and degradation,' Vilar cried and threw himself down on his bed. It was a good ten minutes before he heard the dull beat of a funeral drum. Another ten minutes passed before the shots of the firing squad rang out.

Three days later the general summoned his adjutant.

'It's time we dealt with the case against the engineer. I have reliable reports from rebel territory that the rising is subsiding. The insurgents no longer have a unified command and each unit commander is operating independently. It will be all over in a month's time and the insurgent units will disintegrate into the usual bands of robbers, and they will be a headache for the police and guards for a few years yet. The present generation will know no peace, but the danger is over. I don't know why we should keep the engineer locked up. I regard him as an overwrought idealist, a kind-hearted fellow who can cause us no trouble. There's nothing in all your records that would allow us to lay a finger on him, is there?'

The adjutant's features were contorted in a deferential grimace.

'Yet why should he be observing the proceedings of our court martial from his cell? So that he can write embarrassing memoirs in his old age about the Bosnian business? So that he can rake over and expose so-called atrocities, which are only the unavoidable consequences of martial law and the Bosnian problem? I propose we release him, on condition that he gives his word of honour not to stir from this town until his case is concluded. And meanwhile, Major, would you please get on with it!' The adjutant nodded his assent.

And so Vilar was released with the proviso that he should not leave Tuzla. He found a lodging with Mrs Grgić, who happened to have a room free again. She brought his meals from the Hotel Agular. He avoided company. Just once he happened to meet Hren in the street. The official told him the news of his wife's new baby – 'A real beauty! A delight!' He then peered cautiously around and made his excuses. He was short of time but was very glad his gallant compatriot was out of the mire. He would visit him, he'd certainly come and see him at his lodging, so that they could have a really pleasant chat.

Vilar realized that the bureaucratic soul feared any contact with a man accused of high treason, and did not expect him to come. He ventured out seldom by day, but more frequently in the evenings.

He would visit the Serbian coffee-house which was under strict official surveillance.

One evening as Vilar was making his way back along the deserted street from the Serbian café, he spotted in front of him a strapping Turkish wench in a loose robe. This large woman in front of him proceeded slowly and cautiously, as though seeking something or waiting for someone. Occasionally she would raise her head and stare into the distance like a hen fearing some bird of prey cruising menacingly overhead. She shambled on, awkwardly, with the sluggishness of a bear, but would surprise Vilar by occasionally darting forward, hinting at a more lithe body and a more definite purpose than might have been supposed at first. She puzzled Vilar further by stopping twice, half turning round and, holding her head high, gazing at him from under her veil.

'Strange! What can she want?' Vilar wondered. He had already assumed from her appearance that she must be a married woman. 'Maybe this hot-blooded Muslim has a rendezvous in this deserted street. That would be unusual, and even dangerous in a small Turkish town like this.'

Now he himself slowed his pace and kept his eyes on her movements. There was enough light from the clear sky to make out everything distinctly. The solitary oil street-lamp glimmered weakly, showing her turning off into a secluded side alley bordered on one side by a worm-eaten fence leading uphill to the Turkish cemetery. This was even narrower, even more deserted. As he walked by, Vilar glanced up the alley to see the Turkish woman standing close by the fence, waiting.

'Well, well!' Vilar gulped, as something new occurred to him. He continued straight on for twenty paces or so, but the new idea was becoming an obsession. He had no dishonourable intentions, but an overpowering curiosity made him return. This could be an opportunity to hear from a genuine Muslim woman something of the secrets of life in a harem. The idea that he might be walking into a trap never occurred to him. He was afraid of no man, let alone this Turkish wench in her ankle-length gown.

He made his way back and turned into the narrow alley. She was still there, waiting. He trod softly as he approached the mysterious stranger, trying to think of an appropriate opening gambit. He had scant experience of such late-night assignations. This particular encounter seemed such an unusual adventure that he felt no sense of religious betrayal when, face to face with the heathen charmer, he whispered with a would-be Turkish twang what seemed to him the most appropriate greeting: 'Allahu ekber!' ['Great is Allah!']

'But how much greater is our Orthodox God!' came the booming baritone from behind the thick veil. Vilar, astounded, recognized Milošević immediately. He was so thunderstruck that he missed the next words: 'Come away with me now, Master Frank!'

Jovica gripped him with his right hand and with the other opened a gate in the fence. He led him to a dark yard behind a dilapidated building. Together they stood beneath the branches of a blossoming plum tree. The bandit chief threw off the female robe, revealing a brace of pistols and a dagger tucked in his belt. Keeping his voice down, he said, 'Well, Master Frank, here we are in my citadel.'

TRANSLATED BY HARRY LEEMING

GRIGOR ZOHRAB 1861–1915

'We are struggling against that concept which says that right belongs to the strong.'
From his final letter, 1915

When, as a result of mismanagement and corruption, the Ottoman Empire began to disintegrate in the 19th century, both Russia and Great Britain became interested in the fate of the Armenians. To the Russians, Armenia was the road to India and Egypt; to the British, it was the shield guarding their colonies from Russian expansion. Consequently, both powers became actively involved in 'saving' Armenia from Turkish tyranny, and the 'Armenian question' became a much discussed factor in international politics.

In the words of Sultan Abdul-Hamid II (1876 –1909), 'the way to get rid of the Armenian question is to get rid of the Armenians.' The policy of suppression, which until then had been entrusted to tax collectors, the police and the judges, was now carried out through massacres. Between 1894 and 1896 alone, over 200,000 Armenians were slain. By the end of 1914, the Young Turk triumvirate, who had succeeded in their coup of 26 January 1913, had entered the war on the side of Germany and saw an unrepeatable chance to secure 'Turkey for the Turks'. On 24 April 1915, the holocaust reached Constantinople from the interior provinces and enveloped the intellectuals. The book *Houšarjan* (*In Memoriam*), edited by T'ēodik (Labčinčian T'eodos Grigor, 1873–1928) and published in 1919 when Constantinople was under Allied occupation, lists the names of 761 men and women who were arrested and sent into 'exile' – a euphemism for murder. These were the main leaders of the 2.5 million Armenians in historical Armenia, and comprised poets, publicists, members of the Ottoman Parliament, writers and clergymen – including nine bishops and twelve nuns. The massacre of over one million Armenians during World War I was probably the greatest organized crime in history to that date. 'Who, after all, speaks today of the annihilation of the Armenians?' was the rhetorical question Hitler posed in a speech he gave to his military commanders on 22 August 1939 justifying his plan to annihilate Jews and gypsies during the Second World War.

The foremost personality among the 761 was Grigor Zohrab, born 26 June 1861 and known as the founder of the realistic short story in western Armenian literature, as illustrated in the following 'The Storm' (1889). The Russian–Turkish war of 1877–8 and its legacy, the

Grigor Zohrab.

Congress of Berlin, raised great hopes among the Armenians that the great powers would prevail on Turkey to treat the Armenians on an equal basis with all other citizens. Grigor Zohrab did not believe any changes would occur to better his countrymen's lot, and his editorials and political reviews in *Lragir* (*Newspaper*) and *Erkragound* (*The World*) castigated those who did. In his capacity as member of the Ottoman Parliament Zohrab applied his brilliant oratorical and legal skills to national, social, economic and educational problems. In his many short stories and novellas published during his lifetime – *Anhetac'ac seround mê* (*A Disappearing Generation*, 1887), *Xĭčmtank'i jayner* (*Voices of Conscience*, 1909), *Keank'ê inč'pes or ē* (*Life as It Is*, 1911) and *Louṙ c'aver* (*Silent Griefs*, 1911) – he skilfully analysed the complexities of urban life.

His commitment to the Armenian cause was firm and uncompromising. In 1913, under the pseudonym of Marcel L'eart, he printed in Paris a pamphlet entitled *La Question Armènnienne à la lumière des documents*, in which he predicted the coming catastrophe. 'If, in the next war, Turkey and Germany become allies,' he wrote, 'the fate of the Armenians in Turkey will be in mortal peril.' In his last letter, he said: 'We are struggling against that concept which says that right belongs to the strong.'

On 20 May 1915, Grigor Zohrab and Vartkes, another Armenian deputy, were arrested and sent to Diarbekir. On the road from Aleppo, the two men were set upon by a marauding band who, after murdering Zohrab, crushed his head between two massive rocks.

V. NERESSIAN

The Storm

They stood waiting, trembling with terror, in front of the house on the wharf, while the furious storm rocked the Bosphorus.

It must have been past midnight of a summer night lost in a blackness which the incessant, jagged lines of the lightning vainly tried to penetrate. In the sky, as everywhere else, there was a death struggle between light and darkness, a vengeful combat, and here, too, darkness was winning out, invading everywhere, and piling its folds one upon another, casting its black cloak on the entire horizon and the stormy waters of the sea.

Only the mighty roar of the sea, clear and distinct, pierced the darkness like a wild scream, with intermittent lapses, as if the huge lungs which exhaled the tempest wished to take a fresh breath in order to roar all the more fiercely.

And in the fury of this commotion, the inmates of the house ran helter skelter, not knowing what they did or said, vainly trying to catch sight of the *Dauntless*, the small craft which harboured one of their own, now made the plaything of mighty billows, and perhaps hopelessly lost in them. They were crying, praying, hoping.

'Sahag is with her,' said father, trying to cheer his wife.

'There's nothing to worry about,' added a neighbour. 'They've probably already landed somewhere. The *Dauntless* is not a boat to be afraid for.'

And the storm kept roaring, dissipating these reassuring words, shaving off the tips of the waves as with a sharp dagger, and pushing back the men who had flocked on the beach, as if repelling their intervention.

'Lord, God, be merciful,' they cried, as if trying to project a faint voice and expecting an answer from across the sea.

Durig, who had lived in their house and had grown up with them, loved the sea; and it was her custom to go boat riding every evening after supper. For two years after her marriage, however, she had been away from the sea. Confined in the bustle and the dust of Bera, disgusted with its filthy surroundings, she always longed for her father's seashore home, the wide open spaces and the blue waves of the sea.

She was a bride of two years, when, having become a widow, she was obliged to return to her father's home because she was unable to live with her mother-in-law who had never forgiven her for remaining alive after her son's death.

Many had predicted a new marriage after this return.

'She's still young,' the women commented. 'She is beautiful,' said the men. And indeed she was beautiful and young, but hers was a sullen, manly beauty which confounded the accoster, and forestalled his advances. Her eyes seemed full of hidden lightning, and no one dared look into their depths. Secluded in her widow's mourning, proud and alone, she turned a deaf ear to the idle affections of her suitors. For four years, she had stayed in her father's house, still mourning, while the gossip-mongering women, envious of her exceptional charm, said to one another:

'Black becomes her. No wonder she doesn't take it off.'

And true, black did become her. It emphasized the softness of her milk white skin, it merged into the lustre of her luxurious hair, and accentuated the elegance of her tall, shapely figure. The girls did not care for her, because the youths who swarmed around her made them despair. They felt that this young widow was destroying all their prospects.

'Let her get married so that the rest of us will have a chance with the eligibles,' they protested.

And yet, Durig did her best to discourage all the men. Like a high, haughty peak, she was inaccessible in her beauty and the majesty of her mourning.

Only an hour before, she had started on her customary sail. Sahag had brought the boat and was giving his Hanum lady a ride on the spotless blue sea. Sahag was a lad from Buyoukdere whose powerful figure gave him the appearance of the perfect athlete. For twenty years, his father had served as the house boatman, and now, for about a year and a half, Sahag had been performing his father's duties. Having grown up in this house since his childhood, he was loved by the members of the family as if he were one of their own. Seated across from his Hanum, as he rowed, he recalled his childhood. He recalled the days when, together with his Hanum, he used to go to the house of Varbed Doudou, the house near the butcher's, whence he used to make his escapades to the seashore to play Koukouch and Kaidrak with his Greek playmates.

He contemplated with a tinge of bitterness and pain that he had never beome a useful man, but, instead, had stayed a boatman like his father. While in these thoughts, the mild waves gently caressed the sides of the boat as it drifted away from the shore. Meanwhile the weather, instead of getting cooler as was usual in the evenings, was getting suffocatingly hotter.

Durig made no reply to the boatman's recollections of childhood days, but she too remembered those bygone days, and listened to him without interrupting. Submerged in entirely different thoughts, her gaze wandering between the sea and the skies, she did not see the rowing boy across from her who, in relating their childhood reminiscences, seemed to convey a silent protest against the indifference and the chasm which now separated them.

The sea was spread like a vast, smooth blue sheet, and a hot breeze, as if fanned by an unseen fire, beat against their faces. Far away, on the beaches of

Buyoukdere, the newly lit candles and kerosene lamps flickered like glowing specks. They were now out on the open stretches of Sultaniyeh, and neither the skipper nor the mistress noticed the slowly gathering clouds whose mottled lustre was reflected on the motionless sea. They had already gone much further than usual, and were drifting with the course of the waves. They were now exactly midway between the two shores. A sombre veil descended on the sea, enveloping the two in a cloud of mist. Unable to see anything else any longer, the young woman fixed her gaze on the boatman before her, taking in his youthful, powerful torso which, upon each bending of the back, revealed through his thin bourounkjik shirt the rise and falling of a hairy chest, and through the broad sleeves, his muscular arms.

Durig watched her boatman in the heat of the sea and the air, in this semi-darkness, in this unique solitude and aloneness. He was still a lad. A velvety down was just beginning to sprout on his tanned face; and up from his bare feet, resting on the central supporting board, could be seen his uncovered thighs. There was something fresh, vigorous, and pure about this boy which stirred the young woman.

'How old are you, Sahag?'

'How should I know, Hanum? I must be 17 or perhaps 18, or . . .'

And the young woman reluctantly compared the boy's 17 years with her 22 and was quite satisfied.

'Now let's see. You are old enough, and we must find a girl for you.'

Durig assumed the air of a mother in order to speak all the more freely; moreover, this solitude on the sea enhanced her boldness. She took a secret delight in speaking of his coming betrothal as she spoke about his fiancée, his wife-to-be. Sahag's future wife should be a girl from Buyoukdere, a happy woman in these powerful arms which she was now admiring. And with such talk she drew immense enjoyment from the youth's blushes and embarrassment. Through half-veiled questions she tried to sound the depths of his simplicity, and the more confused and disturbed the youth became, the plainer became her explanations, and the more obvious her words, for she had no fears that this boy would understand her – this boy whose sensitivity seemed calm and solid as a rock. And the young woman, like a curious physician who tries to locate the nerve centre, went deeper and deeper, probing the heart of the lad. But the youth refused to make any replies and, fixing his gaze on the fog of the distant shore, avoided his mistress's curious and imperious eyes. Could it be that he understood such language?

Suddenly there was a downpour. The sea became speckled with small bubbles and darker shades of blue spread over the surface. A strong wind, driven from the distance, tore the misty veil which had shrouded mistress and servant. Over the heights of Oushadedeh, a flash of lightning, followed by a terrific thunder, inundated land and sea with a yellow, dazzling light.

'Hanum, my lady, it's a storm, let's flee!'

The surface of the sea took sail and swelled into a long, endless billow.

They turned back. The skipper accelerated his strokes because he well knew the menace which confronted them. Now they were moving, riding the crest of the billow, rising and falling with it. The south wind was fast rushing on them in all its fury. The boat approached the open spaces of Baykoz, and the sea, no longer able to resist the storm, was being torn asunder into a thousand lashing waves, splintering into white foam.

Sahag gave his all, throwing into the struggle his full might and endurance. The fragile boat bounced perilously on the waves, while the storm kept pushing it from behind. A relentless wind now whipped the young mistress, destroying her beautiful hair-do and slapping it against her temples. Night surrounded them with a terrible melody, stressing the necessity to unite before the dread prospect of drowning at sea. To add to the crisis, the tiny boat was drawing water. The widow had abandoned the steering ropes of the rudder, leaving the helpless craft entirely at the mercy of the storm. She stopped speaking. She was looking death straight in the face – to be drowned in this liquid expanse, so close to his side – and she was afraid.

Her face, now completely drained of all colour, was even more desirable, while the wind with its indiscreet and searching blasts whipped against her skirts, lifting and filling them like a delightful sail. Unable any longer to keep her dress down, she abandoned it to the whim of the wind, exposing her knees, and showing a pair of black stockings clinging to those curves around which the folds of snowy white lingerie played like white foam.

The storm had reached the peak of its fury; and the sea wrapped the little boat, now filled with salty water, in its mountainous billows. Far away in the dark, under the flashes of lightning, one could discern the land, peaceful and tranquil. There, the houses were lit with red cheery lights, while the little boat, now hopelessly lost in the waves, watched the solid security of the land like an unreal dream.

Sahag kept up his superhuman exertions as the imminent danger doubled his strength and skill. All his efforts were bent on avoiding the exposure of the boat's sides to the attacks of the waves, while his left oar deftly controlled his direction. His salvation lay not in fleeing from the waves, but in avoiding a single misstep; and thus, persecuted and obedient, they were driven deeper and deeper between the towering waves and the bottomless deep.

Faint with exhaustion, the young woman lay there, stretched in all the glorious and exciting disorder of her finery. By this time, the boat was entering the Bay of Oumour Nehri, in whose narrow confines the sea was even more furious, more threatening, and deadly. The youth felt that death was inevitable. Both he and his mistress were drenched to the skin. A salty sharpness, bitter and nauseating, saturated his lungs. While he was watching the waves in order to keep his direction, a flash of lightning enabled him to see that his boat was near the shore which stretched its entire length like a vast snowy field, lost in the whiteness of the foam.

It seemed no longer possible to avoid being crushed in this mighty combat between land and sea; it was impossible to turn back to the open spaces. Sahag gave a piercing cry – a sort of call for help, a piteous, despairing shriek – which the sea, as if to prevent a sudden rescue, purposely drowned with its roar. They were about 60 feet from the shore, and the sea, like a cradle, rocked them back and forth, as if trying to lull its doomed passengers into sleep.

At this moment, a huge wave seized the boat and, raising it high on its crest, lingered a moment as if undecided and then, with a terrific force, hurled it up on the sand of the shore, and recoiled. And this was their salvation.

Bounding from the boat, the youth first of all dragged the boat farther inland. Then he tried to help his mistress. And though it was dark, he could clearly discern the pale face and the ravishing outlines of her body, accentuated by her clinging skirts. He held the fulsome, angelic body in his arms, and raised it to shoulder height. His touch, the warmth of it, awakened the young woman. But she was not surprised to find herself in those arms; rather, in her deep exhaustion, she had the sensation of being in a happy, long-cherished dream. And she wished that that dream would linger, that it would never end. And having surrendered herself to this illusion, there under the black skies, in this strange and titanic rhapsody of the storm, and amid the mighty roar of the tempest, she pretended to be still asleep, leaving undefended those slowly colouring cheeks, and that taut body which trembled like a playing lyre, until this dream, which was so like the reality, continued into full consummation.

On the wharf where the young woman set foot, tears, kisses and prayers were freely intermingled.

'You are saved, you are saved.'

'Come, change your clothes, you are drenched, Durig.'

After the general relief, there were many eager questions: 'Where did you get caught?' 'How did you escape?' 'Where did you land?' In the general exultation, the youth had been completely forgotten. But now it was his turn. Durig showed them her saviour.

'I was completely lost. I don't remember a thing, ask Sahag,' she said.

There were thanks and praises for Sahag, and Durig's father gave him a gold piece for reward. 'You are the son of this house,' they all said in one voice. After that, it was natural that the youth became even more devoted to his Lady Hanum who was now thrice his mistress.

But after a while, only the memory of the storm remained. Durig never again took her customary evening boat rides. In vain, the youth offered her every assurance – they would not go very far, no, only along the shore, and the boat was solid and dependable. But Hanum was adamant. From that night on, she did not want to see the youth's face, she avoided meeting him, and whenever she was obliged to speak to him, there was a dry, imperious note in her voice.

There was resentment in her heart for having surrendered herself to this youthful servant. The very moment to which she had looked forward with a flaming passion seemed like a shame and a smudge on her proud heart. She who had refused many a noble suitor could not bear the thought of having been conquered by this common servant. The storm which had roared over her head and in her soul had passed, and she wanted to forget that terrible night; but the youth, on the contrary, tried to recall, and make her recall, those blessed, terrifying moments. He constantly lingered in her presence, insufferable like a living rebuke. He never could speak of his happiness and good fortune, never dared tell his mistress of what happened when she fainted; and that happy fainting engraved deeply in his heart and soul became more of a dream than a reality, but not without deeply stirring his newly awakened spirit.

There were moments when, sitting for hours in his little room near the kitchen, and after reconstructing all the details of his incredible dream, an irresistible something bade him to face his Hanum, and to confess his love and his suffering. After all, had he not saved that ravishing body from a watery grave? It was only just that she should belong to him.

Slowly, he was driven to solitude. He became sullen, self-centred and savage. There was no longer anything for him to do in the house; they would no longer sit in his boat, and they kept him more for the sake of paying him a pittance, rather than from any expectation of real services. He felt all this and was saddened; this patronage weighed heavily on his heart. He would have long since run away from the house, were it not for the mortal dread of being deprived of the presence of his idolized Hanum. It is true that they had been saved from the storm; but coming so close to danger had been judged to be the result of recklessness, and the youth felt that he had fallen out of favour in that house. As if he were guilty, they spared him only out of pity. So, he tried to avoid them, and it never occurred to him that their deserting him was an act of ingratitude, as if he were a dog once serviceable but now useless. They did not drive him away, but they did not want him either. This pain, following upon the storm's terrors, together with the bliss and the yearning it had engendered in him, disturbed his rather fragile mind.

'He's gone mad,' they said, pitying him; to which

the young widow added her indifference and deliberate evasion. Whenever they talked about him, she invariably expressed her fears that his condition would be aggravated. To others, this pessimism seemed like an exaggeration; they even jested over her fears and were greatly amused.

'He might jump on your neck some day,' they taunted her.

'Please, don't say such things. They make me shudder.'

Future events proved that her fears were well-founded. The youth's mental condition slowly deteriorated. As the superstructure of a shaken building falls apart, so in his case did body and soul disintegrate. They brought a physician, but his questions evoked nothing but an incoherent jabber about the storm. Finally, the physician dissipated all doubts by explaining that the storm was the cause of his mental disorder. 'But,' he added, 'there's nothing to fear; his is a case of mere idiocy.'

'No, no, doctor, it would be dangerous to keep him in the house, is it not so?' insisted the widow.

At last they sent the boy away. They sent the idiot to his mother's home.

His life had been saved, but his soul had been hopelessly lost in the storm.

TRANSLATED BY MISCHA KUDIAN

Texts

Erkeri žovacu [*Collected Works*] (Minas Hyusyan (ed.), Erevan, 1962).
Novelner [*Novellas*] (Erevan, 1954).

Translations

Ararat (xvii, no. 4, autumn 1976, New York). A quarterly periodical edited by Leo Hamalian. This issue devoted to Siamant'o, Varoužan, Zohrab and R. Zardarian, all writers killed in 1915. Translation of Zohrab's 'The Storm' reproduced with permission.

Manuscript of the poet Daniel Varoužan. *Museum of Literature, Erévan*

DANIEL VAROUŽAN 1884–1915

'The Armenian nation wept and roared in me and my songs spouted forth under a foreign sky tied to our native land and people only by the links of yearning.'

Letter written from exile, 1908

Daniel Daroužan.

On 26 August 1915, Daniel Varoužan became yet another victim of the Armenian genocide. However, his experience of the persecution of his culture and his people began at an early age. Born in a little village near Sebastia on 20 April 1884, he had 'just barely begun to read the breviary at the village school' when he was taken to Constantinople in 1896 during the massacres of the Armenians. There, he searched for his father, and 'in the horror of blood, I found him in prison [in] those sad days, falsely accused.' In 1902, he went to Venice to the Mourad–Raphaelian school, where he discovered the revolutionary ideas of J. J. Rousseau and Tolstoy. Three years later, he was at the University of Ghent in Belgium, studying political science and sociology. The years 1905–8 were difficult ones. He wrote to a friend:

> I bore the most profound personal sufferings in Ghent. But that was the period . . . when the Armenian nation was drowning in the nightmare of sword and famine, and I did not want to give in to my personal sufferings. I almost silenced my heart, and preferred to sing the 'nation's heart', whose throbbings I felt in the depths of my own blood. The Armenian nation wept and roared in me and my songs spouted under a foreign sky, tied to our native land and people only by the links of yearning.

In 1912 he returned to Constantinople where, in 1914, he founded and edited the literary annual *Nawasard*.

Daniel Varoužan lived during one of the most critical periods in Armenian history. The events of 1894–6, reinforced by his father's incarceration and the misery of his displaced compatriots in Constantinople, had a strong impact on his youthful mind. However, in a letter to an intimate friend, Varoužan described his own development thus: 'Two environments have had a great influence on my artistic maturation: Venice with her Titian and Flanders with her Van Dyck. It was the vivid colours of the former and the barbaric realism of the latter that sharpened my senses.'

Although Varoužan's untimely death limited his literary creativity, nevertheless the quantity and quality of his work, the breadth of his outlook and a rare balance of the national and universal have established him as a poet of the first rank. His collection of poems *Sarsoułner* (*Tremors*, 1906) is a celebration of life and a glorification of love; his second book, *C'ełin sirtê* (*The Heart of the Race*, 1910) is the crystallization of the sorrow, of the blood and of the tears of a relentlessly persecuted people. But Varoužan's most famous book *Het'anos erger* (*Pagan Songs*, 1912) offers a variety of poems in which he expresses his universality, his urbanity and his love of 'pagan beauty' as a sharp rebuke to the conservative, retrogressive, prejudiced and bourgeois Istanbul–Armenian community. The langorous description of bathers reclining on the navelstones, the long slabs of marble, in 'Oriental Bath' is an example.

Between the years 1912 and 1915, just before his death, Varoužan prepared for publication an exquisite collection of poems, the last and the loveliest of his creations, *Hac'in ergê* (*Songs of the Bread*, 1921). Within this, Varoužan creates an atmosphere in which the poet exalts and affirms the tormented and the tormenting life of the ruthlessly exploited common man, the poor, landless peasant. It is a greenhouse wherein, like an exotic, perishable plant, our human dignity, quality and charity are revitalized and preserved quietly, as if a leavening for the humanization of the coming generations.

V. NERSESSIAN

Արեւելեան Բաղանիք

Մորճագմբէթ բաղնիքին ներքնադուռն յո՜յլ կը բացուի,
Երեբնոս դո՛ւռն հաստաբեստ՝ որ կը ծեծուի միշտ թակով,
Եւ անընդհատ կը քրտնի, կը ճռնչէ ուժասպառ
Հուրիներուն ետեւէն՝ որոնք դանդա՜ղ կը մտնեն։
Բոլոր մե՛րկ են ու չքնա՛ղ, — թեւերն իրենց ծալլեր են
Լանջքերնուն վրայ հոյաչէն՝ որոնց վրայ կը դիզուին
Կոյտերն իրենց ծիծերուն, պտուկներով թխագեղ։
Սատափազօծ սանդալներն յատակին վրայ կը հնչեն·
Սրտերնուն հեւքն աղուական, ձայներն իրենց քաղցրանոյշ
Բաղնիքէն ներս կը փոխուին անդնդասոյզ զօղանջի·
Աստղերուն պէս՝ լողացող մառախուղին մէջ աղօտ՝
Իրենց աչքերը խոնաւ նշողիւններ կ'արձակեն,
Եւ գոլորշին, իր տամուկ չղարշներով, կը պատէ
Մարմինն իրենց՝ որ պտղիլ կը սկսի ա՛լ քրտինքով։
Հուրիները կը լոգնա՛ն· — Պորտաքարին կիզանուտ
Ոմանք պառկած նուաղկոտ նայուածքներով կ'երազեն։
Լուսացնցուղ գմբէթէն՝ արեւուն շողը ճերմակ
Ներս կը մաղուի՝ մարգարտեայ յորդ անձրեւի մը նման·
Եւ ծփանուտ գոլորշին կը դառնայ ծով մ'արծաթեայ
Ուր լիւղ կու գան կարապներն Արեւելքի Հեշտանքին·
Ըսպածանին՝ որ կպած է զիստերնուն լօռի պէս,
Ա՛լ կը նետուի· մարմինները կը փոխուին արձանի·
Եւ մազերնին, հիւս առ հիւս, ծովերու պէս կը քակեն,
Ուրկէ երբե՛մըն կ'իյնան գոհարներու հատիկներ։
Օ՜, ծամե՜րն այդ, ծամե՜րն այդ, որոնցմով ա՛լ կը ծփայ
Կարծես բաղնիքը ամբողջ· եւ պորտաքարը մարմար
Կը թխանայ անոնց յորդ սեւափրփուր ալիքով։
Գլուխն իրենց կը սանտրեն ոսկեդրուագ սանտրերով
Երկա՜ր, երկա՜ր, մինչեւ ծայրն անծայրածիր մազերուն
Կ'երթան իրենց մատուըները ծեքծեքուն ու դանդաղ
Միշտ լողալով կայծերու մէջ մատնիի անդամանդ։
Անոնք երբե՛մըն կը զգան նուաղումներ, ու երբեմն
Ցանկարծակի կը սարսռան՝ երբ գմբէթէն կը կաթի
Ցուրտ ցօղ մ'իրենց ծոծրակին հեշտագրգիռ փոսին մէջ։
Ահա հարիւր ծորակնե՜րն, ահա մարմար ծորակնե՜րն
Իրար ետեւ կը բացուին՝ աղմկայոյզ կարկաջով·
Մոխիրի պէս գորշ շոգին կը բարձրանայ ծուփ առ ծուփ·
Դատարկ գուռերը բոլոր կենդանութիւն կը ստանան·
Ջուրը կ'յորդի ամէն կողմ, ջուրը կ'երգէ քաղցրահունչ·
Հուրիները կը լոգնա՜ն· — Գուռերուն շուրջ հաւաքուած
Գանովայի՛ Շնորհներ, կարծես իրար կը փարին,
Եւ կը խառնեն ծիծերնին, կը խառնեն ժիր թեւերնին
Եւ սրունքնին պաղպաջուն, եւ պորտերնին կօշարայ՝

ORIENTAL BATH

The inner door of the green-domed bath opens slowly,
And as it grates and sweats all day,
Against its massive ebony frame pound
Heavy pendant pulley weights,
That now swing into a wide, true arc,
Inviting in a cluster of naked houris,
Who drift in, lingeringly, slowly;
All naked, and all surpassing beautiful,
Their arms folded modestly
Across their gleaming breasts, which swell
Over and on to their forearms, breasts darkly starred
With round brown nipples, swaying breasts;
Their wooden sandals, worked in mother of pearl,
Clink sharply on the damp, cool marble floor;
Inside the bath their low melodious voices
And their soft breath turn to muffled bells.
And as the vapour rises within
The bath, like moistened veils clinging
Along their naked bodies, which now start to pearl
With sweat, their eyes glow with a fine warm lustre,
Like brilliant stars seen through a foggy sky.
Houris at their baths! Some, stretched out
On warm navelstones, dream, smiling languorously,
While from the light-spreading dome the sun
Filters through like pearly rain,
Making a lustrous sea of the dense
Silver vapours in which swim these sinuous
Swans, Oriental maidens; and now they cast
Aside the towels that had clung like seaweed
To their thighs – O, their bodies unadorned as statues!
And now their hair, braid on braid, like waves
On a stormy sea, loosened,
And at intervals precious stones escape,
That hair, O, that hair,
The whole bath seems to undulate, darkening
With its raven sway the white and granite
Navelstones. Their hair, they comb their long,
Long hair endlessly down to the tips
With gold-covered combs, while their fingers
Glitter with the sparkle of their diamond rings.
The houris sometimes feel listless and faint,
And sometimes shiver suddenly when, from
The high vaporous dome above, some cold,
Fresh dew falls straight between their breasts.
Behold! the marble founts, the thousand taps
Now bursting one on the other
Tumultuously, as ashen vapours
Rise towards the dome, rise sinuously and slow;
The water overflows on every side
And winds its way to the empty water troughs.
Houris at their baths! Canova's graces
They all seem to be, and as closely twined,
Gathered round the sparkling marble basins.

Ուրկէ մուշկի հատիկներ, տարրալուծուած, կը բուրեն։
Մարմարներուն վրայ նստած զիստերն իրենց կ'ընդլայնին՝
Ու կը խմեն հեշտութիւնն իրենց տակէն սահող ջրին։
Ոսկի թասերը ահա քարերուն վրայ կը հնչեն,
Տօսա՛խ թասերն, որոնք մերթ սիրտերու պէս կը ճայթին՝
Այդ անպատում մերկութեանց ծառայելու ժամանակ։
Կը քրքըրի կաւն ահա, ծոթրինաբոյր կաւը զով,
Ծաղկահիւթով զանգուած՝ զոր մեր նախնիք կ'ուտէին,
Մազերն անով կը ծեփուին, ու կը դառնան ապրշում,
Լանջքերն անով կ'օծանուին, ու կ'ըլլան նման փրփուրի·
Անոր խիւսովը պաղուկ, եւ լպրծուն շաղախով
Կը զովանան հուրիներն, որովայնին կը յղկեն
Գետի խիճին պէս ողորկ ու թաւշօրէն օծանուտ։
Կ'եռան ջուրերն, կը լուան կըրակներն այդ պաշտելի·
Կը փրփրին օճառներն՝ Մաքրութիւններն անգամ մ'ալ
Իրենց մածան լոյսերուն մէջ մաքրելու ի խնդիր։
Ջուրն, որ ամէն կողմանէ, պորտաքարին շուրջն ի վար,
Կ'հոսի կ'երթայ՝ կոյուղին իսկ բուրումով լեցնելու,
Գո՛րշ է կաւով ու կիրով, լեղի կիրով հերաթափ,
Եւ իր ուխին հետ մէկտեղ մերթ կը գլէ կը տանի
Թխակուտակ թնճուկներ, անութներու գանգուրներ,
Եւ խռիներն աղուամազ այդ կիպերեան լուսեղէն
Արձաններուն կենեղուտ՝ որոնք այլեւս ուժաթափ
Կը լեցնեն հուսկ թասերն, թասերը հուսկ կը պարպեն·
Գուռերն հե՛ղ մ'ալ կը յորդին, բաղնիքն հեղ մ'ալ կ'աղմկի,
Ջուրն եռեփուն կը վազէ, հե՛ղ մ'ալ կ'լողան հուրիներն·
Կը բռնկի մորթերնին վարդի մը պէս բոցավառ·
Եւ նուաղուն բիբերով, թասերն՝ իրենց գլուխին,
Կուրծքերնուն վրայ միշտ գրկած դէզերն իրենց ծիծերուն՝
Այլեւըս դուրս կը փութան, շարան շարան, հեւասպառ,
Անգայտացած շոգիով, կակաչներու պէս բոսոր...
Օ՜, գանգուրներն յորդառատ՝ իրենց կուրծքին վրայ մերկ,
Օ՜, գանգուրները խոնաւ, կաթիլներով ծանրացած,
Որոնք բոբիկ ոտքերնուն՝ սատափ ցօղեր կը ծորեն...,
Ի՜նչպէս պատմել ձեր օծումն, ի՜նչպէս պատմել ձեր զարդերն՝
Երբ մարմիննիդ կը սրբէք, եւ կուռքի պէս կը հագուիք...
Թող համբուրեմ մա'տերնիդ՝ զոր դուք այսօր կը թաթխէք
Հինաներու գուշին խորն՝ իբր արիւնոտ սրտի մէջ,
Թող համբուրեմ մազերնիդ՝ կնդրուկներով օծանուտ՝
Որոնք, գիշերը, լուսնին տակ, կը բուրեն բարձին վրայ,
Եւ յօնքերնիդ ծարուրուած, ամպանման թարթիչնիդ,
Եւ լա՛նջքը ձեր՝ որ փաղփուն մանեակներով ոսկեշար
Ամուսնական անկողնին նշողուն ջա'հը կ'ըլլայ·
Թող համբուրեմ պորտը ձեր՝ ուր ծրարած կը ծածկէք
Թէ' Արաբիոյ հաշիշներն եւ թէ' մուշկերն Ափրիկեան։
Ձեր տուներն ա'յժըմ կ'երթաք գոհարներով բեռնաւոր...
Թո'ղ սալարկները Քաղքին ձեր քայլերէն թարմանա՜ն...

They bathe their breasts, their curving limbs and arms,
All their lovely flesh;
And, seated on the navelstones, their thighs
Spread, spread and taste the delightful
Water which glides by and titillates.
Behold! the golden dippers ring across
The stones; the boxwood dippers sometimes break,
Like hearts, in the hands of these lovely nudes;
The argil-cool, thyme-scented clay dissolves
As they stroke it through their flowing waves of hair,
Transforming them to silk; and the clay
Cleans and anoints their breasts, hiding them in foam;
And, with the coolness of the argil's foam,
Its slippery substance, the houris grow refreshed,
They rub their bellies smooth,
Gleaming as sand on a whitened beach.
The water foams and washes pure
These beautiful maidens of Oriental fire.
And now from every side of the navelstones
The water flows down and away,
Rushing away, towards sewer troughs,
And giving even to these a delicate, perfumed scent.
The water is grey, with lime and argil,
And, as it swells, it carries along
Small hair from under their arms, brown twinings from
Hair, downy leavings from these pale, white
And living statues, who now fill
Their final dippers, slowly,
And slowly pour water down their backs.
The steaming water runs, once more the baths
Roar, the troughs are gorged once more,
Once more the houris bathe, and their skins take fire
Like flaming full-blown roses in the sun.
With languid eyes and the dippers raised high
They bathe clean their full, smooth breasts.
In the rare vapour, red as tulips,
Beauty on beauty, the houris leave the bath.
O the luxurious curls slanting on to their breasts,
O those wet curls heavy with water,
With drops that fall as pearls around
Their groomed and dimpled feet; to sing,
O just to sing of their charms and rare perfume,
The glow of their bodies, the sandals, silks and veils!
Those fingers, that today dipped into
The depths of henna bowls, as into a bloody
Heart, let me just kiss them; and let me
Kiss that hair, silked with sweet oils,
Hair that in the night, beneath the moon,
Gives its scent to the down-filled pillows;
O to kiss, to press against my lips
Their aromatic brows, their curving lashes,
Bosoms dazzling with brilliant jewels,
Whose stones illuminate as torches
Around the bridal bed – O but to press
My lips to their navels, where deeply concealed,
Rests Arabian hashish
And Afric musk! Now bound homeward, and burdened,

Ցուրտը խածնէ՛ թուշերնիդ, ու այտերնիդ բոսորէ՛։
Վարշամակէ՛ն ձեր տամուկ, քղանցքներէ՛ն ծփծփուն
Արտաբուրէ՛ եւ յորդի՛ լոգանքին հոտը ծոթրին·
Եւ լեցընէ գռեհներն, հրապարա՛կն եւ ուղի՛ն·
Աւելցած մասն այն հացին՝ զոր դուք բաղնիք կը տանիք,
Ջոր թասին մէջ կը դնէք, եւ կը ծածկէք ղենջակով,
Թող արձակէ՛ բուրումն իր՝ տարաշխարհիկ համեմով,
Ջի այն ատեն փողոցներն Արեւելեան Քաղաքին
Պիտի զգան թէ Մայիսն հետքերնուդ վրա՛յ կը ծաղկի,
Եւ թարմացած մայթերէն Գարո՛ւն, Գարո՛ւնը կ՚անցնի։ —

So prettily, with precious stones and rare jewels,
Lightly scented with oils and thyme
Whose fragrance clouds their paths,
The city squares, scents the leavings in
Luncheon baskets, and trails its perfumes deep
Inside the folds of undulating skirts –
Now bound homeward they go their different ways,
The cold slapping their cheeks red,
The pavement echoing the sound of their footfalls,
Perfumed footsteps on Orient streets;
And tracing footprints tender as flowers, as blooms
Of May, will make the streets themselves think
That spring, the soul of spring is passing by.

TRANSLATED BY ARAM TOLEGIAN

Առկայծ Ճրագ

Ցաղթանակի գիշերն է այս տօնական· —
Հա՛րս, եղ լեցուր ճրագին։
Պիտի դառնայ կռիւէն տղաս յաղթական· —
Հա՛րս, քիթը ա՛ռ պատրոյգին։

Սայլ մը կեցաւ դրան առջեւ, հորին քով· —
Հա՛րս, վառէ՛ լոյսը ճրագին։
Տղաս կու գայ ճակատն հպարտ դափնիով· —
Հա՛րս, բե՛ր ճըրագը շեմին։

Բայց... սայլին վրայ արի՞ւն եւ սո՞ւգ բեռցեր են...
Հա՛րս, ճրագդ ասդի՛ն երկարէ։
Հերոս տղաս հոն զարնուա՛ծ է սրտէն· —
Ա՛խ, հա՛րս, ճրագդ մարէ՛...

THE FLICKERING LAMP

This is a night for feast and triumph,
Pour oil into the lamp, O Bride,
My boy returns a victor from war –
Trim well, trim well the wick, O Bride.

A waggon stops before the door, beside the well,
Light up, light up the lamp, O Bride,
My boy returns, bay leaves on his brow –
Bring up, bring up the lamp, O Bride.

Lo – with grief and blood the waggon's laden –
Hold up, hold up the lamp, O Bride.
Here lies my valiant son shot through the heart –
O . . . snuff out, snuff out the lamp, O Bride.

TRANSLATED BY ARAM TOLEGIAN

SIAMANT'O 1878–1915

'What a cursèd, what a blood-soaked country; within which even the core of the sun appears bleak and bloody, like a dagger-stabbed eye.'

The third victim among the 761 Armenian intellectuals massacred in 1915 was the poet of protest and rebellion, Siamant'o. Born Atom Earčanian on 1 January 1878 in Akn, near Xarberd, he was educated in Istanbul and at the Sorbonne in Paris (1897–1900), and travelled widely in France, England and the United States. The change in the political scene in his native land – the Second Ottoman Constitution – brought him back in 1908. A year after the Adana massacres of 1909, Siamant'o moved to Boston, and spent a year there as editor of the Armenian paper *Hayrenik'* (*Homeland*), urging Armenians to go back to their homeland because of the apparent dawn of a new era. He himself also returned and as a result, was one of the first to lose his life in 1915.

His works are collected in five books: *Diwc'aznōrēn* (*Triumphantly*, 1901); *Hogevark'i ew yoysi ǰaher* (*Torches of Despair and Hope*, 1907); *Karmir lourer barekamēs* (*Bloody News from My Friend*, 1909), written shortly after, and under the impact of the massacres of Adana; *Hayreni hrawer* (*Call of the Earth*, 1910); and *Sourb Mesrop* (*Saint Mesrob*), considered his masterpiece and written in 1913 on the occasion of the 1500th anniversary of the invention of the Armenian alphabet.

The extremely sensitive Siamant'o weeps over the destruction of his homeland and the suffering of his people, especially during the period from 1890 to 1909. His verses are pessimistic – 'Human justice – I spit on your face' – and he calls upon the Armenians to rebel as did the heroes of the past, confident in achieving victory. This is how Siamant'o describes the climate in which he was destined to live:

> . . . What a cursèd, what a blood-soaked country;
> wherein even the core of the sun appears bleak and
> bloody,
> Like a dagger-stabbed eye.

V. NERSESSIAN

Texts for Varoužan and Siamant'o

Daniel Varoužan, *Erkeri žovacu erek' hatorov* (Erevan, 1986). Complete works in 3 vols.

Daniel Varoužan and Siamant'o, *Erker* (H. Rštouni (ed.), Erevan, 1979). Complete works.

Translations

Aram Tolegian, *Armenian Poetry Old and New* (Wayne State University Press, Detroit, 1979). A bilingual anthology. Translations of 'Oriental Bath', 'The Flickering Lamp' and 'A Handful of Ash' reproduced with permission.

Diana Der Hovanessian and M. Margossian, *Anthology of Armenian Poetry* (Columbia University Press, 1978). The translations of Varoužan and Siamant'o are rather free.

James Etmekjian, *An Anthology of Western Armenian Literature* (Caravan Books, Delmar, 1980).

Secondary sources

D. Varoužan, *Banaste tcout'younner* (Erevan, 1955). Poems compiled and annotated by S. Taronac'i.

Ափ մը Մոխիր, Հայրենի Տուն...

Ա

Աւա՜ղ, ապարանքի մը պէս մեծ էիր եւ շքեղ,
Ու ես՝ երդիքներուդ սպիտակ կատարէն,
Աստղածորան գիշերներու լոյսին հետ,
Վարէն, ահեղավազ Եփրատին կ'ունկնդրէի...։

Բ

Արցունքո՜վ, արցունքո՜վ լսեցի որ աւերակ առ աւերակ
Քու լայնանիստ պատերդ իրարու վրայ կործանեցին,
Սարսափի օր մը, կոտորածի օր մը, օր մը արիւնի...
Զքեզ եզերող պարտէզիդ ծաղկըներուն վրայ։

Գ

Ու մոխրացա՞ւ այն սենեակը կապոյտ,
Որուն որմերուն ետեւ եւ գորգերուն վրայ
Իմ երջանիկ մանկութիւնս կը հրճուէր,
Եւ կեանքս կ'աճէր եւ հոգիս իր թեւերը կ'առնէր...

Դ

Փշրեցա՞ւ, ուրեմն, այն հայելին ոսկեծիր,
Որուն եթերային խորութեանը մէջ,
Երազներս, յոյսերս, սէրերս եւ կամքս կարմիր,
Տարիներով, մտածումիս հետ, ցոլացին...։

Ե

Ու բակին մէջ երգող աղբիւրը մեռա՞ւ,
Ու կոտրտեցա՞ն պարտէզիս ուռին եւ թթենին.
Եւ այն առուակը որ ծառերուն մէջէն կը հոսէր,
Ցամքեցա՞ւ, ըսէ՛, ո՞ւր է, ցամքեցա՞ւ, ցամքեցա՞ւ...

Զ

Օ՛, այն վանդակին կ'երազեմ յաճախ,
Որուն մէջ գորշագոյն կաքաւս, առաւօտուն,
Արեւածագին հետ եւ վարդի թուփերուն դիմաց,
Զարթնումի ժամուս՝ յստակօրէն կը կարգաճէր...։

A HANDFUL OF ASH

[*a*]

Alas, you were a great and beautiful mansion,
And from the white summit of your roof,
Filled with star-flooded night hopes,
I listened to the Euphrates, racing below.

[*b*]

I learned with tears, with tears I learned of the ruins,
Of your broad walls battered down, stone by stone,
On to your fragile border of flowers in the garden . . .
On a terror-filled day, a day of slaughter, of blood.

[*c*]

And charred is the blue room
Inside whose walls, on whose rugs
My childhood delighted,
And where my life grew, where my soul grew.

[*d*]

That gold-framed mirror is shattered, too,
In whose silver depth my dreams,
My hopes, my loves and my burning will
Stood reflected for years, and my musings.

[*e*]

And in the garden the spring song is dead,
The mulberry and the willow there, they have been
blasted, too,
And the brook that flowed between the trees –
Has it gone dry? Tell me, where is it? Has it gone dry?

[*f*]

O I often dream of the cage
From which my grey partridge, mornings
And at sunrise, fronting the rose trees,
Would rise, as I did, and start its own distinct cooing.

Է

Հայրենի՛ տուն, հաւատա՛ որ մահէս յետոյ,
Քու աւերակներուդ սեւին վայ իմ հոգիս
Պիտի գայ, որպէս տատրակ մը տարագիր,
Իր դժբախտի երգն եւ արցունքը լալու...:

Ը

Բայց ո՛վ պիտի բերէ, ո՛վ պիտի բերէ, ըսէ՛,
Քու սրբազան մոխիրէդ ափ մը մոխիր,
Մահուանս օրը, իմ տրտում դագաղիս մէջ,
Հայրենիքս երգողի իմ աճիւնին խառնելու...

Թ

Ափ մը մոխի՛ր աճիւնիս հետ, Հայրենի տուն,
Ափ մը մոխի՛ր քու մոխիրէդ, ո՛վ պիտի բերէ,
Քու յիշատակէ՛դ, քու ցաւէ՛դ, քու անցեալէ՛դ,
Ափ մը մոխիր... իմ սրտիս վրան ցանելու...:

[*g*]

O my homeland, promise that after my death
A handful of your holy ashes
Will come to rest, like an exiled turtledove,
To chant its song of sorrow and tears.

[*h*]

But who will bring, tell me, who is to bring
A handful of your precious ashes,
On the day of my death, to put into my dark coffin
And mingle with my ashes, ashes of a singer of the
homeland?

[*i*]

A handful of ash with my remains, my native home –
Who is to bring a handful of ash from your ashes,
From your sorrow, your memories, your past;
A handful of ash to scatter on my heart?

TRANSLATED BY ARAM TOLEGIAN

CONCLUSION

This war will shake up each individual, will shake up the masses, will shake up humanity. Out of the million deaths will emerge life. Feeling and intellect will be renewed and reborn, words will gain wings.

Editorial from the Hungarian journal
A Tett (*Action*), 1915

By November 11th, 1918, when the combatants in the West laid down their arms, the men commemorated in this volume were all dead, victims of an unprecedented bloodletting that had taken between ten and thirteen million lives. Yet if the Armistice freed the survivors from the service of arms, it by no means freed their minds from the consciousness of war. 'I didn't know,' the Italian writer Curzio Malaparte wrote bitterly, 'that a war has no end for those who fought it.'

Nor was the impact of the war confined to combatants. Those too old or of the wrong sex would spend the rest of their lives under the war's cloud, mourning their missing loved ones or caring for the maimed; those too young to have fought would internalize the war's passions and cultivate its myths. Indeed, no war in modern history has exercised a greater fascination on succeeding generations. Even today when the great majority of the participants have disappeared, the war's memory persists in a myriad of forms and the intensity of this memory shows few signs of fading. If we want to understand why this is so, we must begin by asking what the war meant to those who experienced it most directly, the combatants of 1914-1918.

THE EXPERIENCE OF WAR

I like its [the Army's] manliness, the courage it demands, the fellowship it gives. These are infinitely precious things. But I hate the machine — the thing as a whole and its duty (to kill), its very existence.

Herbert Read, 1918

The poetry that was written during the war, the flood of memoirs, novels and films that came later in the 1920s and 1930s, the documentaries that flash across our television screens – all these have seared into our collective historical memory unforgettable images of mass and senseless destruction whose horror is strangely wedded with romance and nostalgia. No war had ever been fought like this before; no war would ever be fought like this again. Trench-warfare, as it developed on the Western Front in 1914-1915, forced millions of men to take refuge underground where, leaving their pre-war selves behind, they improvised new forms of existence. The war literature shows us how war consumed these men, degraded them, brutalized them, flattened their sense of time, faded their memory of family and loved ones, and transformed them, as Ernst Toller recalled, into 'cogs in a great machine which sometimes rolled forward, nobody knew where, sometimes backward, nobody knew why. . .'

Life in the trenches was dull, monotonous, and dangerous, a strange combination of tedium and horror. The boredom of the trench routine was in some ways worse than the perils of offensive action. While waiting to be ordered 'over the top', trench-soldiers endured eternities of immobility under conditions that shattered the nerves, broke the spirit, deadened the mind, and unleashed every instinct that pre-war civilization had sought to contain. Henri Barbusse, one of the first novelists to explore this subterranean world and expose it to the civilian public, claimed that he had found in its denizens 'wickedness to the point of sadism, egoism to the point of ferocity, the need for pleasure to the point of madness'.

Trench-soldiers lived in 'shrivelling fear' and staggered on, in Peter Baum's poetic phrase, 'attracted magnetically by Death'. The forms death took were usually dehumanized and anonymous, metal projectiles fired by an unseen hand. It was not so much the idea of being killed that was so alarming, T.E. Hulme wrote describing an artillery barrage, '. . . but the idea of being hit by a jagged piece of steel. You hear the whistle of the shell coming, you crouch down as low as you can, and just wait. It doesn't burst merely with a bang, it has a kind of crack with a snap in it, like the crack of a very large whip.' It was not a sound one got used to. Hulme noticed that even the most hardened of regulars collapsed under heavy bombardment. 'One man threw himself down on the bottom of the trench shaking all over and crying. Another started to weep. It lasted for nearly one and a half hours and at the end of it parts of the trenches were all blown to pieces.' The poet Wilfred Owen confessed to his mother that, after being exposed to such shelling continously for fifty hours, 'I nearly broke down and let myself drown in the water that was now slowly rising over my knees.'

Apollinaire assisting in a military barrage, 1915

The war experience, then, was terrifying, dehumanizing, demeaning and in sharp and ironic contrast to the heroic images of war that had circulated before 1914 and that continued to be current behind the lines. 'Glory', a word much in favour with civilians, was hard to come by on the Western Front, unless one was lucky enough to be admitted to the air arm – and once admitted, talented or lucky enough to survive. For the infantrymen, however, war was more like work than combat. 'This magnificent wild beast that we used to imagine,' Paul Reynal's *poilu* explains to his disbelieving and disapproving father in his 1924 play *The Tomb under the Arch of Triumph*, 'is above all a muddy beast of burden.' How strange it was for the young idealists of 1914 to discover that serving in the infantry was essentially a sentence to hard labour.

Yet even in the midst of this industrialized hell, intellectuals and artists discovered values they admired. Among these were manliness and comradeship, the two so closely connected in writings about the war that they can only with great difficulty be separated. Witness the modernist writer Richard Aldington, who cannot be suspected of any underlying love of war or sympathy for those who willed it or defended its necessity. Once at the front, the protagonist of his 1929 novel *Death of a Hero*, George Winterbourne, '. . . hated the war as much as ever, hated all the blather about it, profoundly mistrusted the motives of the war partisans, and hated the Army.'

> But he liked the soldiers, the War soldiers, not as soldiers but as men. He respected them . . . He was with them . . . With them, because they were men with fine qualities, because they had endured great hardships and dangers with simplicity, because they had parried their handicaps and dangers not by hating the men who were supposed to be their enemies, but by developing a comradeship among themselves. They had every excuse for turning into brutes, and they hadn't done it. True, they were degenerating in certain ways, they were getting coarse and rough and a bit animal, but with amazing simplicity and unpretentiousness they had retained and developed a certain essential humanity and manhood. With them, then, to the end, because of their manhood and humanity. With them, too, because their manhood and humanity existed in spite of the war and not because of it. They had saved something from a gigantic wreck and what they had saved was immensely important – manhood and comradeship, their essential integrity as men, their essential brotherhood as men.

In a society whose members lived walled off from one another in tightly-sealed classes, the discovery of comradeship could be exhilarating. So too could the submergence of the self into a tightly-disciplined mass. For many young soldiers, the nation came to take on a new and more concrete meaning. As a French soldier, Marc Boasson, noted in a letter:

> The war is breaking us, but it is also reforging us. Thanks to it, the virtues necessary for national life are being rediscovered and are once more being put into practice. Will they survive the war? Perhaps. In any case, we are witnessing, we are reliving the subordination of the individual to the whole, the rule of the national interest and its domination over petty individual selfishness. A single and strong authority, the re-established unity of wills.

Yet one did not have to be a nationalist to feel the attraction of the front. Many combatants felt that they had shed their pre-war personalities, seen through the superficiality of bourgeois conventions, and gained a rare glimpse of the deepest realities of human existence. Pierre Teilhard de Chardin, priest, stretcher-bearer and intellectual, who spend four years under arms, sought to explain these feelings to a female cousin in September 1917:

> The front cannot but attract us, because it is, in one way, the *extreme boundary* between what you are already aware of, and what is still in the process of formation. Not only do you see there things that you experience nowhere else, but you also see emerge from within yourself an underlying stream of clarity, energy and freedom that is to be found hardly anywhere else in ordinary life – and the new form that the soul then takes on is that of the individual living the quasi-collective life of all men, fulfilling a function far higher than that of the individual, and becoming fully conscious of this new state. It goes without saying that at the front you no longer look at things in the same way as you do in the rear; if you did, the sights you see and the life you lead would be more than you could bear. This exaltation is accompanied by a certain pain. Nevertheless it is indeed an exaltation. And that's why one likes the front in spite of everything and misses it.

UNDERSTANDING THE WAR

> *After the Charleroi affair*
> *And since we waved the Marne goodbye,*
> *I drag my carcass everywhere,*
> *But never know the reason why.*
>
> Marc de Larreguy de Civrieux

Thus though it is correct and necessary to emphasize, as so much of the war literature of the late 1920s and early 1930s did, the terrible disillusionment suffered by the enthusiastic volunteers and conscripts of 1914-1915, it is also — and equally — true that the war was experienced by many intellectuals as a privilege, a rite of passage, and a revelation of mysteries and emotions not available to men in times of peace. Despite the stilted rhetoric and the echoes of stentorian Victorian verse, these lines of the American Alan Seeger, inspired by his experiences in the bloody battles on the Aisne river in 1914-1915, expressed what many felt:

> There we drained deeper the deep cup of life,
> And on sublimer summits came to learn,
> After soft things, the terrible and stern,
> After sweet Love, the majesty of Strife.

Yet whereas many might feel, like Seeger, that on Europe's battlefields they had 'found for all dear things I forfeited/ A recompense I would not now forgo', those who fought the war, even those most well educated and intellectually inclined, often found it difficult to explain to others or themselves why they were there, suffering and dying. The official reasons given for the war seldom had much purchase on the minds of the front soldiers. Indeed, if we are to believe the testimony of the war literature – and many of the texts that appear in this volume – the men in the trenches developed a sense of identification with their adversaries and suspected increasingly, as the war progressed, that they were the dupes of scheming politicians, inept generals and profiteering industrialists.

Scepticism about official war aims in no way meant that soldiers were unwilling to fight. With amazingly few exceptions, given the length and casualty rates of the war and the apparent futility of many of its major battles, they did what they were told to do. They learned to kill and put themselves at risk when ordered into combat. Roland Dorgelès, author of one of the most famous French war novels *The Wooden Crosses*, thought that Edmond Adam's poem 'Gamecocks' caught exactly the mood of the French *poilus*:

> And we'll do as brave gamecocks do, when
> they're thrown into the pit at one another,
> and unflinchingly, heroically
> and ruthlessly fight,
> till they drop and die at nightfall of their wounds,

roared on and clapped by an ecstatic crowd,
for the glory, but the ruin too,
alas,
of unpardonable masters.

Adam's verses capture the combination of feelings typical of French trench soldiers in the later stages of the war: resigned acceptance of a tragic and uncomprehended fate; pride in their ability to fight 'unflinchingly, heroically and ruthlessly . . . till they drop and die at nightfall of their wounds'; anger at the 'ecstatic crowd' at home that cheers them on and applauds the carnage; suspicion that they are fighting for the glory of 'unpardonable masters'; and a veiled threat that the war will bring about their masters' ruin.

Fused with the theme of generational conflict so omnipresent in European culture before the war, such emotions could easily give rise to the suspicion that the war was a plot of the Old Generation against the Young; for was it not true that the fathers of the generations of 1914 were those who had made the decisions that sent the youth of Europe to the slaughter? And was it not also so that the most fervent spokesman for a struggle to the bitter end were to be found, like Maurice Barrès, among the generation of the fathers? Wilfred Owen worked these suspicions into verses that go far to explain the generational tensions of the postwar period:

When lo! an Angel called him out of heaven,
Saying, Lay not thy hand upon the lad,
Neither do anything to him. Behold,
A ram caught, in a thicket by its horns;
Offer the Ram of Pride instead of him.
But the old man would not so, but slew his son,
And half the seed of Europe, one by one.

It was but one short step from sentiments like these to the threats of Gabriel Tristan Franconi who warned that the ghosts of the fallen heroes would come back to rise against the civilian shirkers in the cities; and that 'those who know no gratitude or have grown rich on the War will learn to dread the sight of young veterans who have lost everything in this enormous conflict . . .' They would return, he predicted, ' . . . to swell and organize the ranks of the vagabond army of the Fifth Estate and to endow it with unconquerable militancy and strength.' Though not true of Franconi's own country France, this turned out to be an amazingly accurate vision of what would happen in Italy and Germany.

Anger was an understandable reaction to the front experience, and Franconi was not alone in dreaming that the dead would some day rise to haunt the living and demand atonement from those politicians, speculators and shirkers who had benefited from the sacrifices of the front fighters. But there were also those who took a more detached view of the war's meaning. Some thought, like the Breton poet Jean-Pierre Calloc'h, that the enormous loss of life was a precondition for spiritual renewal. 'The seed must die if it is to spring up and thrive. I see the bodies of my brothers like seeds in the earth: on their ashes wonderful fruit shall thrive.' Others believed, like Walter Flex's friend Ernst Wurche, that it was '. . . God's will that ageing life should become young again in the eternal youthfulness of death'. Out of death would come life. Such thoughts consoled Flex when Wurche died and gave him the mental strength to return to the front where he was killed in October 1917. On the day he died he wrote a letter reaffirming his unshakeable faith that '. . . everything that happens and can happen to me is part of a living development over which nothing dead has any power.' To the end, Flex was convinced 'that the best of our men have not died in order that the living die, but that the dead live. Are there not too many dead among our living'.

Such optimistic and serene visions of the war were rare among those who have left records of their thoughts, as were the sophisticated arguments of the Englishman T. E. Hulme, who held that there were times when 'great and useless sacrifices' may be necessary to prevent an evil like the German domination of Europe. 'These sacrifices,' Hulme wrote in opposition to the pacifism of Bertrand Russel, 'are as negative, barren, and as *necessary* as the work of those who repair sea-walls. In this war, then, we are fighting for no great *liberation* of mankind, for no great jump upward, but are merely accomplishing a work, which, if the nature of things were ultimately "good" would be useless, but which in this actual "vale of tears" becomes from time to time necessary, merely in order that bad may not get worse.'

Few combatants would have been able to muster Hulme's detachment. Few also would have had such a vivid sense of what German 'hegemony' over Europe would mean. Most acknowledged their inability to understand the huge and inscrutable historical event that had swept them up in its maelstrom and that might snuff out their life at any moment. They ascribed it to the will of God, or the 'giant, unseen hand of fate', and they tried, like Edward Thomas, to reconcile their lack of hatred for their enemy with their duty to do everything they could to kill him. Thomas cared nothing for the kind of patriotism being trumpeted daily in the press, nor for the official reasons given for the war:

I hate not Germans, nor grow hot
With love of Englishmen, to please newspapers
Beside my hate for one fat patriot
My hatred of the Kaiser is love true . . .

But England was in danger and, right or wrong in the judgment of future historians:

She is all we know and live by, and we trust
She is good and must endure, loving her so:
And as we love ourselves we hate her foe.

Combatants differed greatly, therefore, in their attempts to make sense out of the war. But there was one idea on which a notable number of them seemed to agree: that the best, the bravest, the noblest, and the purest of heart and spirit had been the ones who died. Given the nature of the war and the role played in it by conscripted troops, this conviction may at first seem surprising. Death often struck at random; and in the later stages of trench warfare, chivalric gestures were frowned upon by troops intent on staying alive. Indeed, one of the most demoralizing discoveries soldiers made upon arriving at the front was that lives were being lost and bodies mutilated in actions that had no apparent purpose. And yet against the evidence of common sense, the idea took root that it was primarily the 'élite souls' that had perished.

Perhaps such thoughts were inevitable. Survivors of the war could not help but wonder why they had been spared. They might suspect, like the German poet Walther Heymann '. . . that those who fell in battle were the best we had'. Yet whatever its origins, this idea would have important cultural consequences. Many survivors returned from the war obsessed by the conviction that they must bear witness for their dead comrades and fulfil the missions which their friends would otherwise have performed. Others were demoralized by the disparity they perceived between the talents and grandeur of the fallen and the moral shortcomings of the pygmies (like themselves) who had survived. In England especially, the idea of a 'lost generation' and a 'missing élite' became a favoured way of accounting for a disappointing history in the circumstances of the 1920s and 1930s when people perceived their lives and the society in which they lived as running downhill. Beginning in the early 1950s, the English writer Henry Williamson spent almost twenty years in a desperate venture to capture the war experience, make sense of it, and place it in a context of English and general European decline. His fifteen-volume saga, *A Chronicle of Ancient Sunlight*, is, with all its defects, the best guide we have to the contradictory feelings inspired by the war and also to the extraordinary difficulty combatants had in comprehending and putting behind them the war experience.

IMPACTS OF WAR ON EUROPEAN CULTURE

The storm has just ended but nonetheless we are worried and anxious, as if the storm were about to break. Almost all human things remain in a state of terrible uncertainty. We reflect on what has disappeared, we are almost destroyed by what has been destroyed; we do not know what is going to come into being, and we have every reason to fear it. We hope vaguely; we fear precisely; our fears are infinitely more precise than our hopes. We confess that the sweetness of life is behind us, that abundance is behind us, but disarray and doubt are in us and with us.

Paul Valéry, 1922

One effect of the war was to provide people with a new way of thinking about their history. After the Armistice, members of the generations of 1914 would divide their lives into a *before*, a *during*, and an *after*; and it became stylish among historians to say that the 20th century had actually begun in 1914. The period before the war could now be looked at with nostalgia as a *belle époque* when life was sweet, worry-free, and easy; and everything unpleasant that happened after 1918 could be accounted for plausibly as a consequence of four years of unprecedented destruction. 'But what an epoch!' Paul Valéry exclaimed in a letter to the Belgian symbolist writer Albert Mockel in May 1918. 'Our generation has had such a strange fate: there never were intellectual intoxications more powerful or more varied than those we knew thirty years ago! . . . and here we are confronted with a catastrophe of indefinite proportions . . .'

No one doubts the impact of the war on the lives of those who lived through it. But today historians are more cautious when assessing the effects of the war on those long-term developments that were transforming the way people were governed, the way they produced goods, the way they used and viewed technology, the way they related to one another in the international arena – in short, the ways they organized their public and private lives. Similar caution also has to be observed when assessing the impact of the war on culture because, like Paul Valéry in 1918, today we perceive connections between pre-war 'intellectual intoxications' and what came after 1918.

Between 1914 and 1918, European intellectuals differed greatly in their expectations of the effects the war would have on culture. Some thought that it would transform and reinvigorate European art and literature. 'Out of the million deaths will emerge life. Feeling and intellect will be renewed and reborn, words will gain wings,' wrote the Hungarian avant-garde jounal *A Tett* (Action) in 1915. Others believed exactly the opposite: they feared that the war would destroy spirit and deaden sensibility. 'Our war,' lamented Gerrit Engelke, is 'lacking in a soul ... War is the negation or at least the undermining of the spiritual, and the furthering of the power of the material world.' Still others, like Renato Serra, warned that war would have no significant effect on culture. 'War is a fact like so many others in this world, just one fact, though an immense one, alongside the others, which have been or are to be. It adds nothing, it takes nothing away. It doesn't change a single thing in the world. Not even literature.' Who among these intellectuals was right?

Viewed from our perspective today, this question does not lend itself to any easy or uncomplicated answers. In the short term, the war dealt a further blow to the official 'bourgeois' culture that was coming under heavy attack during the years before 1914. The institutional bulwarks of that culture – the academies, the scientific institutes, the universities, the schools, the churches – along with its most illustrious representatives, all mobilized themselves to justify their country's actions and to vilify the enemy's. Since no government dared to reveal to its citizens or its armed forces the truth about the progress, costs and realistic prospects of the war, all engaged in a wilful programme of disinformation whose most revolting aspect, from the combatants' point of view, was the translation of the mass and technological slaughter of the battlefronts into a discourse of individual and heroic achievement. Abused in this way, some of the most important concepts of official culture were discredited. Words like 'duty', 'honour', 'glory', and 'democracy', took on double and sinister meanings in the minds of men at the front. Henri Barbusse insisted that: 'The most beautiful words were soiled through such use; and the word 'victory' itself was drummed into us in such a disgusting way that even now (in 1920), we cannot hear it without a feeling of nausea.' Sources as varied as poems, letters and trench newspapers all testify to the disdain, anger and even hate with which front soldiers viewed the products of official culture during the war. Only on the home front was death in combat represented as beautiful or fulfilling. Front soldiers knew better.

The reaction against official culture should have strengthened the adversary culture, modernism, and in many respects it did. The Dadaist movements of 1917–1921 rose in violent reaction against the lies and cultural products of official culture. In their manifestos, their poetry, their paintings, their sculpture and their spectacles, the Dadaists called into question every feature the official culture said a work of art was supposed to have: its seriousness, its coherence, its relationship to the past, even its beauty. Dadaist art was irreverent, incomprehensible, aggressively antagonistic and wilfully ugly.

The war also buttressed modernist culture by confirming and validating its central idea of a cultural rupture or break. Earlier modernist movements had been inspired by the intuition that the old culture was exhausted and that a new culture was coming into being to take its place. The new culture, modernists believed, would be perspectivist in its approach to truth; it would reform the role of reason by revealing the power of subjectivity, imagination, emotion, and irrational drives; and it would replace the concept of a determined and lawfully-governed universe with a vision that gave greater scope for the enjoyment of freedom and the manifestation of individual and collective will.

There were ample signs of cultural renewal before 1914; but they were limited to small circles of intellectuals and artists, and seemed to have little effect on the society as a whole or the way that people lived their lives. The more modernist art and literature diverged from the norms of official culture, the more alienated its makers became from the communities in which they lived. Then came the cataclysm of the war. Small wonder that so many intellectuals interpreted its outbreak as a sign that the cultural and social stalemate had at last been broken. As the carefully segregated classes of pre-war Europe marched together, fought together, worked together, and suffered and died together, it appeared unlikely that the old structures of European life could ever be restored.

At the same time, no one could predict what lay ahead. The tree of European Progress that had seemed so vital and sturdy in 1900 had snapped and broken. The notion of a history that took the form of regular and lawful evolution could no longer convincingly be sustained. The war was a powerful lesson in discontinuity, in perspectivism, and in the limitations of reason. With every nation proclaiming its own truth, and with civilized and humanitarian values unable to prevail over those forces driving Europeans toward mutual destruction, the way seemed open for the European avant-gardes to declare the bankruptcy of their adversaries and to sweep an internally weakened official culture from the scene.

The war thus created a climate within which modernism could flourish; and the twenties witnessed a rapid diffusion and vulgarization of some of the most radical ideas of the pre-war period. The relativity of truth, the subjectivity of time and space, the blurring of the distinction between dreams and reality, the elevation of instinct and unconscious impulses over reason, the rejection of moral codes as repressive and unhealthy – all these conceptions, and many more, burst through the floodgates opened by the earthquake of the war. Sensing victory, modernist art, music and literature now began to assemble its own canon and establish its hierarchy of masterpieces. The poetry of Eliot and Pound, the novels of Proust, Joyce and Mann, the paintings of Picasso and Kandinsky, the music of Schoenberg and Stravinsky, found many champions, especially among the younger members of the generation of 1914. Surrealism, a further development of the French wing of Dadaism, even came close to enjoying a brief moment of cultural hegemony in the Paris of the late 1920s.

But though the war did much to strengthen modernist culture and to create a climate favourable to its diffusion, it also had the effective of depriving it of much of its spirit of youth, optimism and vitality. If it were true that modernist culture was explicitly grounded in the idea of radical discontinuity, it was also indisputable that implicit in the modernist project was the belief that the new culture would not only be more honest and less repressed but also higher, richer, and more fulfilling than the one that had preceded it. But after 1918 who could claim with any certainty that the European culture of the future would necessarily be more organic or more vital than the European culture of the past? On the contrary, many agreed with Oswald Spengler that Western culture had exhausted its creative energies and entered a downward spiral that would lead toward irremediable decline; and even cautious optimists, like Ortega y Gasset, believed that the war had exposed the precariousness, superficiality, and vulnerability of what most Europeans had regarded in 1900 as the most stable and advanced of civilizations. We Europeans, Valéry wrote in a famous essay in 1919, now know that '. . . we are mortal'. This may explain why, already in the 1920s but even more so in the succeeding decade, many intellectuals and artists drew back from the experiments in formal innovation that had been such an important aspect of pre-war modernism and began to gravitate towards more traditional and even classical models of artistic creation.

In attempting to assess the impact of the war on culture, however, it would be a mistake to focus solely or even primarily on the conflicts and interactions of official and modernist culture; for surely the most important *cultural* development of the years after 1914 was the creation of a mass market for new types of cultural products made possible by technological innovation. Mass culture in the form of newspapers, magazines, comic books, films, and later television, displayed an extraordinary capacity to absorb the themes and techniques of official, folk, and modernist culture, to adapt them to its own uses and clientele, and to package the results in ways that appealed to thousands and millions of people. Mass culture offered new opportunities and new publics to intellectuals and artists. But in return for extended influence, greater financial rewards, and higher social status, they paid a heavy price. Increasingly after 1918, the intellectual and the artist became agents of parties, state bureaucracies and corporations. Also by the late 1920s the dialectic of revolution and counter-revolution had reached a point where even the modernist avant-garde was coming under pressure to make political commitments. The closing pincers of politicization and commercialization made it more and more difficult for artists to maintain their independence. In 1927, the Frenchman Julien Benda denounced these developments in *The Treason of the Intellectuals*; but ten years later the organization of political hatreds by intellectuals, and the constraints of the market place on cultural production, had gone far beyond Benda's worst fears when he originally published his book. The Nazi campaign against decadent art, the installation of Socialist Realism in Soviet Russia, and the mobilization of American and European intellectuals and artists for or against the Spanish Republic were all disturbing signs, indicating that the era of modernist avant-garde was drawing to an end.

Did the war contribute in any way to the rise of mass culture and to the commercialization and politicization of the intellectuals? Certainly, it did not set these processes under way. Technological innovation and the creation of ever greater national and international markets were their preconditions. Once in motion, the spread of literacy, the use of national languages, rising standards of living, increases in leisure time, and escalating domestic and international antagonisms were the forces that drove these processes forward. To the extent that the war uprooted people, grouped them together into masses, liberated them from former constraints and customs, exacerbated social and national tensions and antagonisms, it accelerated the formation of a mass culture and the politicization of intellectual life. But these developments would have occurred even if there had been no war.

This, however, is to take the long view, a luxury we can afford today but one that was not available to the generations of 1914. During the two decades that followed the Armistice, the memory of the war obsessed the consciousness of millions of Europeans. Its vestiges were everywhere to see: in the mutilated veterans who begged in city streets; in the scrolls of fallen soldiers and the monuments that were to be found in every European town and village; in the museums created to commemorate the war; in the cemeteries, ossuaries and places of remembrance that dotted every nation's countryside. The war entered into language and helped to shape a politics of 'positions', 'fronts', 'offensive', and 'battles to the bitter end'. How did it affect sensibility? Some, like Herbert Read, no doubt walked away from it determined to wage war on war. But others wrote and spoke of the war with exaltation and nostalgia. Had the war numbed respect for individual human life and accustomed Europeans to accept mass death in the name of abstract political principles? Was it the necessary prelude to the Holocaust? These questions are as important to ask as they are impossible to answer. Still, one cannot help being struck by the fact that the man who plunged Europe into war in 1939 and carried her to the verge of self-destruction, as well as many of his closest lieutenants and followers, was a veteran of the trenches and a member of the generation of 1914. Hitler liked to say that he was an artist who worked on history, recalling paradoxically the modernists' pre-war vision of a cultural revolution. But the revolution Hitler had in mind and set out to realize was far from the one that the modernists had dreamed of during the heady years of 'intellectual intoxications' before 1914.

ROBERT WOHL

APPENDIX

A complete list of all poets, playwrights, writers, artists, architects and composers who died as a result of the First World War is an impossible task. This appendix represents the most comprehensive list compiled to date of these creative artists. There are bound to be omissions, especially from countries whose documentation was haphazard during the upheavals of the post-war era. The purpose is to present a ready reference to those who, having read this anthology, might wish to investigate this subject further. To assist in this research, entries of special interest for either artistic or purely historical reasons have been highlighted in bold type.

Bibliographical abbreviations used in this appendix

AEMG	Thierry Sandre (ed.), *Anthologie des écrivains morts à la guerre 1914-18* (Association des écrivains combattants, Amiens, 1924-26, 5 vols).
Bénézit	Emmanuel Bénézit (ed.), *Dictionnaire critique et documentaire des peintres, sculpteurs, dessinateurs et graveurs de tous les temps et de tous les pays . . .* (Gründ, Paris, 1976, 2 vols).
DTH	Bruno Grabinski (ed.), *Dichtergüße toter Helden*, (Hildesheim, 1917).
Ginisty	Paul Ginisty (ed.), *Les artistes morts pour la patrie* (Alcan, Paris, 1915).
Th.-B.	Ulrich Thieme & Felix Becker (eds), *Allgemeines Lexikon der bildenden Künstler von der Antike bis zur Gegenwart* (E.A. Seeman, Leipzig, 37 vols).

Abonnel, Michel
1881–2 Feb. 1915, exhaustion, St Chamond. French painter, pupil of Cormon, Paris. Exhib. Salons des Artistes Français. (Ginisty.)

Áchim, Géza *see* Gyóni, Géza

Acker, Paul
1874–27 June 1915, car accident on patrol, Neuhausen, Alsace. French writer from Alsace. Prolific writer of 23 novels 1898–1914, e.g. *Les Exilés*, 1911, Paris. Also essayist & critic, contributed to *Revue Bleue*, *Revue des Deux Mondes*, *Revue Hebdomadaire* etc. (Albert-Emile Sorel, 'L'Alsacien Paul Acker, mon ami', *Revue Hebdomadaire*, 29 Sept. 1919; *Bibliographie des Auteurs Modernes de Langue Française*.)

Adam, (Antoine Émile Joseph) **Edmond** (*see entry page **232***)
1889–24 Aug. 1918, wounds, Veuve after †Courmelois-Thuisy, Sub-Lt, Reserve, 1st Regt du Génie. Chevalier Légion d'honneur. French poet & essayist, contrib. to *Les Humbles*.

Adler, Kurd
1892–6 July 1916. German poet, contrib. to *Die Aktion*: 'Das Geschütz', 'Ruhe an der Front'. (*Wiederkehr: Gedichte*, Verlag die Aktion, Berlin-Wilmersdorf, 1918.)

Ajalbert, Charles Jean
1896–28 Mar. 1915, wounds, Argonne. French poet: 'La Maison dans la nuit'. (*AEMG*, ii, 13.)

Akuni, E.
1863–1915. Armenian writer.

Alain-Fournier (pseud. of Henri Fournier) (*see entry page **296***)
1886–22 Sept. 1916 †Marne. French novelist: *Le Grand Meaulnes & Miracles* (Alain Rivière & Daniel Leuwers [eds.], Garnier, Paris, 1986). (Robert Gibson, *Alain-Fournier and 'Le Grand Meaulnes'*, Grant & Cutler, 1986.)

Albrecht, Eugen Franz
1864–1916 †. German conductor & composer. (*Deutsche Tonkünstler Zeitung*, 1916, 109.)

Alexandre, Paul
1884–26 Sept. 1916. †Bouchavesnes. French playwright, contrib. to *Petit Parisien*. Made modern adaptation of *Phèdre: La Ravage*. (*AEMG*, iv, 3.)

Allard-Méus, Jean
1892–22 Aug. 1914, †Meurthe-et-Moselle, Croix de Guerre, Chevalier Légion d'honneur. French poet much influenced by Edmond Rostand: *Polichinelle, comédie en un acte en vers* (Lequesnes, Paris, 1910); *Lettres à You, roman puéril*; *Rêves d'Amour, Rêves de Gloire* (Leclerc, Paris, 1920).

Allfree, Geoffrey S.
1889–29 Sept. 1918, drowned on active service, Lt, RN. British watercolourist of landscapes & dazzleships. Exhib. Medici Gallery, London, 1961.

Allsac, Joseph d' *see* Pradel de Lamaze, Joseph de

Amar, Pierre
1892–22 Aug. 1914 †Charleroi, on first day of combat. French military poet: 'Marie-Louise' (Bouasse-Lebel, Paris, 1916). (*AEMG*, ii, 19.)

Ambrosio-Donnet, Antoine
1887–15 Oct. 1915, Western Front, Sgt, Inf. French sculptor, twice winner of Grand Prix de Rome, 1913–14.

Ancher, Pierre
1893–10 July 1918, wounds, St Louis de Bordeaux. French poet: 'Je connais des chansons' (1911), 'A l'hôpital – Le Réveil' (1915). (*AEMG*, iv, 13.)

André, Marc
1893–28 Apr. 1917 †Cerny, Chemin des Dames. French short-story writer: 'La Tulipe'. (*AEMG*, ii, 23.)

André, Maxime (Ernest Marie Balthazar Vicomte) d'
1864–2 Dec. 1914, †Bixschoolte, Lt-Col., 5th Chasseurs à Cheval. French military poet & novelist: *Dona Galla*, unpubl. verse drama. (*AEMG*, ii, 10.)

Andziej, Vincuk *see* Viasioły, Kas'jan.

Ansorge, Hugo *see* Mrázek, Hugo Klement

Antoine, Georges
1892–15 Sept. 1918, influenza, Belgium, after 4 years' military service. Belgian composer. 14 major works incl. mainly songs: 'Wallonie', 'Cinq petits poèmes de Tristan Klingsor'; 'Mélodies d'après Verlaine'; 'Veillée d'armes: poème pour orchestre', 1918. (*AEMG*, iii, 713.)

Apollinaire, Guillaume (pseud. of Wilhelm de Kostrowitzky)
(*see entry page **200***)
1880–9 Nov. 1918, Spanish influenza, Paris. French avant-garde poet, playwright & art critic: *Œuvres poétiques* (Marcel Adema & Michel Décaudin [eds.], Gallimard, Paris, 1965).

Arbouin, Gabriel
1878–19 Jan. 1917, wounds received in Oct. 1916. French novelist: *Don Pencho* (fragment). Contrib. stories to *Radical*, *Rappel*, *Paris-Journal*. (*AEMG*, ii, 36.)

Arbousset, Jean (Roger)
1895–9 June 1918 †Saint-Maur. French poet: *Le Bivre de Quinze Grammes* (Grès, Paris, 1917).

Arné, Émile
1890–7 Apr. 1915 †Flirey. French poet of Provence influenced by Mistral. Collaborated with Octave de Vitrolles on periodical *Quatre Dauphins* (1913). (*AEMG*, iii, 21.)

Arnold, Paul-A.
1896–16 Apr. 1917 †Craonne. French poet, publ. in *Marches de Flandres*. (*AEMG*, iii, 26.)

Arramond, Dominique
1880–11 June 1918 †Compiégne. French poet of the Gironde, contrib. to *La Vie Bordelaise* & edited *Le Reliquaire Pyrénéen*. (*AEMG*, iv, 18.)

Art-Roë *see* Mahon, Patrice

Asch, Walter
1893–2 May 1915 †Tarnov, Galicia. German composer, pupil of Pfizner. Composed a variety of small-scale works, which he requested not to be publ. after his death.

Audibert, Georges
1885–28 Sept. 1915 †Souchez. French romantic symbolist poet: *Sous les yeux de la Mort – La Source et le Ciel* (Crès, Paris, 1918).

Audigier, René
1894–27 July 1917 †Longueval. French poet; 'Le Manoir de Chateaugay'. (*AEMG*, iv, 23.)

Auster, Philippe *see* Patin, Maurice

Babbage, Herbert Ivan
1875–14 Dec. 1916 †, Cornish Light Infantry. British landscape & genre painter.

Bag, Olivier *see* Olivier-Hourcade

Bagshawe, William Wyatt
1882–1 July 1916 †Serre, Somme, 12th Yorks & Lancs Regt. British artist from Sheffield, prize-winner at Slade School. Spring Exhib., New English Art Club. (Slade School Records.)

Baguenier, Desormeaux, Jacques (Henri Hector)
1888–22 Aug. 1914 †Neufchâteau, Belgium. French poet: 'Recuill pour Ariane', 'Marjolaine ou les Songes au Bois Dormant'. (Marc Leclerc: *Anthologie des Poètes Angevins*, 1922.)

Bail, Paul *see* Desclers, Maurice

Baker, Jack
1897–8 Aug. 1918 †Morlancourt, Signaller, 7th London Regt. British war poet: *Memories of the Line* (Imperial War Museum, London).

Baldacci, Licurgo
1887–1917. Italian architect from Carrara. 1st Prix de Rome, 1909. Influenced by Giuseppe Mancini. (*Emporium*, 1917, xlv, 239.)

Balder, Jacques (pseud. of Georges David)
1885–8 Sept. 1914 †Marne. French poet, publ. in *La Phalange*: 'La Petite Fille sans l'Averse', 'Le Tournant', 'Marlborough Mourant'. (*AEMG*, iii, 41.)

Baldwin, J. Brake
1885–July 1915, exhaustion, Voluntary Aid Detachment of Red Cross. British artist, exhib. Royal Institute of Oil Painters. (*The Studio*, 1916, 282.)

Baley, Ha Hu *see* Leybold, Hans

Bannerot, Georges
French anti-war poet: 'Les Statues mutilées' (Libr. d'Action d'Art de la Ghilde: 'Les Forgerons', Paris).

Barbet, Louis *see* Dulhom-Noguès, Louis

Baron, François
1898–5 May 1918, wounds, after †Moyenneville. French writer publ. posth.: *Sous le Casque loin des Lauriers* (Figuière, Paris, 1918).

Barselian, G.
1883–1915. Armenian writer.

Barthelmess, Hans
1888–11 July 1916 †Verdun. German painter and etcher from Erlangen. Studied with P. Halm, Munich. Portraits, landscapes, circus scenes. (J. A. Stupp [ed.], *Hans Barthelmess*, Ausstellung im Stadtmuseum Erlangen, 1988.)

Basset, Serge
1865–29 June 1917 †Lens. French journalist & playwright, collaborated on 21 adaptations for the stage. (*AEMG*, v, 777.)

Baudet, Marie
1864–6 Apr. 1917, by shell explosion while attending the wounded, Reims. French painter, exhib. Indépendants & d'Automne. (Bénézit.)

Baudot, Émile Marcel
1886–21 Mar. 1916, wounds, Verdun, 44th Batt. Inf. French sculptor, exhib. Indépendants, Beaux-Arts, d'Automne.

Baum, Peter (*see entry page **174***)
1869–6 June 1916, shrapnel wound,

France, stretcher-bearer. German novelist & poet: *Gesammelte Werke* (Rowohlt, Berlin, 1920).

Beaufort, Jean (Louis Henri)
1891–1916. French poet: 'Première Mosaïque' (unpubl.). (*AEMG*, iii, 720.)

Beckh, Robert Harold
1894–15 Aug. 1916, France, 2nd Lt, East Yorks Regt. British poet: *Swallows in Storm and Sunlight* (Chapman & Hall, Manchester, 1917). War poetry incl. 'No man's land', 'Billets', 'A song and a smile'.

Béclu, René
1881–17 Jan. 1915, shell blast, Lorraine, Sub-Lt, 166th Infantry Regt. French sculptor.

Bégarie, Jean-Baptiste
1892–17 Feb. 1915. French poet of the Provence: 'An me fusilh' in *J. B. Bégarie, mort pour la France* (Bibliothèque de l'Ecole Gaston, Fébus.)

Békássy, Ferenc (István Denes Gyula) (*see entry page **346***)
1893–25 June 1915 †Dobronoutz. Hungarian poet: *Adriatica and other Poems* (Hogarth, London, 1915); *Elmerült szigetek*, (Budapest, 1915); *Hátrahagyott irásai, Fantáziák és gondolatok* (Budapest, 1916).

Belval-Delahaye (Francisque-Anatole)
1879–27 Sept. 1918, influenza, Romans, Drôme. French poet & playwright: *Par le Fer et par la Torche* (1908), *La Chanson du Bronze* (1908), *La Colère du Lion, drame revolutionnaire en vers*. (Émile Noël, *Le Dernier Poète Romantique: A. Belval-Delahaye, l'homme et l'œuvre*, 1911.)

Bender, Paul
–Sept. 1917. German architect from Dresden, pupil of Wallots.

Bengoechea, Hernan de
1889–9 May 1915 †Ouvrages Blancs, Arras, 1st Regt. Étranger, Croix de Guerre. French-Colombian poet: *Les Crépuscules du Matin* (*Les Tablettes*, 1921); playwright: *Le Vol du Soir* (*Les Tablettes*, 1922); essayist: *Le Sourire de l'Île-de-France* (*Les Tablettes*, 1924). (*AEMG*, i, 697.)

Benoit, Charles
1888–28 Dec. 1914. French writer of Avignon: *Le Tamaris et l'Olivier – Provence et Languedoc* (1924). (*Trois morts de soldats: les Frères Benoit*, 1918.)

Bernard, Édouard
1888–27 Sept. 1914 †Apremont-la-Forêt. French poet: *Brèves Silhouettes* (Dole, 1911).

Bernard, Jean-Marc (*see entry page **242***)
1881–5 July 1915 †Souchez. French critic & poet. Founder of periodical *Les Guêpes*.

Berneis, Benno
1884–Aug. 1916, France. German painter from Bavaria. Studied with Slevogt & Corinth in Berlin. Portraits of literary personalities in Berlin around the Café des Westens. (Th.-B.)

Berridge, William Eric
–20 Aug. 1916, France, Somerset Light Inf. British poet: *Verses* (Chichester Press).

Bertaux, René
1878–10 June 1917 †Sulzern, Alsace, camouflage unit. French painter, exhib. with Groupe Libre at Indépendants.

Berthiers, Joseph
1879–15 Nov. 1916 †Sailly-Saillisel, Croix de Guerre. French-Breton story writer, publ. in *La Nouvelle Édition Française* (1910): 'Marie-Rose la sinistrée'; 'Le Consentement'; 'Contes Bretons'; 'Jean-Louis, vie d'un Orphelin'.

Berthon, Léon
1893–12 Feb. 1917, illness contracted at front, Clermont, Oise. French story writer, contrib. to *Journal Rose*; & war poet: *Poèmes de la Guerre* (M. Rocher [ed.]). (*AEMG*, v, 580.)

Berthon, Maurice-Alexandre
1888–20 Sept. 1914, wounds from †Cauroy, Berry-au-Bac, 5th Infantry Regt. French portrait painter & of works of Algeria, debut at Salon des Artistes Français. (Ginisty.)

Bertrab, Carl von
1863–26 Oct. 1914 †Eastern Front. German (landscape) painter from Cronberg.

Bertrand, Adrien (*see entry page **221***)
1888–18 Nov. 1917, wounds, Grasse. French poet & novelist: *L'Appel du Sol* (Curandera, Challes-les-Eaux, 1986; Prix Goncourt, 1916).

Bertrand, Henri (occ. pseud.: Henri & Jean Sansterre)
1882–22 Mar. 1916, wounds, Légion d'honneur. French writer of adventure novels: *Les Mémoires d'un Sauvage* (1912). (*AEMG*, i, 83.)

Bertrand, Maurice
1881–7 Oct. 1914 †Colincamps, Somme. French poet, playwright & short-story writer, largely unpubl. (*AEMG*, iii, 47.)

Beslay, Maurice
1877–29 May 1915 †Bonvigny, Chevalier, Légion d'honneur. French playwright: *Le Réussite* (Théâtre Michel, Paris, 1912). ('Vermelles, sur le Front', *Nouvelle Revue*, Paris, 1915; *AEMG*, iii, 51.)

Besnard, Robert
1881–20 Sept. 1914 †Autréches, Aisne. French modernist painter: 'Un Chien Colley', 'Fin de Soirée'. (Ginisty.)

Beury, André
1889–Sept. 1914, disappeared, Champenoux. French novelist: *Le Successeur* (1913), which became a play (Th. Grand-Guignol, 1913). Associate of Charles Müller (q.v.).

Beutler, Gustav
1892–15 July 1918 †Prosnes, Reims. German writer: 'Briefe an Walther Rathenau' (unpubl. in Archiv der Walther-Rathenau-Gesellschaft, Berlin).

Biguet, André
1892–8 Oct. 1918 †Pontgirard, Champagne. French poet: *Goënole* (verse-drama), *Le Feu et la Cendre* (Crès, Paris, 1913).

Bischoff-Culm, Ernst
1870–July 1917. German East Prussian painter, member of the Berlin Secession, in group around Hübner, Bryer & von Kardof. Painted portrait of poet Walter Heymann (q.v.). (Th.-B.)

Blanchard, Marcel
1890–19 June 1915 †Carency, Arras, Sub-Lt, 231st Infantry Regt. French poet: *Les Rumeurs de la Galère* (1910), *La Grande Guerre* (1912). (*AEMG*, iii, 56.)

Bleimor *see* Calloc'h, Jean-Pierre

Bliss, Francis Kennard
1892–28 Sept. 1916 †Thiépval, acting Forward Artillery Observation Officer. English poet, brother of composer Arthur Bliss. (Memorials of Rugbeians, iv.)

Blives, Roger de
1876–9 May 1915 †Loos, Artois, 2nd Artillery Regt. French painter, founder of Soc. des Peintres de Paris.

Blume, Fritz
–1916 †. German war poet: 'Fall ich vor Arras'. (*DTH*.)

Boccioni, Umberto (*page **6***)
1882–17 Aug. 1916, after a fall from his horse during military training nr Verona. (Calvesi & Coen, Boccioni, l'opera completa, Electra, Milan, 1983.)

Bochmann, Gregor
1878–20 Sept. 1914 †Aisne, Landwehr-Regt. German sculptor from Düsseldorf, son of the landscape painter Bochmann the Elder.

Bock, Erwin
–12 July 1916, Italy, Cadet, Tiroler Kaiserjägerregt. Austrian song composer in the manner of Schubert. (*Neue Musik-Zeitung*, 40, 368.)

Böckeler, Bernhard
–1916. German war poet: 'Kampflied', 'Bilder aus Russisch-Polen', 'Germanen – Cäser, Heil!'. (*DTH*.)

Börsch, Rudolf
1895–May 1915, Przemysl. German writer, contrib. to *Die Aktion*: 'Revolution' (16 May 1914, col. 427).

Boine, Jean
1894–16 Apr. 1917. French poet, writer & journalist, contrib. to *La Vie Doloise*. Collected poems: *Poésies* (Dole 1920).

Boinvilliers, Jean
1890–21 Feb. 1915, Capt., Res., 66th Regt. French painter. (Ginisty.)

Boisanger, Henri de
1877–8 Sept. 1914 †Connantray, La Fère-Champenoise. French army novelist & poet from Brittany: 'Merci mon commandant . . . Ah! Merci pour Saint-Cyr!' (*Le Lieutenant de Trémazan*, Perrin, Paris, 1908; 'La Conquête Nouvelle', *Le Correspondant*, 1911.) (*AEMG*, ii, 65.)

Bojić, Milutin (*see entry page **355***)
1892–26 Oct. 1917, tuberculosis, military hospital, Salonika. Serbian poet, writer of verse plays mostly on themes from Serbian history: *Pesme bola i ponosa* (Salonika, 1917).

Bolz, Hans
1887–4 July 1918, exhaustion, Kuranstalt Neuwittelsbach, nr Munich. German avant-garde artist. Contrib. to *Der Sturm*, Berlin. Destroyed most of his work shortly before his death, but collected by Julius Diezel & exhib. Galerie Flechtheim, Düsseldorf with illus. cat., 1922. (H. v. Wedderkop, *Deutsche Graphik des Westens*, Feuer, Weimar, 1922.)

Bonfils, Louis
1891–11 June 1918 †Mélicocq, Oise, Capt., 319th Infantry Regt. French poet of the Provence: *Jout un Balcoun* (comedy play in verse in 1 act, Lon Gal, Montpellier, 1918), *Tableaux de Guerre: Lettres du Front*.

Bonnafont, André
1883–24 Oct. 1916, wounds following raid as aviator at Douaumont. French illustrator, contrib. to *Vie Parisienne*.

Bonneaud, Henri

1884–22 Dec. 1914, typhoid, Verdun. French Catholic poet: 'L'Immortalité'. (*AEMG*, v, 583.)

Bonneton, Eugène
1874–1/5 Nov. 1915, gassed, Argonne, Sgt, 145th Territorials. French painter of old quarters of Paris, courtyards & barren landscapes. Exhib. Artistes français. (Ginisty.)

Bouffanais, Jules-René
1885–1915. French engraver, pupil of Laguillermie. 2nd Prix de Rome, July 1914.

Bouignol, Maurice
1891–26 Apr. 1918 †Rubescourt, Oise. French poet: *Sans Gestes* (Fasquelles, Paris, 1918). *Glaives et Médailles* (Crès, Paris, 1920).

Bouisset, Pierre-Victor-Auguste
1889–1 Mar. 1915 †Notre-Dame-de-Lorette, 10th Batt., Chasseurs à Pied. French sculptor.

Boumal, Louis
1890–22 Oct. 1918, exhaustion. French poet. (*AEMG*, iii, 725.)

Bource, Marcel
1883–3 Mar. 1916 †Douaumont. French poet: 'Les Soirs'; & playwright: *La Récidine*. (*AEMG*, ii, 79.)

Bourcier, Charles
1882–25 Sept. 1914, disappeared, †La Chavatte, Somme. French writer & editor: *La Chimère, revue bi-mensuelle de littérature démocratique*, (1907–10). *Hors des Sentiers Baltus*. (play perf. Paris Mar. 1913). Autobiographical novel: *Paul, mon frère* (Flammarion, Paris, 1923).

Bourgeois, Joseph
1893–9 May 1915 †Souchez, Cpl, 97th Infantry Regt. French poet: 'Les Bœufs', 'Chanson triste'. (*AEMG*, iii, 80.)

Boutet, Pierre
1884–25 Aug. 1914, disappeared, Courbesseaux. French græcophile poet: 'La Ville Heureuse' in *Les Poèmes* (Nouvelle Éd. Françaises, 1913).

Boyd, Stuart
1887–7 Oct. 1916, wounds, Dernancourt after †28 Sept., Lt, 1st Loyal North Lancs Regt. British landscape painter, son of *Punch* contributor Alexander Stuart Boyd. Slade School scholar. Exhib. Royal Academy 1909; memorial exhib. Fine Art Soc. (Slade School Records.)

Boyer, Léon
1883–10 Mar. 1916 †Froide-Terre, Verdun, 153rd Infantry Regt. French pastoral poet of the Auvergne: 'Genêts et Rocailles'. Contrib. to periodicals *Revue des Poètes*, *La Musette*, *La Semaine Auvergne*, *La Veillée d'Auvergne*. (*AEMG*, ii, 89.)

Bras, Jos ar (pseud.: Dirlem)
1889–8 Sept. 1915 †Bar-le-Duc. Breton poet who wrote in Celtic-Breton tongue: 'Ar Beziou'. (Camille Le Mercier d'Erm, *Les Bardes et Poètes nationaux de la Bretagne armoricaine*, Paris, 1919.)

Braun, Otto
1897–29 Apr. 1918 †Marcelcave, Somme. German writer & poet: *Aus den nachgelassenen Schriften eines Frühvollendeten* (Julie Vogelstein [ed.], Klemm, Berlin-Grunewald, 1922).

Bray, Horace (Edgar Kingmill)
1896–9 Aug. 1918, accidental collision on departure for France, Shotwick, England, 2nd Lt, RAF. Canadian poet. (J. W. Garvin, *Canadian Poems of the Great War*, McClelland & Stewart, Toronto, 1918.)

Breuil de Saint-Germain, Jean du
1873–22 Feb. 1915. French anglophile writer, Prix Montyon, Acad. française. (H.-L. Motti, *In Memoriam, Jean du Breuil de Saint-Germain*, Paris, 1916; *AEMG*, iii, 87.)

Bréval, André
1890–24 Jan. 1916, gassed nr Nieuport. French poet: 'Les Colchiques'. Corresponded with Charles Dumas (q.v.). (*Poèmes*, Cluberre, 1923.)

Brine, Everard Lindesay
–1917, illness, Kasvin, Mesopotamia, Lt, 4th Batt., Hampshire Regt. British poet: *Poems* (Blackwell, Oxford, 1920).

Broichsitter, Heinrich
1884–24 Apr. 1915, Flanders. German philosophy student & poet: 'Wir fragen den Weg' in *Lyrik* (Costenoble, Jena, 1920).

Brooke, Brian (pseud.: Korongo)
1889–25 July 1916, wounds after †2 July 1916, Great Rush, Mametz, Capt., 2nd Batt., Gordon Highlanders. Scottish poet, in jingoist vein: *Poems* (Bodley Head, London, 1917).

Brooke, Rupert (Chawner)
(*see entry page 52*)
1887–23 Apr. 1915, blood-poisoning, off Skyros, Sub-Lt, Hood Batt., RND. British poet: *The Collected Poems* (Sidgwick & Jackson, London, 1987).

Brown, John
–1918 †, 9th Seaforths, Royal Scottish Regt., MC. British poet: *Letters, Essays & Verses* (Elliot, Edinburgh, 1921).

Browne, W(illiam) **Denis** (*page 10*)
1888–4 June 1915 †Krithia, Gallipoli, Hood Batt., RND. British composer mainly of songs (Hugh Taylor, *The Life and Work of W. Denis Browne*, diss., Cambridge, 1973.)

Bruant, Aristide-Louis-Armand
1883–16 April 1917. French army captain & poet: 'L'Ame des Fleurs' (1911). (Frédéric Bitton, *Le Capitaine Bruant*, 1919.)

Brulat, Jean
1893–24 Mar. 1916 †Bois Bourrus, Verdun. Sgt, 38th Infantry Regt. French landscape painter of town of Menton.

Brun, Gaston
1873–17 May 1918, wounds after 6 Aug. 1916 †Verdun, Capt., 17th Territorials, Chevalier, Légion d'honneur. French traditional painter of Marne landscapes.

Brunel, Roger
1884–25 Jan. 1917, drowned when torpedoed *Amiral Magon*. French poet of Provence: 'La Provence'. Unpubl. (*AEMG*, ii, 94.)

Brydon, Joseph
1875–15 July 1915 †Bois Blaurain. French novelist: *L'Abbé Guérande* (Union de Littérature et d'Art, Tassel, Paris, 1908), *Dans l'ombre du cœur* (Figuière, Paris, 1912); & portrait painter, exhib. Soc. Artistes français.

Bunbury, H. St Pierre
1883–25 Aug. 1916. British portrait painter.

Burke, Edward Coplays Lardner
–1916, East Africa. South African artist.

Burlyuk, Vladimir Davidovitch
1886–1917 †Salonika. Russian Futurist artist, younger brother of David Burlyuk. Co-founder of group of artists 'Himmelblaue Rose', Munich. Prints in series of Futurist publications, 1914.

Burny, Victor
1893–30 Oct. 1918, influenza, Calais. Belgian war poet, largely unpubl.: 'Il était une Église' (1915), 'L'Observateur' (1915), 'Une Croix dans les Dunes' (1916), in *AEMG*, iii, 735.

Butler, T. O'Brien (pseud. of Whitwell)
c. 1870–7 May 1915, drowned, *Lusitania*. Irish composer of the first opera to be written to a libretto in the Gaelic language: *Murigheis* (perf. Dublin 7 Dec. 1903.)

Butterworth, George (Stainton Kaye)
1885–5 Aug. 1916 †Pozières, 2nd Lt, Durham Light Infantry, MC. English composer & folksong collector. Set Housman's verses: 'A Shropshire lad'. (Ian Copley, *George Butterworth and his music, a centennial tribute*, Thames Press, London, 1985.)

Byram, Léo (pseud. of Capitaine Eugène Drevet)
1872–7 May 1915 †Gallipoli. French adventurer & novelist, a professional soldier who fought against pirates in China: *Petit Jap deviendra grand* (Berger-Levrault, Paris, 1908), *Mon Ami Fou-Than* (Almann-Lévy, Paris, 1910), *Les Amis de mon Ami Fou-Than* (Plon-Nourrit, Paris, 1913).

Čada, Karel *see* Šarlih, Karel

Cadot, (Barthélemy)**-Louis**
1886–3 Sept. 1914 †Ferme Saint-Libraire sur le Grand-Couronné de Nancy, 269th Infantry Regt. French composer, studied under Guy Ropartz: *Lysis et Florie* (ballet, perf. Th. du Moulin Bleu) & piano pieces, operettas, songs: 'Chanson Rustique'. Also painted, exhib. Indépendants 1912–13; & wrote: *La Chimère apprivoisée* (Figuière, Paris, 1913).

Cahn, Joseph
1887–30 Jan. 1917, wounds, after †Biaches, 29 Dec. 1916. French poet: *Au Souffle des Mois* (St Maudé, 1912), *Vers de terre . . . de France* (Deshayes, 1916), *Et puis voici des Vers* (Cahors, 1921).

Calderon, Frederick Elwyn
1874–3 Apr. 1916 †St Eloi, 1st Canadian Contingent. English portrait painter.

Calderon, George (Leslie)
(*see entry page 27*)
1868–4 June 1915, Krithia, Gallipoli, 9th Batt., Oxfordshire & Bucks Light Infantry. English linguist & playwright: *Eight One-Act plays* (Grant Richards, London, 1922); *The Fountain* (Gowans & Gray, London, 1911). (P. Lubbock: *George Calderon: a sketch from memory*, Grant Richards, London, 1921.)

Calloc'h, Jean-Pierre (pseud.: Bleimor)
(*see entry page 270*)
1888–10 Apr. 1917 †. Breton poet: 'Ar En Deulin' & playwright: 'Er Flamaked' (1906), 'El ma pardonamb'. (*Ar En Deulin/A genoux*, Kendalc'h, 1963.)

Cambon, André
1882–27 Mar. 1915. French germanophile writer of a single spy-story: *Courrier*

d'Espionne (Oudin, Paris, 1914).

Campbell, Alan U. ('Beo')
1885–30 Dec. 1917, †La Vacquerie, Lt-Cmdr, Howe Batt., RND. British playwright & son of actress Mrs Patrick Campbell: *The Ambassador's Wife* (perf. Chicago, 1910), *The Dust of Egypt* (perf. Wyndham's Th., London).

Campbell, Ivar
1890–8 Jan. 1916, wounds after †Sheikh Saad, Mesopotamia, 7 Jan., Capt., Argyll & Sutherland Highlanders. Scottish poet: 'Marriage of Earth and Spring', 'London Pride' (unpubl.).

Camuzat, Marcel
1884–7 Mar. 1915 †Argonne, 95th Infantry Regt. French architect: Monument Guiton, La Rochelle.

Candole, Alec (Corry Vully) De
1897–3 Sept. 1918, France, Machine Gun Corps. English poet: *Poems* (Cambridge University Press, 1920); essayist: *The faith of a subaltern, essays on religion and life* (Cambridge University Press, 1919).

Canioni, Georges-Ambroise
1885–Mar. 1915, wounds †Chelles, Oise, Aug. 1914. French painter & lithographer, traditional in style of Millet. Prix Danton at l'École Estienne. (Ginisty.)

Canivet, Auguste (pseud.: Ewa Saens)
1877–31 May 1916, wounds, Armentières. French-Breton novelist: *L'Homme rouge* (1898), *La Fille du Mal* (1900), *L'Enfant de la Segado* (1902); contrib. to periodical *Nouvelliste du Morbihan*. (*AEMG*, iii, 128.)

Capdeville, Eugène
1892–7 May 1917 †Craonnelle. French poet: 'Tel le roman de notre cœur' (1917). (*AEMG*, v, 31.)

Carbaugh, Frank
–Aug. 1918, wounds, France, Sgt, Inf., American Expeditionary Force. American war poet: 'The Fields of the Marne'. (*Yanks' AEF Verse*, Putnam, New York, 1920.)

Carbonnelle, Henri
1872–4 Nov. 1914, wounds, †Gercourt Aug. 1914. French journalist & playwright: *Prostitution* (a social drama perf. Montparnasse, Paris), *Plus Foussard des Deux* (vaudeville), *Démocratie*. Unpubl. (*AEMG*, iv, 151.)

Cardet, Marcel Ferdinand
1876–25 Apr. 1915 disappeared †Éparges. French watercolour painter, esp. of studies of old Paris & Bruges.

Carniel, Riccardo
1867–9 June 1915, Southern Front, cyclist, 1st div. Gênes Regt. Italian painter from Trieste of landscapes of Paris region & of Italy.

Caron, Georges
1883–17 Oct. 1914, POW Nuremberg after capture, 22 Sept. 1914 †Varennes, Argonne. French sculptor in marble. Exhib. Salon National.

Carrau, Charles
1885–12 Jan. 1916 †Maison de Champagne. French poet: 'Carillon Pascal'. Publ. in *La Biche*. (*AEMG*, iv, 159.)

Cartier-Bresson, Louis
1882–11 May 1915, wounds, Frévin-Capelle after †La Targette, 153rd Infantry Regt. French painter. Prix Troyon (1907), Prix de Rome (1910). Exhib. Gallery Richard, London. (Th.-B.)

Cassagnac, Guy (Paul Marie Julien de Granier) de
1882–20 Aug. 1914 †Fonteny. French novelist: *L'Agitateur* (Plon-Nourrit, Paris, 1911), *Quand la Nuit fut venue* (Ollendorff, Paris, 1913); & playwright (in collaboration with brother Paul): *Tout à Coup* (1914), *Le Sang des Vignes* (unpubl.). (*AEMG*, iii, 135.)

Caval, Marcel
1886–10 Oct. 1915 †Souvain. French lyric writer to music by Louis Melrack: 'Gai Moineau de Paris', 'Zorelitta', 'Je ne dois pas t'aimer'. Also wrote short plays. (*AEMG*, iv, 165.)

Cazin, (Jean-) **Michel**
1869–1 Feb. 1917, accidental torpedo explosion while visiting the Cmdr of the *Erzbischoff*. French artist. Drawings of the front, but chiefly a ceramic artist. (Henri Malo: *Critique sentimentale, souvenirs sur les Cazins*, Cluberre, Paris, 1922.)

Červinka, Karel Viktor
1891–1915, †Soč, Gorica. Czech poet.

Chaigne, Georges
1887–5 Apr. 1915 †Bois de Mortmare, Lt, 367th Inf. Regt. French writer: *Sous la robe blanche*, *Mœurs électorales romaines* (Larose, Paris, 1911); & playwright of verse drama: *Nikylla*. (*AEMG*, iv, 169.)

Chalhoub, Maurice *see* Mareil, Maurice

Chambouleron, Maurice Eugène
1897–12 Oct. 1918 †Houdelincourt, Lorraine. French decorative artist.

Champcommunal, Jean-Joseph
1880–5 Nov. 1914 †Andéchy, Roye, Sgt, 101st Infantry. French graphic artist & painter. (Ginisty.)

Champeaux, Louis (pseud. of Georges Babet)
1890–6 May 1917 †Craonne. French author: *L'Expérience du Docteur Forgues* (Thallandier, Paris, 1913).

Champfeu, Jacques de
1896–27 Mar. 1918 †Dancourt, Légion d'honneur. French soldier-poet: 'Un songe'. (Philippe d'Estailleur-Chanteraine [ed.], *Jacques de Champfeu, gentilhomme, poète et soldat français*, Paris, 1922.)

Champollion, André Chéronet
–23 Apr. 1915, †Bois-le-Prêtre. American painter. (Letters reproduced in *Harvard Alumni Bulletin*, 7 & 28 Apr. 1915.)

Chapin, Harold
1886–26 Sept. 1915, †Loos, L/Cpl, RAMC. American-born playwright: *The Comedies of Harold Chapin* (Chatto & Windus, London, 1921) incl. *The New Morality*, *Art and Opportunity*, & an intro. by J. M. Barrie. (Sidney Dark: *Harold Chapin, Soldier and Dramatist*, John Lane, London, 1916.)

Chardon, Ary-Henri
1889–22 Aug. 1918 †Beurraignes. French poet: *Les voix de la forêt* (Libr. Académie, Perrin, 1910).

Charlton, Hugh Vaughan
1884–24 June 1916 †Whytschaete, Flanders, 7th Northumberland Fusiliers. British naturalist & artist.

Charlton, John Macfarlan
1891–1 July 1916 †La Boiselle, Capt., 21st Northumberland Fusiliers. British ornithologist & artist: *British birds* (iv). (E. B. Osborn, *The new Elizabethans: a first selection of the lives of young men who have fallen in the Great War*, John Lane/Bodley Head, London, 1919.)

Chassin, Henri
1890–24 July 1917 †Marnes, 151st Infantry. French poet: 'Les Clameurs et les voix' (1916). (*AEMG*, ii, 128.)

Chervet, Henri
1881–30 Sept. 1915, Lt, 156th Infantry Regt. French critic, playwright & poet: 'Madrigal'. (*AEMG*, iv, 185.)

Chiesa, Édouard
1887–7 Aug. 1915 †Gallipoli. French war poet: 'Au jour le jour'. (*AEMG*, iii, 168.)

Choudens, Jacques de
1887–13 June 1915 †Notre-Dame-de-Lorette (Nord). French war poet: *Poésies de Guerre* (Offenstadt, Paris, 1915).

Chowne, Gerard (Henry Tilson)
1875–2 May 1917, wounds, Salonika, Capt., 9th East Lancs Regt. British artist and decorator. Member, New English Art Club. 1-man show, Carfax Galleries, London: *Paintings and drawings by Gerard Chowne*, 1911. (Slade School Records.)

Civrieux, Marc de Larreguy de *see* Larreguy de Civrieux, Marc de

Clermont, Émile
1880–May 1916. French (mystic Christian) novelist & philosopher: *Amours promis* (1909); *Laure* (1913), *Histoire d'Isabelle* (Grassat, Paris, 1917). (René Doumic, 'Émile Clermont', *Revue des deux Mondes*, Paris, 1 May 1916.)

Cocardas, Henri
1881–26 Apr. 1915, wounds, Saint-Maurice, Meuse. French poet: 'La bonne Auberge' (*Nouvelle Revue*, 15 Mar. 1914).

Codet, Louis (*see entry page **311***)
1876–4 Nov. 1914 †Bridge of Stenstraate, Belgium. French novelist: *La Fortune de Bécot* (Gallimard, Paris, 1921).

Coiquand de Fontanes, Raymond Jean-Jules
1875–16 June 1915 †Labryinthe, Capt, 70th Infantry Regt. French painter of exotic scenes, member of Soc. des Peintres Orientalistes. (Ginisty.)

Colin, Henri
1882–5 Sept. 1915 †Montdidier. French poet: 'Saurez-vous deviner?' (*AEMG*, iii, 191.)

Colin, Maurice
1891–12 Sept. 1914. French poet, collected in *Mes Glanes*. (*AEMG*, iii, 193.)

Collet, Étienne
1885–20 Aug. 1914 †Steige. French poet: 'Ma Maison'. (*AEMG*, ii, 156.)

Collison-Marley, Harold Duke
1878–25 Sept. 1915, †Vermelles, Lt-Col., 19th London Regt. British graphic artist. Contrib. to *Graphic & Daily Graphic*. (Slade School Records.)

Colombe, Christophe
1886–25 Sept. 1915 †Souain, Croix de Guerre. French poet, novelist, & playwright of the Vendée: *Le Trait d'Union* (Revue du Languedoc, 1907). (*AEMG*, iv, 215.)

Compagnon, Auguste
1879–7 Oct. 1915 †Somme-Suippes, Champagne. French war poet: *Poèmes et Lettres des Tranchées* (1916). Posth. awarded Maurice Barrès medal from Soc. des Gens de Lettres.

Compodonico, Charles
1888–19 June 1916, wounds. French poet: *Lettres et Poésies* (Paris, 1924).
Cook, Leonard Niell
–7 July 1917, 2nd Lt, Royal Lancs Regt, MC. British poet: 'Plymouth Sound' in *More Songs by the Fighting Men* (Erskine Macdonald, London, 1917.)
Corbie, Henri de
1895–5 May 1917. French poet, unpubl.: 'Offrande de Printemps'; 'Offrande d'Automne' (1914). (*AEMG*, i, 189.)
Corbin, Pierre
1882–24 Mar. 1917, wounds, Monastir, after †Salonika, 20 Mar. French poets in *Anthologie critique des Poètes* (La Poètique, Paris, 1911).
Corrard, Pierre
1877–21 Nov. 1914 †Bolente. French poet & writer of romantic novels: *La Bohême d'aujourd'hui*. (*AEMG*, iii, 198.)
Cottineau, Raymond
(pseud.: Jean l'Hiver)
1893–10 Feb. 1915, Ypres. French war poet: *Le beau Sacrifice*, Prix Acad. française. (*AEMG*, ii, 169.)
Coulhon, Vital
1871–16 Sept. 1914, wounds, Villers-Cotteret, 42nd Infantry Regt. French sculptor.
Coulson, Leslie
1889–7 Oct. 1916 †Lesbœufs, Somme, Sgt, London Batt., Royal Fusiliers. British poet: 'Who made the Law?' in *From an Outpost and other Poems* (Erskine Macdonald, London, 1917).
Cousinéry, Marcel
1891–29 Apr. 1917 †air combat. French poet of rhymed letters to his mother, the Countess of Noailles & the Duchess of Brissac. (*AEMG*, iii, 204.)
Coutouly, Pierre de
1884–8 Dec. 1914 †Vauquois, 113rd Infantry Regt. French ceramicist & sculptor, mainly humorous portrayals of animals.
Cozic, Amédé (pseud.: Karedik)
1880–14 June 1915 †Haute Chevauchée. Breton poet: 'Buge Ar Menezion'. (Le Mercier d'Erm: *Les Bardes et Poètes de la Bretagne Armoricaine*, Rennes, 1919.)
Craven, A. Scott (pseud. of A. K. Harvey James)
–April 1917, France, Capt., Buffs Regt. English poet: *Alarums and Excursions* (Elkin Mathews, London, 1910); playwright: *The Last of the English or Hereward the Wake* (Elkin Mathews, London, 1910); & lyricist: *Princess Caprice* (a musical comedy by E. Welisch & R. Bernauer, London, 1912).
Crecelius, Gustav
1881–21 Aug. 1914 †Donon, Alsace. German painter of still-lifes, from Karlsruhe. Pupil of Hans Thoma. (*Deutsche Kunst und Dekoration* xxxvii, 1915/16, 213.)
Crenier, Camille (Henri)
1880–5 Mar. 1915 †Notre-Dame-de-Lorette, Cpl, 3rd Batt., Chasseurs à Pied. French sculptor, Prix de Rome with *Salamine*, 1908. (Th.-B.; Ginisty.)
Crisp, Frank E(dward) F(itzJohn)
–5 Jan. 1915. British artist, exhib. Royal Academy.
Crombie, Eugene
–23 April 1917 †Rœux, Somme, Capt., 4th Gordon Highlanders. British poet: *More Songs by Fighting Men* (Erskine Macdonald, London, 1917.)

Dadd, Philip, J. S.
–3 Aug. 1916, France. British painter & illustrator. Exhib. Royal Academy, Walker Art Gallery, Liverpool.
Dalize, René (pseud.: René Dupuy)
1879–7 May 1917 †Cogne-le-Vent. French poet; student associate of Guillaume Apollinaire: 'Ballade du pauvre Macchabé mal enterré' (publ. 1919). Wrote novel: *Le Club des Neurasthéniqes* (Franquevaux, Paris-Midi, 1912); & *Journal d'un Commandant de Compagnie* (now lost). (*AEMG*, v, 73.)
Danselow, Max Berthold
–1916? German war poet from Düsseldorf: 'Mein Eisern' Kreuz'.
Dansette, Charles
1894–25 Sept. 1916, 43rd Infantry Regt. French sculptor, exhib. Artistes Français, 1913.
Darmet, Louis
1890–2 Sept. 1918 †Juvigny, Alsace. French poet: *Près du Piano fermé* (Basset, Paris, 1912).
David, Georges *see* Balder, Jacques
Day, M(iles) Jeffrey Game
1869–27 Feb. 1918, drowned, after shot down in air combat, DSC. British poet: 'On the wings of the morning' in *Poems and Rhymes* (Sidgwick & Jackson, London).
Debelyanov, Dimcho (*see entry page* ***351***)
1887–2 Oct. 1916 †Dolno-Gorno Karadjovo. Bulgarian poet: *Complete Works* (Sofia, 1983).
Debert, Émile
–30 Apr. 1915 †Argonne. French pianist & composer. (Ginisty.)
Déchin, Géry
1882–26 Apr. 1915, wounds, †Saint-Clément, Metz 12 Apr. 1915. French sculptor, pupil of Injalbert.
Dejardin, Adolphe
1892–29 May 1916, †Dixmude. Belgian poet: *Histoires tragiques* (1910); *Frissons, Poèmes* (1910); *Au Gré des Heures* (1912). Contrib. to *Cri de Liège*. (*AEMG*, iii, 742.)
Delafraye, Charles
1875–23 Oct. 1914, wounds, Cologne lazarett after †Bucquoy, 4 Oct. French Catholic poet: 'Rosa Mystica'. Collaborated on *La Revue Picarde et Normande* from 1889. (*AEMG*, v, 83.)
Delahaye, Auguste
1894–15 July 1918 †Cutry, Soisson. French poet of the Vendée: *Les Heures sacrées* (Essaims Nouveaux). (Abbé Bertret, *Auguste Delahaye: Apôtre et Soldat*, Lussand, Vendée.)
Delaherche, Pierre
1895–25 Sept. 1915 †Auberive-sur-Suippe, Champagne, Cpl-Grenadier, Infantry Regt. French painter, son of ceramic artist Auguste Delaherche.
Delarve, André Morize- *see* Morize-Delavre, André
Delaunay, Pierre
1870–7 June 1915 †Hébuterne. French painter of Midi landscapes. (Ginisty.)
Dellys, Lucien (pseud. of Lucien Gunnéguez)
1881–27 Sept. 1915, †Main de Massiges, Braux-Sainte-Coyère. French Breton-born author of popular novels: *Le Maître des Peaux-Rouges* (1913), *Le Bracelet d'Onyx* (1914).
Deluc, Gabriel
1883–1916?, Senegalese Regt. French painter, pupil of Léon Bonnat, exhib. Artistes Français 1906–14. (Ginisty.)
Demouchy, Georges
1891–6 Oct. 1914 †Apremont, 134th Infantry Regt. French painter, pupil of Cormon. Exhib. La Triennale, 1915.
Dennys, Richard (Molesworth)
–24 July 1916, wounds, Rouen after †12 July 1916. British poet: *There is no death* (John Lane, London, 1917).
Desclers, Maurice (pseud.: Paul Bail)
1882–17 Feb. 1915, †Éparges, 106th Infantry Regt. Posth. Croix de Guerre & Légion d'honneur. French writer of theatre revues at Les Mathurins, Les Capucines, La Cigale & La Scala. A lyric 'Jardins sous la Pluie' was set to music by Claude Debussy.
Despax, Émile
1881–Jan. 1915 †Metz. French poet: *Au Seuil de la Lande* (1903), *La Maison des Glycines* (Mercure de France, Paris, 1905).
Desvachez, Alexandre
1893–12 Sept. 1916 †Somme, 110th Regt. French poet, Co-editor of *Les Humbles*. (*AEMG*, iv, 258.)
Détanger, Joseph *see* Nolly, Émile
Devos, Prosper-Henri
1899–1914. Belgian novelist: *Un Jacobin de l'An CVIII*; *Mona Lisa*. Founded periodical *La Belgique française*. (*AEMG*, iii, 757.)
Devred, René
1887–3 Apr. 1915 †Riaville, Meuse. French songwriter, much influenced by Debussy: 'Le Ruisseau', 'Arpège'.
Diaz de Soria, Guido
1877–28 Aug. 1916, wounds, Lavalard, Amiens after †Maurepas, 11 Aug. French novelist: *La première Leçon* (Ollendorff, Paris, 1903).
Dibelius, Franz
1881–19 Aug. 1916 †Thiaumont. German war poet: 'Frühling 1916', 'Das Letzte'. (*Meine Last ist abgelegt: Gedichte und Gedanken*, Verlag für Volkskunst Richard Keutel, Stuttgart, 1917.)
Dickinson, Humphrey Neville
1882–Sept. 1916, Rouen, 3rd Royal West Kent Regt. British novelist: *Keddy, a story of Oxford* (1907), *The Business of a Gentleman* (Heinemann, London, 1914), *Thomson's Friend* (Humphreys, London, 1917).
Diraison-Seylor, Olivier
1873–25 Apr. 1916. French author of novels based on his experiences as sailor: *Les Maritimes* (Juven, Paris, 1901), *L'Amour en croupe* (1912).
Dirlem *see* Bras, Jos ar
Dixon, Clive MacDonnell
1869–5 Nov. 1914 †Ypres, British Expeditionary Force. English artist from Yorkshire, exhib. Royal Academy.
Długosz, Stanisłav
(pseud.: Jerzy Tetera)
1891–6 Sept. 1915, †Samoklęski, Lubartówa, Platoon Cmdr, 1st Brig., Polish Legion, Virtuti Military Order. Polish patriotic poet, politician & historian: *Przed złotym czasem* (1917). Author of

monographic study, *Płk Dionizy Czachovski*. (K. Kosinksi, *Stansav Długosz charakterystyka twerczo'sci poetyckiej*, Warsaw, 1937.)

Döll, Oskar
1886–20 Sept. 1914 †France. German public sculptor & medallist. Pupil of Georg Wrbas. Work in Dresden destroyed.

Doucet, Henri
1883–Mar. 1915 †North French Front. French artist, associated with Berlin Secession 1911 & Omega Workshops 1912. Designed theatre sets for Duhamel's *Combat*, Goloubof's *Source enchantée* & Claudel's *L'Échange*. (A. Salmon, *Le jeune Peinture français*; Th.-B.)

Doumic, Max
1863–11 Nov. 1914. French architect. Prix Nationale, 1894.

Down, (William) Oliphant
–23 May 1917, wounds, Demicourt, Somme, Capt., 4th Batt., Royal Berks Regt, MC. British poet: *Poems* (Gowans & Gray, London, 1921); & playwright: *Three One-Act plays* (Gowans, London, 1923), *The Quod Wrangle* (Lacy's, London, 1914).

Downing, George Guy Barry
1893–4 Sept. 1917, flying accident in training, Scotland. British graphic artist, contrib. to *Colour*. (Slade School Records.)

Drouard, Maurice Edme
1886–28 Sept. 1915 †Perthes-Tahure, Champagne. French decorator & sculptor.

Drouet, Marcel
1888–4 Jan. 1915 †Consenvoye, Woëvre. French poet: *L'ombre qui tourne* (Dorbou, 1912). ('Le Tombeau de Marcel Drouet', *Le Cahier Rouge*, Paris, 1923.)

Drouin, Robert
1893–2 Oct. 1914 †St Marle les Tuots, wounds. French poet: 'Le vieux parc'. (*AEMG*, iii, 243.)

Drouot, Paul
1886–8 June 1915 †Notre-Dame-de-Lorette. French poet, collaborated on many literary periodicals. (*Poèmes choisis*, 1922.)

Dubarle, Robert
1881–15 June 1915 †Schnepfenried. French novelist: *Jean Barral; Lettres de Guerre* (Perrin, Paris, 1918); *Paroles des vivants et des morts: dialogues avec la douleur* (Paris, 1922).

Duchamp-Villon, Raymond
1876–7 Oct. 1918, typhoid, medical auxiliary service. Modernist sculptor. Brother of Marcel Duchamp. (The Duchamp Brothers, New York Graphic Soc., New York, 1977.)

Duflos, Jean
1879–27 Sept. 1915 †Champagne. French war poet: 'Noël 1914'. (*AEMG*, iv, 287.)

Dufner, André
1898–18 July 1918, disappeared †Villers-Cotterets, Faucrolles, Aisne. French poet, only publ. in *La Mouette*: 'Soir gris'.

Duguet, Jean
1886–22 June 1916 †St-Jean, Avocourt, Verdun. French poet: 'Paolina'. (*AEMG*, i, 224.)

Dujardin, Antoine
1887–30 Apr. 1915, wounds, Toul. French war poet: *Dans les tranchées 1914–15* (Mazeyrie, Tulle, 1915).

Dulhom-Noguès, Louis
(pseud. of Louis Barbet)
1889–8 Sept. 1914. French poet of Gascony: *Arretour* (1911); *La première Gerbe* (Girard, Paris, 1914, Prix Acad. française). Also works for theatre.

Dumange, Albert
1894–5 Oct. 1915 †St Hilaire-le-Grand. French poet: 'Les Conchants'. (*AEMG*, i, 235.)

Dumas, André Genès
1880–19 Apr. 1916. French painter of Paris scenes. (Ginisty.)

Dumas, Charles
1881–7 Nov. 1914, wounds. French poet: *L'Eau souterraine* (Ollendorff, Paris, 1903, Prix Sully-Prudhomme), *L'Ombre et les Proies* (Ollendorff, Paris, 1906), *Stellus* (Alphonse Lemerre, 1916, Prix Acad. française, Prix Acad. Beaux-Arts, Prix de Soussay).

Dupin, Jules
1890–26 Aug. 1915. French poet: *Le Journal de Maine de Biran* (Paris, 1912); *Les Ascensions du cœur* (Grasset, Paris, 1913).

Dupin, Léonce
1863–30 May 1918, wounds. French poet: 'Pro Patria', *Les Chants tricolores*, Nov. 1915. (*AEMG*, v, 648.)

Dupuy, René *see* Dalize, René

Dutruel, Paul Alain *see* Pad, Stéphan

Earčarnian, Atom *see* Siamant'o

Egisheim, Artur Freÿburger aus
–5 Mar. 1915 †Rava. German war poet: 'An meine Mutter vor der Schlacht'. (*DTH*.)

Ehrenbaum-Degele, Hans
1889–28 July 1915 †Ostrolenka. German poet: *Gedichte* (Paul Zech [ed.], Insel, Leipzig, 1917); 'Will the succeeding generations also appreciate what we have relieved them of: what we have expended in terms of blood, hatred, disgust, destruction?' Ed. *Das Neue Pathos* with Ludwig Meidner, Berlin 1913–14 & was publ. in *Der Sturm*.

Eng, Roger
1892–6 Dec. 1916, wounds, Bar-le-Duc after accident at the front. French war poet, imprisoned for a year in the Alten Grabow camp where he wrote *Écho d'Alten* & revues & lyrics for the theatre: *Les Âmes Oubliées* (Jonan, Caen, 1913); *Le Voyage* (Figuière, Paris, 1913), *Les pleurants de Saint Michel* (1917).

Engelke, Gerrit (*see entry page **82***)
1890–13 October 1918, wounds, British lazarett. German poet & writer: *Rhythmus des neuen Europa: das Gesamtwerk* (Postskriptum, Hanover, 1979).

Éon, André-Marie
1889–23 Oct. 1918, illness contracted at front, Troyes. French poet, contrib. to *Pan*, *Divan*. (*AEMG*, v, 651.)

Éon, Gabriel
1883–10 June 1915 †Hébuterne. French poet, contrib. to *Poitiers Universitaire*. (*AEMG*, i, 251.)

Erlwein, Hans (Jakob)
1872–Oct. 1914, car accident delivering presents to the troops at the front. German architect in Dresden. (Galerie Arnold exhib., 1913; *Der Baumeister*, xiii, 1915.)

Esmein, Maurice
1888–4 Feb. 1918 †, medical auxiliary, 72nd Infantry Regt. French landscape painter, Indépendants. Exhib. 1919.

Étévé, Marcel
1891–20 July 1916, Estrées, Somme. French poet & writer: *Lettres d'un combattant* (1917).

Evans, Ellis Humphrey (pseud.: Hedd Wyn)
1887–31 July 1917 †Pikem Ridge, 15th Batt. Royal Welsh Fusiliers. Welsh national poet, winner of 'Black Chair of Birkenhead' with heroic poem 'Yr Arwr'. (William Morris, *Hedd Wyn*, 1969; Derwyn Jones, *Ysgrifau Beirniadol*, vi, 1971.)

Exbrayat, Victor-Étienne
1879–1915 †Beauraignes, Somme. French medallist. (Th.-B.; Ginisty.)

Fabre, Marcel
1883–10 Oct. 1914 †Artois. French author of children's fiction: *Dans la Tourmente* (Roulf, Paris, 1911), *Les Mousquetaires de la Mer* (La Vie Mondiale, 1914).

Farrar, Ernest Bristow
1885–18 Sept. 1918. English organist & composer, mainly of songs & choral pieces. Collector of English folksong.

Farusi *see* Saint-Jean Lentilhac, Maurice de

Faure, Maurice
1862–7 Feb. 1915, exhaustion, Villiers-sur-Mer, Capt.-Cmdr, 1st Hussars. French portrait painter in watercolour.

Ferl, Walter
1892–4 Oct. 1915 †. German poet, contrib. to *Die Aktion*: 'Klage an den Mond'. (*Hinter der Front: Sonette*, Xenian, Leipzig, 1914.)

Fernet, André
1886–1 June 1916 †air combat, Viviers, nr Morhange, Lorraine. French critic & dramatist: *La Maison divisée* (Crès, Paris, 1916), *Le Cœur pur* (Crès, 1915).

Ferrat de Gaude, Joseph
1883–11 Oct. 1915 †Tahure, Champagne. French painter.

Ferrés-Costa, Pere
1888–6 May 1916, †Carency, Arras. Catalan poet in the French Army: 'A Na Catarina', 'Arbade'. Wrote under a variety of pseudonyms. (*AEMG*, i, 714.)

Ferrier, Jean André Gabriel
1884–26 Oct. 1916, illness contracted during †Somme. French painter of vast canvas *Endormi par le parfum d'une fleur fanée, j'ai souvenir d'une femme qui je n'ai jamais vue*, hung in Petit Palais des Champs-Élysées, 1919.

Feuillâtre, Paul(-Benjamin)
1881–21 Sept. 1914 †Troyes. French poet: *Écho et Narcisse* (La Belle Éd., Paris), *Le Jeu de l'Amour et du Désespoir* (La Belle Éd., Paris).

Filley, Georges
1882–1914, wounds, Chartres. French painter, d'Automne, Indépendants: *Femme se déshabillant, Mulâtresse*. (Ginisty.)

Fiolle, Paul
1887–2 July 1916 †Somme. French writer: *La Marsonille* (Payot, Paris, 1917); *Lettres, Campagne 1914–16* (Soc. de la Revue le Feu, 1917).

Fischer, Eugen
1891–14 Feb. 1915, wounds, lazaret, Carpathia. German expressionist writer, contrib. to *Die Aktion* (1914, col. 313).

Fisse, Georges

1890–13 Dec. 1914, †Pervyse, Vicogne. Belgian poet, songwriter & humorist. Collaborated on *Cri de Liège* with Paul Dumont & Adolphe Dejardin (q.v.). (*AEMG*, iii, 767.)

Flex, Walter (*see entry page 185*)
1887–13 Oct. 1917 †Ösel. German poet, playwright & novelist: *Gesammelte Werke* (Beck, Munich, 1925).

Florès, George Ricardo- *see* Ricardo-Florès, George

Flower, Clifford
1891–20 Apr. 1917 †France, driver, RFA. British poet, wrote verses in support of striking miners: 'My People's Voice' (1912); & 4 war poems: *Memoir & Poems* (priv.).

Fock, Gorch (pseud. of Johann Kinau)
1880–31 May 1916, drowned †Skagerrak. North German writer of stories concerning lives of Elbe fisherfolk: *Hein Goldenwind*, *Seefahrt ist Not*; & 2 stageworks: *Doggerbank*, *Cilli Cohrs*. Poems: *Sterne überm Meer* (Glogau, Hamburg, 1918). 'One's birthplace is the key to a man's soul. But then there are men who provide the key to their birthplace.'

Fontaine-Vive, Jean
1895–2 Aug. 1917 †. French-Savoyard poet: *Jeunesse ardente* (Riou, Paris, 1918), *Fleurs printanières* (Étampes, 1919).

Fontenay, Charles
1889–10 Jan. 1916 †Massige, Champagne. French poet, musician & painter. (*Deux Frères morts pour la France: Charles et Étienne de Fontenay, lettres du front 1914–16*, Plon, Paris, 1920.)

Forman, Justus Miles
1875–7 May 1915, drowned in the sinking of the *Lusitania*, accompanying theatre producer Charles Frohman & playwright Charles Klein (q.v.), both of whom also drowned. American novelist & playwright: *The Garden of Lies* (1902); *The Hyphen* (1915), a melodrama which deals with hyphenated political allegiance of the German-American in the war. (*Dictionary of American Biography*, John D. Wade.)

Foulon, Maurice
1893–9 July 1915, wounds, from †Neuville-Saint-Vaast, 13 May. French writer of verse, fiction & essays. (*AEMG*, i, 272.)

Fournier, Alain- *see* Alain-Fournier

Fournier, André
1896–1916 †Somme, 149th Inf. Regt. French fresco painter.

Fournier, Henri *see* Alain-Fournier

Foville, Jean de
1877–26 Apr. 1915 †Éparges, Croix de Guerre. French poet, novelist: *Bethsabée* (1913); art historian & numismatic aesthete.

François, Louis-Jean
1893–1914 †Saint-Julien, Belgium. French sculptor.

François-Poncet, Maxime
1898–4 Apr. 1918 †Aisne. French poet, editor of *La Presqu'île*. (*AEMG*, i, 550.)

Franconi, Gabriel-Tristan (*see entry page 238*)
1887–23 July 1918 †Bois de Sauvillers. French (satiric) writer: *Un Tel de L'Armée française* (Payot, Paris, 1918); & poet: *Poèmes* (La Renaissance du Livre, Paris, 1921).

Frank, Ludwig
1874–3 Nov. 1914 †Noissoncourt, Baccarat. German socialist politician & poet. (Carl Schorske: *German Social Democracy* 1905–17, Cambridge, Mass., 1955.)

Frech, Fritz
1894–4 Sept. 1917, air combat †Lens. German poet: 'Schneesturm in Polen'. ('Gefallene Künstler', *Ostdeutsche Monatsheften*, viii, 1921.)

Frenois, André du (pseud. of André Cassinelli)
1887–22 Aug. 1914, disappeared †Courbesseaux. French journalist & poet, disciple of Maurras: 'Le petit Caquois', *Le Divan*, 1913).

Freston, Hugh Reginald (Rex)
1891–24 Jan. 1916 †La Boiselle, 2nd Lt, 3rd Royal Berks Regt. British poet: *Collected Poems* (Blackwell, Oxford, 1916).

Froissart, Jacques
1877–14 Sept. 1918, Vesle, Aisne. French poet: 'Au Gré des Songes' (*La Revue Nationale*, Paris, 1918).

Fuglsaug, Hans
1889–21 June 1917, France. German painter from Schleswig-Holstein. (Hans Vollmer [ed.], *Allgemeines Lexikon der bildenden Künstler des XX: Jahrhunderts*, E.A. Seemann, Leipzig, 1955.)

Gallian, Emmanuel (pseud.: Noël Gaulois)
1867–23 May 1915 †Malembois, Meuse. French playwright: *Leroy s'amuse* (1893), *La Bête noire de Baptistin* (Billaudot, Paris); & story writer: 'Le Secret de la Marinière' (in *Les Veillées des Chaumières*).

Gambey, Léon
1883–1 Dec. 1914 †Bois d'Ailly, Hauts-de-Meuse, 56th Infantry Regt. French graphic artist, noted for his series of drawings of figures from the Napoleonic period in *Giberne*. (Th.B.)

Garçon, Jules *see* Letervanic, Georges

Gardiner, Edwin A.
–1916, while carrying dispatches, France. British artist, exhib. Nottingham Museum & Art Gallery, 1915.

Garrett, Henry Fawcett
1885–22 Aug. 1915, Suvla Bay, Gallipoli, Capt., 6th East Yorks Regt. British decorative wall painter. (Slade School Records.)

Gass, Georges
1884–22 Sept. 1914 †Sapigneul. French landscape painter.

Gaucher, Raymond
1887–19 June 1915 †Labyrinthe, Eulenburg. French poet: *Les Enthousiasmes* (Poisson, Caen, 1913).

Gaudier-Brzeska, Henri (*page 50*)
1891–5 June 1915 †Neuville-Saint-Vaast. French-born modernist sculptor & graphic artist. Friend & associate of Ezra Pound, T. E. Hulme (q.v.), Wyndham Lewis & Jacob Epstein. (Ezra Pound, *Gaudier-Brzeska: a memoir*, 1916: Horace Brodzky, *Henri Gaudier-Brzeska*, 1933; Jeremy Lewison [ed.], Cat. *Henri Gaudier Brzeska, sculptor 1891–1915*, Kettle's Yard, Cambridge, 1983.)

Gauthier-Ferrières, Léon Adolphe Désiré
1880–17 July 1915 †Gallipoli. French editor, biographer, journalist & poet: *Le Miroir brisé* (Paris, 1920). (Henri d'Yvignac, *Un poète mort en Soldat, Gauthier-Ferrières*, Sansot, Paris, 1916.)

Gautier, Philippe (pseud.: Guy Balignac)
1884–7 Nov. 1916 †Pressoir, Somme. French author: *Quatre Ans à la Cour de Saxe* (Perrin, Paris, 1913, Prix Acad. française).

Gaÿl, Gerhard Freiherr von
–9 Mar. 1916 †air combat, Cmdr, Feldfliegerabt. No. 18. German war poet who wrote the flying section's songs: 'Fliegerlied der Abteilung 18', 'Seinem lieben Oskar v. Puttkamer aufs Grab'. (*DTH*, 65.)

Geandreau, Louis
1885–13 Jan. 1915 †Crouy-sur-Aisne, posth. Croix de Guerre. French verse-dramatist: *Jean de la Fontaine* (perf. Comédie-Française, Paris, 31 Oct. 1923, Prix Toirac for best comedy of the year); *Galthier l'Oyseau* (play about Leonardo da Vinci, perf. Bordeaux). (E. Rostand [ed.], *Le Ciel dans l'Eau: poèmes et théâtres*, Paris.)

Gellner, František (*see entry page 336*)
1881–13 Nov. 1914, missing, Galicia. Czech artist, poet, short-story writer & dramatist: *Radosti života* (Prague, 1903); *Cesta do hor a jiné provídky* (Pardubice & Jihlava, Prague, 1914).

Genet, Henri-Émile
1889–4 Sept. 1916. French-Breton poet: *Rêveries Bretonnes* (Brive, Roche, 1909). (*AEMG*, i, 289.)

Genevoix, Gustave
1847–19 Oct. 1915 †Champagne, Capt. French novelist & playwright. Veteran of the Franco-Prussian War of 1870–1, without doubt the oldest writer to fall in the war at the age of 68. Wrote in the tradition of Hervieu, plays: *En appel* (perf. 1903), *Article de Paris* (1905); & novels: *Le Vicomte de l'Aubette* (Calmann-Lévy, Paris, 1880), *Ce qu'elles font* (Plon, Paris, 1896).

Georget, Henri (Alexandre)
–3 Mar. 1915 †Boureuillés, Argonnes. French impressionist painter: *Nymphes dans une Forêt* (1912, Prix Paquin).

Georgin, Anatole
1891–1 May 1916 †Bois de la Caillette, Croix de Guerre. French journalist & story-writer: 'La Quiche Lorraine' etc. (in *Le Pays Lorrain*, 1911). (*AEMG*, iv, 367.)

Géry, Louis
1885–20 Aug. 1918 †Cuts, 366th Regt. French poet: *Quelques Poèmes* (Nice, 1912), *Le Cahier des Poètes* (Nice 1912–13). (*AEMG*, ii, 326.)

Getchev, Albert
–2 Dec. 1915. Bulgarian writer.

Gethin, Percy Francis
c. 1875–summer 1916, 2nd Lt, Devonshire Regt. British painter & etcher. (*The Studio*, lxix, 44.)

Gidony, Francesco
1887–17 Apr. 1917, wounds, Lt, Canadian Infantry. Canadian-born artist. (Slade School Records.)

Gien, Auguste (pseud.: Jean Millery)
1884–25 Aug. 1914, disappeared, †Rozelieures, Meurthe-et-Moselle. French chansonnier: 'Le moulin joi', 'La Bourgogne chante et pleure' etc. Publ. in *La Bourgogne d'Or*.

Gignoux, Gonzague
1886–25 Sept. 1916 †Beach 916, Armensko, Florina. French essayist &

novelist: *Une Ascension au Pelvoix* (Grenoble, 1907). His novel *La Force des Mots* is lost.

Gignoux, Léon
1891–5 Nov. 1914, wounds. French poet: 'Printemps en banlieue'. (*AEMG*, i, 297.)

Gillhausen, Guido von
–1918, wounds, Berlin, from †Eastern Front, Maj.. German military composer. (*Allgemeine Musikzeitung*, 1918, 225.)

Ginisty, Pierre
1884–24 Dec. 1914 †St Julien, Poëcappelle. French playwright, son of Paul Ginisty, the director of Th. de l'Odéon, Paris: *Jour d'Échéance*; *Chambre d'Ami*; *Barnabé*.

Glaize, Raymond
1880–27 Sept. 1914, wounds from †Hargny-aux-Cerises. French painter of Breton landscapes. (Th.B.; Ginisty.)

Godin, André
1883–13 July 1916 †Massiges. French writer, fascinated by Far Eastern religions: *Siddartha, épisode de la vie de Bouddha*. (*André Godin, sa vie, son œuvre*, Berthe de Nyse, 1918.)

Gonnard, Philippe
(pseud.: Claude Lefilleul)
1878–25 Oct. 1916 †Woëvre. French Catholic poet: 'Prière pour les Patries'. (*AEMG*, ii, 346.)

Good, Charles-Gustave
1885–17 Dec. 1914 †Maricourt, Somme. French painter, exhib. Soc. des Artistes Indépendants. (Ginisty.)

Gounelle, Henri
1894–21 June 1915 †Calonne. French poet: 'La Bacchante'. (*AEMG*,v, 386.)

Gourdault, Pierre
1880–5 Jan. 1915, wounds, Givenchy-le-Noble after †Roclincourt, 28 Dec. 1914. French painter of North African scenes. (Ginisty.)

Granados (y Campiña), **Enrique**
1867–24 Mar. 1916, drowned after torpedo attack on SS *Sussex* in English Channel. Spanish-Catalan romantic composer. Composed zarzuelas, orchestral works, songs, piano pieces (*Goyescas*). (Pablo Vila San-Juan, *Papeles Intimos de Enrique Granados*, Amigos de Granados, Barcelona, 1966).

Granier, Albert-Paul (*see entry page **315***)
1888–17 Aug. 1917 †plane crash, Verdun. French poet: *Les Coqs et les Vautours* (Jouve, Paris, 1917).

Granier, Louis
1891–13 Sept. 1914, wounds, Clermont de Besançon. French poet: 'Invocation'. (*Les Essaims Nouveaux*, xx, May 1919.)

Gravier, Joseph
1890–12 July 1916 †Éparges. French poet from Lyon. (*AEMG*, ii, 372.)

Gray, Maurice
1889–8 Aug. 1918, †Beaucourt en Santerre, Capt., Machine Gun Corps, Cavalry. British artist. (Slade School Records.)

Grégoire, Henri-Charles
1882–30 Aug. 1914 †Fossé, Ardennes. French poet: 'Le Concert de la muerte'; & novelist: *Le Vandale du Louvre*, *Le dernier Réveillon*. (*AEMG*, i, 332.)

Gregory, William Robert
1881–32 Jan. 1918, †Italian Front, Maj., 4th Connaught Rangers, MC, Légion d'honneur. Irish painter of West Irish landscapes & set designer: Synge's *Deidre of the Sorrows*, Yeats's *Shadowy Waters*, Augusta Gregory's *The Image*, at the Abbey Th., Dublin. (Slade School Records.)

Grenfell, Julian (Henry Francis) 1888–26 May 1915, wounds, Boulogne after †Railway Hill, Ypres. British soldier-poet: 'Into Battle'. (Nicholas Mosley, *Julian Grenfell: his Life and the Times of his Death 1888–1915*, Weidenfeld & Nicolson, London, 1976.)

Grimbert, Clovis
1887–11 June 1918 †Méry, Somme. French journalist, 'poète de terroir', ed. of one of the major newspapers of the front: *Le 120 Court*. Poems: 'Les Poilus', 'Nos Poux', 'Noël des Gueux de la Guerre'. Wrote soldiers' revue *Haut les Cors!* (perf. 19 May 1917 'dans le bois d'A . . .') (*120 Court*, xl, Dec. 1918.)

Grouiller, Robert Pierre
1886–15 Oct. 1918, wounds, Provins. French etcher & wood carver of old Paris, Rouen, Chartres, etc. (Bénézit.)

Gsell, Hans
1884–30 Apr. 1915 †Savonnières. German animal sculptor from the Alsace. Mainly birds & cats. (*Kunstchronik*, new series, xxvi, 1915, 443.)

Guénard, Albert
1877–17 Dec. 1914, illness, Morlaix. French poet: 'Entre seize et vingt ans' (1897), *Le dernier Jour de Trianon* (drame en un acte en vers, Amiens, 1907). (*AEMG*, v, 661.)

Guerdavid, Yves (Le Rouge) de
1892–28 Feb. 1917, wounds. French-Breton poet: 'Le Menhir' (1911). (*AEMG*, iv, 405.)

Guérin, Gabriel
1869–Feb. 1916, illness. French landscape painter & art critic, exhib. Soc. Artistes français 1896–1914. (Bénézit.)

Guiard, Amédée
1872–28 Sept. 1915 †Bois de la Folie. French novelist & poet: 'L'Enfance'. (Jean des Cognets, *L'un d'eux: Amédée Guiard*, Blond et Gay, Paris.)

Guillez, Arthur Edmond
1885–18 July 1916, wounds & gassing, Saint-Mesmie after †Montagne de Reims. French engraver & painter, winner 2nd Grand-Prix de Rome. War drawings. (Th.-B.)

Guillot, Léon
1882–20 May 1915 †Maison Blance, Bois d'Ailly. French græcophile poet: 'Les Chèvres de Pan'. (*AEMG*, iii, 349.)

Gumpel, Lucien
1880, 25 Sept. 1915 †Aubérive, Champagne. French poet: 'Le circuit du Parnasse'; & playwright: *Monsieur de Prevan*, *Une Vieille contait*, *La Nuit de Racine* (all perf. Th. de l'Odéon, Paris.)

Gunnéguez, Lucine *see* Dellys, Lucien

Gyóni, Géza (pseud. of Géza Áchim) (*see entry page **348***)
1884–25 June 1917, POW, Krasnojarsk. Hungarian war poet: *Lengyel mezökön, tábortűz mellett* (Przemysl, 1914); *Complete Works* (Szépirodalmi Könyvkiadó, 1984).

Halphen, Fernand (Gustave)
1872–May 1917, illness. French composer, pupil of Massenet. 2nd Grand Prix de Rome: *Mélusine*. (*Neue Musik-Zeitung*, xx, 1917, 310.)

Hamonno, Alphonse-Georges
1883–23 Mar. 1916, illness contracted in trenches, Paris. French-Breton poet: *Le Tisseur de Rêves* (Sansot, Paris, 1911).

Hardyman, (John Hay) **Maitland**
1894–24 Aug. 1918 †Biefvillers, Maj., Somerset Light Infantry, DSO, MC. British poet: *A Challenge* (Allen & Unwin, London, 1919).

Harmenon, André d'
1893–5 May 1915 †Artois. French poet, co-founder of literary periodical *Mail*. (*AEMG*, iii, 360.)

Haroutounian, Hovhannes (pseud.: T'lkatinc'i)
1860–1915. Armenian writer.

Hatton, Brian
1887–23 Apr. 1916, Oghratina, Egypt, Worcester Yeomanry. British painter of country scenes & Egyptian landscapes. Exhib. Royal Soc. of Portrait Painters. Member, Chelsea Arts Club. (Churchill Gardens Museum, Hereford.)

Heald, Ivan
1883–4 Dec. 1916, shot down while flying over German lines in France as Observer, RFC. Irish journalist & writer. (Sidney Dark, *Ivan Heald: hero and humorist*, Pearson, London, 1917.)

Heath, Roger Meyrick
1889–16 Sept. 1916, Delville Wood, 9th Batt., Prince Albert's Regt. English scholar & poet: 'Beginnings'. (Memorials of Rugbeians [iv]).

Hecht, Georg
1885–14 May 1915 †St Mihiel. German poet of *Die Aktion*: 'Moseh', 'Leichnam'. Friend of Hugo Ball. Publ. essays, poems, translations together with Eugen Mondt.

Heller, Paul
–13 Oct. 1916. Austrian contributor to *Die Aktion* & poet-editor of *Die Botschaft*.

Hellingrath, (Friedrich) **Norbert** (Theodor) **von**
1888–14 Dec. 1916 †Douaumont, Verdun. German Hölderin scholar & poet: 'Pindar-Übersetzungen'. 'In the depths of my soul I am a philologist, and on the surface only a poet. That is why I will *become* a poet and *be* a philologist.'

Hendry, George E.
–1916, Flanders, Rifle Brig. British landscape & portrait painter. Exhib. Bruton Gallery, London, 1905.

Héneux, Édouard
1880–13 Sept. 1914 †Chelles, Aisne. French architect.

Henseler, Franz (Seraph) (*page 3*)
1883–15 Apr. 1918, exhaustion & insanity after 4 years' military service, Haar, nr Munich. German expressionist painter & illustrator. Member of Werkbundausstellung, Cologne, 1914; Rheinische Expressionisten, Düsseldorf, 1914. (*Die Rheinischen Expressionisten*, Aurel Bongers, Recklinghausen, 1979.)

Hesse, Hermann
–1917 †Western Front. German composer from Hamburg: 'Pro Patria' (symphonic poem). (*Neue Musik-Zeitung*, xxxix, 18.)

Hewett, Stephen Henry Philip
1893–22 July 1916 †Delville Wood, 14th

Warwicks Regt. British scholar & poet: *A Scholar's Letters from the Front* (1918).

Heyman, Charles
1881–15 May 1915
†Ablain-Saint-Nazaire, 226th Infantry Regt. French engraver of Paris scenes. (Ginisty; Th.-B.)

Heymann, Walther
1882–8 Jan. 1915 †Soissons. German short-story writer & poet: *Kriegsgedichte und Feldpostbriefe* (G. Müller, Munich, 1925).

Heymel, Alfred Walter von
1878–26 Nov. 1914, Berlin, illness contracted at front. German publisher (of Insel-Verlag, Leipzig) & poet: *Gedichte und Prosa: Der Tag von Charleroi* (Insel, Leipzig, 1925). Archive held at Schiller Nationalmuseum, Marbach.

Heyne, Ludwig Heinrich
1878–22 Oct. 1914, wounds, Douvrain, †La Bassée, 53rd Inf. Regt. German painter from Düsseldorf. (Th.-B.)

Hillemacher, Jean
1889–6 Sept. 1914 †Blesme, Vitry-le-François, Marne, Sgt, 128th Inf. Regt. French painter. (Th.-B.; Ginisty.)

Hinz, Hugo
1894–7 July 1914 †Eastern Front. German poet, contrib. to *Die Aktion*: 'Verse I & II' (Franz Pfemfert [ed.], *De Aktionslyrik: Anti-Kriegslyrik der Aktion*, Berlin-Wilmersdorf, 1916).

Hirtz, Georges
1893–23 Dec. 1918, influenza, contracted in trenches. French war poet: *Bric à Brac – vers de guerre avec un peu de prose* (1921). (*AEMG*, v, 419.)

Hobson, John Collinson
–31 July 1917, Lt, 116th Machine Gun Coy. British poet: *Poems* (Blackwell, Oxford, 1920).

Hoch, Franz Xaver
1869–17 June 1916, †Vosges. German painter of the Bavarian landscape. (Th.-B.)

Hodgson, William Hope
1878–17 Apr. 1918, 171st Brig., RFA. British author of seafaring mystery & adventure stories: *The Luck of the Strong* (1916), *Men of the Deep Waters* (1914), *Cargunka and Poems and Anecdotes* (1914), *The Calling of the Sea: Poems* (1920). Bibl. Ian Bell, *W.H. Hodgson, Voyager and Visionary*, Antiquarian Book Monthly (1985).

Hodgson, William Noel
(pseud.: Edward Melbourne)
1893–1 July 1916, Somme. British war poet: 'Before Action' (*Verse and Prose in Peace and War*, Smith, Elder, London, 1916).

Hoff, Fernand
1895–14 Feb. 1917 †Südelkopf, Alsace. French war poet: 'En face de la Mort' (Prix Monthyon de littérature, 1920).

Hoffmann, Kurt
–2 Mar. 1915 †St Quentin. German architect & war poet: 'Dem Kaiser'. (*DTH*, 82.)

Hoffmann, Richard
1881–May 1918. German painter from Düsseldorf.

Hombek, Albert
1890–1 Sept. 1914 †Maubeuge, Bonssois. French poet: 'Femme' (1910). (*AEMG*, ii, 384.)

Horne, Cyril Morton
–27 Jan. 1916 †France, Capt., 7th Batt., King's Own Scottish Borderers. Scottish poet: *Songs of the Shrapnel Shell and other Verse* (Harper, New York, 1918).

Houin, Marcel
1887–7 Aug. 1915, disappeared. †Sedul-Bahr, Gallipoli. French poet: 'Pleine Mer'. (*AEMG*, iv, 409.)

Hourcade, Olivier *see* Olivier-Hourcade

Hulin, Ernst
1882–9 Dec. 1918, POW Strasbourg. French sculptor: *Fétiches* (illus. *Les Arts*, cl. 1914, 13.) (Th.-B.; Ginisty.)

Hulme, T(homas) **E**(rnest)
(*see entry page **44***)
1883–28 Sept. 1917, Nieuport, Belgium, Royal Marine Artillery. English aesthete, philosopher & experimental poet: *Speculations* (Routledge, Kegan Paul, London, 1924), *Further Speculations* (London, 1955), *Notes on Language and Style*.

Humières (Vicomte Ayméric Eugène) **Robert d'**
1868–26 Apr. 1915 †Lizerne, 4th Zouaves. French essayist, playwright: *Cœur*, *Les Ailes closes*, *Comme des Dieux*; & ballet librettist: *La Tragedie de Salomé* (to music by Florent Schmitt, 1912); translator of Kipling & Wedekind.

Hutchinson, Henry William
1898–13 Mar. 1917 †France. British war poet.

Hutchison, George Jackson
1869–1918. British painter from Scotland. Exhib. Glasgow Art Gallery.

Ibels, Robert
1895–19 Aug. 1917 †Côte du Poivre, Verdun. French war poet, unpubl.: 'Fusées' (1916). (*AEMG*, i, 368.)

Isræl, Léon
1882–6 Apr. 1916 †. French songwriter & poet: 'Ballade des fiers conscrits', 'La glaise'. (*AEMG*, v, 125.)

Jacques, Raphaël
1882–7 Sept. 1914 †Courbesseaux, Sgt, 269th Regt. French painter & engraver. (Ginisty.)

Jallifier, Joseph-Étienne
1885–28 Sept. 1914 †Linons, Chaulnes, 140th Infantry Regt. French lithographer.

James, A. K, Harvey *see* Craven, A. Scott

Janecke, Wilhelm
1886–Oct. 1916, disappeared †Somme. German poet: *Die Wüste* (unpubl.).

Janowitz, Franz (*see entry page **109***)
1892–4 Nov. 1917, Southern Front. Austrian lyric poet: *Auf der Erde* (1919).

Jaurès, Jean
1859–31 July 1914, assassinated by a fanatic Nationalist. Principal leader of French Socialist movement, co-founder of newspaper *L'Humanité*. (Harvey Goldberg, *The Life of Jean Jaurès*, 1962.)

Jeftić, Branko
–1916 †, squad cmdr. Serbian painter.

Jenkins, Arthur Lewis
1892–31 Dec. 1917, air crash in training, Yorkshire, RFC. British poet from Devon: *Forlorn Adventures* (Sidgwick & Jackson, London, 1918).

Jentsch, Robert
1890–21 Mar. 1918, Western Front, Lt. German poet, associate of Georg Heym & Friedrich Koffka. Printed in *Der Demokrat* & *Die Aktion*.

Jephson, Frank Maurice
1886–20 Apr. 1917, wounds, France. British composer & organist.

Joannis-Pagan, Joseph de
1885–23 Sept. 1914 †Lironville, Lorraine. French melancholic poet: *Les Sous graves et doux* (Paris, 1918, Prix Jacques Normand, 1920).

Job, Cvijeto
–1916 †. Serbian painter.

Jobbé-Duval, Pierre
1887–29 Oct. 1917, illness. French playwright: *L'Occasion*, *L'Étau*; & ballet librettist: *Siang-Sin* (to music by Georges Hüe, perf. L'Opéra, Paris, 1924).

John, Edmund
1883–28 Feb. 1917, heart disease, Italy, after discharge from Artists Rifles. English poet: *Symphonic symbolique and other Poems* (Erskine Macdonald, London, 1919), *The Flute of Sardonyx* (Herbert Jenkins, London, 1913).

Johnson, Donald Frederic Goold
1890–15 July 1916, wounds, Lt, Manchester Regt. British poet: *Poems* (Cambridge University Press, 1919).

Jones, Leslie Phillips
1895–7 June 1915, wounds, Gallipoli, 29th Div., 2nd Hampshire Regt. British poet: *Youth and other Poems* (priv., 1915).

Jordens, Jules-Gérard
1885–26 Apr. 1916 †Pontavert. French poet: 'Voici l'Âme et la Chair' (1909). (*AEMG*, iv, 413.)

Jordic *see* Pignon, Georges

Jost, Walter
–1916 †Somme. German war poet from Saxony: 'Zum Leben'. (*DTH*, 89.)

Jouenne, Charles Célestin
1877–25 Aug. 1914 †Iwuy (Nord). French engraver. (Ginisty.)

Jourdan, Jacques
1880–25 Mar. 1916 †Verdun. French painter, Salon national, 1913. (Ginisty.)

Jürgens, Fritz
1888–7 Sept. 1915 †Champagne. German self-taught songwriter to poems by Gustav Falke & Martin Greif, publ. by Schott, Mainz.

Jung, Moriz
1885–1 Mar. 1915 †Maniłova Heights, Łubne, Carpathia. Austrian graphic designer, caricaturist & illustrator. Contrib. postcards for the Wiener Werkstätte. (Th.-B.)

Jutz, Carl (the Younger)
1873–7 Sept. 1915, Russian Front. German landscape painter, son of the bird painter & etcher Jutz the Elder. (Th.-B.)

Kandt, Richard
1867–29 Apr. 1918, gassing, Dresden. German poet: 'Das neue Reich' (1914) in *Meine Seele klingt* (Reimer, Brelin, 1918).

Kelly, Frederick Septimus
1881–13 Nov. 1916
†Beaucourt-sur-Ancre, Cmdr, 'B' Co., Hood Batt., DSC. Australian-born composer of songs & piano pieces & 'Elegy In Memoriam Rupert Brooke' for stringed orchestra. (*Australian Dictionary of Biography*, ix, 554; *F. S. Kelly Diaries*, Oct.

1907–Apr. 1915, National Library of Australia, Canberra.)

Kershaw, J. Franklin
–14 Oct. 1917. British painter, member, Oldham Soc. of Artists.

Kettle, Thomas M(ichael)
*(see entry page **41**)*
1889–9 Sept. 1916 †Ginchy, Lt, Dublin Fusiliers. Irish politician, essayist & poet: *Poems and Parodies* (London, 1916). (J. B. Lyons, *The enigma of Tom Kettle, Irish Patriot, Essayist, Poet, British Soldier 1880–1916*, Glendale Press, Dublin, 1983.)

Kilmer, (Alfred) **Joyce**
1886–30 July 1918 †Ourcq, Sgt, 165th US Inf., Croix de Guerre. American (Roman Catholic) poet & journalist: 'Prayer of a Soldier in France'. (*Trees and Other Poems*, 1914; *Main Street and Other Poems*, 1917; *The Circus and other Essays*; Robert C. Halladay [ed.], *Joyce Kilmer, Poems, Essays and Letters*, 1918.)

Kinau, Johann *see* Fock, Gorch

King, George
1897–12 Feb. 1917 †, 2nd Lt, 9th Suffolk Regt. British war poet: *Verses* (Mawby, Derby, 1918).

Klein, Charles
1867–7 May 1915, drowned in sinking of *Lusitania*. American playwright & assistant to theatre producer Charles Frohman, also drowned. Numerous plays incl. *The Music Master* (1904); *The Lion and the Mouse* (1905); *The Third Degree* (1909); *The Gamblers* (1910); *Maggie Pepper* (1912); *The Daughters of Men* (1915). (*Who's Who in America*, 1912–13.)

Klés, Petr (pseud. of Vilém Vordren)
1869–2 Oct. 1916 †Bosnia. Czech poet & prose writer.

Klingebiel, Jean
1892–16 Apr. 1917 †Chemins-des-Dames, body unrecovered. French poet & Christian essayist. (*AEMG*, i, 376.)

Kloster, Charles
1884–27 Apr. 1917, POW, captured at †Avocourt. French painter, poet, critic & philosopher. Pupil of Bonnat. (Th.-B.; Ginisty; *AEMG*, ii, 415.)

Knapp, Ludwig
1889–29 Mar. 1918 †Western Front. German poet: 'Septembernacht' in *Gedichte* (Kaiser, Munich, 1918).

Koch, Justus
–31 Oct. 1914 †Flanders. German volunteer from University of Göttingen who wrote jubilant student war & drinking song: 'Das Abschiedslied des Studenten im Felde'. (*DTH*.)

Köhler, Paul Ernst
1890–14 Oct. 1914 †Northern France. German nationalist poet: 'Die Jugend im 1914er Krieg', *Vom Baum des Lebens* (Müller & Fröhlich, Munich.)

Konieczny, Włodzimierz
1886–5 July 1916 †Polska Góra, Volhynia, Wolczesk, Polesia. Polish sculptor & graphic artist. Initiator of the Polish Literary & Art Association in Paris. Member, Polish Artists Association. Established Cracow Workshop. (Th.-B.)

Kostrowitzky, Wilhelm *see* Apollinaire, Guillaume

Kraus, Fritz
1874–Apr. 1918, Western Front. German sculptor of public monuments: Berlin Tiergarten director Geitner, Admiral von Koester, Kiel. (Th.-B.)

Kremer, Louis
1883–18 July 1918, wounds. French poet: 'Le Tribut d'Airain' (1909). (*AEMG*, ii, 425.)

Kühnelt, Hugo
1877–8 Sept. 1914. Austrian sculptor from Vienna. Pupil at the Vienna Academy under Hellmer. Member of Vienna Secession. (Th.-B.; *The Studio*, lvi, 1912, 35.)

Kuřina-Blatnický, Josef
1893–1914, Russian Front. Czech poet.

Kuula, Toivo
1883–18 May 1918, after being shot on eve of Finnish independence, Viipuri. Finnish composer, mainly of songs & works for unaccompanied male choir. Pupil of Järnefelt & Sibelius. (E. Roiha, *Toivo Kuula, a Finnish composer of genius*, Helsinki, 1952.)

La Bonnardière, Dominique
1873–23 June 1915 †La Fontenelle, 257th Inf. Regt. French writer of farces: *Chantecoine*, *La Folie de Guignol*; of a mysterium: *Le Miracle de Saint François* (to music by Pierre Bethenod); & poet: *La Fenêtre en sol-eillée* (Allier, Grenoble, 1913).

Lachasse, Jean
1889–20 Dec. 1914 †Soupir, Chemin-des-Dames. French story writer in the style of Edgar Allan Poe, publ. *Revue de la Vie mondaine* & *Gazette de France*. ('Contes étranges et fantasques', *Images de Paris*, 1921; *AEMG*, iii, 410.)

Lafon, André *(see entry page **276**)*
1883–5 May 1915, scarlet fever, Bordeaux, contracted in Saint-Ciers-sur-Gironde, auxiliary forces. Associated with Jean de La Ville de Mirmont (q.v.). Author of *L'Élève Gilles* (Hôtel de Ville, Blaye, 1987; Prix National de Littérature, 1912) & *La Maison sur la rive* (Perrin, Paris, 1914).

Lafond, François
1899–2 Nov. 1918 †Rethel, 20th Batt., 25th Regt., Chasseur à pied. French poet. (*AEMG*, i, 385.)

Lagardère, Abbé Jean
1861–4 Nov. 1918. French patriotic poet & religious writer: *Haut les cœurs* (1916), *France . . . Demain!* (1917). (*AEMG*, i, 388.)

Laguille, Ernest
1886–27 Sept. 1915 †Maisons de Champagne. French poet & story writer, contrib. to *Revue Méridionale* (1904–14).

Lançon, René
1892–12 Apr. 1915 †Marcheville, Meuse. French poet: *Les Fleurs qui s'ouvrent* (Sansot, Paris, 1912). (*AEMG*, ii, 441.)

Landes, François
1886–6 Aug. 1916 †Bras, Meuse. French poet: *Œuvres Posthumes* (Gautier). (*AEMG*, ii, 446.)

Langstaff, James Miles
1883–1 Mar. 1917 †Vimy Ridge, Maj., 75th Batt., Canadian Expeditionary Force. Canadian war poet: 'The Answer', 'War-Shaped Destiny', in J. W. Garvin, *Canadian Poems of the Great War* (McClelland & Stewart, Toronto, 1918).

Lanoue, Élysée
1883–1 July 1915 †La Harazèe. French poet: 'Appel au rêve' (publ. in *Hermès*, 1913).

Laplace, Gaston
1885–Nov. 1917, accident, Saint-Jean-de-Maurienne. French engraver. Artistes français.

Laporte, André Victor Louis
1889– Mar. 1918, wounds, Val-de-Grâce. French composer, pupil of Paul Vidal: *Mort d'Orphée* (symphonic poem for orchestra & harp solo, 1914, Prix Pleyel).

Larreguy de Civrieux, Marc de *(see entry page **217**)*
1895–18 Nov. 1916 †Froideterre, Verdun. French anti-war poet: *La Muse de Sang* (Libr. du Travail, Paris, 1926).

Lartigue, François de
1893–12 Oct. 1914 †Champagne. French poet of Gascony: *Arrajades Gasconnes* (Marrinpoey, 1920). (*AEMG*, iv, 446.)

La Salle, Louis de
1872–7 Oct. 1915 †Champagne. French poet: *Les vaines Images* (Grasset, Paris, 1911); & novelist: *Le Réactionnaire: Mœurs parisiennes* (1908). (*AEMG*, v, 144.)

La Senne, Émile
1881–11 Nov. 1914. French poet & story writer: *A Voix basse* (Gongy, Paris, 1902), *L'Éternelle Aventure* (Grasset, Paris, 1911), *La Païva* (Daragon, Paris, 1911). Acad. Française Memorial Prix Fabien, 1916. (*AEMG*, ii, 438.)

Lassausaie, Guy
1891–10 Mar. 1915 †St Julien, Ypres. French poet: *Musiques d'Âme* (1914); novelist: *Par delà les Morts* (1914, incomplete); & playwright: *Le Rameau de Jasmin* (incomplete). (*AEMG*, ii, 450.)

Lasserre, Jacques
1894–11 Oct. 1915, air crash, 1st Regt Cuirassiers. French decorator-painter.

Latapie, Georges-Ambroise
1889–1914, tetanus from foot wound †Trouville. French poet: *Une Hirondelle ne fait pas le Printemps* (Ondin, Paris, 1914).

Latil, Léo
1890–27 Sept. 1915. French poet, friend of Darius Milhaud, who collected & publ. *Poèmes* (1917). Milhaud set *Quatres Poèmes de Léo Latil* to music (Durand, 1920). (*Lettres d'un Soldat*, Blond et Gay, Paris, 1916.)

Laurens, (Marius Jean Baptiste) Léopold
1889–8 May 1915 †Sedul-Bahr, Gallipoli. French journalist, story writer & poet. Stories publ. in *Le Radical*, *Le Républicain du Gard*, *Le Journal du Midi*. (*AEMG*, iv, 454.)

Lautrey, Louis
1864–31 Mar. 1915 †Bois le Prêtre, Chevalier, Légion d'honneur. French poet: *Poèmes d'Israel* (1910); & verse-dramatist: *Hélène de Tournon* (1914). (*AEMG*, ii, 471.)

La Ville de Mirmont, Jean de
*(see entry page **303**)*
1886–28 Nov. 1914 †Verneuil. French poet: *L'Horizon chimérique*, later set to music by Gabriel Fauré; & author of novella: *Les Dimanches de Jean Dézert* (Bergue, Paris, 1914). (Michel Suffran, *Jean de La Ville de Mirmont*, Seghers, Paris, 1968.)

Lavoine, Jacques

1896–17 Apr. 1917 †Cornillet. French poet. ('Jacques Lavoine, mort pour la France', *Nouveau Mercure*, 1918.)

Lazarević, Aleksandar
–1915, typhus while on military service. Serbian painter.

Leader, B(enjamin) Eastlake
c. 1878–12 Oct. 1916, Capt., Royal West Surrey Regt. British painter. Exhib. Royal Soc. of Oil Painters.

Léché (Vicomte) Oswald de
1893–18 June 1915 †Liévin, Pas-de-Calais. French poet: *Hymnes Français* (Figuières, Paris, 1916).

Lecomte, Alphonse
1882–14 Oct. 1914 †Godat, Reims. French artist, primarily of ceramics & frescos. (Th.-B.; Ginisty.)

Lederer, Jacques
1894–20 Apr. 1917 †Chavonne, Vailly, Aisne, Cpl, 355th Inf. Regt. French painter.

Ledwidge, Francis (*see entry page 37*)
1887–31 July 1917 †Ypres, Lance-Cpl, Inniskilling Fusiliers. Irish pastoral poet: *The Complete Poems of Francis Ledwidge* (Brian O'Keefe, London, 1974).

Léger, Marcel
1892–9 June 1915 †Perthes-les-Hurlus, Sgt, 53rd Inf. Regt. French sculptor.

Le Goff, Paul-Henri
1883–1915. French sculptor, pupil of Coutan: *L'Hives* (Grand Prix Roux, 1911). (Th.-B.; Ginisty.)

Legrand, Maxence (pseud. of Alexandre Warschawsky)
1882–4 Jan. 1916 †Hartmannswillerkopf. French novelist: *Clair-Obscur* (1913). (*AEMG*, ii, 476.)

Lehmann, Alfred *see* Lemm, Alfred

Lehuédé, Marcel-Pierre
1886–16 Apr. 1918, Oise, after gassed †Grivesnes. French sculptor, 2nd Grand Prix de Rome 1913. Created memorials to 354th Regt, Suippes cemetery.

Leighton, Roland Aubrey
1895–1915 †Plœgsteert Wood. British poet. Fiancé of Vera Brittain. *Roland Leighton* (David R. Leighton [ed.], publ. priv., 1981).

Lemas, Louis
1891–14 Dec. 1914 †Ypres. French poet: 'Les Tumultes' (1911), publ. in *Les Loups*. (*AEMG*, iv, 475.)

Lemercier, Eugène-Emmanuel
1886–6 Apr. 1915 †Éparges. French painter & graphic artist: *Peintures, Dessins et Esquisses*. (André Michel: 'Un Peintre Soldat E.-E. Lemercier', *Revue Hebdomadaire*, 25 May 1918.)

Lemeunier, Carolus-Albert-Denis
1881–30 Oct. 1918, exhaustion & influenza, 117th Infantry Regt. French painter.

Lemm, Alfred (pseud. of Alfred Lehmann) (*see entry page **166***)
1889–autumn 1918. German short-story writer: *Gesammelte Prosa* (Thomas Rietzschel [ed.], Brennglas-Verlag, Assenheim, 1987).

Le Moal, Louis (pseud.: Laouik)
1881–14 Sept. 1918 †Crouy. French-Breton poet: 'De ha Bla'. (*AEMG*, ii, 479.)

Lenoir, August-Henri
1885–1 May 1915 †Bois le Prêtre. French painter: *Faunesse* (1914). (Ginisty.)

Leo, (Hauptmann)
–1916 †Verdun. German war poet: 'An meine vier Jungen: ein Neujahrsgruß'. (*DTH*.)

Leonhardt, Carl F. W.
1881–16 June 1918, Western Front. German architect. (Th.-B.)

Lerichem, Marc
1885–15 Oct. 1918, Lyon, influenza & wounds, received †Metzeral. French sculptor, 1st Grand Prix de Rome, 1914.

Leroux, Jules (*see entry page **292***)
1880–14 June 1915, disappeared †Neuville-Saint-Vaast. French novelist: *Une Fille de rien* (Figuière, Paris, 1911), *Léon Chatry, Instituteur* (1913, Manufacture, Lyon, 1985), *Le Pain et le Blé* (1914, L'amitié par le Livre, Saint-Vaast-la-Hougue, 1947); & poet: *La Muse noire* (Figuière Paris, 1911).

Le Roy, Jean
1894–26 Apr. 1918 †Locre, Belgium. French poet: 'Le Prisonnier des Mondes' (1913). (*AEMG*, ii, 503.)

Lesclot, Auguste
1884–Sept. 1914 †Champagne. French landscape painter. (Ginistry.)

Lesker, Hans
1879–23 Sept. 1914 †Argonnes. German painter from Stuttgart. Exhib. Munich Secession. (*Die Kunst*, xxxi, 1915, 79; Th.-B.)

Lestang, Pierre de
1896–5 Aug. 1917 †Yser canal, Bixschoote. French poet: *Cendres* (1921). Unpubl. essays, diary 1914–17 & novel *L'Abbé Daunon*. (*AEMG*, iii, 445.)

Letervanic, Georges (pseud. of Jules Garçon; also known as Jean Roch)
1888–14 Oct. 1918 †Neuvillette, Aisne. French poet: 'Ballade du vieux Terrien', *La grande Pitié* (unpubl.). Wrote comedy in verse, *L'Obsession*. Collaborated with Clovis Grimbert (q.v.) on *120 Court*. Composed songs under pseud. of Jean Roch: 'Les Chansons de Jacques-le-Poilu'.

Lettov, Michail
–5 Oct. 1915. Bulgarian writer & poet.

Lévêque, Jean
1888–23 July 1918 †Oulchy-la-Ville. French journalist & poet, contrib. to *La Nouvelle Revue*, *La Phalange*, *Gil Blas*. (*AEMG*, iv, 480.)

Leverkühn, Kurt Gustav
1890–22 Mar. 1918 †Western Front. German war poet: 'Zwiegespräch vor der Schlacht' (Gustav Schiesler [ed.], priv. Gesellschaft der Bibliophilen zur Hamburger Tagung, 1918).

Lewis, Frank C.
1898–21 Aug. 1917, air combat, France, Flight Sub-Lt, RNAS. British war poet: 2 sonnets on 'Belgium 1914' in *More Songs by the Fighting Men* (Erskine Macdonald, London, 1917).

Lewis, Tobias
–1916, Royal Sussex Regt. British oil painter from Brighton. (*The Studio*, xxxv, 319.)

Leybold, Hans (pseud. with Hugo Ball: Ha Hu Baley) (*see entry page **149***)
1894–8 Sept. 1914, suicide (?), Itzehoe garrison after †Namur. German avant-garde poet, contrib. to *Die Aktion*. Wrote poems jointly with Hugo Ball.

Libotte, Marcel
1895–25 Mar. 1916, pneumonia on training, Bayeux, Calvados. French poet: *Poèsies* (Bénard, Liège, 1921). (*AEMG*, iii, 784.)

Lichtenstein, Alfred (*see entry page **154***)
1889–25 Sept. 1914 †Vermandovillers, Somme. German expressionist short-story writer, poet & satirist. (Klaus Kanzog [ed.], *Gesammelte Gedichte/Gesammelte Prosa*, Arche, Zurich, 1962/1966.)

Liedke, Alfred
1877–23 Nov. 1914, typhus, Laon. German painter & lithographer. Pupil of Bracht, Berlin Academy. (E. A. Seemanns, *Meister der Farbe*, v, no. 947, 1917.)

Linnemann, Rudolf
1874–19 Mar. 1916, accident, Western Front. German architect, interior designer & glasspainter from Frankfurt. (*Kunstchronik*, xxvii, 1916, 386.)

Lintier, Paul
1893–15 Mar. 1916 †Jeandelincourt. French author of *Ma Pièce: souvenirs d'un canonnier* (posth. Prix Acad. française); *Tube 1233*. (*AEMG*, ii, 520.)

Lintott, Harry Chamen
1880–22 Mar. 1918, wounds, Lt, 5th Batt., Royal Fusiliers. British painter of portraits, specializing in miniatures. (*The Studio*, 1918, lxxiv, 23.)

Lissmann, Fritz
1880–27 Sept. 1915 †Ypres. German painter of bird life. (Hamburg Kunsthalle.)

Littlejohn, W. H.
–10 Apr. 1917 †Arras, Sgt-Maj., Middlesex Regt. British poet: *The Muse in Arms* (John Murray, London.)

Locquin, Maurice
1885–23 June 1915 †Sondernach, Alsace. French painter. (Ginisty.)

Löns, Hermann (Fritz Moritz) (*see entry page **178***)
1866–26 Sept. 1914 †Loivre, Reims. German novelist, short-story writer, poet of the Lüneburge Heide & satirist. (Wilhelm Diemann [ed.], *Hermann Löns: Leben und Schaffen*, Hesse & Becker, Leipzig, 1923.)

Loew, Jean
1886–21 June 1915 †Sedd-el Bahr, Gallipoli, body unrecovered. French writer: *La Passion: Chemin de Croix* (1912). (*AEMG*, iii, 452.)

L'Olagne, Jean (pseud. of Jean-François Angeli)
1886–June 1915 †Hébuterne-Serre, Pte, 140th Regt. French poet of the Auvergne. (*AEMG*, ii, 528.)

Lombardon, Guy de
1883–23 Aug. 1914 †Monfaucon. French poet of Provence. (*AEMG*, iii, 459.)

Lorieux, Julien August Philibert
1876–30 Apr. 1915, wounds after †Bois le Prêtre, 394th Inf. Regt. French sculptor & medallist. (Th.-B.; Ginisty.)

Losques, Daniel Thouroude de
1880–Aug. 1915, air crash, Sgt bombadier, Escadrille V. French cartoonist & satirist, particularly of theatre world. Publ. *Rire*, *Fantasio*. Collected in *Couloirs et Coulisses*. (Th.-B.; Ginisty.)

Lotz, Ernst Wilhelm (*see entry page **98***)
1890–26 Sept. 1914 †Bouconville, Aisne, Lt. German poet: *Wolkenüberflaggt* (Wolff,

Munich, 1917), *Prosaversuche und Feldpostbriefe* (H. Draws-Tychsen [ed.], Huber, Diessen, 1955).
Loysel, René *see* Saint-Laurent, Jean de Thomas de
Lučki, Nespor (pseud.: Proka Janić)
–1915, typhus. Serbian poet.
Lyon, Walter Scott Stuart
1885–8 May 1915 †Ypres, Staff-Capt., Lothian Brigade, 9th Batt., Royal Scots. British war poet: *Easter at Ypres* (Maclehose, Glasgow, 1916).
Łysek, Jan (pseud.: Jan Obuszek)
1887–5 Nov. 1915 †River Styr, Kostiuchnówka, Wolyn. Lt, Polish Legion. Polish playwright. Wrote monologues, verses, dramatic scenes based on folklore in the style of Stanislav Wyspianski: *Jasiyń* (1909); *Duszas ziemi* (1909); *Śpiacy zastep* (1910); *Śpiacy rycerze* (1914). (B. Orszulik, *Jan Łyzek*, Zesz. Nank. WSP, Kat. 3, 1965.)

McCrae, John
1872–28 Jan. 1918, pneumonia & meningitis, France, Lt-Col., medical consultant to British Army in France. Canadian doctor of pathology & poet. Wrote the most famous poem of the war in English: *'In Flanders Fields' and Other Poems* (Hodder & Stoughton, London, 1919).
Mache, André
1890–31 Dec. 1916, illness. French poet. Poems: 'Les Heures dolentes', 'La Promeneuse invisible'; & verse dramas. (*AEMG*, v, 697.)
Macke, August
1887–26 Sept. 1914 †Perthes-les-Hurlus, Champagne, Inf. German modernist painter, associated with Der Blaue Reiter group through friendship with Franz Marc (q.v.). Tunisian watercolours (1914) mark high point of career. (Ernst-G. Güse [ed.], *August Macke, Gemälde, Aquarelle, Zeichnungen*, Bruckmann, Munich, 1987.)
Mackenzie, Herbert *see* Matheson, Herbert Goldstein
Mackintosh, Ewart Alan
1893–21 June 1917 †Cambrai, Lt, Seaforth Highlanders, MC. British poet and songwriter: *A Highland regiment* (Bodley Head, London, 1917); *War, the Liberator, and other Pieces*, Bodley Head, 1918).
MacLaren, Donald Graeme
1886–29 June 1917, France, King's Liverpool (Scottish) Regt. British artist & Slade School scholar. (Imperial War Museum, London; Slade School Records.)
Maczka, Józef
1888–9 Sept. 1918, cholera while on military service, Jakaterynodar (Drasnodar). Polish poet.
Magnard, Albéric
1865–3 Sept. 1914, killed by German troops in his manor house, Baron, Oise, while resisting invasion. French composer, close associate of Guy Ropartz. Composed operas (*Guercœur*), symphonies, chamber music and songs. (*Zodiaque*, Cahiers de l'atelier du cœur Meurtry Abbaye Ste-Marie de la Pierre-qui-vire-Yonne, cxlvii, 1986.)
Mahon (Benjamin Léon Marcelin) **Patrice** (pseud.: **Art Roë**)
1865–22 Aug. 1914, Ste-Marie-aux-Mines, Lt-Col., 62nd Artillery Regt. French militarist who wrote novels based on his experience in the army: *Pingot et moi*, (Académie française prize winner); *Rachté*; *Monsieur Pierre*. (Georges Beaume, 'Art-Roë', *Revue Hebdomadaire*, Paris, 11 Nov. 1916.)
Maillieux, Lucien
–7 Nov. 1914 †Courbesseaux, Meurthe-et-Moselle. French composer & pianist, pupil of Xavier Leroux. Wrote 15 pieces for piano & violin or solo piano & *Naïs et l'Amour*, a ballet, & songs to verses by de Dubor.
Mallet, Gérard
1877–7 Aug. 1918, Vesle nr Bazoche, Aisne, Sub-Lt, Croix de la Légion d'honneur (1920). French war poet: *Poèmes de Guerre* (Soc. Litt. de France, Paris, 1921).
Malzburg, Ewald
1892–20 Sept. 1916 †Verdun. German designer & painter from the Rhineland.
Mann, Arthur James 'Hamish'
1896–10 Apr. 1917, wounds, †Arras, 2nd Lt, 8th Black Watch. British poet: *A Subaltern's Musings* (Long, London, 1918).
Mann, H. W.
–30 Mar. 1918. British painter of landscapes & town scenes & architect. Drew sketches of towns of the Western Front: *Leaves from the Sketch-book of Lieut. H. W. Mann, RFA*. (The Studio, Mar. 1918.)
Manning, William Sinkler
–6 Nov. 1918, Meuse. British poet. (F. W. Ziv [ed.], *The Valiant Muse, an anthology of poems by poets killed in the World War*, G. P. Putnam, New York, 1936.)
Manson, Willie B(raithwaite)
1896–1 July 1916 †Gommecourt. New Zealand-born composer of songs to poems by Longfellow, Rossetti & Housman. Royal Academy of Music, London: Lucas Medal, Battison Haynes Prize.
Marc, Franz (*page 177*)
1880–4 Mar. 1916 †Verdun. German expressionist painter & theorist. Founder with Kandinsky of Der Blaue Reiter group, 1912. Friendship with August Macke (q.v.). (Klaus Lankheit [ed.], *Briefe aus dem Feld*, Piper, Munich, 1982; K. Lankheit, *Franz Marc, Katalog der Werke*, Du Mont, Cologne, 1970.)
Marc de Lummen, Jean van
1875–2 June 1917, on reconnaissance, †Girauvoisin, Saint-Mihiel. French animal and landscape painter, son of Flemish animal & portrait painter Emile Van Marcke de Lummen. Member, Soc. des Artistes français. (*Chronique des arts*, 1917/19, 117, 190.)
Marchal, Robert
1890–1 Nov. 1914, Septsarges, Meuse. French poet, aesthete & literary & music critic: *Poèmes de l'Œillet blanc*; *La Création de l'Homme*.
Maréchal, René
1895–21 June 1915 †Souchez, Cpl, 46th Inf.. French painter-decorator. With his father Olivier, collaborated on décors for La Porte Saint-Martin, La Comédie des Champs-Élysées.
Mareil, Maurice (pseud. of **Maurice Chalhoub**)
1884–6 Feb. 1916, flying accident, Étampes. French-Algerian operetta librettist (*Susie*, 1912) who won 1st prize in the Auteurs du Front contest of 1915 with revue *Coucou, nous voilà!* (*AEMG*, v, 706.)
Marel, Maurice
1895–12 Aug. 1916, grenade, Verdun. French war poet: *Poèmes* (Barlatier, Marseille, 1919).
Marichal, Jean-François
1889–30 Aug. 1914 †Villiers-le-Sec, Aisne, Pte, 4th Zouaves. French poet. Wrote verse drama *Le Trésorier de Florence*, perf. Trocadéro, 10 Mar. 1918. (*AEMG*, i, 434.)
Marie, Lucien
1883–31 May 1915, trench mortar explosion, Mont Sauçon. French poet & composer. Poems publ. in *Nouvelle Revue Française*, (1 Sept 1910; 1 Mar. 1912).
Marriott-Watson, R. B.
–24 Mar. 1918, France. Lt, 2nd Royal Irish Rifles. Irish poet. (J. T. Trotter [ed.], *Valour and Vision*, Longmans Green, London, 1920.)
Marten, Miloš (pseud. of Miloš Šebesta) (*see entry page 342*)
1883–23 July 1917, wounds, Přepeče, Turnau, Bohemia. Czech literary critic & decadent novelist: *Style & Stylization* (1906); *A Book of the Strong* (1910); *Cortigiana* (1911); *Accord* (1916).
Marwitz, Bernhard von der
1890–8 Sept. 1918, wounds, Lazarett Valenciennes, Lt. German writer & poet, devoted to Hölderlin, friend of Paul Claudel & painter Götz von Seckerndorff (q.v.): *Stirb und Werde: aus Briefen und Kriegstagebuchblättern des Leutnants Bernhard von der Marwitz* (Harald von Koenigswald [ed.], Breslau, 1931). (Helmut Wocke, *Zwei Früh-Vollendete*, 1949.)
Masefield, Charles John Beech
1882–2 July 1917, wounds †Lens, Acting Capt., 5th North Staffs. Regt, MC. British poet: *The Season's Difference and other Poems* (Fifield, London, 1911), *Dislikes: Some Modern Satires* (Fifield, London, 1914), *Poems* (Blackwell, Oxford, 1919); & novelist: *Gilbert Hermer* (Blackwood, Edinburgh, 1908).
Maselj-Podlimbarski, Franc
(*see entry page 363*)
1852-September 1917, exiled. Slovene novelist. *Zbrani spisi* (J. Slebinger (ed.), Ljublijana, 1923-31, vols 1, 2, 4).
Massacrier, Auguste
1872–Oct. 1914 †Chavatte. French military writer & composer of soldiers' marching songs: 'Les Conscrits' (Evette, Paris); 'Petit Fantassin' (Dhoudt, Roubais).
Massé, Justin
1890–30 Mar. 1918. French Catholic writer. Wrote story of his conversion & vocation in *Les Deux Rêves*.
Matheson, Herbert Goldstein
1884–23 Mar. 1918, France, 2nd Lt, 13th Kensington Batt., London Regt. British composer of popular songs, incl. 'At the Sign of the Dragon', 'Remembering', 'The Trail that leads to Home', 'Wait for Me' (publ. by West, Cramer, Enoch, London, 1915–20).
Maurice Georges

1882–15 Mar. 1916 †Navarin, Souain. French poet. (*AEMG*, v, 230.)
Maux, André
1886–16 Apr. 1915, Aix-Noulette, Artois, medical corps. French poet, founder of periodical *La Terre Latine* with Guilhem Bercedaque. (*AEMG*, iv, 541.)
Mayer, Pierre
1894–28 May 1915, shot †Beauséjour/Mesnil-les-Hurlus. French composer of chamber music in the style of Franck.
Méjan, Alfred
1886–10 May 1916 †Verdun. French playwright: *Mathurin Régnier* (unpubl.).
Melbourne, Edward *see* Hodgson, William Noel
Ménagé, Louis
1885–13 Oct. 1914 †Vingré, Aisne. French war poet: *Pieusement pour la Patrie* (Prix Archon-Despérouses of Acad. française (Ziller, Paris).
Ménant, Julien
1880–22 May 1915, wounds, Morœuil, after shell blast †Neuville-Saint-Vaast 21 May, 146th Inf. Regt. French sculptor, 2nd Grand Prix de Rome, 1909. (Ginisty.)
Méplain, Anatole
1891–21 Apr. 1917, mine explosion. French poet publ. posth. in *Œuvres de Jeunesse*.
Mercadier, Théodore
1884–24 Jan. 1917 †Kemali, Bulgarian Front. French poet: 'L'Âme en Peine', Prix Jacques Normand 1915. (*AEMG*, iii, 485.)
Meyer-Buchwald, Gustav
1881–14 Oct. 1918, Gits, Roeselare. German portrait painter from Dresden. (Th.-B.)
Michel, Albert
–June 1915 †Western Front. German expressionist writer, contrib. to *Die Aktion*, Berlin: 'Nachtstück'.
Mieille, Lucien
1891–26 Jan. 1915, disappeared, Bois Foulon. French poet & composer. Wrote lyrics to 'Au Drapeau d'un Régiment pyrénéen' (music: Henri Filleul). (*AEMG*, iii, 495.)
Migeon, Georges
1881–13 May 1915 †Notre-Dame-de-Lorette. French architect, Prix Chevayard, École des Beaux-Arts.
Millery, Jean *see* Gien, Auguste
Miquignon, Charles
1882–16 Sept. 1916. French war poet. (*AEMG*, iv, 568.)
Mirland, René-Félix-Henri
1884–2 July 1915 †Bois de la Grurie, Fossé-Vert. French architect. Grand Prix de Rome, 1911.
Mitchell, Colin
–22 Mar. 1918, Sgt, Rifle Brig. British poet: *Trampled Clay* (Macdonald, London, 1917).
Mitton, Thomas Edward
–24 Dec. 1917, France, 2nd Lt, Royal Engineers Signals. British poet: *Poems* (Cornish, Birmingham, 1918).
Moerner, Gerhard
1890–15 Apr. 1917 †Lombartzyde, Western Front. German war poet: *Aus dem Felde* (Kugel, Hamburg, 1918).
Mokel, Charles
1891–30 Aug. 1914 †Faux. French poet. Verse play *Pierrot s'en va* perform 1914 (unpubl.).
Mokranjac, Stevan
–1914. Serbian composer.
Moll, Francis
1896–9 May 1915 †Ouvrages Blancs, Polish & Czech Volunteers. French engraver.
Moncaut-Larroudé, Fernand
1890–4 Aug. 1918, wounds. French poet: 'Les Frissons d'un cœur'; 'La Gerbe rouge'. (*AEMG*, iv, 572.)
Monnier, Jacques
1871–23 Aug. 1917, on military exercise. French playwright of vaudeville comedies *Le Jumeau* (1903); *La Vache, La Revanche de Madame Bidouille* (1904); *Mauvaises passes* (1906). Last work, *Le Boulet*, was a grand-guignol drama. (*AEMG*, v, 714.)
Monti, Jean *see* Montrichard, Jean de
Montrichard, Jean de (pseud.: Jean Monti)
1885–1915 †Brimont, Maréchal-des-Logis, 28th Dragoons. French painter of the Lorraine landscape. (*Chronique des Arts*, 1914/16, 227.)
More, Georges
1891–13 June 1915 †Berry-au-Brac, Sub-Lt, 74th Inf. Regt. French poet from Normandy: *Les Reliques* (Gossez, Rouen, 1922); *La Bravoure, la Mort m'a dit* (Facettes, 1919).
Moreau, Constant
1888–24 Nov. 1918, influenza, Bulgarian Front. French neo-romantic poet & verse-dramatist. (*AEMG*, v, 459.)
Moreau, Philippe
1880–25 Aug. 1914, disappeared nr Dienze, Lorraine. French composer & conductor. Pupil of Xavier Leroux. Composed 'Trois Poèmes pour Ténor et Orchestre' (1912); 1 symphony, 1 *drame lyrique*.
Morgner, Wilhelm
1891–12 Aug. 1917, disappeared †Langemarck. German expressionist painter from Soest, pupil of Georg Tappert. Occ. contrib. to *Die Aktion* & *Der blaue Reiter*. (Ernst-G. Güse, *Wilhelm Morgner*, Westfälisches Landesmuseum, Münster, 1983; Lucja Nerowski-Fisch, *Wilhelm Morgner 1891–1917: ein Beitrag zum deutschen Expressionismus*, Mocker & Jahn, Soest, 1984; Christine Knupp-Uhlenhaut [ed.], *Wilhelm Morgner: Briefe u. Zeichnungen*, Mocker & Jahn, Soest, 1984.)
Morize-Delarve, André
1894–12 Apr. 1915 †Saint-Julien, Ypres. French story writer & poet, publ. chiefly in *La Chronique Versaillaise* 1911–14. (*AEMG*, iv, 583.)
Mormann, Wilhelm
1882–15 Nov. 1914 †Dombrovice. German sculptor of religious figures. Exhib. Düsseldorf Kunstakademie. (Th.-B.)
Morris (Francis) St Vincent
1896–29 Apr. 1917, wounds, after plane crash in a blizzard over Vimy Ridge, RFC. British poet: *Poems* (Blackwell, Oxford.)
Moss-Blundell, Cyril Bertram
1891–26 Nov. 1915, †Loos, 14th Batt., Durham Light Infantry. British draughtsman & caricaturist.
Moulin, Eugène Émile
1880–5 Oct. 1914, disappeared, Somme. French sculptor, pupil of Antonin Mercié.
Mrázek, Hugo Klement
(occ. pseud.: Hugo Ansorge.)
1889–Dec. 1916, †Vladimir, Wolynia, 8th Inf. Regt. Czech lithographer & composer, pupil of Novák. Chamber pieces & songs. (*Hudébní rozhledy*, vii, 1914, 74; *Memorial Book of the Second Czech School in Brno*, 1929, 54–7; *Věra Svobodová* [Moravian Museum magazine], xxxix, 1954; G. Pukl, *H. K. Mrázek and His Compositional Style*, diss., Brno, 1958.)
Müller, Charles (Paul Émile)
1877–1 Oct. 1914, Amiens after †Longueval, Albert. French satirist. Parodies incl. *A la Manière de . . .* & revue *Mille-Neuf-Cent-Douze* (1912). (Edmond Rostand [ed.], *Charles Müller, par ses amis*, Flammarion, Paris, 1918.)
Müller, Ernst
1880–Nov. 1917, Flanders. German architect, worked with Richard Brodersen.
Munnoch, John
–Apr. 1915, Pte, 5th Batt., Royal Scots. British landscape & genre painter from Scotland. Exhib. Royal Scottish Academy.
Munro, H(ector) H(ugh) (pseud.: Saki) (*see entry page **11***)
1870–14 Nov. 1916, by sniper, †Beaumont-Hamel, 22nd Batt., Royal Fusiliers. British satirist, short-story writer, novelist & playwright: *The Complete Works of Saki* (Penguin, London, 1982).
Murray, Dixon, Henry Edward Otto
1885–9 Apr. 1917, Vimy Ridge. British painter of bird subjects: *Illustrated Sporting & Dramatic News*, 1912–15.
Mussakov, Vladimir
–28 Sept. 1916. Bulgarian writer.

Nalepinski, Tadeusz
1885–13 Nov. 1918, influenza & exhaustion from war duties, Berne. Polish poet, novelist, literary critic & playwright: *On idzie! Rzecz o królu* (Duchu Rosji, 1907) in which Dostoevsky is portrayed as a master of a new ideology; *Chrzest*, a Polish fantasy (1910); *Ava Patria*, a chronicle about the Pilsudskii legions; *Spiewnik rozdarty* ([*The Torn Songbook*], 1914).
Naulin, Abel
1895–31 Apr. 1915, hospital at Dunkirk from wounds from patrol †Lizerne, Ypres. French army artist.
Nayral, Jacques
1876–9 Dec. 1914, bullet, †La Bassée. French satiric-comic playwright, poet & novelist: 4 collections of poems; 5 novels (*Germain Saint-Léger*, 1914); short stories; comedies (*Les Camelots du Deux Cent-un*). (*AEMG*, i, 489.)
Nénot, Marcel
1892–27 Sept. 1915 †La Vistule, Champagne. French-Monégasque poet & novelist, contrib. to periodical *Petit Monégasque*. Verse-play *Le Seuil* first perf. in Casino of Nice, 1914. (*AEMG*, i, 497.)
Nessel, Kurt
1880–18 Sept. 1914, †Western Front. German portrait painter. (Th.-B.)
Nölken, Franz
1884–4 Nov. 1918, Western Front. Painter from Hamburg. Influenced by Matisse &

the Dôme group. Centenary exhib., Galerie Herold. Cat.: *Franz Nölken* (Mocker & Jahn, Hamburg, 1984).

Nollat, Jacques Talon
1885–28 Aug. 1914 †Vitrimont, Lunéville, body undiscovered, 23rd Colonial Inf. Regt. French caricaturist, humorist & illustrator. Contributed to *Rire*, *Fantasio* & *Journal*.

Nolly, Émile (pseud. of Joseph Détanger)
1880–3 Sept. 1914, wounds, Lorraine, 43rd Colonial Inf. Regt. French novelist of army life: *Le Chemin de la Victoire*; *La Barque annamite* (1910); *Gens de Guerre au Maroc* (1912). Posth. Grand Prix de littérature, Acad. française, 1915.

Novotný, Jaroslav
1886–1 May 1918 †Miass-Ural, Officer, Czech Legion. Czech composer of songs and choral works. Student of Novák. Songs incl.: 'Věčná svatba', op. 2, 1909; 'Dětské písně', op. 6; 'Ze srdce', op. 9, 1914–15. (Dr Markéta Hallová, *Jaroslav Novotný*, diss. Prague, 1986.)

Nye, Reginald Rayner
1886–17 Dec. 1915, sniper, †Ploegsteert, Flanders, Capt., Royal Scots. British playwright, poet & novelist (*Marthe*), whose short stories were published in *The Bystander*, London.

Obuszek, Jan *see* Łysek, Jan

Olivier-Hourcade (pseud. of August Hourcade, also known as Olivier-Bag)
1892–21 Nov. 1914 †Oulches, Aisne. French-Girodin poet: *Des Ombres tremblantes* (1909). Founder of group Le Coin du Feu, periodical *Les Marches du Sud-Ouest* & Societé des Poètes Girondins et du Sud-Ouest.

Ollone, Charles d'
1865–15 July 1918, exhaustion on active service, Somme. French poet: *Heures chantantes* (1908), *Nouvelles Heures chantantes* (1913), *Dernières Heures chantantes* (1919); & novelist: *Sœur Marie-Odile* (1909), *La Victoire ailée* (1911).

Orcelle, Charles-Jules
1878–1915. French lithographer of series of portraits after Greuze, 1914.

Orchardson, Charles M. Q.
1873–26 Apr. 1917, Near East. British oil painter, son of Sir William Q. Orchardson, RA. Exhib. Royal Academy.

Orlov, Michal *see* Palát, Antonín

Ostendorf, Friedrich
1871–17 Mar. 1915, †Loretto Heights. German architect. Pupil of Karl Schäfer. (Th.-B.)

Owen, Wilfred (Edward Salter) (*see entry page **75***)
1893–4 Nov. 1918, †Sambre & Oise Canal, Coy. Cmdr, Manchester Regt. British poet. (Jon Stallworthy [ed.], *The Complete Poems and Fragments*, Chatto & Windus, 1983, 2 vols.)

Oxland, Nowell
–9 Aug. 1915 †Suvla Bay, Gallipoli, Lt, 6th Border Regt. British poet. (F. W. Ziv [ed.], *The Valiant Muse*, Putnam's, New York, 1936.)

Pad, Stéphan (pseud. of Paul Alain Dutruel)
1892–24 Mar. 1918, collision of a troop transport train, Gondrecourt, Meuse. French writer. Stories, notes and poems publ. in *L'Éffort social* as 'La Route', 1912–14. (*AEMG*, i, 519.)

Palát, Antonín (occ. pseud.: Michal Orlov)
1899–1918, †Adameli. Czech poet.

Palmer, Robert (Stafford Arthur)
1889–1916, wounds, in a Turkish camp, †Umm-Al-Hannal, Tigris, 21 Jan. 1916. British poet, younger son of Earl of Selborne. (E. B. Osborn, *The Muse in Arms*, John Murray, London, 1917; L. Ridding, *The Life of Robert Palmer*, Hodder & Stoughton, London, 1921.)

Palussière, Julien
–24 Nov. 1914 †Cuffies, nr Soissons, 231st Inf. Regt. French designer of jewellery, exhib. Artistes français.

Pancol, Georges
1888–25 Nov. 1915. French poet & novelist. Unpubl. autobiographical novel: *L'Échec*. (*G. Pancol*, Sansot, Paris, 1923.)

Paoli, Marcel
1891–16 Nov. 1914, disappeared, Malancourt. French poet from Provence. (*AEMG*, v, 261.)

Paréra, Maurice
1888–5 Aug. 1916, wounds, Fleury, Lt, 4th Zouaves. French landscape & portrait painter.

Parizelle, Jean (Charles Alfred Louis)
1883–10 Sept. 1914, wounds after shell blast, Ligny-en-Barrois, Meuse, 254th Infantry Regt. French painter, pupil of Bonnat. (Ginisty; Th.-B.)

Parr, George Roworth
1891–19 Dec. 1914 †Ploegsteert Wood, Prince Albert's Somerset Light Infantry. British short-story writer: 'The Soldier's Reward'; 'A Dream on the Tunnel Hill'. (Cuthbert Headlam, *G. R. Parr, A short Memoir together with his letters written while on active service during the Great War, and some other of his writings*, Edinburgh, 1915.)

Parry, Harold
1897–6 May 1917, 2nd Lt, 17th King's Royal Rifles. British poet, purposely avoided writing about the war: *Letters and Poems* (Smith, Walsall.)

Patin, Maurice (pseud.: Philippe Auster)
1883–7 Sept. 1914, disappeared, †Ramberout aux Pots, Meuse. French verse-dramatist: *La Faute de David* (perf. 1909, publ. 1914); *La Première Aventure* (1913).

Patriarche, André-Henri
1894–23 Feb. 1915, wounds, †Argonne, 4th Inf. Regt. French sculptor, Salon National des Arts Décoratifs.

Pégot, (Jan-Bertrand) Ogier
1878–2 Oct. 1915, shell blast †Affichy, 265th Inf. Regt. French painter of scenes in Brittany, Soc. des Artistes Indépendants. (Ginisty; Bénézit.)

Péguy, Charles (*see entry page **248***)
1873–5 Sept. 1914 †Valleroy. French poet & philosopher: *Œuvres Complètes* (NRF, Paris, 1916–55).

Peignot, Rémi
1888–17 June 1915, patrol, Western Front, 57th Artillery. French painter & draughtsman. (Ginisty.)

Pemberton, V. T.
–7 Oct. 1918, Capt., Royal Garrison Artillery, MC. British poet: *Reflections in Verse* (Grant Richards, 1919).

Penrose, Claude
1893–Aug. 1918, †Somme, Maj., MC. American-born poet in British Army: *Poems* (Harrison, London).

Pergaud, Louis (*see entry page **283***)
1882–8 Apr. 1915 †Marcheville, Lorraine. French novelist & story writer, chiefly about animals. Winner Prix Goncourt (1910): *De Goupil à Margot*. (*Œuvres complètes*, Mercure de France, Paris, 1987.)

Périer, Joseph
1881–1917, influenza. French poet. (*AEMG*, v, 726.)

Perović, Miloš (pseud.: Pietro Kosorić)
1874–1918, wounds, Paris. Serbian poet from Belgrade whose poetry reflects metaphysical debates of life & death. Best known for prize-winning verse-tragedy *Karadjordje*, 1906. (*Ženomrzac, pozorišna šala*, Skoplje, 1914; *Misli*, Belgrade, 1934.)

Perréoux, Robert (pseud. of Vicomte Marie-Charles-Roger de Ferré de Péroux)
1882–20 Aug. 1914 †Nomény, Nancy. French poet: *Ombres, poèmes* (Grasset, Paris, 1912); *Le Mariage de Jean, simple histoire en vers* (Impr. Réunies, Boulogne-sur-mer). (*AEMG*, v, 268.)

Perrot, Charles
1887–13 Oct. 1914 †Arras, Sub-Lt, Infantry Regt. French man of letters & poet. Wrote a psychological study of pre-war youth, *Le printemps sans Soleil* (Renaissance du Livre, Paris, 1918); complete poems in *Les Éfforts et le Destin*, (Renaissance du Livre, Paris, 1918).

Person, Paul
1886–27 Oct. 1917 †Verdun. French poet. (*Paul Person*, Paris, 1918.)

Petković-Dis, Vladislav (*see entry page **359***)
1880–16 May 1917, drowned off Corfu after ship was torpedoed. Serbian poet of patriotic lyrics of Balkan Wars. His best poems (e.g. 'Tamnica' – 'The Prison' – and 'Nirvana') express agony of tormented existence & also aspiration for unknown ideal worlds. (J. Lavrin [ed.], *An Anthology of Modern Yugoslav Poetry*, Državna Založba Slovenije/Calder, Ljubljana/London, 1962.)

Petrenz, Adolf
1873–9 Feb. 1915, wounds, Western Front. German satirical journalist, poet & writer. Patron of Walther Heymann (q.v.). (Goetz Otto Stoffregen, 'Adolf Petrenz', *Die Unvergessenen*.)

Petrović, Nadežda (born Čačak)
1873–1915, typhus, Valjevo, serving as a nurse. Female Serbian painter greatly influenced by Matisse and les Fauves. (*Bibliografski Zavod*, Zagreb.)

Petitpoisson, Lucien
1893–1 July 1916 †Curlu, Somme. French war poet: 'Adieux'. (*AEMG*, iv, 605.)

Peyron, Alexandre
1889–Apr. 1916. French poet of Provence. (*AEMG*, v, 730.)

Pfannschmidt, Friedrich (Johannes)
1864–7 Sept. 1914 †Pierre-Morrains, Chalons. German memorial sculptor from Berlin, president of the Künstlerverband deutscher Bildhauer. (Th.-B.)

Philipps, Colwyn (Erasmus Arnold)
1888–13 May 1915, †Ypres, Capt., Royal Horse Guards. British poet: *Verses, Prose, Fragments, Letters* (London, 1915).

British poet & graphic artist: *Selected Poems & Drawings* (1918).
Slapater, Scipio (*see entry page **320***)
1888–3 Dec. 1915 †Mt Podgora. Italian novelist, critic & essayist: *Il mio Carso* (Mondadori, Milan, 1958).
Smith, Geoffrey Bache
1894–3 Dec. 1916, wounds, Warlencort, Lt, 19th Lancs. Fusiliers. British romantic poet: 'Glastonbury', 'We who have bowed ourselves to time', etc.; *A Spring Harvest* (Macdonald, London, 1918).
Solomon, Louis B.
1896–12 Apr. 1918, Lt, Royal Fusiliers. British poet: *Wooden Crosses and other Verses* (Fountain, Roehampton, 1918).
Soltau, Franz
–May 1915, Galicia, Lt. German artist from Berlin.
Somerhausen, Léo
1894–28 Sept. 1918, shell blast †Blankaert, Dixmude. Belgian war poet: 'Proses et Poèmes écrits au Front 1914–18', in *La Renaissance d'Occident* (Bruxelles, 1921).
Sorge, Reinhard (Johannes)
(*see entry page **144***)
1892–20 July 1916, †Belgium. German playwright & mystic poet: *Werke* (Hans Gerd Rötzer [ed.], Nuremberg, 1962–7, 3 vols.)
Sorley, Charles Hamilton
(*see entry page **59***)
1895–13 Oct. 1915, †Loos. Capt., Suffolk Regt. British poet: *The Collected Poems of Charles Hamilton Sorley*; *The Collected Letters of Charles Hamilton Sorley* (Jean Moorcroft Wilson [ed.], Cecil Woolf, London, 1985).
Souquières, André
1885–8 Oct. 1917 †Douaumont. French war poet: 'Les Champs rouges'. (*AEMG*, iv, 710.)
Spiess, Robert
1886–17 Sept. 1914 †Juvincourt, Lt, Res. 182nd Saxon Infantry Regt., Iron Cross. German artist from Dresden: ink drawings in Frédéric Chopin, *The XXIV Preludes* (Tischer u. Jagenberg, Cologne, 1914). (Th.B.)
Stables, J. Howard
1895–17 Feb. 1917, wounds, †Kut, Mesopotamia, Lt, Gurkha Rifles. British poet: *The Sorrow that whistled* (Elkin Mathews, London).
Stadler, Ernst (*see entry page **101***)
1883–30 Oct. 1914 †Zandvoorde, Ypres. Lt. German expressionist poet & essayist: *Dichtungen, Schriften, Briefe* (Hurlebusch/Schneider [eds], Beck, Munich, 1983).
Stenner, Hermann
1891–4 Dec. 1914 †Ilov, E. Poland. German expressionist painter from Bielefeld. (Hans Georg Gmelin, *Hermnn Stenner*, Hans Thoma-Gesellschaft/Karl Thiemig, Reutlingen, 1975.)
Stephan, Rudi
1887–29 Sept. 1915 †Tarnopol, Galicia. German composer: Musik für Orchester, Musik für Geige u. Orchester, *Liebeszauber* & opera *Die ersten Menschen* (perf. Frankfurt, 1920). (Juliane Brand, *Rudi Stephan*, Komponisten in Bayern, 2, Hans Schneider, Tutzing, 1983.)
Stephen, Adrian Consett
(*see entry page **20***)
1892–14 Mar. 1918 †Zillebeke, Ypres, 2nd Lt, Royal Field Artillery, MC, Croix de Guerre. Australian playwright: *Anchored* (1913); *Echoes, Futurity* (1914); *The Victor* (1915). (*Four Plays*; *Stories, Burlesques & Letters from 'Hermes'*; *An Australian in the RFA*, Penfold, Sydney, 1918.)
Sterling, Robert (William)
1893–23 Apr. 1915, Lt, Royal Scots Fusiliers. British poet: *The Poems* (Oxford University Press, 1915).
Stewart, John E.
–26 Apr. 1918, Maj., Staffs. Regt, MC. British war poet: *Grapes of Thorns* (Macdonald, London, 1917).
Stitt, Innes d'Auvergne Stewart
1898–28 Mar. 1918, missing †Arras, Queen's Westminster Rifles. British religious poet: (with Leo Ward) *Tomorrow and Other Poems* (Longman, London, 1917).
Stoyanov, Georgy
–5 Dec. 1917. Bulgarian writer.
Stramm, August (*see entry page **124***)
1874–1 Sept. 1915 †Rokitno marshes, Brest-Litovsk, Batt. Cdr, Iron Cross 1st class. German poet: *Das Werk* (René Radrizzani [ed.], Limes, Wiesbaden, 1963).
Streets, John William
–1 July 1916, wounded & missing †Somme, Sgt, 13th Yorks & Lancs. Regt. British war poet: *Truth! An Allegory* (Stockwell, London, 1912), *The Undying Splendour* (Macdonald, London, 1917).
Striepe, Kurt
–spring 1917. German writer. Contrib. to *Die Aktion*.
Stuart, Andrew John
–26 Sept. 1915. British war poet. (J. W. Cuncliffe [ed.], *Poems of the Great War*, Macmillan, New York, 1916.)
Šubrt, Emil
1893–1918 †Oslavija, Gorica. Czech poet.
Suchet, Gabriel
1894–8 May 1916 Sonville. French poet: 'Les Genévriers'. (*AEMG*, ii, 643.)

Tassot, Fabien (pseud.: F. Roger-Hugues)
1885–24 Oct. 1918, influenza, air force. French comic playwright & poet: *Attelage à trois* (1905), *L'heureuse Mésaventure*; collection of poems: *Le Rachat du Canal du Midi* (Toulouse, 1912).
Tauzin, Henri Alexis
1879–11 Oct. 1918, pneumonia after active service, Lyon. French architect & decorator. Pupil of J. L. Pascal. 2nd Prix de Rome, 1904. (Ginisty.)
Taufer, František
1885–1915, missing, Eastern Front. Czech poet & short-story writer.
Tavan, Ludovic
1888–1917, shell †Vardar. French puet of Provence. (*AEMG*, iv, 716.)
Taylor, Luke
1876–1916, wounds. British etcher; member of Ridley Art Club.
Teed, Samuel H.
1883–25 July 1916 †Pozières, Lt, Royal Berks Regt. British painter. Exhib. Baillie Gallery.
Tennant, E(dward) Wyndham
1897–22 Sept. 1916 †Somme, Lt, Grenadier Guards. Son of Lord Glenconner. British poet: *Worple Flit and other Poems* (Blackwell, Oxford), *Songs, Plays, Ballads*. (Pamela Glenconner, *Hon. E. W. Tennant, a Memoir*, John Lane, London, 1919.)
Terlikowski, Stefan
1883–15 May 1916, wounds, Douai. Polish painter, graphic designer & caricaturist. Exhib. Beaux-Arts, Paris, 1914.
Tetera, Jerzy *see* Długosz, Stanisław
Thellier de Poncheville, Georges
1877–18 June 1915 †Cote 119, Souchez, Pas-de-Calais. French poet: *Le Chapelet des Souvenirs* (Messein, Paris, 1904) & playwright *Flagrant délit* (unpubl., but perf.: 1910); *L'Augmentation* (1912). (*AEMG*, ii, 651.)
Thierry, Albert
1881–26 May 1915 †Noulette. French poet, story writer & educationalist. (*AEMG*, i, 629.)
Thiesen, Jakob
1884–Dec. 1914, France. German portrait & landscape painter. (Memorial exhib., Städtische Galerie, Düsseldorf, 1913.; Th.-B.)
Thiessig, Florian
1856–1916, Russian civil POW camp, Pensa. German composer and conductor. Works incl. operas, oratorios, orchestral pieces. (*Neue Zeitschrift für Musik*, 1916.)
Thiriet, Robert
1895–25 Aug. 1915 †Maison-de-Champagne. French poet. (*AEMG*, ii, 655.)
Thomas, Paul-Marie
1896–25 Nov. 1914 †Jonchery-sur-Suippe, Marne. French poet: *Les Gerbes* (Paris, 1914). (*AEMG*, iv, 722.)
Thomas, (Philip) **Edward**
(*see entry page **62***)
1878–9 Apr. 1917, †Arras, Royal Garrison Artillery. British prose writer and poet: *The collected Poems of Edward Thomas* (R. George Thomas [ed.], Oxford University Press, 1985).
Thurin, Robert
1896–21 Feb. 1915 †Artois. French poet. (*AEMG*, ii, 663.)
Thylmann, Karl
1888–29 Aug. 1916, wounds, Gross-Anheim. German etcher & lithographer from Darmstadt. (C. Thylmann, *Gesamtwerk*, 1968, 4 vols.)
Todd, Herbert Nichols
–7 Oct. 1916, Queen's Westminsters. British poet & playwright: *Poems and Plays* (Jackson, Sedbergh, 1917).
Tombs, Joseph Simpkin McKenzie
1889–11 Sept. 1915, wounds. British journalist & poet: *Critical Moments* (Fisher Unwin, London, 1917).
Torre, Michel della
1890–29 Apr. 1915 †Vauquois. French poet: 'Le Bouquet de Floréal'. (*AEMG*, ii, 666.)
Touron, Marius
1882–24 Apr. 1915 †Éparges. French poet: *Glanes et Copeaux* (Revue Picarde et Normande, Caen, 1917, winner, Prix Capuran, Acad. française).
Toussaint(-Collignon), **Marcel**
1882–13 Oct. 1916 †Sailly-Saillisel. French poet: *Le Sculpteur de sable – Le Drapeau* (Lemerre, 1909, winner, Prix

Sully-Prudhomme), *Les Taciturnes* (Prix Archon-Despérouses), *Le Dard et l'Épée* (1917), *Les Cils baissés*. (Maximilian Buffenoir, 'Un poète mort pour la France: Marcel Toussaint', *Revue Bleue*, Paris, 10–17 Nov. 1917.)

Trakl, Georg (*see entry page 112*)
1887–3 Nov. 1914, after †Grodek, from overdose of cocaine, Cracow military hospital, Lt, Austrian Medical Corps. Austrian expressionist poet: *Dichtungen und Briefe* (Otto Müller, Salzburg, 1969).

Tripet, Louis Justin
1888–4 Sept. 1916 †Denicourt, Somme. French painter, exhib. in Memorial Exhib., Grand Palais, 1919. (Ginisty.)

Trotter, Bernard Freeman
1890–7 May 1917, France, 2nd Lt, 11th Leicesters. Canadian war poet: *A Canadian Twilight & other poems of War & of Peace* (McClelland, Goodchild & Stewart, Toronto, 1917).

Troufleau, Charles
1878–27 Sept. 1916, wounds. French humanist poet: *Ici commence* (1910), *Entre des Murs* (1912). (*AEMG*, i, 662.)

Troyen, Michel
1875–14 Feb. 1915, shell blast †Prunay, Marne, 1st Regt Étranger. Russian painter of rustic Russian portraits & scenes. Exhib. at the Indépendants. (Joseph.)

Truchet, Abel
1857–9 Sept. 1918 †Auxerre, Lt, 1st Regt du Génie. French impressionist painter of the Paris *vie mondaine*, particularly Montmartre scenes. (Bénézit; Joseph.)

Tuaillon, Jules-Joseph
1884–9 Apr. 1915, wounds at †Bois-Leprêtre 24 Mar. 1915, 346th Inf. Regt. French engraver.

Umbricht, André
1889–26 June 1918 †Maignelay, Oise. French war poet from the Alsace: 'Printemps de Guerre', 'Un Soir près de Verdun'. (*AEMG*, iii, 697.)

Valmont, Gustave
1881–6 Sept. 1914 †Courgivaux, Ésternay, Marne. French paleographer & poet: *L'Áile de l'Amour* (Calmann-Lévy, Paris, 1911).

Varoužan, Daniel (*see entry page 373*)
1884–26 Aug. 1915, executed by the Turks prior to the Armenian massacre. Armenian nationalist poet: *The Trembling* (1906); *The Heart of a Nation* (1909); *Pagan Songs* (1912); *The Song of Bread* (publ. 1921). (Minas Hysyan [ed.], *Erkeri žołovacu*, Erevan, 1962.)

Verlet, Paul
1890–23 Oct. 1923, wounds, bullet lodged in chest. French war poet. (*De la Boue sous le Ciel: Esquisses d'un Blessé*, 1919.)

Vernède, Robert Ernest
1875–9 Apr. 1917 †Havrincourt Wood, Lt, Rifle Brigade. British poet: *War Poems and other Verses* (Heinemann, London, 1917); & novelist: *The Judgement of Illinborough* (1908); *The June Lady* (1912), *Meriel of the Moors* (1906), *The Port Allington Stories and Others* (Heinemann, London, 1921), *The Pursuit of Mr Faviel* (Nelson, 1907), *The Quietness of Dick* (Collins, London, 1919); & travel writer: *The Fair Dominion, a record of Canadian impressions* (1911), *An Ignorant in India* (1911).

Viasioły, Kas'jan (pseud. of Vincuk Andzeij)
1886–1916. Byelorussian writer. (A. B. McMillin, *A History of Byelorussian Literature*, Schmitz, Giessen, 1977.)

Villepique, René
1894–4 Apr. 1918 †Moreuil, Somme. French poet. (*AEMG*, iv, 746.)

Villermin, Antoine
1889–20 Aug. 1914 †Gosselmingen, Lorraine. French poet: *Les chants quotidiens*, 1910; *La Jeunesse du Cœur*, 1911. (*AEMG*, i, 683.)

Villiers, Paul-Edmond
1883–29 Aug. 1914. French painter, first of historical subjects (*Le Procès de Jeanne d'Arc*) & then of pastoral scenes (*Bergère aux Champs*). Pupil of Cormon.

Vincent, Roger
1886–9 May 1915 †Neuville-Saint-Vaast. French writer, contrib. to avant-garde periodicals *Chimères*, *Poèmes*, *Double Bouquet*, *Les Facettes*. (*AEMG*, ii, 685.)

Violand, Camille
1891–4 Mar. 1915 †Côte 196, Perthes-les-Hurlus. French poet. Contrib. to *La Revue Hebdomadaire*, 1914, 1915. (*AEMG*, iv, 755.)

Vollet, Gaston
1887–16 Dec. 1916. French poet of the Gironde, publ. in *La petite Gironde*. (*AEMG*, v, 333.)

Vordren, Vilém *see* Klés, Petr

Wagon, Florimond
1895–20 May 1916, disappeared †Mort-Homme, Cpl, 151st Inf. Regt. French writer & poet. Contrib..to *Les Humbles*: 'Deux Sonnets', 'Les soirs se suivent', 'La Marne' (June 1916). (*AEMG*, iii, 702.)

Walsey, Léon-John
1880–25 Mar. 1917 †Verdun, Sgt, 13th Artillery Regt. French sculptor & painter, member of Salon d'Automne. Memorial Exhib., Feuilles d'Art, Nov. 1919. (*Art et Décoration Chronique*, Nov. 1919.)

Warren, Francis Purcell
1895–3 July 1916 †France, 2nd Lt, S. Lancs Regt. British composer of music for strings from Royal College of Music, London.

Weisgerber, Albert (*page 356*)
1878–10 May 1915 †Fromelles, Ypres. German poet-impressionist painter, president of New Munich Secession. (Askia Ishikawa-Franke, *Albert Weisgerber: Leben und Werk*; Wilhelm Weber, *Albert Weisgerber, Zeichnungen*, 1958.)

West, Arthur Graeme
(*see entry page 67*)
1891–3 Apr. 1917, by sniper, Bapaume, 6th Oxford & Bucks Light Infantry. British war poet. (*The Diary of a Dead Officer*, Allen & Unwin, London, 1918.)

White, Bernard Charles de Boismaison
1886–1 July 1916 †Somme, Lt, 1st Tyneside Scottish Regt. British poet: *Remembrance and other Verses* (Selwyn & Blount, London, 1917), *Parodies and Imitations* (London, 1912).

Whyte, Robert Bardour
1892–25 Sept. 1915 †Nigg, 2nd Lt, 3rd Black Watch. British writer of commentaries: 'Foundations of the State', 'Military Interludes'; verses & letter. (*Robert Bardour Whyte*, Constable, Edinburgh, 1918.)

Wibaux, Édouard
1892–27 Apr. 1917, illness contracted at front, Val-de-Grâce. French poet & playwright: *Un Frisson passe* (Paris, 1914), *La Rencontre amoureuse* (Paris, 1914).

Wiegand, Hans
1890–Feb. 1915. German landscape painter. Pupil of Adolf Lins in Düsseldorf. (Th.-B.)

Wilkinson, Eric Fitzwater
1891–9 Oct. 1917 †Passchendaele Ridge, Capt., West Yorks Regt, MC. British poet: *Sunrise Dreams and other poems* (Erskine Macdonald, London, 1918).

Wilkinson, (George) **Jerrard**
1885–1 July 1916 †Beaumont Hamel, Somme. Duke of Cambridge's Own, Middlesex Regt. British song composer: 'From a Distance', 'Choric Song', 'Four Songs about Children', 'A Country Cradle Song', 'Suzette', 'Nine Songs & Duets from the Ancient Japanese'.

Wilkinson, Walter Lightfowler
1886–9 Apr. 1917 †Vimy Ridge, Lt, 8th Argyll & Sutherland Highlanders. British war poet. (*More Songs by the Fighting Men*, Erskine Macdonald, London.)

Wilson, Ronald W.
1896–28 Feb. 1915, meningitis, France, Army Medical Corps. British poet: *Poems* (Temple, Letchworth, 1915).

Wilson, T(heodore) **P**(ercival) **Cameron**
–23 Mar. 1918 †Somme, Capt., Sherwood Foresters. British war poet: *Magpies in Picardy* (Poetry Bookshop, London, 1919), *Bolts from the Blue* (Wells Gardner, London, 1929), *The Friendly Enemy, being the history of one who cried for the moon* (Mills & Boon, London, 1913).

Winterbotham, Cyril W(illiam)
1887–27 Aug. 1916. British religious poet: *Poems* (Banks, Cheltenham).

Wolter, W.
–16 April 1915 †Champagne. German philosophy student & war poet: 'Furor teutonicus'. (*DTH*.)

Wordsworth, Osmund Bartle
1887–2 Apr. 1917, †Hénin-sur-Cojeul, Arras, 2nd Lt, Machine Gun Corps. British novelist: *The Happy Exchange* (1914).

Wurm, Miloš
1892–1918, †Vozières. Czech poet.

Wyn, Hedd *see* Evans, Ellis Humphrey

Xažak, K.
1867–1915. Armenian writer.

Yvan, Antoine
1880–30 Aug. 1914, †Cour-des-Rois, Guincourt, Ardennes. French poet, writer & dramatist. Poetry: *Poèmes d'autrefois et d'aujourd'hui* (Charles, 1902), *Les Rendez-vous* (Rudeval, 1907). Novels: *L'Homme seul* (Vanier, Paris, 1910); *L'Amie des Jeunes* (Ollendorff, Paris, 1911); *Les Gédéons* (Plon-Nourrit, Paris, 1913). Plays: *Le Révolté* (1912); *Le petit Corot*; *Le Jardin de Molière* (1910, perf. Comédie-Française); *L'Île déserte*. Opéras-comiques: *Le Testament de Scapin*; *Mademoiselle Don Juan* (1910).

Zacharias, David
1871–5 Aug. 1915. German painter from Düsseldorf. Painted groups, interiors, still-lifes & landscapes. Memorial exhib. Kunstsalon Teichert, Königsberg, March 1917. (Th.-B.)

Zardarian, Ṙuben
1874–1915. Armenian writer.

Zellermayer, Robert
–5 Feb. 1917, air crash nr Trieste. German writer, contributed to *Die Aktion*.

Zirner, Josef
1891–1916. German *Kapellmeister* & composer in Breslau. (*Deutsche Tonkünstler Zeitung*, 1916.)

Zohrab, Grigor (*see entry page **368***)
1861–20 May 1915, murdered while under arrest during Armenian massacres, Aleppo. Armenian short story writer & nationalist. (*Novelner*, Erevan, 1954.)

Zuckermann, Hugo
1881–1915, wounds, Carpathia. Austrian (Zionist) poet. (*Gedichte*, Löwit, Vienna, 1915.)

Żuławski, Jerzy
(*see entry page **330***)
1874–9 Aug. 1915, wounds & typhus, military hospital, Dębica, Tarnóv. Polish poet, playwright, novelist & translator of Hindu poetry. Drama: *Eros and Psyche* (1904). Science fiction: *Na srebrym globie* ([*On the Silvery Globe*], 1903); *Zwyciezca* ([*The Champion*], 1910); *Stara ziemia* ([*The old Planet*], 1910). Editor of army journal *Do Broni*.

ADDENDA

Battisti, Cesare
1875–1916, captured and hung by the Austrians. Italian journalist and literary critic born in Trento. Founded the arts review *Vita trentina* (1903). Joined Italian army in 1915 and was executed by the enemy after the ill-fated attack on Monte Corno, 1916.

Borsi, Giosué
1888–Nov. 1915, †Zagora. Italian journalist and poet from Livorno associated with the Florentine review *La Voce: Scruta obsoleta* (1910), *Confessioni a Giulia* (1915), *Colloqui* (1916), *Lettere dal fronte* (1916).

Ellis, Ellis Humphrey
1887–31 July 1917, †Pilken Ridge, Private, 15th Batt., Royal Welsh Fusiliers. Pastoral and lyrical poet who wrote in Welsh: *Cereddis Bugail* (1918).

Locchi, Vittorio
1889–1917, lost when ship torpedoed in the Aegean. Italian poet, celebrated particularly for *Sagra di Santa Gorizia* (1916), one of the most remarkable poems of the Great War, *Canzoni del Giacchio* (1914), *Testamento poetico* (posth.).

Oxilia, Nino
1888–June 1918 by an Austrian grenade. Italian poet, playwright and film director. Plays: *La zingara* (1909), *Addio giovinezza* (1911), *La dama e lo specchio* (1914). Poetry: *Gli orti* (posth.). Films: *Veli di giovinezza. Rapsodia satanica. Sangue blu. Addio giovinezza.*

Stuparich, Carlo
1894–1916. Shot himself to avoid capture after single-handed defence of a forward position on Mount Cengio. Italian poet whose works are gathered in *Cose ed ombre di uno* (1921).